THIRD EDITION

FUNDAMENTALS OF REAL ESTATE INVESTMENT

AUSTIN J. JAFFE

PENNSYLVANIA STATE UNIVERSITY

C. F. SIRMANS

UNIVERSITY OF CONNECTICUT

SOUTH-WESTERN
™
THOMSON LEARNING

Australia · Canada · Mexico · Singapore · Spain · United Kingdom · United States

Fundamentals of Real Estate Investment, 3e
by
Austin J. Jaffe
C.F. Sirmans

Printed in the United States of America
1 2 3 4 02 01

For more information contact South-Western/Thomson Learning, 5191 Natorp Boulevard, Mason, Ohio, 45040. Or you can visit our Internet site at http://www.swcollege.com

For permission to use material from this text or product contact us by
• telephone: **1-800-730-2214**
• fax: **1-800-730-2215**
• web: **http://www.thomsonrights.com**

ISBN

0-324-13992-6

CONTENTS

PREFACE

As in our earlier editions, the third edition of *Fundamentals of Real Estate Investment* is intended to provide an introduction to the real estate investment process. This process may be viewed as a series of organized and coordinated steps that investors can follow to systematically analyze potential real estate investments in the real world. Numerous topics are discussed throughout as they apply to the real estate investment process; indeed, the book uses this paradigm as a foundation. Topics discussed include the basics of the investment decision, the environment in which the investment decision is made, the development of cash flow statements, and the application of various investment criteria. By the end of any investment analysis, the investor must make a choice between various alternatives. This choice is what real estate investment is all about. By following the investment process developed in this book, we believe that the choice can be made easier and that the results will be more consistent with expectations.

The basis for the book remains the equity valuation model. Developed in the late 1960s and early 1970s, this approach effectively changed real estate investment analysis. This approach served as a turning point for the modern analysis of real estate investments. The use of discounted cash flow models permitted the explicit modeling of many factors relevant to the investor that had previously been neglected or only grossly approximated. By using the equity valuation model, investors were able to include within the analysis several parameter values and, more importantly, to alter and test their estimates to evaluate the various impacts of these parameters on their results. With the rise of computerized analysis in the 1970s and 1980s, and especially with the increased use of electronic spreadsheets in the 1980s, computerized real estate investment analysis has become relatively common in the field. In the 1990s, investors are more technically competent and "cash flow literate" than they have ever been. This edition tries to capture these developments and build on the foundation of the previous editions.

In addition to the rise of computerized analysis, over the past 30 years observers of this field have witnessed several other major changes. One highly noticeable area is that of tax law. Rules governing the treatment of depreciation, capital gains, minimum taxes, recapture of excess (or other) depreciation, treatment of financing costs, and other items have been changed throughout the years. Tax legislation affecting real estate has occurred in 1976, 1981, 1984, 1986, and, most recently, in 1993. This edition of *Fundamentals of Real Estate Investment* provides the latest tax treatment of real estate investments. In addition, there have been new research findings and developments in real-world markets in areas including real estate finance, land use law, financial applications, and portfolio analysis applied to real estate. This third edition includes the results of recent research findings in many of these areas, although we can only provide an overview of several important topics here.

Those students interested in a more detailed analysis are referred to a new edition of the predecessor of this book, *Real Estate Investment Decision Making* by Jaffe and Sirmans (second edition, forthcoming, 1996). In this book, the reader will find more extensive treatment of market, legal, financial, and tax analyses. In addition, a broader discussion of real estate as an investment is provided, including real estate as an institutional investment vehicle, the history of real estate investment analysis, portfolio theory and evidence in real estate markets, and several other advanced tools in the field.

Fundamentals of Real Estate Investment is divided into six parts. Earlier editions had only five parts; we have expanded our number of examples and case studies in this edition, in response to reader comments. Part I provides a discussion of some basic concepts, including an overview of the real estate investment process, the importance of risk, and the time value of money. The real estate investment process using the equity valuation model forms the foundation of the book. An extended example throughout Part I illustrates the basic approach. Part II describes the environment in which investment occurs. Separate chapters are provided for each of the major environments: market analysis, legal analysis, financing analysis, and tax analysis. In this new edition, we illustrate some of the latest research findings about key questions for these environments.

Part III outlines the financial analysis requirements for real estate investors and forms the core of the book. There are three types of decisions the investor confronts: operating decisions, financing decisions, and reversion decisions. While some of these decisions are made prior to the acquisition of the investment, several are required subsequent to purchase. Part IV is devoted to several investment criteria and the production of financial output to assist in making the investment decision. These chapters are generally introduced in the order in which the methods and techniques were developed and applied. First, traditional investment criteria (so-called "rules of thumb") ratios as investment methods and appraisal techniques are illustrated and discussed. Second, two of the most well-known discounted cash flow models are developed and applied to real estate. These models are called "net present value" and "internal rate of return." Within the last several years, these methods have become *the* standard forms of real estate investment analysis in many markets. Third, several additional techniques attempt to analyze the risk associated with real estate investing. Recent years have produced a number of extensions, and in this edition we have expanded this treatment.

Part V is devoted to illustrating the principles, methods, and techniques shown previously in this book. Chapter 14 is an extensive case study, updated and expanded to take into account the 1993 tax law changes, that provides a "hands-on" illustration of a real-world example of how this analysis may be directly applied to making investment decisions. Chapter 15 is new to this edition and provides several additional applications to numerous similar but related areas of analysis. Part VI provides a brief, updated conclusion, emphasizing several important points in the book and raising key questions and issues of importance to real estate investors for the remaining years in the 1990s.

One of the principles of this revision is to expand the number of examples and illustrations in most chapters of the book. In addition to Part V, readers should feel comfortable with most, if not all, of the calculations due to our heavy use of examples. In many places, we also have included special expanded examples as special illustrations. When added to our choices of illustrations of current issues in real estate investment analysis, the reader should be able to read about numerous recent events and be familiar with most of the applications discussed in the book.

This edition has also expanded the number of questions and problems at the end of each chapter. Real estate investing is a "numbers game" in some respects, and students must be prepared to "get their hands dirty" by doing the calculations. Describing what is being computed is not enough; learning is by doing. Therefore, it is intended that students be able to calculate many of the measures by hand and rely on spreadsheets to assist with many of the more tedious calculations. We have included references, updated for recent findings, for those who seek additional reading material and a broader exposure to the field.

Although real estate investing is arguably achieved by calculating a series of numbers, it is also a type of applied economic analysis. Therefore, for the first time in this edition, we have included at the opening of each chapter a series of principles that govern the analysis in that chapter. This inclusion is intended to signal the importance we place on viewing the process of real estate investment as stemming from a series of economic, financial, legal, and perhaps mathematical principles to arrive at an enhanced set of decisions. Real estate investing is sometimes argued to be an art form; we prefer to think of it more as a part of social scientific analysis useful in the real world.

As before, we support this book with a revised Instructor's Manual containing a variety of resources to assist in the teaching of this material. Suggested answers to the questions and problems are provided therein. We also include overheads for transparencies, sample test questions, and other items of assistance. As described in Appendix B, we also make available some supporting Lotus 1-2-3 diskettes. For this edition, an additional set of templates is now available with more sophisticated applications and techniques.

Students using this book should have an introduction to economics, if possible, before enrolling in this course. In addition, it is helpful if students are familiar with a first course in financial management, although this is not a requirement. Some math is used, but only basic algebra. Experience with calculators is expected since some of the applications are detailed and extensive. Experts in spreadsheet analysis might find some new ideas for development, but computer wizardry is not a prerequisite. Indeed, the available templates described in Appendix B shift the development burden of computer expertise off the novice computer user; prepared templates can save literally hundreds of hours!

The authors wish to thank colleagues at various universities and in various real estate firms for their numerous suggestions, criticisms, and error discoveries on this and earlier versions of the manuscript. It is especially gratifying when others offer compliments based on portions that were helpful in actual real estate practice. The authors are also indebted to scores of classes over the past 15 years at six nationally known universities where our students have demanded high-quality treatment of a complex and interesting subject. This ongoing process has led to a better manuscript.

For this edition, we are indebted to several colleagues. Special thanks goes to Bert Kruijt and Jacco Hakfoort of the University of Amsterdam in The Netherlands whose "bugs committee" helped us to further "de-bug" this edition. Thanks also to Ernie Wittich, Clyde Richey, Ken Lusht, and many others we somehow have forgotten to name here for their comments and criticisms. The authors also wish to thank Tim Womeldorf, Jim Valente, Jonathan Dombrow, Randy Guttery, Mauricio Rodriguez, Kim Figiela, Melissa Pember, Al Keshvarzian, Scott Beggs, Scott Sumner, Todd Goulet, Maria Nate, Denise Rowe, Dave Birkhahn, and Michele Morin for their help with the computational material in the book, including the testing and verification of the solutions to the problems. Finally, thanks also to our supportive wives and children, who have long put up with our late nights, weekends, and even weekend late nights at the office so that we could complete this revision.

While every effort has been made to ensure that this manuscript is error-free, we know that somehow, some errors go undetected. Hopefully, we have caught those from the earlier editions, especially with help of our readership. Of course, any remaining errors are the sole responsibility of the authors. As in earlier editions, finders of mistakes are encouraged to send their troves to the authors with sincere thanks.

Austin J. Jaffe   C. F. Sirmans
University Park, PA   Storrs, CT

PART I

BASIC CONCEPTS

CHAPTER 1

THE INVESTMENT DECISION

PRINCIPLES

1. There is a systematic process of making real estate investment decisions.
2. The investment process is applicable for property throughout the world.
3. Investing is the sacrifice of certain cash outflows for uncertain cash flows.
4. The success of any real estate investment depends upon the timing, magnitude, and riskiness of its expected cash flows.
5. Real estate involves risky investments.

Value is at the heart of the real estate investment decision. The main question to be answered in this text is: *How do real estate investors determine the price they are willing to pay for a property they want to buy and how is the investment decision made?* The *value* of an investment can be broadly defined as the present worth of the future benefits from owning an investment. Thus value represents the present worth of the income that an investment is expected to generate.

We must analyze the real estate project to determine the present worth of the benefits in view of our objectives, goals, and constraints. This is called the *investment value* of property. We compare this investment value with the *market value* of the investment, the price that participants in the marketplace are willing to pay for the investment, in order to make the investment decision.

This chapter gives an overview of the real estate investment decision. The *real estate investment process* provides the real estate investor with a systematic method for considering the many contingencies on which the value and thus the investment decision in income-producing property depend. This investment process applies to *all* types of income-producing real estate, including, for example, apartment complexes, office buildings, income-producing single-family projects, shopping centers, industrial properties, and vacant land. This process takes the investor through the acquisition phase, the operations phase, and the disposition phase. Within each of these various stages, decisions that have an impact on the overall investment decision must be made.

SOME BASIC INVESTMENT CONCEPTS

This section introduces some basic investment concepts: the definition of investing, the risk-return trade-off underlying investment decisions, the investor objectives, and the concept of value.

INVESTING: A DEFINITION

The investment decision is essentially a choice between consumption in the present and consumption at a future time. Investment is, in essence, present sacrifice for expected future benefit. Because the present is relatively well known and the future is uncertain, investment decisions represent *certain sacrifices* for *uncertain benefits*. In the case of income-producing real estate, these benefits take the form of future cash flows or increases in property values or both. As will be demonstrated later, the possibility of maximizing wealth motivates the purchase of property rights in an income-producing asset.

Real estate valuation involves the problem of evaluating alternative future cash flows and converting these flows into value estimates. The investment decision is based on expectations regarding

1. The timing of the expected cash outflows and inflows
2. The magnitude of the expected cash outflows and inflows
3. The riskiness of the expected cash outflows and inflows.

Timing is important because the inflows or outflows that occur affect the investment value and thus the wealth position of the owner, who trades present money for future money. To induce this trade, however, there must be compensation for the "time value of money." Of course, the rate of compensation varies from investor to investor. The mechanics of compound interest demonstrate the precise effects that cash flows have on value as a result of differences in timing. The time element for investment decisions is thus easily captured through the "discounting" of the expected future inflows.

THE RISK-RETURN TRADE-OFF

Another key factor influencing the investment decision is risk. Real estate investment decisions involve many complex, dynamic, and uncertain elements. The degree of uncertainty can range from the deterministic situation where all variables are known to highly probabilistic situations where little information is available about many variables. The time dimension can range from static to dynamic, with complexity measured in terms of the number of variables to be analyzed in the investment decision.

There are two basic sources of financial returns from owning income-producing real estate: the annual cash flow from operations and the cash flow from the disposition of the investment at the end of ownership (typically, sale). Estimates of both the annual income and the receipts from disposition are necessary in order to determine the value of the asset. Both are seldom precisely known. Future operating cash flows are uncertain and a real estate investment has no fixed future price.

The model of real estate investment decision making presented in this text rests on the assumption that cash *flow*—the dollars remaining after all prior claims are met—serves as the basis for investment decisions. Claims include operating expenses, financing costs, and taxes. This after-tax cash flow is the one valued by investors in the market.

The investor tries to (1) evaluate the circumstances that affect a real estate investment's cash flows and (2) enumerate the key events on which such cash flows are contingent. For example, the cash flow from an apartment project depends on the rents that can be charged, which in turn is related to supply and demand conditions in the apartment rental market. These contingencies must be taken into account in order to value an investment project properly.

Obviously, many potentially relevant events may affect an investment. Since the analyst must focus on the most relevant, three problems arise, including how to

1. Identify the contingencies on which cash flows are dependent
2. Estimate the cash flow from a real estate project once the contingencies have been identified
3. Convert the cash flow estimates into a value.

INVESTOR OBJECTIVES

Every investor should have an overall financial plan based on current financial resources and on reasonable expectations of future financial position and income. It is important to prepare an investment plan that correlates with the other segments of the investor's financial plan and incorporates strategies, goals, and objectives to meet potential requirements and any legal restrictions.

Real estate investing that can satisfy objectives includes one, all, or any combination of the following:

1. Means of building an estate
2. Pride of ownership
3. Hedge against inflation
4. Desired rate of return on equity invested
5. Diversification of investor objectives.

Investment opportunities in real estate vary enough in size and character to meet almost every financial constraint and investment objective.

The identification of the appropriate objective or objectives is crucial to effective decision making. It is clear that all investment opportunities will not appeal to all investors. A major downfall is the failure to understand and specify objectives prior to the commitment of funds to an investment. As we will see in Chapter 2, *we assume that the basic investor objective is wealth maximization.*

Often the investor perceives only the rewards associated with a real estate investment and ignores the risks. However, because the risk-return trade-off is faced in all investment decisions, the following basic definitions are important:

Risk is the variation in the expected future benefits.

Return is the amount of inflow generated by an investment each year. There are numerous levels of return. The most important from the equity investor's viewpoint is the after-tax cash flows.

Rate of return is the relationship between the cash flows and the amount invested, typically measured in a percentage per year on the equity.

Risk analysis is the orderly process of identifying the contingencies on which the success of an investment depends.

There are several general categories of risk associated with a real estate investment, as we will see. In addition, there is a positive relationship between the amount of risk and the expected return. It is difficult to determine the level of risk to assume. However, a general principle applies to investment decision making: *Risk and expected return are directly related to each other.* The primary task of the real estate investor is to identify and evaluate the major factors contributing to expected risk and return.

VALUE

Value is defined as the present worth of rights to future benefits arising from ownership. This definition implies the necessity to express the future benefits in dollars and then discount them to a present amount at the appropriate rate, a capitalization process most commonly known as the income approach to value. To apply this technique correctly, two elements are imperative: (1) an accurate forecast of the future benefits expressed in terms of dollars and (2) the selection of the appropriate rate at which to discount the benefits.

There are two major value concepts of concern: market value and investment value. *Market value* represents the present value of the anticipated benefits from the market's perspective. The various investors in the marketplace view the risk-return trade-off and arrive at expectations of the returns and the risks associated with an investment. The expectations are then converted into a value.

Because value depends on the discounted future benefits, it is affected by expectations. So value can be defined in terms of the present worth of the rights to the income stream. It is therefore assumed that the property is bought for the right to the income stream that will be generated.

Because this text is particularly concerned with *investment value*, we must determine the maximum price for a particular interest that an investor is willing to pay. Turvey called investment value the "ceiling price" and asked:

> What determines a purchaser's ceiling price for a particular interest? In the case of a purchaser who an investor and buys the interest for the income he expects to receive from it, his ceiling price will equal the present value to him of the anticipated net income discounted at a rate of interest equal to the yield obtainable on alternative investments with similar characteristics. This rate of interest will thus reflect not only the riskiness of the investment, the expected duration of the income and so on, but also the price at which alternative investment interests can be acquired. The present value of the interest to the purchaser consequently reflects the attraction of investment in alternative properties.[1]

To summarize the basic investment principles, we have defined *investing* as the sacrifice of certain outflows for expected, but risky, inflows. Obviously there is particular concern with the expected after-tax inflow in relation to the amount of outflow (equity). Risk and return tend to go hand in hand, as investments with high expected returns typically have high expected risks. So it is wise to evaluate the expected risk-return trade-off for an investment according to subjective preferences and arrive at an investment value. This investment value is then compared with the market value of the investment.

THE REAL ESTATE INVESTMENT PROCESS

Any successful real estate investment requires careful analysis of the many contingencies on which the decision depends. Figure 1–1 outlines the *real*

[1]Ralph Turvey, *The Economics of Real Property* (London: Allen & Unwin, 1957), pp. 8–9.

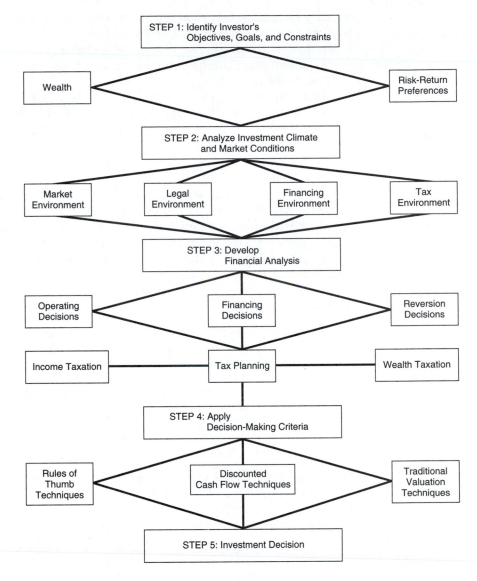

FIGURE 1-1
Real Estate Investment Process

estate investment process. The five basic steps that lead to the final investment decision can be summarized as follows:

1. Identify the goals, objectives, and constraints of the various partici-
    pants in the investment process which an investment must satisfy in
    order to be acceptable.

2. Analyze the overall investment environment—market, legal, financing, and tax—in which the investment decision must be made.

3. Forecast the expected future benefits and costs (cash flows) arising from the ownership of the investment. This analysis involves four types of decisions: operating, financing, and reversion decisions, as well as tax planning.

4. Apply appropriate decision-making criteria to compare the benefits with the costs of the investment. An analysis must be carefully developed to be relatively certain of the investment's ability to meet the constraints and objectives of *all* the participants in the investment process.

5. Accept or reject the investment under the assumptions of the input variables.

The purpose of the investment process is to discover whether a specific investment is feasible. A real estate investment is feasible when the investor determines that there is a reasonable likelihood of satisfying explicit investment objectives, which must be tested against a specific set of constraints.[2] Thus the investment process is simply a structure in which the expected risks and expected returns can be analyzed.

STEP 1: IDENTIFYING INVESTOR OBJECTIVES

The *first step* in the investment process is to identify the goals, objectives, and constraints of the four major participants in a real estate investment: the equity investor, the mortgage lender, the user of the real estate (the tenant), and the government (federal, state, and local). Figure 1–2 outlines some of the relationships between them.[3]

Each participant has different, and often conflicting, objectives for entering into the investment. And, each participant places constraints and restrictions on the feasibility (the probability of financial success) of a real estate investment. All the constraints must be carefully analyzed when considering a real estate investment because failure to do so will be potentially disastrous.

❐ **THE EQUITY INVESTOR.** The equity investor is the decision maker who chooses the specific form of business entity appropriate for the ownership of an investment. These forms include ownership as an individual, a partnership (limited or general), a corporation, a real estate investment trust, a

---

[2]James A. Graaskamp, *A Guide to Feasibility Analysis* (Chicago: Society of Real Estate Appraisers, 1980).

[3]It should be noted that there are a few other participants in the real estate investment process with secondary rules. These include property managers, real estate brokers, attorneys, tax assessors, and real estate appraisers, among others.

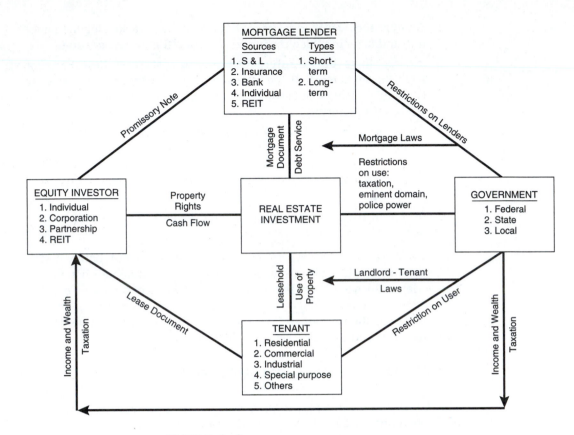

FIGURE 1–2
Participants in the Real Estate Investment Process

syndication, and so forth. All of these business entities have various advantages and disadvantages, which we will examine later.

The equity investor is interested in the amount of cash flow from an investment and must be certain of having the legal right to the cash flow. The legal viewpoints related to ownership of real estate rights are extremely important in investment decision making.

☐ **THE MORTGAGE LENDER.**   The second major participant in the real estate investment process is the mortgage lender. Most real estate investments use a substantial amount of borrowed funds. In order to borrow a substantial amount of funds, the borrower (equity investor) typically has to pledge the real estate as security for the debt. The mortgage lender is obviously interested in the recovery of the amount lent, as well as in earning a rate of return on the loan. To the mortgage lender, the mortgage is an investment.

❐ **THE TENANT.** The third major participant is the user of the real estate—the tenant who buys the immediate right of possession from the landlord (equity investor) in exchange for the payment of consideration (rent). The tenant's requirements must be carefully analyzed, for without the tenant, there is no income from the real estate investment.

The *lease* is the document that links the equity investor, the investment, and the tenant. The laws governing leases differ substantially between states, and therefore no legal decision should be made without specific counsel in the jurisdiction in which the property is located.

❐ **THE GOVERNMENT.** The fourth major participant in a real estate investment is the government. All levels—federal, state, and local—have an impact on the real estate investment decision-making process. The government not only influences the relationships between the equity investor, the mortgage lender, and the tenant but also places restrictions on the use of the real estate investment.

STEP 2: ENVIRONMENT FOR DECISION MAKING

The *second step* in the investment process involves analysis of the overall climate affecting the investment. This step encompasses four distinct areas of analysis: the market environment, legal environment, financing environment, and tax environment.

More specifically, this step is concerned with the examination of business risk for a specific investment. As one of the major categories of risk to which a real estate investor is exposed, *business risk* is defined as the variability of the expected net income from a real estate investment. An investment produces two potential sources of net income: the annual flow from operations and the flow from the reversion (typically, sale). Market analysis is aimed at identifying the factors, and the probability of their occurrence, that influence net income. The key factors are rents, vacancies, operating expenses, and expected future selling price at the end of the holding period.

❐ **THE MARKET ENVIRONMENT.** An understanding of the supply and demand forces that influence the feasibility of a particular investment is extremely important. Market analysis must take into account these forces at the national, state, and local levels.

The demand for real estate is derived from the demand for the goods and services that it provides. For example, the demand for residential properties is derived from the demand for housing services; the demand for shopping centers is derived from the demand for retail goods, such as clothes and shoes that the stores will provide; the demand for office buildings is derived from the demand for professional services, such as medical and dental care.

Real estate investors often believe that the real estate itself has an intrinsic value. However, value comes from the services that a real estate investment provides. Therefore, the lesson is to analyze the correct source of demand. If the investor knows six dentists who demand an office building, the task is much easier. All that is necessary is to determine the specific characteristics that they require in their offices. If tenants are not known, the analyst might infer that there is a demand for office buildings because of increases in aggregate statistics, such as population, income, and employment. Obviously, the latter situation entails substantially more uncertainty than the former. All too often *secondary data* are used to infer demand conditions.

The real estate market is divided into numerous submarkets, such as the residential, industrial, commercial, and vacant land markets. Obviously, even these groups can be subdivided further. The market can also be divided by size of project, by location, or by type of structure. All of these constitute the market environment and should not be overlooked.

Another common error that the analyst makes is the failure to consider *both* sides of the market. Often the analyst will consider only the demand side while ignoring the supply side. *The analyst must identify the appropriate submarket in which a real estate investment is competing or will compete (as in the case of a proposed development) and identify the supply and demand influences operating in that market.*

Market analysis is frequently concerned with a reduction of aggregate data such as population, employment, and income to factors that are more relevant to a particular project. To a great extent, however, it deals with factors beyond the investor's control.

One of the purposes of market analysis is to identify the user of the services provided by the investment. The characteristics and preferences of potential tenants must be carefully analyzed to identify the demand for any given real estate project appropriately. Other factors to be considered are the physical and structural characteristics of the site, the condition of improvements, transportation access, and personal-response factors such as security. All of these attributes are part of the "service" that the project supplies to meet the potential demand.

❒ **THE LEGAL ENVIRONMENT.** The legal environment plays a major role in investment analysis. Whereas market analysis is concerned with the economic constraints on an investment, analysis of the legal environment examines the legal constraints. From a legal perspective, real estate is a complex commodity. As Figure 1–2 indicates, the real estate investment process involves many legal relationships between the various participants. Legal constraints are imposed on the real estate, the equity investor, the mortgage lender, and the tenant. All levels of government impose different legal constraints on the investment.

One of the major legal decisions concerns the choice of business entity for undertaking the investment. The most popular forms are individual ownership, the partnership, and the corporation. Since most real estate investments involve large sums of capital, investors typically form a business entity. Each entity has advantages and disadvantages, and factors such as liability, management, ease of transferability, and taxation greatly influence the decision.

The ownership of real estate provides certain property rights. Examples are the right to use and the right to sell the property. The quality and quantity of property rights associated with the ownership of real estate are of great concern because these rights are valued in the real estate market. Any limitation on these rights reduces the investment's value.

Limitations on property rights may stem from public and private sources. Public influences on property rights are the result of some governmental action. At the federal government level, the greatest impact consists of income and wealth taxation. At the local government level, the greatest impact consists of various forms of land-use controls. Private sources may curtail property rights by placing deed restrictions to limit the use of the real estate. The property rights in real estate can be "sold" separately. In the case of income-producing real estate, the owner "sells" the right of use to the tenant. In return, the tenant pays the owner a price (rent). A potential investment should be carefully investigated as to limitations on the property rights in order to preclude eventual losses.

Another major area of concern is the relationship with the user of the real estate—the tenant. This relationship is specified in the *lease document*. Here the investor must be aware that the lease covers a great deal more than simply the amount of rent due each month. To be feasible, an investment must satisfy the constraints of the legal environment.

One of the most difficult areas in real estate investing is the analysis of the sociopolitical aspects of the legal environment. Any real estate investment (particularly a large-scale development) can affect the well-being of society as a whole. While there may be a demand for a particular project and while the project may be "legal," public sentiment against the project may be a complicating factor.

The relationship of real estate investment to the community as well as the environment within the realm of the community's own interests should be carefully analyzed, as these values must be dealt with in the decision-making process. In many cases, the investor must be prepared to comment on the compatibility of an investment with community standards and expectations. What is technically legal at any given time may not be politically permissible. Such considerations can place constraints on the total feasibility of a particular real estate investment.

❐ **THE FINANCING ENVIRONMENT.** Every real estate investment involves the use of money. There are two sources: debt and equity. A real estate investor could use all equity or all debt or some combination of the two. This last situation is the typical case.

To be feasible, a real estate investment must provide enough income to cover the cost of debt and equity. The cost of borrowing is generally referred to as the interest rate. The cost of equity is the required rate of return on equity. This *equity yield* could be measured on either a before-tax or after-tax basis. We will argue that the after-tax basis is the more appropriate.

On the debt side, the mortgage lender has traditionally accepted a fixed rate of interest and a sinking fund payback of the amount lent over the mortgage maturity, i.e., fixed-rate, level-payment, fully-amortized loan commonly known as a *fixed-rate mortgage*. In recent years, there have been numerous variations in mortgage-lending practices, such as adjustable-rate loans and equity participation loans. The changes have been prompted, for the most part, by unexpected inflation in the economy.

On the equity side, real estate investors have used a wide variety of techniques to obtain the necessary equity funds. The equity position in a real estate investment is presumed to have more risk exposure than the mortgage position because the equity claim is, in essence, the "residual" claim associated with the investment. The equity investor receives funds only if there are any resources left over after all other claimants have been paid. The equity position could receive cash inflow in the form of either periodic cash flow or an expected capital gain (or some combination).

Both debt and equity capital tend to flow into those sources that have the highest expected rate of return for a given level of risk. For example, if the return on capital increases in some segment of the financial market, lenders (or equity) investors may move funds out of real estate into this other segment. As a result of these shifts in financial markets, we see movements upward and downward in the amount of funds (both debt and equity) invested in the real estate market.

☐ **THE TAX ENVIRONMENT.** One of the most important governmental influences in investment decisions is the power of taxation. Taxation of the incomes of individuals and businesses by the federal government was not permitted under the U.S. Constitution until the passage of the Sixteenth Amendment in 1913.[4] The Congress enacts the tax laws that specify how the tax liability is to be determined. The Internal Revenue Service (IRS) administrates the laws, collects taxes, and issues regulations implementing and interpreting the tax laws. There exists a special court, the Tax Court, in which taxpayers may contest the rules and decisions of the IRS.

The influence of taxes is important in making the investment decision, since taxes influence the amount of cash flow from an investment. Recall that we defined *investing* as the outflow of cash (equity from the investor's perspective) in return for expected, but uncertain, cash inflow. The important cash inflow is the amount left after taxes have been paid.

The government is interested in the amount of taxable income (and thus taxes), whereas the investor is interested in the after-tax cash flow. These are not measured in the same way. An investor must carefully analyze the tax environment in order to make correct investment decisions.

STEP 3: CASH FLOW FORECASTING

As outlined in Figure 1–1, the *third step* in the real estate investment process is to forecast the expected cash flows from an investment. The cash flows must be forecast for the period of time during which the investment is expected to be held. Because cash flows from the investment are not known, the investment decision is based on reasonable expectations.

There are two major sources of cash flows from a real estate investment—*the annual cash flow from rental collections* and *the cash flow from the disposition (typically, sale) of the investment.* The cash flow figure that is of most interest is the amount left after all costs of operating and selling the investment have been paid. These costs include operating expenses, payments on mortgage debt, and income taxes.

[4]However, an earlier federal income tax had been passed in 1894 but was ruled to be unconstitutional.

TABLE 1–1
EXPECTED CASH FLOW FROM OPERATIONS FOR EACH YEAR

	Potential gross income (PGI)
minus	Vacancy and bad debt allowance (VBD)
plus	Miscellaneous income (MI)
equals	Effective gross income (EGI)
minus	Operating expenses (OE)
equals	Net operating income (NOI)
minus	Debt Service (DS)
equals	Before-tax cash flow (BTCF)
minus	**Taxes (savings) from operations (TO)***
equals	After-tax cash flow (ATCF)

* See Table 1–2.

❐ **CASH FLOW FROM OPERATION.**   Table 1–1 measures the *expected annual cash flow* from the operation of a real estate investment. Table 1–2 measures the *expected taxable income* from operation. *The equity investor is interested in the cash flow, whereas the government is interested in the taxable income.* The two income streams are related by the taxes due from operation. They are *not* the same.

POTENTIAL GROSS INCOME.   The starting point in calculating the cash flow from operation each year is the *potential gross income (PGI)*. PGI is the estimated rent per unit for each year multiplied by the number of units available for rent. For example, if an income-producing, residential four-plex rents two units for $800 per month, one unit for $567 per month, and one unit for $500 per month, the PGI would be $32,000 for that year.

EFFECTIVE GROSS INCOME.   Since it is unlikely that an investment will be completely occupied all year round or that all rents will be collected, an allowance for vacancy and bad debt should be deducted. There may also be miscellaneous income from other types of operation, such as parking space rentals. This miscellaneous income would be added to the cash flow statement. The net effect of these items results in *effective gross income (EGI)*. If the four-plex above averages vacancies of only 3 percent of PGI, then the annual vacancy would be $960, and if there is no miscellaneous income, this would result in an EGI of $31,040.

NET OPERATING INCOME.   From the EGI, the operating expenses are deducted to result in *net operating income (NOI)*. Operating expenses include those items associated with operating the investment, such as repairs, management fees, property taxes, insurance, advertising fees, and utilities. Assuming operating expenses for the four-plex are $7,500, NOI would be $23,540.

BEFORE-TAX CASH FLOW.   The debt service (payment on mortgage debt is subtracted from net operating income to yield *before-tax cash flow (BTCF)*. The final step in the calculation of the *after-tax cash flow (ATCF)* is the subtraction of the income taxes due on operation from the BTCF. The ATCF is what concerns the equity investor. Based on a $128,000 loan at 12 percent interest for 25 years with monthly compounding, the annual debt service on the four-plex would be $16,174, so BTCF would be $7,366.

AFTER-TAX CASH FLOW.   Table 1–2 calculates the *ordinary taxable income (OTI)* and *taxes from operation (TO)*.[5] The calculation of taxable income differs in several ways from the calculation of cash flow. For tax purposes, the investor is allowed to deduct the operating expenses from the gross income. While interest on mortgage debt is tax deductible, the principal portion of any debt service is not. A deduction for depreciation of the improvements is also permitted to be amortized on a straight-line basis over a 27.5 year period for residential income-producing property and over 39 years for nonresidential income-producing property. This is not a cash outlay, however; it is simply an allowance for tax purposes.

The next item in the calculation of taxable income is the amortized financing costs, or the costs associated with placing a mortgage against an investment. Although these costs cannot be deducted in the year incurred, they can be amortized (written off) over the life of the mortgage debt. The final adjustment is the replacement reserves. These represent an allowance

TABLE 1–2
EXPECTED TAXES FROM OPERATIONS FOR EACH YEAR

	Effective gross income (EGI)
minus	Operating expenses (OE)
equals	Net operating income (NOI)
minus	Interest on debt (I)
minus	Depreciation deduction (D)
minus	Amortized financing costs (AFC)
plus	Replacement reserves (RR)
equals	Ordinary taxable income (OTI)
times	Investor's marginal tax rate (τ)
equals	**Taxes (savings) from operations (TO)**

[5]A real estate investment can also generate other types of taxes from operation. These will be examined in Chapter 7.

for the replacment of personal property. While these reserves may represent cash flow items, they are not deductible for tax purposes. Assuming the four-plex's loan had a first year interest charge of $15,310, a depreciation deduction of $5,273, amortized financing costs of $154, and no replacement reserves, ordinary taxable income to the owner would be $2,803.

The taxes from operation are estimated by multiplying the taxable income by the marginal tax rate. Should the investor be in a 28 percent marginal tax bracket, taxes from operations would be $784. Therefore, ATCF in year 1 would be $6,582, the difference between BTCF of $7,366 and taxes from operations or $784. In addition to these ordinary income taxes, there may be some minimum tax due on what is known as "tax-preference income." These concepts will be examined in other chapters.

CASH FLOW FROM REVERSION. The second source of cash flow comes from the disposition (typically, sale) of the investment. Since real estate is usually held for a limited period, this cash flow must be forecast in addition to the cash flow from operation. Table 1–3 measures the cash flow from the sale. Table 1–4 measures the taxable income and taxes due on the sale.

As we will discuss in upcoming chapters, there are other methods of disposition (such as tax-deferred exchanges), but the primary method is that of sale. These other methods of disposition simply complicate the investment model; however, we will outline these other methods and demonstrate their impact on the investment decision.

SELLING PRICE. The starting point in the calculation of both cash flow and taxable income is the expected future selling price. Remember that because the investment decision is being made now, it is based on the expected inflows. So we must forecast the expected change in value to determine the anticipated selling price at the end of the holding period.

NET SALES PROCEEDS. Selling expenses associated with the disposition of the investment are deducted from the expected selling price. Selling ex-

TABLE 1–3
EXPECTED CASH FLOW FROM SALE OF AN INVESTMENT

	Expected selling price (SP)
minus	Selling expenses (SE)
equals	Net sales proceeds (NSP)
minus	Unpaid mortgage balance (UM)
equals	Before-tax equity reversion (BTER)
minus	Taxes due on sale (TDS)*
equals	After-tax equity reversion (ATER)

* See Table 1–4.

TABLE 1–4
EXPECTED TAXES DUE ON SALE OF AN INVESTMENT

	Taxable Income
	Expected selling price (SP)
minus	Selling expenses (SE)
equals	Amount realized (AR)
minus	Adjusted basis (AB)
	Total gain on sale
	Taxes Due on Sale
	Total gain on sale (TG)
times	Investor's marginal tax rate (τ)
equals	Taxes due on sale (TDS)

penses include brokerage fees, legal fees, and other costs associated with the disposition (sale) of the property. The result is the net sales proceeds (NSP). Assuming the four-plex sold after a holding period of three years for $175,000 and the investor incurred $17,000 in selling expenses, NSP would be $158,000.

BEFORE-TAX EQUITY REVERSION. The before-tax equity reversion (BTER) is the net sale proceeds minus the unpaid mortgage (UM) balance. Most mortgage loans call for the repayment of the loan when an investment is sold. So if the investment is sold prior to the mortgage maturity, the outstanding balance must be paid. The four-plex's loan balance at the end of three years would be $125,065, so BTER is $32,935.

AFTER-TAX EQUITY REVERSION. The final step in calculating the cash flows from sale is the deduction of any taxes that are due.

Table 1–4 shows how to calculate taxes due on the sale of an investment. To begin, we deduct expected selling expenses from the selling price to obtain the amount realized. Then we deduct the adjusted basis from the amount realized to arrive at the total gain on sale. The adjusted basis is the original cost plus the cost of capital improvements minus the total cumulative depreciation deductions. The adjusted basis in the four-plex would be $144,181 ($160,000 pruchase price minus accumulated depreciation of $15,819, or $5,273 times 3); hence, the total gain on sale would be $13,819.

The taxable income from sale is the amount of the total gain. This taxable income is then multiplied by the investor's marginal tax rate to result in the taxes due on sale. At a 28 percent marginal tax rate, the four-plex investor's taxes due on sale would be $3,869, resulting in an ATER of $29,066.[6]

Referring again to Table 1–3, we see that the taxes due on sale are then subtracted from the before-tax equity reversion to result in the after-tax cash flow from the sale (ATER) of the investment.

Using these estimates of the expected cash flow from operation and the cash flow from sale, the investor is now prepared to apply various criteria to examine the relationship between cash inflows and cash outflows.

---

[6]Although preferential capital gains treatment was removed from the tax law in recent years, the current law places an upper limit on the maximum tax rate of 28% to be applied to the total gain on sale.

STEP 4: CRITERIA FOR DECISION MAKING

The *fourth step* in the investment process is to apply the decision-making criteria. Compare the benefits with the costs and ask: *How much should be paid?* Alternatively, if a certain price is paid, what is the expected rate of return from the investment? Does the expected rate of return compensate for the risks?

The decision-making criteria fall into three broad categories: rules-of-thumb techniques, traditional valuation techniques (or real estate appraisal methods), and discounted cash flow (DCF) models. Each of these methods has advantages and disadvantages.

❐ **RULES-OF-THUMB TECHNIQUES.** Many investors employ rules of thumb in making decisions. These techniques are fairly simple and have a number of limitations which make them, at least from a theoretical viewpoint, less desirable as decision-making criteria. We will deal more fully with these limitations in Chapter 11.

Some of the more popular rules of thumb are the gross income multiplier, the overall capitalization rate, and the equity dividend rate. The *gross income multiplier* simply measures the relationship between value (selling price) and gross income from operations. This is analogous to a price/earnings (P/E) ratio used in corporate finance. The *overall capitalization rate* (or its reciprocal, the *net income multiplier*) is the ratio of net operating income to value. The *equity dividend rate* is the ratio of before-tax cash flow (typically for the first year) to the amount of equity invested. All of these are useful criteria for the initial screening of prospective investments.

❐ **TRADITIONAL APPRAISAL METHODS.** The second major set of techniques for estimating value consists of the traditional appraisal models: direct sales comparison approach, cost approach, and income approach.

Using the *direct sales comparison approach,* we estimate the value of an investment by comparing it with similar properties that have recently been sold. The pertinent question is, How much would the comparable property have sold for if it were similar to the investment under consideration? Then, by adjusting for differences, an indicated value for the investment can be obtained.

Another traditional appraisal method is the *cost approach,* where an estimate of the value of an investment is made based on the cost of reproducing the property using the current construction costs and considering the condition and location of the property. If the investment involved is an existing building, for example, the investor would compare this estimated value with the selling price to make the investment decision.

A third appraisal method is the *traditional income approach,* where *value* is defined as the present worth of the expected income stream. Using this method, the value is estimated by "discounting" the net income from operations and revisions at an appropriate "capitalization" rate.

❏ **DISCOUNTED CASH FLOW (DCF) MODELS.** The third and final major set of decision-making criteria for real estate investment analysis consists of discounted cash flow (DCF) models. These are based on the concept that the value of a real estate investment is equal to the present worth of the future cash flows.[7] To use DCF models, we first forecast the expected cash flows and then discount future cash flows at the investor's required rate of return. Discounted cash flow models recognize that a dollar today is worth more than a dollar tomorrow: the essence of the concept of present value and the time value of money.

There are two basic DCF models: net present value and internal rate of return. To use the *net present value method*, we discount the expected cash flows using the required rate of return based upon the perceived risks of the investor. If the present value of the cash inflows exceeds the present value of the cash outflows, the investment is accepted. If the present value of the cash inflows is less than the present value of the outflows, the investment is not accepted.

With the *internal rate of return method,* we compare the inflows with the costs and calculate the rate of return. The internal rate of return (IRR) is the rate that equates the present-value of the cash flows with the present-value costs of investing. Once the IRR has been calculated, it is compared with the required or "hurdle rate" of return. If the calculated rate of return is greater than or equal to the desired rate of return, the investment is made. If it is less than the desired rate, the investment is not made.

The discounted cash flow models can be used with either before-tax or after-tax inflows in relation to the cost (equity) of investing. The DCF models may also be used to test the sensitivity of the rate of return, and hence the investment decision, to the various assumptions that must be made in forecasting the cash flows for a real estate investment.

STEP 5: THE INVESTMENT DECISION

Now that all of the considerations have been analyzed, a decision must be made. The various assumptions and estimates have been reviewed and checked for accuracy and potential white elephants have been discarded. Therefore, we are ready to make a wealth-maximizing investment in real estate.

[7]To be technically correct, the income approach is also a type of DCF model.

SUMMARY

This chapter introduced some basic investment concepts. Because real estate investing requires the outflow of a *certain* amount of money in return for an expected, but *uncertain,* cash flow, we are concerned with determining the value.

In Chapter 1, the real estate investment process was outlined as a step-by-step framework for decision making. Each step was discussed in the light of its importance to the total process. The following chapters focus on the more intricate details of each of these steps. Chapter 2 examines the investor's objectives.

QUESTIONS

1–1. What is investing?

1–2. What is the relationship between risk and return?

1–3. Why is the risk-return relationship important for investors?

1–4. *Value* can have various meanings. How is value defined for real estate investment analysis?

1–5. What is the relationship between market value and investment value? How are they distinguished?

1–6. Describe the real estate investment process. What is its purpose?

1–7. Who are the major real estate investment participants?

1–8. There are four major environments in which real estate investment decisions are made. Describe each of these and discuss how each might have an important impact on the investment.

1–9. How is *after-tax cash flow* defined? What is its relationship to taxable income?

1–10. What are the two basic discounted cash flow models?

PROBLEMS

1–1. A real estate investment has the following inputs:
Asking price: $900,000
Rentable area: 10,000 square feet
Rent per square foot: $15 per year
Vacancy losses: 7 percent per year
Operating expenses: $42,000
Debt service: $85,300, of which $81,000 is interest
Depreciation deduction: $42,500
Investor's marginal tax rate: 28 percent
Compute the expected after-tax cash flow (ATCF) from operation for year 1.

1–2. You have recently sold your apartment building for $500,000. It was purchased for $400,000 five years ago. You have taken depreciation deductions of $18,462 per year. The unpaid mortgage balance is $325,000. Your marginal tax rate on ordinary income is 28 percent. Compute your after-tax equity reversion (ATER).

1–3. Using the information in Problem 1–1, compute the following:
a. Gross income multiplier
b. Net income multiplier
c. Overall capitalization rate.

1–4. Using the facts from Problem 1–1, suppose the appropriate overall capitalization rate was 10.5 percent. What is the indicated value of the property using the estimated net operating income?

1–5. A real estate investment has the following inputs:

Purchase price: $2,000,000
Original mortgage balance: $1,500,000
Rentable area: 18,000 square feet
Rent per square foot: $20 per year
Vacancy losses: 7 percent per year

Operating expenses: $50,000
Debt service: $180,631, of which $127,501 is interest
Depreciation deduction: $51,282
Investor's marginal tax rate: 31 percent.
Compute the following based on this information:

a. After-tax cash flow (ATCF) for year 1
b. Gross income multiplier
c. Overall capitalization rate
d. Equity dividend rate
e. Loan-to-value ratio.

SELECTED REFERENCES

Brown, Robert K., "The Investment Counselor's Role in the Development Process," *Appraisal Journal*, 39 (July 1971), 225–36.

Firstenberg, P. M., Stephen A. Ross, and Randall C. Zisler, "Real Estate: The Whole Story," *Journal of Portfolio Management*, 3 (1987), 22–34.

Friedman, Jack P., "Olde Tyme Religion Returns to Real Estate," *Real Estate Finance*, 9 (Summer 1992), 34–38.

Jaffe, Austin J., and C. F. Sirmans, "Improving Real Estate Investment Analysis," *Appraisal Journal*, 49 (January 1981), 85–94.

Landauer, James D., "Real Estate as an Investment," *Appraisal Journal*, 28 (October 1960), 426–434.

Miles, Mike, "What is the Value of U.S. Real Estate?" *Real Estate Review*, 20 (Summer 1990), 69–77.

Turvey, Ralph, *The Economics of Real Property*. London: Allen & Unwin, 1957.

Wendt, Paul, and Alan Cerf, *Real Estate Investment Analysis and Taxation*, 2nd ed., New York: McGraw-Hill, 1979.

CHAPTER 2

RISK, RETURN, AND DECISION MAKING

PRINCIPLES

1. While there are numerous alternative investor objectives, the appropriate goal is wealth maximization for most real estate investors.
2. There exists a trade-off between risk and return.
3. The efficient market hypothesis is a central idea in modern real estate analysis.
4. A good real estate investment is one that promises an abnormally high rate of return.
5. The equity valuation model is the most effective valuation model currently available for real estate investors.

In Chapter 1 we outlined the real estate investment process. The initial step in the process required an analysis of the investor's objectives regarding risk, return, and other dimensions. In this chapter we introduce some additional principles about real estate as an investment and discuss some popular reasons why real estate continues to be an attractive investment vehicle.

This chapter builds on the framework developed in Chapter 1 in a number of ways. First, some basic principles are examined in addition to those introduced previously. We discuss the difference between speculation and investment, the special attributes of real estate as an investment, and the expected relationship between risk and return. We also discuss some of the reasons why investors are attracted to real estate and the extent to which these reasons are likely to result in financial gain for the investors.

Although there are several possible objectives for real estate investors, this book argues that with the exception of special cases, the presumed objective of real estate investors is to become as wealthy as possible through investment acquisition, operation, and disposition decisions. Therefore, the goal of wealth maximization is assumed to be the investment objective of the typical investor.

The concept of market efficiency is introduced and is shown to be one of the more useful notions for modern real estate investment analysis. With these concepts, it is then possible to define a "good investment" and to introduce a model that can be used to identify such investments. This model is called the *equity valuation model*, and it is the heart of the decision-making process. The final section discusses the reasons why the model is useful for solving the problem of choosing real estate investments.

SOME CHARACTERISTICS OF REAL ESTATE INVESTMENTS

In Chapter 1, *investment* was defined as the present sacrifice of resources for the expected future benefits of resources. Typically, the resources involved refer to cash of the equity investors as well as debt financing of the lender. Because equity investors reap the benefits of financing success, however, the risk of loss is borne by them, also, even if mortgage or other debt financing is employed.

Because the definition of investing is quite broad, it is useful to refine the concept of investing to illustrate the following items: (1) the relationship between investment and speculation, (2) the main parts of real estate as an investment, and (3) the relationship between risk and return. This discussion will lead us to the investment model used throughout this book: the *equity valuation model*. This technique will permit a systematic analysis of potential real estate investment projects, taking into account, in an orderly and logical way, all the considerations indicated in the real estate investment process in Chapter 1.

This method will also provide clear but general decision rules so that an investor can decide which, if any, investments should be acquired of those available and which should be avoided. Clearly, unlike some approaches, this analysis implies that some real estate projects are unattractive as investment vehicles, especially for certain investors, whereas others provide opportunities to increase investors' wealth positions. The analysis and techniques discussed in this book provide tested methods of achieving financial success as a real estate investor.

SPECULATION VERSUS INVESTMENT

Some individuals like to distinguish between two types of economic activity: speculation and investment. To these individuals, *speculation* involves the acceptance of large risks and unsecured gambles with borrowed funds for the sole purpose of fast returns in ventures of dubious activity. This line of thinking has also associated "speculators" with such epithets as sneaky, immoral, corrupt, and nonproductive. On the other hand, individuals who saved their own funds and who, over time, without as much risk and with less fanfare, slowly acquired interests in real estate were said to engage in the process of *investment.* These investors were the "good guys" and were thought to provide economic benefits to society. Speculators supposedly harmed society and thus became known as the "bad guys."

It is surprising that this distinction continues to be shared by many people today. In many ways, it is difficult if not impossible to distinguish between investors and speculators. Furthermore, even if such a distinction can be made, it is doubtful whether it is useful for any productive purpose. For example, if an individual acquires a parcel of real estate, whether his or her intentions are to develop the land and live there for forty years or to hold the land undeveloped for two years and then resell it should make little difference to society.[1] In both cases, the real estate is acquired by the highest bidder and is used in the manner the investor chooses. If, subsequently, another investor would like to use the real estate in a more productive manner, the second investor could outbid the "speculator" and redevelop the property. In any case, with each subsequent purchase, the real estate is used as productively as possible by everyone involved.

Does it make any difference to society if the investor has a long planning horizon or a short one? Does it matter if all cash is used to finance the investment or if a lender willingly agrees to lend the investor money to help finance the investment? Does the reason why an individual buys property make any difference? If the answer to any of these questions is yes, then it follows that an individual or a group of individuals would be interested in acquiring the real estate from the investor or speculator and using the property in a way they would prefer. If so, society in general benefits, as each transaction helps to ensure that the property goes to the user who values it the highest.

Therefore, not only is the historical distinction between investment and speculation immaterial, it can be argued, also, that "speculators" *aid* society by helping to make markets clear at *better* (and often higher) prices. Without such activity, it would become more difficult to transact real estate, and market prices would be less representative of the value placed on the property by society at that point in time.

---

[1]The concept of ownership of land in the United States includes several property rights including the "right of use." A decision by a legitimate owner not to develop a parcel of land is perfectly consistent with the long-held right of use available under Anglo-American law.

The Uniqueness of Real Estate as an Investment

Real estate as an investment consists of several parts. Each part provides a separate reason why real estate continues to be attractive as an investment. Each part, when added to the others, gives investors an opportunity that is unique across a wide spectrum of investments available. Therefore it is important to be able to identify the major parts of real estate investments and to be able to account for each part systematically when doing a financial analysis.

The benefits of owning real estate as an investment can be divided into seven parts.

Rental income is one of the principal benefits for many types of projects. The payment made by users of the land to the owner of the land is called "economic rent." Whether or not the land is rented to a tenant, an economic rent accrues to the owner. If the owner chooses to rent the land, the contract rent that is agreed upon is a function of the economic rent the market is willing to pay for the space. Therefore, the investor benefits from owning the real estate by collecting the rental income if the economic rent on the property is high, relative to that of other properties in the area.

Appreciation refers to changes in the value of the real estate over time. Some of the change in the property's value may be due to inflation; some may result from changes in the supply and demand forces in the market for the real estate. As will be shown in Chapter 4, changes in value due to inflation do not affect the wealth of the investor. Only changes in the relative value of the land are of interest to the investor. These relative price changes may occur for a variety of reasons including growth in the community, specific improvements on the land, restrictions on the supply of competing properties, shifts in the tastes and preferences of consumers, and changes in the needs of society regarding property and the use of land.

Financial leverage is often considered to be one of the principal benefits of real estate investing. It is said that investors benefit by using debt financing if the cost of financing is less than the rate of return earned by owning the real estate. Because interest payments are tax deductible, the appropriate comparison should be the after-tax cost of borrowing relative to the after-tax rate of return on the investment. Many investors feel that because a large percentage of the typical real estate investment is financed with debt, the opportunities for gains from leverage are greater in real estate than in other areas of investment.

Control of the investment is another reason why real estate is an attractive area for investing. Many investors are interested in the managerial aspects of the investment. Rather than desiring a passive investment where managerial decisions are made for the investor, such as in common stocks or corporate bonds with publicly traded firms, some investors want to manage their own investments directly. For such investors, the opportunity to develop, modify, manage, and change real estate is precisely what they are seeking.

Real estate as an *inflation hedge* is a concept that has become increasingly popular since the early 1970s. It has frequently been alleged that real estate is as fine an inflation hedge as any other vehicle available to investors. An inflation hedge is an investment whose return equals or exceeds the rate of inflation over long periods of time. Such an investment is of interest to investors to the extent that some investments fail to keep pace with inflation and, over time, the real wealth of investors falls due to the reduction in the purchasing power of the dollar. It has often been alleged that real estate as an inflation hedge is superior to other investments.

Security is another reason why investors seek real estate. Land is fundamental to modern living, not because urban society requires the soil for crop yield but because the city remains the center of modern economic life. As such, land situated in prime locations will retain its importance in years to come.

Real estate may also provide benefits to investors who seek real estate as a *portfolio asset*. It is well known that the risk of loss can be reduced by diversification into investments with different financial characteristics than those currently in an investor's portfolio. Increasingly, real estate projects are being evaluated as a portfolio asset by life insurance companies, pension funds, bank holding companies, and other large firms. With real estate's other attributes, the potential as a diversification asset has attracted a host of new investors in recent years.

THE RELATIONSHIP BETWEEN RISK AND RETURN

The relationship between risk and return is one of the most important relationships for the real estate investor. It is important for two reasons. First, if the relationship is maintained, the investor knows that expected high rates of return are likely to be accompanied by equivalent high levels of risk. Second, if the relationship is weakened, the investor knows that in some cases high rates of return are possible with lesser amounts of risk. Thus, the strength of this relationship also tells the investor about the degree of market efficiency that exists. Therefore, a basic understanding of risk and return is essential.

In market economies, some investors prefer safe investments while others prefer riskier ones. In order for investors to accept riskier investments, however, they must be promised a higher expected rate of return. If not, no rational investor would accept the riskier investment; the investor would be better off with the safer investment earning the same level of return.

Therefore, it is likely that a positive relationship would exist between expected (or required) rates of return and risk. Figure 2–1 illustrates the relationship between risk and return. The figure indicates that the higher the level of risk (σ), the higher the required rate of return on equity (k_e). When there is no risk associated with the investment, it is reasonable to expect to earn the risk-free rate (k_f). At point *A* there is no risk to the investment, and the risk-free rate is expected to be earned.

However, if a rate of return is desired that is greater than the risk-free rate (the lowest rate of return available), then the investor necessarily has to take on some risk. This amounts to moving up the risk-return trade-off. Note that Figure 2–1 indicates two combinations of risk and return. Points *B* and *C* indicate two levels of risk and return possibilities. Also, note that

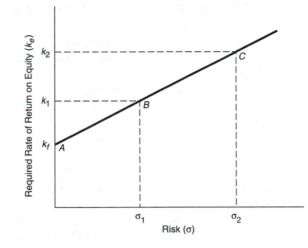

FIGURE 2–1
The Relationship Between Risk and Return

at point B, the investor requires a lower rate of return than at point C, because the risk is much less at point B than at point C.

There are several types of risk in the world of real estate investment analysis. These include *financial risk,* or the risk of defaulting on borrowed funds; *business risk,* or the risk of income losses resulting from changes in economic conditions; *inflation* (or *purchasing power*) *risk,* or the risk of losses in real value due to changes in the nominal prices of goods and services; and others. Each type of risk can be represented, conceptually, as a premium that must be added to the risk-free rate to compare it with the required rate of return by the investor.

The important point here is that the analysis of return necessitates the analysis of risk. The two are inseparable and, as a result, it is essential that investors study both when making investment decisions.

INVESTOR OBJECTIVES

To enable the investor to choose projects among several alternatives, one of the first steps in the investment process is the choice of investment objective. Although there are likely to be differences between investors regarding interests, risk preferences, and tastes, it is argued that the objective of most investors is *wealth maximization*. This objective is broad and general, but it provides a conceptual framework for real estate investment analysis.

The Choice of Investor Objectives

Investors often say that they have several different reasons for investing in real estate. Some of the more frequently cited reasons are listed in Table 2–1.

Some investors seek income; some seek appreciation. Others purchase real estate as an inflation hedge; others purchase it to gain from leverage. Still others have nonfinancial objectives, such as control over tangible assets and power to build structures on the site. Some investors may purchase real estate in an attempt to avoid paying rent to a third party. All of these reasons may be part of the same story. And all of them are consistent with the fact that real estate provides a host of opportunities for various types of investors.

Another issue deals with the behavior of investors. Traditionally, it has been assumed that investors are interested in maximizing some type of combination of benefits. For example, an investor may be interested in choosing the project with the greatest amount of after-tax cash flow.

TABLE 2–1
POSSIBLE INVESTOR OBJECTIVES

1. Maximization of gross income
2. Maximization of net income
3. Maximization of taxable income
4. Maximization of before-tax cash flow
5. Maximization of after-tax cash flow
6. Maximization of income after taxes
7. Maximization of leverage gains
8. Maximization of depreciation write-offs
9. Maximization of interest deductions
10. Maximization of appreciation
11. Minimization of operating expenses
12. Minimization of negative before-tax cash flow
13. Minimization of negative after-tax cash flow
14. Minimization of income taxation
15. Minimization of management expenses
16. Minimization of financing expenses
17. Minimization of required equity down payment
18. Achievement of an "acceptable rate of return"
19. Achievement of "sufficient returns to pyramid"
20. Achievement of "satisfactory" results
21. Maximization of profits
22. Maximization of rate of return
23. Maximization of social benefits
24. Maximization of wealth

Some analysts, however, may not use a maximization objective; they may be "satisfied" with a certain level of cash flow. These investors would be interested in securing projects that meet certain criteria. Once such projects had been found, they would be deemed acceptable and the searching for other projects would cease.

Finally, there may be investors who are interested in a different type of objective. These investors seek to minimize some cost. For example, an investor interested in minimizing tax liability or minimizing required equity contributions might choose a different project than an investor who follows a different objective. In these cases, the investor's specific circumstances may dictate the choice of investment project.

THE GOAL OF WEALTH MAXIMIZATION

It is argued in this book that the appropriate goal for most investors is to maximize investor wealth. As will be shown in Chapter 12, this goal is not the same as maximization of rate of return. However, the goal *is* consistent with choosing projects using the net present value of equity technique.

There are several attractive features of the goal of wealth maximization. It is general, so it can be applied to a wide range of investors and types of investments. It is broad, so it can take into account several of the attributes that go into real estate as an investment. It is consistent with the well-being of investors in that the project that increases the wealth of the investor the most is the project that makes the investor best off.

Suppose an investor wanted cash flow and inflation hedge from an investment. The investor might consider a number of projects that are expected to yield these benefits. If the investor were to select a project based on only those two characteristics, considerations such as appreciation, management concerns, and leverage choices might be neglected. Even though the investor was concerned primarily with only two of the aspects of real estate as an investment, it is reasonable to presume, for example, that the investor would prefer more appreciation to less, fewer management problems to more, and greater leverage gains to less, for the same amount of cash flow, inflation hedge, and risk. Therefore, it is important that the investor's objective take all those things into account.

The objective of wealth maximization does precisely that if the measurement of additions to wealth is robust enough. As will be shown later in this chapter, the net present value of equity is a model that indicates how much wealth the investor receives as a result of purchasing the investment. Therefore, with a model such as the net present value of equity, the investor can feel confident that choosing projects according to the results of the model will yield the highest returns possible, on an expected basis, taking into account cash flow, appreciation, leverage, managerial expenses, inflation, and other concerns. In addition, the model can take into account risk preferences of different investors, as well as various risk levels of different projects. Therefore, the model is well suited for investors seeking to maximize their wealth positions through investment in real estate.[2]

THE STORY OF REAL ESTATE: A PARABLE

> *Once upon a time, in a land not so far away, there was a unique asset called real estate. It was widely heralded as being the very best investment in the world. It promised the highest income for its owner, and the highest rates of appreciation, throughout the land. It also kept up with or exceeded the rate of inflation in most years, could be financed with "other people's money" to a large extent, and provided*

[2]It should be noted that these statements held true only for the analysis of individual real estate investments. In a portfolio context, the goal of wealth maximization continues to hold, but the choice of individual investments may vary.

opportunities for direct management and control. And it also came in several sizes and shapes for investors with different preferences, expectations, and budgets.

With such credentials, it did not take very long for real estate to become the most active and most talked about investment in the land. Fewer and fewer investors looked elsewhere; everyone became interested in owning real estate. Indeed books were written at a rapid pace in those days. Advertisements appeared in all newspapers and bulletins. People gave up their full-time jobs to become investors. Few members of the town were unaware of these developments.

But in a matter of weeks, it seemed, trouble began. Despite all the interest in real estate, it became increasingly difficult to find property for sale. At the time, this seemed illogical. In retrospect, however, this development occurred for two reasons. First, with everyone wanting to buy and few individuals wanting to sell real estate, it is not surprising that it was difficult to find real estate for sale. Second, when someone did want to sell (generally, that person didn't "want" to sell, instead "had" to sell for some reason unrelated to the attractiveness of the property), the property was on the market for only a very short period of time. (This was often as little as a few days in the beginning, but by the end of this period it had dropped to only a few hours! It had been rumored that if this kept up, property would be sold within minutes!)

Everyone thought the world was doomed because unless you knew someone with "too much" real estate (an unlikely prospect for most people), you were likely to, as it was said, "never get your hands on some." However, it didn't take very long before a new development took place which led to a new complaint that was heard throughout the land. Not only was it difficult to find property for sale—and if you were so lucky, you had to buy it immediately before someone else bought it—but one day the leaders of the town observed that real estate was beginning to sell for increasingly higher prices. This was thought to be a terrible development in the overall scheme of things, since real estate was so very important to the people of this town. It had become the focus of their lives.

Indeed, as more parcels were sold, it became clear to everyone that the price of real estate was steadily rising. This development was generally condemned by all, but the real estate buying continued at a rapid pace. Landowners were accused of being greedy and sinful. Investors were threatened by governmental officials and their jealous neighbors. Potential investors were also angry, but this was probably because they were too late to get in on the action.

It didn't take long before the price of real estate was quite high. Real estate became known as a great thing to own but something that was impossible to buy. Investors began to return to stocks, bonds, and other types of investments. People began to think about other things, once again.

Something else happened, as well. The rate of return from holding real estate began to fall. The income and appreciation that was expected now became increasingly a matter of concern because without them the investors would lose money. The most recent investors made the most noise because they seemed to accept the facts the hardest: They weren't going to get rich by owning real estate. In addition, lenders saw that they could make a lot more money by charging increasingly higher and higher rates on their loans, especially on long-term mortgages. Some lenders even invested in real estate themselves. The tax law hadn't changed, but it seemed that new investors couldn't benefit as much as in the old days.

In the end, some investors never quite recovered from these developments. They seemed to spend the rest of their lives telling stories about the "good old days" when real estate was "selling for a song." Other investors could never understand what had happened to the real estate market. They often blamed the "developers from the East" and the "greed of the bankers" for ruining the opportunities for investors.

And, there was another group who never really said much about the changes except that one could tell that they had changed as well; they were never quite as interested in real estate again. Some became interested in oil and gas technology; others invested in computer firms and microcomputer software. They seemed happy enough and they seemed to make just as much money, but they never talked about real estate again.

Simply because real estate possesses several investment attributes does not mean real estate is a good investment. In the beginning of time it may have been true, but in modern times there is a different story to tell.

THE CONCEPT OF MARKET EFFICIENCY

The attractiveness of real estate as an investment vehicle is well known. The special features of the asset, such as a fixed supply, longevity, and the heterogeneity of each parcel, suggest that real estate would be of special interest to numerous investors. In addition, governmental policies traditionally have been favorable to real estate since the founding of our nation and especially during the present century. Finally, several institutions have emerged to deal with real estate. These institutions not only finance complex investments, but offer very specialized and highly professional management services. There are also highly specialized brokerage firms that facilitate the buying and selling details in the real estate business. As a result, there is an extraordinary amount of interest in real estate markets.

The concept of *market efficiency* refers to the extent to which market prices reflect available information about buyer and seller behavior. This notion of efficiency does not refer to how well the market works in terms of enabling investors, for example, to sell as quickly and as cheaply as possible, or how long it takes or how difficult it is for a local banker to approve a borrower's application for a 30-year mortgage. This definition of market efficiency refers to how rapidly public information about the attractiveness (or unattractiveness) of market investments affects the market's price.[3] If the market price quickly and accurately reflects the available information, the market is said to be *efficient*. If the market price does not reflect the information (that is, the price is slow or very slow to adjust to the new information), the market is said to be *inefficient*.

[3]This concept of efficiency refers to *informational* efficiency rather than economic, operational, or other types.

Whether or not the market meets the efficiency test is an important determination. If the market is found to be relatively efficient, then it is unlikely that investors, using market information, will be able to earn high rates of return with low levels of risk on a consistent basis (sometimes called "abnormal returns"). The reason is that in such a market, the attractive attributes about the investment are likely to be reflected in the price prior to the investor's purchase.

If the market is not very efficient, some investors may be able to use favorable (unfavorable) information to buy (sell) real estate before others know about the information and adjust their expectations upward (downward). If so, trading in an inefficient market suggests the possibility of such abnormal returns for investors. All one has to do is find such a market and obtain new information before others do and exploit this information so as to make better investment decisions as a result.

This approach becomes an important part of the method in this book. The real estate investment process can be used to ensure that real estate parcels are selling for their "correct" (that is, efficient) prices. If a parcel of real estate is available for a different price than the investor believes is the efficient one, the investor may be in a position to buy it and earn an abnormal return on the investment.

WHAT IS A GOOD INVESTMENT?

It is now quite easy to define a good investment. A *good investment* is *one that promises an abnormally high rate of return*. Stated another way, a good investment is one that is "worth" more than it "costs." Such an investment expects to yield a high rate of return relative to an expected small amount of risk. Clearly, every investor would be interested in investments with a weak and favorable relationship between the expected rate of return and the expected level of risk.

Unfortunately, (but not unexpectedly!) in many markets in the real world, it is difficult to find investments that promise high returns and low risks. (After all, if they were readily available, who wouldn't buy them!) Indeed, it is unlikely that available information would not affect prices of real estate. The only question is, How rapidly are such prices affected?

In real estate markets, researchers do not know enough about the extent to which markets meet the efficiency test. There is some evidence that in the long run, risk and return are closely related. There is also some evidence that the returns from investing in real estate and in unimproved land approximate the returns from investing in other areas, once risk is adjusted for. This is precisely what would be expected in a market economy with numerous participants, considerable interest, and a healthy flow of market information.

CAN WE MEASURE A GOOD INVESTMENT?

There is an excellent way of testing to see if real estate is a good investment or not, using the definition above. A well-known investment model called the equity valuation model can be used to identify potentially good investments. The equity investment model has two forms: the net present value of equity (NPV_e) and the internal rate of return on equity (IRR_e). Both can be used to select good investments. However, as will be shown in Chapter 12, these models are not interchangeable, and care should be used when selecting between the two.

The *net present value of equity* is defined as the difference between the investment value of equity and the required equity outlay. Mathematically, this model can be represented as follows:

$$NPV_e = \sum_{t=1}^{n} \frac{ATCF_t}{(1 + k_e)^t} + \frac{ATER_n}{(1 + k_e)^n} - (MV - MD) \qquad (2\text{--}1)$$

where:

$$NPV_e = \text{net present value of equity,}$$
$$ATCF_t = \text{after-tax cash flow in the } t\text{th period,}$$
$$ATER_n = \text{after-tax equity reversion in the } n\text{th period,}$$
$$n = \text{expected holding period,}$$
$$k_e = \text{required rate of return on equity,}$$
$$MV = \text{current market value of the property, and}$$
$$MD = \text{current market value of the debt.}$$

If the net present value of equity is greater than zero, this tells the investor that the present value of equity (the present value of the after-tax cash flows each tth period plus the present value of the after-tax equity reversion at the end of the nth period, discounted by the required rate of return on equity) is greater than the required equity outlay (the difference between the market value of the property at the time of acquisition and the mortgage used to finance the purchase, or the equity down payment). In such cases, the investor should buy the property.

If the net present value of equity is less than zero, the investor should avoid the property because the investor would be buying a parcel of real estate where the cost of the investment (that is, the down payment) is expected to exceed the present value of the benefits (that is, the investment value of equity). If so, the investor would be worse off by purchasing the investment.

There is also a similar rate-of-return calculation. This approach is called the *internal rate of return on equity*. The *IRR* is defined as the rate that will make the present value of the cash inflows equivalent to the present value of the outflows. Another way to define the IRR is to say that it is the rate that will make the NPV of an investment equal to zero. This measure is defined as the rate, IRR, such that Equation (2–2) holds true:

$$0 = \sum_{t=1}^{n} \frac{ATCF_t}{(1 + IRR_e)^t} + \frac{ATER_n}{(1 + IRR_e)^n} - (MV - MD) \qquad (2\text{--}2)$$

where:

$$IRR_e = \text{internal rate of return on equity.}$$

In this case, a comparison is required between the expected rate of return on equity and the required rate of return on equity. If the internal rate is not less than the required rate, the investment is an attractive one for the investor.

To illustrate how the equity valuation model can be used by real estate investors and is related to our discussion in Chapter 1, Example 2–1 is provided for a small, income-producing, residential investment.

Why the "Efficient Market Hypothesis" Is Important
The concept of market efficiency is often referred to as the "efficient market hypothesis," or EMH. Based on the research in financial markets in the 1960s, this name was given to a method of approaching the analysis of assets and prices in various types of markets. The text briefly describes the central idea of the concept of market efficiency. Interested readers are referred to any modern corporate finance or investment text for additional discussion.

The EMH is important for real estate as well as other analyses because it provides a basis for the analysis of market prices and investor behavior. If this approach is adopted, investors can assume that when, for example, a real estate investment is sold, both the buyer and the seller, using market and perhaps other kinds of information, come to an agreement (a "meeting of the minds"). As a result, unless there is evidence to the contrary, it may be presumed that the value of the property is the sale price as of the date of the transaction. The EMH tells us that available information affecting the value of the asset now and in the future is likely to be used by market participants when making actual transactions.

Note that the EMH does not require that investors predict the future. Nor does it presume that all investors earn the same rate of return. In fact, the EMH may be useful even if the particular real estate market is sometimes slow to adjust to new information that subsequently affects actual prices. The EMH permits the analysis of market behavior under the belief (and, it is hoped, evidence) that, in general, available information is used by market participants such that eventual sales prices will reflect available information *before* the sale takes place. If so, the EMH will serve as a valuable framework for understanding market activities as a conceptual basis for making real-world, normative investment decisions.

In recent years, there is a growing body of evidence about the degree of efficiency in real estate markets. A recent survey found considerable evidence about the appropriateness of the EMH for real estate. Despite data problems and the complexity of real estate markets, the EMH remains a central concept for real estate investors.

EXAMPLE 2–1. THE EQUITY VALUATION MODEL

The basic model in this chapter is referred to as the *equity valuation model*. This example illustrates how to implement the model using the small, income-producing, residential property described in Chapter 1.

Suppose Patricia is considering investing in a four-unit residential dwelling. After investigating market conditions and comparable real estate in the area, she concludes the following:

$160,000	Purchase price
$145,000	Building value
80%	Loan-to-value ratio
12%	Interest rate
25 years	Loan term, monthly compounding
$32,000	First-year gross income, increasing $1,500 each year
3% of PGI	Vacancy and bad debt allowance
$7,500	First year operating expenses; $7,800 in year 2; $8,200 in year 3
$175,000	Resale price
$17,000	Selling expenses
3 years	Holding period
28%	Marginal tax rate
14%	Required rate of return on equity
3% of loan	Financing costs

First, Patricia calculated the expected after-tax cash flows for each year and the expected after-tax equity reversion in year 3 following the tables in Chapter 1. Then she compares the present value of these cash inflows, given her required rate of return on equity of 14%, to her cash outflows at the time of purchase. This results in the net present value of equity, as depicted in Equation (2–1). From this analysis, she can then calculate the expected rate of return, as depicted in Equation (2–2).

TABLE A
EXPECTED CASH FLOW FROM OPERATIONS

	Year 1	Year 2	Year 3
Potential gross income	$32,000	$33,500	$35,000
− Vacancy and bad debts	960	1,005	1,050
Effective gross income	31,040	32,495	33,950
− Operating expenses	7,500	7,800	8,200
Net operating income	23,540	24,695	25,750
− Annual debt service	16,174	16,174	16,174
Before-tax cash flow	7,366	8,521	9,576
− Taxes from operations*	784	1,139	523
After-tax cash flow	$ 6,582	$ 7,382	$ 9,053

* See Table B.

	Year 1	Year 2	Year 3
Effective gross income	$31,040	$32,495	$33,950
− Operating expenses	7,500	7,800	8,200
Net operating income	23,540	24,695	25,750
− Interest on debt	15,310	15,200	15,077
− Depreciation deduction	5,273	5,273	5,273
− Financing costs	154	154	3,532
+ Replacement reserves	0	0	0
Ordinary taxable income	2,803	4,068	1,868
× Investor's marginal tax rate	0.28	0.28	0.28
Taxes from operation	$ 784	$ 1,139	$ 523

At the end of year 3, Patricia expects to sell the four-plex for $175,000 and incur $17,000 in selling expenses. She must pay the unpaid mortgage balance at the end of year 3 and pay any taxes due on sale. This yields the after-tax equity reversion (cash flow from sale).

TABLE C
EXPECTED CASH FLOW FROM SALE

Expected selling price	$175,000
− Selling expenses	17,000
Net sales proceeds	158,000
− Unpaid mortgage balance	125,065
Before-tax equity reversion	32,935
− Taxes due on sale*	3,869
After-tax equity reversion	$ 29,066

* See Table D.

TABLE D
EXPECTED TAXES DUE ON SALE

Expected selling price	$175,000
− Selling expenses	17,000
Amount realized	158,000
− Adjusted basis	144,181
Total gain on sale	13,819
× Investor's marginal tax rate	0.28
Taxes due on sale	3,869

Patricia is now positioned to calculate whether she should invest in the project, *given her required rate of return on equity and other assumptions.*

TABLE E
NET PRESENT VALUE OF AN INVESTMENT AT 14%

Year	Equity	ATCF	ATER	PVF @ 14%	NPV
0	$(35,840)	—	—	1.00000	$(35,840)
1		6,582	—	0.87720	5,774
2		7,382	—	0.76947	5,680
3		9,053	29,066	0.67497	25,729
				NPV of equity =	$ 1,343
				IRR on equity =	15.7%

Because Patricia's net present value of equity is greater than zero, she should invest in the project. In other words, this investment is "worth" $1,343 more to her than it "costs." The internal rate of return on the project is approximately 15.7%, which is greater than her required rate of return of 14%. In later chapters, we will examine in more detail all of the calculations shown in this simple example.

WHY THE EQUITY VALUATION MODEL WORKS

The equity valuation model is an extremely useful tool for real estate investors because it identifies for each investor, at any point in time, (a) those investments that are expected to make the investor wealthier and (b) those investments that are expected to make the investor poorer. A frequently accepted goal for investors is to increase their wealth as much as possible by investing in real estate. If this is accepted as a goal, the equity valuation model shows clearly whether potential investments are acceptable or not. However, if the question is which of several investments should be chosen, the investor *cannot* use either the net present value or the internal rate of return versions of the equity valuation model. (This issue is addressed at length in Chapter 12.)

The equity valuation model provides answers to the central question in real estate investment analysis, Will the acquisition of the parcel of real estate under consideration be likely to make the investor richer or poorer in a world of risk and uncertainty? This model enables the investor to identify in a systematic fashion the parameters that affect the answer to the question and quantify several of the important parts of the question. While good judgment is always required, the model enables the investor to come to terms with the central issue and make a decision of critical importance to the success of the venture.

SUMMARY

Real estate investment analysis involves the analysis of several things. First, many attributes of real estate make it a potential investment for many people. Second, in well-functioning markets, it is reasonable to expect a close relationship between risk and return. Third, the concept of market efficiency is important in that the degree of efficiency is likely to affect the potential opportunities for real estate investors. Fourth, a good investment is one that increases the wealth of the investor on a risk-adjusted basis. Fifth, the equity valuation model can be used to identify potential investments that are expected to add to the wealth of specific investors. Finally, the equity valuation model has two formats: the net present value of equity and the internal rate of return on equity. Both can be used to identify good investments, but there are some critical differences between the models.

QUESTIONS

2–1. Is there a difference between *speculation* and *investment*? Explain.

2–2. What characteristics of real estate help to distinguish it from other investments?

2–3. Do you think there is a precise trade-off between risk and return in real estate mar-

kets? What are the implications of your answer?

2–4. The text provides a list of several investor objectives. Is the goal of wealth maximization superior to many of these objectives? Why or why not?

2–5. What does the concept of market efficiency mean for real estate investors?

2–6. The text defines a *good investment* as one with an expected abnormally high rate of return. Do you think real estate markets frequently provide these types of opportunities? Why or why not?

2–7. Demonstrate how the use of the equity investment model can be used by real world investors.

PROBLEMS

2–1. Suppose you had the following choices:
a.

Investment	Expected Rate of Return	Standard Deviation
A	15%	2%
B	15%	3%

Which investment would you prefer?
b.

Investment	Expected Rate of Return	Standard Deviation
C	15%	3%
D	16%	3%

Which investment would you prefer?
c.

Investment	Expected Rate of Return	Standard Deviation
E	15%	3%
F	16%	4%

Which investment would you prefer?

2–2. An investment has a total value of $200,000. The investor can borrow $150,000. The present value of the expected after-tax cash flow (from operation and reversion) is $40,000. Is this a good investment?

2–3. Suppose you have the following information:

Investment	NPV
A	$5,000
B	8,000

Which investment would you prefer?

2–4. A particular real estate investment was purchased for $500,000 (all cash). It was sold one year later for $525,000. It also generated $50,000 in income during that year. What was the investor's actual rate of return?

2–5. You have been given the opportunity to invest in a parcel of vacant land. The price is $100,000. You expect to sell the land for $120,000 one year from now. Given the riskiness of this type of investment, you feel that the required rate of return should be 25 percent. Is this a good investment?

2–6. Using Equation (2–1) in the chapter, compute the net present value of equity given the following:

Year	Market Value	Mortgage Debt	ATCF	ATER
0	$500,000	$400,000		
1			$10,000	
2			12,000	
3			18,000	
4			13,000	
5			8,000	$100,000

The investor's required rate of return is 15 percent.

2–7. Illustrate that as the required rate of return on equity increases, the NPV of equity decreases.

2–8. Using the facts in Problem 2–6 and Equation (2–2) in the chapter, compute the internal rate of return on equity.

2–9. Using Figure 2–1, what happens to the risk-return trade-off if:
   a. Expected inflation suddenly increases?
   b. There is an increase in the risk premium?

2–10. Given the information in Example 2–1, Patricia is forced to choose between the investment opportunity in the chapter and one with the following cash flows.

Year	Equity	ATCF	ATER
0	(40,000)	—	
1		11,000	
2		9,000	
3		8,000	28,500

   a. Calculate the NPV for this project.
   b. If Patricia's investor goal is to maximize after-tax cash flows, which opportunity would she choose? Why?
   c. If Patricia's goal is to maximize wealth, which opportunity should she choose? Why?
   d. If Patricia's goal is to minimize her required equity down payment, which opportunity should she choose? Why?

SELECTED REFERENCES

Bedford, E. W., "Why Buy Real Estate?" *Appraisal Journal*, 13 (April 1945), 135–37.

Gau, George W., "Efficient Real Estate Markets: Paradox or Paradigm?" *American Real Estate and Urban Economics Association Journal*, 15 (Summer 1987), 1–12.

Lusht, Kenneth M., "The Real Estate Pricing Puzzle," *American Real Estate and Urban Economics Association Journal*, 16 (Spring 1988), 95–104.

Miles, Mike, Rebel Cole, and David Guilkey, "A Different Look at Commercial Real Estate Returns," *Journal of the American Real Estate and Urban Economics Association*, 18 (1990), 403–431.

Miles, Mike, and Thomas McCue, "Historical Returns and Individual Real Estate Portfolios," *American Real Estate and Urban Economics Association Journal*, 10 (Summer 1982), 184–199.

Ross, Stephen A., and Randall C. Zisler, "Risk and Return in Real Estate," *Journal of Real Estate Finance and Economics*, 4 (June 1991), 175–190.

Scott, Louis W., "Do Prices Reflect Market Fundamentals in Real Estate Markets?," *Journal of Real Estate Finance and Economics*, 3 (March 1990), 5–24.

Sirmans, C. F., and James R. Webb, "Investment Yields in the Money, Capital, and Real Estate Markets: A Comparative Analysis for 1951–1976," *Real Estate Appraiser*, 44 (November–December 1978), 47–51.

Sirmans, G. Stacy, and C. F. Sirmans, "The Historical Perspectives of Real Estate Returns," *Journal of Portfolio Management*, 4 (Spring 1987), 22–31.

Wendt, Paul F., and Sui N. Wong, "Investment Performance—Common Stocks versus Apartment Houses," *Journal of Finance*, 20 (December 1965), 633–46.

Zerbst, Robert H., and Barbara R. Cambon, "Real Estate: Historical Returns and Risks," *Journal of Portfolio Management*, 10 (Spring 1984), 5–20.

CHAPTER 3

REAL ESTATE INVESTMENT MATHEMATICS

PRINCIPLES

1. Modern real estate investment analysis requires some mathematical technology.
2. Mastering this technology is essential and far from impossible.
3. The mathematics of real estate investment involves only simple algebra and relates directly to the tables in Appendix A.

In this chapter we review some of the basic mathematical mechanics for making real estate investment decisions. Specifically, we discuss how to calculate the following:

The future value of a lump-sum present amount.

The future value of a series of payments.

The necessary payments to accumulate a future amount.

The present value of a lump-sum future amount.

The present value of a series of unequal future amounts.

The rate of return on an investment. This rate is generally referred to as the *internal rate of return.*

The mechanics of a mortgage.

Compound Interest Tables

The compound interest tables in Appendix A are used in making real estate investment decisions. There are three sets of tables:

Table 1—Present Value of $1.00 Factors

Table 2—Mortgage Constant (Monthly Payments)

Table 3—Proportion of Mortgage Outstanding

Table 1 provides the factors for finding the present value of a payment to be made in the future at various rates of discount. Table 2 provides the mortgage constant factors for monthly payments. The mortgage constant, when multiplied by the amount borrowed, tells the investor the payment necessary to fully amortize (pay off) the loan. Table 3 provides the proportions outstanding on mortgages. These are useful in determining the interest-principal amounts on mortgages.

Table 3–1 provides the equations necessary to calculate these values. The equations in this table calculate the values on an annual compounding basis. The period of compounding may also be on a quarterly, monthly, or daily basis. In order to calculate the values with alternative compounding periods, the annual interest rate must be divided by the number of periods and the number of years multiplied by the number of periods.

How to Calculate Future Value

The future value of $1.00 factor (FVF) is calculated using the following equation:

$$FVF_{i,n} = (1 + i)^n \qquad (3\text{–}1)$$

where:

$FVF_{i,n}$ = future value of $1.00 factor at rate i for n periods

i = rate of interest

n = number of periods

The future value of any present amount is calculated by multiplying the future value factor by the present amount. In equation form:

$$FV = (FVF_{i,n})PV \qquad (3\text{–}2)$$

TABLE 3–1
COMPOUND INTEREST FUNCTIONS

Function	Symbol	Equation	Description
Future value of lump sum factor	FVF	$FV_{i,n} = PV(1 + i)^n$	Amount that will accumulate by investing a present amount today for n periods at i interest rate
Future value of an annuity factor	FVAF	$FVA_{i,n} = ANN \dfrac{(1 + i)^n - 1}{i}$	Accumulated value of annual payments for n years at i interest rate
Sinking fund factor	SFF	$ANN_{i,n} = FVA \dfrac{i}{(1 + i)^n - 1}$	Amount needed to invest annually at i interest rate to accumulate a desired future amount at the end of n years
Present value of lump sum factor	PVF	$PV_{i,n} = FV \dfrac{i}{(1 + i)^n}$	Worth today of a future lump sum to be received n periods in the future at i interest rate
Present value of an annuity factor	PVAF	$PVA_{i,n} = ANN \dfrac{1 - \dfrac{1}{(1 + i)^n}}{i}$	Worth today of a series of equal amounts to be received at the end of each year for n years at i annual interest rate
Mortgage constant	MC	$ANN_{i,n} = PVA \dfrac{i}{1 - \dfrac{1}{(1 + i)^n}}$	Payment necessary for n years at i annual interest rate to amortize a present amount

where:

$$PV = \text{present value}$$

$$FV = \text{future value}$$

❒ **EXAMPLE 1: FUTURE VALUE OF A PRESENT AMOUNT.** What is the future value of $1.00 six years from now, compounded at 12 percent per year?

$$\text{Future value} = FVF_{i,n} \text{ (present value)}$$

$$= (1 + .12)^6 \ (\$1.00)$$

$$= 1.97382 \ (\$1.00)$$

$$= \$1.97382$$

Thus, $1.00 six years from now is worth about $1.97, at a compounded rate of 12 percent. The factor, 1.97382, at 12 percent interest for six years, can be found by solving Equation (3–1).

Stated differently, if an investor pays $1.00 for an investment and sells it six years later for $1.97, the investor will earn a 12% rate of return.

❐ **EXAMPLE 2: FUTURE VALUE OF A LUMP SUM.**   Suppose a real estate investor is considering purchasing a parcel of vacant land. The investor borrows $25,000 today and wants to repay the loan in a lump sum (with 12 percent interest) five years from now. How much would the investor owe after five years?

The future value of $25,000 five years from now at a rate of 12 percent is

$$\text{Future value} = \text{Present value } (\text{FVF}_{i,n})$$

$$= (\$25,000)(1.12)^5$$

$$= \$25,000 \ (1.76234)$$

$$= \$44,059$$

Thus if the investor borrowed $25,000 for the investment, a payment of $44,059 would be due five years later at an interest rate of 12 percent.

❐ **EXAMPLE 3: FUTURE VALUE OF A REGULAR ANNUITY.**   Suppose you want to save for the down payment on a piece of real estate. If you can deposit $10,000 at the end of each year into a savings account, how much will you accumulate at the end of five years if the account pays 8 percent interest compounded annually?

$$\text{Future value of annuity } (\text{FVA}_{i,n}) = \text{ANN}(\text{FVAF}_{i,n})$$

where:

$\text{FVA}_{i,n}$ = future value of an annuity

$\text{FVAF}_{i,n}$ = future value of an annuity factor at rate i for n periods

ANN = series of equal payments

$$\text{FVA}_{i,n} = \text{ANN} \left(\frac{(1 + i)^n - 1}{i} \right) \tag{3–3}$$

$$= \$10,000 \ (5.8666)$$

$$= \$58,666$$

The future value annuity factor, 5.8666, can be calculated by using the FVAF equation found in Table 3–1. Multiplying this factor by the expected $10,000 results in a sum of $58,666. Thus, if the investor deposits $10,000 annually at a rate of 8 percent for 5 years, a down payment of $58,666 would be accumulated five years later.

❏ **Example 4: Calculating a Regular Payment to Earn a Specified Amount.** Suppose you own an apartment complex and you would like to start a replacement reserve account to buy new stoves and refrigerators three years in the future. You estimate that you will need $33,100 by the end of 3 years. You want to know how much you must set aside in an account paying 10 percent interest per year.

We can rewrite the SFF equation in Table 3–1 to solve for the unknown, which is the annuity:

$$ANN_{i,n} = FVA(SFF_{i,n})$$

where:

$ANN_{i,n}$ = amount needed to invest annually

$SFF_{i,n}$ = sinking fund factor at rate i for n periods

$$ANN_{i,n} = FVA \left(\frac{i}{(1 + i)^n - 1} \right) \tag{3–4}$$

$$= \$33,100 \, (.30211)$$

$$= \$10,000$$

How to Calculate Present Value

The present value of $1.00 factors in Table 1 of Appendix A are constructed using the following equation:

$$PVF_{i,n} = \frac{1}{(1 + i)^n} \tag{3–5}$$

where:

$PVF_{i,n}$ = present value of $1.00 factor at rate i for n periods

i = rate of discount

n = number of periods

The present value of any future amount is calculated by multiplying the present value factor by the future amount. In equation form:

$$PV = (PVF_{i,n})FV \tag{3-6}$$

where:

PV = present value

FV = future value

❏ **EXAMPLE 5: PRESENT VALUE OF A FUTURE AMOUNT.** What is the present value of $1.00 to be received six years in the future, discounted at 12 percent per year?

$$\text{Present value} = PVF_{i,n} \text{ (future value)}$$

$$= \frac{1}{(1 + .12)^6}(\$1.00)$$

$$= .50663 (\$1.00)$$

$$= \$.50663$$

Thus, $1.00 to be received six years from now is worth about 51 cents today, at a discount rate of 12 percent. The factor, .50663, for 12 percent interest for six years, can be found in Table 1 of Appendix A by using the column labeled 12 percent for six years.

Stated differently, an investor could pay 51 cents today for an investment that would sell for $1.00 six years in the future and earn a rate of return of 12 percent.

❏ **EXAMPLE 6: PRESENT VALUE OF A LUMP SUM.** Suppose a real estate investor is considering purchasing a parcel of vacant land. The investor expects to sell the parcel for $25,000 five years from now. How much could be paid today for the investment if the investor wants to earn a return of 15 percent per year?

The present value of $25,000 five years from now at a rate of 15 percent is

$$\text{Present value} = \text{Future value } (PVF_{i,n})$$

$$\text{Present value} = (\$25,000)\frac{1}{(1.15)^5}$$

$$= \$25,000 (.49718)$$

$$= \$12,430$$

The present value factor, .49718, can be found in Table 1 of Appendix A by using the column labeled 15 percent for five years. Multiplying this factor by the expected $25,000 results in a price of $12,430. Thus if the investor paid $12,430 for the investment and sold it for $25,000 in five years, the rate of return would be 15 percent per year.

❑ **EXAMPLE 7: RATE OF RETURN.** Suppose the investor in Example 6 paid $13,570 for the parcel of land and sold it five years later for $25,000. What would be the rate of return on the investment?

In this type of situation, we know the present value ($13,570) and the future value ($25,000). What we do not know is the rate that will make the two values equal after a five-year period of time. The answer can be found as follows:

$$\text{Present value} = \text{Future value } (PVF_{i,n})$$

$$\$13,570 = \$25,000 \ (PVF_{i,5})$$

$$.5428 = (PVF_{i,5})$$

The question is, What rate (i) will make this equation true?

One solution is to simply choose an i and solve the equation. Suppose, for example, we were to "guess" 12 percent. Solving the equation yields:

$$.5428 = \frac{1}{(1.12)^5}$$

$$.5428 \neq .5674$$

Obviously the equation does not hold at 12 percent. Thus we must pick another rate. Should it be larger or smaller than 12 percent. It should be larger. Why? Because the larger the rate, the smaller the number yielded by the right-hand side of the equation. (The reciprocal of 1.12 raised to the fifth power is larger than, for example, the reciprocal of 1.15 raised to the fifth power. Try it and see.)

Thus, suppose we select 13 percent. Solving the equation:

$$.5428 = \frac{1}{(1.13)^5}$$

$$.5428 = .5428$$

Thus the correct rate is 13 percent. If the investor paid $13,570 for an investment and sold it five years later for $25,000, the rate of return would be 13 percent per year.

Another solution is to take the equation

$$.5428 = \frac{1}{(1 + i)^5} = PVF_{i,5}$$

and look through the factors in Table 1 of the Appendix for five years until the factor .5428 is found. This factor is found in the 13 percent column for five years.[1]

☐ **EXAMPLE 8: PRESENT VALUE OF AN UNEQUAL SERIES.** A real estate investment is expected to produce the after-tax cash flows (ATCFs) shown in Table 3–2. What is the present value of these cash flows at a rate of 12 percent? The present value factors (PVF) from Table 1 in Appendix A at 12 percent are shown in column 3. Multiplying these factors by the yearly ATCF yields the present value of each cash flow. Adding the present values results in a total present value of $85,498.68. What does this mean to the investor? It means that the investor can pay up to $85,498.68 for the investment and, assuming the investment generates the expected ATCF, earn a rate of return of 12 percent per year.

Suppose the investor pays more than $85,498.68 for the investment. What would happen to the rate of return? It would be lower. For example, if the investor paid $90,289.55, the rate of return would be 10 percent. Should the opposite occur and the investor pays $79,032.51, the rate of return rises to 15 percent. Thus, the lower the price, the higher the rate of return for a given set of cash flows. Note, however, that these changes are based on the assumption that the estimated ATCFs are correct. The *actual* (realized) rate of return may be different from the *expected* if the actual cash flows are different from the expected. The actual return cannot be calcu-

TABLE 3–2
EXAMPLE OF PRESENT VALUE OF AN UNEQUAL SERIES

(1)	(2)	(3)	(4)
		Present Value	
Year	ATCF	Factor @ 12%	Present Value
1	$20,000	.89286	$17,857.20
2	20,400	.79719	16,262.68
3	30,000	.71178	21,353.40
4	20,600	.63552	13,091.71
5	20,200	.56743	11,462.09
6	10,800	.50663	5,471.60
		Total present value =	$85,498.68

[1]Alternately, the rate of return may be solved for directly: $i = \sqrt[5]{\$25,000/\$13,570} - 1$, or 13%

lated until an investment is bought, operated, and sold. The actual income streams would then be known with certainty. *Investing, however, requires the investor to commit the outflow in the present in return for the expected (but risky) inflows in the future.*

HOW TO FIND NET PRESENT VALUE

□ **EXAMPLE 9: NET PRESENT VALUE OF AN INVESTMENT.** The net present value (NPV) of an investment is equal to the present value of the inflows minus the present value of the outflows. Suppose an investor pays $97,175 in equity for an investment. The expected cash flows from operations are shown in Table 3–3. What is the *net present value* of the investment? The concept behind NPV is very simple: If an investment is "worth" more than it "costs," then accept it. If not, reject it.

Assuming that the investor requires a 12 percent after-tax rate of return, the net present value is $3,016. The decision rules are:

$$\text{Accept if NPV} \geq \$0, \quad \text{and}$$
$$\text{Reject if NPV} < \$0 \tag{3-7}$$

At a rate of return of 12 percent, the present value of the cash inflows exceeds the present value of the outflows by $3,016. Thus the decision would be to invest. In this example, the cash inflows are "worth" $100,191, but they only "cost" $97,175.

Suppose, however, that the investor requires a higher rate of return. Will the decision still be to invest if the required rate is 14 percent? To find the NPV at 14 percent (PV of cash inflows minus PV of cash outflows), we discount all the cash flows at 14 percent (see Table 3–4).

TABLE 3–3
NET PRESENT VALUE OF AN INVESTMENT AT 12%

Year	Equity	ATCF	ATER	PVF @ 12%	Present Value
0	−$97,175	—		1.00000	−$97,175
1		$20,000		.89286	17,857
2		20,400		.79719	16,263
3		30,000		.71178	21,353
4		20,600		.63552	13,092
5		20,200		.56743	11,462
6		10,800	$29,000	.50663	20,164
				Net present value =	$ 3,016

TABLE 3–4
NET PRESENT VALUE OF AN INVESTMENT AT 14%

Year	Equity	ATCF	ATER	PVF @ 14%	Present Value
0	−$97,175	—		1.00000	−$97,175
1		$20,000		.87720	17,544
2		20,400		.76947	15,697
3		30,000		.67497	20,249
4		20,600		.59208	12,197
5		20,200		.51937	10,491
6		10,800	$29,000	.45559	18,132
				Net present value =	−$ 2,865

The NPV of −$2,865 indicates that an investor requiring a 14 percent rate of return should not invest in this project. As the required rate of return goes up for a given set of cash flows, the NPV decreases.

It seems intuitive that there must be a rate at which the present value of the inflows is equal to the present value of the outflows. This rate is called the *internal rate of return (IRR)* and is illustrated in Example 10.

HOW TO CALCULATE THE RATE OF RETURN

❏ **EXAMPLE 10: RATE OF RETURN ON AN INVESTMENT WITH AN UNEQUAL SERIES.** Continuing with the numbers developed in Examples 8 and 9, what is the expected rate of return? As explained in Chapter 2, the *IRR* is defined as the rate that will make the present value of the cash inflows equivalent to the present value of the outflows. Another way to define the IRR is to say that it is the rate that will make the NPV of an investment equal to zero. There is no simple way to compute the IRR directly without a calculator that performs the function. The alternative is a trial-and-error (or iterative) approach. When a rate of return is tried and the resulting NPV is positive, the rate should be raised. If the NPV is negative, the rate should be lowered.

Returning to Example 9, the foregoing analysis indicates that 12 percent is too low a rate, since the NPV was a positive $3,016, and that 14 percent is too high, since the NPV was a negative $2,865. Therefore, let us try 13 percent (see Table 3–5).

The resulting NPV is a positive $7.00, indicating that the IRR is very close to 13 percent; in fact, it is just above 13 percent (13.0022 percent). This rate, 13.0022 percent, will make the present value of the cash inflows equal

TABLE 3–5
EXAMPLE OF CALCULATING THE INTERNAL RATE OF RETURN (IRR)

Year	Equity	ATCF	ATER	PVF @ 13%	Present Value
0	−$97,175	—		1.00000	−$97,175
1		$20,000		.88496	17,699
2		20,400		.78315	15,976
3		30,000		.69305	20,792
4		20,600		.61332	12,634
5		20,200		.54276	10,964
6		10,800	$29,000	.48032	19,117
				Net present value = $	7

to the cash outflows. Therefore the expected rate of return on the investment of $97,175, assuming the expected cash flows will be realized, is approximately 13 percent. Under these assumptions, the IRR on this investment is 13 percent.

THE MECHANICS OF MORTGAGES

THE MORTGAGE CONSTANT

Table 2 of Appendix A gives the "mortgage constant." The mortgage constant, when multiplied by the amount borrowed, results in the amount of debt service (payment) to be made each period. In equation form:

$$\text{Payment} = \text{Amount borrowed } (MC_{i,n}) \tag{3–8}$$

where:

MC is the mortgage constant at interest rate i for a maturity of n periods.

Table 2 in Appendix A relates to payments made monthly.

❐ **EXAMPLE 11: CALCULATING PAYMENTS ON MONTHLY MORTGAGE.** Mr. B borrows $75,000 from the City Bank. The loan is at 12 percent interest with payments to be made *monthly* over a period of 20 years (240 monthly payments). What is the monthly debt service? Table 2 in Appendix A gives the mortgage constant under monthly payments. At 12 percent interest for 20 years, the monthly mortgage constant is .01101. The monthly payment is thus:

$$\text{Payment} = \text{Amount borrowed } (MC_{i,n})$$

$$= \$75,000\ (.01101)$$

$$= \$825.75$$

The annualized payment is 12 times the monthly payment:[2]

---

[2]Note that the "annualized" payment (the monthly payment times 12) does *not* equal the annual payment that results from compounding of monthly payments within each year.

$$\text{Annual payment} = \$825.75 \ (12)$$

$$= \$9,909$$

Mr. B must make a payment of $825.75 each month for 240 months (or 20 years). At the end of 20 years, he will have amortized (paid off) the entire loan.

☐ **EXAMPLE 12: DETERMINING THE OUTSTANDING BALANCE (MONTHLY PAYMENTS).** What amount of the $75,000 would be outstanding after six years of monthly payments?

There are two procedures that can be used to determine the proportion outstanding.

Under the first approach, the numbers would be calculated as follows. The original amount outstanding is $75,000. The debt service is a constant amount of $825.75 each month. Since the interest rate is 12 percent annually (or 1 percent monthly), the amount of interest in month 1 is $750 ($75,000 × .01). The total payment is $825.75 and the interest payment is $750; thus the principal amount is $75.75 ($825.75 − $750.00). At the end of month 1, the amount outstanding is $74,924.25. This is the original balance, $75,000, minus the principal payment in month 1, $75.75. Using this new balance, the interest payment in the second month is $749.24 ($74,924.25 × .01). The principal payment in the second month is $76.51 ($825.75 minus $749.24). The amount outstanding at the end of the second month is $74,847.74. This process is continued each month.

Note that at the end of six years (72 months), the amount outstanding is $67,061. The original amount was $75,000. This is a proportion of:

$$\text{Proportion outstanding after 6 years} = \frac{\$67,061}{\$75,000}$$

$$= .89415$$

The second approach would use the mortgage constant tables to calculate the proportion outstanding.

$$\text{Proportion outstanding} = \frac{\text{Mortgage constant total term}}{\text{Mortgage constant for remaining term}} \qquad (3\text{--}9)$$

Using the 12 percent, monthly mortgage constant in Table 2 in Appendix A:

$$\text{Proportion outstanding} = \frac{.01101}{.01231}$$

$$= .89439$$

The two methods yield slightly different results due to rounding.

The proportion outstanding after 6 years is found by dividing .01101, the mortgage constant for the total term (12 percent for 20 years, monthly payments), by .01231, the mortgage constant for the remaining term (12 percent for 14 years, monthly payments).

Multiplying the proportion outstanding, .89439, by the original amount, $75,000, yields the amount outstanding after six years:

$$\text{Amount outstanding} = \$75,000\,(.89439)$$

$$= \$67,079.25$$

Table 3 of Appendix A gives the proportion outstanding on mortgages at various interest rates, maturities, and holding periods. These proportions *assume monthly compounding* and are very helpful in setting up the mortgage amortization schedules when monthly payments are made.

☐ **EXAMPLE 13: CALCULATING THE AMORTIZATION SCHEDULE (MONTHLY PAYMENTS).** Allocate the payment in Example 11 between interest and principal for years 1 through 6.

If a mortgage calls for monthly amortization, the first approach in Example 12 for allocating between interest and principal payments each month is a tedious task. The allocation has to be made for each month. Using the proportion outstanding (in Table 3 of Appendix A), the investor can easily allocate between interest and principal as shown in Table 3–6.

The numbers were calculated as follows. The proportion outstanding at the end of each year is found by using Table 3 under 12 percent, 20 year (240 months) maturity. The amount outstanding at the end of each year is found by multiplying the amount borrowed ($75,000) by the pro-

TABLE 3–6
AMORTIZATION SCHEDULE FOR $75,000 MORTGAGE AT 12% RATE FOR 20 YEARS, MONTHLY PAYMENTS

(1)	(2)	(3)	(4)	(5)	(6)
	Proportion	Amount	Annual		
Year	Outstanding*	Outstanding	Debt Service	Interest	Principal
0	1.0000	$75,000			
1	.98718	74,039	$9,909	$8,948	$ 961
2	.97273	72,955	$9,909	8,825	1,084
3	.95646	71,735	$9,909	8,689	1,220
4	.93811	70,358	$9,909	8,532	1,377
5	.91744	68,808	$9,909	8,359	1,550
6	.89415	67,061	$9,909	8,162	1,747

* From Table 3 of Appendix A.

portion outstanding at the end of each year (column 2). The amount of principal each year is found by subtracting the amounts outstanding at the end of each year. For example, the principal payment in year 1 ($961) was calculated by taking the difference between the $75,000 and the amount outstanding at the end of Year 1 ($74,039). The difference between the debt service each year ($9,909) and the principal payment ($961) results in the amount of interest paid in year 1 ($8,948). This process is continued for each year.

EXAMPLE 3–1 USING COMPOUND INTEREST CONCEPTS

Recall from Example 2–1 in Chapter 2 that Patricia was considering investing in a four-unit residential dwelling. This example illustrates how to use the mathematics of compound interest to derive some of the solutions to the cash flow analysis.

ANNUAL DEBT SERVICE

Patricia will borrow 80% of $160,000, or $128,000. Monthly debt service equals the original loan amount multiplied by the monthly mortgage constant, or

$$MC = \frac{\dfrac{i}{m}}{1 - \dfrac{1}{\left(1 + \dfrac{i}{m}\right)^{n \times m}}} = \frac{\dfrac{.12}{12}}{1 - \dfrac{1}{\left(1 + \dfrac{.12}{12}\right)^{25 \times 12}}}$$

$$= \frac{.01}{1 - \left(\dfrac{1}{(1.01)^{300}}\right)} = 0.01053$$

The annual mortgage constant, therefore, is 0.12636. Hence, annual debt service is $16,174 ($128,000 × .12636).

AMORTIZATION SCHEDULE

The proportion outstanding for Patricia's mortgage is

$$\text{Yr 1:} \frac{MC_{(300,.01)}}{MC_{(288,.01)}} = 99.325\%$$

$$\text{Yr 2: } \frac{MC_{(300,.01)}}{MC_{(276,.01)}} = \frac{0.010530}{0.010686} = 98.564\%$$

$$\text{Yr 3: } \frac{MC_{(300,.01)}}{MC_{(264,.01)}} = \frac{0.010530}{0.010780} = 97.707\%$$

Now, she can complete her amortization schedule for a $128,000 mortgage at 12% compounded monthly for 25 years.

(1) Year	(2) Proportion Outstanding	(3) Amount Outstanding	(4) Annual Debt Service	(5) Interest	(6) Principal
0	1.00000	$128,000	—	—	—
1	0.99325	127,136	$16,174	$15,310	$ 864
2	0.98564	126,162	16,174	15,200	974
3	0.97707	125,065	16,174	15,077	1,097

Notice column 6, principal reduction, is calculated by subtracting the amount outstanding this year from the amount outstanding the previous year. For example, principal reduction in year 1 equals $864 ($128,000 − $127,136). Also, annual debt service equals principal plus interest, so interest equals debt service minus principal. Hence, for interest in year 1, subtract $16,174 − 864 to obtain $15,310.

DEPRECIATION

Annual depreciation equals the depreciable asset (that is, the improvements) divided by the useful life of 27.5 years for residential income-producing real estate, or $5,273 ($145,000/27.5).

FINANCING COSTS

Patricia will incur financing costs equal to 3% of the $128,000 loan, or $3,840. This cost cannot be deducted as an expense; rather, it must be amortized over the life of the 25-year loan, so $154 is deductible each year ($3,840/25 = $154). The tax law provides for all amortized financing costs to accelerate in the year that the loan is paid off. So in year 3, Patricia can deduct $3,532 [$3,840 − (154 × 2 years)].

UNPAID MORTGAGE

At reversion, Patricia must pay off the lender the unpaid mortgage. Fortunately, we have already calculated this; it is simply the amount outstanding in year 3, the year of reversion. From the amortization schedule, this equals $125,065.

ADJUSTED BASIS

Recall the adjusted basis equals the original purchase price minus accumulated depreciation. Accumulated depreciation for three years is $15,819 ($5,273 × 3). Therefore, Patricia's adjusted basis is $144,181 ($160,000 − $15,819).

NET PRESENT VALUE

Patricia must discount the after-tax cash flows and after-tax equity reversion at her required equity rate of return of 14%. Example 2–1, Table E shows an NPV_e of $1,343. Because her net present value of equity is greater than $0, she should invest in the project, *given her assumptions*.

GROWTH RATES

Patricia is able to calculate the growth rate of various inputs. For example, if she pays $160,000 for the project and sells it three years later for $175,000, she projects the four-plex to grow in value (g) 3.03% per year. This can be shown easily as follows:

$$PV = FV/(1 + g)^n$$

$$\$160,000 = \$175,000/(1 + g)^n$$

$$1.09375 = (1 + g)^3$$

$$(1.09375)^{1/3} = (1 + g)$$

$$1.0303213 = 1 + g$$

$$g = 3.03\%$$

Similarly, growth in PGI (that is, rents) is:

$$\$32,000 = 35,000/(1 + i)^2$$

$$i = 4.58\%$$

Notice this compounds for only two years, not three years as in the case of growth in value. This is because Patricia expects to receive the PGI at the end rather than the beginning of year 1.

SUMMARY

A thorough understanding of the methods discussed in this chapter can make them a useful tool for real estate investors. Our discussion has centered on the key areas for real estate investment decision making. These include how to (1) calculate the present value of future cash inflows, (2) calculate the net present value, and (3) calculate the internal rate of return. It is also important that the investor understand the mechanics of mortgages. The basic elements are how to calculate the debt service and the mortgage amortization schedule. The amortization schedule is necessary in order to determine the amount of interest deductible for tax purposes.

QUESTIONS

3–1. Why are the mathematical techniques described and illustrated in this chapter important for real estate investors?

3–2. There are three sets of tables in Appendix A in this book. Describe how each type is calculated.

3–3. How do present and future values differ?

3–4. "The calculation of the rate of return is actually similar to the present value calculation." True or false? Explain.

3–5. What is an amortization schedule and how is it derived?

3–6. Why is the calculation of the proportion of loan outstanding a useful result?

PROBLEMS

3–1. A real estate investor is considering the purchase of a parcel of vacant land that is expected to have a value of $500,000 five years from now. The investor's required rate of return is 15 percent per year. How much should the investor pay for the land?

3–2. An apartment building has a current market value of $750,000. If the value of the property is expected to increase by 5 percent per year, how much will the property be worth in three years?

3–3. You promise to pay a lender $631.93 per month for 25 years. The lender wants to earn 12 percent per year. How much will the lender loan you today? How much would he loan at an interest rate of 8 percent?

3–4. Using the facts in Problem 3–3, how much will you owe at the end of five years? Ten years?

3–5. Using the facts in Problem 3–3, suppose you wanted to borrow $65,000. What is the lender's net present value? What is the lender's internal rate of return? Would the lender make the loan?

3–6. A real estate investment was purchased for $1,000,000 and sold six years later for $1,340,000. What was the percentage increase in the property's value per year?

3–7. A mortgage loan of $1,000,000 was made at an interest rate of 12.5 percent with monthly payments for 20 years.
   a. What is the monthly payment?
   b. What is the annual payment?
   c. Allocate the payments for years 1 through 5 between interest and principal.
   d. What is the amount outstanding at the end of eight years?

3–8. A mortgage loan of $450,000 was made with payments of $5,417 per month for 25 years. What is the interest rate on the loan?

3–9. A real estate investment has the following cash flows:

Year	Cash Flow
0	−$100,000
1	15,000
2	20,000
3	18,000
4	12,000
5	85,000

If the investor's required rate of return is 15 percent, what is the net present value?

3–10. Using the facts in Problem 3–9, compute the internal rate of return.

3–11. An investor recently purchased a large apartment complex. Upon further inspec-tion of heating system, he determined that it most probably will need to be re-placed in seven years. Further, he has re-ceived several estimates indicating that the replacement cost will be $47,000. How much money would this investor need to deposit in a sinking fund, on an annual basis; this account will earn interest at a rate of 8 percent.

3–12. An investor is considering purchasing an apartment building for $1,500,000. If she does, the bank is requiring that her loan to value ratio be no more than 73 percent, and that the mortgage be amortized for 15 years at 10 percent.
   a. Calculate the monthly mortgage constant, using the formula from the chapter.
   b. What will the monthly debt service be? The annual debt service?
   c. During the first year, how much of the debt service will be applied toward in-terest? Toward principal?

SELECTED REFERENCES

Ellwood, L. W., *Ellwood Tables for Real Estate Ap-praising and Financing*, (3rd ed.). Chicago: American Institute of Real Estate Appraisers, 1970.

Jaffe, Austin J., and C. F. Sirmans, *Real Estate In-vestment Decision Making*, Englewood Cliffs, N.J.: Prentice Hall, 1982.

Mason, Robert C., "Comprehending Compound-ing," *The Appraisal Journal*, 62 (April 1994), 234–239.

THE INVESTMENT ENVIRONMENT

CHAPTER 4

THE MARKET ENVIRONMENT

PRINCIPLES

1. Since real estate investments are fixed in location, the analysis of the market environment is essential.
2. The market study can be the most important aspect of the real estate investment process.
3. Estimation of market rents is a key element in an investment study.
4. Inflation is an important factor in analyzing real estate markets.
5. Business risk stems from developments in the market environment.

In this chapter we begin our analysis of the second step in the investment process—analyzing the environment in which the investment decision is being made. One of the most important aspects is market analysis. The real estate market represents the interaction between the demand for and the supply of real estate. The market determines the price (rent) to be charged on various types of real estate in different locations. The locational aspect is very important in market analysis.

The market environment is also concerned with analyzing the demand for ownership and the way the value of an investment is determined. Obviously, the economic factors create risks that must be considered in the decision making process. This chapter examines the market environment and describes how the investor uses this information to make investment decisions.

Purpose of Market Analysis

We have defined *real estate investing* as the sacrifice of certain outflows for uncertain inflows. Forecasting the future inflows from an investment is risky. The investor must examine the factors influencing the inflows and formulate expectations from this analysis. To begin, the investor must carefully analyze the market forces influencing the investment decision. This analysis is critical: A mistake in the identification of present or future market forces can be costly or result in project failure.

The critical elements of an investment include the quantity and certainty of gross income, operating expenses (operating ratio), and resultant net income over some future time period. Value is a reflection of future income expectations (benefits), and such estimates are risky. The only insurance against risk—and the only clarification (to a limited degree) of uncertainty—is an in-depth market study with a principal thrust concerning supply and demand. Perhaps the most neglected area of real estate investment theory and practice is the requisite market study as a first step in value estimation.

The purpose of the market analysis is simply to reduce the risk associated with investing. One of the major risks is economic or business risk. Business risk is related to such factors as

1. National economic trends, such as unemployment or recession
2. A deteriorating economic base
3. Economic obsolescence, perhaps due to a changing neighborhood
4. Flood, fire, and other natural or man-made disasters
5. Functional obsolescence, lack of quality construction, or age
6. Properties having high operating expense ratios and requiring very specialized kinds of management (i.e., nursing homes, hotels)
7. Legal restrictions, such as zoning changes
8. Population and sociodemographic trends
9. Changes in income levels, tastes, and preferences of tenants.

These are only some of the factors that influence the business risk to which an investment is exposed. Obviously some types of real estate investment are subject to more business risk than others. All involve risk, however, and the purpose of market analysis is to analyze this category of risk.

Business risk is a function of general economic conditions and characteristics of the investment and is not related to the financial structure (debt-equity mix). Therefore, the variability of net income is generally the most appropriate measure of this type of risk. A real estate investment produces two potential sources of net income: the annual net operating income and the net income from the future disposition (typically, sale). Because market analysis identifies the variability of net income from these

Current Issue 4–1
Where Is the Real Estate Market?

Despite the considerable attention that most real estate texts devote to "the real estate market," students may be surprised to learn that the market is difficult to find. Most markets have a central location and a formal, physical site, but real estate markets rarely do. Such characteristics assist market participants in buying, selling, or collecting information about the economic qualities of the assets and rights traded.

In the case of real estate, there is no central market. There is no building such as the New York Stock Exchange for trading real estate investments. (For some, this means that real estate investing is more fun!) Although real estate is often sold at security markets as a financial claim, there are several reasons why real estate investments lack a central clearinghouse.

For example, since real estate investments are tied to a particular site, it is difficult to interest buyers who are unfamiliar with the locale of the investment. The locale is not only critical to the success of the investment, but each locale may exert a different influence on real estate investment returns. These factors retard the ability of market makers to extend the scope of the market beyond the local investment community. In addition, the uniqueness of the parcels precludes easy property descriptions for those parcels that come "on the market." If a national real estate market is ever to exist, it is essential that a standard information form be developed in order to facilitate the conveyance of information for trading. With the wide variety of real estate and the difficulties involved in adequately describing it, the prospects for a fully developed national real estate market are not great. Finally, the thinness of most real estate markets suggests that it would be difficult to maintain active trading, since most parcels come on the market so infrequently that it makes more sense to "make a market" when the asset needs to be sold.

In recent years, the use of real estate auctions has increased such that the closest thing currently available to a supermarket in real estate might very well be the auctioneer's block. In some countries, (for example, Australia), auctions are used in conjunction with direct sales on a regular basis. In the United States, real estate auctions tend to be used in distressed markets, with foreclosed properties, in agricultural land sales, and for some nonprofit purposes.

It should be noted, however, that recent developments in some financial markets have increased the marketability of some forms of real estate investments. These include such investments as mortgage-backed bonds, REITs, and mutual funds secured by mortgages. They are helping to make a type of national real estate market. In the future, it may be easier for someone in Pennsylvania to buy real estate in California, and it will probably be in the form of a financial claim such as a bond or a mutual fund share.

two sources, the investor should know which factors influence the variability. There are several factors, including rent per unit, vacancy level, operating expenses, estimated selling price at the end of the holding period, and selling expenses.

AN ILLUSTRATION

To illustrate the sensitivity of value estimates to changes in rents, suppose an investor is considering a building with 100 units. Market analysis indicates a range in rents from $175 to $200 per month per unit. Therefore, the potential gross income will vary between $210,000 to $240,000 per year, a considerable difference.

An analysis of competing properties indicates a value estimate of five times the potential gross income (PGI). This is referred to as the gross income multiplier (GIM). The investor would thus obtain an estimated value between $1,050,000 and $1,200,000:

$$\text{Value} = \text{PGI (GIM)} \tag{4–1}$$

$$\text{Value} = \$210,000 \ (5) = \$1,050,000$$

$$\text{Value} = \$240,000 \ (5) = \$1,200,000$$

This is a range in value of $150,000, which is a sizable difference in value for only a $25 range in rents. Therefore, investment values are very sensitive to errors or bad estimates.

Market analysis helps narrow the range in the key factors influencing net income—rents, operating expenses, vacancies, and future selling price. Small changes in these inputs to the investment process can make a disproportionate difference in the estimated value for an investment and in the expected rate of return.

THE REAL ESTATE MARKET

The real estate investor must focus considerable attention on the real estate market. The *real estate market* can be defined as a mechanism by which real estate goods and services are exchanged—a mechanism influenced by the wants of the participants in the market, as well as by political and governmental intervention in the marketplace.

The purpose of the real estate market is to allocate a scarce commodity. This scarce commodity is real estate, which includes both land and improvements to the land and the property rights associated with the ownership. The real estate market, like any market, allocates this scarce resource by using the price mechanism. Generally we find that the person willing to pay the most for the real estate acquires the rights associated with that ownership. In some instances, the public has decided that the scarce resource should be allocated by the government. The implementation of land use controls such as zoning ordinances can be viewed as an example of this type of allocation.

The real estate market links the supply and the demand for real estate. There are two types or categories of supply and demand with which the investor must be concerned. The first is the supply and demand for the use of the real estate; this involves the tenant's perspective. The second is the supply and demand for the ownership of an investment, or the equity investor's perspective. The equity investor must consider both of these.

THE TENANT'S PERSPECTIVE

The demand for a real estate investment is based on the flow of services that it produces. For example, the demand for an apartment from the tenant's perspective is based on the housing services provided. Some of these services include shelter, comfort, prestige, access to work or shopping, safety, and social opportunities. Thus, the tenant is buying a set of services, not merely a physical living unit.

For these services, the tenant pays a "price" called rent. The greater the demand for the services, the greater the rent. Generally, we do not observe the rent per unit of services; rather, the rent per physical unit—for example, the rent per apartment or the rent per square foot of retail space. Remember, however, that the tenant is really buying the services. So the investor must be certain that the investment provides the level of services demanded.

THE EQUITY INVESTOR'S PERSPECTIVE

The second type of supply and demand analysis involves the buying and selling of the ownership of the investment. For example, suppose that 50 apartment buildings were bought in a particular real estate market during a given period. We would conclude that there had been a total demand for 50 apartment buildings. This buying and selling involves placing a value (or selling price) on the expected future income (from rental and future disposition).

The value represents the present worth of the expected future income. To illustrate, suppose an investment is expected to produce $10,000 in net income per year for 10 years. In addition, the investment has an expected selling price of $100,000 at the end of the 10 years. The investor requires a 12 percent return per year on the investment. What is the value of the investment?

To find the value, take the forecasts of income from operation and sale and discount them at the appropriate rate. The present value of $10,000 received at the end of each year for 10 years, with an investor's required rate of return of 12 percent, is $56,502. The present value of $100,000 received at the end of year 10, discounted at 12 percent, is $32,197. Therefore, the value of this investment, *given these assumptions*, is $88,669.

However, this valuation process raises several questions. How is the expected income determined? What is the risk associated with future income, that is, how certain are we that the investment will generate the expected cash flows? How is the appropriate rate of discount determined?

All of these questions (and others) must be answered from the equity investor's perspective. This is what market analysis is all about. Viewing the investment from the tenant's perspective helps the investor determine the expected net income and variations over the holding period. Market analysis from the equity investor's perspective helps determine the relationship between value, risk, and cash flow from the investment.

Therefore, market analysis identifies supply and demand factors from both the tenant's and the landlord's (equity investor's) perspective. It also helps to consider market conditions from the seller's and the equity investor's perspective. Changes in factors that influence the number of tenants and the rents tenants are willing to pay will also affect the expected income from an investment. These changes can have an impact on the value of the investment from the equity investor's perspective. Likewise, various factors can influence the equity investor's behavior in the marketplace. For example, if equity investors perceive a particular real estate investment as becoming more risky because of international, urban, or neighborhood trends, this increased risk would be reflected in the valuation of the investment.

DECISIONS FROM THE MARKET STUDY

The market study analyzes the likely present and future demand for an investment and the existing and likely future supply of closely competitive facilities. From this, the investor formulates four conclusions:

1. The various prices and their probabilities at which the particular investment (existing or proposed) might be rented and expected future changes in rents
2. An estimate of the quantity (occupancy ratio or, conversely, vacancy ratio), such as apartment units or square feet of office space, likely to be sold or rented per year at those prices
3. A discussion of the specific conditions such as financing terms, sales techniques, or certain amenities that are required for sale or rental
4. An estimate of the probable future trends in selling price for the type of investment under consideration in its market environment.

It is obvious that the market study determines the first inputs to the cash flow statement. Remember that cash flow from a real estate investment can arise from two sources: the annual cash flow from operating the investment and the cash flow from the future disposition (usually sale) of the investment.

The market study also shows future trends in the expected market value (or selling price) of the investment. Increases (or decreases) in market value are caused by relative price changes or inflation. It is also possible to have both simultaneously. *Inflation* is defined as increases in all prices at the same rate of change. A *relative price change* is one in which the price or value of an investment rises (or falls) relative to prices of the other goods (investments) in the economy.

The investor must understand that the present investment value is not influenced by inflation. Although inflation affects the future value, it does not affect the present value of an investment. On the other hand, expected relative price changes affect both the future and the present value of an investment.

EXAMPLE 4–1   DETERMINING RENT

A real estate investor is considering the development of an apartment project. The building will cost $1,000,000 and the land costs are $250,000. Market analysis indicates that the project would sell for $1,500,000 at the end of the five-year holding period (about a 3.75% increase in value per year). The project will consist of 50 units, the expected vacancy rate (VAC) is 7 percent per year and the operating expenses (OE) will be 45 percent of the potential gross income each year. The investor's required rate of return is 12 percent.

The investor has asked you to determine the rent per unit necessary to make this a feasible project.

To answer the investor's concerns, recall that the value of the project is equal to the present worth of the income stream.

$$V = PVAF_{(i,n)}[PGI - VAC - OE] + PVF_{(i,n)}[\text{Selling price}]$$

$$\$1,250,000 = 3.6048[\text{Rent}(50) - .07(\text{Rent})(50) - .45(\text{Rent})(50)] + .56743[1,500,000]$$

Solving for rent:

Unit rent per year = $4,611

Unit rent per month = $384

The project must rent for at least $384 per month per unit in order to be feasible.

RISK VERSUS UNCERTAINTY

A distinction is sometimes made between risk and uncertainty. *Risk* is associated with situations in which a probability distribution of the returns from investment can be estimated. *Uncertainty*, on the other hand, is associated with situations in which estimates of probability distribution are impossible. This distinction is not made in our discussion: Risk and uncertainty are used synonymously.

However, we realize that probability distributions of expected returns can be estimated with some precision. Some investments may have distributions that can be estimated objectively with statistical techniques. When such methods are used, risk is said to be measured by objective probability distributions.

On the other hand, there are many investment situations in which statistical data cannot be used. The investor may have few or no historical data to use, particularly when the investment is a new project. However, the investor may rely heavily on historical data for similar projects and personal judgment. This is called *subjective probability distributions*. Thus, *risk* (or uncertainty) refers to an investment whose return cannot be predicted with certainty, but for which an array of alternative outcomes and their probabilities can be estimated. This is a major purpose of market analysis.

RISK OVER TIME

How does the risk for an income stream change over time? Figure 4–1 shows the distribution of expected cash flow from an investment for years 1, 5, and 10. The distribution becomes flatter over time, indicating that there is more uncertainty about expected cash flows in later years. The dashed lines show the standard deviation, a well-known measure of risk, attached to the cash flow each year. The lines diverge from the expected cash flow over time, which indicates that the riskiness is increasing. If the cash flow in later years could be estimated equally, as well as the cash flow

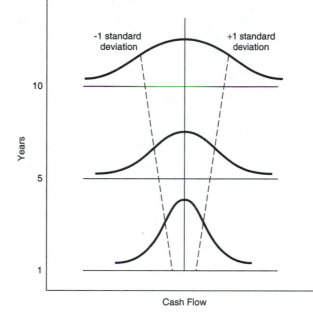

FIGURE 4–1
Risk as a Function of Time

in earlier years, that is, if risk were constant through time, the standard deviation would be constant and the dashed line would not diverge from the expected value.

In setting up the expected cash flow for each year, some factors are probably the key to riskiness over time. For example, it is relatively easy to forecast the depreciation deduction and debt service with a fixed-rate mortgage in later years, but much harder to forecast the expected rents, vacancies, or selling price. The market forces that cause these factors to vary are difficult to forecast as time increases.

This fact makes the investor base judgments on short-term holding period forecasts of cash flows. It has been argued that, on the average, income-producing properties typically are sold or refinanced within 10 years or less of purchase. Longer-term forecasts of the expected cash flows should generally be used only in such cases as long-term leases.

INFLATION, RELATIVE PRICE CHANGES, AND MARKET ANALYSIS

Market analysis is particularly aimed at identifying potential relative price changes in an investment. These price changes are caused by shifts in supply or demand or both for a particular investment, including real income changes, population growth (or decline), changes in neighborhood characteristics, or changes in tax laws.

It is important to understand the impact of relative price changes. The price of a particular investment can increase or decrease relative to other goods. Unexpected relative price declines have a negative impact on the rate of return for a particular investment. Likewise, unexpected relative price increases have positive effects on rates of return.

To illustrate relative price changes, consider the following simple example. An investor purchases a parcel of land for $10,000. One year later the land is sold for $12,000 (ignoring all holding costs and assuming no inflation). The investor has thus earned a 20 percent return.

$$\$10,000 = \frac{\$12,000}{(1 + R)^1}$$

$$R = 20\%$$

But how is the investor able to sell the investment for a higher price? Figure 4–2 illustrates this for the simple case. The curves S and D represent the supply and demand curves for land. Suppose that population growth shifts the demand curve for land to D'. The price then rises from P to P' in real terms.

The present value of an investment depends on two factors: the estimated future value and the rate of return. Obviously, if the rate of return is held constant and the estimated future value is increased, the present value will be higher. In the simple example, the present value would be $12,000 instead of $10,000 if the expected future value is increased to $15,000 because of a relative price change. If the price is higher because of neutral inflation (or an equal percentage change in all prices), the present value would not be higher because the required rate of return must be increased to compensate for the purchasing power risk to which the investor is exposed.

If we view the required rate of return, k, as the sum of the risk-free rate, k_f, the market risk premium, k_m, and the inflation premium, k_p, then

$$k = k_f + k_m + k_p \tag{4–2}$$

If there is no inflation, $k_p = 0$. In the example above, if the risk-free rate is 5 percent and the market risk is 15 percent, the required rate of return is 20 percent.[1]

---

[1]This type of analysis is generally attributed to Irving Fisher, a forefather of many ideas in modern economic analysis.

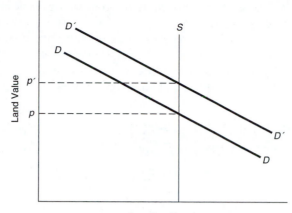

FIGURE 4–2

A Shift in the Demand for Land

$$k = k_f + k_m + k_p \tag{4–3}$$
$$k = .05 + .15 + .00$$
$$k = .20$$

Assume that inflation now increases from 0 percent annually to 5 percent annually. In our example, the land that sold for $10,000 a year ago would sell for $12,000 without inflation. With inflation, however, it sells for an additional $500, or $12,500. The question is whether the investor is any better off due to this inflationary effect. The answer is no.

If inflation is 5 percent, then $k_p = .05$. The required rate of return, k, becomes

$$k = k_f + k_m + k_p$$
$$k = .05 + .15 + .05$$
$$k = .25$$

The present value of the investment is

$$PV = \frac{\$12,500}{(1 + .25)^1}$$
$$PV = \$10,000$$

This may seem surprising, because inflation increases the future, rather than the present value of the land. However, the important point is that it also increases the required rate of return to keep the real value constant.

Because financial markets anticipate inflation, inflation premiums, k_p, are incorporated into market interest rates. Therefore, since inflation affects all assets in nominal dollars equally, a higher required rate of return means that the real value (and return) stays constant.

EXAMPLE 4–2   GROWTH RATE IN PROJECT'S VALUE

A real estate investor is considering the development of an apartment project. The building will cost $1,000,000 and the land acquisition costs will be $250,000. The project will consist of 50 units. Market analysis indicates that comparable rents per month per unit are $384. The investor's expected holding period is 5 years, and the required rate of return is 12%. The expected vacancy rate is 7% per year, and operating expenses will be 45% of the annual potential gross income.

The investor has asked you to determine the growth rate in value that would be necessary for this to be a feasible project.

Recall that the value of the project is the present worth of the expected income:

$$V = PVAF_{(i,n)}[PGI - VAC - OE] + PVF_{(i,n)}[\text{Selling price}]$$

$$\$1,250,000 = 3.6048[230,400 - 16,128 - 103,680] + .5674[\text{Selling price}]$$

$$\$1,500,000 = \text{Selling price}$$

The investor must sell the project for at least $1,500,000 at the end of the holding period to earn the required rate of return of 12%. In other words, the property must increase in value from $1,250,000 to $1,500,000, a growth rate of about 3.75% per year, in order to be a feasible project.

Obviously, some changes in the value of real estate have occurred due to increasing demand for, or perhaps supply restrictions of, property during recent years. Although accumulated wealth is largely attributed to inflation, it is actually due to changes in demand or supply or both in the real estate market and to changes in the value of indebtedness assumed by borrowers prior to rising interest rates. Market analysis is aimed at trying to uncover these potential relative price changes. To understand the investment process, one must understand the impact of inflation and relative price changes on present values and required rates of return.

MEASURING RISK AND RETURN

Modern real estate investment analysis defines *risk* as the dispersion of an investment's returns—the positive and negative deviations from the expected return. The most widely used method of risk analysis utilizes the expected (mean) rate of return as an indication of an investment's profitability, and the variance (or standard deviation) as an indication of its risk.

Business risk, broadly defined, is the risk inherent in investing in real estate, as measured by the variability in the rate of return for an all-equity financed investment.[2] A general way of viewing the rate of return, k, that should be required on an investment is

$$k = k_f + k_m$$

The term k_f is the risk-free rate, and k_m is the premium for business risk. The risk-free rate applies to an investment where there is no chance that the realized rate of return will be less than the expected rate of return. The risk-free rate is simply compensation for postponing current consumption plans. The risk premium is the additional return necessary to compensate investors for bearing the risk that the realized rate could be lower than expected. Thus k is the required rate of return and reflects compensation for both waiting and risk.

EXPECTED RATE OF RETURN

A simple measure of the overall rate of return from an investment is calculated as follows:

$$R = \frac{NOI}{Value} \qquad (4-4)$$

where:

R = overall rate of return (sometimes called the overall capitalization rate)

NOI = expected net operating income

$Value$ = value of the investment

[2]In addition to business risk, several other types of risk face real estate investors including *financial risk, purchasing power risk, legal risk, exchange-rate risk,* and others.

TABLE 4-1
ILLUSTRATION OF EXPECTED RATE OF RETURN FOR INVESTMENT A

Value	Net Operating Income (NOI)	Probability (p_i)	Overall Rate (R)	$(R_i \times P_i)$
$1,000,000	$ 80,000	.25	.08	.0200
1,000,000	100,000	.60	.10	.0600
1,000,000	110,000	.15	.11	.0165
				$E(R_A) = .0965$

For example, an investment under consideration is expected to generate $100,000 per year. The value is $1 million. The overall rate, R, is thus 10 percent ($100,000 divided by $1,000,000).

There is the possibility, however, that the net operating income will not be as expected. Suppose an investor decides that there are 6 chances out of 10 that the actual net operating income will be $100,000. The investor also feels that there is a .25 probability that the investment will generate $80,000 and a .15 probability that $110,000 will be realized. These outcomes are summarized in Table 4–1.

$E(R)$ denotes the expected rate of return, which is the weighted average of possible rates of return using the probabilities (p_i) as the weights. Thus $E(R)$ can be written as follows:

$$E(R) = R_1 \times p_1 + R_2 \times p_2 + R_3 \times p_3 + \ldots + R_m \times p_m \qquad (4\text{–}5)$$

$$= \sum_{i=1}^{m} R_i \times p_i$$

where R_i represents the overall return from the ith "state of the world," m is the number of "states of the world," and p_i represents the probability of the ith "state of the world."

For investment A, the expected rate of return is

$$E(R_A) = .08(.25) + .10(.60) + .11(.15)$$

$$= .0965, \text{ or } 9.65\%$$

MEASURING RISK

To measure risk, investment analysis uses *variance* or *standard deviation*. These measure the dispersion of the expected return around the mean (expected) value and provide information on the extent of possible deviations of the actual return from the expected return. The greater the variance in expected return, the greater the risk.

The variance (σ^2) of the mean is given by

$$\sigma^2 = \sum_{i=1}^{m} [R_i - E(R)]^2 p_i \qquad (4\text{--}6)$$

(σ is the Greek letter sigma. The variance is thus read "sigma squared.")
To calculate the variance:

1. Calculate the deviation of each possible outcome from the expected value $[R_i - E(R)]$
2. Raise this deviation to the second power $[R_i - E(R)]^2$
3. Multiply this term by the probability of getting R_i (that is, p_i) $[R_i - E(R)]^2 \times p_i$
4. Sum these products, $\sum_{i=1}^{m} [R_i - E(R)]^2 p_i$

Note that the distribution of returns is measured in percentages. The dimension of σ^2 is in "percentages squared," which, of course, is economically meaningless. Thus we take the square root of the variance, which results in the standard deviation (σ) in "percentages":

$$\sigma = \sqrt{\sigma^2} \qquad (4\text{--}7)$$

Because standard deviation also measures the variability of the distribution, it is stated in percentages. For ranking investment proposals, however, either the variance or the standard deviation can be used, because both are always greater than or equal to zero.
The standard deviation for investment A is

$$\sigma_A = \sqrt{.00010275}$$

$$= .01014$$

Thus, for investment A, the expected overall return $E(R_A)$ is 9.65 percent with a standard deviation, σ_A, of 1.014 percent.

THE DECISION RULES FOR MEAN-VARIANCE ANALYSIS

To evaluate investments using the expected return and variance (or standard deviation), apply the following decision rules:
Investment A is preferred to investment B if one of the following two conditions holds:

1. The expected return of A exceeds (or is equal to) the expected return of B *and* the standard deviation of A is less than the standard deviation of B.

or

2. The expected return of A exceeds that of B *and* the standard deviation of A is less than (or equal to) that of B.

In equation form, the "mean variance" decision rules can be written as follows:

$$E(R_A) \geq E(R_B), \quad \text{and}$$

$$\sigma_A < \sigma_B,$$

or

$$E(R_A) > E(R_B), \quad \text{and}$$

$$\sigma_A \geq \sigma_B$$

In the example, the expected return, variance, and standard deviation for investment A are

Expected return: $E(R_A) = .0965$

Variance: $\sigma_A^2 = .00010275$

Standard deviation: $\sigma_A = .01014$

Suppose the expected return, variance, and standard deviation for investment B are

Expected return: $E(R_B) = .0965$

Variance: $\sigma_B^2 = .00015$

Standard deviation: $\sigma_B = .01225$

Note that both investments have the same expected return of 9.65 percent. However, investment A is preferable to B under condition 1. The expected return from both investments is the same, but investment A has a smaller variance (or standard deviation). Investment B is thus riskier in terms of variance from the expected return.

FURTHER EXAMPLES

The mean-variance decision rules help the investor select and, more importantly, understand the relationship between expected returns from an investment and the risks. To further illustrate these decision rules, suppose an investor has the investment opportunities shown in Table 4–2.

Which of these should the investor select? Using the decision rules, compare investments C and E. Both have the same expected return, but C has less risk because the standard deviation is smaller. Thus C is pre-

TABLE 4-2
ILLUSTRATION OF RISK AND RETURN

Investment	Return E(R)	Risk (σ)
C	.11	.02
D	.13	.02
E	.11	.03

ferred to E. Now compare investments C and D. These have the same risk, but D has a higher expected return. Therefore D is preferred to C. Since D is preferred to C and C is preferred to E, investment D is preferred to E. Now, if the investor were to choose among the three, investment D would be selected.

However, sometimes there are problems with the mean-variance decision rules. Suppose an investor has the choices shown in Table 4–3. Which should the investor select? We cannot use the mean-variance rules because, in this case, the expected risk and expected return are greater for investment G than for investment F. The question that the investor must answer is, Does the increase in return "compensate" for the increase in risk? If it does, then choose G over F. If it does not, the investor would prefer investment F. This is a major reason why the investor must identify his or her particular preference on the risk-return trade-off.

Current Issue 4–2
Capitalization of Inflation into Discount Rates
The text argues that real estate market participants evaluate expected inflation when pricing real estate investments such that inflation is expected to have a neutral impact on investor's well-being. This is the theoretical proposition; it is also important to examine the evidence.

There is a considerable body of literature regarding the effects of inflation in markets and the speed at which inflationary expectations impact prices. Most empirical evidence on financial markets shows that inflationary expectations are adequately captured in borrowing rates, consistent with the notion that the EMH applies to estimating inflation premia in investment markets.

Empirical studies on inflation in real estate markets sometimes find conflicting results. However, in the absence of solid evidence to the contrary, it seems reasonable to assume that inflationary expectations are likely to be incorporated into discount rates, and cash flow forecasts as well, *prior* to purchase by investors.

TABLE 4-3
ANOTHER ILLUSTRATION OF RISK AND RETURN

Investment	Return E(R)	Risk (σ)
F	.11	.02
G	.13	.03

COMMON ERRORS IN ANALYZING MARKETS

A survey of real estate market analyses examined the question, What have been the deficiencies of real estate market and investment analyses that have been prepared, and what can be done to improve them? This survey examined 45 feasibility reports prepared by consultants, appraisers, and market analysts with established national or regional reputations.[3] It found that the caliber of market analysis reports was substantially below the "state of the art." Six of the most common errors made in analyzing real estate markets are summarized in Table 4-4.

UNSPECIFIED RESEARCH DIRECTION

The appropriateness of any investment decision can be evaluated only when the investor's goal or objective is known. As noted previously, the analyst must determine what decision the investor is trying to make.

STATISTICS WITHOUT EXPLANATION

Nearly all market analysis reports contain large amounts of statistics on such factors as population growth, employment levels, income levels, and

TABLE 4-4
COMMON ERRORS IN ANALYZING MARKETS

Type of Error	Percentage of Reports
1. Unspecified research direction	73%
2. Statistics without explanation	82
3. Misspecification of supply and demand	67
4. Failure to correlate supply and demand	60
5. Inattention to economic indicators	76
6. Omission of primary data	49

[3]Gary W. Eldred, and Robert H. Zerbst, "A Critique of Real Estate Market and Investment Analysis," *Appraisal Journal*, 46 (July 1978), 443–52.

transportation facilities. The purpose of the market analysis is not to describe but to explain how these relate to the problem at hand.

MISSPECIFICATION OF SUPPLY AND DEMAND

As noted previously, market analysis centers on understanding supply and demand for a given investment. What is the market for the investment under consideration? What segment of the market is being served by the project? How does this project compare with competing projects?

FAILURE TO CORRELATE SUPPLY AND DEMAND

The investor must carefully analyze supply and demand to determine expected vacancy rates for the investment under consideration. From this the investor must make quantitative decisions regarding the ability to rent the investment.

INATTENTION TO ECONOMIC INDICATORS

The investor must also analyze the possible effects of the regional and national economic climate on local economies and decide how possible downturns will affect the investment. Leading economic indicators may be used in investment decision making.

OMISSION OF PRIMARY DATA

Data can be classified as primary or secondary. *Secondary data* are collected for some purpose other than the study at hand. This type of data is available from such sources as the U.S. Bureau of Census, trade associations, and planning agencies. While typically cost-free, these frequently do not fit the investment process very precisely.

Primary data, on the other hand, are gathered specifically for the investment decision. Primary data help determine the tastes and preferences of the particular segment of the real estate market to which an investment is aimed. Types of data include vacancy surveys, rental rates, and operating expense levels of competing investments.

FACTORS TO CONSIDER IN ANALYZING MARKETS

The general factors influencing real estate investments can be broadly classified as those influencing demand and those influencing supply. Table 4–5 illustrates the various types of factors that should be considered in analyzing the real estate market. First, delineate the market area. Second, analyze its demographic characteristics, including population

TABLE 4–5
REAL ESTATE MARKET ANALYSIS FOR AN INVESTMENT

I. Delineation of the market area
  A. Metropolitan area
    1. Name of standard metropolitan statistical area (SMSA)
    2. Identification of entire area
    3. Geography
    4. Climate
    5. General urban structure; location of facilities
    6. Direction of city growth
    7. Commuting patterns (journey to work)
    8. Any major community developments and/or special features or characteristics germane to the market analysis
II. Demographic analysis
  A. Population
    1. Most recent estimate for total population
    2. Past trends in population growth
    3. Estimated future population
    4. Distribution by age groups
  B. Households
    1. Most recent estimates for household formations
    2. Past trends in household formations
    3. Estimated future total households and average annual rate of growth
    4. Current trends in household size (increasing, decreasing)
III. Economy of the market area (demand-side analysis)
  A. Economic history and characteristics
    1. General description
    2. Major economic activities and developments
  B. Employment, total and nonagricultural
    1. Current estimates
    2. Past trends
    3. Distribution by industry groups
    4. Estimated future employment
    5. Trends in labor participation rate
    6. Trends in female employment
  C. Unemployment
    1. Current level
    2. Past trends
  D. Economic-base analysis
    1. Metropolitan area compared with national and state employment data
    2. Discussion of principal employers
    3. Payroll data (census of manufacturers, trade, services, governments)
  E. Income data
    1. Personal income by major sources
    2. Per capita personal income
    3. Family-income distribution
    4. Projections for growth in personal income

IV. Construction and real estate activity (supply-side analysis)
   A. Building and construction industry
      1. Residential building by type (single-family, multifamily, rental or sales)
      2. Nonresidential construction
      3. High-rise building activity (minimum height of five stories above ground)
      4. Heavy engineering construction
   B. Demand-and-supply analysis for properties other than residential
      1. General demand factors in metropolitan area
      2. Existing inventory, by property type
      3. Projected production, by property type
   C. Housing inventory, by type (single-family, multifamily)
      1. Most recent estimates
      2. Past trends including 1980 census
      3. Principal characteristics
   D. Residential sales and rental markets
      1. General market conditions
      2. Major subdivision activity
      3. Trends in sales prices or monthly rentals
      4. Unsold inventory of new sales housing
      5. New rental housing
      6. Residential units under construction
   E. Other housing markets
      1. Public and governmental subsidized housing
      2. Specialized submarkets for housing demand and supply
   F. Real estate loans and mortgage markets
      1. Sources and availability of funds
      2. FHA, VA, FNMA, GNMA
      3. Interest rates and terms of mortgages
      4. Recordings of mortgages and/or deeds of trust
      5. Foreclosures
V. Political and legal aspects (Legal Environment Analysis)
   A. Land-use planning
      1. Regional
      2. County (counties)
      3. Incorporated cities in SMSA
   B. Zoning
      1. Review of present zoning ordinances for county (counties) and cities
      2. Zoning history and present attitudes of zoning authority
      3. Identify raw land presently zoned for land use of subject property
   C. Ordinances, codes, regulations
      1. Subdivisions
      2. Building codes
      3. Health and public safety
      4. Allocation of land for schools, recreational areas, open space
   D. Municipal services
      1. Public safety
      2. Hospitals and health care
      3. Utilities

E. Ecological
   1. Environmental impact studies
   2. Limited growth policies
   3. Floodplains and flood control
   4. Solid-waste disposal
F. Property taxation
   1. Tax rate per $1,000 valuation
   2. Assessment ratio as percent of market value
   3. Special assessment districts
VI. Sources of information
   A. Types of data
      1. Population
      2. Employment
      3. Personal income
      4. Planning
      5. Building
      6. Zoning
      7. Other pertinent
   B. Sources of data
      1. Secondary data sources
      2. Primary data sources

Source: U.S. Dept. of Housing and Urban Development, *FHA Techniques of Housing Market Analysis.* (Washington, D.C.: August, 1970).

growth, estimated future population growth, age distribution, and number of households. Third, consider those factors influencing the demand for a real estate investment, including employment trends, income data, and the economic base of the neighborhood. Fourth, analyze the supply side of the market. This includes examining the building and construction industry, analyzing housing market and mortgage market trends, and inventorying existing competition. Fifth, analyze the political and legal areas. These include land-use planning, zoning, building codes, municipal services, property taxation, and other aspects of the legal environment. Finally, identify the types and sources of data for market analysis.

INCOME

Because the demand for real estate is dependent on income, and real estate is used to produce products and services, the investor must carefully consider the demand for the products or services produced using the real estate. For example, the demand for residential units is derived from the demand for housing.

The level of income determines the demand for real estate and indicates the ability to obtain financing.

DEMOGRAPHIC FACTORS

Demographics, or population characteristics, are one of the major determinants of the long-term direction of real estate markets. Profiles of age and rates of family formation, fertility, mortality, and migration are extremely important. Migration trends are probably the most difficult to forecast but have the most impact on real estate markets.

SUPPLY FACTORS

The existing supply of real estate includes structures that have been built over a long period of time. New structures added in any one year may exceed the old structures torn down, but seldom is the net increase a very large proportion of the total supply. Thus the supply of real estate at any point in time is relatively fixed. The characteristics of existing and new supply such as age, location, and physical conditions should be compared with the investment under consideration. These give the investor some idea of how his or her investment would compete in the market.

ECONOMIC TRENDS

The real estate investor should monitor the important indicators of economic activity that forecast recessions or growth. Some good indicators are interest rates, construction activity, and unemployment levels. The key factor for successful analysis is not what the investor can find out about the market, but which of all these factors will have a significant impact on the investment decision.

PHYSICAL CHARACTERISTICS

The physical attributes of land and improvements play a crucial role in the overall feasibility of an investment. These attributes may limit utility or provide opportunities to create competition.

The physical attributes include

1. Size and shape of the site
2. Topography
3. Storm-water drainage
4. Watersheds, springs, or other water factors·
5. Soil and subsoil characteristics
6. Utilities
7. Functional layout of the improvements
8. Personal-response factors, such as security

9. Transportation access

10. Physical condition of improvements.

The investor is obviously concerned with matching the demands in the marketplace to the supply. The key question is whether the investment under consideration provides the services demanded by prospective users.

SOCIOPOLITICAL ENVIRONMENT

As we have stated, the purpose of market analysis is to help the investor identify the degree of business risk for an investment. All real estate investments are subject to business risk, since the net income is not known with certainty.

Another important set of factors that influences the decision-making process is referred to as the sociopolitical environment. Whereas market analysis is aimed at identifying the demand and supply factors, the sociopolitical environment is concerned with the relationship between an investment and the neighborhood (or community).

While an investment may be legal (say, in terms of zoning), it may not be perceived as "good" by a given neighborhood or community. All real estate investments, and particularly large-scale projects such as shopping centers, create "external" influences on a neighborhood. These externalities—increased property values, increased traffic, noise—must be dealt with by the investor. External effects can be both positive and negative, and a neighborhood may perceive that an investment imposes more negative influences than it does positive. The investor may have to face these questions (and other constraints) in the decision-making framework.

Adverse public reaction to potential investments is as serious a constraint as the possibility of lack of demand or competition. Business risk should thus be viewed in a much larger framework than just supply and demand (economics). The sociopolitical environment is as important, though often much more difficult, to identify. A cursory review of any newspaper will reveal articles related to this environment.

RENTAL AND VACANCY FORECASTS: AN ILLUSTRATION

One of the key purposes of market analysis is to determine the expected rental for the investment under consideration. The major technique for determining expected rents and vacancies is to compare similar properties. Using an apartment investment as the subject property, Table 4–6 shows how this is done by listing the data on six comparable properties.

In the analysis, the investor first determines the current rental income of the comparable properties. The rent is given per apartment unit, per square foot, and per room. Note that although the rent per apartment varies from $260.00 to $477.00 per month and the variation per room is

Current Issue 4–3
Leading Issues in the Sociopolitical Environment
During the past several years, the public has continued to take an active role in the redefinition and reregulation of real property rights. In many ways, the sociopolitical environment is often the most important area for real estate investors, especially real estate developers.

For example, although land-use controls through zoning date back to the beginning of the twentieth century in the United States, modern local governments have often gone far beyond the adoption of a comprehensive zoning plan for the primary purpose of separating inharmonious land uses. Some cities have regulations on the size and shape of commercial signs, on the types of advertisements, and on the nature of permitted activities on the property. In addition, local ordinances frequently require investors to obtain numerous permits before building additions, making alterations, extracting tree stumps, and even excavating swimming pools. Some cities require that builders refrain from casting shadows on their neighbors; others forbid any new construction at all. Some cities, in fact, now possess a bundle of property rights that resemble the private bundle of the property owner of only a few years ago.

In recent years, the NIMBY ("Not-In-My-Backyard") phenomenon has gained more and more attention. Citizens want control of land use matters, including the citing of various activities which have potential conflict with residential usage. Citizens seem to want to ensure that certain activities are placed *elsewhere* away from their own properties. For example, the decision to place a drug halfway house in a residential neighborhood would, at the same time, endorse the idea of halfway houses somewhere in the community. In this case, the ability to employ the state to keep certain land uses away from their surroundings is a hot sociopolitical issue. In 1991, the Advisory Commission on Regulatory Barriers to Affordable Housing, a blue-ribbon governmental commission appointed by then-President Bush, attributed a large part of the affordability problem in middle-class America to the NIMBY syndrome.

While it is important to identify the leading sociopolitical issues of the local community *before* large amounts of resources are committed, it is essential that the investor develop a high level of political acumen regarding land-use issues in communities with active state and local governments. The specialists in this area are usually attorneys and, sometimes, former political officials. It may be worthwhile to employ the services of these experts for certain real estate investments, since this area is a growing aspect of real estate investment decision making.

TABLE 4–6
MARKET ANALYSIS OF A POTENTIAL APARTMENT INVESTMENT

Apartment Project	No. of Units	Apartment Mix					Estimated Occupancy	Comments
		Type	Sq. Ft. Floor Area	Rent per Month	Sq. Ft. Rent Per Month	Rent Per Room		
1. Oakbrook Village	52	1BR, 1BA, ST	453	$260	$.57	$ 86.67	98%	Student-oriented, well landscaped, two miles from university on student bus route, drapes and carpet, completely furnished, quiet
	55	2BR, 2BA, F	939	400	.43	100.00	99%	
	49	1BR, 1.5BA, TH	729	325	.45	108.33	97%	
2. Tiger Plaza	68	1BR, 1BA, F	709	294	.41	98.00	97%	Large complex, student-oriented, drapes and carpets, completely furnished, tennis court and pool, one mile from university, on student bus route
	79	2BR, 1BA, F	893	354	.40	88.50	99%	
	73	3BR, 1.5BA, F	1,044	468	.45	93.60	98%	
3. Plantation Trace	23	1BR, 1BA, 2nd Fl, F	676	295	.44	98.33	97%	Student-oriented, drapes and carpets, large closets, washer-dryer connections, pool, tennis court, club house site needs additional landscaping
	24	1BR, 1BA, 1st Fl, F	742	318	.43	106.00	97%	
	24	1BR, 1BA, TH	796	319	.40	106.33	97%	
	25	1BR, 1BA, 1st Fl, F	796	337	.42	112.33	98%	
	27	2BR, 2BA, F	931	397	.43	99.25	99%	
	25	2BR, 1BA, F	864	367	.42	91.75	99%	
	21	2BR, 1.5BA, TH	890	377	.42	94.25	98%	
	21	3BR, 2BA, F	1,168	477	.41	95.40	98%	

4. Place du Plantier	28	1BR, 1.5BA, TH	633	280	.44	93.33	98%
	31	1BR, 1BA, F	633	295	.47	98.33	97%
	30	2BR, 1BA, F	873	350	.40	87.50	99%
	30	2BR, 1.5BA, TH	963	360	.37	90.00	99%
	29	2BR, 2BA, F	962	375	.39	93.75	98%
	32	3BR, 2BA, F	1,136	440	.39	88.00	98%

Student oriented, well-maintained landscape, pets allowed, tennis court, clubhouse, well-lighted, drapes and carpets, completely furnished, on student bus route

5. Embassy	40	1BR, 1BA, F	735	320	.44	106.67	97%
	44	1BR, 1BA, F	595	290	.49	96.67	97%
	47	2BR, 1.5BA, F	935	400	.43	100.00	99%
	44	2BR, 1BA, F	727	335	.46	83.75	98%

Student-oriented, half-mile from university, site needs additional landscaping, very small kitchen space, drapes and carpets, completely furnished

6. Sharlo/Sharlo Terrace II	78	1BR, 1BA, F	614	280	.46	93.33	97%
	74	2BR, 2BA, F	838	370	.44	92.50	99%
	73	3BR, 2BA, F	980	440	.45	88.00	98%

Large complex, student-oriented, drapes and carpet need replacing, large closets, pool

Definitions: BA = Bathroom
BR = Bedroom
F = Flat
FL = Floor
ST = Studio
TH = Townhouse

from \$83.75 to \$112.33, in terms of square footage, the variation is much lower. The mean rent per square foot is \$0.43, with only a \$0.06 deviation in either direction (excluding the 1BR, 1BA studio in Oakbrook, which is not typical of market rent). The mean rent per room is \$95.95, with a deviation of approximately \$12.00 in either direction. This points out the necessity of measuring rent in various units and of comparing rent on a basis most similar to the market.

In the analysis, it is also important to determine who the tenants are and what special services or amenities are necessary to secure this rent. Obviously, in a student market, proximity to the university and the availability of public transportation are necessary. Although the apartments usually have identical layouts or floor plans, are there additional features in the subject property, such as an extra bath, that will make it more appealing? Or are there missing features that will make it less appealing?

Table 4–6 also gives the occupancy rates for the various comparables. This is important in establishing the expectations regarding vacancies for the investment under consideration. The same process is used to forecast rent and vacancies for other types of investments. If the subject property is 100-percent occupied when other similar properties have vacancies, the rent may be underpriced, or vice versa if the subject property is underoccupied.

SUMMARY

This chapter outlines the critical elements in valuing an investment: quantity and certainty of gross income, operating expenses, and new income over some future time period. Since value is a reflection of future income expectations, and such estimates involve risk, the most important aspect in reducing this risk is to perform market analysis. The real estate market links the supply and demand for real estate. This is measured from two perspectives: the tenant's and the equity investor's. A market study involves the careful consideration of numerous factors. The most common errors in analyzing markets are reviewed. The chapter concludes with a simple illustration of how to perform a market study. Analyzing the market environment is an important component of the real estate investment process.

QUESTIONS

4–1. What is the purpose of market analysis?

4–2. What is business risk? How is it measured?

4–3. What is the relationship between *risk* and time?

4–4. "Inflation has no effect on equity values; only relative price changes do." True or false? Explain.

4–5. Can real estate investors benefit from expected inflation? Unexpected inflation?

4-6. How is the expected rate of return measured? How is the variance of the expected return measured?

4-7. Illustrate how the decision rules for mean-variance analysis can be used when an investor tries to decide between two alternative investments.

4-8. What are the most common errors found in real estate market studies?

PROBLEMS

4-1. An investment with a value of $500,000 has the following expected NOI:

State of World	NOI	Probability
1	$50,000	.05
2	55,000	.80
3	65,000	.15

a. Calculate the expected overall rate of return.
b. Calculate the variance and standard deviation.

4-2. An investor is considering the purchase of a parcel of land.
a. Suppose there was no expected inflation and the required rate of return was 10 percent. Suppose also that the investor expected to sell the parcel for $100,000 after a three-year holding period. How much should be paid now?
b. Suppose the investor paid $75,132 for the investment and sold it for $110,000. Relative to the required rate of return of 10 percent, would the earned rate of return be higher or lower?
c. Suppose there was inflation at a rate of 5 percent and the investor expected to sell the land for $114,266. How much should be paid today?

4-3. Under what situations would an investor be able to benefit from the following?
a. Expected relative price increase
b. Expected relative price decrease
c. Expected inflation (neutral; all prices increasing)

d. Expected deflation
e. Unexpected relative price increase
f. Unexpected relative price decrease
g. Unexpected inflation
h. Unexpected deflation.

4-4. Suppose an investor faces the following choices:

Investment	Expected Return E(R)	Risk (σ)
A	.15	.02
B	.15	.03
C	.15	.03
D	.14	.03
E	.15	.02
F	.16	.03

Which should the investor select between
a. Investments A and B?
b. Investments C and D?
c. Investments E and F?

4-5. A developer asks your advice on a proposed 75-unit apartment building.
a. Based on the following assumptions, what is the minimum rent that would make this a feasible project?

Construction Costs
    of Building = $1,500,000
    Land Costs = $350,000
    L/V Ratio = 75%
Mortgage Interest
    Rate = 10%
Mortgage Maturity = 25 years with monthly payments
Holding Period = 10 years

Expected
Appreciation in
Property Value = + 2%/year
                   compounded
Required Equity
Rate of Return = 15%
Operating
Expense Ratio = 35%
Vacancy Rate = 5%

30	1BR, 1BA
28	2BR, 1BA
17	2BR, 2BA

Based on the information gathered in the sample market analysis in Table 4–6, would the market support the developers required average rent determined in problem 4 –5a, given the preferred apartment mix?

b. The developer has decided on the following apartment mix for the proposed project:

SELECTED REFERENCES

Anderson, Austin, "Common Pitfalls in Real Estate Market Research," *Real Estate Finance*, 6 (Spring 1989), 77–81.

Bowes, W. A., "What *Is* Market Analysis?" *Real Estate Appraiser*, 34 (July–August 1968), 11–14.

Carn, Neil, Joseph Rabianski, Ronald Racster, and Maury Seldin, *Real Estate Market Analysis: Techniques and Applications*, (Englewood Cliffs, N.J.: Prentice Hall, 1988).

Clapp, John M., *Handbook for Real Estate Market Analysis*, (Englewood Cliffs, N.J.: Prentice Hall, 1987).

Eldred, Gary W., and Robert H. Zerbst, "A Critique of Real Estate Market and Investment Analysis," *Appraisal Journal*, 46 (July 1978), 443–52.

Graaskamp, James A., *A Guide to Feasibility Analysis*. Chicago: Society of Real Estate Appraisers, 1970.

Jaffe, Austin J., and Robert G. Bussa, "Using a Simple Model to Estimate Market Rents: A Case Study," *Appraisal Journal*, 45 (January 1977), 7–13.

Myers, Dowell and Phillip S. Mitchell, "Identifying a Well-Founded Market Analysis," *The Appraisal Journal*, 61 (October 1993), 500–508.

Pearson, Thomas D., "Location! Location! Location! What Is Location?," *The Appraisal Journal*, 59 (January 1991), 7–20.

Redman, Arnold, and C. F. Sirmans, "Regional/Local Economic Analysis: A Discussion of Data Sources," *Appraisal Journal*, 45 (April 1977), 261–72.

Sirmans, C. F., *Data Sources for Real Estate Market Analysis*. Glastonbury, Conn.: Pension Real Estate Association, 1994.

Sirmans, C. F. and Krisandra A. Guidry, "The Determinants of Shopping Center Rents," *Journal of Real Estate Research*, 8 (Winter 1993), 107–115.

Sirmans, G. Stacy, C. F. Sirmans, and John D. Benjamin, "Determining Apartment Rent: The Value of Amenities, Services, and External Factors," *Journal of Real Estate Research*, 4 (Summer 1989), 33–43.

Vandell, Kerry D., "Market Analysis: Can We Do Better?" *The Appraisal Journal*, 56 (July 1988), 344–350.

Vernor, James D., *Readings in Market Research for Real Estate*. Chicago: American Institute of Real Estate Appraisers, 1985.

CHAPTER 5

THE LEGAL ENVIRONMENT

PRINCIPLES

1. Real estate investments are subject to legal risk.
2. The four major real estate participants may have different organizational forms.
3. The relationships between participants are property rights relations and are often specified by specific legal rules.

In the real world, there is a certain amount of risk associated with the legal environment. As a result, an investor must pay attention to the local, state, and federal laws that affect the environment. *Legal risk* is the possibility that the government will alter the laws that affect the real estate investment.

There are many effects of legal risk. For example, if a property owner is interested in converting his or her property to a condominium in the near future, this action will affect several groups of people. For instance, current tenants will be affected by the change because their leaseholds will not be available in the future. In addition, tenants in other buildings may be affected because the supply of rental space will be less than in the past. Prospective purchases of condominium units may also be affected by the new project. Mortgage lenders who have creditor interests in the apartment building have an interest in the outcome of the conversion because the mortgage note must be satisfied before the conversion is complete. Finally, various units of government are interested in the outcome. In every case, each participant has an economic interest in the "property rights" that have been developed and are protected by the legal system. Therefore a complete real estate investment analysis requires a basic understanding of the modern legal environment. Note, however, that this chapter is not intended to be an all-inclusive summary or substitute for legal counsel.

SOME BASIC DEFINITIONS

In order to study the legal environment in real estate, it is necessary to learn a number of basic definitions. These include the doctrine of property as a "bundle of rights," real estate, realty, real property, personalty, personal property, and fixtures.

It is sometimes said that real estate consists of a set of rights. These rights may be linked together by size, shape, nature, or duration. They may be vast and all-inclusive or few and limited. The complete set of rights is often referred to as the entire bundle of rights.[1] In Anglo-American law, this bundle is called "fee simple absolute." In actuality, the study of real estate is the study of the bundle of rights.

In order to apply the doctrine of the bundle of rights, it is necessary to distinguish between real estate and real property. Although these terms are often used synonymously, there are distinctions between them. *Real estate* refers to (a) the physical object (land and its improvements), (b) the profession of brokers, appraisers, counselors, and others concerned with the land and its usage, and (c) the academic field of study interested in the process and institutions dealing with land usage and alteration among several interested parties in society. *Real property* refers to the rights associated with the *realty*, or the physical real estate. Therefore, while *realty* and *real estate* are synonymous terms, *real property* and *real estate* differ. It is apparent, then, that the rights in the assets and not merely the assets are of particular interest in examining these resources for investment purposes.

A similar distinction is made between personalty and personal property. *Personalty* is defined as movable objects. Since land and permanently attached structures are fixed, personalty can be viewed as any other objects except realty. On the other hand, *personal property* consists of the rights associated with the personalty. Although these distinctions are not as general as real property rights, they are basic to our legal system. For example, the right of possession exists for both realty and personalty.

It is also possible for an object to become permanently attached to the real estate. Such an object is then called a *fixture*. Although the law provides some guidelines in these cases, it is sometimes difficult to determine whether an object that formerly was personalty is now a permanent attachment to the real estate and thus a fixture. It is important to recognize that fixtures become a part of the real estate and are therefore valued with the real estate for nearly every economic purpose.

[1]The concept of "bundle of rights" is attributed to William Blackstone, a prominent English legal scholar.

THE REAL ESTATE INVESTMENT PARTICIPANTS

There are four major real estate participants in the real estate investment process: the equity investor, the mortgage lender, the tenant, and the government. Each has a particular interest and specific legal environment in which to operate. (The relationships between these participants were outlined in Figure 1–2, "Participants in the Real Estate Investment Process.")

The equity investor must decide on the appropriate organization form. The mortgage lender will be one of several types, using various types of instruments. The tenant is likely to vary with the type of property. The government may be at the federal, state, or local level.

THE EQUITY INVESTOR

The equity investor is faced with several choices regarding the type of business organization. The decision is to choose the one that is best for the investor, given the specific objectives of the owner. In the typical case, the equity investor is usually concerned with taxation, liability, marketability, method of creation, and expected duration of the organization. After considering all of these, the investor decides on the best organizational form for each investment. Table 5–1 illustrates the various forms of ownership.

❒ **INDIVIDUAL (PROPRIETORSHIP).**   Individual ownership is very simple to form and operate for a small enterprise. The transferability of assets is easy and inexpensive, and management of the company remains a personal responsibility. For some types of operation, this form is suitable. However, for many small operations, it may not be the most advantageous ownership form. The taxation treatment is according to regular, individual tax rates. Proprietorships have unlimited liability, which permits suitors seeking damages to have access to personal, nonbusiness assets. The aspects of unlimited liability and sole responsibility for decisions may be an incentive to use one of the other forms.

TABLE 5–1
SELECTED ALTERNATIVE FORMS OF OWNERSHIP

Individual (Proprietorship)
General partnership
Limited partnership
Ordinary corporation
Subchapter S corporation
Land trust
Real estate investment trust (REIT)
Joint venture
Syndication

❐ **GENERAL PARTNERSHIP.** This is very similar to proprietorship. General partnerships are created by agreement of the parties. In general, partnerships offer individual proprietors the advantages of joint decision making and risk sharing with the disadvantage of potential management disagreements and differences of opinion. Tax treatment is according to individual rates, but each partner applies the investor's individual tax rate. Potential liability remains unlimited. Although marketability and disposition can be complicated, it is fairly simple in most cases.[2]

❐ **LIMITED PARTNERSHIP.** Limited partnership is a relatively popular type of business entity. It attempts to secure the best of both worlds: limited liability on the part of limited partners and taxation at personal rates.

This form also requires a general partner (or partners) to serve as managing agent for the entire operation. In addition, termination provisions are typically provided in the agreement. However, marketability is somewhat difficult due to problems with transfer of ownership, and withdrawal of the general partner can terminate the partnership agreement.

[2] However, there are a number of concurrent estates available which can result in significant differences at the time of disposition.

Therefore, this form would be attractive to investors who seek a passive investment, free of management problems and obligations, and one in which liability is limited to the amount invested, tax losses offset ordinary income, and where marketability is not the most important consideration.

❑ **ORDINARY CORPORATION.** The well-known corporate form is often viewed as "the only realistic business form" by many investors. There are, of course, advantages such as limited liability, ease of marketability of ownership "shares," generally centralized and constant management, and a perpetual life for the business. However, other factors are less favorable. Income earned by the corporation is taxed twice, once at the corporate rate and again when dividends distributed to shareholders are taxed at ordinary rates. In addition, tax losses can only offset previous tax payments at the corporate rate. Finally, for some small companies, it may be more expensive and time consuming to form a corporation or to dissolve one than to use the partnership forms.

❑ **SUBCHAPTER S CORPORATION.** The Subchapter S corporation is a special form allowed by the 1958 Technical Amendments Act to the Internal Revenue Code. It was designed to avoid the double taxation provision of corporate income yet retain the other provisions of corporate treatment. Subchapter S corporations may not have more than 35 shareholders. In addition, all shareholders must be individuals (partnerships and their corporations are specifically excluded) and residents of the United States. There are some additional income requirements, but the basis of this form permits limited liability with tax treatment preferable to the double taxation of corporations. Management considerations depend on the specific organizations, and marketability is somewhat affected by the additional requirements and the upper limit on partners. Recent changes in the tax law are likely to make Subchapter S elections a more viable option.

❑ **LAND TRUST.** The land trust is only available in a few states. It was created in Illinois and enjoys its widest usage there. Under this arrangement, title passes to a trustee who holds the title to property only for the purpose of carrying out the wishes of the owners or beneficiaries. Therefore the trustee does not take over the operations of the property without the written permission of the beneficiaries.

The land trust has been criticized by tenant groups as being a form that serves no particular purpose except to hide the true ownership of property. If a dispute arises between a tenant and the owner, the land trust becomes a shield between the often angry tenant and the true owner. The trustee, of course, may not be able to make many operating decisions without the permission of the owner.

On the other hand, proponents have argued that there is more substance to a land trust. This form permits limited liability on the part of the owners, enables tax treatment at ordinary rates, and offers considerably more ease in marketability than partnerships or Subchapter S corporations. There are other advantages also. Thus, the land trust remains an attractive option in some states despite legal struggles to prohibit its usage.

❏ **REAL ESTATE INVESTMENT TRUST (REIT).**   The REIT is a special version of an equity trust. It is governed by specific rules and regulations that permit limited liability, tax treatment based on ordinary income, and good marketability. Management is typically handled by an advisory board, since an REIT must have at least 100 shareholders. However, tax losses may not be "passed through" to shareholders as in partnership forms. In addition, poor performance in the late 1960s and 1970s, and then again in the late 1980s, has soured many individuals on REIT ventures. It remains, however, a viable form, given the limitations of small investors seeking passive interests in real estate. There has been renewed interest in REITs in the 1990s.

❏ **JOINT VENTURE.**   This form is a special arrangement that, unlike most of the previous forms, is not expected to be an ongoing concern. Two or more parties are needed to create a joint venture, which can take on any legal ownership form. Real estate development is a good example, since the developer may need to offer additional incentive to equity holders in order to interest them in somewhat risky ventures. Therefore, joint ventures are the legal arrangement for some real estate investment.

❏ **SYNDICATION.**   Syndication, like the joint venture, is not truly an ownership form; rather, a technique to raise capital for investment purposes. The organizer or syndicator is frequently the general partner in a limited partnership and often benefits from management fees and an active role in the operation. Syndicates are really associations for conducting business and thus differ from legal forms of ownership. However, a potential investor may wish to organize a syndicate for investment in larger projects or to attract capital for limited partnerships. Table 5–2 summarizes the major characteristics of the business organizations discussed in this chapter. It should be emphasized that each investor will have different objectives in selecting the appropriate business organization. Therefore, no single organization is "best" for real estate investing.

THE MORTGAGE LENDER

The second participant in the real estate investment process is the mortgage lender. An investor seeking sources of funds for investment has a growing number of financial institutions from which to choose. Table 5–3 presents the breakdown of outstanding mortgage debt by institution. As indicated, nearly three-fourths of all mortgages were on small (one-to-

TABLE 5–2
SUMMARY OF CHARACTERISTICS OF BUSINESS ORGANIZATIONS

	Taxation Status	Investor's Liability	Transferability	Management	Method of Creation	Duration
Individual	Flow through (single)	Unlimited	Transferable	Personal	Individual	Terminated by death or agreement; deceased interest
General partnership	Flow through (single)	Unlimited	Not transferable	All partners in absence of agreement have equal voice	Created by agreement of the parties	Terminated by death, bankruptcy, or withdrawal of a partner
Limited partnership	Flow through (single)	Limited	Transferable	General partners have equal voice; limited partners have no voice	Created by agreement of the parties	Termination provided in the agreement
Corporation	Non-flow through (double)	Limited	Transferable	Shareholders elect directors who set policy	Charter issued by state	Perpetual
Subchapter S corporation	Non-flow through (double)	Limited	Limited by maximum number of shareholders	Varies with specific organization	Charter issued by federal authority	Terminated by actions of shareholders
Land trust	Flow through (single)	Limited	Very transferable	Beneficiaries	Created by trust document if permitted by state law	Terminated by trustees, beneficiaries, or terms of agreement
Real Estate Investment Trust (REIT)	Modified flow through (tax losses cannot exceed cash distribution)	Limited	Modified	Trustees	Created by agreement of the parties and charter issued by state	Perpetual

TABLE 5–3
TOTAL MORTGAGE DEBT OUTSTANDING BY MAJOR TYPE OF LENDER (IN MILLIONS OF DOLLARS)

Lender	1–4 Family ($)	(%)	Multifamily ($)	(%)	Nonresidential ($)	(%)	Farm ($)	(%)	Total ($)	(%)
Savings Institutions[1]	480,636	78.49	68,325	11.16	63,096	10.30	322	0.05	612,379	15.46
Commercial Banks	526,800	57.83	38,064	4.18	325,485	35.73	20,595	2.26	910,944	23.00
Life Insurance Companies	11,195	4.63	27,174	11.24	194,012	80.26	9,348	3.87	241,729	6.10
Mortgage Pools & Trusts[2]	1,278,726	95.83	55,552	4.16	19	*	16	*	1,334,313	33.69
Federal & Related Agencies	211,868	70.81	41,003	13.70	11,190	3.74	35,154	11.75	299,215	7.55
Individuals & Others[3]	372,699	66.27	86,083	15.31	88,357	15.71	15,372	2.73	562,511	14.20
Total	2,881,924	72.8	316,121	7.98	682,159	17.22	80,807	2.04	3,961,091	100

[1]Includes savings banks and savings-and-loan associations.
[2]Outstanding balances of mortgage-backed securities insured or guaranteed by government agencies and private conduits.
[3]Other holders include mortgage companies, real estate investment trusts, state and local credit agencies, state and local retirement funds, noninsured pension funds, credit unions, and finance companies.
*Denotes percentages that are insignificant.
Note: Amounts may not add to total due to rounding.
Source: Federal Reserve Bulletin, March, 1994.

four-family) residential units. This indicates the predominance of mortgage finance for residential property. While savings institutions, until recently, had held a large percentage of all outstanding mortgages, they are currently in third place (15.46 percent) behind commercial banks (23.0 percent) and mortgage pools and trusts (33.69 percent) for the percentage of mortgage debt held. Most savings institution mortgages consisted of single-family residences and small income-producing buildings (78.5 percent). On the other hand, life insurance companies placed a majority of their funds in mortgages on nonresidential property such as shopping centers and office buildings. Federal and related agencies such as the Veterans Administration, Small Business Administration, and Farm Credit Administration appeared as the sixth-largest supplier of mortgage funds to the market. In contrast, there is an increasing interest in mortgage securitization as evidenced by the large portion of mortgage debt held by mortgage pools and trusts (33.69 percent of total mortgage debt outstanding). This is a change from the recent past, when mortgages tended to be concentrated in savings institutions and commercial banks.

The following discussion highlights the major financial institutions and the prospect of each institution as a source of funds for the real estate investor.

❒ SAVINGS-AND-LOAN ASSOCIATIONS. Savings-and-loan associations, often called "thrift institutions," specialize in making single-family loans based on time and passbook deposits at their institutions. However, the investor in income-producing real estate may also view savings-and-loans as a source of funds, because many small income-producing properties are financed with loans from these institutions. In recent years, savings-and-loans have taken a much more active role in the financing of multifamily and commercial mortgages. The savings-and-loan association of the future may be much more conservative than in the recent past due to problems incurred as a consequence of high-risk commercial loans originated in the 1980s that experienced abnormally high default rates.

❒ COMMERCIAL BANKS. Historically, commercial banks have been more diversified than savings-and-loan associations, mutual savings banks, or mortgage companies. In recent years, commercial banks have expanded their operations to include more multifamily and commercial mortgages. They have also been active in short-term construction loans for multifamily housing. The investor in income-producing real estate may use a commercial bank as a source of long-term credit and particular short-term credit such as construction funds.

❒ LIFE INSURANCE COMPANIES. Life insurance companies are well-established real estate lenders, although this does not appear to be true to the casual observer. Despite the fact that these companies have declined in importance in terms of residential loans in recent years, they continue to be a major source of capital for multifamily property and large commercial projects. A real estate developer may find life insurance companies a sound source of long-term permanent financing.

☐ **MORTGAGE POOLS AND TRUSTS.** Mortgage pools and trusts have become the largest single holder of mortgage debt (Table 5–3). This has resulted from the increased level of liquidity and higher returns in relation to levels of risk. Although the majority of mortgage-backed securities currently cover residential properties, there has been a growth in interest in commercial mortgage-backed securities (CMBS) in recent years. This has been in large part due to the success of the Resolution Trust Corporation in issuing CMBSs.

☐ **FEDERAL CREDIT AGENCIES.** Federal credit agencies play an important role in the market for single-family loans, multifamily loans, and farm credit. Because most of their assets are held in the form of mortgages, some of the agencies may assist in supplying funds. The available federally subsidized programs are numerous and frequently very detailed regarding qualifications and program changes. However, for some investors in multifamily housing, the federal agencies may be a viable credit source.

☐ **INDIVIDUALS AND OTHERS.** The final category consists of two groups. The first includes those few individuals with enough liquid money willing to lend it to a real estate investor in the form of a mortgage over a long-term period. A common example is the seller who takes back a purchase-money mortgage or one who accepts a second or junior mortgage in lieu of cash at the time of sale. The second includes such institutions as mortgage companies, state and local credit agencies, pension funds, credit unions, and REITs. Each has particular interests and legal requirements. Many may provide funding for certain types of investment projects for a particular investor. Further, institutions such as mortgage companies service and originate loans for governmental agencies in the secondary mortgage market.

THE TENANT

The third participant is the immediate user of the real estate—the tenant. The tenant in feudal times had very few rights for the duration of the leasehold. However, the development of landlord-tenant law is evidence of the shift toward protection and existence of the rights of tenants. A brief overview of this law will be presented later in this chapter.

There may be different legal ramifications for each type of tenant. One classification divides various leaseholds according to expected duration of the estate. In nearly every case, the legal differences between the tenancies will be directly related to the rights associated with the document (lease) between the equity investor (or agent) and the tenant (or agent).

❐ **RESIDENTIAL USERS.** This is the most commonly encountered type of tenant for most small income-producing real estate. Residential users consist of tenants in single-family dwellings, small apartment buildings, six-flat apartment buildings, garden-type apartments, large complexes, and others. Residential tenants are primarily interested in suitable living conditions. Depending on the geographical area of the country and on local market conditions, the typical lease for a residential property will extend from a monthly leasehold up to two years or longer. Compared with long-term commercial leases, these are quite short.

Compared with other types of tenants, residential tenants are more concerned with the physical amenities within the building. In most agreements, maintenance is expected to be performed by the lessor on a regular basis and, for serious problems, at the notice of the tenant. Failure to provide these services often results in management problems, tenant turnover, and landlord-tenant disputes. In fact, most of the new landlord-tenant laws enacted during the past 15 years are a result of problems encountered with residential property.

In addition, items such as groundskeeping, snow removal, and the overall maintenance of the property's grounds are important to residential tenants. Since residential tenants view their leaseholds as their "homes," management should treat the property accordingly. Effective property management is essential in assisting the investor to maintain a good rapport with tenants.

The problems of management are well known to many investors in residential real estate. However, these problems can be minimized if prudent management techniques are followed. The residential tenant may be one of the most difficult management problems for the unsuspecting investor, but without the property manager, income-producing apartment buildings would be less valuable.

❐ **COMMERCIAL USERS.** There are several types of commercial tenants, or users, involved in a commercial or business activity. These include wholesale and retail stores, office buildings, and shopping centers. Commercial tenants tend to be larger, more sophisticated, and often more financially secure. In addition, leases for commercial use frequently involve percentage *leases*. These leases allow for the remittance of a percentage of sales or income for the rental payment. In some cases, this percentage is in addition to a minimum guaranteed rent.

Although some commercial leases are not percentage leases, most are long-term. It is possible to find commercial leases for 30 or 40 years for large firms or *anchors* in some shopping centers. Commercial leases are also frequently quoted on a square-foot (or sometimes front-footage) basis. This unit of measurement enables quick comparisons in what are often highly competitive markets.

Commercial leases may also have specific clauses that are characteristic of this type of lease. There may be restrictions and requirements regarding the number of hours the firm must be open for business. This is especially common if the percentage lease is in use and gross income is applied as a measure of volume sales. In addition, there may be some specific requirement regarding business records and audit procedures, another frequent provision in commercial leases. Finally, the commercial tenant may be limited to only performing certain activities while on the lessor's premises.

❏ **INDUSTRIAL USERS.** Industrial tenants are generally users of property in which the interior of the buildings is unfinished. Warehouses, plants, utilities, and factories are typical examples. Since this type of property tends to be quite large, industrial leases tend to be quite extensive and are often specially designed for the user. The growth of industrial parks has led to much more careful analysis of the economics of leasing industrial space versus an outright purchase of the property.

Industrial tenants are concerned with access, production efficiency, and safety conditions in the facility. Their leases tend to be long term and are typically net of maintenance, utilities, and other operating expenses. Because industrial real estate is very competitive, leases must be negotiated very carefully. Since many of the facilities are large, a small error in negotiation may result in a very expensive leasing obligation.

❏ **SPECIAL-PURPOSE USERS.** There are a number of other tenants that lease space for other specific purposes. Some examples of special-purpose users are theaters, assembly halls, and sports arenas. Leasing arrangements and terms vary with each specific use. The requirements of the lessor (landlord) to the lessee (tenant) depend on the value of the economic activity to be performed on the property. Each industry tends to have its own institutional standards regarding leasing terms. For example, a lease for a movie theater may specify a percentage rate with a minimum per-seat guarantee. In addition, the revenue from the concessions may also be included in the lease.

Special-purpose buildings require a much more critical analysis of the activity performed on the premises. Furthermore, more information may be needed to ascertain the riskiness of the tenant and the tenant's ability to make the rental payments. In some cases, however, the profitability of a successful enterprise may result in a very successful real estate investment for the building's owner.

One of the more interesting forms of business organization in the United States is the real estate investment trust (REIT). Although similar versions exist elsewhere, REITs have special tax provisions and ownership requirements that make it very different from other forms of ownership.

The history of REITs is an interesting and colorful one. During the late 1960s and early 1970s, there was a boom cycle in the market for REITs, driven largely through the financing motivations of increasingly aggressive investors. When interest rates began to rise in 1974, the beginning of the end was in sight. Soon, a financial crunch was underway for REITs and many mortgage trusts were forced into bankruptcy. Developers with forward commitments were also in trouble. Share prices of REITs plummeted; investors swore never to invest in these "crazy" real estate vehicles again.

Time heals all wounds and by the mid-1980s, there were several new trusts and a new generation of REITs investors. There was also considerable interest in the initial public offerings (IPOs) of REITs in financial markets. As real estate markets weakened in the late 1980s, REIT share prices fell faster. Once again, this volatile vehicle has claimed a new set of victims.

By the early 1990s, a third generation of REITs have appeared. This time, REITs are often used to restructure existing real estate debt and more than ever before, REITs are viewed as a financial vehicle for existing real estate operations. Despite the financial difficulties in most institutional real estate markets, new IPO offerings for REITs attract considerable attention on Wall Street. REITs are an interesting aspect of real estate investment and finance.

THE GOVERNMENT

The final primary participant in the real estate investment process is the government. Generally, the impact of government regulation and influence is felt by all the other participants. Typically, government influence is divided into three categories: federal, state, and local governments. Together these three "public sectors" greatly affect real estate investment decisions.

❐ FEDERAL.   The most visible impact that federal government has on a real estate investment is its ability to tax the income from real estate. Chapter 7 is devoted to an analysis of taxation and tax planning to assist the investor in legally avoiding unnecessary tax payments. However, other federal regulations on the use of real estate can be equally important. For example, the right of *eminent domain* rests with the federal as well as with state governments. This right permits the taking of private real estate for public purposes as long as "just compensation" is paid. Therefore, if the government decides that your property is needed for a public purpose, it may be obtained through this right, or limitation of your rights of eminent domain.

Federal land-use regulations have resulted from a growing public awareness of conservation and environmental impacts that occur during some uses of land. The federal government has taken an active stance in this area, and the future appears to hold an even greater participation by federal authorities.

Finally, the federal government also retains the right of *escheat,* or the taking of property when no heirs or will can be found after the death of the owner(s). Further, estate taxes can dramatically affect the returns and worth of property at the time of death.

☐ **STATE.** Property law varies from state to state. Although modern property law comes from early English common law and is generally followed throughout the United States,[3] differences occur as courts and legislatures attempt to deal with various issues. Therefore, *most of property law comes from state law.*

Various states have defined different estates and interests. Some states have adopted the title theory of mortgages. Others have followed the lien theory. Certain states have created new laws to meet changing conditions in the area of consumer protection of urban tenants in landlord-tenant law or, in some of the western states, in dealing with water rights. Finally, each state has various income, property, and estate tax laws which can significantly affect the value and return of real estate. In general, there are many areas where real estate is affected by state government and its law. Many of these considerations are treated below.

☐ **LOCAL.** Local government may be the municipality, county, or other political boundary. It is characterized by smaller and more-detailed concerns. Examples of local government action include building codes, zoning ordinances, and set-back requirements. The local government can have a significant influence. Recent moves toward rent-control ordinances have been controversial in many communities. Some local governments have also attempted to deal with growth and expansion by limiting (or in some cases forbidding) the issuance of new housing permits. Another example is the recent interest in condominium conversions. Although many

[3]This is not true of Louisiana, which follows the French or Napoleonic legal system. Also, certain elements of Spanish law are found throughout the state laws in the southwestern portion of the United States.

real estate developers and investors view local government as an obstacle to their objectives, it is becoming an ever-increasing political force.

RELATIONSHIP BETWEEN THE REAL ESTATE INVESTMENT AND THE PARTICIPANTS

We have described some of the legal aspects of the primary participants in the real estate investment process. Now let us focus on the relationship between the participants and the investment vehicle: the land, improvements, and the property rights associated with the realty.

PROPERTY RIGHTS OF THE EQUITY INVESTOR

The equity investor, as we have already said, acquires a bundle of rights as an investor in real estate. These entitle the investor to a cash flow. The magnitude and safety of the cash flow is directly related to the magnitude and quality of the bundle of rights and interests that the investor acquires in taking title to the property. Sometimes the rights are present interests; other times they involve future interests. Some rights are concurrent interests; others are rights in the land of others. All interests that entitle rights to valuable property are presumed to have value. It is important that the investor understand the basic differences between the many forms of property interests or *estates*.

❐ **FREEHOLD ESTATES.** Freehold estate interests are widely held and represent the most complete interests available in many cases. With the exception of life estates, freehold estates are potentially infinite in duration. The name *freehold* comes from the common law, where it referred to the interests in land that were associated with free men. Because they were the only estates that were given full protection of law, they are large and powerful interests today. There are basically four types of freehold estates: fee simple absolute, defeasible fees, fee tail, and life estates.

The largest and most complete estate available is called *fee simple absolute,* or *fee simple.* Potentially infinite as long as heirs can be found, it can be passed on to future heirs without restriction or limitation. A fee simple estate is the complete bundle of rights (subject to the traditional government limitations).

The second category of fee estates consists of *defeasible fees.* These are identical with fee simple estates, except they are defeasible depending on the occurrence of some event. An example would be a grant of property to "Mr. Jones and his heirs as long as the property would be used for the benefit of the children in the community." This is called a *fee simple determinable* or a *qualified fee,* since the existence of the fee estate is determined by the event that the property is used "for the benefit of the children in the community." Another example would be if Mr. Brown grants to "Mr. Smith and his heirs but if smoking is permitted on the premises, then Mr. Brown has the right to reenter and repossess the property." Such a grant creates a *fee simple subject to condition subsequent* for Mr. Smith. Clearly, if the specific condition (that is, smoking) occurs (with "permission"), then the grant dictates that Mr. Smith may lose his interest and the estate may "revert" to Mr. Brown if he elects to take the property. A final example is a *fee simple subject to executory limitation* or *devise*. This is really either of two estates. If it is subject to limitation, it is created by deed. If it is subject to devise, it is a creation by last will and testament. As an example, assume Mr. White by deed conveys his property to "Mr. Black and his heirs, but if Mrs. Black remarries, then the property goes to Mr. Green and his heirs." In this case, Mr. Black is said to have a *fee simple subject to executory limitation*. The limitation, of course, is that if Mrs. Black remarries, then Mr. Green will take title to the property in fee simple.

A third category of freehold estate, which in modern law is unenforceable or viewed as a modified fee simple estate, is called the *fee tail*. This estate specifies that the property would pass according to the "heirs of his body." If the holder of the fee tail produced a male[4] heir, then at the time of his death,[5] the property would pass to the lineal heir. If the line were to be stopped, the property would, by design, revert to the original grantor (or his heirs). As one can imagine, there were so many problems with this estate that modern law has attempted to eliminate its usage, and, in most cases, states will not enforce a fee tail conveyance. Though rarely seen today, it is a reminder of the common law heritage.

The final freehold estate is a *life estate*. There are basically two types of life estates: *conventional life estates* and *legal life estates*. The first is characterized by the words in the deed "for the term of his natural life." The grantee in this case would have a conventional life estate that would entitle him or her to use the property (but not damage it), take "fruits" from it, and even sell the interest to other parties. However, at the time of the life tenant's death, the grantor (or heirs) would get back the interest in the property.

It is also possible for the life estate to be measured by the life of someone other than the recipient of the grant. In this case, the life estate is called *pur autre vie* ("for another's life").[6] For example, assume Mrs. Howard grants her property to Mrs. Roberts for the life of Mr. Howard. When Mr. Howard dies, Mrs. Roberts's interest is extinguished and the property reverts to Mrs. Howard.

A common form of *legal life estates* refers to wives' interests in their husbands' property called *dower rights* and husbands' interests in their

---

[4]In medieval times, only males could hold title to property at the sufferance of the king. Later, the estate known as *fee tail female* was introduced to specify a line of female descendants.
[5]It was assumed that only males could hold property interests.
[6]The name of this estate is taken from Old French.

wives' property called *curtesy rights.* These rights are in disfavor with courts and in many states are no longer enforceable. However, in the states where they are, these estates refer to rights that may result in surprises at the time of the spouse's death if the grantee is not careful. In many cases, title assurance methods have eliminated much of the risk of "legal life estate surprises."

Clearly, the analysis of freehold estates is complex and intricate. This review exposes the reader to some of the terminology and concepts of estates in land. It is not intended to be a substitute for legal counsel. It should be apparent, however, that there are many kinds of estates available for interests in property.

❑ **CONCURRENT ESTATES.** Concurrent estate interests are used when more than one person desires joint ownership of property. There are four types of concurrent estates: joint tenancy, tenancy in common, tenancy by the entirety, and tenancy in coparcenary. It is important to distinguish between these estates.

Joint tenancy is an estate that specifies that the surviving tenants will divide the property of the deceased cotenant equally, immediately upon the death of the cotenant, and without entering the estate of the deceased cotenant. All tenants are said to own the entire property as joint owners. The right of survivorship (by the surviving cotenants) is a characteristic of this estate. Finally, in order to create a joint tenancy, one must meet the "four unity tests." This requires that all the cotenants enter the agreement at the same time (unity of time), all acquire their interests by a single conveyance (unity of title), all interests are of the same type and duration (unity of interest), and all have an undivided right to use the property (unity of possession). If one or more of these unities cannot be met or are broken over time, the property is not a joint tenancy but a tenancy in common.

A *tenancy in common* is a concurrent ownership form where each tenant owns an undivided portion of the property but not necessarily in equal amounts. Further, a tenant may sell his or her interest at will and not disturb the estate. Finally, a tenancy in common permits the passage of property to heirs rather than automatically to cotenants, as in joint tenancy. For several reasons, tenancy in common is preferred by courts and state lawmakers over joint tenancy. The opposite was true in common law, but in modern courts the complications that arise through the use of joint tenancies (and concurrent tenancy in common) have led some states to abolish joint tenancies and still others to apply a very strict interpretation of the four unities test.[7]

For some husbands and wives, the joint tenancy may seem to be the preferred concurrent estate. However, the estate known as tenancy by the

---

[7]For example, the concurrent use of joint tenancies and tenacy in common can render unsuspecting partners unhappy with the premature death of one of the partners.

entirety was specifically designed for husbands and wives. A *tenancy by the entirety* is very similar to a joint tenancy except it requires an additional fifth unity (unity of person). This means that the husband and wife during marriage are viewed as one legal person in this estate. If one dies, the property automatically goes to the survivor. In addition, neither spouse can voluntarily dispose of an interest in the property without the permission of the other. In a joint tenancy, any tenant can act and be held responsible for the whole tenancy. Finally, in the event of a divorce, the tenancy by the entirety is destroyed and a tenancy in common remains.

The final tenancy is the *tenancy in coparcenary*. It is really an extinct estate which, if found, is typically viewed as a tenancy in common. It was the estate left without male heirs but with at least two female heirs. The female heirs are said to be tenants in coparcenary. Thus, this estate was created by the law of inheritance and receives virtually no legal usage today.

❒ **FUTURE INTERESTS.** These estates are interests in existing property which will not begin until some future date. These acknowledge that the holder of the future interest has an estate presently: the right to use and enjoy property at some time in the future. In addition, some future interests may never become possessory interests if certain events do not occur. These are called *contingent estates*. These may be contrasted with future interests that are known to occur at some definite point in time, or *vested estates*.

All future estates can be classified as one of five types: reversions, possibilities of reverter, rights of reentry, remainders, and executory interests. *Reversions* are future interests that entitle the holder to recover a possessory interest at a future time. An example is the interest at the time of the death of the life tenant. Because all life tenants will die, reversions are said to be vested interests. *Possibilities of reverter* are future interests associated with a determinable fee. Recall that in a determinable fee, the owner of the fee may retain the interest for life and pass it to his or her heirs and they to theirs, "as long as" the event specified occurs (or does not occur). Because the future interest may never become a possessory estate, it is classed as a "possibility of a reverter."

A *right of reentry* is also the future interest associated with a determinable fee but specifically with a fee simple subject to condition subsequent. The right of reentry gives the original grantor the "right to reenter" the property if certain conditions occur (or do not occur). As noted earlier, the grantee has the right to take back the property. In the case of nearly all of the other future estates, they become possessory estates automatically.

Remainders are the granting away of the reversionary interests. Remainders typically follow life estates but may also follow some fees, fee tails, or terms for years. Remainder interests must become possessory interests. Finally, *executory interests* are technical future interests that may be created by deed or will and that permit transfer of property rights after the death of the grantor. It is an interest that may become a possessory interest at some future date or due to the occurrence of some event. Courts tend to prefer remainders, contingent on some event occurring, rather than executory interests for the reason of freer alienation of land.

☐ **INTERESTS AND RIGHTS IN THE LAND OF OTHERS.** The final area of property rights of the equity investor consists of a set of related rights of nonpossessory interests. There are four main types: easements, profits, licenses, and covenants.

An *easement* is interest in someone else's land that entitles the holder to use and enjoy the land in some manner. A common example is a utility easement for running underground water pipes over a portion of another property owner's land. For investors in real estate, it is important to identify any easements that may stop the usage of land in some way and thereby have an adverse effect on the value of the property.

A *profit* is very similar to an easement, but in addition to permitting the use of another's land, it grants the holder of the profit the right to take away the soil or raw materials from the land. Clearly, a profit implies an easement, since it encompasses all the interests of an easement and more. A profit may also be a valuable property right depending on the type of property and the value of the soil and natural resources.

A *license* is a personal privilege granted to the holder to go on another's land without being a trespasser. A license is not an interest in land, nor is it a possessory estate. As a mere permission, it is limited in the extent of its rights. Frequently, a license may be revoked by the licensor at his or her discretion.

Finally, a *covenant* is a promise to do or not to do a specific thing. In terms of real estate, a covenant may restrict the building of auxiliary buildings in a certain subdivision. Conceptually, covenants are restrictions that stop the owner from using his or her land as he or she pleases. In some cases, this might be a critical factor in the valuation of property. In that event, the existence of a covenant is an important factor for the real estate investor.[8]

THE MORTGAGE LENDER AND THE MORTGAGE DOCUMENT

The relationship between the mortgage lender and the real estate investment is spelled out in the mortgage document. Although there is a brief discussion regarding the use of mortgages for real estate finance in Chapter 6, the discussion in this section centers on two main parts. The first part reviews the concept of the mortgage instrument as security and the second part highlights the requirements for a valid mortgage.

[8]Restrictive covenants are extensively used as private land-use controls in Houston, Texas, the only major US city without a comprehensive zoning ordinance.

Suppose a fee simple estate is worth $100. The law permits the grantor to divide inheritable estates into smaller bundles. For example, suppose the fee simple is divided into a conventional life estate with a remainder interest. If the expected life of the life tenant is known, then it is possible to estimate the value of the remainder interest (that is, the future interest will be the difference in value between $100 and the present value of the benefits for the remainder of the life's tenant's expected life).

As another example, suppose a leasehold is created by the owners of the fee simple estate above. Specifically, suppose a tenancy for 20 years is created and the reversion is granted to another person. What is the value of the future interest, if the fee simple estate is known to be worth $100? Mathematically, the estate would be expected to sell for the present value of a deferred annuity beginning twenty years hence.

Finally, a defeasible fee could be created out of the fee simple estate. The likelihood of the future interest (generally a possibility of a reverter or a right of reentry) will be determined by the probability of the event occurring (or not occurring) as specified in the grant. Thus, the probability of occurrence times the value of the estate discounted to the present will provide a sound estimate of the value of the estate.

❐ NATURE OF THE MORTGAGE INSTRUMENT. The mortgage process technically contains a *mortgage* or the written instrument that pledges real property as security for an obligation, and a *promissory note,* or the written promise of one person to repay an amount of money according to agreed terms and conditions. It is important to recognize that the financing process involves both a mortgage and a note. If the note were to be written without a mortgage, it would be, in effect, unsecured. Therefore both are essential ingredients for the functioning of the mortgage as a secured instrument. Once the note is repaid, a *release is* sought from the lender in order to free the property that was held as security.

The concept of the mortgage instrument has a long history in common law. Over time, however, two "theories" of mortgage law developed: the *title theory* and the *lien theory*. Basically, because states that have adopted the title theory view the adoption of a mortgage as a change in possession and a conveyance of title, the use of a mortgage in a title state is paramount to a conveyance of property rights between the equity holder (mortgagor) and the mortgage lender (mortgagee). In states that have adopted the lien theory, by far the majority, different results occur. In lien theory states, the existence of a mortgage implies that the mortgagee merely has a claim against the property in the event of a default.

Therefore, there is no conveyance of title and fewer property rights have been transferred.

Finally, in some states, a device that is quite similar to a mortgage is used for security. This device is called a *deed of trust* (or *trust deed*). Unlike the ordinary mortgage, the deed of trust involves a third person. In using it, the borrower (or *trustor*) transfers the title to the real estate to a *trustee* who holds it in trust for the lender (or *beneficiary*) for performance of the obligation owed by the borrower to the lender. When the obligation is fulfilled, the title is reconveyed to the trustor by the trustee.

❐ **REQUIREMENTS FOR A VALID MORTGAGE.** A number of elements are necessary for a mortgage to be free of defects. However, in some cases, the law may hold that certain defects in the mortgage document can result in the mortgage remaining as a so-called equitable mortgage. A valid mortgage must name the mortgagor and the mortgagee. It must contain the words of conveyance to clearly indicate that a mortgage is being agreed upon. It must specify the debt to be secured, and it must be recorded.

The mortgage must adequately describe the realty being mortgaged. In title states, the mortgage must clearly state the conditions upon which the title will be "defeated." This is called the *defeasance clause.* The mortgage must be signed by the mortgagor and in some states must be sealed and witnessed. The document must also be delivered and accepted.

Finally, mortgage law has specified other requirements regarding satisfaction of the mortgage, acceleration of the note, possible extensions of the mortgage, assignment of the mortgage, and release of the mortgage. A full discussion of these clauses is beyond the scope of this book, but in many cases, the advice of experienced counsel is very helpful. These instruments are the only way the mortgage lender can specify his or her legal rights to the real estate.

THE TENANT AND LEASEHOLDS

The tenant also acquires a set of legal rights that include more than the use of the property for the period of the lease. The tenant has a legal interest in the real estate called a *nonfreehold* or *leasehold estate.* Each is frequently classified according to its expected duration.

❐ **NONFREEHOLD (LEASEHOLD) ESTATES.** Generally there are four types of tenancy: tenancy for years, tenancy from period to period, tenancy at will, and tenancy at sufferance. With the exception of the last one, all are estates because they represent interests and rights in land.

A *tenancy for years* is a leasehold estate in which the beginning and end of the estate are clearly specified. For instance, if you have an estate for 20 years, at the end of that period, the property would automatically revert to the lessor.

A *tenancy from period to period* may last as long as a tenancy for years, but implies that the tenant may stay on the premises for consideration of rent according to the terms stated in the original tenancy. This implied tenancy may be terminated with sufficient notice given by either party. Sufficient notice may be defined within the document or measured by local law or tradition. A typical period of notice is six months.

A *tenancy at will* is the least structured. In this leasehold, the lessor offers the lessee (tenant) to continue the estate "for as long as the lessee wishes." Thus a tenancy at will is an estate of indeterminate duration and involves fewer restrictions on either party than any of the other leasehold estates. The notice period for termination is typically stated in the lease or is determined by state statute or state court precedent.

Tenancy at sufferance is the legal term for the tenant who remains after the expiration of a previous lease. The tenant who continues without the consent of the lessor is "at the sufferance" of the lessor. Thus, it is not an estate but a possession without legal right. It is said that a tenancy at sufferance differs from a trespasser only because the original entry was legal. Although tenants at sufferance possess civil and human rights, they have no real property rights.

❏ **LEASE ANALYSIS.**   The lease is the legal document that conveys a legal interest (leasehold) in real property. However, as we will see, the lease also represents a contract between landlord and tenant that contains a set of express and implicit conditions that bind the parties.

It should be pointed out that the major legal difference between a leasehold and other interests where the owner conveys rights (such as licenses, easements, or profits) is that the lease conveys the right of exclusive possession. Interests in the land of others convey the right to *use* the land but do not convey the right of possession. The legal test to determine if a conveyance is a leasehold is whether or not the transaction of rights results in a transfer of possession. If so, then a leasehold state has been created.

The essential elements of a lease include identification of landlord and tenant, both of whom must be of legal age and otherwise capable of entering the agreement; identification of the leased premises with sufficient precision to avoid ambiguity; specification of the amount of rent to be paid and the time and method of payment; and an indication of the term or length of the leasehold to which the parties have agreed. In some leaseholds the term is not specifically agreed upon at the time of signing.

In addition, and depending on the legal requirements of the state, other clauses are also found in most leases. A frequently used covenant describes the permissible uses allowed under the lease. For commercial property, this clause specifies what types of activities will be permitted by the lessor. In the case of a shopping center, this clause is critical because the selection of tenants is made according to economic function as well as risk and safety of the lessee. In residential leases, this clause ensures a minimum amount of conflict between tenants, since all are presumed to want peaceful and quiet usage of their rental space.

Another important covenant specifies the maintenance and repair responsibilities of the landlord. However, consistent with recent changes in landlord-tenant law, landlords are held responsible for physical maintenance and repair of appliances and urban services even if these promises are not expressly provided.

Leases also have provisions for assignment and subleasing, specifying the rights of the lessee should he or she wish to convey the rights of the leasehold before the end of the lease.

Finally, leases frequently include clauses concerning the status of the leasehold in the event of condemnation, casualty loss, or destruction. Although the outcomes may vary according to express covenants and state laws, the typical result is that the lessee is freed from rental obligation if the physical premises are "uninhabitable."

❏ **OTHER CONSIDERATIONS.** The development of landlord-tenant law during the past two decades is one of the major changes in property law. As a result, the landlord is now required to deliver possession to the tenant at the beginning of the lease.[9] In a famous New Jersey case, the court ruled that the "covenant of quiet enjoyment" was implied by all leases and if the landlord failed to provide this provision, the tenant could argue that he or she could not enjoy the premises and, in effect, that the leasehold was being terminated by "constructive eviction."[10]

Additional responsibilities of the landlord include the landlord's duty to deliver habitable premises. This shift from common law was based on the doctrine held by the court for all urban dwellings of the "implied warranty of habitability."[11] Courts also shifted the burden of repair and maintenance more squarely on the shoulders of the landlord. Now, landlords have a larger responsibility than ever for repairing "defects that interfere with basic habitability."

GOVERNMENTAL LIMITATIONS ON PROPERTY RIGHTS

Government laws and regulations can have a dramatic impact on real estate investments. Much of this area remains controversial and deals with politically sensitive issues. Resolution of conflicting land uses and

[9]Whether this consists of "actual" or "legal" possession varies according to state. According to the majority view, the English rule is followed, which requires actual possession to be delivered to the tenant.
[10]See *Reste Realty* v. *Cooper* (1968).
[11]See *Javins et al.* v. *First National Reality Corp.* (1970).

protection of public interests by land-use control[12] are two areas that merit discussion.

❐ **CONFLICTING LAND USES.**   The law attempts to resolve matters where a conflict of usage creates a problem. Four common types of conflicts concern nuisance, lateral support, water rights, and air rights.

The law of *nuisance* requires that a user of property operate in such a way that the use does not interfere with neighboring usage or with the public's right to use the property. Public nuisances are of particular concern, since such an activity can cause "injury to the public health, morals, safety or general welfare of the community." Nuisance doctrine is much less specific, and often the rulings are based on a case-specific analysis. In general, it protects holders of property interests from injury due to interference from others.

Lateral support is a property right that entitles the owner of property to have his or her land supported by adjoining land.[13] For example, the owner of an apartment building that begins to lean due to a weakening of the lateral support from the adjacent land is entitled to seek legal remedies. Although the property holder does not own the adjacent land, his or her right to receive lateral support is "an absolute right inherent in the land itself."

Water rights and *air rights* are two of the most visible areas in which interests may conflict. However, each area has developed a body of case law regarding the central question, Who owns what? Water rights refer to the title of lands under water and the rights of the water itself. This is clearly an important area in some of the arid states, and also where two adjoining land owners share a water supply or rely on a common water source for their livelihood. Many of the problems regarding water rights arise from the differences between two conflicting theories of water usage: the *riparian rights theory* and the *prior appropriation doctrine*. The riparian rights theory holds that the water rights belong to the adjacent landowner and no one can use water at the deprivation of others with an equal opportunity to use it. This theory has been rejected by many western states in favor of the prior appropriation doctrine that establishes a

[12]Many potential conflicting land uses involve private property rights exclusively, and thus no government activity is necessary. However, many of these disputes seek governmental authority to rectify the issue, often by taxing the wrongdoer based on a measure of the damages to the plaintiff. Economists have shown that governmental action may not be needed in many of these disputes, because the conflicting parties can negotiate the damages between themselves. This was illustrated in 1960 by Ronald Coase in his famous article, "The Problem of Social Cost," *Journal of Law and Economics* 3 (October 1960), 1–44.

[13]A similar notion is the doctrine of subjacent support that gives property holders the right to expect support from beneath the surface of the land once a structure is erected. In fact, the legal issue in the famous U.S. Supreme Court case of *Pennsylvania Coal Co.* v. *Mahon* (1922) is based upon the need for lateral and subjacent support.

priority schedule for users. Those there first have the best claim to use of the water.[14]

Air rights also involve conflicts of usage. Traditionally this was an area of torts, but with the development of technology, these property rights are becoming more important. Formerly, planes had free access to the "paths in the sky," since the sky was considered to belong to the public. However, if damage is done to property on earth, modern property law holds that this is a taking of property and that compensation must be paid to the property owner. This area is also controversial, and the courts will probably provide more rulings and precedent in the next few years.

❏ **LAND-USE CONTROL.** For the urban property holder, land-use control has become one of the most important legal areas of interest. As noted earlier, some of the limitations result from local governmental action, while others are due to state or local law. In many urban areas land-use control has been a hotly contested issue and one that will be important for years to come.

Some of the main techniques and methods that the public sector uses for land-use control include (but are not limited to) zoning laws, regulation of land development, urban land-use planning, eminent domain takings, environmental controls, and aesthetics as a land-use goal.

Zoning laws have been passed by most municipalities throughout the United States. These local ordinances typically provide a "master plan" by which the urban and nearby rural land will be utilized in a systematic and organized fashion. The issues of the value of zoning ordinances, their implementation, the costs of their usage, and the changes in property rights associated with the adoption of zoning ordinances have become well known to economists, city planners, and politicians and to many potential investors in real estate. The issues are far too complex for a cursory treatment here, but it is apparent that zoning and other land-use planning programs are becoming an increasingly important consideration for real estate development and investment.[15]

Other *regulations of land development* have also emerged in recent years. Some cities hope to limit the extent of urban growth by refusing to issue building permits or by limiting the number to be issued each year.[16] Another method is to limit the "urban service boundary" outside of which police, fire, water, and other local services will not be extended. Once

---

[14]A well-known study of water rights is H. Stuart Burness and James P. Quirk, "Water Laws, Water Transfers, and Economic Efficiency: The Colorado River," *Journal of Law and Economics,* 23 (April 1980), 111–34.

[15]For a general treatment, see Martin A. Garrett, Jr., *Land Use Regulations.* New York: Praeger, 1987. See also William A. Fischel, *The Economics of Zoning Laws.* Baltimore: The Johns Hopkins University Press, 1985.

[16]See *Construction Industry of Sonoma Country v. City of Petaluma* (1976).

again, the issues can become complex and often raise the emotional levels of those involved. To some, this activity is called economic (or legal) extortion, since builders and developers are frequently asked by the local municipalities to pay "development fees" to help offset the additional costs to the city of having to provide extra urban services. To others, this type of regulation appears to be the only hope for rationing growth in urban areas among potential users.[17]

The government may also take property by condemning it and using it for public purposes. This power, called *eminent domain,* requires that *just compensation,* or an amount in dollars equal to the market value of the loss, be paid to the former holder of the real property. Frequently, eminent domain proceedings are controversial and make headlines. However, empirical studies have shown that just compensation is not always equal to the owner's loss in market value.[18]

Environmental controls are also becoming a relevant issue for much real estate development. Many municipalities now require environmental impact statements prior to the approval of large developments. These concerns have become more prevalent as cities pay more attention to growing problems in areas of energy, resource demands, and urban structure.

Finally, a new movement has argued for *aesthetics as a land-use goal.* Although traditionally the law of nuisance failed to uphold "unsightliness" as a legal nuisance, recent municipal ordinances have sought, in the interest of society's welfare, to limit the use of billboards, signs, and other "visual pollution." This is a relatively new and highly controversial area for government intervention and indicates the extent to which the investor must examine the role of governmental influence before investing in real estate.

Figure 5–1 classifies the major property rights of real estate participants. Nearly all the property rights that appear in the figure were discussed in this chapter.

RELATIONSHIPS BETWEEN PARTICIPANTS

Each of the four primary participants in the real estate investment process has a specific legal relationship with the real estate investment itself. In this section we will look at the linkages between each of them.

---

[17]The use of exactions, impact fees, and other charges remain an important but controversial area in many communities today. See G. Bauman and W. Ether, "Development Exactions and Impact Fees: A Survey of American Practices," *Law and Contemporary Problems,* 51 (Winter 1987), 50–65.

[18]See Patricia Munch, "An Economic Analysis of Eminent Domain," *Journal of Political Economy,* 84 (1976), 473–97.

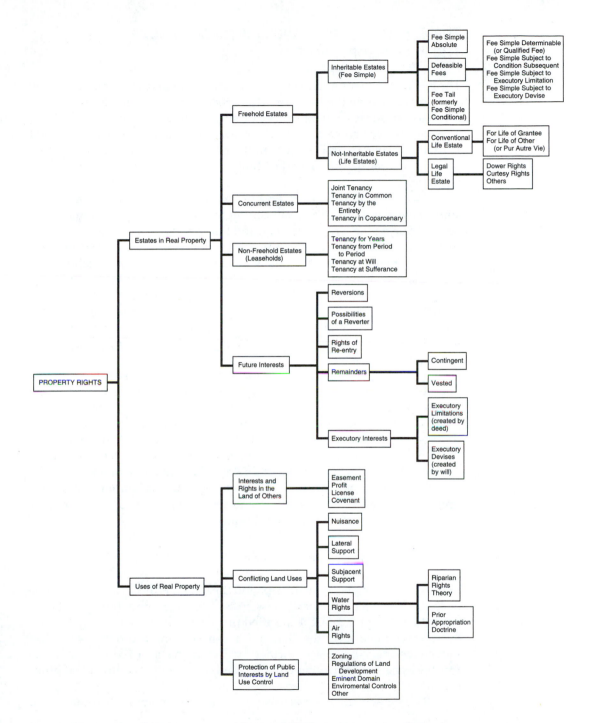

FIGURE 5–1
Property Rights in Land

The Equity Investor and Mortgage Lender: The Promissory Note

The link between the equity investor and the mortgage lender is *the promissory note* signed by the investor. This specifies that the maker of the note (investor) promises to repay a specific sum of money to the payee (lender). The note can be *negotiable* or *nonnegotiable*. Negotiable notes can be passed to other persons for cash or sold in the market for negotiable notes. Nonnegotiable notes lack this marketability and, for this reason, are used less frequently.

Two common types of promissory notes are used in real estate: *straight notes* and *installment notes.* Straight notes require that only interest be paid during the term of the note and that principal be repaid at the end. Installment notes require periodic interest and principal reduction payments. In the usual case, the note is repaid in the level amortization payment plan, which enables a decreasing portion of a given level periodic payment to be attributed to interest and an increasing portion to principal reduction. It is also possible to only partially amortize the note and make the final payment larger to cover the remaining balance. This final payment is called a *balloon payment,* and the mortgage in which it appears is called a *balloon mortgage.*

There are a number of common provisions in promissory notes. Frequently, the same provisions appear in the mortgage (or deed of trust). Together the note and the mortgage make up the agreement between the parties. Some of the provisions typically included are the date and place of the creation of the note, the amount of the note, the names of the payee and the maker, the time in which interest will begin and the effective rate to be charged, the results in the event of a default, and a statement regarding the use of a mortgage as security. Other issues include acceleration provisions, prepayment clauses and penalties, and the use of escrows. In general, for complex transactions, legal counsel is advisable.

The Equity Investor and the Tenant: The Lease

The legal link between the investor and the tenant is the *lease.* This is a type of contract in which one party (lessor) conveys to another (lessee) for consideration the right to use a specified property for a period of time. However, as we have seen, the changing nature of landlord-tenant laws has moved the analysis of leases further away from the law of contracts. Therefore the lease is an instrument that is based on a blend of contract and property law.

To create a valid lease, at least six essential elements must be included:

1. A statement of the correct names and the signatures of the competent parties.

2. An identifiable description of the leased premises, typically including but not limited to the address of the location.

3. A statement of the consideration to be paid.

4. A statement of the purpose(s) for which the premises are expected to be used.

5. A statement of the beginning and ending dates of the leasehold.

6. A statement of the rights and obligations of each party. This may be a simple statement or many pages of clauses and covenants.

Many of the clauses are important for specifying the rights of the lessor and lessee. A well-written lease will help to prevent potential problems. Finally, it is necessary to spend some time carefully examining the clauses in the lease used in the real estate. If real estate is to be viewed as a bundle of rights, then the establishment of leasehold extends certain rights to the lessee. It is of paramount importance to know what right the lessee possesses.

THE EQUITY INVESTOR AND GOVERNMENT: TAXATION

All levels of government have the authority to impose the burden of taxes. Taxation may consist of taxes on income; taxes on real property, typically used for local purposes; and taxes on the gain from selling assets. In "income tax" systems at the federal and most state levels, the government taxes both income and wealth.

Chapter 7 focuses on the complex and detailed tax system. We will see that not only is tax planning useful, but in many cases it is necessary in order to earn a competitive return. Tax avoidance is expected; tax evasion is illegal and punishable by law.

However, there are other taxes that affect real estate investment. These include personal property taxes, payroll taxes, estate taxes, and others. One of the more controversial issues in recent years has been the extent to which property taxes should be used to finance public expenditures such as schools. The Proposition 13 revolt in California made the clear point that in the minds of many homeowners and real estate investors, the tax burdens had grown significantly, often to 3 percent or more of market value per annum.

Another way to view taxation is the *tax capitalization theory*. This notion argues that if, for example, many investors believe that property (or other) taxes will increase in the near future, they will evaluate that expectation in analyzing investments. Thus, their investments and the values placed on property will take the tax burden into account.

Whether most or all of the tax burden is "capitalized" into the value of investment property is an empirical question that remains unanswered. Evidence indicates that at least some of the tax burdens on real property are capitalized into selling prices by investors in the real estate market. At the same time, however, the investor is also concerned with the influence of various government programs on the investment's value. For example, the monies collected from the property tax are used to support schools, build roads, support police and fire protection, and so forth. These programs could very well increase the property value. So the investor should be concerned with the net effect: the decrease associated with the property tax and the increase from "quality" neighborhoods.

THE MORTGAGE LENDER AND THE TENANT: LENDER REQUIREMENTS

The link between the mortgage lender and the tenant is perhaps the weakest of all the legal links between the participants. The lender never encounters the tenant directly. However, if the tenant is not financially secure, this may result in default on the promissory note. Poor tenant selection by the equity investor or management agent may therefore directly affect the mortgage lender.

A major part of the mortgage lender's review of the investor's application for funds is an analysis of the investor's projected income statement. Because the income to be generated from the real estate is directly a function of the tenants' willingness and ability to pay rent, the lender ought to analyze the financial position of major tenants. The lender's willingness to make the loan may be contingent on the type and quality of tenants in the property, particularly in large-scale projects where long-term financing becomes available after the leases are signed.

The lender may require tenants to pass certain income and credit tests. This is especially true in residential income-producing real estate where tenants may not have as easy access to credit markets as large corporations in commercial and industrial property.

THE MORTGAGE LENDER AND GOVERNMENT: RESTRICTIONS ON LENDER BEHAVIOR

The mortgage lender is linked to the government by a set of legal restrictions placed on the lender. Clearly, the nature of these restrictions depends on the lender involved. Those placed on savings and loan associations, for example, will differ from those placed on commercial banks or life insurance companies. Federally chartered savings and loan associations are largely confined to lending on residential real estate. There are also limits placed on the maximum amount that may be lent on any particular property, as well as restrictions on maximum loan-to-value ratios, the length and amount of term loans, and requirements regarding the geographic locations of properties held as loan security.

Commercial banks, however, are permitted to engage in many more financial services. Although banks were not permitted to make real estate loans until after 1913, their interest has since grown to where they represent a major source of real estate loans (Table 5–3). However, there are regulations regarding the use of deposits for real estate loans, including limits on the ratio of mortgages to deposits and loan-to-value restrictions. Banks also do a good deal of short-term (construction) and interim financing which have other requirements.

THE TENANT AND GOVERNMENT: EVALUATING LESSEE'S RIGHTS

The final link is between the tenant and government. This link involves further restrictions on tenant usage as well as an ongoing interpretation of the lessee's rights. The changing nature of landlord-tenant law has forced many governments to pass new laws to reflect the new legal environment. Laws such as those requiring itemized lists of damages for which charges were deducted when returning security deposits, or those requiring fire alarms and smoke detectors in apartment buildings in some cities and towns, exemplify the changing legal emphasis.

Some observers feel that the government has no business in some of these areas. Builders frequently argue that although the intention may be good, many of the new laws result in higher construction costs and often higher rents charged to tenants. The problem for builders and investors, of course, is that the rents are not always increased in proportion to the increased costs. Sometimes only part of the additional cost is "passed on" to the tenant.

Proponents of government intervention in these areas argue that there is no market mechanism to correct safety, health, or other hazards. Therefore they view the problem as a governmental duty. Whether either side is correct more often than the other is a matter of conjecture. What is clear is that the lessee's rights are continually being refined and reinterpreted with each new governmental action.

OTHER ISSUES IN THE LEGAL ENVIRONMENT

The legal environment extends far beyond the topics discussed in this chapter so far. During the latter half of the twentieth century, state and local governments took an increasingly active stance in the areas of land-use control under the authority of police power. The real estate investor must take the government's role in this area into account when making investment decisions. The private bundle of rights has become more and more limited by governmental involvement in how real estate may be used.

Land-use control extends beyond resolution of conflicts through zoning and comprehensive planning. Recently, local governments have sought to regulate land on the basis of aesthetic requirements such as sign ordinances, architectural review procedures, and the specification and unique treatment of historically important properties. These areas have traditionally been left to the private market for allocative decisions.

In addition, extensive regulations on the extent, timing, size, and type of urban growth have become a part of the political scene. Courts have consistently sided with local governments who are seeking to plan or limit how their real estate is to be used. These regulations have also included ordinances that put restrictions on types of tenants, unrelated co-inhabitants, and absentee owners. The recent drive to stop condominium conversions is further evidence of the active role government plays in these areas. Finally, rent control is the ultimate example of governmental limitations on the rights of property owners. Although certain municipalities have had a long history of rent control (most notably New York City), there is a rapidly growing rent control movement spreading throughout the United States. In some states (for example, New Jersey), several cities and towns have implemented rent control ordinances. In others, there is considerable political sentiment for this type of regulation. This development will have a dramatic impact on real estate as an investment if more communities implement such plans. This an area for real estate investors to keep a careful eye on in the future.

SUMMARY

Because real estate investment analysis is a legal process, a large portion of investing in income-producing real estate in an effective manner involves the use of sound legal advice and planning. Furthermore, because many transactions are or become quite complex, legal problems may easily arise, especially if ownership forms, financing arrangements, tax status, or governmental attitudes change during the life of the investment. Finally, there may be many legal decisions and choices that must be made beyond those briefly discussed in this chapter. This includes various types of transfers of ownership such as wills and inheritance laws, sales contracts, deeds, the use of escrows, gifts, and estate planning, and title assurance and insurance.

It is necessary to have a basic understanding of the legal environment prior to analyzing the financial opportunities associated with the investment. However, merely to possess a descriptive understanding of the various partnership forms or the breakdown of estates is rarely sufficient. *The real estate investor must understand the impact of the legal environment on the decisions he or she faces.* Only then will the legal environment "matter" to the decision maker.

QUESTIONS

5–1. Real estate has long been defined as a "bundle or rights." Why is this useful for analysis purposes?

5–2. What is the difference between *real estate* and *real property*? *Personalty* and *personal property*?

5–3. Various business organizations possess different characteristics according to a number of important variables. Distinguish the major ownership forms according to these variables.

5–4. Name the different types of tenants.

5–5. How do the different levels of government affect real estate investments?

5–6. What are estates? Why are estates valuable?

5–7. What is the difference between *freehold* and *leasehold estates*?

5–8. In recent years, the legal environment has become more important for investors. In what ways can real estate investors benefit from understanding the legal environment before investing?

PROBLEMS

5–1. Suppose two houses of identical size, quality, and condition are for sale in the same neighborhood. One house, however, consists of a fee simple estate as the set of property rights available to a potential buyer. The other is a defeasible fee estate. If the fee simple estate is worth $50,000, how much do you think the defeasible fee estate is worth if there is a 95 percent probability that it *will not* "revert" and become a possessory estate? How much is the defeasible fee worth if there is a 95 percent probability that it *will* "revert" and become a possessory estate?

5–2. "Imagine that you are holding a set of colored pencils bound together with a rubber band. Assume that these pencils represent a bundle of rights. The pencils are of different colors, and if they were of different lengths and thicknesses, made of different materials, and were not all pencils, they would more closely resemble the 'bundle or rights' called real property. But even then the simile would be imperfect. Property rights are not sticks, they are more like amoebas, ever-changing in their physical and legal entities." What is the author's main point? Is this a useful view of real property? How does the "bundle of rights" influence the real estate investment decision?

5–3. While discussing "Interests and Rights in the Land of Others," four main types of rights are identified: easements, profits, licenses, and covenants. Indicate, for each of the following scenarios, which type of interest or right the individual holds.
   a. Tom lives near a farmer who has a well stocked fishing pond located on his property. The farmer has given Tom permission to fish in the pond at any time.
   b. Ed recently purchased a house in a subdivision. Upon moving in, Ed realized that he was unable to build a barn in his backyard as a result of a restriction placed in his deed.
   c. Kim purchased a parcel of land that did not adjoin a public road. As a result of this, she was granted a right of way through the property in between hers and the road on which to build an access road and lay power lines.
   d. As it turns out, the farmer in part a. is also a major stockholder in the development company which built Ed's house and he loves barns. When he found out that Ed was unable to build a barn on his property, he not only allowed him to use some of his land to build one on, but also allowed him to remove and sell any minerals he located on the property.

5–4. A property containing 10,000 square feet sold for $950,000. The property was leased at a contract rate of $10.00 per square foot with 10 years remaining on the lease. The estimated market rent was $12.00 per square foot with a market vacancy rate of 5%. The property was leased on a net basis. The only operating expense to the owner was a management fee of 5% of effective gross income. The required rate of return on the leasehold is 12%. What is the value of the property if it was not encumbered by the lease?

Selected References

Clauretie, Terrence M., and James R. Webb, *The Theory and Practice of Real Estate Finance*. Fort Worth, Tex.: The Dryden Press, 1993.

Hamill, James R., "Incentive Problems and General Partner Compensation in Limited Partnership Real Estate Investments," *Journal of the American Real Estate and Urban Economics Association*, 21 (Summer 1993), 131–140.

Haney, Richard L., Jr., "Adverse Environmental Conditions: Their Impacts on Real Estate Values," *Journal of Real Estate Research*, 7 (Summer 1992), 235–238.

Kratovil, Robert, and Raymond J. Werner, *Real Estate Law* (10th ed.). Englewood Cliffs, N.J.: Prentice Hall, 1993.

Nelson, Theron R., and Thomas A. Potter, *Real Estate Law: Concepts and Applications*. St. Paul, Minn.: West Publishing, 1994.

Siedel, George J., III, *Real Estate Law*. St. Paul, Minn.: West Publishing, 1993.

Wright, Robert R., and Susan Webber, *Land Use in a Nutshell*. (3rd ed.). St. Paul, Minn.: West Publishing, 1994.

CHAPTER 6

THE FINANCING ENVIRONMENT

PRINCIPLES _____

1. The financing environment for real estate investment has undergone considerable change in recent years.
2. Financing of real estate involves both debt and equity claims.
3. There are numerous sources of financing for real estate investors.
4. New developments in capital markets has transformed the instruments used in the financing of commercial real estate projects.

Capital markets in the United States, including mortgage markets, despite their problems and shortcomings, are undoubtedly the most extensively developed results of financial intermediation in the world. It is consistent that the emphasis on financing aspects in American real estate markets is quite pronounced and has been throughout this century. When compared to the rest of the world, real estate finance in the United States is often viewed as more critical to the success of real estate investment projects than other aspects of the real estate investment process.

In terms of the commercial mortgage market, the United States is in a leadership role here as well. Innovation is the key concept and the market for commercial real estate finance has undergone tremendous changes and extensive new developments. Real estate finance is essential for commercial real estate development and investment in the United States. Investors throughout the world look to the United States for new ideas, mortgage instruments, and financial innovations. In recent years, there has been much to evaluate; in the future, there is likely to be even more developments.

It is a misleading presumption to conclude that real estate finance refers *only* to debt sources of finance. *Equity* financing must also be considered, especially in the commercial real estate market. Examples of equity financing vehicles include limited partnerships, syndications, and (equity) real estate investment trusts (REITs). *Financing* refers to the use of capital for acquisition or other purposes. Strictly speaking, real estate finance is not limited to the analysis of the priority of claims (that is, the seniority of debt versus equity claims). Financing is important because of the ability to use accumulated capital for investment decisions now, given the promise to "service" the capital (both debt and equity) in the future. The promised servicing of debt is often a repayment of the amount borrowed (principal) and a payment for the use of the funds (interest). The promised servicing of equity funds is a periodic return on capital (cash flow), and an anticipated growth in cash flow during future years.[1]

This chapter provides a brief overview of commercial real estate finance. In addition, we provide a brief history of debt financing. The chapter also outlines the mortgage lending process. Finally, a survey of several new developments in the financing environment is provided.

While considerable real estate investment activity takes place in residential markets, especially when viewing single-family housing or condominium ownership as an investment decision, as is typically the case, these purchases are financed through depository institutions. The reader is referred elsewhere for overviews of the history of residential real estate finance in the United States. This history parallels the evolutionary development of the commercial real estate finance market discussed here, but residential real estate finance is not the focus of our study. Rather it is to the development and history of commercial real estate finance that we now turn.

THE FINANCIAL SYSTEM FOR COMMERCIAL PROPERTY FINANCE

As in the residential financing system, the commercial property finance system consists of sources (suppliers) and uses (investors) of funds. The sources of capital include life insurance companies, banks, savings and loan associates, pension funds, commingled real estate funds, REITs, foreign investors, as well as private investors in the United States. It is an important characteristic of the flexibility and efficiency of the American mortgage market that so many sources of capital feed the user in the real estate finance market.[2]

[1]Some readers might think that appreciation in price would be the second component of the expected cost of equity finance. It can easily be shown that the growth in cash flow component is equivalent to the expected rate of return from appreciation, if future selling prices are a function of anticipated cash flows subsequent to the purchase.
[2]Compare the American mortgage finance system to that of many other countries, especially to those where government financing is the critical supplier of capital. Such a comparison reveals a greater choice of instruments and a wider range of financing strategies in the United States. Historically there has been minimal government involvement in commercial real estate financing, except for regulations for lenders.

Demanders of mortgage finance capital in commercial markets are typically one of two main parties: investors or developers of commercial real estate. The list of investors is varied (see Chapter 5), but virtually all require mortgage finance in order to be successful ventures. Real estate developers also require access to mortgage finance both for construction and development loans, and sometimes, for permanent financing.

FINANCIAL INTERMEDIATION IS THE GOAL

The bringing together of sources and uses of capital is the core to the finance function. In a world of costless transactions, suppliers of capital would be able to identify and meet users in need of debt and equity to carry out their investment objectives or development plans. These meetings would occur continuously and the terms of their agreements would be worked out instantaneously. Risk would not exist long in this world, since, if risk did exist, an assessment would be appropriately and properly made and prices would adjust accordingly.

Of course, the real world of real estate finance and investment is far different from the world described above. First, suppliers and users of capital often do not know each other; in fact, there may be several different parties on either side of the transaction, often spread out geographically throughout the country (or even the world). One of the enormous benefits of a well-developed mortgage finance system is that parties to financing transactions need not worry about meeting the other parties. Intermediaries assist by bringing together the interested parties.

Second, formal meetings to exchange economic claims (that is, financial securities) are logistically impossible to arrange. Financial instruments and other devices have been developed by financial intermediaries to facilitate the necessary transactions.

Third, there are numerous items to be arranged regarding the terms of any financing arrangement; for many transactions, the documents may cover scores of pages. The evaluation of real estate financing documents reveals a number of interesting observations. For example, both parties can be expected to benefit from a contract which provides for outcomes based upon various contingencies. If so, it is reasonable to expect that financing agreements will become increasingly complicated as more and more contingencies are anticipated.

Finally, in the actual world of real estate investing, risk is very real. In fact, the assessment of risk in commercial real estate finance is a major activity, involving thousands of individuals throughout the world. The type of risk referred to here is generally called *default risk*, or the likelihood that the borrower will not or cannot complete the terms of the note on the mortgage. If not, the property may be foreclosed on by the lender, or alternative courses of action may be elected. Note that there are also other types of risk in commercial real estate finance such as interest rate risk, exchange rate risk, and others.

THE ROLE OF FINANCIAL INNOVATIONS

The thrust of development in the area of real estate finance has been in terms of innovations by various intermediaries. Some innovative practices have occurred by banks and savings and loan associations during the 1980s when the regulatory environment permitted some additional activities on the part of thrift institutions. In commercial markets, the innovative players have not been depository institutions. Rather, the new developments have tended to come from mortgage brokers and investment bankers, who began to consider commercial real estate finance as a serious market opportunity during the mid-1980s. Innovations such as mortgage-backed securities have changed the nature of real estate financing forever.

Securitization occurs when mortgages are pooled and ownership in the pool is sold as a "pass-through security" with investment-grade credit rating.[3] The credit rating is based on either the cash flows from the real estate and/or credit enhancement. The enhancement is usually provided by subordinated debt and/or equity. The attractiveness of this instrument is that it allows nonliquid real estate loans to be pooled and issued as marketable securities.

While much of the "securitization" of mortgage assets has been in residential finance, the development of securitization of commercial real estate debt has now become a reality. The size of the commercial mortgage market is quite large.[4] Figure 6–1 illustrates the number and dollar volume of commercial mortgage loans made by insurance companies during the 1951–1993 time period. Figure 6–2 shows the average interest rate on commercial mortgage loans.

Beginning in 1984, the market for securitized commercial real estate debt was $1.2 billion. By 1986, the market had grown to over $6 billion. By the mid-1980s, the maturity of the market for securitized commercial mortgages was similar to that for residential mortgages in the early 1970s. With a commercial real estate mortgage market of about $800 billion by 1987, only about 3% of the outstanding mortgages had been securitized. By 1990, there were approximately $1 trillion in outstanding commercial mortgages.[5] There is considerable reason to believe that the market will continue to grow.

[3]A mortgage-backed security is considered a "pass-through" security because the originator continues to service the mortgages in the pool while passing through the collected payments of principal and interest, less a servicing fee, to the investor.
[4]For more discussion of the history of the commercial mortgage market, see William M. Wendt, "Evidence of Change," *Mortgage Banking* 6 (November 1993), 52–66.
[5]See Laura Quigg, *Commercial Mortgage-Backed Securities*, (New York: Lehman Brothers Fixed Income Research, December 1993).

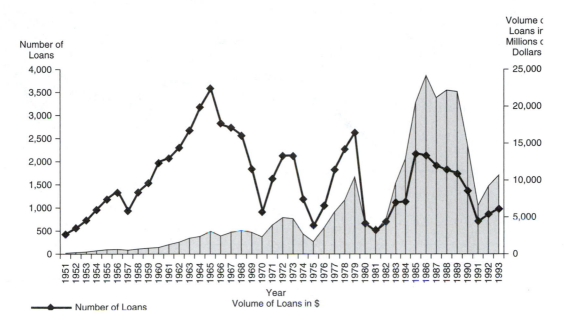

FIGURE 6–1

Commercial Mortgage Loan Commitments: 1951–1993.
Source: Data from American Council of Life Insurance, Washington, D.C.

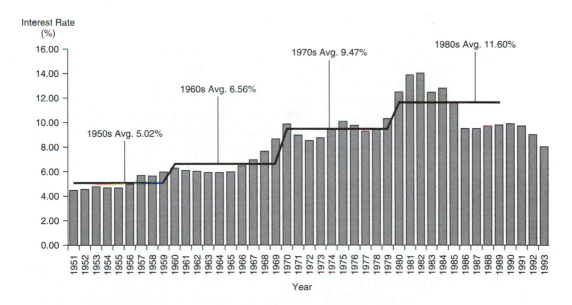

FIGURE 6–2

Average Commercial Mortgage Loan Interest Rate: 1951–1993.
Source: Data from American Council of Life Insurance, Washington, D.C.

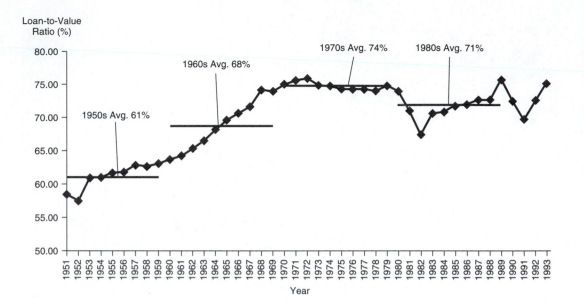

FIGURE 6–3
Average Commercial Mortgage Loan-to-Value Ratio: 1951–1993.
Source: Data from American Council of Life Insurance, Washington, D.C.

TYPICAL CAPITAL STRUCTURE

Typical loan-to-value ratios for commercial property were considerably lower in the 1950s and 1960s than in recent years. Figure 6–3 shows the average loan-to-value ratio on commercial mortgages.

Figure 6–3 shows a steady increase in the amount of debt relative to equity throughout the 1970s. During periods of credit tightening (for example, 1980–82), loan-to-value ratios fell dramatically. In addition, during the period of oversupplied real estate markets in the early 1990s, the percentage of debt borrowed fell sharply. Real estate financing is sensitive to economic changes affecting the macroeconomy as well as local conditions in real estate markets.

HOW HAS MORTGAGE TERM VARIED OVER THE YEARS?

It is also interesting to examine variations in mortgage maturity. Figure 6–4 provides the data.

During the 1970s, the typical repayment period (that is, *mortgage term*) was extended towards and beyond 20 years for institutional commercial mortgages. It should be noted that these years were characterized by increasingly underestimated rates of inflation. With the tight monetary

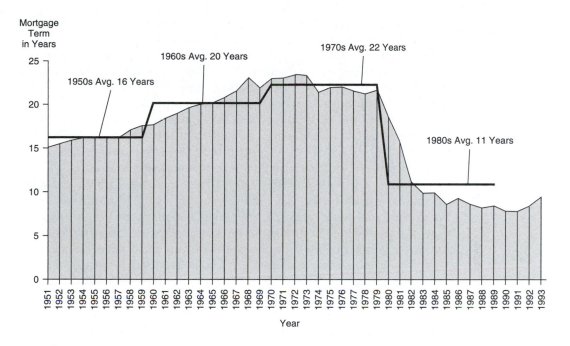

FIGURE 6–4
Average Commercial Mortgage Loan Term: 1951–1993.
Source: Data from American Council of Life Insurance, Washington, D.C.

policy begun by the Reagan Administration in 1980, inflation began to slow down, and with this slowing, borrowers began to repay their loans over shorter periods. It is interesting to note that the 1980s and early 1990s has been characterized by relatively short repayment periods.

THE RELATIONSHIP BETWEEN MORTGAGE FINANCE AND THE MACROECONOMY

Real estate finance is an activity that grows and shrinks with economic conditions in the real estate market. This is only natural since the production of debt or equity claims is always reversible. One of the fundamental principles in financial markets is that the capital structure decision (that is, the determination of the debt-equity mix for an investment) is subject to change by management decision at any point during the holding period. Therefore, it is critical to monitor financing options throughout the holding period of any investment. As economic activity strengthens, there is likely to be a growth in commercial mortgages. During declining periods, mortgage markets get tighter and shrink. One of the mistakes in the late 1980s was a belief that real estate (and therefore, commercial mortgage) markets would not decline.

During periods of economic slowdown or even decline, the financial health of borrowers weaken. Vacancies rise as some firms shut down. There may be an oversupply in commercial space if the preceding period of growth was long and extended. Vacancies might appear in this case as tenants seek better terms with owners of competing projects. Rent concessions might be required to keep tenants on your property. All of these conditions lead to the same conclusion for commercial mortgage markets: borrowers become delinquent in making debt service payments. In addition, foreclosures (or the legal process of lenders obtaining control of the properties after formal default by the borrower) begin to rise.

During the period of the early 1990s, these conditions prevailed throughout much of the U.S. A huge supply of office and retail space flooded the real estate market. Commercial tenants could become increasingly aggressive in their demands, and landlords were forced to deal with the real possibility of large vacancy rates, despite prudent real estate practices. In addition, since real estate markets are localized, difficulties in mortgage markets may vary from location to location.

Figure 6–5 shows the dramatic differences in delinquency rates over the past 25 years. Notice that the peaks in the data correspond to the periods of turmoil in financial markets. During the 1970s, there were tight

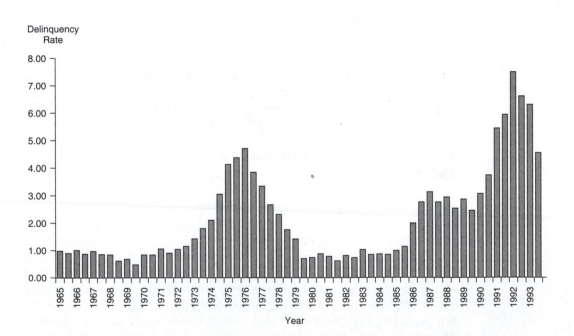

FIGURE 6–5
Commercial Mortgage Delinquencies: 1965–1993.
Source: Data from American Council of Life Insurance, Washington, D.C.

PART II THE INVESTMENT ENVIRONMENT

How Important is the Financing Environment?
Investments in real estate typically use both equity and debt financing. The ability to purchase an ownership interest with only a fraction of the equity capital required means there will always be a demand for debt financing in real estate. Alternatively, if long-term debt financing did not exist, real estate development and investment would be but a small fraction of the level that exists today.

In the formal socialist countries, the development of real estate was a bureaucratic decision made by the state. The *financing* of the state projects was similarly carried out by the state workers: wheelbarrows of money were ordered from the finance ministry to the construction ministry to pay for materials and labor. Of course, the construction ministry was not the only bureau seeking funds. In the former Soviet Union, for example, there were at least 100 ministries, all trying to attract "capital" to build monuments for the state.

In nonmarket economies, there is little household savings and no market for financial capital. Banks are extensions of the state and not financial intermediaries in the Western sense. When the state ran out of money (in the U.S.S.R., they literally ran out of paper to print rubles), there was simply no money available for development. Real estate finance in the U.S.S.R. was reduced to competing political pleas for Soviet rubles.

Once of the underappreciated aspects of modern financial systems is the efficiency with which financial resources are accumulated from savers and utilized by investors. As financial markets have developed, become broader and more flexible, the strength of mortgage finance has been enhanced. Further, the allocative price of finance (that is, the cost of credit) is a modern marvel relative to a generation ago. Real estate finance is undoubtedly, an essential ingredient for modern investment analysis.

credit market conditions during 1973–1974 and again in 1976–1977. Throughout the beginning of the 1980s, real estate markets were expanding rapidly. By 1987, the boom was over and many borrowers began to feel the pinch. In hindsight, it is easy to see that the "bull market" in real estate was over by the late 1980s. However, look at the data for the 1990s. Delinquency rates are at an all-time high in 1991, 1992, and 1993, almost twice as high as during previous periods. Clearly, delinquencies are a major problem for lenders in the 1990s; real estate has fallen from grace after many years of superior financial performance.

Delinquency rates on commercial mortgages were far from uniform throughout the United States during recent years. Despite the development of national databases, mortgage backed-securities, and the beginnings of a national real estate market for institutional grade properties, there remains substantial differences in various real estate markets and the risk of finance by location. In addition, financial difficulties in declining markets vary with property type. For example, delinquency rates for mortgages on office buildings are likely to be different from rates for retail or industrial property. Real estate finance remains a specialized area in that expertise is needed for each sector of the market, given the different instruments employed and the different market experiences. Construction cycles vary by type of property as well, making an accurate assessment of commercial real estate finance even more difficult.

Changing economic conditions directly affect the market for commercial mortgage finance. There are interrelationships between macroeconomic variables and decisions required by investors in real estate markets using commercial mortgages. Recent trends have demonstrated the importance of changes required by investors as economic conditions change. In recent years, volatile economic conditions have meant that there is a new financial environment facing real estate investors. There have been several important turning points in the market for commercial real estate finance: 1958, 1968, 1979, and 1986.[6] No doubt there will be others in the future.

THE MORTGAGE LENDING PROCESS

Although each mortgage loan is different, there are some basic steps or stages in the mortgage loan process that are common to all. This section outlines the steps an investor would take in order to obtain debt financing. Although the process differs slightly depending on the type of project, the end result is to obtain permanent financing. The process for obtaining financing for such projects as new construction, or the rehab of an existing project which involves both permanent and temporary financing, can for our purposes, be viewed as four steps:

STEP 1: *The Application:* The borrower submits in writing a formal request for a specific type of mortgage on a specific property.

STEP 2: *Underwriting/Analysis:* The lender analyzes the borrower, the project, and other market conditions using various criteria and makes a decision to lend or not.

STEP 3: *Commitment:* Assuming that the decision is made to lend, the lender submits a formal commitment to the borrower.

STEP 4: *Closing:* After all parties meet the various requirements, the loan is closed.

[6]See Wendt, op. cit.

In principle, the mortgage lending process appears to be straight-forward and uncomplicated. Of course, in practice, especially with complex financing arrangements, nothing could be further from the truth. The four basic steps outlined above, and discussed in detail below, are a part of every financing agreement.

APPLICATION STAGE

During the application stage of the mortgage lending process, the borrower submits a formal application for monies to a lender. The actual application is often referred to as a loan package, and usually consists of some or all of the following items.

A SPECIFIC DESCRIPTION OF THE PROJECT. This part of the application explains why the loan is needed: to finance a new construction project, a renovation, or purchase an existing building.

A DESCRIPTION OF THE TYPE OF LOAN REQUESTED. This would include such items as the amount requested, repayment schedule, maturity date, and interest rate schedule. The applicant also indicates whether he is requesting a temporary or permanent loan.

BORROWER'S FINANCIAL STATEMENTS. The lender usually requires the financial statements and tax returns from not only the borrower, but any co-borrowers or guarantors for the last three to five years. This enables the lender to analyze the financial condition of the borrower to help make a lending decision.

INFORMATION ON THE BORROWER'S BACKGROUND. The lender especially looks to see how the borrower has paid past obligations, and if he has any experience in the type of project under consideration. As a result of the problem real estate loans many lender's have had in the recent past, this information has become more important in the decision-making process.

PROJECT PRO FORMA FINANCIAL STATEMENTS. If the main source of repayment of the obligation is cash flow from operations of the proposed investment, the lender wants to know if there is enough cash flow to cover the debt service. These would also include cost breakdowns in the event that any improvements were to be made.

ANY EXISTING LEASES OR LETTERS OF INTENT. If the investment is an existing project, the lender verifies income through existing leases. If the investment is a new construction project, pre-lease agreements for the proposed site must be included.

APPRAISAL OF THE PROPERTY. The appraisal is an important part of the application package. Primarily, it gives an identification of the property and the local neighborhood and community. The appraisal also addresses zoning (this is important if improvements are planned), and gives an analysis of the highest and best use of the property. The appraisal also provides estimates of the value of the project using the cost approach, the market approach, and the income approach.

ENVIRONMENTAL STUDY.   The environmental site assessment has become more important in the lender's decision-making process as a result of recent federal and state regulatory changes. Because of these changes, as well as recent court rulings finding lenders liable for clean-up costs on contaminated properties, lenders have begun to look more closely at environmental studies.

An environmental site assessment consists of different stages. In the first stage, examination of existing records of past uses of the property, as well as regulatory compliance and visual inspection of the property, take place. In the second stage, the assessor monitors ground water and/or soil if concerns were identified in the initial stage. The goal of this is to confirm the absence or presence of hazardous wastes on the site. The final stage occurs if contamination requiring further investigation or remediation is found. The goal of this is to determine the extent and rate of migration of the contamination. This stage also includes clean-up and/or removal actions.

UNDERWRITING/ANALYSIS STAGE

A thorough analysis of the mortgage loan application concentrates on two areas: the property and the borrower. The primary source for repayment is the cash flow from the project. If the loan is "recourse" debt, the borrower would also be liable for repayment. Since the property is pledged as collateral, the value of the property is also of major importance. It is only after detailed analysis has been completed, that the lender makes a decision of what type of mortgage, for how much, and under what conditions she is willing to commit to the borrower.

ANALYSIS OF THE PROPERTY.   An analysis of the property should begin with a review of the appraisal and environmental studies, the title search, and the project financial statements—both historical and proforma. The goal of the review of each of these being to insure value, true ownership, debt coverage ability, and that the property is environmentally clean.

REVIEW OF THE APPRAISAL.   Upon receiving a current appraisal, the lender reviews the appraisal to assure that the appraiser has used generally accepted methods in estimating value. The lender compares the current appraised value with those of the past to look for any significant changes in value, as well as to compare overall changes in value to those of the local market. Further, the lender would check for accuracy and make sure that there are no conflicts between the information on the property he or she already has and the appraisal. For example, she would check that the effective gross income and operating expenses under the income approach are similar to what appears in the tax returns or pro-forma statements provided by the borrower; any variances should be identified and explained.

The goal of this review is to determine the adequacy of the property as a source of repayment. One method of measuring the adequacy is the loan-to-value ratio. Each lending institution sets guidelines depending on the type of property and the current market conditions for that type of property. The greater the perceived risk, the more stringent the loan-to-value requirements. For example, a lending institutions guideline's may set raw land at a 50 percent loan-to-value maximum while an apartment building may have a 80 percent loan-to-value maximum.

ANALYSIS OF PROJECT FINANCIAL STATEMENTS. The review of the project's financial statements are important in order to determine whether the cash flows are adequate to cover the debt service. The measure used to determine the adequacy is called the *debt coverage ratio*, calculated by dividing net operating income by the debt service. In general, lenders look for a debt coverage ratio greater than or equal to 1.2. Figure 6–6 illustrates average debt coverage ratios for commercial mortgage loans that have existed over the years.

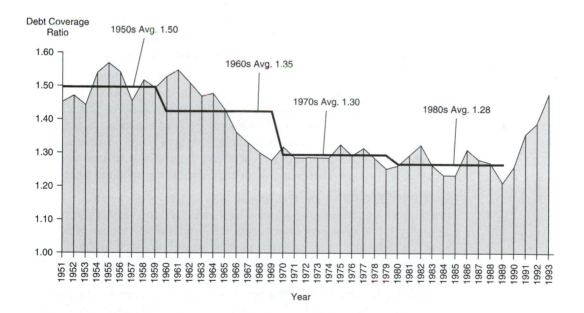

FIGURE 6–6
Average Commercial Mortgage Debt Coverage Ratio: 1951–1993.
Source: Data from American Council of Life Insurance, Washington, D.C.

The lender would begin his or her analysis by looking at the historical performance of the property through a review of the operating statements and/or tax returns and lease agreements with the intention of determining the trends of rental rates, vacancy factors, and operating expenses. These are compared with those of the market to see how the property compares with similar properties. Determination of the trend helps the lender make reasonable assertions as to the expected future performance of the project and the impact of the proposed loan on that trend.

REVIEW OF THE TITLE.   The focus of a title search is to ensure that at a closing, clear title is passed on, in the case of a purchase, or that the ownership name is the same as that of the borrower or guarantor who is pledging the property. The search also identifies the existence of any prior liens such as tax liens or a previously filed mortgage. In order to hedge against any mistakes, lenders usually require "title insurance." By doing this, the lender is protected from someone making a priority claim which would either erode or eliminate their collateral coverage.

REVIEW OF THE ENVIRONMENTAL STUDY.   Lenders typically require environmental studies on most commercial properties that they finance because of the increasing emphasis placed on environmental concerns, especially with respect to lender liability issues. These issues can arise if the lender is forced to take possession of the property, and there are environmental violations for which the lender could then become responsible. If there are environmental concerns, such as underground storage tanks or contaminated well water, the lender wants to ensure remediation prior to or as a condition of the loan.

ANALYSIS OF THE BORROWER.   The analysis of the borrower, like the analysis of the property, focuses on several different aspects. In each case, the lender's analysis focuses on the integrity of the borrower and experiences in similar projects, and on financial strength. The end result of this analysis is to determine if the borrower has the ability and knowledge to successfully manage a property while servicing the associated debt.

EXPERIENCE/INTEGRITY OF THE BORROWER.   Lenders carefully analyze the integrity and experience of their borrowers prior to financing real estate projects. They perform a background search to determine how the borrower has repaid obligations in the past. Although this does not guarantee that the borrower will repay this obligation as agreed, past performance is a good indication of future behavior.

The lender also looks at the borrower's experience in similar projects to ensure that he or she is competent to manage this property. For example, if a potential investor approached a lender to finance the purchase of a strip shopping center, and all of his past experience has been with office buildings, the lender would want to ensure that the borrower's knowledge of this type of investment is adequate enough for him to be successful.

ANALYSIS OF THE BORROWER'S FINANCIAL STATEMENTS.   A lender can receive several different types of financial statements from several different types of borrowers, but in the end the analysis is still the same; the lender is going to focus his or her analysis on the ability of the borrower to repay the loan.

In order to determine if the borrower has the ability to make the debt service payments if he or she is the primary source of repayment, or to cover any shortfall from cash flows from an income-producing property, the lender will focus on the borrower's debt service coverage ratio.

COMMITMENT STAGE

During the commitment stage, the lender sends the borrower a commitment letter that outlines the terms under which the lender would make the loan. This sets the guidelines for expected performance of both lender and borrower during the term of the loan. Most of the sections of the commitment letter are common to all while others are particular to the situation.

COMMON SECTIONS.   All commitment letters begin by identifying the lender, the borrower(s), and the guarantor(s). For legal reasons, the legal names of all parties are used in this section. For example, if the borrower is a corporation, the lender would use the name as it appears on the articles of incorporation filed in the corporation's home state.

The commitment letter discusses in detail the amount of the loan and the purpose for which the loan is being granted. The importance of identifying the purpose of the loan occurs when individuals borrow for business purposes. Since there are different laws governing consumer borrowers and commercial borrowers, this is important from the standpoint of possible collection activities, reporting requirements, and lender liability suits.

Further, the lender outlines the actual mechanics of the loan, which include the interest rate to be charged, any prepayment penalty which may exist, the maturity date, the principal repayment schedule, late fees, the default rate, the security for the loan, insurance requirements, and underwriting fees.

Finally, the commitment includes requirements for financial statements (how often and of what type), an expiration date for the borrower's acceptance of the commitment, and an eventual closing date.

OTHER COVENANTS.   Other covenants cover a wide variety of issues. These are all to ensure that the lender is able to protect its interest in the property and that the borrower operates his or her business in a responsible way. They can also act as warning signs to both the lender and the borrower when events begin to occur that may hinder the borrower's ability to meet scheduled debt payments. There are basically two types of covenants that the lender incorporates into the commitment letter: negative covenants and financial covenants. *Negative covenants* are established by the lender to govern the business actions of the borrower. Typically, negative covenants would prevent the borrower from taking such actions as pledging the collateral for this loan for another loan without the lender's permission, assuming more debt without the lender's permission, or paying off loans to officers prior to paying the debt to the lender. *Financial covenants* establish such guidelines as high-low ranges within which specified performance ratios occur and requirements for reporting the financial condition to the lender. The goal of these, once again, is for the lender to establish guidelines in which the borrower can operate and service the debt without putting a strain on the project and enable the lender to monitor the borrower's financial position adequately. The lender will also identify what level of financial statements are required, such as accountant-compiled, -reviewed, or audited.

CLOSING STAGE

The closing stage of the mortgage lending process consists of three parts; the preclosing, the actual closing, and the post-closing.

PRECLOSING STAGE. The lender at this point prepares all of the documents necessary to close the loan. These include a note, a mortgage deed, possibly a security agreement, subordination agreements, term loan agreement, and so on. The lender will provide the lender and/or his attorney with copies of the documents to review prior to the actual closing.

CLOSING. At this point, the lender, the borrower, and their respective legal counsel meet to sign the documents that establish the obligation. At this stage of the closing process, the borrower pays any fees that are due the lender.

POSTCLOSING. Finally, the lender enters the mortgage loan on his or her loan-tracking system and has the appropriate documents recorded. These documents would include the mortgage deed, deed, and any other security agreements.

NEW DEVELOPMENTS IN THE FINANCING ENVIRONMENT

During the late 1980s and early 1990s, several new developments have occurred in the area of real estate finance. Many of these developments are likely to have permanent impacts on the real estate financing environment for years to come.

As indicated earlier in this chapter, the securitization of real estate has been a major change in some real estate markets. Residential securitization has grown dramatically since the 1970s and is now viewed as a maturing feature of the financial system. Many observers expect that the securitization of commercial mortgages will continue to grow. By the year 2000, we should expect to see commercial mortgage-backed securities as a viable type of security with an active level of trading in national security markets. The real estate equity markets are also looking at the reemergence of REITs, while both real estate lenders and investors find themselves at the forefront of developing environmental law.

COMMERCIAL MORTGAGE-BACKED SECURITIES

The initial explosion in growth of the CMBS market has been tied to the distress of the commercial real estate market in the late 1980s and the early 1990s, and the bail out of the savings and loan institutions by the resolution Trust Corporation (RTC) during that same period. Figure 6–7 shows the issuance of CMBSs from 1987 through 1993 by the RTC and non-RTC issuers.

In the early 1990s the explosion began with the large issuances by the RTC who originated 48.5 percent of all CMBSs in 1992, but only 17.2 percent in 1993. Based on current trends, the possibilities for sustained growth in this market are excellent. For example, in 1993, of the $700 billion in outstanding nonresidential commercial mortgages, approximately 2.7 percent were securitized. Further, of the $291 billion in outstanding multifamily mortgages during the same period, approximately 10.3 percent were securitized. If only 20 percent of this total debt is resecuritized, this would translate to approximately $200 billion in commercial mortgage-backed securities.

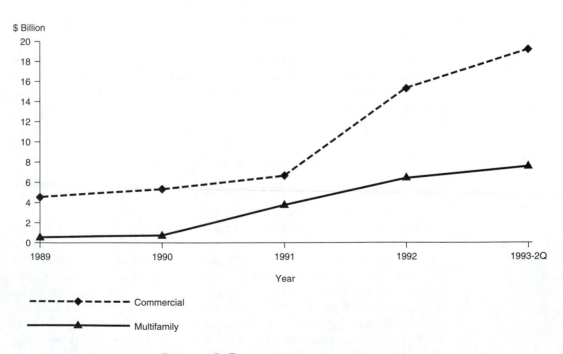

FIGURE 6–7
Nonagency CMBS Outstanding: 1989–1993-2Q.

Growth in the CMBS market is further strengthened by the restructuring of commercial mortgage portfolios by institutional investors. They are finding that the pooling of loans to be sold as securities is a means by which to clear their books of troubled loans. Further, while federally regulated commercial banks must maintain capital reserves equal to 100 percent of commercial mortgages outstanding, they are only required to reserve 20 percent of the mortgage-backed securities. At the same time, the National Association of Insurance Commissioners has adopted a new risk-based capital requirement for life insurance companies that is 10 times greater for commercial mortgages than for a single-A-rated or higher bond.

The development of MBSs for commercial mortgages is a story worth following in the next few years. As new sources of capital for real estate investors, commercial MBSs will be competing with equity sources, especially given the new set of REITs available.

SECURITIZATION OF EQUITY CAPITAL

There has been a history of raising equity capital for real estate ventures for many years. Often as master limited partnerships or as syndication units, deal makers have used these devices during various periods to raise funds for investment. Sometimes the choice of financing vehicle was determined by the federal tax climate; other times, the demand was driven toward one instrument or another depending upon changes in the financial system affecting real estate. In recent years, markets have witnessed the return of REITs as financing vehicles, especially during the early 1990s.

The hottest investment vehicle for equity securitization in real estate markets in the 1990s are REITs. After a checkered period of booms and busts in the 1970s, the late 1980s and early 1990s have witnessed the return of equity (and other) REITs as favorable financing mechanisms. Given the difficulty in many real estate markets (and thus, the unwillingness of financial institutions to finance real estate investments), REITs have come during a period when capital is often needed most. Sometimes the influx of funds is used to restructure existing financial arrangements. Other times, the funds raised in the new REITs have been used to acquire new investments (in the early 1990s, so-called "bottom fishing"). The use of REITs is rapidly becoming a specialized and permanent form of financing of real estate projects.

ENVIRONMENTAL REGULATION

Commercial mortgage lenders find themselves at the forefront of hazardous waste law. This is the result of federal environmental regulation and court rulings which provides for the assessment of financial liability for the clean-up of contaminated property. There are three general areas of concern that lenders must consider prior to making a lending decision: lender liability issues, federal legislation authorizing a lien on the contaminated property equal to the cost of clean-up, and federal legislation requiring that the associated parties meet certain requirements before the transfer of contaminated property.

The Comprehensive Environmental Response, Compensation, and Liability Act of 1980, As Amended (CERCLA)—"Superfund,"—is intended to remediate already-contaminated property rather than establish guidelines for current conduct. This legislation provides for financial liability for four types of potentially responsible parties:

1. Present owners or operators of a facility regardless of when the hazardous condition was created

2. Owners or operators of a facility at the time the hazardous condition was created

3. Any person who by contract, agreement or otherwise arranged for disposal or treatment of hazardous substances

4. Any person who accepts or accepted hazardous substances for transport or disposal at treatment facilities or other sites from which there is a release.

The courts have used Superfund to establish strict liability for owners or operators of contaminated properties. They have further established joint and several liability in the case of multiple parties where fault cannot be assigned proportionately.

Liability is shifted to a lender when the lender subsequently forecloses on a property without performing the appropriate due diligence. Environmental concerns are likely to be of increasing importance to real estate lenders in the future.

SUMMARY

The financing of commercial real estate has always been an important part of the real estate investment process. As the financial system has changed, so have the opportunities for new financing mechanisms and vehicles. While the primary motivation for using debt or equity may be similar now as in the past, current methods are likely to be much different now and in the future from their former methods.

The changes in the financial system stemming from the deregulated financial system in the 1980s has given rise to a new set of institutional vehicles for real estate finance. Financing methods have always been complicated to the novice; the new methods will increase the complexity. Increasingly, mortgage-backed securities, limited-partnership units, and REITs will become mainstays in institutional real estate finance markets.

Understanding the financing environment is essential to successful real estate investing in most countries, but especially in the United States. Financing plays a very important role in the American real estate investment community since a wide range of choices and instruments are available. In addition, as real estate becomes increasingly integrated into capital markets in the U.S. and worldwide, there will be continuing opportunities for innovation and money making in the area of real estate finance. Regardless of the rate of appreciation in real estate markets, there continue to be tremendous opportunities for individuals interested in the area of real estate finance.

QUESTIONS

6–1. What are the two components of real estate financing, and what is involved in the servicing of each?

6–2. Discuss three reasons why financial intermediation is necessary to the continued growth of the commercial real estate market.

6–3. Why are mortgage-backed securities considered a "pass-through" security, and

what makes them so attractive to both lenders and investors?

6–4. What are the four basic steps in the mortgage lending process? Give a brief description of each.

6–5. What is the lender's goal when reviewing the appraisal during the underwriting/analysis stage?

PROBLEMS

6–1. A lender who has a minimum debt-service-coverage ratio requirement of 1.25 times and a loan-to-value maximum of 70 percent for commercial office buildings is reviewing an application for permanent financing with the following specifications:

Loan:	Amount	$1,000,000
	Term	25 years; fully amortized
	Interest	8.5 percent
Property:	Appraised value	$1,400,000
	Environmental concerns	none
	After-tax cash flows	$45,000 annually
Borrower:	Annual income	$81,000

Based on the above information, should the lender make the loan? If not, what should be changed in the application so that the lender would accept the application?

6–2. Using the information from Problem 6–1, assume that: (1) the term has been modified to 20 years/fully amortized, and (2) a new appraisal has valued the property at $1,500,000. Will the lender now make the loan? Why? Why not? If not, what modifications would you suggest to the applicant so that the lender would make the loan?

Selected References

Brueggmann, William B., and Jeffrey D. Fisher, *Real Estate Finance and Investments*, 9th ed. Homewood, Ill.: Richard D. Irwin, 1993.

Fergus, James T., and John L. Goodman, Jr., "The 1989–92 Credit Crunch for Real Estate: A Retrospective," *Journal of the American Real Estate and Urban Economics Association*, 22 (Spring 1994), 5–32.

Graff, A., and D. M. Cashdan, Jr., "Some New Ideas in Real Estate Finance," *Journal of Applied Corporate Finance*, 3 (Fall 1990), 77–89.

Kuhle, James L., Carl H. Walther, and Charles H. Wurtzebach, "The Financial Performance of Real Estate Investment Trusts," *Journal of Real Estate Research*, 1 (Fall 1986), 67–75.

Maisel, Sherman J., *Real Estate Finance*, 2nd ed. Orlando, Fla.: Harcourt, Brace Jovanovich, 1992.

Perry, Harold W. ("Skip"), Jr., "Commercial Mortgage Securitization: An Overview," *Real Estate Issues* 19 (April 1994), 7–12.

Wendt, William M., "Evidence of Change," *Mortgage Banking*, 37, (November 1993), 52–66.

CHAPTER 7

THE TAX ENVIRONMENT

PRINCIPLES _____

1. Real estate analysis requires a knowledge and an assessment of the tax laws affecting each real estate investment.
2. Tax shelter benefits available for real estate investors are the key factor when distinguishing between income and cash flow.
3. There is a step-by-step process for analyzing tax effects.
4. The evaluation of tax consequences can be an important element in a proper real estate investment analysis.

In the previous chapters we discussed the importance of the market, legal, and financing environments in real estate investment decision making. This chapter analyzes the tax environment for real estate decision making. We concentrate on the impact of the federal income tax laws on investor behavior, cash flows, and valuation.

Recall our discussion of the major participants in the investment decision in Chapter 1. The government, through the tax laws, plays a major role in the overall feasibility of an investment. Real estate has received widespread attention as a "tax shelter." In this chapter we take the government perspective on the tax laws and show how to calculate the government's claim (taxes) on the expected income from operations and sale of real estate investments.

CASH FLOW VERSUS TAXABLE INCOME

It is important to understand the difference between the *cash flow* from a real estate investment and the *taxable income* from the investment. The investor is interested in cash flow—the amount of income after all expenses,

TABLE 7–1
MEASUREMENT OF CASH FLOW FROM OPERATIONS
FOR EACH YEAR

	Estimated rent per unit per year
times	Number of units
equals	Potential gross income (PGI)
minus	Vacancy and bad debt allowance
plus	Miscellaneous income
equals	Effective gross income (EGI)
minus	Operating expenses (OE)
equals	Net operating income (NOI)
minus	Debt service (DS)
equals	Before-tax cash flow (BTCF)
minus	Taxes from operations (TO)*
equals	After-tax cash flow (ATCF)

* See Table 7–2.

including taxes, from the investment. An investment generates two potential sources of cash flow: the after-tax cash flow from operation and the after-tax cash flow from sale, referred to as the after-tax equity reversion. On the other hand, the taxing agency (government) is interested in the taxable income from both operation and reversion (sale or exchange).

Table 7–1 shows how to measure the expected after-tax cash flows from operation. The investor forecasts these cash flows for each year of operations: the holding period. Table 7–2 measures the expected ordinary in-

TABLE 7–2
MEASUREMENT OF TAXABLE INCOME AND TAXES
FROM OPERATIONS FOR EACH YEAR

	Effective gross income (EGI)
minus	Operating expenses (OE)
equals	Net operating income (NOI)
minus	Interest on debt (I)
minus	Depreciation deduction (D)
minus	Amortized financing costs (AFC)
plus	Replacement reserves (RR)
equals	Taxable income (TI)
times	Investor's marginal tax rate (τ)
equals	Taxes from operations (TO)

TABLE 7–3

MEASUREMENT OF EXPECTED CASH FLOW FROM THE
SALE OF AN INVESTMENT

	Estimated selling price (SP)
minus	Selling expenses (SE)
equals	Net sales proceeds (NSP)
minus	Unpaid mortgage balance (UM)
equals	Before-tax equity reversion (BTER)
minus	Taxes due on sale (TDS)*
equals	After-tax equity reversion (ATER)

* See Table 7–4.

come taxes for each year of operations. Table 7–3 measures the after-tax equity reversion from the sale of an investment at the end of the expected holding period. Table 7–4 shows how to calculate taxes due on sale when straight-line depreciation is used.

TABLE 7–4

TAXES DUE ON SALE IF STRAIGHT-LINE
DEPRECIATION METHOD IS USED

	Taxable Income
	Selling price (SP)
minus	Selling expenses (SE)
equals	Amount realized (AR)
minus	Adjusted basis (AB)
equals	Capital gain (CG)
	Taxes Due on Sale
	Capital gain (CG)
times	Investor's marginal tax rate (τ)
equals	Taxes due on sale (TDS)

REAL ESTATE AS A TAX SHELTER

As Table 7–2 illustrates, the ordinary taxable income (*TI*) from operating a real estate investment is:

$$TI_t = NOI_t - INT_t - DEP_t + RR_t - AFC_t \qquad (7–1)$$

where:

TI_t = ordinary taxable income from operations in year t

NOI_t = net operating income from the investment in year t

INT_t = interest on debt

DEP_t = depreciation deduction in year t

RR_t = allowance set aside for replacing personal property (replacement reserves) in year t

AFC_t = costs of borrowed funds, such as fees and points, deductible over the life of the mortgage

Taxes from operations are equal to taxable income (*TI*) multiplied by the marginal tax rate.

It is easy to see how a real estate investment shelters taxes. If the depreciation deduction, interest, and amortized financing costs are equal to the net operating income plus replacement revenues, taxes are equal to zero, since taxable income is zero. Taxes are equal to the taxable income multiplied by the tax rate. If the net operating income and replacement reserves are greater than the depreciation deduction, interest, and amortized financing costs, taxable income is greater than zero. Some of the cash flow is sheltered, but not all of it. If the net operating income and replacement reserves are less than the depreciation deduction and interest costs, the taxable income is negative. This does not mean that cash flow from the investment is negative; instead it means that for *tax purposes*, the investment is generating a loss. Under certain forms of ownership, this loss can be used to offset the investor's other taxable passive income.

ANALYZING TAX IMPACTS

To analyze the expected taxes from a real estate investment, the investor must do the following:

1. Determine the tax classification of the investment
2. Determine the status of the investor, that is, corporate or noncorporate
3. Estimate the investor's marginal rate by examining the investor's taxable income
4. Estimate the taxable income that arises from both operations and disposition (such as sale, exchange, and so on)
5. Compute the estimated taxes using the expected tax rate and the expected taxable income

Current Issue 7–1

Who Benefits from Real Estate as a Tax Shelter?

Many people believe that the existence of real estate tax shelter provisions in the federal tax code suggests that real estate as an investment is subsequently enhanced. There are two problems with this approach. First, the tax shelter aspects of the investment are likely to be priced into the asset by the *present* owner such that the *future* investor seeking an investment will be too late. Second, even if the tax shelter benefits are not completely "capitalized" into the market price of the investment before the investment is sold, higher-income investors can place a greater value on the tax shelter than can lower-income investors. This is because of the progressive tax rate schedule that applies to current United States taxpayers.

If the favorable tax provisions of real estate (depreciation write-off, expensing of such items as property taxes and business expenses, and so on) are well known to the clientele of investors interested in certain types of property, it is likely that present prices reflect the tax shelter provisions. For the future investor, this means that the price will be higher than it would be without the favorable tax law. As such, any advantage to the tax shelter accrues to the "seller" rather than the "buyer," once the law is in place. In fact, if all the tax shelter benefits are capitalized, the only investor who would benefit would be the investor who owned the property prior to the discussion and passage of the new tax law.

Similarly, the fact that a higher tax rate is applied to income for certain individuals suggests that tax savings also vary according to individuals' income. In some cases, we would expect that low-income investors would not be able to "afford" some investments (such as tax-sheltered limited partnerships), since their prices would be determined by high-income investors. This is because the high-income investors would drive up the price based on the value placed on the tax savings; the higher their tax rates, the greater the tax savings. Thus it is expected that investors in the highest tax brackets would value tax shelter vehicles the most. In the real world, this is frequently the case.

Note that these results occur even though low- as well as high-income investors deduct interest, depreciation, and business expenses when calculating their tax liabilities. The point is not that these deductions are not permitted, but that the investor has already paid for the right to claim the deductions at the time of purchase.

The first step is to determine the tax classification of the investment. For tax purposes, two types of classifications exist. The first classifies real estate into four categories: property held as personal residence, property held for sale to customers, property held for use in a trade or business, and property held for investment. Each of the categories has different tax rules. It should be noted that within the tax code's definition, most real estate investments are classified as trade or business property and *not* investment property.

The second classification comes from recent tax changes that require a taxpayer's income to be subdivided into three categories: active, portfolio, and passive income. Table 7–5 depicts the three categories. The basic implication of this categorization is that losses derived from passive activities cannot be used to offset income from either active or portfolio activities. Thus, passive losses may only be used to offset passive income; however, these losses may be carried forward (termed "suspended losses") to offset future passive income. Passive activities are defined as activities in which the investor does not materially participate; specifically included in this are rental and limited partnership activities.

Under the 1993 tax revisions, rental activities are always treated as passive activity, regardless of the level of the taxpayer's participation. In general, rental activities can't be considered as part of a greater activity that includes nonrental activities. A special rule allows up to $25,000 of losses from real estate rental activities for taxpayer's with adjusted gross incomes under $150,000. The taxpayers must actively participate in these activities.

The next step is to determine the tax status of the investor. This is important since both tax rates and taxable income are determined differently for the corporate and the noncorporate investor. Certain business organizations, such as partnerships, are not taxed separately. The income from a partnership is taxed on the individual partner's tax return.

Next, estimate the investor's marginal tax rate. Tax rates vary depending on the taxable income of the taxpayer. The crucial one for making investment decisions is the *marginal* rate. Under the 1993 tax law revisions, marginal tax rates are as high as 39.6 percent for the noncorporate investor, while corporate investors face marginal tax rates as high as 35 percent. This means, for example, that the noncorporate taxpayer in a 39.6 percent bracket would owe almost 40 cents in taxes out of every

TABLE 7–5
CLASSIFICATION OF TAXPAYER'S INCOME

1. Active income
   a. Wages
   b. Salaries
2. Portfolio income
   a. Interest
   b. Dividends
3. Passive income
   a. Trade or business in which the investor does not materially participate
   b. Rental activities
   c. Limited partnership activities

$1 increase in taxable income. Likewise, a $1 decrease in taxable income would save the investor 40 cents in taxes. State tax laws increase the marginal tax rates even more.

The fourth step is to estimate taxable income. The operation and sale of real estate produces two types of income taxes: tax on ordinary income and capital gains and taxes on preference and adjustment items in the computation of the taxpayer's alternative minimum tax (discussed later). Taxable income is also measured according to the investment's tax classification and the investor's tax status.

The final step is to estimate the taxes using the tax rates and the taxable income. These estimates are then subtracted from the before-tax cash flow (from operation or reversion) to arrive at the estimated after-tax cash flow. We will examine each step in the following sections.

CLASSIFYING REAL ESTATE FOR TAX PURPOSES

The tax classification of a taxpayer's real property controls the tax influence on the investment. The four classifications are property for personal use, property for sale to customers, property for use in a trade or business, and property for investment (for the production of income). Table 7–6 outlines some of the key differences in the tax treatment of each of these.

One distinguishing characteristic of property held for personal use is that all expenses incurred for personal, living, or family purposes as well as expenses for repair or maintenance are nondeductible. Nor is the owner permitted to deduct an allowance for depreciation. In the case of sale, any loss incurred is nondeductible, but a gain is taxed as a short- or long-term capital gain, depending on the holding period. Interest paid on a mortgage loan and real property taxes incurred on a home, however, are deductible if the owner itemizes deductions. The owner of a personal residence is also permitted to defer all or part of the gain realized on a sale if the purchase of another home is made within a specified period of time.

Table 7–6 also shows some important differences between property held for sale to customers and investment property. When the owner of a real estate investment holds it "primarily for sale to customers in the ordinary course of his trade or business," the owner is a *dealer*. On the other hand, if the owner holds property primarily as an investment for the production of income or for use in trade or business, the owner is an *investor*. There are several differences in the treatment of the investor and the dealer in real estate. One key difference is the treatment of income from sales. The dealer's sales are taxed as ordinary income. The investor's sales are classified as capital gains income. In addition, the dealer is not allowed a deduction for depreciation.

One of the major drawbacks on property held for investment purposes is that the interest paid on mortgage indebtedness is subject to limi-

TABLE 7-6
CHARACTERISTICS OF VARIOUS CLASSIFICATIONS OF REAL ESTATE FOR TAX PURPOSES

Tax Classification	Depreciation Allowance	Treatment of Characteristic for Tax Purposes						
		Treatment of Gain from Sale	Treatment of Loss from Sale	Operating Expense Deduction	Property Tax Deduction	Interest Deduction	Tax-Deferred Exchange	Selling Expenses
1. Personal residence	No	Capital gain (can be deferred)	Loss not deductible	No	Yes	Yes	No	Yes
2. For sale to customers	No	Ordinary income	Ordinary loss	Yes	Yes	Yes (limited)	No	Ordinary business expense
3. Trade or business	Yes	Capital gain (Section 1231)	Fully deductible	Yes	Yes	Yes	Yes	Deductible from sales price
4. Investment	Yes	Capital gain	Deductible (limited)	Yes	Yes	Yes (limited)	Yes	Deductible from sales price

tations for the noncorporate taxpayer. *Investment interest* is defined as interest paid or accrued on indebtedness incurred or continued to purchase or carry property for investment.

Generally, the tax code considers real estate owned and operated for the purpose of deriving rental income to be property used in a trade or business and a passive activity. Transient lodging such as hotels and motels are excluded from this passive activity classification. As previously mentioned, losses derived from passive activities are generally not deductible against active and portfolio income. However, upon the sale of such an activity, any "suspended losses" would be allocated in the following order:

1. Gain from the sale of the passive activity

2. Income from other passive activities

3. Active or portfolio income.

Thus, upon the sale of a passive activity, the investor may be able to use some losses against active or portfolio income.

Real estate held for use in a taxpayer's trade or business receives the most favorable treatment. The owner is entitled to deduct all operating expenses related to the investment, as well as an allowance for depreciation.

On the sale of trade or business property held for more than six months, the investor is entitled to treat the gain or loss as a Section 1231 transaction. As we will see, Section 1231 transactions enjoy the greatest tax benefits with respect to capital gains and losses. Also, all interest expenses are deductible, and the investor can take advantage of the tax-deferral exchange provisions.

Both the courts and the Commissioner of the Internal Revenue Service agree that any owner who devotes a substantial amount of time to the operation and management of rental units is engaged in a trade or business. Accordingly, a real estate investment will probably be classified as held for use in a trade or business. Most real estate investors, therefore, will enjoy maximum tax benefits.

TAX STATUS AND TAX RATES

Various types of taxes can influence the real estate investment decision. Particularly important are the ordinary income tax, the capital gains tax, and the minimum tax. A real estate investment may generate income that is subject to these taxes. To forecast the expected tax implications of an investment, the investor must know the taxable income and the applicable tax rates. This section discusses the various types of taxes and the tax rates.

TABLE 7–7
1993 NONCORPORATE INCOME TAX RATES

Married Taxpayers Filing Jointly	
$0–$36,900	15%
$36,900–$89,150	28%
$89,150–$140,000	31%
$140,000–$250,000	36%
$250,000 and above	39.6%
Single Taxpayers	
$0–$22,100	15%
$22,100–$53,500	28%
$53,500–$115,000	31%
$115,000–$250,000	36%
$250,000 and above	39.6%
Individuals Filing as Head of Household	
$0–$29,600	15%
$29,600–$76,400	28%
$76,400–$127,500	31%
$127,500–$250,000	36%
$250,000 and above	39.6%

NONCORPORATE TAX RATES

Table 7–7 shows the personal tax rates for 1993 taxable income. Table 7–8 shows an example for an individual married filing jointly. Marginal tax rates on personal income range from 15 percent to 39.6 percent, with higher incomes taxed at 39.6 percent. All taxpayers are categorized as either married filing a joint return (or surviving spouse), single, or head of household.

For example, suppose a taxpayer, married filing a joint return, has a taxable income of $70,000. The taxes due are computed as shown in Table 7–8.

TABLE 7–8
TAXES FOR MARRIED FILING JOINTLY

Taxes on income up to $36,900 at 15%	$ 5,535
Taxes on $33,100 at 28%	9,268
Taxes due	$14,803

CORPORATE TAX RATES

The investor may also use the corporate form of ownership, which is a separate taxable entity. The income distributed to the investor by the corpora-

TABLE 7-9
CORPORATE TAX RATES

$0 to $50,000	15%
$50,001 to $75,000	25%
$75,001 to $10 million	34%
$10 million to $15 million	35%
$15 million and above	35%*

*Additionally required to increase tax liability by the lesser of 3 percent of the excess or $100,000.

tion would also be taxed on the investor's individual return. This "double taxation" aspect of the corporation has made it less desirable for investing in real estate. There are, however, other advantages of using the corporate form that may outweigh the double taxation disadvantage. Table 7–9 lists the corporate tax rates beginning July 1, 1987 and after. The 1986 Tax Act reduced the corporate tax rates to relieve some of the double taxation burden but broadened the base to which the rates are applied. The 1993 tax laws increased taxes for higher-income corporations.

TAXABLE INCOME FROM OPERATIONS

The taxable income from operations is calculated as shown in Table 7–2. The gross income is adjusted for operating expenses, financing costs, and depreciation deductions. The following sections discuss each of the categories as they relate to the determination of taxable income from operations.

OPERATING EXPENSES AND TAXES

In general, the expenses of operating, maintaining, and repairing real estate investments are deductible in the year that such expenses are paid or incurred. However, operating expenses are cash outflows, which makes them less valuable to the equity investor compared to the depreciation deduction.

Suppose the investor is in a 28 percent marginal tax bracket. Suppose that the net operating income is $50,000 that year. The investor incurs an unexpected operating expense of $5,000. This reduces the NOI to $45,000. The deductibility of this operating expense reduces the after-tax cost to the investor to $1,400 (28 percent of $5,000). While the expense generated a "tax savings" of $1,400, it cost the investor $3,600.

The test of whether an expenditure is an operating expense or a capital expenditure depends on the nature of the expenditure and its relationship to the operating, care, and maintenance of the property. A repair

Current Issue 7–2

Tax Treatment of Owner-Occupied Housing

The tax code differentiates between owner-occupied housing and real estate as an investment asset. This is not surprising, given the importance placed on the single-family home in our society. It is necessary, however, to recognize some of the major differences.

First, expenses associated with ownership of a home are not tax deductible to the homeowner, where as for the investment, expenses incurred in its renting or maintenance may be used to reduce the tax liability from the investment. Two exceptions to this rule include the deductibility of interest from a homeowner's mortgage and the deductibility of local property taxes on owner-occupied property. As in the case of real estate investment property, homeowners share in this benefit for these two items under the current tax law.

Second, homeowners may not claim depreciation deductions. This is not because owner-occupied housing is physically different from any other type of housing regarding depreciation, but because the law provides depreciation allowances only for real estate investment property.

Third, homeowners may defer capital gains from the sale of their homes indefinitely so long as homes of equivalent value are owned and the new home is purchased within 24 months of the sale of the former residence. In addition, there is a special once-in-a-lifetime exclusion of capital gains income for homeowners. At present, if the homeowner is at least 55 years old, he or she may claim up to $125,000 of capital gains income as tax-free, if the gains accrued from the sales of former residences. Thus, for many owners, this means the elimination of capital gains treatment for owner-occupied homes. While real estate investors may defer capital gains treatment through tax-deferred exchanges, they are not afforded this special rule under the current tax code.

Finally, and perhaps the greatest advantage afforded owner-occupied homes by the tax code, is the omission of the stream of benefits from housing (so-called housing services) from the tax base under the federal tax code. While rent is a taxable item from investment property, the "imputed rent" that accrues to homeowners avoids the tax code. Thus housing services received by owners are untaxed; housing services received by tenants are taxed. This omission emphasizes not only the importance placed on owner-occupied housing in this society but also the special treatment afforded owners of housing compared with renters under the last, current, and, most likely, future tax codes.

is deductible, whereas the cost of a capital addition is depreciable over the improvement's useful life. A repair is an expenditure that only maintains the value or useful life of real property. A capital expenditure, on the other hand, increases the useful life or the value of the property, adding to the owner's basis for the property. The costs for capital expenditures can be recovered through a depreciation allowance or upon a taxable disposition of the investment. Since the owner's basis (cost) has increased through the capital expenditure, the tax due on the sale as a result of capital gain would be lowered.

Because repairs and capital improvements are similar, it is often difficult to distinguish between them. The itemization in Table 7–10 shows how general types of expenditures are treated for tax purposes.

The same problem occurs in the case of an expenditure made in protection of income versus defense of title. Only expenditures to conserve income are deductible. The costs of protecting title must be capitalized as part of the cost of the property and are thus depreciable. The costs of acquiring an investment, such as legal costs and appraisal fees, also are not deductible in the year paid but are added to the depreciable basis and thus are depreciable.

Real estate taxes are deductible by the owner in the year paid or incurred, even on property held for personal use. In the case of a personal residence, however, the taxes are deductible only if the owner forgoes the use of the standard deduction.

Another category that the investor must consider is allowance for replacements. In some instances, the investor should set aside an allowance for the replacement of personal property, such as carpets and appliances. Such reserves, while treated as operating expense for cash flow purposes, are not operating expenses for tax purposes. Therefore replacement reserve allowances must be added to taxable income from operations. Personal property in the investment can be depreciated.

TABLE 7–10
CLASSIFICATION OF EXPENDITURES

Type of Expenditure	Repair	Capital Addition
Roofing	Patching leaks and replacing a limited number of shingles	Installing a new roof or replacing major parts
Wiring	Mending or replacing temporarily	Installing new wiring or replacing most of it
Plumbing	Mending and replacing minor parts	Replacing major units
Fire damage	Cleaning up, removing, and replacing temporarily	Restoring or modernizing damaged facilities

FINANCING AND TAXES

Mortgage financing of real estate investments has four fundamental tax consequences: (1) the mortgage debt is included as part of the depreciable basis; (2) the interest costs are, in general, deductible; (3) borrowed money does not represent taxable income; and (4) the costs associated with placing the mortgage are, in general, not deductible in the year in which they are paid but can be amortized over the life of the loan.

❒ **DEPRECIABLE BASIS AND THE MORTGAGE.**   First, if an investment is being purchased, the investor can include the amount of any borrowed money used to finance the purchase as part of his or her cost basis when computing the allowance for depreciation. Although only a part of the money is equity, the investor is entitled to take the entire price paid for his or her cost basis. This includes the investor's own money as well as the borrowed money. Thus a substantial portion of the net income from a property may be received as a tax-free allowance for depreciation. The investor is also in a position to increase his or her equity in the investment by paying off the mortgage debt out of the monies contributed by the depreciation allowance.

Suppose an investor is purchasing a property valued at $500,000. Suppose also that the property has a $350,000 mortgage that the investor assumes and in addition invests $150,000 in equity. The total cost of the investment is $500,000 on which the investor would calculate his or her basis for depreciation purposes. The depreciable basis is independent of any mortgage amount. The result is the same regardless of whether an investor buys a property and takes out a new loan, buys a property and assumes an old loan, or buys a property subject to an existing loan.

❒ **INTEREST DEDUCTIBILITY.**   What are the tax effects of various payments and charges made or received by the mortgagor or mortgagee during the life of the mortgage? Repayment of the principal of the mortgage debt is neither income to the mortgagee nor a deductible expense to the mortgagor. However, the payment of interest on a debt is both income to the mortgagee and a deductible item to the mortgagor.

Interest paid by an investor on a mortgage debt is deductible even though the investor might not have assumed personal liability for the debt, as in a purchase subject to an existing loan. The distinction between investment property and property held for trade or business is important because the interest expense paid on a mortgage is subject to limitation if the property is for investment purposes. The limit on the deductibility of investment interest—defined as interest paid or accrued on indebtedness incurred or continued to purchase or carry "property held for investment"—is equal to the sum of net investment income. This applies only to the noncorporate investor.

Real estate investments classified as portfolio activities encompass this deduction, but it does not include interest from passive activities or a personal residence that are basically fully deductible.

☐ **REFINANCING AND TAX.**   The third major advantage of using a mortgage is that borrowed money does not represent taxable income to the borrower. Thus an investor who wishes to liquidate a portion of an investment in real property can do so by borrowing against the property. Unlike personal property, the cash received on borrowing for nonpersonal-use property is not taxable, even though the amount borrowed is in excess of the property's basis. The investor's price for borrowing is the payment of interest, an expense that is normally deductible.

☐ **DEDUCTIBILITY OF FINANCING COSTS.**   The costs of placing a mortgage on nonpersonal-use property are not deductible as expenses in the year in which they are paid. The investor may, however, be entitled to amortize these costs over the life of the mortgage loan. These costs include commissions, brokerage fees, points, and any other expenses of obtaining the loan.

The deduction of the financing cost is taken as an annual amount over the mortgage maturity. For instance, suppose an investor borrows $500,000 against an office building. The investor pays a $1,500 commission for arranging the loan, $1,000 for title insurance in favor of the lender, $750 in legal fees related to the loan, and $10,000 in points to the lender. The loan maturity is 20 years. The total loan costs are $13,250, of which one-twentieth (5 percent) can be deducted each year. Thus the amortized financing costs for annual tax purposes are $662.50.

The unamortized remainder of the costs is deductible in full in the year of sale if the investment is sold prior to the mortgage maturity. Using the same example, suppose the investor sells the property after eight years. The total amount amortized is $5,300 ($662.50 times 8), with a balance of $7,950 ($13,250 minus $5,300) that can be deducted in the year of sale. Any prepayment penalties associated with a mortgage loan are also deductible against operating income in the year paid.

If the loan is taken out against nonbusiness property, such as a personal residence, the financing costs cannot be deducted or amortized. Except for points paid, the costs are not added to the owner's basis. These points are deductible as interest in the year paid.

☐ **AT-RISK LIMITATIONS.**   One additional exception to the deductibility of real estate losses besides passive activities has resulted from the TRA 1986 inclusion of real estate as being subject to at-risk rules. At-risk rules limit the amount of losses an investor may deduct to the amount he or she actually has at risk or for which he or she is personally liable. Usually loans in which the investor was not liable (nonrecourse) were excluded; however, with respect to real estate, certain types are included in the amount an investor is at risk. Loans must be from a qualified lender who may not have an equity interest but may be a related party so long as the terms of the loan are similar to others without these relationships. Loans that are acquired from the seller, which may be the bank itself, cannot qualify as at-risk amounts. Therefore, an investor buying property must be careful when securing a mortgage.

DEPRECIATION DEDUCTION

The third item in the calculation of taxable income from operations is the depreciation deduction. This is the key to the "shelter" aspect of real estate investing. In order to calculate the depreciation deduction in any year, the taxpayer must determine three factors: the amount being depreciated, the useful life of the asset, and the depreciation method.

❏ **WHAT IS DEPRECIATION?** The depreciation deduction allows the taxpayer to recover the costs of the depreciable property from taxable income. Depreciation produces tax deductions *without* any cash outlay. A maximum depreciation deduction reduces taxable income, which in turn reduces tax liability and increases after-tax cash flow.

Cumulative depreciation deductions usually bear little or no relationship to the *actual* change in the value of the property. Typically, the situation is such that the taxpayer has a deduction for depreciation while the property value is rising. The net result is the creation of a tax-free cash flow.

Two types of property are allowed depreciation deductions:

1. Property used in trade or business
2. Property held for production of income (investment).

Property used by the taxpayer for personal purposes, such as the taxpayer's residence, is not depreciable.

Depreciation is only allowed on property with a limited useful life, such as buildings and machines. Land is not depreciable since it has an infinite useful life. Although certain land improvements such as paving, curbs, and gutters may be depreciable, the depreciation of land improvements in general depends on whether they permanently improve the land or improve it only as long as a particular building remains useful.

The depreciation deduction in any year is the aggregate amount set aside over the useful life of the asset to equal the cost or basis of the property. Therefore, the depreciation deduction depends on:

1. Costs or basis (that is, the amount to be depreciated)
2. The period of time over which the asset is to be depreciated
3. The classification of the asset for depreciation purposes.

Since much of the investment in a real estate asset is depreciable, the deduction may have three results:

1. All the before-tax cash flow from an investment may be sheltered from taxes.
2. Part of the before-tax flow from an investment may be sheltered.

3. More than the before-tax cash flow from the investment may be sheltered from income taxes. This reduces the taxpayer's other taxable income and other income taxes.

All real estate investments create a tax shelter to some degree. The amount of the tax shelter is determined by the relationship between the depreciation deduction and the net operating income from the investment, the interest payment on mortgage debt, the amortized financing costs, and any adjustment for replacement reserves. The depreciation deduction affects the operating taxable income as well as the taxable income from the sale of the investment.

❏ **DETERMINING THE DEPRECIABLE AMOUNT.** The first step in estimating the depreciation deduction is to determine the amount to be depreciated. *Basis*, the term used to describe the value of property for income tax purposes, generally means the cost of the property. The basis is important for determining the amount of annual depreciation deductions and for determining the investor's gain or loss on the property at the time of sale. The total depreciable amount is generally the original cost *plus* the cost of any capital improvements *less* the cost of the land.

Basis includes cash, mortgages, and other real estate given in exchange for the investment. For example, if an investor purchases a property for cash and also assumes a mortgage, the cash and the mortgage amount are combined to form the basis of the investment.

Certain items may affect the cost of an investment and change the depreciable basis. These include expenditures for capital improvements, certain legal fees, and the cost of title insurance. Other items, such as financing costs, do not affect the basis. However, these financing costs are deducted over the life of the mortgage.

To determine the depreciable amount, the investor must allocate the total cost between land and building.

❏ **BASIS ALLOCATION.** From a tax perspective, a real estate investment consists of a depreciable building and nondepreciable land. The allocation between land and building is based on the market value of each at the time of acquisition. You can determine the allocation by using a professional appraisal or by other methods. For example, suppose you make an investment for a total cost of $100,000. If the building to total value ratio is 75 percent, the depreciable amount is $75,000. On the other hand, if the ratio were to increase to 85 percent, the depreciable amount would increase to $85,000. The increase or decrease in depreciable amount represents a considerable increase or decrease in depreciation deductions, which in turn translates into savings or losses in taxes.

A second means of allocation is to use tax assessor estimates. For instance, suppose the tax assessor has assessed the value of the building at

$50,000 and the value of the land at $15,000. This represents a building to total assessed value ratio of $50,000/$65,000, which is equal to 77 percent. Using the ratio, the investor would allocate $77,000 of the $100,000 cost to the building and the remaining $23,000 to land value.

☐ **TIME DEPRECIATED.**   Another major factor influencing the depreciation deduction is the length of time over which an investment is to be depreciated. The 1993 tax laws have modified the depreciable lives for real estate. Under the new law, real estate has been divided into two categories: residential real property, which has a life of 27.5 years (including low-income housing), and nonresidential real property, which must be depreciated over 39 years. Both types must also be depreciated on a straight-line basis. The effect of this has been to substantially reduce the amount of depreciation deduction the taxpayer is allowed to take.

Depreciation in the year the property is placed in service is based on the mid-month convention. This assumes that an asset is placed in service on the fifteenth of the month regardless of the actual day. Table 7–11 shows the percentage deduction for residential property depreciated on a 27.5-year basis for the years in service. To use this table, choose the vertical column which shows the recovery year and move across to the month of depreciation. The percentage will be applied to the total amount to be depreciated. For example, if a real estate investment was placed in service in June, the first year's proportion would be .020 and the second year would be .036. A similar proportion would be used over the balance of the life. If the property is sold before the end of the life, the deduction for the year of disposition is based only on the number of months the property was in service during that year.

☐ **CLASSIFICATION OF ASSETS.**   The final step in determining the depreciation deduction is to select the method. The 1993 tax revision allows real estate investors to use the straight-line method to depreciate residential rental property over 27.5 years and nonresidential real property over 39 years.

TABLE 7–11
MID-MONTH CONVENTION FOR RESIDENTIAL REAL PROPERTY DEPRECIATION (27.5 YEARS)

| Year of Recovery | Month Placed in Service | | | | | | | | | | | |
	JAN	FEB	MAR	APR	MAY	JUN	JUL	AUG	SEP	OCT	NOV	DEC
1	.036	.032	.029	.026	.023	.020	.017	.014	.011	.008	.005	.002
2–27	.036	.036	.036	.036	.036	.036	.036	.036	.036	.036	.036	.036
28	.029	.032	.035	.036	.036	.036	.036	.036	.036	.036	.036	.036
29	0	0	0	.002	.005	.008	.011	.014	.017	.020	.023	.026

TABLE 7–12
CLASS LIVES FOR CERTAIN REAL ESTATE RELATED ASSETS

3 year	Property with class lives of 4 or less years (includes such items as carpeting, draperies, furnishings)
5 year	Property with class lives between 4 and 10 years (includes cars, energy-saving devices)
7 year	Property with class lives between 10 and 16 years (includes office equipment, fixtures)
10 year	Property with class lives between 16 and 20 years (includes mobile homes and "prefab" houses)
15 year	Property with class lives between 20 and 25 years (includes landscaping, sidewalks, improvements)
20 year	Property with class lives of 25 years and over (includes sewer pipes and farms)

Certain other types of assets, such as improvements, are subject to accelerated methods of depreciation based upon their ACRS class lives. Table 7–12 depicts the types of real estate assets that would fall into this category. The investor also has the option of depreciating these assets on a straight-line rate. The ACRS methods are applied using a mid-year convention; however, if 40 percent of the assets are acquired in the last quarter of the year, the taxpayer must follow a mid-quarter convention.

Table 7–13 shows the accelerated depreciation percentages for these class lives using the mid-year convention.

The depreciation deduction is computed by multiplying the proportion each year by the depreciable basis. This process is continued for each year.

COMPONENT COST DEPRECIATION

Due to the changes in depreciation from the TRA 1986, the effect of lengthening the recovery periods for depreciation has resulted in lower depreciation deductions, and thus less of a tax savings. One solution to this lower deduction is a concept of component cost depreciation.

Real estate is a combination of assets including land, buildings, land improvements, and personal property. If these can be segregated, both land improvements and personal property may be subject to shorter depreciable recovery periods. Land improvements are items such as sidewalks, landscaping, or parking lots. Personal property includes all property contained in or attached to a building but does not include structural components such as heating, wiring, or lighting. Specific recovery periods for these assets can be found in the Internal Revenue Code under the asset depreciation range (ADR) system; however, land improvements generally fall into the 15-year, 150-percent declining-balance category, and

TABLE 7-13
DEPRECIATION RATES FOR CERTAIN ASSET CLASS LIVES

Year of Recovery	Class Life					
	3	5	7	10	15	20
1	.33	.200	.143	.100	.050	.038
2	.45	.320	.245	.180	.095	.072
3	.15	.192	.175	.144	.086	.067
4	.07	.115	.125	.115	.077	.062
5		.115	.089	.092	.069	.057
6		.058	.089	.074	.062	.053
7			.089	.066	.059	.049
8			.045	.066	.059	.045
9				.065	.059	.045
10				.065	.059	.045
11				.033	.059	.045
12					.059	.045
13					.059	.045
14					.059	.045
15					.059	.045
16					.030	.045
17						.045
18						.045
19						.045
20						.045
21						.017

personal property falls into the seven-year, 200-percent declining-balance category. Table 7–14 demonstrates the benefits of using component cost depreciation. In the example illustrated by this table, if component cost depreciation had not been used, the entire amount of capitalized costs would have been subject to a recovery period of 27.5 years. However, $42,600 (the total capitalized costs for 7-year property and 15-year property) is subject to shorter recovery periods if component cost depreciation is used.

ALTERNATIVE MINIMUM TAX

In addition to generating ordinary taxable income, a real estate investment also has the potential to generate tax-preference income, which is subject to the minimum tax.

There are two sources of tax preference income from real estate investments: (1) appreciated property given to charities, and (2) accelerated depreciation on property in service prior to 1987. For appreciated property that is donated, the excess appreciation of all donated property is a tax

TABLE 7–14
COMPONENT COST DEPRECIATION APPLIED

Property Description	7-Year Property	15-Year Property	27.5-Year Property
Foundation			$ 60,000
Framing			70,000
Roofing			10,000
Doors			1,000
Windows			2,500
Sidewalks		$ 2,700	
Landscaping		10,000	
Parking Lot		5,800	
Fencing		2,500	
Intercom	$ 900		
Security equipment	2,500		
Carpeting	3,000		
Cabinets	5,000		
Shelves	1,200		
Kitchen fixtures	9,600		
Total Capitalized Cost	21,600	21,000	143,500

preference item and thus is added back to taxable income. For property in service prior to 1987, an accelerated method of depreciation is available. In the computation of alternative minimum tax, the excess of the accelerated method of depreciation over the straight-line method is a tax preference

TABLE 7–15
CALCULATION OF MINIMUM TAXES ON PREFERENCE INCOME (AMT)

	Taxable Income
plus:	Tax preferences
plus or minus:	Adjustments
equals:	Alternative minimum taxable income
minus:	Exemption
equals:	Tax Base
times:	21%
equals:	Minimum tax before reduction
minus:	Regular income tax
equals:	Alternative minimum tax

item. In addition to real estate, there are five other types of tax preferences. As shown in Table 7–15, these are added back to taxable income to arrive at the alternative minimum tax.

Table 7–15 shows how to compute the alternative minimum tax. To calculate this, tax preferences are added to taxable income. Certain adjustments are either added or subtracted to this sum depending on their tax treatment. These adjustments include among others, depreciation of real and personal property in service after 1986, passive activity losses, installment sales of dealer property, alternative net operating loss deduction, and certain itemized deductions.

For depreciation of real property in service after 1986, depreciation must be calculated on a 40-year life. When subtracted from the regular depreciation, any excess must be added back; however, following the 27.5-year or 39-year life to which the property applies, the amount will result in a reduction of taxable income. Additionally, an exemption is allowed to reduce the minimum tax liability under the TRA of 1986. This amount is $30,000 for single taxpayers and $40,000 for married taxpayers; however, a phase-out of 25 percent over certain levels of alternative minimum taxable income is applied. These levels are $112,500 for single and $150,000 for married taxpayers. Thus, when these incomes exceed $232,500 and $310,000, respectively, no exemption will be allowed.

To illustrate, suppose a married real estate investor had taxable income of $150,000. He also had property in service prior to 1986 with an excess of accelerated depreciation over straight-line depreciation of $25,000 and positive adjustments of $40,000. The amount of alternative minimum tax would be as shown in Table 7–16.

TABLE 7–16
CALCULATION OF ALTERNATIVE MINIMUM TAX

	Taxable income	$150,000
plus	Tax preferences	25,000
plus/minus	Adjustments	40,000
equals	Alternative minimum taxable income	$215,000
minus	Exemption*	23,750
equals	Tax base	$191,250
times	21%	.21
equals	Minimum tax before reduction	$ 40,163
minus	Regular tax[†]	35,000
equals	Alternative minimum tax	$ 5,163

* $40,000 − .25 ($215,000 − $150,000).
[†] Assume the taxpayer's regular tax was $35,000.

Therefore, in addition to the taxpayer's regular tax, he must pay an additional $5,163. This would then reduce the investor's after-tax cash flow.

TAXES ON THE SALE OF AN INVESTMENT

The disposition of a real estate investment is generally referred to as the reversion. The tax impact on the sale of the real estate investment depends on its tax classification and form of ownership. We have already discussed the four tax classifications of property in relation to federal income taxes. This section deals primarily with the tax impact on the individual and the corporate investor from the sale of property held for investment purposes or for use in a trade or business.

For the individual taxpayer, capital gains and losses must be netted together; short-term and long-term gains or losses are computed separately. If a capital gain results, it is subject to tax at the investor's ordinary rate or a maximum of 28 percent. However, if a capital loss is the result, the deduction in the year of sale is limited to $3,000. This must first be used against short-term losses and then long-term losses. Any loss in excess of $3,000 may be carried forward indefinitely, but the distinction between short-term and long-term must remain.

For the corporate taxpayer, capital gains and losses are also netted together and short-term and long-term are kept distinct. However, they are not subject to a minimum tax of 28 percent and losses may only offset gains. Thus, the corporate taxpayer is not allowed to deduct $3,000 of loss against regular income and is further limited in the respect of carrying forward his or her losses. A corporate taxpayer is subject to a three-year carryback and five-year carryforward. Additionally, these corporate carryovers and carrybacks are then classified as short-term. Thus, the taxpayer cannot offset them against future long-term gains.

Table 7–4 illustrates the calculation of taxes due on the sale of the real estate investment. The selling price less selling expenses results in the *amount* realized. Subtract the *adjusted basis* from the amount realized in order to arrive at the *total gain* from the sale. The adjusted basis is the original total cost of the property plus the cost of capital improvements made to the property, less the accumulated depreciation deduction over the holding period. For any nondepreciable investment, such as unimproved land, the adjusted basis equals the original cost.

After arriving at the total gain from the sale, the *capital gain* (loss) on the sale of a real estate investment is multiplied by the investor's marginal tax rate to compute the taxes due on sale. Under the 1993 tax law, capital gains are taxed at a maximum rate of 28%.

CAPITAL GAINS AND LOSSES

Gains or losses from sale are treated as either short-term or long-term depending on the length of time the investment is owned. If the period of ownership is more than six months, the gain or losses will be long-term. Holding periods of six months or less are short-term and are taxed as ordinary income.

If there are both long-term gains and losses, the investor must compute the net long-term gain. If there are short-term gains and losses, the investor must compute the net short-term gain and loss. A net short-term is treated as ordinary income. A net short-term loss may be used to offset a long-term gain.

All real estate qualifies for capital gains treatment unless it is held primarily for sale to customers in the ordinary course of business. Real estate used in trade or business and held for more than six months qualifies as Section 1231 property. Within the tax guidelines, Section 1231 property receives more favorable tax treatment than other investment real estate, referred to as capital assets. Sale of real estate held as neither a capital asset nor Section 1231 asset results in an ordinary gain or loss, whereas Section 1231 and capital assets receive more favorable tax treatment of gains but have different guidelines for losses.

The disposition of Section 1231 assets can result in more favorable tax treatment than that given to capital assets because (1) a net gain from all sales of Section 1231 assets is taxed as a long-term capital gain, and (2) a net loss from such sales is fully deductible against other income without the limitations imposed on the deductibility of losses of capital assets.

Net long-term losses on capital assets may be deducted from ordinary income. There is a limitation of $3,000 on the deductibility of long-term losses from individuals. Per-year short-term losses for the individual are used dollar for dollar to offset taxable income, subject to the $3,000 limitation. The benefits of the carryforward of a capital loss are available to an individual taxpayer until used up or until his or her death.

For the corporate investor, the full amount of the capital gain is included in a corporation's taxable income before the corporate tax rate is applied. Capital losses can only be deducted against capital gains. A corporation can carry back capital losses for three years to obtain a refund on taxes paid during that period, or it may carry losses forward five years for the same purpose. The benefit of any capital loss must be used in this carryback or carryforward period, or it is lost to the corporate taxpayer.

MINIMUM TAXES ON SALE

The second type of taxes to consider on a sale is minimum taxes. The following section discusses minimum taxes for corporate entities.

❐ **MINIMUM TAXATION OF CORPORATIONS.** The corporate investor calculates the tax preference income by the formula in Table 7–17. Assume the corporation has taxable income of $350,000, including a charitable contribution of appreciated property of $200,000, which had a cost of $50,000.

TABLE 7–17
CORPORATE ALTERNATIVE MINIMUM TAX

	Taxable income
plus	Tax preferences
plus or	
minus	Adjustments
minus	AMT net operating loss
	Alternative minimum taxable income
minus	Exemption
	Net alternative minimum tax
times	.20
	Alternative minimum tax before credits
minus	Foreign tax credit
	Alternative minimum tax
minus	Regular tax
	Additional tax due (credit carryover)

They also have excess depreciation on personal property of $20,000 and a carryforward net operating loss of $70,000. Their regular tax liability for the year amounted to $119,000. The additional taxes due would be computed as shown in Table 7–18. Since the alternative minimum tax did not exceed the corporation's regular tax liability, no additional tax is imposed. The purpose for establishing the alternative minimum tax is to ensure that everyone will pay some amount of tax on income generated throughout the year.

Corporate tax preference items must be added back to taxable income. These include, among others, bad-debt reserves, tax-exempt interest, and charitable contributions of appreciated property. These will all increase the base upon which the corporation is taxed. Adjustments may be either added to or subtracted from taxable income. One of the major new items included as a result of TRA 1986 is the depreciation on all of a corporation's personal property. In the computation of AMT, personal property that may have been subject to higher ACRS percentages must be computed using the 150-percent declining-balance method over the asset's class life. The treatment of depreciation of real property acquired after 1986 is handled in the same manner as the noncorporate taxpayer.

In computing alternative minimum taxable income, the new tax law allows a special AMT net operating loss to be deducted from the sum of taxable income and tax preferences. However, it limits the deduction for the AMT net operating loss to 90 percent of that sum. This deduction produces alternative minimum taxable income (AMTI) from which an exemption is subtracted to arrive at net AMTI. The exemption for corporations is $40,000;

TABLE 7–18
COMPUTATION OF TAX LIABILITY

	Taxable income	$350,000
plus	Tax preference	150,000
plus	Adjustments	20,000
minus	Net operating loss	(70,000)
	Alternative minimum taxable income	$450,000
minus	Exemption	0*
	Net alternative minimum taxable income	$450,000
		.20
	Alternative minimum tax	$ 90,000
minus	Regular tax	(119,000)
	Additional tax due	0

* Exemption is phased out for incomes over $310,000.

however, for corporations with net AMTI between $150,000 and $310,000, the exemption is subject to a phase-out of 25 percent, which is calculated similarly to the noncorporate phase-out. From this the allowable foreign tax credit and regular tax are subtracted to arrive at the additional tax the corporation must pay.

However, unlike the noncorporate taxpayer, this amount may be used in future years as a credit to offset future alternative minimum taxes.

To summarize briefly, the sale of a real estate investment creates two potential sources of tax liability: capital gains taxes and "minimum" taxes. The investor must carefully analyze the expected tax consequences *before* undertaking an investment. These taxes are subtracted from the before-tax equity reversion (BTER) to arrive at the after-tax equity reversion (ATER), as shown in Table 7–3. The investor makes the investment decision based on the expected cash flow after taxes from operations and sale.

METHODS OF DEFERRING TAXES ON DISPOSITION

The two most common methods of deferring taxes on the disposition of a real estate investment are *the installment sale* and the *tax-deferred exchange.*

THE INSTALLMENT SALE

When the seller does not receive the entire amount at sale and provides some financing for the buyer, it is possible to defer the tax liability. The installment sale allows the seller to spread the gain from the sale over a period of time instead of reporting it all in the year of the sale. However, tax laws affecting the installment sale have recently been changed. Anyone considering such a sale should seek the most current information.

The installment method of reporting taxable income has advantages over the ordinary method of reporting the entire gain in the year of sale. Some of these considerations follow:

1. Only a pro rata share of the down payment is needed to pay the tax due in the year of sale; if the entire gain were taxable in the year of sale, most of the down payment, or more, might be used in payment in tax on the gain.

2. The seller may postpone the payment of tax on part of the gain until the time in which he or she receives payments that include the proportionate share of the gain.

3. The seller may save some of the total tax if he or she uses the installment method, and if the gain on the sale is taxed as ordinary income. Due to the progressive tax rate structure, the seller's gain will be taxed at lower rates if reported over a period of years than if it is reported all in one year.

4. The seller risks the possibility of changing tax rates. Since taxes are computed according to the tax rates in effect in the year in which the gain is reported, if tax rates decrease in the future, the total tax will be less if the sale is spread out. On the other hand, if the tax rates increase, so will the total tax liability.

❐ **BASIC REQUIREMENTS.**   Basically, in the installment sale method, the buyer pays the seller in a series of payments. The investor is relieved of the obligation to pay tax on income not received and is allowed to include only the "gain" portion of the principal in his or her gross income.

The effect of an installment sale is to spread the gain and tax over the years during which the installment payments are received. This is achieved by applying a gross profit percentage (gain divided by contract price). Losses may not be reported on the installment method. The contract price is the sale price reduced by mortgages or other indebtedness assumed (or taken subject to) by the buyer and payable to a third party. The interest portion of each installment payment is reportable in its entirety as ordinary income, and if no interest is provided for in the agreement, the IRS will impute interest.

Commissions and other selling expenses incurred by the seller are not deducted in determining the sale price, contract price, or payments in the year of sale. The selling expense should be added to the seller's basis. If a minimum amount of interest is not provided for, the IRS will impute interest—each installment payment is divided between interest and principal, and the interest portion will be ordinary income to the seller and deductible interest to the buyer.

With this method of financing, the seller of installment sale property is able to defer tax on the gain received to later years rather than paying the entire amount in the year of sale.

TAX-DEFERRED EXCHANGES

Section 1031 of the Internal Revenue Code provides an exception to the general rule requiring recognition of gain or loss upon the sale or exchange of property. Under this section, no gain or loss is recognized if the property held for productive use in a trade or business or for an investment is exchanged solely for property of a like kind to be held for productive use in a trade or business or for investment. The application of the section for deferring the taxes due on the disposition of a real estate investment is referred to as the deferred exchange.

❐ **WHY EXCHANGE?**   Exchanging real estate rather than selling it and reinvesting the proceeds stems from two basic motivations. The first is that exchanging an investment is an attractive method of marketing real estate when a sale does not appear possible. The second, and probably the more important motivation, is the availability of income tax deferral. Thus taxes that would be paid on an outright sale may be postponed under the use of the exchange.

To illustrate the importance of the tax deferral concept of the exchange, consider the following simple example. Suppose an investor has a property with a market value of $250,000 and an adjusted basis of $150,000. If the property is sold for an amount realized in cash of $250,000, the taxable income (assuming all capital gains) from the sale is $40,000 (40 percent of the $100,000 total gain). If the investor is in a 40 percent marginal tax bracket, the tax on the taxable capital gain is $16,000. Thus, as a result of the taxes, the investor is left with less capital to reinvest.

The investor, however, must ask the question, Am I better off by selling, paying the tax due on sale, and reinvesting, or by avoiding current taxation by means of the tax-deferred exchange? Since the exchange has other important tax implications (the most important of which is that, in general, the basis of the property given up becomes the basis of the property acquired by the exchange), there is no simple answer to the question.

❐ **BASIC EXCHANGE REQUIREMENTS.** Under Section 1031, no gain or loss is recognized if property held for use in a trade or business or for investment is exchanged solely for property of "like kind" to be held either for productive use in a trade or business or as an investment. The *first requirement* of a tax-deferred exchange is that property must be held for productive use in a trade or business or for an investment.

The exchange qualifies for Section 1031 treatment as long as the properties involved fit into either class. Therefore property held for use in a trade or business may be exchanged for property held for investment, and vice versa. Recall that for tax purposes, real estate is divided into four categories. Property held as a personal residence and property held primarily for sale do not qualify under Section 1031. On the other hand, investment property and property for use in a trade or business may be exchanged and may qualify in any combination: investment for investment, investment for business, or business for business.

The *second requirement* for tax-deferred treatment under Section 1031 is that the properties involved in the exchange must be of "like kind," which refers to the nature or character of the property and not to its grade or quality. Under Section 1031, one kind or class of property may not be tax-deferred exchanged for property of a different kind or class. The fact that any real estate involved is improved or unimproved is immaterial because this relates only to the grade or quality of the property and not to its kind or class.

In general, *like kind* refers to the distinction between real and personal property. Real property may be exchanged for real property as long as the first requirement is met. The exchange of real property for personal property does not qualify under Section 1031 for nontaxable treatment. For example, an exchange of an apartment building will qualify even if it was exchanged for a farm. Also, a commercial building for business use could be exchanged for an apartment building. However, an exchange of an apartment building for government bonds would not qualify under Section 1031 for tax-deferred purposes.

Few real estate exchanges are completely nontaxable for all participants. Property value differences usually require the balancing of the equities with what is known as "boot." Boot can take several forms and, by definition, does not qualify as like-kind property. The *third requirement* of a real estate exchange is the identification of the amount of boot and the amount of taxes due on the exchange.

Boot includes such items as stocks, bonds, cash, notes, or personal property received in a real estate exchange. Boot may also be received in the form of relief from indebtedness, which is treated as a receipt of cash. While boot is generally perceived as value given to entice the other investor to trade, its meaning has greater impact when it is considered in the light of tax consequences to the party who receives it.

SUMMARY

This chapter focuses on the effect of tax laws on the real estate investment decision. We begin by differentiating between cash flow and taxable income from operations and from sale, and how the difference between the two enables real estate to act as a tax shelter. Next we discuss the various tax rates and the factors that determine the amount of taxable income from an investment. The chapter concludes by providing some examples for deferring taxes in the disposition of property.

QUESTIONS

7–1. Distinguish between *cash flow* and *taxable income*. Why should the real estate investor be more concerned with cash flow than with taxable income?

7–2. What are the main elements of a tax shelter?

7–3. Discuss the key differences between the four types of real estate for tax purposes. Which enjoys the most favorable tax rules?

7–4. How are corporations subject to "double taxation"?

7–5. What are the tax consequences of the financing decision?

7–6. How does depreciation affect after-tax cash flow? Illustrate with an example, using the current tax rules.

7–7. What is the alternative minimum tax and how is it calculated?

7–8. What are the two most common methods of deferring taxes on the disposition of real estate investments?

7–9. Should the marginal or the average tax rate be used in making cash flow projections? Explain.

7–10. How have recent tax law changes limited the attractiveness of real estate as a tax shelter?

PROBLEMS

7–1. An investor is considering purchasing an apartment building with the following conditions:

Total Value	$1,300,000
Loan-to-Value	70%
Interest Rate	10%, compounded annually
Term	20 years
Number of Units	20
Annual Rent per Unit	$8,000
Appreciation Rate	2% annually
Building to Value Ratio	85%
Depreciation Method	Straight-line
Holding Period	5 years
Vacancy Rate	5%
Operating Expenses	10% of PGI
Replacement Reserves	$2,000
Selling Expenses	7.5% of selling price
Investor's Marginal Tax Rate	28%

a. Calculate the after-tax cash flow for year 1.
b. Calculate the after-tax equity reversion if the property is sold in 5 years.

7–2. Set up the depreciation schedule using the following inputs:

a. | | |
|---|---|
| Depreciable basis | $5,000,000 |
| Recovery period | 39 years |
| Depreciation method | Straight-line |
| Marginal tax rate | 28 percent |
| Placed in service | January |

b. What is the present value of the tax savings discounted at 12 percent?

7–3. An investor has purchased an office building for $2,000,000 with the following conditions:

Total Value	$2,000,000
Loan-to-Value	70%
Interest Rate	10%, compounded monthly
Term	20 years
Building-to-Value Ratio	85%
Holding Period	3 years
Appreciation Rate	1.75%, annually
Selling Expenses	8% of selling price
Investor's Marginal Tax Rate	28%

After purchasing the building, the investor incurred losses of $10,000 in the first year, $11,000 in the second year, and $5,000 in the third year. Taking into account these passive losses, compute the investor's ATER from a sale in year three.

7–4. An investor who is married and filing joint tax returns and whose annual taxable income is $310,000 has purchased an apartment building on 10 acres of land. The purchase price of the investment was $7,500,000. The building-to-total-investment-value ratio is 65 percent. For tax purposes, the straight-line depreciation method is used.

a. What is the investors' marginal tax rate?
b. What is the depreciable life of the building?
c. What is the annual depreciation allowance?
d. What is the annual tax savings?

SELECTED REFERENCES

Follian, James R., Patric H. Hendershott, and David C. Ling, "Understanding the Real Estate Provisions of Tax Reform: Motivations and Impact," *National Tax Journal,* 40 (September 1987), 367–372.

Henderson, Glenn V., and William H. Walker, "Analysis of Installment Sales," *Appraisal Journal*, 47 (October 1979), 485–9.

Kau, James B., and C. F. Sirmans, *Tax Planning for Real Estate Investors,* 3rd ed. Englewood Cliffs, N.J.: Prentice Hall, 1985.

Ling, David C., "Probabilistic Valuation Models and Income Tax Asymmetries with an Application to the Analysis of Passive Loss Restrictions," *Journal of Real Estate Research,* 8 (Spring 1993), 205–220.

Milburn, Robert D., and Steven F. Holub, "How the Deficit Reduction Act of 1984 Affects Real Estate," *National Real Estate Investor* (special edition), September 15,1984.

Turnbull, Geoffrey K., "Land Markets and Tax Reform: The Effects of Passive Loss Limitations," *Land Economics,* 65 (1989), 118–130.

Valachi, Donald J., "The Tax-Deferred Exchange: Some Planning Considerations," *Appraisal Journal,* 47 (October 1979), 76–85.

PART III

FINANCIAL ANALYSIS

CHAPTER 8

OPERATING DECISIONS

PRINCIPLES

1. Operating decisions are those which investors need to monitor and manage affecting gross income, vacancies, and operating expenses.
2. For most investments, there are several required operating decisions.
3. The analysis of operating expenses is an important aspect of real estate investment analysis.
4. Income and expense analysis has produced a series of ratios.
5. Break-even analysis is an accounting tool which may be useful for real estate investors.

One of the major decisions facing investors is the set of operating decisions. These decisions occur throughout the holding period of the investment. As a result, they are often as important as or more important than any of the other decisions the investor is forced to make in real estate investment analysis.

In many real estate investment projects, a careful analysis is frequently overlooked by the investor, the presumption being that the property will manage itself. Although these investors concentrate on the "more glamorous" aspects of real estate investing, such as financing, tax planning, or improvements analysis, few considerations affect the investor's rate of return as much as operating decisions. Since operating decisions are fundamental to successful real estate investing, they affect income and cash flows directly. It is therefore imperative that a careful analysis of operating expenses and the decisions associated with the operation of the project be made. In addition, these decisions must take place periodically throughout the holding period.

Operating decisions affect gross possible income, vacancies, bad debts, and operating expenses. Therefore these items are reflected in net operating income. Determining the rent roll, analysis of vacancies, collection policies, operating expense programs and policies, and some related decisions is the subject of this chapter.

ESTIMATION OF POTENTIAL GROSS INCOME

The rent roll, or the expected rental stream for a specific project, comes from the market analysis discussed earlier in Chapter 4. This "top line" is the beginning of the cash flow statement and is therefore one of the major steps in successful real estate investment analysis.

It is particularly important in real estate to identify the demand forces for the property. The demand will help to determine the economic rent associated with the location of the real estate. Next, the supply must be identified, as the competition will provide valuable information about other projects available for tenants. Together, the forces of supply and demand—the market—will dictate the price the owner can expect for leaseholds for the subject property.

In addition to the base rent, there are a number of other revenue sources for various property classifications. Many office leases include clauses that allow owners to recover "Common Area Maintenance" (CAM) charges. Owners of office buildings incur many expenses not attributable to any one tenant. These expenses are often "passed-through" to the tenant based on the proportion of total space occupied. If the lessor is responsible for expenses, the lease is termed a *gross lease*; when expenses are paid by the lessee, the lease is referred to a *net lease*.

Retail leases often include provisions for "Overage Rent" which allow owners to receive additional rent based on the tenants gross sales volume. Such a lease calls for the payment of a minimum or base rent. In addition, if the tenant's sales volume exceeds an agreed-upon minimum amount, the tenant pays overage rent based on a percentage of the difference between the actual sales volume and the agreed-upon minimum sales amount. Another common revenue category is a CPI increase. CPI stands for *consumer price index*, and CPI increases allow rents to increase based on the index.

Sources of gross income are shown, by type of property, in Table 8–1.

TABLE 8–1
TYPICAL REVENUE CATEGORIES FOR VARIOUS TYPES OF INVESTMENT PROPERTIES

Office	*Retail*	*Apartment*	*Industrial*
Base rent	Base rent	Base rent	Base rent
+ Escalation income	+ Percentage rent	+ Parking income	+ Escalation income
+ CAM revenue	+ CAM recovery	+ Late charges	+ CPI increases
+ CPI increases	+ Escalation income	+ Deposit forfeit	+ Parking income
+ Parking income	+ CPI increases	+ Laundry	+ Tenant services
+ Other revenue	+ Other revenue	+ Other revenue	+ Other revenue
Gross income	Gross income	Gross income	Gross income
− Vacancy allowance	− Vacancy allowance	− Vacancy allowance	− Vacancy allowance
Effective gross income	Effective gross income	Effective gross income	Effective gross income

ESTIMATION OF OPERATING EXPENSES

Another important area in real estate investment analysis is the estimation of the types and amounts of operating expenses associated with the property. Errors in forecasting operating expenses can have a substantial impact on the real estate investment. This is true not only of current owners of property, but also of prospective real estate investors.

A SURVEY OF TYPICAL OPERATING EXPENSES

Traditionally, for valuation purposes, all the required outlays associated with the regular operation of the property have been called the *operating expenses* of the investment. Expenditures of a more permanent and larger nature that improve, upgrade, or rehabilitate the property are called *capital improvements* and are not regarded as operating expenses.

It is sometimes useful to separate the various operating expenses into categories: variable expenses, fixed expenses, and the reserve for replacement. *Variable expenses* differ from *fixed expenses* in that the former varies with the occupancy and general operation of the property. These items include electricity and water, garbage removal, supplies, repairs, bookkeeping services, management fees, and others. *Fixed expenses* are periodic in nature, and in the short run remain constant or level throughout the period, independent of the operation of the property. The best-known fixed expenses are property taxes and property insurance. Recent dramatic changes in property values and thus in property taxes suggest that, in some cases, taxes may not be fixed for the relevant period. In the long run, or course, all expenses tend to vary. However, this categorization is based on the income-reporting period, typically one year. Traditionally, however, since property taxes are based on the tax rate and assessment base, these taxes are treated as fixed each period (year). Other fixed expenses include additional taxes and local fees.

The final expense category is the *reserve for replacement*. This category is frequently misunderstood by beginning investors because it does involve an immediate outflow of cash and is not deductible for tax purposes. It is really a reserve account that is used to set aside funds that will eventually be used to replace worn-out appliances, furniture, or machinery. This reserve adjusts the value of the cash flow to reflect the fact that some of the appliances will need to be replaced in the near future. This is one of the ways that cash flow differs from income for accounting purposes.

Since the funds are not spent each period (monthly, quarterly, semi-annually, or annually) like other expenses, the Internal Revenue Services will not permit their deduction from gross income for tax purposes. However, they should be included as an expense item for investment purposes (that is, when calculating cash flow). By assuming either that the assets to be replaced have economic lives equal to the building (which in most cases is unlikely) or that these assets will not wear out (which in most cases is unlikely, if not impossible for most items), failure to include this reserve would result in overstating the value of the property. In any event, inclusion of this expense gives the investor an accurate net operating income figure at each point in time. (This argument can still be made *even* if the investor does not set aside funds for this purpose. The point is that the income and cash flow streams must be evaluated under the realistic assumption that expenditures will be required to replace some of these short-term assets.)

Table 8–2 outlines typical operating expense categories for various types of income-producing real estate projects. In valuing the property, the investor would estimate future expenses and use these to gauge net operating income. It should be quite reasonable to forecast changes in certain expense items for future periods. It should also be noted that items such as management fees and the reserve for replacement may not be included on past operating expense statements, especially if these were made by the previous owners. This would be true if the previous owner personally managed the property or if he or she failed to establish a reserve for replacement. As already noted, the replacement reserve is not a true expense but rather an account established for valuation purposes. Table 8–3 presents a sample replacement reserve account for an apartment investment.

Data compiled by the Institute of Real Estate Management (IREM) show that the average operating expenses as a percentage of gross possible income per room for residential properties were 13.9 percent for utilities, 5.0 percent for repairs and maintenance, 2 percent for decorating, and

TABLE 8–2
TYPICAL OPERATING EXPENSE CATEGORIES FOR VARIOUS TYPES OF INVESTMENT PROPERTIES

Office	Retail	Apartment	Industrial
Management fees	Management fees	Management fees	Management fees
Property insurance	Property insurance	Property insurance	Property insurance
Administration	Administration	Administration	Administration
Security	Security	Security	Security
Ads and promotion	Ads and promotion	Ads and promotion	Ads and promotion
Parking expense	Utilities	Utilities	Utilities
Maintenance and repair	Maintenance and repair	Maintenance and repair	Maintenance and repair
Utilities	CAM expense		Parking expense
Cleaning and janitorial work		Payroll and fringe benefits	Cleaning and janitorial work
Real estate tax	Real estate tax	Real estate tax	Real estate tax
Replacement reserves	Replacement reserves	Replacement reserves	Replacement reserves
Other expense	Other expense	Other Expense	Other expense
Total OE&T	Total OE&T	Total OE&T	Total OE&T

TABLE 8–3
REPLACEMENT RESERVE ACCOUNT

Asset	Number	Cost ($)	Expected Economic Life (Yrs.)	Annual Reserve Amount ($)
Refrigerators	24	350	15	560
Stoves	24	300	15	480
Air conditioners	48	150	8	900
Carpeting	24	500	6	2,000
Drapes	24	150	6	600
			Total replacement reserve	$4,540

about 9 percent for payroll and management. Total variable expenses averaged about 33.2 percent of gross possible income and about 34.5 percent of the effective gross income. Total fixed expenses averaged nearly 15 percent. Therefore, for this type of property, total operating expenses averaged about 48 percent of potential gross income and about 50 percent of effective gross income.

Another study by IREM indicated that rent collected for suburban office buildings was typically allocated as shown in Table 8–4.

The study was based on a sample of data from 332 suburban office buildings. The occupancy level for the entire sample was 94 percent. These buildings were within a 30-mile radius of a metropolitan location, outside the central business district, and had a minimum floor area of 5,000 square feet, at least 80 percent of which was occupied by office space.

Another significant property classification is retail or shopping centers. The International Council of Shopping Centers (ICSC) has compiled data on mean shopping center revenues and expenses throughout the country. The ICSC divides this property classification into two sub-

TABLE 8–4
EXPENSE/RENT RATIOS FOR SUBURBAN OFFICE
BUILDINGS

Type of Expense	Percent of PGI
Utilities	15.8%
Janitorial, maintenance, repair	14.6
Real estate taxes	10.2
Insurance and services	3.5
Administration and payroll	5.5
Total expense ratio	49.6%

Source: Institute of Real Estate Management, 1993.

TABLE 8–5
MEDIAN OPERATING EXPENSE PER SQUARE FOOT

Expense Category	Enclosed Malls	Strip Centers
Maintenance & Repair	$0.86	$0.45
Utilities	0.44	0.13
General & Administrative	0.81	0.48
Security	0.24	0.09
Marketing	0.47	0.05
Insurance	0.15	0.13
Taxes	0.85	0.88
Total	4.07	2.23

divisions: enclosed malls and strip centers. Table 8–5 shows the median operating expense per square foot for each of the two subclasses.

VARIABLE EXPENSE ITEMS

❏ **UTILITIES.** Utility expenses include most power and water services found in most urban properties, including electricity, gas, heating fuels, telephone charges, sewer or other sanitary system charges, and water. Although many utility expenses are relatively fixed in nature, an investor may be able to restrict unnecessary usage of some of these items by following recommended management prevention techniques. For example, the investor may be able to reduce electricity usage by checking and replacing worn or insufficient insulation in the walls and ceilings and by installing energy-efficient storm windows and thermopane glass. The caulking and weather stripping of windows and doors may further reduce unnecessary electrical usage. Similarly, the investor should regularly check plumbing fixtures for work rings and seals. As energy becomes more expensive, it will be to the investor's advantage to make the most efficient use of utility services.

❏ **REPAIRS AND MAINTENANCE.** There are two types of repairs and maintenance expenses: those that are minor and are expected to occur at various intervals and those that are potentially more costly and mostly unexpected. Items typically classified as repairs include breakdowns of elevators, heating and cooling systems, refrigerators and stoves, and other mechanical items. Maintenance items include the general upkeep of the building's common space and the exterior grounds, minor maintenance of appliances on a regular basis (preventive maintenance), and regular maintenance of equipment. When cash flow problems occur in residential income property, some owners tend to postpone certain maintenance and repair items. This deferred maintenance strategy often results in even greater maintenance expenses in the future, falling property values, and very unhappy tenants.

❐ **SERVICES.**   Many items can be better handled by outside professional services. The more obvious ones are garbage removal, regular extermination and pest control, building security, and fire safety control. However, some investors may also be interested in other services such as professional bookkeeping and accounting, maintenance and building cleaning, and window washing. In many ways, the benefits of professional services accrue to both owners and renters. The owners may wish to employ specialists who are more familiar with the problems of the job and are trained to handle various situations. Tenants will appreciate the results.

❐ **ADMINISTRATIVE AND PAYROLL.**   Administration and payroll expenses encompass employees who have been hired by the investor (or the management firm) for various tasks. These people include regular maintenance staff, secretarial assistance, groundskeepers, and others. Administrative expenses consist of small operating expenses such as the costs of preparing credit reports on prospective tenants, legal expenses, and petty cash items.

❐ **SUPPLIES.**   This item refers to materials and small items incidental to the operation of the property. Hardware items and other minor maintenance items purchased by the investor or manager fall into this category. Although supplies constitute a very small percentage of expenses, the owner or manager who neglects this part of the upkeep is inviting trouble in the future.

❐ **DECORATING.**   Sometimes included in services, decorating is listed separately here because it is an important way to ensure an investment's success. The newly redecorated income-producing building allows the investor to attract tenants at the highest rents. It is also regarded as a sign of good management. In many cases, the expenses can easily be justified by the increases in rental receipts.

❐ **MANAGEMENT.**   This is one of the more controversial expense items. If the owner manages the property himself or herself, then for accounting purposes, there are no management expenses. Since the owner provides the service, he or she would not pay a monthly management fee.

Traditionally, management is compensated on a percentage of gross income. Therefore the management firm is useful to reduce vacancies and maximize potential gross income. Management fee percentages vary between 5 and 8 percent for smaller and problem properties. The rate is largely determined by custom and local market conditions.

It is up to the investor to decide whether to hire a management company. Such a company can run the property efficiently and, in the long run, will make more money for the investor.

FIXED EXPENSE ITEMS

❐ **REAL ESTATE TAXES.** Real estate taxes are one of the more permanent expenses that owners of real property must pay. Based on local assessment, these taxes are *ad valorem*, or "according to value." Each state defines the relationship between *assessed value* and *market value* (which requires all property to be assessed at the same percentage). The total amount of tax liability is determined by the tax rate times the assessed value. If the owner feels that the property assessment is too high relative to his or her estimate of market value and the state's assessment-to-market-value ratio, he or she may request a reassessment.

❐ **INSURANCE.** Property insurance is another important area for analysis. Although entire books are available on the subject, the basic purpose for acquiring insurance protection is to reduce or limit unforeseen casualty losses. Insurance firms offer various packages of protection including fire insurance, extended coverage policies (with additional protection against floods, hail, tornadoes, and other disasters), casualty coverage against robbery, theft, and on-the-job accidents, and liability. Property insurance is a fixed expense. In addition, other taxes may be included as fixed expenses. Examples of these are franchise taxes, personal property taxes, or similar levies or fees.

EXAMPLE 8–1 PRO-FORMA OPERATING STATEMENT

An investor has enlisted your services to help analyze his property. Suppose the investor owned a 20,000-square-foot office building, of which 95 percent is leasable. There are presently three leases covering the property. Specifics of the three leases are as shown in Table 1.

While the office is currently 100 percent occupied, you anticipate that the typical vacancy for each of the five years is 5 percent. There are a number of operating expenses associated with the property: management fees are 5 percent of collected income, property taxes are $20,000 per year for the next two years and $22,500 thereafter, utilities are $1.50 per square foot of building area and are growing at 4 percent per year, insurance is $4,000 per year, janitorial expenses are projected at $.75 per square foot and increasing at 6 percent per year, and reserve requirements for the property total $5,000 per year.

The owner asks you to set up a pro-forma operating statement Table 2) covering the next five years to help him analyze the property. He asks that you show the expected revenue to be received from each tenant as well as the total potential gross income, vacancy and credit loss allowance, and the total effective gross income. Operating expenses are to be separated into variable expenses, fixed expenses, and replacement reserves.

TABLE 1
LEASE CHARACTERISTICS

Tenant	Square Footage	Rent per Square Foot	CPI Increases
Bank of Arcadia	8,500 SF	$12.50	N/A
Pasadena Insurance	6,500 SF	$12.85	3% per Year
Hardy Law Firm	4,000 SF	$13.15	3% per Year
Total	19,000 SF	N/A	N/A

TABLE 2
PRO-FORMA OPERATING STATEMENT

Year	One	Two	Three	Four	Five
Revenues					
Bank of Arcadia	$106,250	$106,250	$106,250	$106,250	$106,250
Pasadena Insurance	$ 83,525	$ 86,031	$ 88,612	$ 91,270	$ 94,008
Hardy Law Firm	$ 52,600	$ 54,178	$ 55,803	$ 57,477	$ 59,202
Potential gross income	$242,375	$246,459	$250,665	$254,997	$259,460
Vacancy & credit loss	$ 12,119	$ 12,323	$ 12,533	$ 12,750	$ 12,973
Effective gross income	$230,256	$234,136	$238,132	$242,248	$246,487
Expenses					
Variable expenses					
Management fees	$ 11,513	$ 11,707	$ 11,907	$ 12,112	$ 12,324
Utilities	$ 30,000	$ 31,200	$ 32,448	$ 33,746	$ 35,096
Janitorial	$ 17,000	$ 18,020	$ 19,101	$ 20,247	$ 21,462
Total variable	$ 58,513	$ 60,927	$ 63,456	$ 66,106	$ 68,882
Fixed expenses					
Property taxes	$ 20,000	$ 20,000	$ 22,500	$ 22,500	$ 22,500
Insurance	$ 4,000	$ 4,000	$ 4,000	$ 4,000	$ 4,000
Total fixed expenses	$ 24,000	$ 24,000	$ 26,500	$ 26,500	$ 26,500
Replacement reserves	$ 5,000	$ 5,000	$ 5,000	$ 5,000	$ 5,000
Total operating expenses	$ 87,513	$ 89,927	$ 94,956	$ 97,606	$100,382
Net operating income	$142,743	$144,209	$143,176	$144,642	$146,105

THE ROLE OF PROPERTY MANAGEMENT

Property management is one of the frequently misunderstood areas of analysis. Typically defined as "the branch of real estate composed of renting, supervising, collecting, paying and the overall maintaining and managing of real estate for others,"[1] many investors believe that the expense associated with professional property management is unnecessary. After all, many of the managerial duties and activities may be undertaken by the equity investor. However, since the amount of time required and the types of skills needed may be more than some investors possess, professional property management is a service that warrants consideration. Too, there are other investors for whom the employment of professional management firm arises out of choice, not necessity.

The decision of whether to employ a management firm is often difficult. The advantages are there, however, for the firm may be more familiar with the market and with the latest construction and maintenance procedures to help increase the efficient use of property. Finally, it may have more resources available for bookkeeping, advertising, and preparing financial reports.

Although these factors and others are helpful, the investor does not acquire them without expense. The decision, then, is whether the services are worth the cost. In many cases, they are.

EVALUATING THE IMPACT

One way to determine whether the employment of one or more professional services is "worth it" is to measure its potential impact on the return and value of the investment. For example, if the advice and policies of the property management firm increased the value of the property significantly, it is easy to justify its employment. If, on the other hand, it could not do so and the other services offered were either too expensive or unnecessary, the investor would do better by acquiring the services of others, or of none at all.

Studies have shown that property management significantly influences investment values. Since the professionally trained property manager can best deal with factors affecting income and *operating expenses*, he or she is quite valuable to the investor. The following discussion demonstrates some of the other ways in which professional property management may be of considerable help.

---

[1]Jerome S. Gross, *Illustrated Encyclopedic Dictionary of Real Estate Terms* (Englewood Cliffs, N.J.: Prentice Hall, 1969).

EXAMPLE 8–2 **OPERATING STATEMENT ANALYSIS**

Suppose a real estate investor is considering the purchase of an apartment complex. The property has 30 one-bedroom units with an average of 650 square feet per unit and 60 two-bedroom units with an average of 950 square feet per unit.

In Chapter 4 we illustrated how an investor can use comparable data to determine rents and vacancy rates. Using the information given in Table 4–6 of Chapter 4, the investor concludes that the expected rental rates are $0.44 per square foot for one-bedroom units and $0.40 per square for the two-bedroom units. Therefore, rents per month per unit is approximately $285 for the one-bedroom apartments and $380 for the two bedroom units. The expected vacancy rates are 4 percent for the one bedroom units and 5 percent for the two-bedroom units. In addition to the apartment rent, the complex received other miscellaneous income. Parking spaces were rented totaling $15,000 per year and vending machines in the complex earned $5,500 per year. Table 1 outlines the forecasted gross income for the project.

TABLE 1
FORECASTED GROSS INCOME FOR APARTMENT INVESTMENT

Two-bedrooms		
60 2-bdrm units @ $380 per month	$273,600	
(Less) vacancy & credit loss	$ 13,680	
Rent collections		$259,920
One-bedrooms		
30 1-bdrm units @ $285 per month	$102,600	
(Less) vacancy & credit loss	$ 4,104	
Rent collections		$ 98,496
Total forecasted annual rent		$358,416

The current owner provided a annual operating statement for the property. This statement is given in Table 2. This statement does not conform to the concept of cash flows that represents "income" in valuation analysis. The investor must "reconstruct" the operating statement to yield a correct measurement of income and expenses for valuation purposes.

TABLE 2
APARTMENT OWNER'S INCOME STATEMENT

Receipts		
Rent collections	$358,416	
Parking & concession receipts	$ 20,500	
Total receipts		$378,916
Expenses		
Property taxes	$ 90,000	
Mortgage payments	$157,175	
Management fees	$ 16,500	
Resident manager—salary	$ 19,425	
Water	$ 23,550	
Electricity	$ 2,950	
Legal fees	$ 22,850	
Insurance premium (3 years)	$ 19,200	
Supplies	$ 950	
Pool & grounds maintenance	$ 14,000	
Advertising	$ 2,700	
Building maintenance & repairs	$ 17,700	
Replace two ovens	$ 900	
Replace three refrigerators	$ 1,650	
Depreciation	$ 44,825	
Total expenses		$434,375
Income (loss) for the year		($ 48,959)

In addition to the annual operating statement, the owner has provided explanations and clarifications for many of the line items included in the statement. Total property taxes paid during the year were $90,000; however, this was for a two-year period. One-half of this amount went toward current-year taxes. Similarly, insurance was prepaid for three years; only one-third of the payment is attributable to the current year. The income statement included mortgage payments and depreciation which should not be part of the reconstructed cash flow statement. The resident manager's salary totaled $25,900 for the year, but due to accounting delays, only three-fourths of the manager's total salary was included in the income statement. The line items outlining the replacement of two ovens and three refrigerators are capital improvements and should not be included in the operating statement. However, replacement reserves should be included, and they are estimated to be $8,450 for the year. Some categories included in the income statement could be merged into one line item in the operating statement; for example, water and electricity could be added together and labeled Utilities, while legal fees, advertising, and supplies could be merged into an account labeled Administration and Marketing. Table 3 shows the "reconstructed" operating statement

TABLE 3
APARTMENT OPERATING STATEMENT

Income
Apartment Rent:

60—2 Bdrm. Units @ $380 per month		$273,600
30—1 Bdrm Units @ $285 per month		$102,600
Total Rent		$376,200
(Less) vacancy & credit loss		$ 17,784
Total Rent		$358,416
Other Income:		
Parking Space Rental	$15,000	
Concession Income	$ 5,500	$ 20,500
Effective Gross Income		$378,916

Expenses

Operating Expenses		
Salaries & Personnel	$25,900	
Property Taxes	$45,000	
Insurance	$ 6,400	
Utilities	$26,500	
Management Fees	$16,500	
Admin. & Mktg.	$26,500	
Repairs & Maint.	$17,700	
Contract Services	$14,000	
Replacement Reserves	$ 8,450	
Total Operating Expenses		$186,950
Net Operating Income		$191,966

ANALYSIS OF THE IMPORTANCE OF OPERATING EXPENSES

Given that the investor is able to carefully forecast expected operating expenses, there are a number of ways to analyze the relationships between income, expenses, value, return, and risk. These techniques aid in the investment decision-making process and are discussed next.

OPERATING EXPENSES AND VALUE

One of the most common ways of valuing property is to estimate an average (or "stabilized") net operating income figure based on market and investment analyses and capitalize this amount by the appropriate "discount or capitalization rate." If the investor wanted to find out how much value he or she placed on the property, this approach suggests that

In most European countries, property managers are viewed as more important to the success of real estate investments than are their counterparts in the United States. The function of property management in Europe is often viewed as a critical one; the European property manager is thought to be a valuable professional and important member of the team.

Perhaps one reason for the perceived importance of property management in Europe compared to the United States is the longer holding periods for most real estate investments in Europe compared to the U.S. In the United States, 6 to 10 years is often viewed as a typical holding period; sometimes, even shorter time periods are planned. In countries such as Sweden, The Netherlands, France, the U.K., and elsewhere, holding periods are often 15, 20, or 25 years. In some instances, the holding periods are even longer—the ultimate "buy and hold" strategy!

Some countries (for example, Sweden) have a strong cultural heritage of safe and clean buildings, very well-maintained common spaces, and extremely well-maintained property. It is not surprising then that Swedish real estate investors spend a higher percentage of revenue on maintenance than do investors in other countries.

If an investor expects to acquire the property and not sell it in the near future, effective property management becomes critical. And, since there is often status associated with owning "trophies," maintenance programs for such properties will be developed with considerable care and attention. Property managers in societies with differing interests in maintenance and care of tenants will monitor operating expenses very closely. It would be interesting and perhaps profitable to spend some time and compare property management practices outside the United States with others in differing countries.

the investor would make a reliable estimate of net operating income and divide it by the capitalization rate for projects of this risk class and type of investment. The result is an estimate of investment value. Another measure of how a property is performing is the operating expense ratio. This ratio measures the relationship between operating expenses and income. This measure is useful when comparing the operating efficiency of different properties.

The *operating expense ratio* is defined as follows:

$$OER = \frac{TOE}{EGI} \qquad (8\text{--}1)$$

where

OER = operating expense ratio

TOE = total operating expenses

EGI = effective gross income

Net operating income is determined by multiplying effective gross income by $(1 - \text{OER})$:

$$\text{NOI} = \text{EGI} \times (1 - \text{OER}) \qquad (8\text{--}2)$$

where

NOI = net operating income

Net operating income is "capitalized" into value by dividing the capitalization rate into the net operating income figure:

$$V = \frac{\text{NOI}}{R} \qquad (8\text{--}3)$$

where

V = investment value

R = (overall) capitalization rate

For example, using an operating expense estimate of $25,000, if effective gross income is expected to be $50,000, the operating expense ratio would be .50 and net operating income would be $25,000:

$$\text{OER} = \frac{\$25,000}{\$50,000}$$

$$= .50$$

and

$$\text{NOI} = \$50,000(1 - .50)$$

$$= \$25,000$$

Finally, if the capitalization rate is 10 percent, the investment value is $250,000:

$$V = \frac{\$25{,}000}{.10}$$

$$= \$250{,}000$$

Suppose the effective gross income increases to $55,000 due to increased demand for rental space. The analysis shows that the investment value would increase from $250,000 to $302,500, holding everything else constant:

$$\text{OER} = \frac{25{,}000}{55{,}000}$$

$$= .45$$

and

$$\text{NOI} = \$55{,}000(1 - .45)$$

$$= \$30{,}250$$

Therefore,

$$V = \frac{\$30{,}250}{.10}$$

$$= \$302{,}500$$

The same result would occur, of course, if total operating expenses decreased $5,250 to $19,750, *without an accompanied change in income*. In this case, net operating income would also be $30,250 ($50,000 minus $19,750) and the investment value would also be $302,500.

Finally, the investor could forecast changes in income and expenses and translate these combinations of changes into capitalized value. This is shown in the next section. It is important to emphasize that the calculation of investment value using net operating income as well as other measures of income and an overall capitalization rate is very sensitive to changes in operating expenses.

EXAMPLE 8–3   OPERATING EXPENSES AND VALUATION

The investor introduced in Example 8–1 would like to extend that analysis. Given the information provided, the owner would like to determine the operating expense ratio and the value of the subject property. To help in the analysis, information was provided on other recently sold properties, as shown in Table 1.

TABLE 1
RECENTLY SOLD PROPERTIES

Property	Sales Price (V)	Net Operating Income (NOI)	Total Operating Expenses (TOE)	Effective Gross Income (EGI)
Premier Office Building	$1,579,000	$150,000	$ 92,500	$255,000
Santa Anita Offices	$1,526,000	$145,000	$ 87,500	$227,000
Hastings Office Complex	$1,685,000	$160,000	$102,000	$261,000
Glendale Square Offices	$1,420,000	$135,000	$ 81,000	$217,000

These properties are all similar in size and location to the subject property. The indicated Cap Rate (R) can be calculated for each property by dividing Net Operating Income (NOI) by the Sales Price (V). The Operating Expense Ratio (OER) is simply the Total Operating Expenses (TOE) divided by the Effective Gross Income (EGI). Table 2 outlines the results.

TABLE 2
OER AND R FOR PROPERTIES

Property	Cap Rate (R)	Operating Expense Ratio (OER)
Premier Office Building	9.50%	0.362
Santa Anita Offices	9.50%	0.385
Hastings Office Complex	9.49%	0.391
Glendale Square Offices	9.51%	0.373

The listed comparable sales indicate a market capitalization rate of 9.5%. The year-1 operating income taken from Example 8–1 is $142,743. The indicated cap rate can be applied to the year-1 operating income to calculate the indicated value for the subject property.

$$V = \frac{NOI}{R}$$

$$V = \frac{\$142,743}{9.5\%}$$

$$V = \$1,502,558$$

The result is a range of operating expense ratios from .362 to .392. The operating expense ratio for the subject can be calculated from the information provided in Example 8–1 and compared to the comparable properties. The total operating expenses and effective gross income from 8–1 are $87,513 and $230,256 respectively. Therefore, the subject OER is .380 ($87,513/$230,256). This ratio falls within the range of values derived from the comparable properties and would seem to indicate that the operating expenses for the building are in line with the market.

Although income capitalization is only one method of valuation, operating expenses play a major role in the value of an investment. Since net operating income is the difference between effective gross income and total operating expenses, changes in total operating expenses affect the estimated size of net operating income. Sizable changes in net operating income when divided by the overall capitalization rate result in significant changes in investment value. Therefore, a careful analysis of the changes in operating expenses over time is vital to ensure that the investment (and market) values of the property are not seriously damaged.

Similarly, the investor who is able to eliminate unnecessary expenses, or who is able to raise rents by making significant improvements in the physical facilities, can greatly increase the value of the property. One of the benefits of professional property management firms is their ability to eliminate unnecessary expenses and recommend programs for upgrading and rehabilitation that may result in higher rent schedules despite additional outlays. These actions raise net operating income and therefore the value (and return) of the investment.

OPERATING EXPENSES, THE OPERATING EXPENSE RATIO, AND VALUE

A question that frequently arises in estimating net operating income is the relationship between changes in operating expenses, changes in the operating expense ratio, and the value of property. This is a very important area, since changes in the operating expense ratio directly result from change in income as well as expenses.

The operating expense ratio is a key factor in making real estate investment decisions. As a rule of thumb, the investor can predict whether the value of the property will change by comparing the expected changes in rents and expenses with the operating expense ratio. For example, suppose income is only expected to increase at a rate of 5 percent annually but expenses are expected to increase at a rate of 10 percent annually. If the *operating expense ratio* (total operating expenses divided by effective gross income) was less than .50, then investment value would still increase.

The basic relationship is:

If a = expected growth rate in (effective gross) income

b = expected growth rate in (total operating) expenses

Then, OER = operating expense ratio, and

value will increase when $\dfrac{a}{b} >$ OER   (8–4)

value will remain the same when $\dfrac{a}{b} =$ OER   (8–5)

value will decrease when $\dfrac{a}{b} <$ OER   (8–6)

In this example, a/b = .50. If OER < .50, the value will increase. If OER is greater than .50, the value will decline.

This result may seem paradoxical to some readers. In this example, expenses are expected to rise twice as much as income, and yet if the OER was less than .50, the investment value would rise. The explanation is that the investor must pay careful attention to the relationship between operating expenses and the operating expense ratio and determine how these items affect the value of property. The investor simply cannot make a property decision by only looking at changes in income and expenses.

Gross and Net Income Multipliers

Gross and net income multipliers are reasonably simple investment measures that relate value and effective gross or net operating income. Each has a particular meaning in relation to the analysis of operating expenses. The *gross income multiplier* technique is more commonly used. However, since operating expense levels and, thus, ratios vary among different pieces of property, this technique may be less useful for comparative purposes. However, a well-known article suggests that this technique may be very reliable in making investment decisions.[2]

[2]Richard U. Ratcliff, "Don't Underrate the Gross Income Multiplier," *Appraisal Journal*, 39 (April 1971), 264–71. See also Boykin, James H., and Margaret T. Gray, "The Relevance and Application of the Gross Income Multiplier," *Appraisal Journal*, 62 (April 1994), pp. 203–8.

The *gross income multiplier* (GIM) is defined as follows:

$$GIM = \frac{MV}{EGI} \tag{8-7}$$

where

MV = market value

EGI = effective gross income

GIM = gross income multiplier

For example, if the effective gross income of an income property is $15,000 per year, and the market value of the property is $100,000, the gross income multiplier would be 6.67:

$$GIM = \frac{\$100,000}{\$15,000}$$

$$= 6.67$$

The investor would then compare this GIM with others for sale in order to evaluate investment alternatives.

The *net income multiplier* (NIM) is defined as value divided by net operating income. It is not used much because the capitalization rate is more commonly used in valuation.

Since $V = NOI/R$, value is also equal to $NOI \times 1/R$. The net income multiplier (NIM) is defined as $1/R$. For example, if value is equal to $200,000 and net operating income is $20,000, the net income multiplier is 10.0:

$$NIM = \frac{MV}{NOI}$$

$$= \frac{\$200,000}{\$20,000} \tag{8-8}$$

$$= 10.0$$

The net income multiplier is also equal to $1/R$:

$$NIM = \frac{1}{R} \tag{8-9}$$

In addition, R, the capitalization rate, may be expressed as the NIM reciprocal:

$$R = \frac{1}{\text{NIM}} \qquad (8-10)$$

Using the same numbers as in the above example of $V = \$200,000$, $\text{NOI} = \$20,000$, and $\text{NIM} = 10.0$, then R is .10, since the capitalization rate is the reciprocal of NIM:

$$R = \frac{1}{10.0}$$

$$= .10$$

In any event, real estate writers and experienced investors urge that a great deal of judgment be used when developing multipliers. Since these measures are relatively simple to compute, the data requirements minimal, and the results easy to interpret, care must be taken to avoid inaccuracies.

To the extent that the gross income multiplier technique is preferred to the net income multiplier, the investor is minimizing the impact that *different sets of operating expenses* can have on various properties. Although comparable properties may vary significantly, comparisons on the basis of gross income multipliers may not pose any significant problems for some income-producing real estate. The problem is when operating expenses vary for other comparable properties. In this event, the net income multiplier (or its reciprocal) is a better measure.

Consider the following alternatives in Table 8–6: Projects A and B. Although both have identical expected selling prices and annual effective gross income, the NIM method or direct capitalization using R gives different results. Obviously, an investor would not be indifferent to each project, despite the same GIM. The example shows that Project B requires a greater NIM (or lower R) than Project A. Stated differently, if the capitalization rate, R, was chosen to be 12 percent for both investments, Project B would be valued at $416,667. Therefore, Project A would be preferred if both were viewed as equally risky. Only after the net income multiplier

TABLE 8–6
COMPARISON OF PROJECTS A AND B

	A	B
Expected selling price	$500,000	$500,000
Effective gross income	$100,000	$100,000
Total operating expenses	$ 40,000	$ 50,000
Net operating income	$ 60,000	$ 50,000
GIM	5.00	5.00
NIM	8.33	10.00
R	12%	10%

(and the capitalization rate) is considered is the analyst able to choose Project A over Project B as shown in Table 8–6. Using the gross income multiplier, the investor does not consider differences in expenses among alternatives.

FINANCIAL RATIOS

Some well-known financial ratios involve operating expenses directly or indirectly. Three of the more common ones are the *operating expense ratio,* the *break-even cash flow ratio,* and the *debt coverage ratio.* Each of these measures is important in the analysis of income, expenses, and productivity of real estate.

A high *operating expenses ratio* may indicate that some expenses currently being charged against the property are unnecessary or that rent levels are too low compared with similar property on the market. The investor should carefully monitor this ratio over time to pick up any danger signals in low or falling net operating incomes.

The *break-even cash flow ratio* is similar to the operating expense ratio except that the debt service is added to expenses as a percentage of gross income. This measure indicates the extent to which the investment is able to provide enough cash flow to pay all the required expenses and financial obligations. If the break-even cash flow ratio approaches 80 to 85 percent, this indicates that the required obligations relative to gross income are reasonably high. Since financial expenses (principal and interest payments) tend to be fixed when a level-payment amortization is used, changes in the break-even cash flow ratio reflect changes in operating expenses, in gross income, or in both of these. In any event, this ratio may help identify periods of tight cash flow and years when the operation of the real estate may require further attention.

The *debt coverage ratio* is net operating income divided by the debt service. A measure of financial risk, it determines the ability of the investment to cover the fixed mortgage payment. Typical ratios for large income-producing properties range from 1.2 to 1.5. The importance of this ratio in terms of operating expenses is that if operating expenses are forecast to increase in the near future, this may result in a lower net operating income (dependent on any expected changes in rental income). If the net operating income falls sharply, the debt coverage ratio may fall dangerously close to 1.00 (or perhaps even less, which would mean serious cash flow problems for the investor. This might occur if operating expenses rose rapidly relative to rental income or if rents fell suddenly due to increasing market risk.

For example, if effective gross income was expected to be $40,000 for the upcoming year, and total operating expenses were estimated to be $20,000, net operating income would be expected to be $20,000. If the debt service for the year is $14,500, the debt coverage ratio is 1.38:

$$\text{Debt coverage ratio} = \frac{\text{Net operating income}}{\text{Debt service}} \qquad (8\text{–}11)$$

$$= \frac{\$20,000}{\$14,500}$$

$$= 1.38$$

Suppose operating expenses were expected to increase by 25 percent (to $25,000) for next year without any increase in income. The new debt coverage ratio would be:

$$\frac{\$15,000}{\$14,500} = 1.03$$

A debt coverage ratio of 1.03 indicates the lack of safety available to the investor to meet the debt service requirements from net operating income.

1. Net Operating Income and Value

$$\text{Investment value} = \frac{\text{Net operating income}}{\text{Capitalization rate}}$$

2. Operating Expenses, Operating Expense Ratio, and Value

Increase in investment value	if $\dfrac{\Delta \text{ Effective gross income}}{\Delta \text{ Operating expenses}} > \text{OER}$
No change in investment value	if $\dfrac{\Delta \text{ Effective gross income}}{\Delta \text{ Operating expenses}} = \text{OER}$
Decrease in investment value	if $\dfrac{\Delta \text{ Effective gross income}}{\Delta \text{ Operating expenses}} < \text{OER}$

3. Gross and Net Income Multipliers

$$\text{Gross income multiplier} = \frac{\text{Market value}}{\text{Effective gross income}}$$

$$\text{Net income multiplier} = \frac{\text{Market value}}{\text{Net operating income}}$$

4. Financial Ratios

$$\text{Operating expense ratio} = \frac{\text{Operating expenses}}{\text{Effective gross income}}$$

$$\text{Break-even cash flow ratio} = \frac{\text{Operating expenses} + \text{Debt service}}{\text{Effective gross income}}$$

$$\text{Debt coverage ratio} = \frac{\text{Net operating income}}{\text{Debt service}}$$

Therefore, analysis of the debt coverage ratio can help identify a changing operating expense position. Table 8–7 summarizes the basic measures and relationships of operating expense analysis.

FINANCIAL ANALYSIS OF OPERATING EXPENSES

One of the more vital areas in the analysis of operating expenses is the relationship between fixed expenses, variable expenses, and income. If there are no fixed expenses associated with the property and rents are greater than variable expenses, net operating income will always be positive. However, it is unrealistic to assume that real estate investments will have no fixed expenses. Most have sizable mortgage payments as well. Therefore it is wise to determine how much rental income is needed to "break even" in order to cover variable and fixed expenses. *Break-even analysis* provides this information.[3]

[3] For recent applications, see Lawrence F. Sherman, Jae K. Shim, and Mark Hartney, "Short Run Break-Even Analysis for Real Estate Projects," *Real Estate Issues,* 18 (Spring/Summer 1993), pp. 15–20.

BREAK-EVEN ANALYSIS

Since most income-producing properties have fixed expenses, the investor wants to be able to identify the amount of income needed (and, therefore, the number of apartments that must be occupied) in order to break even. The break-even point is the amount of income where revenues would just cover all costs (variable, fixed, and financial expenses). To use this type of analysis, one must make some assumptions about the revenues and expenses of the property.

First, assume that all the rental units are rented at the same rates. Second, estimate the ratio of variable expenses per rental unit and assume that this ratio will be constant for each additional rental unit occupied. Finally, assume that the fixed expenses remain constant throughout the analysis.

❐ **BREAK-EVEN FOR NUMBER OF UNITS.** To find the minimum number of rental units that must be occupied in order to break even, we can perform the following analysis.

The following definitions are used:

$$GI = gr \times Q$$

$$TC = OE + DS$$

$$OE = VE + FE$$

$$VE = ve \times Q$$

where:

GI = Gross income

TC = Total costs

OE = Operating expenses

VE = Total variable expenses

FE = Fixed expenses

DS = Debt service

Q = Number of rental units occupied

gr = Gross rent per unit

ve = Variable expenses per unit

By substitution, total costs may be written as:

$$TC = VE + FE + DS \tag{8–12}$$

The break-even point for occupied units, BEP(Q), is where gross income equals total costs:

$$\text{Gross income} = \text{Total costs}$$

$$(\text{gr} \times Q) = (Q \times \text{ve}) + \text{FE} + \text{DS} \tag{8–13}$$

By algebra:

$$Q = \frac{\text{FE} + \text{DS}}{\text{gr} - \text{ve}} \tag{8–14}$$

For example, assume an investor is considering investing in ABC Properties, a 50-unit, two-bedroom apartment building. Each apartment can be rented at $250 per month. Variable expenses are estimated to be $100 per month per unit, fixed expenses are estimated to be $1,250 per month, and the monthly debt service is $4,000. How many apartments must be rented in order to break even?

$$\text{BEP(Q)} = \frac{\text{FE} + \text{DS}}{\text{gr} - \text{ve}}$$

$$= \frac{\$1,250 + \$4,000}{\$250 - \$100}$$

$$= 35 \text{ units}$$

Therefore, the owners of ABC Properties must rent 35 of the 50 available units (a 70 percent occupancy rate) to break even (that is, achieve a zero cash flow). These results are demonstrated in Table 8–8.

❑ **BREAK-EVEN FOR RENTAL INCOME.** It is also possible to calculate break-even points for rental income. This can be useful in cases where there is more than one type of rental unit in a particular investment.

TABLE 8–8
ABC PROPERTIES ANALYSIS OF BREAK-EVEN CASH FLOW

Gross income ($250 × 35)		$8,750
Less expenses		
Variable expenses ($100 × 35)	$3,500	
Fixed expenses	1,250	
Operating expenses		$4,750
Net operating income		$4,000
Less debt service		$4,000
If zero, break-even cash flow is correct		$ 0

If the break-even point in total income, BEP($), is to be consistent with BEP(Q), then gross income must equal total costs:

$$(Q \times gr) = FE + (Q \times ve) + DS$$

Since $Q = GI/gr$, then by algebra:

$$\frac{GI}{gr}(gr - ve) = FE + DS$$

$$GI = \frac{(FE + DS)}{gr - ve} \times gr \tag{8-15}$$

Using the same numbers from the ABC Properties example, we get results consistent with those in Table 8–8:

$$BEP\,(GI) = \frac{(\$1{,}250 + \$4{,}000)}{(\$250 - \$100)} \times 250$$

$$= \$8{,}750$$

In other words, $8,750 is needed in rental income per month to break even for this property.

❏ **BREAK-EVEN FOR RENTAL INCOME PER UNIT.** In addition, it may be useful to derive the break-even point in dollars per unit. The algebra is as follows:

$$Q \times gr = FE + Q \times ve + DS$$

$$gr = \frac{FE + Q \times ve + DS}{Q} \tag{8-16}$$

In this case, the results are consistent because the break-even point in dollars per unit is $250:

$$BEP\,(gr) = \frac{\$1{,}250 + 35(\$100) + \$4{,}000}{35}$$

$$= \frac{\$8{,}750}{35}$$

$$= \$250$$

Although all the results deal with hypothetical *monthly* income statements, the break-even analysis will work for other periods (that is, annually) as well. However, the ability to perform useful break-even analysis for annual periods is based on access to annual data. If such data are available and forecasts can be made for the upcoming year, the break-even analysis will work.

Of course, the usefulness of the different break-even methods discussed here vary among analysts, situations, and types of property. The break-even analysis for number of units is best suited for residential income-producing real estate in which all the units are identical in rental price. The methods that measure break-even in dollars and dollars per unit enable the investor to select any gross income and variable expense combination and get a break-even point in dollar terms. Since fixed expenses and debt service are constant, the denominator is always constant for break-even analysis for rental income (in this example, .60) with correct combinations of gross income and variable expenses. Finally, the last method solved for a break-even amount per unit when the number of units was known.

OPERATING LEVERAGE

Operating leverage[4] is the concept that a relatively small increase in gross income can result in a large increase in net operating income. Using the example of ABC Properties again, we have seen that if 35 units are rented at $250 per month, the cash flow will be equal to zero. Similarly, Table 8–9 demonstrates changes in net operating income as a result of changes in occupancy rates.

If, for example, the investor were to increase occupancy from 40 to 45 units (or increase gross income from $10,000 to $11,250), a 12.5 percent increase, the resulting net operating income would increase from $4,750 to

TABLE 8–9
ABC PROPERTIES ANALYSIS OF OPERATING LEVERAGE

Number of units occupied	30	35	40	45	50
Gross income	$7,500	$8,750	$10,000	$11,250	$12,500
Less expenses:					
Variable expenses	$3,000	$3,500	$ 4,000	$ 4,500	$ 5,000
Fixed expenses	1,250	1,250	1,250	1,250	1,250
Operating expenses	$4,250	$4,750	$ 5,250	$ 5,750	$ 6,250
Net operating income	$3,250	$4,000	$ 4,750	$ 5,500	$ 6,250

Assumptions: Rent per unit = $250
Variable expenses per unit = $100
Fixed expenses = $1,250
Income taxes and bad debts = $0

[4]This term, although somewhat related in concept, should not be confused with the term *financial leverage,* which we discuss in Chapter 9.

$5,500, or 15.79 percent. Therefore a small percentage change in occupancy (or gross income) *levers* net operating income into a larger amount. All of this is due to the manner in which the investor uses fixed expenses. As long as the rent per unit is larger than the variable cost per unit, favorable operating leverage will magnify the changes in occupancy into larger changes in income.

Specification of the percentage change in net operating income resulting from a percentage change in occupancy or gross income is called the *degree of operating leverage* (DOL) and can be calculated at any occupancy level. If the change in net operating income is equal to $\Delta Q(gr - ve)$, since FE is constant, the net operating income at any Q occupancy level is $Q(gr - ve) - FE$, so the percentage change in net operating income is:

$$\text{Percentage change in NOI} = \frac{\Delta Q(gr - ve)}{Q(gr - ve) - FE} \qquad (8\text{--}17)$$

If the percentage change in occupancy is $\Delta Q/Q$, the percentage change in net operating income to occupancy is defined as follows:

$$\text{DOL (at occupancy level, Q)} = \frac{\dfrac{\Delta Q(gr - ve)}{Q(gr - ve) - FE}}{\dfrac{\Delta Q}{Q}}$$

$$= \frac{\Delta Q(gr - ve)}{Q(gr - ve) - FE} \times \frac{Q}{\Delta Q} \qquad (8\text{--}18)$$

$$= \frac{Q(gr - ve)}{Q(gr - ve) - FE}$$

For example, the degree of operating leverage at forty units is 1.26:

$$\text{DOL at Q} = 40 = \frac{40(250 - 100)}{40(250 - 100) - 1250}$$

$$= 1.26$$

Therefore, for each 1 percent increase in occupancy after 40 units, net operating income will increase by 1.26 percent.

SUMMARY

The analysis of operating expenses and their impact on investment decisions is one of the critical elements in successful real estate investment analysis. Surprisingly, this aspect is overlooked by many novice investors, except for periods of declining cash flows. This chapter has provided several types of analysis which investors may employ using readily available data. As markets become increasingly competitive, the management of operating expenses may prove to be the difference between success and failure in many real estate markets.

QUESTIONS

8–1. Why should investors analyze gross income and operating expenses?

8–2. "The Internal Revenue Service does not permit investors to subtract the reserve for replacement from effective gross income when calculating taxable income. Therefore, a wise investor will omit the reserve from the analysis of cash flow." True or False? Explain.

8–3. What are the typical operating expense items in investment real estate? Over which items do investors usually have control?

8–4. How can property managers be valuable to real estate investors?

8–5. What is the relationship between *operating expenses*, the *operating expense ratio*, and *value*?

8–6. A comparison between gross and net income multipliers reveals potential conflicts in ranking preferences. What implications does this result have for real estate investments analysis?

8–7. What is break-even analysis, and how can it be useful for real estate investors?

PROBLEMS

8–1. Using the facts in Table 8–3, set up the replacement reserve account assuming that the investor will invest the annual reserve in an account earning 7 percent interest per year.

8–2. Calculate the operating expense ratio, gross income multiplier, and overall capitalization rate using the following:

Investment value	$1,500,000
Potential gross income	$ 250,000
Vacancy and bad debt losses	5 percent
Operating expenses	$ 110,000

8–3. Using the facts in Problem 8–2 and the following:

Debt service	$105,000

calculate the
  a. Break-even cash flow ratio
  b. Debt coverage ratio
  c. Net income multiplier.

8–4. If effective gross income is $10,000 and is expected to increase at the rate of 6 percent per year, and if the operating expense ratio is .60, how high does the expected growth rate in total operating expenses have to be in order for the value of the property to decline? Increase? Stay the same?

8–5. If the rent per unit is $500 per month and variable expenses per unit are $150 per month, what is the break-even number of units if the sum of fixed expenses and debt service is $5,250 per month? What is the break-even point in dollars? Prove your results.

8–6. For the investment in Problem 8–5, what is the degree of operating leverage at 10 units? Twenty units? (Note: Assume that the fixed expenses per month are $2,000.) What does the degree of operating leverage tell the analyst?

8–7. You have been hired to develop a pro-forma operating statement for the next five years on a 40,000-square-foot office building. You are given the following information:

a. 92% of the building is leasable
b. Management fees will be 6 percent of EGI
c. Utilities are $1.50 per square foot of building area, and growing at 3.5 percent per year
d. Janitorial, maintenance, and repair expense are 14 percent of PGI
e. Property taxes are 10 percent of PGI
f. Insurance expense is $5,000 per year
g. Reserve requirement is $6,500 per year
h. Although building is currently 100 percent occupied, you anticipate 5 percent vacancy over the five-year period
i. There are currently four tenants with the following leases:

Tenant	SF	$/SF	CPI Increase
ABC Consultants	6,800 SF	$13.20	2.5% per year
Credit, Inc.	12,000 SF	$12.30	N/A
Camby Insurance	9,000 SF	$12.70	3% per year
EK Productions	9,000 SF	$12.70	2% per year

SELECTED REFERENCES

Downs, James C., Jr., *Principles of Real Estate Management*, 13th ed. Chicago: Institute of Real Estate Management, 1991.

Institute of Real Estate Management, *Income/Expense Analysis: Apartments*. Chicago: Institute of Real Estate Management, 1993.

_____, *Income/Expense Analysis: Office Buildings, Downtown and Suburban*. Chicago: Institute of Real Estate Management, 1993.

Jaffe, Austin J., and C. F. Sirmans, "The Relationship between Growth Factors, Operating Expense Ratio, and Valuation," *Real Estate Appraiser*, 44 (July–August 1978), 30–34.

Kelley, Edward N., *Practical Apartment Management*. Chicago: Institute of Real Estate Management, 1976.

Sherman, Lawrence F., Joe K. Shim and Mark Hartney, "Short Run Break-Even Analysis for Real Estate Projects," *Real Estate Issues*, 18 (Spring/Summer 1993), 15–20.

CHAPTER 9

FINANCING DECISIONS

PRINCIPLES

1. The decision to substitute debt for equity is a fundamental decision for real estate investors.
2. The standard mortgage instrument contains a set of provisions which must be understood.
3. Loan provisions can dramatically affect the effective cost of borrowing on a mortgage.
4. The analysis of financial leverage is basic to the real estate investment decision.
5. Financial leverage increases the riskiness, not the value, of the investment.
6. There are several alternative financing methods.

Real estate financing has become increasingly complex in recent years as the number and types of instruments have proliferated. This chapter deals with several of the financing decisions facing investors. The chapter begins by analyzing the reasons why real estate investors borrow. It is often said that the typical real estate investor has an advantage over other types of investors in that an amount of funds is borrowed with only a relatively small amount of cash. In such a case, the investor finances a large portion of the investment by borrowing, pays the cost of obtaining outside debt sources out of the income stream from the investment, and therefore acquires ownership of the property with only a small percentage of equity.

The second part of this chapter explains the simple mechanics of mortgage calculations and then discusses such aspects as the analysis of various mortgage terms and the impact of the financing decision on the net present value of the investment. The financing decision can be evaluated in numerous ways, since a number of financing methods are popular in real estate. Some of the more popular methods are described, along with examples to show how the investor can explicitly evaluate various financing choices.

WHY BORROW?

An individual who wishes to invest in real estate (or other assets) and has enough cash to pay for the investment outright has two choices: pay cash for the entire property or borrow a portion and pay cash for the remaining amount. What should this potential investor do?

Analysis shows that even if individuals have enough cash for this particular investment (but not enough to satisfy all needs), the value of the funds an individual has may be viewed as more valuable than the cost of borrowing. In other words, the investor can acquire more assets by using debt because the same equity can be "stretched" into more investments, more assets, or more consumption. So individuals (and firms) borrow because they believe they will be better off as a result.

In order to consume goods and services *now* rather than wait, investors must pay a price: the *interest* is the price paid for the use of the money over the period. It is clear, then, that investors would only borrow if it is perceived to be in their best interests. However, if these situations exist, we would expect to see them borrowing as much as possible all of the time. The problem is that the gains from leverage are associated with increasing amounts of *financial risk*—the probability of defaulting on financial obligations. Obviously, the more debt that is acquired, the higher the required interest payments and the greater the probability of not having enough income to cover obligations. Thus financial leverage is not free or riskless, although no investor borrows without expecting *favorable financial leverage.*

In general, financial leverage is the major reason for borrowing. When the expected rate of return from the investment is greater than the cost of borrowing, favorable financial leverage exists for those who have borrowed to finance the project. If, however, the returns fall short of expectations and yield less than the cost of debt used to finance the investment, *unfavorable financial leverage* exists. Not even the most optimistic real estate investor is happy about unfavorable leverage.[1]

EVALUATING FINANCING ALTERNATIVES

If the key financing decision involves the measurement of financial leverage and its impact on the wealth of the investor, it is necessary to compare various financing alternatives in order to decide which would be preferable.

[1]The financial leverage decision rules are provided later in this chapter.

Current Issue 9–1

Should an Investor Borrow as Much as Possible?

Many real estate investment books tell readers that the biggest advantage to investing in real estate is the use of "OPM" (other people's money). These books provide stories and methods for increasing the return on equity with the use of *financial leverage.* The basic idea is that an investor can "lever" upward the return on the investment by borrowing funds at rates lower than the rate earned on the investment itself. If so, the return on the investor's equity will be higher than if no debt financing were used.

It is quite correct that the use of leverage can increase the rate of return to the equity investor. In fact, if a large percentage of total financing is debt (as opposed to equity) financing *and* the leverage is *favorable* (that is, the return on the investment exceeds the cost of debt financing as measured by the effective interest rate on the loans), the return to the equity investor may be astronomical. In this manner, the rate of return from investing in real estate could be as high as 400 or 500 or 700 percent or more!

Does this mean that wise investors should borrow as much as possible when making real estate investment decisions? No, at least not without considering a few additional items. For example, it is important to recognize that the potential gains from financial leverage are not free; the price is additional risk. The risk occurs due to the increased likelihood of default on the debt service payments as a result of unexpected reductions in net operating income. This risk can be expected to result in higher interest costs charged by lenders to investors. If so, there will be a price charged for the ability to lever the investment.

It is also true that the financing choice has an impact on the amount of income taxes the investor will pay. If a large amount of debt is used to finance the investment, the investor will have considerable interest expense. Under the current tax law, interest paid by the investor is a tax-deductible item and may be used to reduce the amount of tax liability owed by the investor. (Note also that homeowners can reduce their taxes in the same manner, so long as the "itemization threshold" is satisfied. This threshold is currently $3,000 for single taxpayers and $5,000 for married taxpayers who file jointly.)

However, simply borrowing money for debt financing (or any other reason) because the interest is tax deductible will not ensure financial success. Like any other market-traded asset, money has its cost. It is likely that the cost of borrowing reflects the deductibility of interest such that the before-tax interest rate would fall substantially if interest deductibility were not allowed by a subsequent change in the tax code. As such, especially for low-income taxpayers, borrowing for tax deductibility reasons is not likely to pay off.

Finally, by the very nature of their existence, owners of corporations (shareholders) receive tax shields from borrowing. First, the interest payments made by the corporation are subtracted from their income when figuring out their taxable income. Second, owners who borrow to finance the purchase of the shares in the corporation receive another round of tax deductions. Dividends that are paid to owners are taxable (after the initial exclusion) and can be reduced through borrowing to finance the purchase of the shares. In this manner, tax shields are valuable to owners, since they will be able to outbid others by borrowing to finance the shares in the firm. Real estate investors can do the same as long as the corporate ownership form is elected.

For instance, you could compare the monthly debt services of each loan plan. (This is similar to using the mortgage constant as a cost of borrowing, since the mortgage constant is the proportion of debt service to the original loan.) *The problem with this method is that it is possible to mistakenly choose the more expensive alternative.*

For example, suppose a loan from Bank A is available for $1,000,000 at a rate of 10.5 percent for 20 years. If the loan is to be repaid in equal monthly payments using a regular amortization schedule, the monthly payment will be $9,984. However, you could borrow the same amount, $1,000,000, from Bank B at a rate of 11.5 percent for 30 years. The monthly payment would be $9,903. By comparing the monthly debt service of the loans, we conclude that the loan from Bank B has a lower debt service. Accordingly, Bank B's loan also has a lower mortgage constant (.00990) compared with Bank A's (.00998). The problem is that despite widespread use by real estate investors, the proper analyses shows that the loan from Bank B is *not* cheaper than that from Bank A. Simply look at the present value cost of each loan.

Another way to see that the loan with the lower debt service is not automatically cheaper is to compare the investor's position at the end of the shorter of the two loans. If the loan from Bank A was accepted, it would be repaid at the end of 20 years. However, if the investor borrowed at Bank B, 10 more years of debt service would remain. This situation causes problems for those evaluating alternative financing "packages" by debt service (or mortgage constant).

A better method is one that measures the true cost of the loan or the *effective cost of borrowing.* This net cost distinguishes loans on the basis of the annual interest cost on a time-adjusted basis of borrowing and repaying interest.

A final method evaluates the impact that various loan arrangements can have on the investment value and/or rate of return of the investment. Sometimes this can be done by using the effective cost of borrowing.[2]

2A spreadsheet template that calculates the effective cost of borrowing is available from JS & Associates; see Appendix B for details.

Mechanics of the Financing Decision

The most commonly used financial debt instrument associated with the investment in income-producing real estate is the *mortgage*. Its use has a long tradition in English common law. In addition, the reliance on the level-payment, fixed-rate, fully amortized loan by many investors has made this method of amortization standard throughout the industry.[3] However, modern real estate finance has expanded the choices available to real estate investors and, in many ways, the methods of obtaining financing for investing in real estate in the future may be significantly different than in the past.

The Mechanics of the Mortgage

After deciding to borrow, an investor must become familiar with the mortgage, since it is the most commonly used financial debt instrument. We might point out that the word *mortgage* can be used as a noun or a verb. The *instrument* of a *mortgage* is the document that provides security to the lender who seeks repayment of a note. In many states, the typical instrument is a trust deed rather than a mortgage, but the results are almost identical. However, an investor may also mortgage a piece of property. In this sense, the investor pledges the property as security in order to receive cash for some purpose. Both uses are permissible and the reader should not be confused.

History of the Mortgage Instrument

The formal use of mortgages began during the fourteenth century in England, although its roots can be traced to the first century B.C. The mortgagee (lender) had most of the property rights. If the mortgagee wished to evict the mortgagor (borrower), it could generally be done. However, the development of common law resulted in more rights for the mortgagor. The mortgage instrument consisted of a description of the property held as security in order to satisfy the note owed. It also specified the one day each year upon which the mortgagor could pay the debt. This was known as *Debt Day*, and the law permitted the satisfaction of the note and the canceling of the mortgage according to the *defeasance clause*.

If the mortgagor failed to pay the debt, any interest in the land was forfeited. This led to the development of the *equitable right of redemption* in the beginning of the seventeenth century. This permitted mortgagors to

[3]It was used exclusively in residential finance from the mid–1930s until the end of the 1970s.

regain their interests during a grace period after the default. The mortgagors could pay interest and costs to the mortgagee and redeem the property. If the grace period expired, then the mortgagee *foreclosed* and took the property.

This common law led to modern foreclosure practices. Foreclosure today limits the period of redemption of the mortgagor by the mortgagee's action. In modern law, there are two doctrines that may be followed: *strict foreclosure* and *statutory foreclosure.* Strict foreclosure is observed by only a few states and closely resembles common law treatment of mortgagors. Statutory foreclosure permits a taking by the mortgagee only to the extent of the debt, and court proceedings are usually required before an exchange of title can take place.

ANALYSIS OF MORTGAGE TERMS

The common terms in a mortgage loan are the *interest rate* on the mortgage, the amount borrowed relative to the total value (or the *loan-to-value ratio*), the period over which the borrower repays the loan (or the *maturity* or *amortization* period of the loan), and the method (or *amortization* or the *repayment*) of the loan. The relationship between these factors determines the amount of *debt service* required each period in order to repay the loan.

Two other concepts are also associated with the mortgage. The *mortgage constant* is a measure of the combined effect of the interest rate and expected maturity of the loan. The *debt coverage ratio* is a measure of the riskiness of the investment from the lender's point of view based on the investment's ability to cover the debt service by its income stream.

❐ **INTEREST RATE.** The *interest rate* is the most commonly recognized mortgage-lending term. During the past few decades, the use of fixed-rate mortgages (FRMs) emphasized the extent to which the interest rate was relied on as the important measure and the basis of the cost of borrowing for the mortgagor and as the basic yield for the mortgagee.

However, with unexpected price changes for real property and unexpected inflation throughout the economy during the 1970s, fixed-rate mortgages posed serious problems for mortgage lenders. Since allowances for inflation might be taken into account by lenders prior to lending funds for mortgages, it has become increasingly difficult for lenders to forecast inflation and "price" the standard fixed-rate mortgage.

This, in turn, has led to the growth of many financing alternatives in recent years. For example, the variable-rate mortgages, currently referred to as adjustable-rate mortgages or ARMs, allow lenders to alter the mortgage interest rate as market conditions adjust to changes in supply and demand. The adjustable-rate mortgages and other new financing options, some of which are discussed later, suggest dramatic changes in the financing of real estate investments in the future.

As a final word on the interest rate, it is clear that a change in the interest rate directly affects debt service. A review of the mathematics of finance in Chapter 3 shows that as interest rates increase, so does debt service, assuming the amortization period and the amount borrowed are held constant. Therefore, changes in interest rates translate into changes in the mortgage constant, the debt coverage ratio, and before-tax cash flow.

❒ **LOAN-TO-VALUE RATIO.**   The amount borrowed as a proportion of total property value is called the *loan-to-value ratio*. For example, if a loan of $400,000 is obtained, against which a property valued at $500,000 is held as security, the loan-to-value ratio is .80.

The loan-to-value ratio is subject to state and federal regulations that may vary for different types of lenders and for different types of properties. Frequently, the investor wishes to maximize the loan-to-value ratio because this will maximize the amount of debt used and, therefore, the amount of financial leverage. Although increased financial leverage increases the financial risk of the investment, many investors seek higher amounts of leverage.

The lender, on the other hand, seeks lower loan-to-value ratios because the lower the ratio, the lower the lender's risk. Since the loan-to-value ratio and the *equity-to-value* ratio must equal 100 percent, a lower loan-to-value ratio implies a higher equity-to-value ratio. In other words, the higher the equity-to-value ratio, the greater the equity down payment of the investor. (Another risk measure, the debt coverage ratio, is also used by the lender to assess the risk of various investments. It is discussed later in this chapter and in Chapter 11.)

For a given investment, the higher the loan-to-value ratio, the greater the debt service, assuming a fixed interest rate and amortization period. For instance, consider two loan-to-value ratios of 70 percent and 80 percent on a $500,000 investment. Both loans carry a 12 percent interest rate and both are fully amortized over 30 years. The debt annual service of the 70 percent loan-to-value ratio loan is $43,202. The debt service of the loan at 80 percent loan-to-value is $49,373, or $6,171 per year higher. The difference is due to the required repayment of $50,000 in additional principal and more interest in the latter case.

❒ **AMORTIZATION PERIOD.**   Also called the maturity of the loan, the *amortization period* is the length of time over which the loan is to be repaid. For example, a 20-year loan is one that must be repaid at the end of 20 years. Like loan-to-value ratios and interest rate levels, amortization periods are frequently limited by state and federal regulations. Lender policies also dictate appropriate amortization periods.

Although many traditional investors regard fully amortized loans as the only debt source available, there are three general categories of amortized loans. The first consists of loans for which interest only is paid and no amortization of the principal takes place. The entire principal is due at maturity of the loan. This type of loan is called an *interest-only loan*. In using this loan, the borrower is not required to provide additional amounts of equity capital. Therefore, assuming all else constant, the interest-only debt service is less than the debt service under the amortized loans.

The second category includes loans of various repayment schemes, but all require a larger than typical payment at maturity. A loan of this type is called a *partially–amortized loan*, since the final payment includes a large repayment of principal.[4] This final payment is less than the amount borrowed and represents the percentage value of the remaining payments. The final payment is called the *balloon payment*.

The final category is the *fully–amortized loan*, which is the major repayment plan for much real estate. The most familiar example is the *level-payment amortized loan* in which debt-service payments are constant throughout the life of the loan, although the breakdown between principal and interest changes each period. For income-producing real estate, the reliance on the level-payment, fully amortized loan is lessening due to a wider choice of instruments.

With respect to the amortization period, if all the other mortgage terms are held constant, the greater the maturity of the loan, the lower the debt service. Suppose a loan of $100,000 was made at an interest rate of 15 percent, with monthly payments for 20 years. The annual debt service is $15,801. If the amortization term is extended to 25 years, the debt service would fall to $15,370. By extending the term of the loan, the debt service is reduced by $431 ($15,801 minus $15,370). The amortization period is measured in years or months, depending on how often payments are made.

☐ **MORTGAGE CONSTANT.**   The payment on a mortgage is generally referred to as the *debt service*. One way to compute the debt service is to multiply the *mortgage constant* by the amount borrowed. The mortgage constant is the factor that relates the interest rate and the amortization period. Mortgage constants are provided in the tables in Appendix A or can easily be calculated with the following equation:

$$MC = \frac{\dfrac{i}{m}}{1 - \dfrac{1}{\left(1 + \dfrac{i}{m}\right)^{n \times m}}} \tag{9–1}$$

where

[4]Partially amortized loans are simply hybrids between interest-only and fully amortized loans.

MC = mortgage constant

i = rate of interest per year

n = number of years

m = frequency of compounding per year

Although the mortgage constant is useful in calculating debt service and for developing amortization schedules, the reader is cautioned about its application. Use of the mortgage constant as a cost of borrowing and as a measure of financial leverage can lead to serious errors in analysis.

☐ **AMORTIZATION SCHEDULE.**   In analyzing real estate, it is necessary to allocate the periodic debt service between interest and principal repayments. The investor can use the mortgage constant to develop the *amortization schedule*. This schedule is often used in the calculation of after-tax cash flow because only the interest portion of the debt service is deductible for tax purposes. Principal repayments offset cash flow but have no effect on taxable income. Thus it is necessary to allocate the debt service between principal and interest.

To develop an amortization schedule, consider the following example. Suppose a loan is made for $100,000 at a 10 percent interest rate, requiring annual payments for a period of 20 years. Using Equation (9–1), the mortgage constant is .11746 and the debt service is $11,746 per year. Table 9–1 illustrates the distribution of debt service between interest and principal.

TABLE 9–1
AMORTIZATION SCHEDULE FOR A $100,000 LOAN AT 10 PERCENT INTEREST FOR 20 YEARS WITH ANNUAL PAYMENTS

Year	Mortgage Balance of Year)	Debt Service	Interest Payment	Principal Payment	Mortgage Balance (End of Year)
1	$100,000.00	$11,746.00	$10,000.00	$ 1,746.00	$98,254.00
2	98,254.00	11,746.00	9,825.40	1,920.60	96,333.40
3	96,333.40	11,746.00	9,633.34	2,112.66	94,220.74
4	94,220.74	11,746.00	9,422.07	2,323.93	91,896.81
5	91,896.81	11,746.00	9,189.68	2,556.32	89,340.49
•	•	•	•	•	•
•	•	•	•	•	•
•	•	•	•	•	•
16	44,525.22	11,746.00	4,452.52	7,293.48	37,231.74
17	37,231.74	11,746.00	3,723.17	8,022.83	29,208.91
18	29,208.91	11,746.00	2,920.89	8,825.11	20,383.80
19	20,383.80	11,746.00	2,038.38	9,707.62	10,676.18
20	10,676.18	11,743.80	1,067.62	10,676.18	0.00

What Is the APR?

The annual percentage rate, or APR, is the official name for the stated interest rate required by federal law on most financial contracts. It became required on contracts during the 1960s as a result of a series of consumer protection laws aimed at providing a better flow of consumer finance information to borrowers. The idea is that when a borrower sees the APR rate on the contract, he or she will be aware of the "true" cost of borrowing.

The APR has also moved toward standardizing the way in which interest is charged on contracts. While there are still various methods of charging interest, the APR rate must be calculated in a prescribed manner (actually, according to prescribed tables) and requires that such items as payment frequency, compound interest, rate per annum, and certain accompanying charges be evaluated. In this way, the APR seeks to provide a common measure of comparison for consumers who may wish to comparison-shop between more than one financing source.

Note, however, that despite the application and enforcement of the APR legislation, a comparison of APRs on mortgages, for example, will not be sufficient to ensure comparisons of equal costs of borrowing. This is because some items are *not* reflected in the APR rate!

This is due to the fact that in some cases, some charges are not required to be included in the APR calculation, and in other cases, it may not be possible to include them because the amounts are not known when the loan is originated. For example, many of the typical closing costs of a mortgage are required to be included when the lender calculates the APR. However, some are not. These include some expenses associated with credit verification, appraisal fees, and others. In addition, special expenses are rarely included.

Perhaps even more important are the expenses that are expected to occur but are not included in the APR rate because it is difficult or impossible to know their precise amount when the loan is originated. For example, prepayment penalties may be known to exist but are not included because the timing of the charge is unknown. Or, as discussed in the text, the impact of early repayment of the loan with closing costs has an impact on the true cost of borrowing, and yet, since the timing of the early repayment is unknown when the loan is made, there is not any treatment of this issue in the APR. This is because the amount and the timing of the charge have impacts on the borrower's cost of funds.

The amortization schedule is calculated as follows. The beginning outstanding balance of $100,000 is multiplied by the interest rate of 10 percent to get the first year's interest payment, $10,000. Since the total payment is $11,746, the difference of $1,746 represents the repayment of principal. Therefore the outstanding balance at the end of the first year (and the beginning of the second year) is $98,254.00. At the 10 percent interest rate, the second year's interest charge is $9,825.40, leaving a principal reduction of $1,920.60. The mortgage balance at the end of the second year is $96,333.40. This process is repeated until the outstanding balance is zero (that is, at loan maturity).

❑ **DEBT COVERAGE RATIO.**   The *debt coverage ratio*, or the ratio of net operating income to debt service, is a measure of the risk of an investment. This ratio is used to evaluate the ability of the income stream to cover the debt service (that is, provide a positive before-tax cash flow to the investor). Traditionally, lenders required debt coverage ratios of 1.15 to 1.50. Now, with debt coverage ratios falling very close to 1.0, current values of this ratio are a lot lower than historical standards and have come under careful scrutiny.[5]

For example, if interest rates rise due to expected inflation, debt service will also rise, assuming everything else is held constant. If net operating income fails to rise or does not rise sufficiently to offset the increased cost of finance, the debt coverage ratio will fall. If this happens, the investor will have difficulty finding financing during periods of tight money.

ANALYSIS OF LOAN PROVISIONS ON COST OF BORROWING

Modern mortgages contain many specific clauses that greatly affect the cost of borrowing. Some clauses require that the mortgagor pay additional fees, penalties, or charges. Others require that payment be made at specific times. The investor must be able to evaluate the effects of special loan provisions on the cost of borrowing. The key question is: *How do mortgage clauses affect the rate of return or value of the investment?*

EARLY REPAYMENT

Although many mortgages extend to 25 or 30 years, few income-producing investments are held for that long a period. In many instances, the investor would like to prepay the loan and satisfy the lien against the property in order to convey a clear title when selling the property after a shorter period of time. In other instances, an investor may wish to accelerate payments (on a promissory note, for example) before the due date. The question is: *What effect does early repayment have on the cost of borrowing?* Note that we discussed the tax consequences in Chapter 7.

[5]For research on the use and importance of debt coverage ratios, see Kenneth M. Lusht and Robert H. Zerbst, "Valuing Income Property in an Inflationary Environment," *Real Estate Appraiser and Analyst*, 46 (July–August 1980), 11–17.

Let us assume that the decision about whether to borrow has been made and that the investor wishes to repay the loan before it is due for reasons other than altering the financing mix of debt and equity. If the loan is a level-payment, fully amortized mortgage, early repayment has no effect on the cost of borrowing and no effect on investor wealth.

This is true because the outstanding balance consists of a set of debt-service payments calculated by using the interest rate and amortization period. In accelerating the payments, the investor takes the present value of the stream of remaining payments from the "acceleration date" until the end of the amortization period. The present value represents the outstanding balance at the acceleration date. Since the amount to be repaid consists of the present value of the outstanding balance, the investor bears no additional costs.

Therefore, for a mortgage without closing costs, prepayment penalties, or other provisions, the possibility of early repayment does *not result* in any financial cost to the mortgagor. Since the payment due at the acceleration date is the present value of future debt service payments, discounted by the interest rate that amortized the loan, the proceeds to be paid have been reduced by the savings of future interest charges. However, this does not occur if closing costs were paid when the loan was originated.

CLOSING COSTS

Closing costs are charges assessed by the mortgagee against the mortgagor when the loan is made. Typical closing costs include loan origination fees, appraisal fees, recording fees, title insurance, pest inspections, credit reference expenses, and other similar charges. Other expenses, such as discount points, are sometimes included and we will treat these separately.

Closing costs are divided into two general categories: (1) costs incurred in placing the mortgage and (2) costs incurred in acquiring the property. The first category must be amortized on a straight-line basis over the life of the mortgage for tax purposes. The second type can be capitalized and increases the depreciable basis of the property. Neither type may be deducted for tax purposes in the year paid.

If the costs are incurred and the funds paid, the timing of the payment (i.e., at the time of either the creation of the mortgage or the acquisition of the property) is important. The magnitude and timing of the outflows affect the cost of borrowing.

In common arrangements, the lender charges the going rate of interest, depending on the availability of funds and the attractiveness of the client as a mortgagor. The lender then calculates the monthly (or yearly) debt service, assuming a fully amortized loan, the yield-to-maturity of the loan, and as required by the Truth in Lending Act, the annual percentage rate (APR). The APR is said to reflect the true cost of borrowing.

For example, if the mortgagor borrows $50,000 for 30 years and agrees to repay an annual debt service of $5,500 at the end of each of those years, the effective cost of borrowing is 10.44 percent. If closing costs amount to $2,000, paid when the loan is originated, the borrower's cost is viewed differently. The borrower pays $5,500 per year for 30 years as before, but the proceeds borrowed are now reduced to $48,000 ($50,000 minus $2,000). Therefore, since the borrower receives less money but is required to repay according to the schedule *as if* $50,000 were received, the effective cost of borrowing increases.

The effective cost of borrowing $50,000 to be repaid with annual payments of $5,500 for each of 30 years, with $2,000 closing costs paid at the time of loan origination, is 10.95 percent. This rate is more than one-half of 1 percent higher than the rate without the closing costs. Thus closing costs make the true cost of borrowing higher than the stated rate.

By law, the APR must include some of the closing costs in order to better represent the cost of borrowing. However, certain fees and expenses are not necessarily included in the APR, so the investor may not really be paying the rate believed. It is important to be able to measure the actual cost of borrowing before any comparisons and decisions can be made.

Finally, some of the closing costs may not result in actual outlays for the mortgage. Loan origination fees, for example, may be charged by the mortgagee's institution to raise the yield of the loan. At this point, it is easy to understand how loan origination fees can dramatically increase the lender's yield. This is further emphasized by the fact that if early repayment occurs and closing costs were assessed to the borrower, the early repayment increases the cost of borrowing. In addition, we must note that *the reported APR does not take into account the likelihood of early repayment.*

Continuing the previous example, suppose the investor wished to repay the loan at the end of year 5. What is the effective cost of borrowing for the loan? The effective cost of borrowing now becomes 11.55 percent, or 60 basis points higher than if the loan were held to maturity. This is because the impact of the closing costs is only spread over 5 years instead of 30. Therefore the effective cost of borrowing is directly related to the probability of early repayment, given that closing costs are paid at the beginning of the loan.

The importance of these results should be apparent. Assuming closing costs, it has been shown that not only is the cost of borrowing higher than is stated by the interest rate and possibly the APR, but also that if the loan is expected to be repaid earlier than at maturity, the cost rises even more. It can be shown that the earlier the repayment, the greater the rise in effective borrowing cost as a result of the closing costs. It also becomes apparent that the probability of early repayment is a very important estimate, since it can have a dramatic impact on the cost of borrowing. Historical evidence also suggests that only a small portion of the mortgages for income-producing real estate are held to maturity!

PREPAYMENT PENALTIES

Some loans also require that prepayment penalties be assessed to the mortgagor if the decision is made to prepay. Prepayment penalties are typically included in mortgages on income property investments. These penalties often are measured by a flat percentage (usually 1 to 3 percent) of the remaining loan balance. An alternative method is to charge six or nine months' interest at the time of prepayment.

Prepayment penalties, however charged, increase the cost of the loan to the mortgagor and raise the yield to the mortgagee. In our example, if the prepayment penalties were 3 percent of the outstanding balance, the amount charged would be $1,448. This payment must be made, but unlike closing costs, prepayment penalties are not paid until the prepayment date. However, this also affects the cost of borrowing.

In the example, the fee of $1,448 paid at the prepayment date increases the effective borrowing rate to 12.02 percent, assuming the same terms, closing costs, and early repayment date. In this case, the prepayment penalty increases the cost of borrowing by 47 basis points, so the impact of such penalties may not be as inconsequential as investors presume.

PREPAID INTEREST

In some transactions, the mortgagee may seek prepaid interest at the time of the origination of the loan. This income to the lender ensures that a buffer is established in the beginning period of the loan. Prepaid interest is frequently used for short-term loans and construction financing. It is often included as part of closing costs, although technically it is not.

The total amount of interest paid to the mortgagee may be the same under a prepaid interest provision, although prepayment of interest clearly affects the cost of borrowing and yield of the loan.

Using the continuing example, if we assume that the lender also required prepaid interest of $1,000, the outstanding balance to be paid at the early repayment date is $49,919 (instead of $48,281). Assuming that the closing costs remained at $2,000, and the prepayment penalties were now 3 percent of $49,919, or $1,498 (instead of $1,448), the new effective rate of borrowing is 12.09 percent.

DISCOUNT POINTS

Discount points are another typical charge used in the mortgage market. These "points" effectively raise the cost of the loan to the borrower by creating additional finance charges. These charges are often added to the loan origination fees but have a similar effect if treated separately. Of course, points charged to borrowers increase the yield to the lender.

For example, suppose the discount points amount to $2,000. When this is considered with all the other special provisions, the cost of borrowing increases to 13.26 percent.

MORTGAGE INSURANCE

Finally, if the loan-to-value ratio of the loan is relatively high, the lender may require private mortgage insurance. This is particularly true of single-

TABLE 9–2

SUMMARY OF IMPACT ON COSTS OF BORROWING BY VARIOUS LOAN PROVISIONS

Description	Effective Cost of Borrowing (%)
1. Basic example:	
$50,000 mortgage, payable in $5,500 annual payments for 30 years	10.44
2. Impact of closing costs:	
$2,000 paid at time of loan origination	10.95
3. Additional impact of early repayment:	
Repayment of note at end of 5 years	11.55
4. Additional impact of prepayment penalty:	
Penalty of 3 percent of outstanding balance, paid at time of prepayment	12.02
5. Additional impact of prepaid interest:	
$1,000 paid at time of loan origination (affects outstanding balance and prepayment penalty)	12.09
6. Additional impact of discount points:	
$2,000 paid at time of loan origination	13.26
7. Additional impact of mortgage insurance:	
Annual premium of one-fourth of 1 percent of original mortgage loan	13.56

Each provision assumes that the previous impacts are applicable. Therefore, if some of the provisions do not apply, the effective costs of borrowing are altered. And, all tax effects are ignored.

family residential loans. Although the mortgage insurance premium is small, typically about one-fourth of 1 percent of the original loan, this, too, increases the effective cost of borrowing.

To conclude our example, since the amount borrowed is $50,000, if the mortgage insurance premium is one-fourth of 1 percent of the loan per year, this amounts to an additional required premium of $125 per year. (We assumed only a yearly premium. Usually, a front-end initial premium of about 1 percent is also included.)

The effect of this provision is clear. Mortgage insurance also results in a higher effective cost for borrowers. If we include the one-fourth of 1 percent premium charge in the analysis with all the other charges, the effective cost of borrowing becomes 13.56 percent.

OTHER PROVISIONS

Many other provisions could be analyzed. These include acceleration clauses, assignments and assumptions, and the use of alternative amortization schedules. In addition, there are different tax effects. Certain closing costs and interest are tax deductible. Prepayment penalties reduce taxable income from operation. Discount points may qualify as tax-deductible items.[6] While similar analysis on an after-tax basis would yield different results, the major point is that it is imperative to compare various financing alternatives and to evaluate the impact of the special loan provisions on the cost of borrowing.

Table 9–2 summarizes our cost-of-borrowing example. It is clear that the actual cost of borrowing is directly related to the factors that apply to the investor's mortgage agreement. In this case, assuming that all the factors applied, what appeared to be a relatively low cost of borrowing (10.44 percent) has increased to 13.56 percent. *This represents a 30 percent increase in the actual cost of borrowing to the mortgagor.* This illustrates the importance of mortgage loan provision analysis.

FINANCIAL LEVERAGE

One of the attractions of income-producing real estate is the ability to finance a large portion of the investment with debt. However, the reason why this is so advantageous to the investor is often misunderstood. As we suggested previously, the investor uses debt with the belief that the rate of return earned by the investment will be greater than the cost of borrowing. This important factor is called *financial leverage.*

CONDITIONS FOR FAVORABLE LEVERAGE

As discussed earlier in the chapter, if the analysis of financial leverage requires that the investor compare favorable opportunities with the costs of debt financing, it is also necessary to consider the impact of taxes on the financing decision, since income from real estate investments is taxable and the costs of borrowing are tax deductible. Therefore one must decide whether leverage will be favorable or unfavorable.

If an investor anticipates a gain as a result of borrowing, *favorable financial leverage* exists. If the opportunity rate of return from real estate investments is not expected to be greater than the costs of borrowing, favorable financial leverage will not exist. In this case, *unfavorable financial leverage* exists and the investor is better off by minimizing the amount of debt used to finance the investment. Not even the most optimistic real estate investor is happy about negative leverage.

Unfavorable leverage means two things. First, the investor would be better off by not borrowing and by using cash (or perhaps by not investing until later). Unfavorable leverage means that the investor is paying

---

[6]Discount points must be amortized if the property is not owner-occupied.

more for the use of funds than the investment is expected to return. Second, no investor would knowingly undertake unfavorable financial leverage to achieve wealth maximization. In other words, if the cost of borrowing is higher than the expected return, the investor would *lose* by borrowing. To borrow under these circumstances means that the investor is willing to pay more for "other people's money" than for personal funds.

The conditions for favorable leverage can be represented as follows:

If

$$r_a \gtrless k_d(1 - \tau)$$

then

$$r_e \gtrless r_a \qquad (9\text{--}2)$$

where:

r_a = expected after-tax return on investment

k_d = expected pretax cost of borrowing

τ = marginal income tax rate

r_e = expected after-tax return on equity

If the after-tax return on the investment is greater than the after-tax cost of borrowing, favorable financial leverage exists because the after-tax return on equity is greater than the after-tax return on the overall investment. If the after-tax return on investment is less than the after-tax cost of borrowing, unfavorable financial leverage exists because the after-tax return to the equity holders is less than the after-tax return on the investment. Finally, leverage is "neutral" when the after-tax return on assets is equal to the after-tax cost of borrowing. In this case, the returns on equity and the investment would be identical.

Real estate finance becomes an important part of the analysis because financing decisions play a large part in the investment decision. This determination is made by comparing the impact of the financing option on the rate of return (yield) or investment value of the property.

ANALYSIS OF IMPACT OF FINANCIAL LEVERAGE

There are several ways of analyzing financial leverage and its impact on rates of return, risk, and value. We illustrate the most useful methods of analysis in this section.

IMPACT ON REQUIRED RATE OF RETURN

One of the ways to demonstrate the effect of financial leverage on the return on equity is to isolate the impact of debt financing and study the potential effects of various financing decisions. The following demonstration illustrates the impact of financial leverage.

We can measure the overall required rate of return from a real estate investment as follows:

$$k_o = k_d(L/V) + k_e(E/V) \qquad (9\text{--}3)$$

where:

k_o = overall required rate of return

k_d = cost of debt financing

k_e = required rate of return on equity

L = amount of debt

E = amount of equity

V = value of investment

Using algebra, we get:

$$k_e = \frac{k_o - k_d(L/V)}{E/V} \qquad (9\text{--}4)$$

Since the value of the investments must be the sum of the amounts of debt and equity, it follows that:

$$k_e = k_o + (k_o - k_d)L/E \qquad (9\text{--}5)$$

Equation (9–5) demonstrates the impact of different combinations of rates of return and costs of borrowing and their effects on the return on equity. This approach also shows the differing impacts of various combinations of debt and equity sources. Alternative combinations of debt and equity can be measured by L/E, which is frequently called the *debt-to-equity ratio*. It is a well-known measure of the amount of leverage.

For example, assume that $k_o = 15$ percent, $k_d = 12$ percent, but $L/E = 0$. In this case, the rate of return on assets is greater than the cost of borrowing (.15 > .12), but no debt was used (that is, it is totally financed with equity). The rate of return on equity would be:

$$k_e = .15 + (.15 - .12).00$$

$$= .15$$

The rate of return on equity is identical to the overall rate of return on investments, which means that there is no leverage effect because no debt is used (that is, $L/E = 0$).

However, consider the case in which $L/E = .25/.75$, or a 25 percent loan-to-value ratio. The rate of return on equity would be 16 percent:

$$k_e = .15 + (.15 - .12)\,\frac{.25}{.75}$$

$$= .15 + .01$$

$$= .16$$

In this case, because 25 percent of the value of the investment is borrowed, the return on equity increased 6.67 percent as a result of favorable financial leverage.

If the investor were to acquire a relatively large amount of debt, say 80 percent of the total value of the investment, the loan-to-value ratio would be .80 and the debt-to-equity ratio (L/E) would be 4.00. Assuming that k_o and k_d remain the same, k_e would be 27 percent:

$$k_e = .15 + (.15 - .12)\,\frac{.80}{.20}$$

$$= .15 + .12$$

$$= .27$$

Therefore, by increasing the amount of debt borrowed at a constant rate of k_d, the rate of return on equity increases substantially. This example illustrates the "levering" of returns available in real estate investing as a result of the investor's ability to use only small amounts of equity.

However, as the loan-to-value ratio and the debt-to-equity ratio increase, the cost of borrowing also increases. This is because lenders view the investment as more risky, since additional debt must now be satisfied out of the net operating income of the investment. For purposes of illustration, suppose that for loans with loan-to-value ratios of .80, lenders would require a 14 percent interest rate. If the expected rate of return on the overall investment remains at 15 percent, the gains from financial leverage would be less than when the cost of borrowing was only 12 percent. The rate of return on equity is now 19 percent instead of 27 percent:

$$k_e = .15 + (.15 - .14)\frac{.80}{.20}$$

$$= .15 + .04$$

$$= .19$$

It is possible to analyze the case in which the cost of borrowing exceeds the overall rate of return on the investment. Next, suppose the cost of borrowing, k_d, is .16, k_o remains at .15, and L/E is 4.00. The return on equity would drop to 11 percent:

$$k_e = .15 + (.15 - .16)\frac{.80}{.20}$$

$$= .15 - .04$$

$$= .11$$

In this case, unfavorable leverage exists. Because the cost of borrowing is greater than the return on assets, unfavorable leverage lowers the rate of return on equity from 15 percent to 11 percent. Furthermore, if the actual return on assets falls short (so that the rate of return is only 10 percent), the impact of borrowing at 16 percent translates into a *negative* rate of return:

$$k_e = .10 + (.10 - .16)\frac{.80}{.20}$$

$$= .10 - .24$$

$$= -.14$$

In this case, the investor loses money because the rate of return is -14 percent.

Therefore, leverage can increase rates of return and change investors wealth very rapidly when it is favorable and can decrease them just as rapidly when it is unfavorable.

IMPACT ON EXPECTED RATE OF RETURN AND RISK

The financing of a real estate investment involves the use of two types of funds: debt (mortgage) and equity. The use of debt to finance an investment can have two impacts: the rate of return to the equity position can be increased and so can the expected risk of the equity position. Thus the investor must face this question: *Does the increase in the expected return offset the increased risk?* If it does, the investor should use the debt. If it does not, the debt should not be used.

EXAMPLE 9–1 **THE IMPACT OF BORROWING ON EXPECTED RISK AND RETURN**

An investor has the opportunity to invest in an apartment building. The cost of the investment is $500,000. The investment is expected to produce the net operating incomes as shown in Table 1.

TABLE 1
POSSIBLE NOIS

State of the World	NOI	Probability
Pessimistic	$55,000	.2
Most likely	60,000	.6
Optimistic	65,000	.2

The investor has two financing options:

1. Financing with 100 percent equity and no debt.
2. Financing with 75 percent debt, 25 percent equity. The debt has an interest rate of 10 percent with a maturity of 25 years, monthly payments. The debt service is $40,905 per year.

☐ **IMPACT ON RATE OF RETURN.** To illustrate the impact of two financing options in Example 9–1 on the rate of return, the following simple rate-of-return measure is used:

$$EDR = \frac{BTCF}{Equity}$$

(9–6)

EDR = Equity divided rate

The equity dividend rate is a simple, but widely used, measure of the rate of return from an investment. BTCF is the before-tax cash flow. Equity is the amount of cash required for the investment.

Now look at Example 9–1. The *expected* rate of return is the weighted average of the return, using the EDR, for each "state of the world" multiplied by the probability for each "state." Thus, in equation form, the expected rate of return is:

$$E(EDR) = \sum_{i=1}^{s} p_i(EDR_i) \qquad (9\text{--}7)$$

where E(EDR) is the expected equity dividend rate, p_i is the probability under each "state of the world," EDR_i is the equity dividend rate under each "state," s is the number of states of the world, and Σ is the summation symbol.

To implement this equation, look at the first financing option. If the investor uses the first option (financing with equity only), the outcomes for each "state" are shown in Table 9–3. Under the pessimistic state of the world, the investor feels that the NOI would be $55,000. The debt service is zero, since option one involves no debt. The equity investment is thus the total cost of $500,000. The before-tax cash flow (BTCF) is the NOI minus the debt service, or $55,000. The equity dividend rate (EDR) for the pessimistic outcome is:

$$EDR = \frac{BTCF}{Equity}$$

$$= \frac{\$55,000}{\$500,000}$$

$$= .11, \text{ or } 11\%$$

The probability of this outcome is 20 percent. Likewise, the EDRs for each of the other possible states of the world are calculated as 12 percent for the most likely state and 13 percent for the optimistic state.

Using Equation (9–6), the expected EDR is:

$$E(EDR) = \sum_{i=1}^{s} p_i(EDR_i)$$

$$= .2(.11) + .6(.12) + .2(.13)$$

$$= .12, \text{ or } 12\%$$

TABLE 9–3
EQUITY FINANCING OPTION

State of the World	NOI	Debt Service	BTCF	EDR	Probability
Pessimistic	$55,000	$0	$55,000	11%	.2
Most likely	60,000	0	60,000	12	.6
Optimistic	60,000	0	65,000	13	.2

TABLE 9–4
DEBT-PLUS-EQUITY OPTION

State of the World	NOI	Debt Service	BTCF	EDR	Probability
Pessimistic	$55,000	$40,905	$14,095	11.28%	.2
Most likely	60,000	40,905	19,095	15.28	.6
Optimistic	60,000	40,905	24,095	19.28	.2

So the investor *expects* the investment to generate a 12 percent EDR if the first financing option (all equity) is used.

What is the expected EDR if the second financing option is employed? This is illustrated in Table 9–4.

Under the second financing option, the investor borrows 75 percent, or $375,000, of the total cost. The equity investment is thus $125,000. Under pessimistic state, the NOI is $55,000. The debt service is $40,905, which leaves $14,095 in BTCF. The equity dividend rate is 11.28 percent ($14,095 divided by $125,000). The probability is 20 percent. The EDR for the most likely outcome is 15.28 percent and is 19.28 percent for the optimistic outcome.

The expected equity dividend rate is:

$$E(EDR) = \sum_{i=1}^{s} p_i(EDR_i)$$

$$= .2(.1128) + .6(.1528) + .2(.1928)$$

$$= .1528, \text{ or } 15.28\%$$

Now let us compare the rates of return expected for each financing option:

Financing Option	E(EDR)
Option 1	11.00%
Option 2	15.28

Note that by borrowing money, the expected rate of return on the equity investment increased from 11 to 15.28 percent.

Does this mean that the investor should always use debt? No; the answer lies in understanding that the risk of the investment has also increased.

☐ **IMPACT ON RISK.** The risk associated with the use of debt is called *financial risk*. This refers to the probability that the debt obligations will not be met. Note that in the preceding examples, the debt claim has priority over the equity position. Thus, the equity position is the "residual" and bears the impact of the risk of investing.

To illustrate the impact of borrowing on the risk, let us define *risk* as the *variation* around the expected rate of return. A measure of variation is the standard deviation, abbreviated by the Greek letter sigma, σ. The equation for calculating the standard deviation, σ, is:

$$\sigma = \sqrt{\sum_{i=1}^{s} p_i[EDR_i - E(EDR)]^2} \tag{9-8}$$

The steps for calculating σ are:

1. Calculate the deviation of each possible outcome from the expected EDR $[EDR_i - E(EDR)]$.

2. Raise this deviation to the second power, $[EDR_i - E(EDR)]^2$.

3. Multiply this term by the probability of getting EDR_i (that is, p_i), $p_i[EDR_i - E(EDR)]^2$.

4. Sum these products, $\sum p_i [EDR_i - E(EDR)]^2$.

5. Take the square root of this sum.

To illustrate, let us first calculate the standard deviation for the first financing option. This is shown in Table 9-5. The equity dividend rate under each state of the world (EDR_i) was calculated previously. The expected equity dividend rate, $E(EDR)$, was 12 percent under the first financing option. Using the steps outlined, the resulting standard deviation is .0063, or .63 percent.

For the second financing option, the same procedure can be followed, as shown in Table 9-6. Thus, for the second financing option, the risk is .0253, or 2.53 percent.

TABLE 9-5
STANDARD DEVIATION FOR EQUITY FINANCING OPTION

State of the World	EDR_i	$EDR_i - E(EDR)$	$[EDR_i - E(EDR)]^2$		p_i
Pessimistic	.11	−.01	.0001	.2	.00002
Most likely	.12	.00	.0000	.6	.00000
Optimistic	.13	.01	.0001	.2	.00002
				$\Sigma =$	.00004

$$\sigma = \sqrt{.00004}$$
$$\sigma = .0063$$

TABLE 9–6
STANDARD DEVIATION FOR DEBT-PLUS-EQUITY OPTION

State of the World	EDR_i	$EDR_i - E(EDR)$	$[EDR_i - E(EDR)]^2$	p_i	
Pessimistic	.1128	−.04	.0016	.2	.00032
Most likely	.1528	.00	.0000	.6	.00000
Optimistic	.1928	.04	.0016	.2	.00032
					$\Sigma = .00064$

$$\sigma = \sqrt{.00064}$$
$$\sigma = .0253$$

What do these numbers mean? Let us summarize as follows:

Financing Option	Expected Return	Risk (σ)
1	11.00%	.63%
2	15.28	2.53

Note that the use of debt increased the expected return on equity from 11 to 15.28 percent. But also note that the risk increased from .63 to 2.53 percent. *Thus expected return and expected risk increased by the use of debt.*

Should the investor use the debt? To answer this question, the investor must ask himself or herself if the increase in return is enough to cover the increased risk. The answer would vary depending on the preference of each investor. For some investors, the answer is yes—meaning that the debt should be used. For others, the answer is no—indicating the debt should not be used.

EXAMPLE 9–2   BELOW-MARKET FINANCING AND VALUE

A real estate investor is considering the purchase of a small office building. The project has an expected net operating income of $25,000 per year and is expected to be worth $300,000 at the end of the five-year holding period.

The investor has two financing options for a $200,000 mortgage on the property:

1. Typical market financing is at 10 percent, interest-only, with a balloon payment in five years.

2. The seller will finance the project at 8%, interest-only, with a balloon payment in five years.

If the investor wants to earn a 14 percent rate of return, how much could be paid under the two financing options? Which is the best choice?

With market financing, the project would have a value as follows:

$$V = \$200,000 + PVAF_{14\%,5\ yrs}[\$25,000 - \$20,000]$$
$$+ PVF_{14\%,5yrs}[\$300,000 - \$200,000]$$

$$V = \$269,102$$

With seller financing, the project would have a value as follows:

$$V = \$200,000 + PVAF_{14\%,5\ yrs}[\$25,000 - \$16,000]$$
$$+ PVF_{14\%,5yrs}[\$300,000 - \$200,000]$$

$$V = \$282,835$$

Note that the investment is "worth" about $13,700 more under the seller financing because the interest rate is lower. Which is the best choice? If the investor could buy the project for less than $282,835, the seller-financing option is the optimal choice.

Current Issue 9–4
How Leverage Affects Real Estate Investments
The use of debt financing, or *financial leverage,* affects real estate investments in several ways. The first reason generally given is that the substitution of debt for equity sources (often the investor's own equity) can magnify the rate of return on the investor's equity position. Of course, simply because the investor borrows does not automatically mean that the rate of return will be magnified. The determination that needs to be made so that an investor can decide whether financial leverage will cause a favorable or unfavorable impact is a comparison between the after-tax cost of borrowing and the after-tax rate of return on the project.

If the after-tax cost of borrowing is less than the after-tax rate of return on the project, the investor achieves a favorable result: a financing gain. This is equivalent to saying that the investor's after-tax rate of return on equity exceeds the after-tax rate of return on the investment. In effect, it means the investor is able to "lever upward" the rate of return as a result of borrowing.

Note, however, that if the after-tax cost of borrowing exceeds the after-tax rate of return on the project, an unfavorable result obtains. In this case, the after-tax rate of return on equity will be less than the after return on the investment. The investor would have earned a higher rate of return if more equity instead of debt financing had been used. No borrower is happy about a lower rate of return on equity than that earned on the entire project; no investor will employ debt financing if this condition is expected.

Another impact of leverage is that the greater the amount an investor borrows, the greater the interest that is paid to the lender(s). This is important because, unlike the situation with equity financing, debt financing receives special treatment by the IRS. All interest is tax-deductible from ordinary income for both corporations and individuals (assuming the deduction threshold is met by individuals or married taxpayers who file jointly). For corporations, this provides a special feature, since interest expenses reduce taxable income at the company level and owners of the corporation may further reduce their taxable incomes from dividends (or other income) by financing the ownership interest with debt. Once again, the investor may subtract out the interest costs. This type of double counting creates incentives for heavy debt financing in real estate and helps to explain the high loan-to-value ratios of many real estate firms.

For individuals, there is also another reason for the use of debt financing. The ability to diversify an individual's equity into several properties may enhance the investor's portfolio of investments by reducing investment risk and by providing the investor with the opportunity to exert greater control over more real estate than if only equity financing were employed. This reason suggests that investors may borrow funds for real estate acquisitions, especially if they are small, noncorporate investors, in order to spread out their interest into as wide a number of properties as possible.

It is often said that "leverage is the prime mover" of real estate. Few acquisitions are made without it. The cost of mortgage finance is a major concern for builders, large-scale developers, and households. The supply of funds for real estate is generally thought to be an important variable in understanding mortgage and housing markets. Leverage is an important part of modern real estate investment analysis.

ALTERNATIVE FINANCING METHODS

Despite the widespread use of conventional fixed-rate, amortized mortgages, modern financing techniques offer several alternatives. Table 9–7 outlines some of the questions which the investor should answer before using any creative financing method. To correctly apply and understand each financing method, the investor should understand the implications for all involved, particularly the lender and the borrower.

The following areas must be carefully analyzed before using any financing method: the mechanics of the technique, the tax implications, the legal aspects of the method, and the decision-making implications.

TABLE 9–7
ANALYSIS OF CREATIVE FINANCING METHODS

The following are some basic aspects to consider before using any creative financing method. It is important to analyze both the lender's and the borrower's perspectives.

1. *The mechanics of the technique.* How does it work? What is the expected yield (from the borrower's perspective—the cost of borrowing) both before- and after-tax?
2. *The tax implications.* What are the tax rules related to this financing method? What are the implications for both the lender and the borrower? Are there unique tax implications in the event of default? What unique tax problems does this method create?
3. *The legal aspects of the method.* What legal problems does the method create? How is the legal instrument different from the traditional? What are the typical clauses in such an instrument?
4. *The decision-making implications.* When would such a financing method be used? Under what investment situations would it be more advantageous than other financing methods?

CONSTRUCTION LOANS

Construction loans are usually negotiated between the developer and lender after the developer has already obtained a committment for a permanent loan on a proposed project. The construction lender is often different from the permanent lender because construction lenders are typically more knowledgeable of local market conditions.

The typical construction loan is dispersed in intervals over time with the total of the draws and interest on the draws making up the loan balance. For instance, a lender may commit a $1,335,000 loan to a developer over a one-year period with the developer drawing a portion of the loan each month over the one-year period. The balance of the loan at the end of the one-year period will be equal to the sum of each month's draw plus the interest accrued on each draw from the time it was dispersed by the lender. This process is illustrated in detail in Example 9–3. Construction lenders will rarely advance loan funds in excess of the value of the property. That is, the lender never wants the developer's total draws to exceed the cost of the construction improvements made to date. The interest rate on the loan during the construction period is usually based on a floating rate. This causes interest-rate risk for the developer in that the actual interest expense during this period may exceed the budgeted amount.

At the end of the construction period, the construction loan—or *interim loan*—is paid off with funds from the *permanent loan,* and the developer begins payments on the permanent loan with funds from rental revenues.

EXAMPLE 9–3 CONSTRUCTION LOAN EXAMPLE

An investor is considering the construction of an office building for a site. The project is estimated to take one year to complete. The costs are:

> Land acquisition costs = $300,000
>
> Site preparation expenses = $100,000
>
> Total hard (construction) costs = $1,200,000
>
> Total soft (interest, etc.) costs = $35,000

Total costs excluding land acquisition are estimated to be $1,335,000. The developer plans to purchase the land with cash as his equity interest in the project. The lender will fund the remaining development costs. The lender will dispense $1,335,000 in development expenses over a 12-month period at a 10 percent contract rate (.10/12 = .833 percent monthly) with 2 percentage points at the end of the loan. Table 1 shows the predicted loan draws and repayment schedule.

TABLE 1
LOAN DRAWS AND REPAYMENTS

Loan Month	Draw Amount	Interest	Balance Interest
1	$ 225,000	$ 1,875	$ 226,875
2	110,000	2,807	339,682
3	100,000	3,664	443,346
4	100,000	4,528	547,874
5	100,000	5,398	653,272
6	100,000	6,277	759,549
7	100,000	7,163	866,712
8	100,000	8,056	974,768
9	100,000	8,956	1,083,724
10	100,000	9,864	1,193,588
11	100,000	10,779	1,304,367
12	100,000	11,703	1,416,070
Loan fees			28,321
Totals	$1,335,000	$81,070	$1,444,391

The developer makes loan draws at the beginning of each month. At the beginning of the first month, the developer draws $225,000. At the end of the month, the balance due reflects the first month's draw and the .833 percent monthly interest on the loan. At this time, the second month's draw is made for $110,000. The balance due at this point is $226,875 +

$110,000 = \$336,875$. This sum accrues interest at the .833 percent monthly rate so the balance due at the end of month 2 is $\$336,875 \times 1.00833 = \$339,682$. This process continues and the balance of the loan at the end of 12 months is $\$1,416,070$.

Another way to arrive at this figure is to compute, for each draw, its future value at the end of 12 months and sum these values. The calculation would be as follows:

$$225,000(1.00833)^{12} + 110,000(1.00833)^{11}$$
$$+ \ldots + 100,000(1.00833) = \$1,416,070$$

The lender would add 2 percent of this amount, or $\$28,321$, to arrive at the balance due, $\$1,444,391$.

In the end, the capitalized value will be the balance due plus the land acquisition cost or $\$1,744,391$. In this case, the loan-to-value ratio at the end of 12 months will be $1,444,391 / 1,744,391 = 82.8$ percent.

YIELD CALCULATION

The lender's rate of return can be determined by finding the rate that equates the present value of the draws to the present value of the loan repayment. The calculations are as follows:

$$\$225,000 + \$110,000/(1+r)^1 + \$100,000/(1+r)^2 + \ldots + \$100,000/(1+r)^{11}$$
$$= \$1,444,391/(1+r)^{12}$$

Solving for r, we find the lender's internal rate of return to be 1.11 percent monthly or 13.34 percent annualized.

PURCHASE-MONEY MORTGAGE

In a *purchase-money mortgage,* the seller takes back a note from the buyer and retains a lien against the property until the value of the note is satisfied. The major difference between this and a conventional mortgage is that the purchase-money agreement is between the buyer and the seller only. Therefore purchase-money mortgages have very high legal priority in the event of a default. This technique is often used, since financing can affect an offer's attractiveness. Sometimes the investor may lack the necessary equity. However, through negotiation, the seller may accept a purchase-money mortgage with a balloon payment or a second mortgage.

INSTALLMENT LAND SALES CONTRACT

The *installment land sales contract* is used when the buyer can provide only a low down payment. It is similar to the purchase-money mortgage because the financing arrangements are made exclusively between the buyer and the seller. However, the major difference between these two arises in the event of a default. In this method, if the buyer defaults prior to fulfillment of the contract, the seller can recover the full value of the property under contract law. Under a purchase-money mortgage, the defaulting buyer is liable (in most states) for only the balance on the note.

BALLOON PAYMENT MORTGAGES

The balloon payment mortgage is a very general financing technique that requires a large outlay as a final payment (hence the term *balloon payment*). In some forms, the balloon payment amounts to an agreed-upon sales price in a future year, after a period of interest payments. In others, the balloon payment takes place at the end of some period of time over which regular amortized payments were made. This accelerates the repayment of the loan but keeps the level of the repayment of principal plus interest at the original term. This form is sometimes called a *balloon mortgage*.

JUNIOR LIENS

Junior liens are claims by creditors against the asset(s) pledged as security for which there exists a senior or prior lien (typically, a first mortgage). These are also called second mortgages and result in a secondary satisfaction in the event of a default and subsequent foreclosure. It should be noted that a purchase-money mortgage may be a junior lien.

Junior liens are inherently riskier from the borrower's point of view due to their secondary priority in claims against the secured assets. To compensate for this risk, lenders often seek higher rates of interest. However, the availability of second mortgages opens up new avenues of finance for the investor. If investment opportunities develop, investors with equity in their properties can acquire additional real property interests by using second mortgages and increasing their wealth through favorable financial leverage.

SALE-LEASEBACK

A *sale-leaseback* is a special financing technique that is used in some markets when more traditional financial arrangements are not acceptable. It is often used between large investors and large manufacturing firms. In a sale-leaseback, the investor purchases real estate that is owned and operated by a well-established income-producing firm. At the same time, the investor leases property back to the firm.

In recent years, this form of financing has become quite popular because equity capital is either more expensive or unavailable for commercial real estate investment. In addition, there are advantages to both sides of the transaction. For the leasing firm, this arrangement frees equity for other uses. For the investor, the expected returns from the leaseback are relatively long in term and typically large in size. There are other advantages if the value of the property appreciates at a higher rate than expected. Finally, there are income tax advantages for both sides.

INCOME AND EQUITY PARTICIPATIONS

Income and equity participations allow the institutional lender to acquire an interest in the equity reversion from the property. In these arrangements, the lender participates in future income in addition to receiving the contracted debt service repayment. For this benefit, the lender often accepts a less secure financial position.

The income-property mortgage market has developed a wide variety of ways of participating in the income. Examples include taking a percentage of the gross income, net operating income, or the before-tax cash flow and/or a percentage of the income from sale. This participation by the lender increases the yield to the lender on the mortgage loan. Conversely, it increases the cost of borrowing to the investor.

For tax purposes, the payment to the lender under the participation agreement is generally treated as interest paid by the borrower/investor. As such, it is deductible as interest from the investor's taxable income from operations. If the agreement is written as interest payments, the payment due in the year of sale would be deductible like a prepayment penalty.

To illustrate a participation loan, consider the following example. A real estate investor is considering the purchase of a small shopping center. The lender has agreed to make a mortgage for $200,000 at an interest rate of 12.5 percent with monthly payments over 20 years. The mortgage constant is .13632 per year. The annual debt service is $27,264. In addition, the lender requires a participation of 2 percent of the annual effective gross income (EGI). The expected cash flow for years 1 through 5 is shown in Table 9–8.

Table 9–8 also contains the EGI for each year, the operating expenses, and the resulting net operating income. From this the investor subtracts the $27,264 payment on the debt service and the participating interest of 2 percent of EGI each year. The result is the before-tax cash flow.

For tax purposes, the participating amount each year is deductible from the investor's taxable income from operations. While we have constructed this example as participation in the effective gross income, the

TABLE 9–8
A PARTICIPATING MORTGAGE EXAMPLE

Year	Effective Gross Income	Operating Expenses	Net Operating Income	Debt Service	Participation Interest	BTCF
1	$55,000	$22,000	$33,000	$27,264	$1,100	$4,636
2	57,750	23,100	34,650	27,264	1,155	6,231
3	60,600	26,000	34,600	27,264	1,212	6,124
4	63,600	28,600	34,980	27,264	1,272	6,444
5	66,750	30,000	36,750	27,264	1,335	8,151

loans have been written for net operating income or before-tax cash flow participation as well.

WRAPAROUND MORTGAGE

A *wraparound mortgage* is a loan that is subordinated to an existing first mortgage and is of a greater amount than the first mortgage. The seller of the real property continues to make payments on the first mortgage using the debt-service payments made on the "wrap" by the buyer.

A wraparound mortgage usually will be of benefit to both buyer and seller. First, because of the lower interest rate on the first mortgage, it is often in the best interest of both parties to preserve this mortgage, if possible. However, there are situations in which the existing first mortgage should not be kept. If the current loan constant on the first mortgage is higher than the loan constant available on new loans from conventional sources, the first mortgage should not be retained. Second, since the seller often provides the wrap, more liberal financing terms may be offered than institutions. This should make the property more marketable for the seller since it will be more attractive to potential buyers. Obviously, the holder of the existing low-interest-rate first mortgage is the losing party in the use of the wraparound mortgage.

The following is an example of a situation in which a wrap may be used to the advantage of both buyer and seller. Suppose the owner of a property is interested in selling an investment for $2 million. A buyer is interested in the property but is only willing to make a $400,000 down payment. Suppose more traditional lenders are only willing to lend $1.4 million at a rate of 13 percent. On the basis of this alternative, it does not seem that the deal will go through.

However, the owner has a mortgage on the property that can be "wrapped." The mortgage was originally for $1 million at 8 percent over a 25-year term. Monthly payments on this loan are $7,718. The loan has been in existence for 7 years, so the current balance is $882,057.

TABLE 9–9
A WRAPAROUND EXAMPLE: AMORTIZATION SCHEDULE*

Year	Annual Payment	Principal Payment	Interest Payment	Amount Outstanding
0	—	—	—	$1,600,000
1	$202,212	$10,714	$191,498	1,589,286
2	202,212	12,197	190,015	1,577,089
3	202,212	13,753	188,459	1,563,336
4	202,212	15,366	186,846	1,547,970
5	202,212	17,434	184,778	1,530,536

* See text for assumptions.

Because of the existing mortgage, the seller is willing to offer a wrap for $1.6 million at 12 percent with a 25-year amortization schedule with a balloon payment required at the end of 5 years. Since the wrap is for $1.6 million and the balance on the first mortgage is $882,057, the seller is, in essence, financing $717,943.

The buyer will make monthly payments of $16,851 on the wrap. This is shown in Table 9–9. The total annual payment is $202,212. Table 9–9 also contains the interest-principal split for each payment over the five-year life of the mortgage. From the total payment, the seller must cover the debt service on the existing first loan. The amortization schedule for the existing first loan is shown in Table 9–10.

To calculate the seller's before-tax yield on the wraparound, it is necessary to calculate the before-tax cash flow to the seller. This is shown in Table 9–11. From the total payment of $202,212 on the wraparound, the seller must pay $92,616 on the debt service of the first mortgage. Thus the net to the seller is $109,596. Remember that the seller financed $717,943 for

TABLE 9–10
AMORTIZATION SCHEDULE FOR THE EXISTING FIRST MORTGAGE*

Year	Annual Payment	Principal Payment	Interest Payment	Amount Outstanding
0	—	—	—	$882,057
1	$92,616	$22,879	$69,737	859,178
2	92,616	24,800	67,816	834,378
3	92,616	26,803	65,813	807,575
4	92,616	29,801	63,535	778,494
5	92,616	31,423	61,193	747,071

* See text for assumptions

TABLE 9–11
BEFORE-TAX CASH FLOWS TO SELLER
FROM THE WRAPAROUND MORTGAGE

Year	Amount Financed	Before-Tax Cash Flow
0	$717,943	$109,596
1	—	109,596
2	—	109,596
3	—	109,596
4	—	109,596
5	—	893,601*

* This includes the $109,596 from debt service plus the $783,465 net difference between the amount outstanding on the wrap and the first mortgage.

the buyer. The yield on the wrap is approximately 16.3 percent. This is calculated by finding the rate that will equate to expected before-tax cash inflows to the amount financed.

ADJUSTABLE-RATE MORTGAGE

Another common alternative financing method is the so-called *adjustable-rate loan* (also known as the variable-rate loan or the renegotiable-rate loan). As the name implies, the interest rate is subject to adjustment, and thus the debt service is subject to the change in some index to which the interest rate is tied.

These types of loans create no unique tax problems for the investor. They do, however, create cash-flow forecasting problems, since the investor must forecast the interest rate on the loan for future time periods. In effect, the risk of changes in interest rate is shifted from the lender to the equity investor.

EXAMPLE 9–4 AN ADJUSTABLE-RATE MORTGAGE EXAMPLE

A real estate investor is considering the purchase of a duplex for $70,000. The lender has agreed to loan 75 percent of the purchase price with a maturity of 25 years with the interest rate adjusted every year. Debt service is payable on a monthly basis. The initial interest rate is 12.5 percent per year for the first year. The investor/borrower expects the interest rate to be as follows for the first five years of the loan:

Years	Interest Rate per Year
1	12.5%
2	13.5%
3	14.0%
4	12.0%
5	11.0%

To illustrate the mechanics of such a loan, consider the facts in Example 9–4. The investor is borrowing on an adjustable-rate loan of $52,500 (75 percent of $70,000) with the interest rate adjustable every year. The payments on the loan are monthly with a maturity of 25 years.

The first year's mortgage constant is .010903. This mortgage constant is then multiplied by the loan amount ($52,500) to result in the monthly payment of $572.44. At the end of year 1, the borrower has an outstanding balance of $52,175.44.

Now we must recalculate the mortgage constant using an annual interest rate of 13.5 percent since this is what the investor expects. What is the maturity of this "new" loan? It is 24 years, or 288 six-month periods. The new mortgage constant is .01172. This is multiplied by the amount outstanding ($52,175.44) to result in the new debt service of $611.35 for each month of the second year. At the end of year 2, the borrower has a balance of $51,863.76.

This process is continued for each year. The final result is shown in Table 9–12. This table shows the amortization schedule for the adjustable-

TABLE 9–12
AMORTIZATION SCHEDULE FOR AN ADJUSTABLE RATE LOAN

Year	Mortgage Constant	Amount Outstanding	Annual Debt Service	Interest	Principal
0		$52,500			
1	.010903	52,175.44	$6,869.28	$6,544.72	$324.56
2	.011720	51,863.76	7,336.20	7,024.52	311.68
3	.012162	51,238.25	7,569.20	6,943.69	625.51
4	.010779	50,729.98	6,627.57	6,119.30	508.27
5	.010189	50,076.88	6,202.65	5,549.55	653.10

Current Issue 9–5
Is the Measurement of Leverage Consistent with
Wealth Maximization?

An important issue in theoretical real estate discussion is the impact of real estate finance on the value of the investment. In addition, given the discussion in the chapter about analyzing the impact of financial leverage, it is essential to consider the possibility that wealth maximization *can* be achieved through proper decisions regarding the capital structure for the real estate behavior.

Modigliani and Miller's seminal 1958 article challenged the conventional views about the relationship between the value of a firm and its choice of capital structure. Essentially, they showed that under limiting conditions, the capital structure determination becomes irrelevant to the wealth of the shareholders. Gains expected from additional financial leverage are offset by higher required rates of return by equity investors. The value of the investment remains the same for all combinations of debt and equity.

The discussions in this chapter involving the analysis of financial leverage employs one of the basic results from Modigliani and Miller's article. The required rate of return on equity is viewed as a function of the overall required rate of return plus the difference between the overall rate and the cost of debt times the debt-to-equity ratio. This idea has become known as Proposition II from the 1958 article. This proposition is essential to obtain the "irrelevancy of capital structure" result.

However, real estate markets do not *automatically* price equity claims precisely the way Modigliani and Miller suggested they do. In fact, many people believe it might be more difficult to observe the degree of efficiency in real estate markets than in securities markets. For example, suppose the equity market assigned a *lower* required rate of return for a specific investment than the theory would predict. If so, the value of the property would be enhanced by the use of debt, Proposition II would not be supported by this example, and the investor would be richer as a result of this specific choice of capital structure. The challenge for real-world investors is to see if they can identify situations in which the required rate of return will be less than what would be expected by the theory. In such cases, there is an inefficiency in the market and an opportunity to increase investor wealth.

rate loan: the debt service for each six-month period at the assumed interest rates, the amount outstanding at the end of each six months, and the allocation between interest and principal for each payment.

As a final note, adjustable-rate mortgages may also include points, fees, and prepayment penalties as in a fixed-rate mortgage. For tax purposes, the items are treated as in the fixed-rate mortgage.

OTHER MORTGAGE INSTRUMENTS

Depending on the plan selected, alternative mortgage instruments allow the investor to acquire a mortgage with a variable interest rate, mortgage term, or debt-service repayment schedule. Because these vary with interest rates, the price of the alternative mortgage instrument may be higher or lower than the price of a conventional mortgage.

OTHER FINANCING DECISIONS

There are several other types of financing decisions that have not yet been discussed. These include many types of financing devices used by commercial investors. For example, the use of wraparound mortgage financing is a well-established method of financing in commercial and industrial markets although it has only recently been used in residential markets. In addition, however, the implementation of the due-on-sale clause has removed the possibilities of wraparound financing in many residential markets.

Many seasoned investors frequently note that financing is *the* major part of real estate investing. The basis of their belief lies not in the availability of "cheap" debt financing, but rather in the gains available to creative investors who learn how to structure debt and equity financing packages to solve problems. These problems include cash flow problems, tax motivations, and timing considerations. In this sense, financing methods are always likely to be a major part of real estate investing.

One of the most common financing decisions that investors face is whether to replace an existing mortgage. The investor may have the opportunity to reduce his debt service by *refinancing* at a lower *interest rate* or may *refinance* to generate cash by increasing the *loan-to-value ratio*. The following example illustrates the decision of whether to refinance or not to refinance.

A real estate investor owns an investment that was purchased five years ago for $500,000. The depreciable basis was $400,000. The investor has been using the straight-line depreciation method with a 27.5-year life. The investment was financed with a $375,000 fixed-rate mortgage at an interest rate of 10 percent with monthly payments for 25 years. The investor is in a 28 percent tax bracket. The estimated current selling price is $625,000. Selling expenses would be 7 percent of the selling price.

The investment is expected to generate $68,750 in net operating income next year. The NOI is expected to increase 2 percent per year. The investor expects to sell the investment for $675,000 five years from now with selling expenses of 7 percent.

The investor is considering refinancing the investment. The new loan would be for $468,750 (75 percent of current value) with a 13 percent interest rate, 25-year term, with monthly payments. There are origination fees of three points (3 percent of the loan amount) if the investor refinances. The proceeds could be reinvested at an opportunity rate of 15 percent. Should the investment be refinanced?

CASH FLOWS WITHOUT REFINANCING

Tables 9–13 and 9–14 calculate the ATCF without refinancing. Table 9–15 computes the ATER from future sale without refinancing, and Table 9–16 calculates the taxes due on sale.

CASH FLOWS WITH REFINANCING

Table 9–17 computes the ATCF from operations with refinancing by deducting the debt service and the taxes (from Table 9–18) from the NOI. Table 9–18 computes the taxes from operations with financing by first de-

TABLE 9–13
MEASUREMENT OF EXPECTED CASH FLOW FROM OPERATIONS WITHOUT REFINANCING

		Years				
		1	2	3	4	5
	Net operating income (NOI)	$68,750	70,125	71,528	72,958	74,417
minus	Debt service (DS)	$40,892	40,892	40,892	40,892	40,892
equals	Before-tax cash flow (BTCF)	$27,858	29,233	30,636	32,066	33,525
minus	Taxes (savings) from operations (TO)*	$ 5,364	5,920	6,502	7,112	7,751
equals	After-tax cash flow (ATCF)	$22,494	23,313	24,134	24,954	25,774

* See table 9–14.

TABLE 9–14
MEASUREMENT OF TAXABLE INCOME AND TAXES FROM OPERATIONS WITHOUT REFINANCING

		Years				
		1	2	3	4	5
equals	Net operating income (NOI)	$68,750	70,125	71,528	72,958	74,417
minus	Interest on debt (I)	$35,048	34,437	33,761	33,014	32,189
minus	Depreciation deduction (D)	$14,545	14,545	14,545	14,545	14,545
minus	Amortized financing costs (AFC)	$ 0	0	0	0	0
plus	Replacement reserves (RR)	$ 0	0	0	0	0
equals	Ordinary taxable income (OTI)	$19,157	21,143	23,221	23,399	27,683
times	Investor's marginal tax rate (τ)	0.28	0.28	0.28	0.28	0.28
equals	Taxes (savings) from operation (TO)	$ 5,364	5,920	6,502	7,112	7,751

TABLE 9–15
MEASUREMENT OF EXPECTED CASH FLOW FROM SALE WITHOUT
REFINANCING

	Expected selling price (SP)	$675,000
minus	Selling expenses (SE)	$ 47,250
equals	Net sales proceeds (NSP)	$627,750
minus	Unpaid mortgage balance (UM)	$317,105
equals	Before-tax equity reversion (BTER)	$310,645
minus	Taxes due on sale (TDS)*	$ 76,497
equals	After-tax equity reversion (ATER)	$234,148

* See table 9–16.

TABLE 9–16
MEASUREMENT OF TAXABLE INCOME AND TAXES DUE ON SALE

Taxable Income		
	Expected selling price (SP)	$675,000
minus	Selling expenses (SE)	$ 47,250
equals	Amount realized (AR)	$627,750
minus	Adjusted basis (AB)	$354,545
equals	Capital gain on sale (CG)	$273,205

Taxes Due on Sale		
	Capital gain on sale (CG)	$273,205
times	Investor's marginal tax rate (τ)	0.28
equals	Taxes due on sale (TDS)	$ 76,497

ducting interest, depreciation, and amortized financing costs from NOI to
derive the taxable income. The taxable income is multiplied by the marginal tax rate to compute the taxes (or savings). Table 9–19 computes the
cash flow from sale in year 5 with refinancing. This is accomplished by deducting selling expenses, unpaid mortgage, and taxes due on sale (from
Table 9–16) from the selling price to arrive at the ATER. Notice that the
taxes due on sale are the same under both options.

DIFFERENTIAL CASH FLOWS

Table 9–20 computes the net proceeds from refinancing by subtracting the
origination fees and unpaid existing mortgage from the new loan amount.
This difference equals the net proceeds from refinancing of $101,572.

TABLE 9–17
MEASUREMENT OF EXPECTED CASH FLOW FROM OPERATIONS: WITH REFINANCING

		Years				
		1	2	3	4	5
	Net operating income (NOI)	$68,750	70,125	71,528	72,958	74,417
minus	Debt service (DS)	$63,441	63,441	63,441	63,441	63,441
equals	Before-tax cash flow (BTCF)	$ 5,309	6,684	8,087	9,517	10,976
minus	Taxes (savings) from operations (TO)*	(2,000)	(1,512)	(1,002)	(469)	(3,057)
equals	After-tax cash flow (ATCF)	$ 7,309	8,196	8,089	9,986	14,003

* See table 9–18.

TABLE 9–18
MEASUREMENT OF TAXABLE INCOME AND TAXES FROM OPERATIONS: WITH REFINANCING

		Years				
		1	2	3	4	5
	Net operating income (NOI)	$ 68,750	70,125	71,528	72,958	74,417
minus	Interest on debt (I)	$ 60,786	60,416	59,999	59,524	58,982
minus	Depreciation deduction (D)	$ 14,545	14,545	14,545	14,545	14,545
minus	Amortized financing costs (AFC)	$ 563	563	563	563	11,810
plus	Replacement reserves (RR)	$ 0	0	0	0	0
equals	Ordinary taxable income (OTI)	$(7,144)	(5,399)	(3,579)	(1,674)	(10,920)
times	Investor's marginal tax rate (τ)	0.28	0.28	0.28	0.28	0.28
equals	Taxes (savings) from operations (TO)	$ (2,000)	(1,512)	(1,002)	(469)	(3,057)

TABLE 9–19
MEASUREMENT OF EXPECTED CASH FLOW FROM SALE: IN YEAR 5
WITH REFINANCING

	Expected selling price (SP)	$675,000
minus	Selling expenses (SE)	$ 47,250
equals	Net sales proceeds (NSP)	$627,750
minus	Unpaid mortgage balance (UM)	$451,249
equals	Before-tax equity reversion (BTER)	$176,501
minus	Taxes due on sale (TDS)*	$ 76,497
equals	After-tax equity reversion (ATER)	$100,004

* See Table 9–16.

Table 9–21 illustrates the differential cash flows of refinancing versus not refinancing. The ATCF and ATER from not refinancing is deducted from the ATCF and ATER from refinancing to reach the differential. The year-0 differential (from Table 9.16) is the net proceeds from refinancing

TABLE 9–20
CASH INFLOW FROM REFINANCING

	New loan amount	$ 468,750
minus	Origination fees	$ −14,063
equals	Net new loan proceeds	$ 454,687
minus	Unpaid existing mortgage	$−353,115
equals	Net proceeds from refinancing	$ 101,572

TABLE 9–21
DIFFERENTIAL CASH FLOW OF REFINANCING VERSUS NOT REFINANCING

	With Refinancing		Without			Present-Value Factor at 15%	Present Value
Year	ATCF	ATER	ATCF	ATER	Differential		
0	$101,572*		0		$101,572	1.00000	$101,572
1	7,309		$22,495		−15,186	0.86957	−13,205
2	8,196		23,314		−15,118	0.75614	−11,431
3	8,089		24,134		−16,045	0.65752	−10,550
4	9,986		24,955		−14,969	0.57175	− 8,559
5	14,032	$100,004	25,775	$185,021	−96,760	0.49718	−48,107
					IRR = 11.96%	NPV =	$ 9,720

* This is the net proceeds from refinancing in Table 9–20.

($101,572). These differentials represent the net inflows from refinancing. In essence, the differential cash flow can be interpreted as follows: In year 0, the investor receives a net (after-tax) cash inflow of $101,572 from refinancing for which he must "pay" $15,186 in year 1, $15,118 in year 2, and so on.

NPV AND IRR FOR REFINANCING

Table 9–21 contains the computation of the NPV of refinancing at a 15 percent rate. The differential after-tax cash flows are multiplied by the appropriate present-value factors to find the present value. The sum of these present values is the net present value (+$9,720 in this case). This positive net present value indicates that the decision to refinance should be accepted. The IRR is found to be 11.96 percent, which can be interpreted as follows:

1. If the opportunity rate is greater than 11.96 percent, then refinance.
2. If the opportunity rate is less than 11.96 percent, then don't refinance.

SUMMARY

This chapter addresses the rewards and risks associated with substituting debt for equity when making a financing decision. It illustrates how various financing decisions affect the net present value of the investment, and describes what to evaluate when making a financing decision. The components that determine the "true" cost of borrowing and the ways in which financial leverage affects the financing decision are also discussed. In conclusion, we address some alternative financing decisions and methods, with an example analyzing the decision of whether or not to refinance a current investment.

QUESTIONS

9–1. Explain why investors use debt to finance real estate investments.

9–2. What is the debt coverage ratio and how is it used by lenders and investors?

9–3. What is the mortgage constant?

9–4. What are discount points? What impact do they have on the cost of borrowing? Explain.

9–5. What is the effect of early repayment of a mortgage if closing costs are zero? If closing costs are significant?

9–6. What is the necessary condition for leverage to be favorable? Unfavorable?

9–7. The overall required rate of return can be split into debt and equity components. Illustrate how the required rate of return on equity can be used to show the impact of financial leverage.

9–8. The text shows how the use of debt financing can increase both the expected return and the expected risk. Therefore, how can the investor determine if debt financing should be used and, if so, how much should be used when making the investment acquisition?

9–9. What are some of the other methods of financing real estate investments?

PROBLEMS

9–1. Using Equation (9–1), what happens to the mortgage constant if
  a. The interest rate increases? Decreases?
  b. The mortgage maturity increases? Decreases?
  c. Annual compounding is used instead of monthly compounding?

9–2. Using the following facts, set up the amortization schedule for years 1 through 5:

  Mortgage amount $1,250,000
  Interest rate   12.5 percent
  Maturity   20 years/monthly
                    compounding

9–3. A mortgage loan has the following terms:

  Amount $250,000
  Interest rate   12 percent
  Maturity   20 years with monthly
                  payments

  a. What is the monthly payment?
  b. Set up an amortization schedule for years 1 through 5.
  c. What is the effective yield if the loan is repaid after five years?
  d. How many "points" would the lender charge if the required yield was 12.5 percent?

e. Suppose the lender charged the points calculated in part d and the loan was repaid after five years. What is the effective borrowing cost?

f. Assume that in addition to the points, the lender also charged a prepayment penalty of 6 percent of the outstanding balance. What is the effective borrowing cost?

9–4. A lender makes a loan with the same facts as in Problem 9–3 except that the loan has a variable interest rate that adjusts at the end of each year. The interest rates are expected to be as follows:

Year	Rate
1	11.5%
2	12.0
3	13.0
4	12.5
5	11.5

a. Calculate the payment for each year.

b. Set up an amortization schedule for years 1 through 5.

9–5. Using the facts in Problem 9–2, calculate the effective borrowing cost under the following:

a. Financing cost of 4 percent of the mortgage amount and the loan is held to maturity.

b. Financing cost of 4 percent of the mortgage amount and the loan is prepaid after five years.

c. Same as part b, but there is also a prepayment penalty of 6 percent of the outstanding mortgage balance.

9–6. If the after-tax return on an investment is 8 percent, what is the effect of financial leverage in each of the following conditions?

a. Pretax cost of borrowing 10 percent; marginal tax rate is .30.

b. Pretax cost of borrowing 10 percent; marginal tax rate is .20.

c. Pretax cost of borrowing 12 percent; marginal tax rate is .20.

d. Pretax cost of borrowing 12 percent; marginal tax rate is .40.

e. Pretax cost of borrowing 15 percent; marginal tax rate is .40.

f. Pretax cost of borrowing 16 percent; marginal tax rate is .50.

9–7. Which loan for $30,000 has lower effective cost of borrowing: a loan at 10.5 percent monthly for 20 years or a loan at 11 percent monthly for 30 years? Which has the lower monthly debt service? Which loan would you prefer as an investor?

9–8. Consider an investment with a market value $30,000. How does the annual debt service using a 12 percent loan for 30 years fluctuate with a loan-to-value ratio of 50 percent? 75 percent? 90 percent?

9–9. A mortgage loan of $250,000 is made at the rate of 8 percent annually for 20 years.

a. What is the annual debt service?

b. What is the breakdown interest and principal for the first five years?

c. Suppose the lender wants to earn 9 percent. How much must the lender discount the loan?

d. What is the yield, assuming no early repayment with the discount in part c?

e. Suppose the loan is repaid after three years with a repayment penalty of 3.5 percent of the outstanding balance and the discount from part c. What is the yield to the lender?

SELECTED REFERENCES

Clauretie, Terrence M., and James R. Webb, *The Theory and Practice of Real Estate Finance*. Fort Worth, Tex.: The Dryden Press, 1993.

Gau, George W., and Ko Wang, "Capital Structure Decisions in Real Estate Investment," *American Real Estate and Urban Econom-*

ics Association Journal, 18 (Winter 1990), 501–521.

Gaumnitz, Jack E., "Leverage and the Rate of Return on Equity in Real Estate Investments: A Note," *Journal of Economics and Business*, 30 (Winter 1978), 155–157.

Jaffe, Austin J., and Kenneth M. Lusht, "Debt and Value: Issue and Analysis," *Real Estate Appraiser and Analyst*, 49 (Fall 1983), 5–18.

Lusht, Kenneth M., "A Note on the Favorability of Leverage," *Real Estate Appraiser*, 43 (May–June 1977), 41–44.

Lusht, Kenneth, and Robert H. Zerbst, "Valuing Income Property in an Inflationary Environment, *Real Estate Appraiser and Analyst*, 46 (July–August 1980), 11–17.

Sirmans, C. F., *Real Estate Finance*. 2nd ed., New York: McGraw-Hill, 1989.

CHAPTER 10

REVERSION DECISIONS

PRINCIPLES

1. Since real estate investors usually have planning horizons that are shorter than the economic life of the improvements on the property, there are a set of decisions involving the disposition of the property at the end of the investment.
2. The reversion can have a large impact on the success of any investment.
3. Using the technology from Chapter 3, there are several types of reversion decisions that can be evaluated.

In the previous chapters we examined the operating and financing decisions that investors must make in analyzing real estate investments. This chapter discusses the other major area of decisions—those involving the future disposition of an investment. One of the major sources of cash flow is that from future disposition.

To make the investment decision, the investor must make assumptions regarding the expected future value of an investment, how long the investor expects to hold the investment, what method of disposition is to be used, how much the taxes from disposition will be, and others. Thus, the expected future disposition influences the decision to invest today.

Reversion decisions must also be made after an investment has been acquired. For example, suppose an investor purchased an apartment building. The investor is constantly reevaluating whether to continue to own or not. The decision is further complicated by the fact that there are various alternative methods of disposition, such as sale, exchange, installment sale, and sale-leaseback. The real estate investor is obviously interested in making the choice that maximizes his or her wealth.

Impact of Reversion Decision on Investment Decision

Reversion decisions must be considered when making investment decisions. The assumptions made concerning property disposition are an integral part of the investment decision. The investor studies the market and from this analysis assesses the likely return on the investment not only from cash flows during the holding period but from disposition at the end of the holding period as well.

There are various methods of forecasting the probable sale price of the investment at the end of some holding period. One common method is to determine a growth rate and assume the investment will increase by that amount annually throughout the holding period. For example, Mr. X is considering purchasing an apartment building for $100,000. After thorough market analysis, he has determined an expected annual growth rate throughout the five-year period of 1.5 percent. If his expectations are correct, he will be able to sell the property for $100,000 \times (1 + .015)^5$, or $107,728.

Another method of forecasting expected sales price is to derive a market capitalization rate. The property value is determined using the following equation:

$$V = \frac{NOI}{R}$$

where:

V = market value

NOI = expected net operating income

R = capitalization rate

Assume that Mr. X expects net operating income to be $11,000 at the end of the holding period and has derived a market capitalization rate of 10 percent. The property value can be determined as follows:

$$V = \frac{\$11,000}{.10}$$

$$= \$110,000$$

Expected sales price can also be forecast using the market gross income multiplier (GIM). Property value is determined using the following equation:

$$V = EGI \times GIM \tag{10-1}$$

TABLE 10-1
IMPACT OF SALES PRICE ON IRR AND NPV

Sales Price	IRR	NPV	N
$115,000	10.55%	$2,828.95	7
110,000	10.05	263.16	7
105,000	9.53	−2,302.63	7

where:

$$V = \text{expected value}$$

$$EGI = \text{expected effective gross income}$$

$$GIM = \text{expected gross income multiplier}$$

If the expected effective gross income for Mr. X's property is $13,000 and the expected gross income multiplier is 8.5, then Mr. X should expect the value of the apartment building to be $13,000 × 8.5, or $110,500 at the end of the holding period.

Now assuming that Mr. X has forecast the expected sales price for the investment and has a required rate of return of 10 percent, what will happen to the NPV of the investment if the actual sales price varies from the forecast? For illustration purposes, assume that Mr. X has decided to purchase the apartment building for $100,000. Annual after-tax cash flows are expected to be $9,000. After analyzing the market, Mr. X reasonably expects to be able to sell the property for $110,000 (net) at the end of the seven-year holding period. Table 10–1 shows the impact of various sales prices on NPV. Note that if Mr. X were overly optimistic in his assumptions and had to sell the investment for only $5,000 less than expected, the NPV would be negative and the return would be less than 10 percent. On the other hand, though, if Mr. X can sell the apartment building for $5,000 more than he expects, the NPV will be $2,829.

In Table 10–1 we assumed that seven years was the optimal holding period for the investment. Could we increase (decrease) our returns by changing the holding period? Holding the sales price ($110,000) constant, what happens to the NPV and IRR if we dispose of the property at the end of five or nine years instead of seven? Table 10–2 illustrates how the return

TABLE 10-2
IMPACT OF HOLDING PERIOD ON IRR AND NPV

Sales Price	IRR	NPV	N
$110,000	10.62%	$2,418.43	5
110,000	10.05	263.16	7
110,000	9.74	−1,518.05	9

on investment is affected by the holding period. Note that Mr. X can increase his expected returns if he disposes of the property at the end of five years instead of seven.

Thus far we have looked at the impact of reversion decisions on investment decisions assuming *sale* of the property for some amount at the end of some holding period. We have looked at the effects of changes in these assumptions on our rate of return. What if instead of *selling* the property we were to choose some alternative method of disposition? How will this affect the rate of return? Some of the other methods of disposition are discussed in this chapter. Each of these methods involves different investment analysis. We will examine the decision-making implications of these alternatives.

SALE VERSUS CONTINUING TO OPERATE

An important decision facing the real estate investor is that of continuing to operate versus sale. In this section, we illustrate how to make this decision.

Consider a real estate investor (in a 28 percent tax bracket) who owns an apartment investment that was purchased five years ago for $500,000. The depreciable basis was $400,000. The investor has been using the straight-line method with a 27.5-year life. The investment was financed with a $375,000 fixed-rate mortgage at an interest rate of 10 percent with monthly payments for 25 years. The investor estimates that the current selling price is $625,000. Selling expenses would be 7 percent of the selling price.

The investor is trying to decide whether to sell or continue to operate for five more years. The NOI next year is expected to be $68,750 and is expected to increase 2 percent per year. The value of the investment is expected to be $675,000 at the end of this additional five years with selling expenses of 7 percent.

Which option should the investor select (to sell or continue to operate) if the required after-tax rate of return is 15 percent?

ATER FROM SALE TODAY

To determine whether to sell or continue to operate, the investor must first compute the after-tax cash flow from sale (or ATER) *now*. This is illustrated in Table 10–3 by subtracting the selling expenses, unpaid mortgage (from Table 10–4), and taxes (from Table 10–5) from the selling price. Table 10–4 is an amortization schedule for the loan that was originated *five years ago*. In other words, the amount outstanding today is the unpaid mortgage in year 5 of the loan ($353,115). Table 10–5 computes the taxes using the standard equations.

TABLE 10-3
EXPECTED CASH FLOW FROM SALE TODAY

	Expected selling price (SP)	$625,000
minus	Selling expenses (SE)	− 43,750
equals	Net sale proceeds (NSP)	581,250
minus	Unpaid mortgage balance (UM)	−353,115
equals	Before-tax equity reversion (BTER)	228,135
minus	Taxes due on sale (TDS)*	− 43,113
equals	After-tax equity reversion (ATER)	$185,022

*See Table 10–5.

CASH FLOWS FROM CONTINUING TO OPERATE

Tables 10–6 and 10–7 compute the after-tax cash flows and taxes from continuing to operate. Table 10–6 computes the after-tax flows (for years 1 through 5) by subtracting debt service and taxes (Table 10–7) from net operating income.

ATER FROM CONTINUING TO OPERATE

Table 10–8 computes the after-tax cash flow (ATER) from sale five years from now. The ATER is equal to the selling price, minus the selling expenses, unpaid mortgage ($317,104), and taxes (from Table 10–9).

TABLE 10-4
MORTGAGE AMORTIZATION SCHEDULE*

Year	Proportion Outstanding	Amount Outstanding	Debt Service	Interest	Principal
0	1.0	$375,000	—	—	—
1	.99053	371,449	$40,892	$37,341	$3,551
2	.98007	367,526	40,892	36,969	3,923
3	.96851	363,191	40,892	36,557	4,335
4	.95574	358,403	40,892	36,104	4,788
5	.94164	353,115	40,892	35,604	5,288
6	.92606	347,273	40,892	35,050	5,842
7	.90884	340,815	40,892	34,434	6,458
8	.88983	333,686	40,892	33,763	7,129
9	.86882	325,808	40,892	33,014	7,878
10	.84561	317,104	40,892	32,188	8,704

*$375,000 loan at 10% with 25-year maturity, monthly payments.

TABLE 10-5
EXPECTED TAXES DUE ON SALE TODAY

	Taxable Income	
	Expected selling price (SP)	$625,000
minus	Selling expenses (SE)	− 43,750
equals	Amount realized (AR)	581,250
minus	Adjusted basis (AB)	−427,275
equals	Total gain on sale (TG)	$153,975
	Taxes Due on Sale	
equals	Total gain on sale	153,975
times	Investor's marginal tax rate (τ)	× .28
equals	Taxes due on sale (TDS)	$ 43,113

TABLE 10-6
EXPECTED CASH FLOW FROM OPERATIONS

		Year				
		1	2	3	4	5
	Net operating income (NOI)	$68,750	$70,125	$71,528	$72,958	$74,417
minus	Debt service (DS)	−40,892	−40,892	−40,892	−40,892	−40,892
equals	Before-tax cash flow (BTCF)	27,858	29,233	30,636	32,066	33,525
minus	Taxes (savings) from operations (TO)*	− 5,363	− 5,921	− 6,502	− 7,112	− 7,752
equals	After-tax cash flow (ATCF)	$22,495	$23,312	$24,134	$24,954	$25,773

*See Table 10-7.

TABLE 10-7
EXPECTED TAXES FROM OPERATIONS

		Year				
		1	2	3	4	5
	Net operating income (NOI)	$68,750	$70,125	$71,528	$72,958	$74,417
minus	Interest on debt (I)	−35,050	−34,434	−33,763	−33,014	−32,188
minus	Depreciation deduction (D)	−14,545	−14,545	−14,545	−14,545	−14,545
minus	Amortized financing costs (AFC)	− 0	− 0	− 0	− 0	− 0
plus	Replacement reserves (RR)	+ 0	+ 0	+ 0	+ 0	+ 0
equals	Ordinary taxable income (OTI)	19,155	21,146	23,220	25,399	27,684
times	Investor's marginal tax rate (τ)	× .28	× .28	× .28	× .28	× .28
equals	Taxes (savings) from operations (TO)	$ 5,363	$ 5,921	$ 6,502	$ 7,112	$ 7,752

TABLE 10-8
EXPECTED CASH FLOW FROM SALE

	Expected selling price (SP)	$675,000
minus	Selling expenses (SE)	− 47,250
equals	Net sale proceeds (NSP)	627,750
minus	Unpaid mortgage balance (UM)	−317,104
equals	Before-tax equity reversion (BTER)	310,646
minus	Taxes due on sale (TDS)*	− 76,496
equals	After-tax equity reversion (ATER)	$234,150

*See Table 10-9.

TABLE 10-9
EXPECTED TAXES DUE ON SALE

Taxable Income

	Expected selling price (SP)	$675,000
minus	Selling expenses (SE)	− 47,250
equals	Amount realized (AR)	627,750
minus	Adjusted basis (AB)	−354,550
equals	Total gain on sale (TG)	$273,200

Taxes Due on Sale

equals	Total gain on sale (TG)	$273,200
times	Investor's marginal tax rate (τ)	× .28
equals	Taxes due on sale (TDS)	$ 76,496

DIFFERENTIAL CASH FLOWS

Table 10–10 illustrates the differential after-tax cash flows of continuing to operate versus selling. The cash flows from selling today are subtracted from the flows of continuing to operate to reach the differential flows. Note that the differential at year 0 is negative, which symbolizes the foregone flow from sale if the investor decides to continue to operate.

NPV AND IRR OF CONTINUING TO OPERATE

Table 10–11 illustrates the calculation of the NPV (at 15 percent) and the IRR of continuing to operate. This is done by multiplying the differential after-tax cash flows by present-value factors. The NPV is found to be a positive $11,590, which indicates continued operation. The IRR is calculated to be 16.75 percent, and with this information, we can formulate the decision criteria:

TABLE 10-10
DIFFERENTIAL AFTER-TAX CASH FLOWS OF CONTINUING TO OPERATE VERSUS SALE

Year	ATCF From Continue to Operate	ATCF From Sale Today	Differential Cash Flows
0	$ 0	$185,022	−$185,022
1	22,495	0	22,495
2	23,312	0	23,312
3	24,134	0	24,134
4	24,954	0	24,954
5	259,923	0	259,923

TABLE 10-11
NET PRESENT VALUE AND IRR OF CONTINUING TO OPERATE

Year	Differential After-Tax Cash Flow	Present-Value Factor at 15%	Present Value
0	$(185,022)	1.0	$(185,022)
1	22,495	.86957	19,561
2	23,312	.75614	17,627
3	24,134	.65752	15,869
4	24,954	.57175	14,267
5	259,923	.49718	129,228
	IRR = 16.75%	Net Present Value =	$11,590

1. If the required rate is less than 16.75 percent, then continue to operate.

2. If the required rate is greater than 16.75 percent, then sell (do not continue to operate).

The *required rate* to which we refer here is merely that rate of return an investor can receive on an alternative investment of equal risk. Since the NPV in this case is positive, the investor can conclude that continuing to operate is the best option, since the present value of the inflows from operating exceed the present value of the outflows from not selling.

INSTALLMENT SALE VERSUS OUTRIGHT SALE

An *installment sale* is the sale of property in which the buyer agrees to pay the seller in a number of installments rather than in a lump sum at the time of purchase.

To understand how an installment sale works, consider the following example: A real estate investor (in the 28 percent marginal tax bracket) is considering the installment sale of a small apartment building. This complex was purchased eight years ago at a total price of $124,000. The investor's depreciable basis was 85 percent of total cost. The straight-line method of depreciation has been used with a recovery life of 27.5 years. The investment was financed with a 12 percent mortgage of $112,500, with monthly payments for 25 years.

The installment sale offer that the investor is considering is as follows: a sales price of $250,000 with the buyer assuming a balance of $102,924 of the existing mortgage, making a cash down payment of $37,076, and the seller taking a purchase-money mortgage of $110,000 for the remainder at 13 percent interest and annual payments over 15 years, with a balloon payment for the balance at the end of year 5. The annual payment will be $17,022. Table 10–12 gives the amortization schedule for this purchase money mortgage. The selling expenses are $12,500.

Alternatively, the investor could sell the investment outright for a price of $250,000 with selling expenses of 5 percent of the selling price. At a required rate of return of 12 percent, which is the better offer: installment or outright sale?

ATCF IN YEAR OF INSTALLMENT SALE

Table 10–13 shows the after-tax cash flow in the year of installment sale. This is computed by subtracting the selling expenses and the taxes (see Table 10–14) from the amount of the down payment. Table 10–14 computes the taxes in the year of installment sale by deriving the taxable gain using the profit percentage (from Table 10–15) and multiplying this gain by the investor's marginal tax rate. Table 10–15 computes the profit percentage by dividing the total gain (selling price minus selling expenses and the adjusted basis) by the contract price (sale price plus the excess mortgage over basis and selling expenses minus the assumed mortgage balance).

TABLE 10–12
MORTGAGE AMORTIZATION SCHEDULE PURCHASE-MONEY MORTGAGE

Year	Amount Outstanding	Debt Service	Interest	Principal
0	$110,000	—	—	—
1	107,278	$17,022	$14,300	$2,722
2	104,202	17,022	13,946	3,076
3	100,726	17,022	13,546	3,476
4	96,798	17,022	13,094	3,928
5	92,360	17,022	12,584	4,438

TABLE 10–13
AFTER-TAX CASH FLOW IN YEAR OF INSTALLMENT SALE

	Down payment	$37,076
minus	Selling expenses	−12,500
minus	Taxes*	−10,174
equals	ATCF	$14,402

*See Table 10–14.

TABLE 10–14
TAX IN YEAR OF INSTALLMENT SALE

	Taxable Income	
	Excess of mortgage over adjusted basis and selling expenses	$0
plus	Down payment	+37,076
equals	Payment in year of sale	37,076
times	Profit percentage*	× .98
equals	Taxable portion of principal	36,334

	Tax:	
	Taxable income	36,334
times	Tax rate	× .28
equals	Tax	$10,174

*See Table 10–15.

ATCF FROM INSTALLMENT RECEIPTS

Table 10–16 computes the after-tax cash flow from the installment receipts for years 1 through 5. This after-tax cash flow is simply the before-tax cash flow (or debt service) plus the balloon payment (in year 5), minus the taxes from Table 10–17.

Table 10–17 computes the taxes required to calculate the ATCF from installment receipts. The first step in this computation is to derive the total principal by adding the amount of principal payment (Table 10–12) each year and any balloon payment (Table 10–12). This total is multiplied by the profit percentage (Table 10–15) to derive the taxable income. The tax is the taxable income times the investor's marginal tax rate.

ATER FROM OUTRIGHT SALE

Tables 10–18 and 10–19 are needed to compare an outright sale with the installment sale. This is done by first computing the after-tax equity re-

TABLE 10–15
PROFIT PERCENTAGE ON INSTALLMENT SALE

Total Gain

	Sale price	$250,000
minus	Selling expense	− 12,500
minus	Adjusted basis	− 93,336
equals	Total gain	$144,164

Contract Price

	Sale price	$250,000
plus	Excess mortgage over basis and selling expenses	+ 0
minus	Mortgage balance assumed	−102,924
equals	Contract price	$147,076

Profit Percentage

	Total gain	$144,164
divided by	Contract price	÷147,076
equals	Profit percentage	98%

TABLE 10–16
AFTER-TAX CASH FLOW FROM INSTALLMENT RECEIPTS

				Year		
		1	2	3	4	5
	BTCF (debt service)	$17,022	$17,022	$17,022	$17,022	$17,022
plus	Balloon payment	0	0	0	0	92,360
minus	Tax*	4,751	4,749	4,747	4,744	30,085
equals	ATCF	$12,271	$12,273	$12,275	$12,278	$79,297

*See Table 10–17.

version from the outright sale (selling price, $250,000). The after-tax equity reversion (Table 10–18) is selling price less selling expenses, unpaid mortgage, and taxes due on sale (Table 10–19).

DIFFERENTIAL CASH FLOWS

Table 10–20 computes the differential after-tax cash flows of installment sale versus outright sale. This differential is simply the installment sale cash flows minus the outright sale cash flow (for each year). Note that at year 0, the differential is a negative because with the installment sale, the investor loses the net of the outright-sale proceeds and the installment-sale proceeds.

TABLE 10–17
TAX DUE ON INSTALLMENT RECEIPTS

		Taxable Income				
	Principal portion*	$ 2,722	$ 3,076	$ 3,476	$ 3,927	$ 4,438
plus	Balloon payment*	0	0	0	0	92,360
equals	Total principal	2,722	3,076	3,476	3,927	96,798
times	Profit percentage†	× .98	× .98	× .98	× .98	× .98
equals	Profit	2,668	3,014	3,406	3,848	94,862
plus	Interest*	+14,300	+13,946	+13,546	+13,094	+12,584
equals	Taxable income	16,968	16,960	16,952	16,942	107,446
times	Tax rate	× .28	× .28	× .28	× .28	× .28
equals	Tax	$ 4,751	$ 4,749	$ 4,747	$ 4,744	$ 30,085

*See Table 10–12 for the mortgage amortization schedule.
†See Table 10–15 for the profit percentage.

TABLE 10–18
EXPECTED CASH FLOW FROM SALE

	Expected selling price (SP)	$250,000
minus	Selling expenses (SE)	− 12,500
equals	Net sale proceeds (NSP)	237,500
minus	Unpaid mortgage balance (UM)	−102,924
equals	Before-tax equity reversion (BTER)	−134,576
minus	Taxes due on sale (TDS)*	− 40,366
equals	After-tax equity reversion (ATER)	$ 94,210

*See Table 10–19.

TABLE 10–19
EXPECTED TAXES DUE ON SALE

	Taxable Income	
	Expected selling price (SP)	$250,000
minus	Selling expenses (SE)	− 12,500
equals	Amount realized (AR)	237,500
minus	Adjusted basis (AB)	− 93,336
equals	Total income on sale (TG)	144,164
	Taxes Due on Sale	
equals	Taxable income from sale (TIS)	144,164
times	Investor's marginal tax rate (τ)	× .28
equals	Taxes due on sale (TDS)	$ 40,366

TABLE 10–20

DIFFERENTIAL AFTER-TAX CASH FLOW OF INSTALLMENT SALE
VERSUS OUTRIGHT SALE

Year	Installment Sale Cash Flow	Outright Sale Cash Flow	Differential
0	$14,402	$94,210	$(79,808)
1	12,271	0	12,271
2	12,273	0	12,273
3	12,275	0	12,275
4	12,278	0	12,278
5	79,297	0	79,297

NPV AND IRR OF INSTALLMENT SALE

Table 10–21 calculates the NPV and IRR of the installment sale versus the outright sale. The NPV, $2,468, is calculated by multiplying the differential flows (from Table 10–20) by their respective present-value factors at the 12 percent required rate of return. Thus, given the 12 percent required rate, since the NPV is positive, the investor should pursue the installment sale but should not sell outright. The IRR is computed to be 12.90 percent. From this we conclude:

1. If the required rate is less than 12.90 percent, then select the installment sale.

2. If the required rate is greater than or equal to 12.90 percent, then select the outright sale.

TABLE 10–21
NET PRESENT VALUE AND IRR OF INSTALLMENT SALE
VERSUS OUTRIGHT SALE

Year	Differential After-Tax Cash Flow	Present-Value Factor at 12%	Present Value
0	$(79,808)	1.0	$(79,808)
1	12,271	.892857	10,956
2	12,274	.797194	9,785
3	12,275	.711780	8,737
4	12,278	.635518	7,803
5	79,297	.567427	44,995
	IRR = 12.90%	Net Present Value =	$2,468

Comparing Installment-Sale Offers

In the preceding example, since the required rate of return was 12 percent and the return on the investment was only 12.90 percent (see Table 10–21), the installment was preferable. What happens, though, if the terms of sale are changed? The investor can change the sales price. The down payment can increase, decrease, or remain the same. The purchase-money mortgage terms can be altered. As well as changing the amount of the purchase-money mortgage, the interest rate and payout period can change. The terms of the loan can be longer or shorter. Payments can be made monthly instead of annually. The balloon payment or mortgage balance can become due after a shorter or longer period of time. The investor's tax rate can change. The required rate of return can increase or decrease. It is necessary to analyze the effect any of these changes would have on the investment decision. For illustration purposes, continuing with the same installment-versus-outright-sale example, let us analyze what would happen, holding all other variables constant, if the installment-sale price was changed to $235,000 from $250,000.

ATCF in Year of Installment Sale

Table 10–22 shows the after-tax cash flow in the year of installment sale. Note that this amount ($3,518) differs from the amount in the original example ($14,402) by $10,884. Table 10–23 computes the taxes in the year of installment sale.

ATCF from Installment Receipts

Since the purchase-money mortgage amount remains the same ($110,000), the after-tax cash flow from the installment receipts for years 1 through 5 will not change (see Table 10–16).

TABLE 10–22
AFTER-TAX CASH FLOW IN YEAR OF
INSTALLMENT SALE

	Down payment	$22,076
minus	Selling expenses	−12,500
minus	Taxes*	− 6,058
equals	ATCF	$ 3,518

*See Table 10–23.

TABLE 10–23
TAX IN YEAR OF INSTALLMENT SALE

	Taxable Income	
	Excess of mortgage over adjusted basis and selling expenses	$ 0
plus	Down payment	+22,076
equals	Payment in year of sale	22,076
times	Profit percentage	× .98
equals	Taxable portion of principal	21,634

	Tax	
equals	Taxable income	21,634
times	Tax rate	× .28
equals	Tax	$ 6,058

ATER FROM OUTRIGHT SALE

Tables 10–24 and 10–25 are necessary to compare the outright sale with the installment sale. The after-tax equity reversion is the same as the original example since the terms of the outright sale remain the same.

DIFFERENTIAL CASH FLOWS

The differential after-tax cash flow of installment sale versus outright sale is computed in Table 10–26.

NPV AND IRR OF INSTALLMENT SALE

Table 10–27 calculates the NPV and IRR of the installment sale versus the outright sale. The NPV is $(8,417). Thus, given a 12 percent required rate, since the NPV is negative the investor should pursue that outright sale. The

TABLE 10–24
EXPECTED CASH FLOW FROM SALE

	Expected selling price (SP)	$250,000
minus	Selling expenses (SE)	− 12,500
equals	Net sale proceeds (NSP)	237,500
minus	Unpaid mortgage balance (UM)	−102,924
equals	Before-tax equity reversion (BTER)	134,576
minus	Taxes due on sale (TDS)*	− 40,366
equals	After-tax equity reversion (ATER)	$ 94,210

*See Table 10–25.

TABLE 10–25
EXPECTED TAXES DUE ON SALE

	Taxable Income	
	Expected selling price (SP)	$250,000
minus	Selling expenses (SE)	− 12,500
equals	Amount realized (AR)	237,500
minus	Adjusted basis (AB)	− 93,336
equals	Total income on sale (TG)	144,164

	Taxes Due on Sale	
equals	Taxable income from sale (TIS)	144,164
times	Investor's marginal tax rate (τ)	× .28
equals	Taxes due on sale (TDS)	$ 40,336

TABLE 10–26
DIFFERENTIAL AFTER-TAX CASH FLOW OF INSTALLMENT SALE VERSUS OUTRIGHT SALE

Year	*Installment Sale Cash Flow*	*Outright Sale Cash Flow*	*Differential*
0	$ 3,518	$94,210	$(90,692)
1	12,271	0	12,271
2	12,273	0	12,273
3	12,275	0	12,275
4	12,278	0	12,278
5	79,297	0	79,297

TABLE 10–27
NET PRESENT VALUE AND IRR OF INSTALLMENT SALE VERSUS OUTRIGHT SALE

Year	*Differential After-Tax Cash Flow*	*Present-Value Factor at 12%*	*Present Value*
0	$(90,692)	1.0	$(90,692)
1	12,271	.892857	10,956
2	12,273	.797194	9,784
3	12,275	.711780	8,737
4	12,278	.635518	7,803
5	79,297	.567427	44,995
	IRR = 9.19%	Net Present Value = $(8,417)	

IRR is computed to be 9.19 percent. The investor should change the terms of the agreement such that his or her required rate of return is satisfied.

Tax Deferred Exchange

The tax-deferred exchange is another method of property disposition. The importance of this method is indicated in Section 1031 of the Internal Revenue Code, which provides an exception to the requirement of recognition of gain or loss upon sale or exchange of property. According to this section, no gain or loss is recognized if the property held for productive use in a trade or business or for an investment is *exchanged solely for property of a like kind* to be held for productive use in a trade or business or for investment. The application of the section for deferring the taxes due on the disposition of a real estate investment is referred to as the *deferred exchange*. There are two basic motivations for exchanging real estate rather than selling it and reinvesting the proceeds. One is that the exchange is attractive as a method of marketing real estate when a sale does not appear possible. The other motivation is the availability of income-tax deferral.

To illustrate an exchange, the following steps are used:

Step 1: Balance equity positions.

Step 2: Calculate the realized gain in an exchange.

Step 3: Calculate the recognized gain in an exchange.

Step 4: Identify the taxable gain.

Step 5: Calculate the ATCF and equity position after exchange.

To illustrate these concepts, assume that a two-party exchange is being considered by Mr. Dunn and Mr. Roe. Mr. Dunn owns an apartment building with a market value of $660,000 and an outstanding mortgage of $240,000. The adjusted basis of the property is $300,000. Mr. Roe owns an office building with a market value of $750,000 and an outstanding mortgage debt of $450,000. The adjusted basis of the property is $525,000.

Mr. Dunn and Mr. Roe have decided to exchange their investments. Mr. Dunn's transaction costs are $49,500, while Mr. Roe's are $57,000. This includes brokerage fees, legal fees, appraisal fees, and other costs of the exchange. The differences in equities will be balanced by cash.

BALANCING EQUITY POSITIONS

The alternatives for balancing the equities in an exchange include the following:

1. Add cash to investor with lower equity.
2. Add note and mortgage to investor with lower equity.
3. Refinance the property with the higher equity.
4. Add another like-kind investment.
5. Add unlike-kind property (bonds, stocks, and so on).
6. Investor with least equity could pay down the outstanding mortgage, thus increasing equity.
7. Any combination of the above that is acceptable and meets the objectives of each party.

Tables 10–28 and 10–29 explain the method of balancing the equities. The first table lists the pertinent data on each property. The second table computes the equity for both parties by deducting the mortgage debt from the market value. The net equity position is then computed for both parties by

TABLE 10–28
EXCHANGE PROPERTY DATA

Property 1	Mr. Dunn's Property
Market value	$660,000
Mortgage debt	240,000
Adjusted basis	300,000
Transaction costs	49,500

Property 2	Mr. Roe's Property
Market value	$750,000
Mortgage debt	450,000
Adjusted basis	525,000
Transaction costs	57,000

TABLE 10–29
BALANCE EQUITIES ON EXCHANGE

	Mr. Dunn's Equity	
	Market value	$660,000
minus	Mortgage debt	−240,000
equals	Equity	$420,000

	Mr. Roe's Equity	
	Market value	$750,000
minus	Mortgage debt	−450,000
equals	Equity	$300,000

	Net Equity Position	

Mr. Roe owes Mr. Dunn the difference in equity of $120,000, to be paid in cash:

		Mr. Dunn	Mr. Roe
	Equity given	$420,000	$300,000
minus	Equity received	−300,000	−420,000
equals	Net equity	$120,000	$(120,000)

subtracting the equity received from the equity given. Note that Mr. Roe owes Mr. Dunn $120,000.

CALCULATION OF REALIZED GAIN

Table 10–30 shows how to calculate the realized gain. The realized gain is the gain that the investor would have had if the property had been sold

TABLE 10–30
REALIZED GAIN ON EXCHANGE

	Mr. Dunn's Realized Gain	
	Market value	$660,000
minus	Adjusted basis	−300,000
minus	Transaction costs	− 49,500
equals	Realized gain	$310,500

	Mr. Roe's Realized Gain	
	Market value	$750,000
minus	Adjusted basis	−525,000
minus	Transaction costs	− 57,000
equals	Realized gain	$168,000

rather than exchanged. It is the market value minus the adjusted basis and the transactions costs. The realized gain is computed in Table 10–30 for both parties.

CALCULATION OF RECOGNIZED GAIN

The recognized gain and taxable gain are calculated in Table 10–31 by subtracting the boot (or cash) given and the transactions costs, and adding the net loan relief to (or from) the boot (or cash) received. The net mortgage re-

TABLE 10–31
RECOGNIZED GAIN ON EXCHANGE*

	Mr. Dunn's Recognized Gain	
	Boot (or cash) received	$120,000
minus	Boot (or cash) given	− 0
plus	Net loan relief	+ 0
minus	Transaction cost	− 49,500
equals	Recognized gain	$ 70,500

	Mr. Roe's Recognized Gain	
equals	Boot (or cash) received	$ 0
minus	Boot (or cash) given	−120,000
plus	Net loan relief	+210,000
minus	Transaction costs	− 57,000
equals	Recognized gain	$ 33,000

*The recognized gain is the taxable gain because it is less than the realized gain.

lief is considered unlike property only to the extent that the difference between the two mortgage balances is positive. Thus there is no "negative" net mortgage relief. *The investor pays tax on the lower of the recognized gain or the realized gain.*

ATCF AND POSITION AFTER EXCHANGE

The ATCF is computed in Table 10–32. Mr. Dunn receives a positive cash flow of $50,760 while Mr. Roe pays out $186,240. Table 10–33 shows the amount of taxes both investors owe as a result of the exchange.

The equity positions after the exchange are shown in Table 10–34. Mr. Dunn received an office building with a market value of $750,000, with equity of $300,000, and an after-tax cash inflow from the exchange of $50,760. Thus, his new equity position is $350,760 after the exchange. Mr. Dunn has deferred taxes on the unrecognized gain (the realized gain minus the recognized gain). Had the investment been sold outright, Mr. Dunn would have had to pay tax on the total recognized gain of $310,500.

Also after the exchange, Mr. Dunn's adjusted basis has risen from $300,000 to $510,000. This adjusted basis would be allocated to the land and building; since Mr. Dunn's adjusted basis has increased, he will have a larger depreciation deduction after the exchange, thus generating more tax shelter. The new adjusted basis is the value of property received plus taxable gain minus realized gain.

TABLE 10–32
AFTER-TAX CASH FLOW FROM EXCHANGE

		Investor	
		Mr. Dunn	Mr. Roe
	Cash outflow	0	−$120,000
minus	Transaction costs	− 49,500	− 57,000
plus	Cash inflows	+120,000	+ 0
minus	Tax on gain 28% bracket*	− 19,740	− 9,240
equals	After-tax cash flow (ATCF)	$ 50,760	−$186,240

*See Table 10–33.

TABLE 10–33
TAXES DUE ON EXCHANGE

		Mr. Dunn	Mr. Roe
	Taxable gain	$70,500	$33,000
times	Marginal income tax rate	× .28	× .28
equals	Tax on gain	$19,740	$ 9,240

Mr. Roe has acquired an apartment building from the exchange with a market value of $660,000, with equity of $420,000. His original equity position in the office building was $300,000. His new equity position is shown in Table 10–34.

SALE-LEASEBACK

Another method of property disposition is the *sale-leaseback*. This is an arrangement under which a property owner sells the property and simultaneously takes back a lease. The terms of such a lease are generally written to the requirements of the parties involved. The lease is typically for a number of years, with renewal options. The rental payments are typically sufficient to amortize the price of the property over the term of the lease and yield a desired rate of return to the investor.

To illustrate, assume that as a real estate developer, you have just been approached by a representative of Dixieland Incorporated (DI), a na-

TABLE 10-34
EQUITY POSITION AFTER EXCHANGE

| | | Investor | |
		Mr. Dunn	Mr. Roe
	Market value of property given	$660,000	$750,000
minus	Mortgage debt	−240,000	−450,000
equals	Original equity	$420,000	$300,000
minus	Transaction: costs	− 49,500	− 57,000
minus	Taxes on recognized gain	− 19,740	− 9,240
plus	Cash given	0	+120,000
equals	New equity position	$350,760	$353,760

tional convenience store chain, about constructing a Dixieland convenience store. DI has purchased a site for $30,000, will construct the store at a cost of $60,000, and desires to sell the land and its improvements to you for $100,000. So, under the terms set forth in a fifteen-year lease, you will lease the property to DI for $17,000 per annum. DI will pay all costs related to maintaining the store, but you must pay the $2,000 per annum property taxes and you retain ownership of the land and building at the end of the 15 years. You estimate that at the end of year 15, the building and the land will be worth $105,000. Selling expenses at that time will be $7,000. You have decided to use the straight-line depreciation method with a zero salvage value, and the useful life is 39 years. The current value (for depreciation purposes) of the building is $60,000. Your tax rate is currently 28 percent and you plan to finance with your own equity (100 percent) and desire a 10 percent after-tax rate of return. Should you accept DI's offer?

ATCF FROM LEASE

The first step in solving this problem is to determine the annual cash flows to the lessor (buyer). These cash flows are computed in Table 10–35 by subtracting the debt service (0) and operating expenses ($2,000) from the lease revenues ($17,000) to obtain the before-tax cash flows ($15,000). The after-tax cash flows ($11,231) are found by subtracting the taxes (Table 10–36) from the before-tax cash flows. The taxes are computed by deducting depreciation and interest expenses from the NOI and then multiplying this figure (taxable income of $13,462) by the investor's tax rate (28 percent). The annual cash flows are $11,231 for fifteen years.

ATER FROM SALE

The second step (Table 10–37) is to compute the after-tax equity reversion from the sale in year 15. This figure is found to be $92,100 by deducting

TABLE 10-35
EXPECTED CASH FLOW FROM OPERATIONS

	Effective gross income (EGI)	$17,000
minus	Operating expenses (OE)	− 2,000
equals	Net operating income (NOI)	15,000
minus	Debt service (DS)	− 0
equals	Before-tax cash flow (BTCF)	15,000
minus	Taxes (savings) from operations (TO)*	− 3,769
equals	After-tax cash flow (ATCF)	$11,231

*See Table 10–36.

TABLE 10-36
EXPECTED TAXES FROM OPERATIONS

	Effective gross income (EGI)	$17,000
minus	Operating expenses (OE)	− 2,000
equals	Net operating income (NOI)	15,000
minus	Interest on debt (I)	− 0
minus	Depreciation deduction (D)	− 1,538
minus	Amortized financing costs (AFC)	− 0
plus	Replacement reserves (RR)	+ 0
equals	Ordinary taxable income (OTI)	13,462
times	Investor's marginal tax rate (τ)	× .28
equals	Taxes (savings) from operations (TO)	$ 3,769

TABLE 10-37
EXPECTED CASH FLOW TO DEVELOPER FROM SALE IN YEAR 15

	Expected selling price (SP)	$105,000
minus	Selling expenses (SE)	− 7,000
equals	Net sales proceeds (NSP)	98,000
minus	Unpaid mortgage balance (UM)	− 0
equals	Before-tax equity reversion (BTER)	− 98,000
minus	Taxes due on sale (TDS)*	− 5,900
equals	After-tax equity reversion (ATER)	$ 92,100

*See Table 10–38.

selling expenses, the unpaid mortgage, and taxes of $5,900 (from Table 10–38) from the selling price of $105,000. Table 10–38 computes the taxes due on sale by deducting the selling expenses and adjusted basis from the selling price to calculate the total gain. The total gain ($21,070) is then taxed at the investor's marginal tax rate (28 percent) to yield the taxes ($5,900).

TABLE 10–38
EXPECTED TAXES DUE ON SALE

	Taxable Income	
	Expected selling price (SP)	$105,000
minus	Selling expenses (SE)	− 7,000
equals	Amount realized (AR)	98,000
minus	Adjusted basis (AB)	− 76,930
equals	Total gain on sale (TG)	$ 21,070

	Taxes Due on Sale	
	Total gain on sale (TG)	21,070
times	Investor's marginal tax rate (τ)	× .28
equals	Taxes due on sale (TDS)	$ 5,900

NPV AND IRR OF SALE AND LEASEBACK

In the third step (Table 10–39), the net present value is computed by subtracting the present value of the investment from the sum of the present value of the cash flows and reversion. If this figure is negative, then a reject decision is made, and the reverse is true if it is positive. In this project,

TABLE 10–39
NPV AND IRR OF SALE AND LEASEBACK

Year	Equity (E)	After-Tax Cash Flow (ATCF)	After-Tax Equity Reversion (ATER)	Present-Value Factor at 10%	Present Value
0	−$100,000			1.0	−$100,000
1		$11,231		.90909	10,210
2		11,231		.82645	9,282
3		11,231		.75132	8,438
4		11,231		.68301	7,671
5		11,231		.62092	6,974
6		11,231		.56447	6,340
7		11,231		.51316	5,763
8		11,231		.46651	5,239
9		11,231		.42410	4,763
10		11,231		.38554	4,330
11		11,231		.35049	3,936
12		11,231		.31863	3,579
13		11,231		.28966	3,253
14		11,231		.26333	2,957
15		11,231	$92,100	.23939	24,736
			IRR = 11.00%	NPV =	+ $ 7,472

the NPV was positive, so the developer accepted the project. If the annual lease revenue had been negotiated at a lower amount, one might have rejected the project (since this may have made the NPV negative). The IRR turned out to be 11.00 percent, which is above the required 10 percent, and further substantiates that the decision to buy and lease back is worthwhile.

SALE-LEASEBACK VERSUS CONTINUING AS IS

Continuing with the previous sale-leaseback example, assume that Dixieland Incorporated *also* has the option to build the convenience store, occupy it for 15 years, and then sell it. Construction costs will not change. DI will use straight-line depreciation with a zero salvage value, and the useful life is 39 years. The basis is $60,000. DI's tax rate is 28 percent. DI plans to finance with its own equity (100 percent) and requires a 10 percent after-tax rate of return. Should DI sell and lease back the property or retain ownership for 15 years?

ATER FROM SALE TODAY

The first step in solving this problem is to determine the cash flow that DI receives for disposition of the property in year 0. DI sells the property at a $10,000 pretax gain ($100,000 − $90,000). The gain is taxed as ordinary income at the investor's 28 percent rate. The after-tax proceeds from sale are, therefore, $10,000 × .72, or $7,200.

ATCF FROM LEASE

The second step is to compute the annual cash flows to DI from the lease. DI leases the property for $17,000 per annum. The annual ATCF from the lease is calculated by multiplying the lease expense ($17,000) by one minus the tax rate (1 − .28), which amounts to $12,240 per year.

ATCF FROM CONTINUING TO OPERATE

The third step (see Table 10–40) is to compute the ATCF from retaining ownership and continuing to operate for 15 years. The cash flow in year 0 for the construction of the building is − $90,000. The cash flows in years 1 through 15 (Table 10–44) are computed by adding the property tax expense ($2,000) to the depreciation deduction ($1,538) and multiplying by the investor's marginal tax rate (.28) (see Table 10–41).

TABLE 10–40
EXPECTED CASH FLOW FROM OPERATIONS

TABLE 10–40
EXPECTED CASH FLOW FROM OPERATIONS

	Effective gross income (EGI)	$ 0
minus	Operating expenses (OE)	− 2,000
equals	Net operating income (NOI)	(2,000)
minus	Debt service (DS)	− 0
equals	Before-tax cash flow (BTCF)	(2,000)
minus	Taxes (savings) from operation (TO)*	−(991)
equals	After-tax cash flow (ATCF)	$ (1,009)

*See Table 10–41.

TABLE 10–41
EXPECTED TAXES FROM OPERATIONS

	Effective gross income (EGI)	$0
minus	Operating expenses (OE)	−2,000
equals	Net operating income (NOI)	(2,000)
minus	Interest on debt (I)	− 0
minus	Depreciation deduction (D)	−1,538
minus	Amortized financing costs	− 0
plus	Replacement reserves (RR)	+ 0
equals	Ordinary taxable income (OTI)	(3,538)
times	Investor's marginal tax rate (τ)	× .28
equals	Taxes (savings) from operations (TO)	$(991)

ATER FROM DISPOSITION IN YEAR 15

The fourth step is to compute the after-tax equity reversion to DI from the sale in 15 years. This is found to be $89,300 by deducting the selling expenses, the unpaid mortgage, and taxes from the selling price (this is calculated in Tables 10–42, and 10–43). Note that the only difference between

TABLE 10–42
EXPECTED CASH FLOW TO DI FROM SALE IN YEAR 15

	Expected selling price (SP)	$105,000
minus	Selling Expenses (SE)	− 7,000
equals	Net sales proceeds (NSP)	98,000
minus	Unpaid Mortgage balance (UM)	− 0
equals	Before-tax equity reversion (BTER)	98,000
minus	Taxes due on sale (TDS)*	8,700
equals	After-tax equity reversion (ATER)	89,300

*See Table 10–43

TABLE 10–43
EXPECTED TAXES DUE ON SALE IN YEAR 15

		Taxable Income
	Expected Selling Price (SP)	$105,000
minus	Selling expenses (SP)	− 7,000
equals	Amount realized (AR)	98,000
minus	Adjusted basis (AB)	− 66,930
equals	Total gain on sale (TG)	31,070

		Taxes Due on Sale
	Total gain on sale (TG)	31,070
equals	Investor's marginal tax rate (t)	× .28
equals	Taxes due on sale (TDS)	8,700

TABLE 10–44
NPV AND IRR OF SALE-LEASEBACK VERSUS CONTINUING TO OPERATE

Year	Sale-Lease	Occupy-Sale	Differential	Present Value Factor at 10% (PVF)	Present Value
0	$ 7,200	$(90,000)	$97,200	1.0	$97,200
1	(12,240)	(1,009)	(11,231)	.90909	(10,210)
2	(12,240)	(1,009)	(11,231)	.82645	(9,282)
3	(12,240)	(1,009)	(11,231)	.75132	(8,438)
4	(12,240)	(1,009)	(11,231)	.68301	(7,671)
5	(12,240)	(1,009)	(11,231)	.62092	(6,974)
6	(12,240)	(1,009)	(11,231)	.56447	(6,340)
7	(12,240)	(1,009)	(11,231)	.51316	(5,763)
8	(12,240)	(1,009)	(11,231)	.46651	(5,239)
9	(12,240)	(1,009)	(11,231)	.42410	(4,763)
10	(12,240)	(1,009)	(11,231)	.38554	(4,330)
11	(12,240)	(1,009)	(11,231)	.35049	(3,936)
12	(12,240)	(1,009)	(11,231)	.31863	(3,579)
13	(12,240)	(1,009)	(11,231)	.28966	(3,253)
14	(12,240)	(1,009)	(11,231)	.26333	(2,957)
15	(12,240)	88,291*	(100,531)	.23939	(24,066)
			IRR = 11.32%		NPV = $(9,601)

*This is equal to the ATER ($89,300) less the cash outflow ($1,009) for DI in year 15.

this and the ATER calculated for the developer is that the adjusted basis is lower for DI since their original basis was $90,000 compared to the developer's original basis of $100,000.

NPV and IRR of Sale-Leaseback versus Continuing to Operate Differential

The final step (Table 10–44) is to compute the net present value (at 10 percent) of the differential cash flows. The cash flows from continuing to operate are subtracted from the flows from the sale-leaseback to reach the differential after-tax cash flows, which are multiplied by present-value factors to compute NPV. The NPV is found to be − $9,601. Thus, given the 10 percent required rate, since the NPV is negative, the investor should not continue to operate and should not sell and lease back.

Summary

This chapter examined the reversion decisions that the real estate investor must make. Reversion decisions deal with future expectations of an investment's value, such as when to dispose of an investment, how much the property is expected to increase or decrease in value over the holding period, and which method of disposition to choose. All of these decisions are made by calculating the net present value (or internal rate of return).

In the next part we explore in more detail the various investment criteria for investment decisions and the risk associated with real estate investments.

Questions

10–1. How does the reversion affect the investment decision?

10–2. The discussion in the chapter demonstrates that investment analysis continues after the property has been purchased, since the investor must constantly decide whether to sell the property or continue to hold it. How does the after-tax equity reversion affect the investor's decision?

10–3. What is an installment sale? Under what conditions would an installment sale be a possibility?

10–4. Tax-deferred exchanges are a method of property disposition. What are the basic steps in exchanging real property?

10–5. What is the most important consideration for a tax-deferred exchange?

10–6. What is a sale-and-leaseback arrangement?

10–7. In several examples in this chapter, the analysis concentrated on the difference in cash flows between the options under study. Why is this approach often useful in real estate decision making?

PROBLEMS

10–1. Using the sale-versus-continuing-to-operate example developed in the chapter, what would happen to the decision if:

    a. The estimated current selling price is higher than $625,000? Lower?

    b. The expected NOI grows at a lower rate than 2 percent? Higher?

    c. The expected value at the end of the holding period is lower than $675,000? Higher?

    d. The required after-tax rate of return is 12 percent? 20 percent?

10–2. Using the installment-versus-outright-sale example developed in the chapter, what would happen to the decision with the following changes?

    a. The installment sale has a price greater than $250,000.

    b. The interest rate on the purchase-money mortgage was greater than 13 percent.

    c. The outright selling price was less than $250,000.

10–3. Using the tax-deferred exchange example developed in the Chapter, how would the following changes affect Mr. Dunn and Mr. Roe?

    a. If the market value of Mr. Dunn's property was $700,000, how would his tax burden change as a result of the exchange? What would his new equity position be?

    b. Assuming the market value of Mr. Dunn's property is still $700,000 and that both Mr. Dunn's and Mr. Roe's marginal tax rates are 28%, what are the deferred taxes for both as a result of the exchange over an outright sale?

SELECTED REFERENCES

Gau, George W., and Ko Wang, "The Tax-Induced Holding Periods of Real Estate Investors: Theory and Empirical Evidence," *Journal of Real Estate Finance and Economics*, 8 (January 1994), 71–85.

Henderson, Glenn V., and William H. Walker, "Analysis of Installment Sales," *Appraisal Journal*, 47 (October 1979), 485–89.

Jaffe, Austin J., and C. F. Sirmans, *Real Estate Investment Decision Making*. Englewood Cliffs, N.J.: Prentice Hall, 1982.

Pellechio, A. J., "Taxation of Rental Income and Optimal Holding Periods for Real Property," *National Tax Journal*, 41 (March 1988), 97–107.

Sirmans, C. F., *Real Estate Finance*, 2nd ed. New York: McGraw-Hill, 1985.

Valachi, Donald J., "The Tax-Deferred Exchange: Some Planning Considerations," *Appraisal Journal*, 47 (October 1979), 76–85.

PART IV
INVESTMENT CRITERIA

CHAPTER 11

TRADITIONAL INVESTMENT CRITERIA

PRINCIPLES

1. There are two types of traditional measures that have been used as investment criteria: rules-of-thumb criteria and appraisal techniques.
2. Rules-of-thumb are old, time-tested measures that are often easy to calculate, understand, and use.
3. Ratio analysis has been adapted from financial statement analysis for use by real estate investors.
4. The three traditional appraisal methods may also be used for investment purposes.

In this chapter we begin our analysis of the various criteria used in making investment decisions. The previous chapters discussed how to forecast the expected outflows and inflows, measured in terms of cash flows. Our task now is to apply some criteria so that we can compare these cash flows. We analyze the various traditional measures—rules-of-thumb and appraisal techniques. The next chapter discusses the more sophisticated discounted cash flow models.

To make the investment decision we have two methods: compare what the investment is worth with what it cost or compare the expected rate of return with that required. All the criteria are simply techniques for obtaining measures of worth or rates of return. We now consider the various rules of thumb used to measure value and rate of return.

RULES-OF-THUMB CRITERIA

The rules-of-thumb criteria fall into two classes: the payback methods (or their reciprocal, rates of return) and the average rate-of-return methods (see Table 11–1). Note that the overall capitalization rate is simply the reciprocal of the net income multiplier. Likewise, the equity dividend rate and the after-tax rate are reciprocals of the before-tax and after-tax cash flow multipliers, respectively.

TABLE 11–1
RULES OF THUMB: A SUMMARY

Payback Methods

A. Multipliers

1. Gross income multiplier (GM) $= \dfrac{\text{Total Investment}}{\text{Gross income (potential or effective)}}$

2. Net income multiplier (NIM) $= \dfrac{\text{Total investment}}{\text{Net operating income}}$

3. Before-tax cash flow multiplier $= \dfrac{\text{Equity investment}}{\text{BTCF}}$

4. After-tax cash flow multiplier $= \dfrac{\text{Equity investment}}{\text{ATCF}}$

B. Rates of return

1. Overall capitalization rate (R) $= \dfrac{\text{Net operating income}}{\text{Total investment}}$

2. Equity dividend rate (EDR) $= \dfrac{\text{BTCF}}{\text{Equity investment}}$

3. After-tax return (ATR) $= \dfrac{\text{ATCF}}{\text{Equity investment}}$

Average Rates of Return

1. Average return on net operating income $= \dfrac{\text{Average net operating income}}{\text{Total investment}}$

2. Average return on before-tax cash flow $= \dfrac{\text{Average before-tax cash flow}}{\text{Equity investment}}$

3. Average return on after-tax cash flow $= \dfrac{\text{Average after-tax cash flow}}{\text{Equity investment}}$

GENERAL CHARACTERISTICS

These rules of thumb have a number of general characteristics in common. First, all these measures can be derived from data available from the forecast cash flow for the investment. The necessary cash flow items include gross income, net operating income, and before-tax and after-tax cash flow. Other items required are total investment costs and total (or initial) equity. All of these measures are easily found by calculating the ratios of costs to cash flow (or income) or the ratios of cash flow (or income) to costs.

Second, many of these rules attempt to measure the same conceptual item: either as a multiplier or as a rate of return. The difference is that each measure relates different levels of expected cash flow to equity or to total investment. For example, the equity dividend rate (EDR) is similar to the after-tax return (ATR) except that the cash flow of the former is before-tax while the latter is after-tax. With the same denominator (equity), the after-tax return will obviously be different from the before-tax equity dividend rate as long as there are tax consequences. The point is that these measures produce different results that may precipitate different investment decisions.

Third, these techniques are unadjusted for the time-value of money. Typically, these are "single-period measures." This means that the multipliers and rates of return are calculated using only a single-period measure of income or cash flow, which severely constrains their usefulness because income (or cash flow) typically changes over time.

In the case of the average rate of return, the average income and cash flow (see Table 11–1) are (1) only averages and thereby prone to significant undervaluing in some periods and overvaluing in others; (2) unadjusted for the timing of the cash flows and, therefore, less useful from an investment standpoint; and (3) inconsistent with investment criteria using the time-value-of-money concept. Finally, because none of these criteria measures change in the expected future income of cash flow streams, they are generally imprecise and subject to error.

PAYBACK-PERIOD METHODS

The *payback period* is simply the number of years necessary to recover the initial investment from an investment's future cash flow. It is often expressed in reciprocal form, that is, as a rate of return.

In equation form, the payback method is expressed as

$$\text{Payback period} = \frac{\text{Investment cost}}{\text{Income}} \qquad (11\text{--}1)$$

Alternatively, in the rate form:

$$\text{Rate of return} = \frac{1}{\text{Payback period}} \qquad (11\text{--}2)$$

$$= \frac{\text{Income}}{\text{Investment cost}}$$

As we noted earlier, there are five measures (or levels) of income from the operation of a real estate investment:

1. Potential gross income

2. Effective gross income

3. Net operating income

4. Before-tax cash flow

5. After-tax cash flow

Payback periods (or rates of return) for these five types of inflow can be calculated by using Equations (11–1) and (11–2).

APPLICATION OF TRADITIONAL INVESTMENT CRITERIA: AN EXAMPLE

To illustrate the various traditional investment criteria, consider an investor interested in buying a four-plex (four-unit) rental housing property. The asking price is $160,000. The investor is in a 28 percent marginal tax bracket and anticipates owning the property for five years, at which time the property is expected to be sold for $175,000, with $17,000 in selling expenses.

The present rent per unit is $667 per month. The potential annual gross income, therefore, is roughly $32,000 and is expected to increase by $1,500 each year throughout the holding period. Vacancy and bad debt allowance are estimated at 3 percent of potential gross income. First-year annual operating expenses are estimated as shown in Table 11–2. Operating expenses are expected to grow to $7,800 in year 2, $8,200 in year 3, $8,800 in year 4, and $9,400 in year 5 of the project. The depreciation schedule is shown in Table 11–3, assuming a total basis of $160,000, a depreciable basis of $145,000, the use of the straight-line method of depreciation, and a recovery period of 27.5 years. The amortization schedule is shown in Table 11–4 using the following information: the mortgage amount is $128,000, the interest rate is 12 percent, the maturity is 25 years (monthly), and fi-

TABLE 11–2
FIRST-YEAR OPERATING EXPENSES

Management fees	$1,595
Property taxes	1,300
Utilities (water and sewer)	975
Maintenance	1,550
Replacement reserves (constant)	1,105
Insurance	975
	$7,500

TABLE 11–3
DEPRECIATION SCHEDULE

Year	Basis	Straight-Line Depreciation
0	$145,000	
1	139,727	5,273
2	134,454	5,273
3	129,181	5,273
4	123,908	5,273
5	118,635	5,273
		$26,365

TABLE 11-4

Year	Proportion Outstanding	Amount Outstanding	Debt Service	Interest	Principal
0	1.00000	$128,000	—	—	—
1	.99325	127,136	$16,174	$15,313	$ 861
2	.98564	126,162	16,174	15,204	970
3	.97707	125,065	16,174	15,080	1,094
4	.96741	123,829	16,174	14,941	1,233
5	.95653	122,436	16,174	14,785	1,389

nancing costs are $3,840, estimated at approximately 3 percent of the mortgage amount.

❐ **GROSS INCOME MULTIPLIER.** One of the most widely used payback methods for estimating both market and investment value is the *gross income multiplier* (GIM). The GIM can be expressed as

$$\text{GIM} = \frac{\text{Total investment}}{\text{EGI}} \tag{11-3}$$

The GIM simply tells the analyst how many years it would take to recover the total investment cost (purchase price) if all the gross income were allocated to recovery. The GIM is analogous to a price: earnings ratio in corporate finance; in essence, the GIM measures the price of the investment (total investment or value) divided by its earnings (EGI).

Referring to our example, with a $160,000 purchase price and an EGI of $31,040 in year 1, the GIM is

$$\text{GIM} = \frac{\$160,000}{\$31,040}$$

$$= 5.0$$

Hence, if all the effective gross income were used and were constant each year, it would take approximately 5.0 years to recover the total cost of the investment.

❐ **NET INCOME MULTIPLIER (OVERALL RATE).** A second type of payback criteria is calculated by using net operating income (NOI) instead of gross income. The method is typically called the *overall capitalization rate,* or *overall rate.* Using Equation (11-2), the overall rate in equation form is

$$\text{Overall capitalization rate } (R) = \frac{\text{NOI}}{\text{Investment cost}} \qquad (11\text{--}4)$$

This overall capitalization rate is sometimes called the "free and clear" rate of return.

Again referring to our example, the investment considered has a purchase price of $160,000 and a net operating income (see Table 11–5) in the first year of $23,540. The overall rate is

$$R = \frac{\$23{,}540}{\$160{,}000}$$

$$= 14.71\%$$

Note that the NOI varies every year in our example, so the overall rate will change, as well.

In payback form, the net income multiplier (NIM) is the reciprocal of the overall rate, using Equation (11–1):

$$\text{NIM} = \frac{\$160{,}000}{\$23{,}540}$$

$$= 6.80$$

It would take almost seven years to recover the total investment cost if all of the net operating income were allocated to recovery.

TABLE 11–5
EXPECTED CASH FLOWS FROM OPERATIONS

		Year				
		1	2	3	4	5
	Potential gross income (PGI)	$32,000	33,500	35,000	36,500	38,000
minus	Vacancy and bad debt allowance (VBD)	$ 960	1,005	1,050	1,095	1,140
equals	Effective gross income (EGI)	$31,040	32,495	33,950	35,405	36,860
minus	Operating expenses (OE)	$ 7,500	7,800	8,200	8,600	9,000
equals	Net operating income (NOI)	$23,540	24,695	25,750	26,805	27,860
minus	Debt service (DS)	$16,174	16,174	16,174	16,174	16,174
equals	Before-tax cash flow (BTCF)	$ 7,366	8,521	9,576	10,631	11,686
minus	Taxes (savings) from operations (TO)	$ 1,093	1,447	1,777	2,112	1,591
equals	After-tax cash flow (ATCF)	$ 6,273	7,074	7,799	8,519	10,095

EXAMPLE 11–1 **ESTIMATING VALUE WITH DIRECT CAPITALIZATION: MARKET-EXTRACTED OVERALL RATE APPROACH**

An apartment property is producing an annual NOI of $190,000. Three similar apartment properties in close proximity to the subject property, offering essentially the same amenities and the same services as the subject, have recently sold. All were market transactions with typical financing and terms of sale. Their sale prices and net operating incomes were:

	Sales Price	Net Operating Income
Sale 1:	$1,200,000	$144,000
Sale 2:	$1,900,000	$235,000
Sale 3:	$1,650,000	$194,700

You, as a real estate adviser, have been asked to determine the indicated overall rate for this property and the indicated market value of this property, based on direct capitalization using a market-extracted overall rate.

The indicated overall rates for the comparable sales properties are simply the NOI divided by the sales price.

Sale 1: $144,000/$1,200,000 = .1200

Sale 2: $235,000/$1,900,000 = .1237

Sale 3: $194,700/$1,650,000 = .1180

The indicated overall rate applicable to the subject property is 0.12. Therefore, value equals the ratio of NOI to the overall rate, or

$$V = I/R$$

$$V = \$190,000/.12 = \$1,583,333 \text{ (say, } \$1,585,000)$$

☐ **BEFORE-TAX CASH FLOW MULTIPLIER (EQUITY DIVIDEND RATE).** The third payback-period method is the *equity dividend rate* (EDR), or the *cash-on-cash return*. The before-tax cash flow (BTCF) is used to calculate the rate. In equation form, the equity dividend rate is

$$EDR = \frac{\text{Before-tax cash flow}}{\text{Equity investment}} \qquad (11\text{--}5)$$

Note that with this method, the cost of the investment is measured by the amount of equity, rather than by the total investment costs. Excluded are the mortgage, financing costs, and acquisition costs.

In our example, the investment has a total cost of $160,000, of which $128,000, or 80 percent, is financed with a mortgage and $32,000 with equity. The BTCF is $7,366 in the first year. The equity dividend rate is

$$EDR = \frac{\$7,366}{\$32,000}$$

$$= 23.02\%$$

In multiplier form, the reciprocal of the EDR is

$$= \frac{\$32,000}{\$7,366}$$

$$= 4.34$$

❐ **AFTER-TAX CASH FLOW MULTIPLIER (AFTER-TAX RETURN).** The final payback rate of return is calculated by using the after-tax cash flows rather than before-tax cash flows. In equation form, the *after-tax return* (ATR) is

$$ATR = \frac{\text{After-tax cash flow}}{\text{Equity investment}}$$

Because the ATCF is $6,273 (Table 11–5) in the first year, the ATR is

$$ATR = \frac{\$6,273}{\$32,000}$$

$$= 19.60\%$$

AVERAGE RATE OF RETURN METHODS

The second major category of rules-of-thumb techniques—the *average* (or accounting) *rates of return*—is not as popular. An average rate of return is calculated by dividing an investment's average annual income (or average before- or after-tax cash flow) by the total investment or equity costs. In equation form, the average rate of return is expressed as

$$\begin{array}{l} \text{Average rate of return} \\ \text{on total investment} \end{array} = \frac{\text{Average cash flow}}{\text{Investment cost}} \qquad (11\text{--}7)$$

The three common forms of the average rate of return method are described next.

☐ **AVERAGE RETURN ON NET OPERATING INCOME.** This is very similar to the overall capitalization rate. For example, if the net operating income of the investment is constant each period, the average rate on net operating income and the overall capitalization rate are identical. The average rate on net operating income is expressed as

$$\text{Average rate on net operating income} = \frac{\text{Average NOI}}{\text{Total investment}} \qquad (11\text{--}8)$$

This measure gives the average rate of return on net operating income to investment cost over an expected number of years.

In our example, using the figures from Table 11–5, the average NOI is computed as follows:

Year	NOI
1	$ 23,540
2	24,695
3	25,750
4	26,805
5	27,860
	$128,650

$$\text{Average NOI} = \frac{\$128,650}{5}$$

$$= \$25,730$$

Therefore, the average return on net operating income is

$$\text{Average return on net operating income} = \frac{\$25,730}{\$160,000}$$

$$= 16.08\%$$

Note that this differs from the overall capitalization rate of 8.4 percent calculated earlier in the chapter. This method averages yearly NOI, whereas the previous example was calculated using NOI from the first year's operations.

☐ **AVERAGE RETURN ON BEFORE-TAX CASH FLOW.** This calculates the average before-tax cash flow as a percentage of equity investment. Therefore the average return on before-tax cash flow is defined as

$$\text{Average return on before-tax cash flow} = \frac{\text{Average BTCF}}{\text{Equity investment}}$$

$$(11-9)$$

Using the figures from Table 11–5, the average BTCF is computed as follows:

Year	BTCF
1	$ 7,366
2	8,521
3	9,576
4	10,631
5	11,686
	$47,780

$$\text{Average BTCF} = \frac{\$47,780}{5}$$

$$= \$9,556$$

We can get the following result:

$$\text{Average return on before-tax cash flow} = \frac{\$9,556}{\$32,000}$$

$$= 29.86\%$$

☐ **AVERAGE RETURN ON AFTER-TAX CASH FLOW.** This average rate of return is calculated in the same way as the before-tax cash flow but on an after-tax basis. This measure is defined as

$$\text{Average return on after-tax cash flow} = \frac{\text{Average ATCF}}{\text{Equity investment}}$$

$$(11-10)$$

Continuing with the four-plex example, using the figures from Table 11–5, the average ATCF was computed as follows:

Year	ATCF
1	$ 6,273
2	7,074
3	7,799
4	8,519
5	10,095
	39,760

$$\text{Average ATCF} = \frac{\$39,760}{5}$$

$$= \$7,952$$

Thus, we can get the following results:

$$\text{Average return on after-tax cash flow} = \frac{\$7,952}{\$32,000}$$

$$= 24.85\%$$

Note that it requires more calculations to determine the average rate on after-tax cash flow, as Table 11–6 shows. Interest payments on the loan decrease as the loan is being amortized. Because the interest portion is deductible, taxable income varies each period. Depreciation is also deducted, assuming that $145,000 is depreciable over 27.5 years. The straight-line method is used, so the amount deductible from taxable income is constant each year. Taxable income or loss multiplied by the tax rate (28 percent) is equal to the tax liability or savings. The tax savings is added to the BTCF to yield annual ATCF.

❐ **ADJUSTING FOR REVERSION.** The average rate of return methods can be modified to adjust the average income and cash flow figures to reflect the fact that the selling price is expected at the end of some holding period. Although this adjustment is an improvement, the adjusted average rates of return still contain several problems.

TABLE 11–6
EXPECTED TAXES FROM OPERATIONS

		Year				
		1	2	3	4	5
	Effective Gross Income (EGI)	31,040	32,495	33,950	35,405	36,860
minus	Operating expenses (OE)	7,500	7,800	8,200	8,600	9,000
equals	Net operating income (NOI)	23,540	24,695	25,750	26,805	27,860
minus	Interest on debt (I)	15,313	15,204	15,080	14,941	14,785
minus	Depreciation deduction (D)	5,273	5,273	5,273	5,273	5,273
minus	Amortized financing costs (AFC)	154	154	154	154	3,224
plus	Replacement reserves (RR)	1,105	1,105	1,105	1,105	1,105
equals	Ordinary taxable income (OTI)	3,905	5,169	6,348	7,542	5,683
times	Investor's marginal tax rate (τ)	0.28	0.28	0.28	0.28	0.28
equals	Taxes (savings) from operations (TO)	1,093	1,447	1,777	2,112	1,591

Using the preceding example, we see that the property sale has the effect on the average return on net operating income, as shown in Table 11–7.

If we include the impact of the before-tax equity reversion on the average rate on before-tax cash flow, the result is shown in Table 11–8.

Finally, if we include the impact of the after-tax equity reversion on the average rate on after-tax cash flow, we calculate the after-tax equity reversion as shown in Tables 11–9 and 11–10.

Therefore we conclude that the adjusted average rate on after-tax cash flow is 22.81%, as shown in Table 11–11.

Table 11–12 summarizes the results of this example. Note that the rates of return decrease if taxes are considered.

USING RULES-OF-THUMB CRITERIA

How does the investor use the rules-of-thumb criteria to make an investment decision? For example, an investment with a gross income multiplier of 5 for an investment means nothing by itself. The investor must compare this with something in order to make the decision.

In using the payback methods, the investor wants to minimize the payback period. If expressed as a rate, the investor wants to maximize this

TABLE 11–7
ADJUSTED AVERAGE RATE ON NET INCOME

	Total net operating income (over 5 years)	$128,650
plus	Net sales proceeds (after 5 years)	+158,000
	Total cash return	286,650
minus	Cost of total investment	−160,000
	Income	$126,650
	Average income: $126,650/5 = $25,330	
	Adjusted average return on net income =	$ 25,330
		$160,000
	=	15.83%

TABLE 11–8
ADJUSTED AVERAGE RATE ON BTCF

	Total before-tax cash flow	$47,780
plus	Before-tax equity reversion	+ 35,564
	Total cash return	83,344
minus	Cost of equity investment	− 32,000
	Cash flow: Average	
	cash flow $51,344/5 = $10,269	$51,344
	Adjusted average rate on before-tax cash flow =	$10,269
		$32,000
	=	32.09%

TABLE 11-9
EXPECTED CASH FLOW FROM SALE

	Expected selling price (SP)	$175,000
minus	Selling expenses (SE)	− 17,000
equals	Net sale proceeds (NSP)	158,000
minus	Unpaid mortgage balance (UM)	−122,436
equals	Before-tax equity reversion (BTER)	35,564
minus	Taxes due on sale (TDS)*	− 6,822
equals	After-tax equity reversion (ATER)	$ 28,742

* See Table 11–10.

TABLE 11-10
EXPECTED TAXES DUE ON SALE

Taxable Income

	Expected selling price (SP)	$175,000
minus	Selling expenses (SE)	− 17,000
equals	Amount realized (AR)	158,000
minus	Adjusted basis (AB)	−133,635
equals	Total gain on sale (TG)	$ 24,365

Taxes Due on Sale

	Total gain on sale (TG)	24,365
times	Investor's marginal tax rate (τ)	× .28
equals	Taxes due on sale (TDS)	$ 6,822

TABLE 11-11
ADJUSTED AVERAGE RATE ON ATCF

	Total after-tax cash flow (over 5 years)	$39,760
plus	After-tax equity reversion (after 5 years)	+ 28,742
	Total cash return	68,502
minus	Cost of equity investment	32,000
	Cash flow	36,502
	Average cash flow:	$36,502/5 = $ 7,300
	Adjusted average return on after-tax cash flow	= $32,000
		= 22.81%

rate of return. In our example, the investment has a calculated net income multiplier of 6.80, so the investor compares this with multipliers of rates on similar investments. If similar properties have multipliers of 9, the investor may conclude that the first project is preferable because it has the shorter payback period. However, whether the investment is "acceptable" or not is a more difficult question.

TABLE 11-12
SUMMARY OF AVERAGE RATES OF RETURN FOR FOUR-PLEX INVESTMENT

	Without Reversion	With Reversion
Average return on net operating income	16.08%	15.83%
Average return on before-tax cash flow	29.86%	32.09%
Average return on after-tax cash flow	24.85%	22.81%

In using the average rate of return measures, the investor prefers investments with the highest expected rates of return. A rate of return of 9 percent for the four-plex investment is preferred to another with a return of 8 percent, using the same measure.

Perhaps a more important consideration is the fact that there are no standards against which the analyst may gauge the acceptability of a particular investment. In the case of payback methods, what is the maximum acceptable payback period? How is it determined? In the case of rates of return, what is an acceptable rate of return? How is this determined? Also, how can an investor account for differences in risk?

LIMITATIONS OF RULES OF THUMB

One of the most serious problems with these measures is that the rate of return varies according to the measure used. Furthermore, we could compare these rates of return with better measures, such as the internal rate of return, and get totally different results.

The most serious defect in both the payback methods and the average rate of return measures is that no provision is made for the discounting of the future cash flow: Consider the hypothetical investments in Table 11-13. The investor can acquire only one project and each costs $100,000.

Each investment expects to return the effective gross income during the years indicated. If the investor were to use the gross income multiplier to decide which investment is preferable, investments A, B, and C would all be equally attractive, since each has a GIM of 4 ($100,000/$25,000). However, a more careful look indicates that as long as there is a time-value of money, investment B would be preferable to C, and both would be preferable to A, if acceptable at all. The time-value of money consideration implies that for the same amount, the investor prefers income (or cash flow) in the present rather than the future. In this example, investments A, B, and C are expected to return $25,000 at the end of year 1. However, investments B and C promise $125,000 in returns over four years while investment A promises only $100,000. Even if a "zero capitalization rate" is used, investment A is unacceptable for a four-year holding period because it promises to return only $100,000 over four years for a $100,000 outlay.

TABLE 11–13
EXPECTED BEFORE-TAX CASH FLOWS FOR INVESTMENTS A, B, C, AND D

	Alternative Investments			
Year	A	B	C	D
0	($100,000)	($100,000)	($100,000)	($100,000)
1	25,000	25,000	25,000	—
2	25,000	50,000	—	—
3	25,000	—	—	—
4	25,000	50,000	100,000	—
5	—	—	—	150,000

However, the GIM method fails to distinguish investment A from investment B or investment C.

The GIM approach also views investments B and C as identically attractive. A closer look indicates that investment B is preferable to investment C for any positive time-value of money. This is because, for identical amounts of income, we prefer to have the cash now rather than later. Therefore, the GIM approach fails to select investment B over C, even though the former is clearly preferable. Finally, if we use the GIM, investment D is never really considered, since it "pays back" after the other three. Therefore, there are serious doubts about the use of payback methods as investment criteria.

Moreover, the rules-of-thumb are inappropriate when cash flows change over the investment holding period. To illustrate this point, consider the investments in Table 11–14. The positive numbers represent the before-tax cash flows for each investment. Each investment requires $150,000 equity, and only one can be selected. The cash flows from investment R are expected to increase as shown. The before-tax cash flows are constant for investment S and are decreasing for investment T.

The average rate on before-tax cash flow is clearly identical for all the investments: $50,000/$150,000 = 33.33 percent. Using this measure, the

TABLE 11–14
EXPECTED BEFORE-TAX CASH FLOWS FOR INVESTMENTS R, S, AND T

	Alternative Investments		
Year	R	S	T
0	($150,000)	($150,000)	($150,000)
1	25,000	50,000	75,000
2	50,000	50,000	50,000
3	75,000	50,000	25,000

investor may conclude that all are equally attractive. A more careful examination suggests that if money has a time value, investment T is the most attractive because it returns more cash flow more quickly, and investment R is the least attractive for the same reason.

RATIO ANALYSIS

The financial feasibility of a real estate investment can also be measured, to a limited extent, by several ratios. These ratios show relationships between the various parts of the cash flow statement. From the investor's standpoint, analyzing the cash flow statement is useful both as a way to anticipate future conditions and as a starting point for planning action that will influence the future cash flow.

Ratios in real estate investment analysis fall into two groups: leverage and operating activity ratios and profitability ratios. Table 11–15 lists the various ratios that we will now discuss.

LEVERAGE AND OPERATING RATIOS

One of the investor's major concerns is the liquidity of the investment. Will the investment be able to meet the financial obligations related to operating and debt costs? There are five useful ratios for this type of analysis.

TABLE 11–15
RATIO ANALYSIS

Ratio	Equation	Four-plex Example[†]
A. Leverage and operating ratios		
1. Mortgage debt to property value ratio (loan-to-value ratio)	$= \dfrac{\text{Mortgage outstanding}}{\text{Property value}}$	$\dfrac{128{,}000}{160{,}000} = .80$
2. Debt coverage ratio	$= \dfrac{\text{NOI}}{\text{Debt service}}$	$\dfrac{23{,}540}{16{,}174} = 1.45542$
3. Default ratio	$= \dfrac{\text{Operating expenses plus debt service}}{\text{Effective gross income}}$	$\dfrac{7{,}500 + 16{,}174}{31{,}040} = 0.76269$
4. Total asset turnover ratio	$= \dfrac{\text{Effective gross income}}{\text{Property value}}$	$\dfrac{31{,}040}{160{,}000} = 0.194$
5. Operating expense ratio	$= \dfrac{\text{Operating expenses}}{\text{Effective gross income}}$	$\dfrac{7{,}500}{31{,}040} = 0.24162$
B. Profitability ratios*		
1. Profit margin	$= \dfrac{\text{ATCF}}{\text{EGI}}$	$\dfrac{6{,}273}{31{,}040} = 0.20209$
2. Return to equity on total investment	$= \dfrac{\text{ATCF}}{\text{Total investment}}$	$\dfrac{6{,}273}{160{,}000} = 0.03921$
3. Return on equity	$= \dfrac{\text{ATCF}}{\text{Equity}}$	$\dfrac{6{,}273}{32{,}000} = 0.19603$
4. "System of financial analysis"	$= \dfrac{\text{EGI}}{\text{Property value}} \times \dfrac{\text{ATCF}}{\text{EGI}}$	$\dfrac{31{,}040}{160{,}000} \times \dfrac{6{,}273}{31{,}040} = 0.03921$

* Also see the ratios in Table 11.1
†These are calculated using the first year's estimated cash flows.

❏ **MORTGAGE DEBT TO PROPERTY VALUE RATIO (L/V).** One of the most commonly used financial leverage measures is the mortgage debt to property value ratio (also known as the loan-to-value ratio). This measures the relationship between the mortgage debt outstanding and the property value. In equation form:

$$L/V = \frac{\text{Mortgage debt outstanding}}{\text{Property value}} \qquad (11\text{--}11)$$

❏ **DEBT COVERAGE RATIO (DCR).** The debt coverage ratio (DCR) measures the extent to which net operating income can decline and still cover the financial obligations (debt service). In equation form, the debt coverage ratio is

$$DCR = \frac{\text{Net operating income}}{\text{Annual debt service}} \qquad (11\text{--}12)$$

This ratio is widely used by lenders to measure the financial feasibility of an investment. If the debt coverage ratio falls below 1, the investment is unable to meet the obligation from operating income. The investor must take remedial action by investing more equity or borrowing to meet the financial obligation.

❏ **DEFAULT RATIO (DR).** This also measures the financial feasibility of an investment from the lender's perspective. In equation form:

$$DR = \frac{\text{Operating expenses plus debt service}}{\text{Effective gross income}} \qquad (11\text{--}13)$$

The default ratio (also called the break-even ratio) measures an investment's ability to cover all the expenses of operations and the debt service.

❏ **TOTAL ASSET TURNOVER RATIO (TAT).** This measures the ratio of effective gross income (EGI) to the total value of the investment. In equation form:

$$TAT = \frac{\text{EGI}}{\text{Property value}} \qquad (11\text{--}14)$$

The TAT is also the reciprocal of the gross income multiplier that we discussed in the previous section.

☐ **OPERATING EXPENSE RATIO (OER).** The operating expense ratio (OER) measures the relationship between total operating expenses and effective gross income (EGI). In equation form:

$$\text{OER} = \frac{\text{Operating expenses}}{\text{Effective gross income}} \qquad (11\text{–}15)$$

The greater the OER, the greater the proportion of effective gross income used to cover operating expenses.

PROFITABILITY RATIOS

A number of profitability ratios were discussed earlier in the chapter. Profitability is the net result of a number of policies and decisions. Profitability ratios show the combined effects of liquidity, management, and debt on operating results. In addition to the ratios discussed previously (see Table 11–1), there are ratios for profit margin and the return to equity on total investment.

☐ **PROFIT MARGIN RATIO.** Computed by dividing after-tax cash flow by effective gross income, this ratio gives the profit per dollar of gross income:

$$\text{Profit margin} = \frac{\text{ATCF}}{\text{EGI}} \qquad (11\text{–}16)$$

A low profit margin relative to other properties could indicate that an investment's rents are relatively low or that its operating costs are relatively high, or both.

☐ **RETURN TO EQUITY ON TOTAL INVESTMENT.** The ratio of after-tax cash flow to total investment measures the return on the total investment:

$$\text{Return on total investment} = \frac{\text{ATCF}}{\text{Total investment}} \qquad (11\text{–}17)$$

However, this ratio is not as appropriate for the investor as the return on equity.

☐ **RETURN ON EQUITY.** The ratio of after-tax cash flow to equity also provides a rate of return measure:

$$\text{Return on equity} = \frac{\text{ATCF}}{\text{Equity}} \qquad (11\text{–}18)$$

This is precisely the same measure as the after-tax return discussed as one of the payback period methods.

❑ **"SYSTEM OF FINANCIAL ANALYSIS."**   It is possible to break down the return to equity on total investment into the product of two ratios: the total asset turnover ratio and the profit margin ratio:

$$\text{System of financial analysis} = \text{Total asset turnover} \times \text{Profit margin}$$

$$= \frac{\text{EGI}}{\text{Property value}} \times \frac{\text{ATCF}}{\text{EGI}}$$

$$= \frac{\text{ATCF}}{\text{Property value}} \qquad (11\text{--}19)$$

Therefore, the product of the total asset turnover and the profit margin is another way of calculating the return to equity on total investment.

LIMITATIONS OF RATIO ANALYSIS

Although the ratios discussed are widely used in investment decision making, they are subject to the following limitations:

1. The ratios can be distorted by many factors. For example, understating operating costs (such as excluding management fees) can deflate the operating expense ratio.
2. It is difficult to generalize about whether a particular ratio is "good" or "bad." For example, a high debt coverage ratio may look good to the lender but may indicate that the investor is underleveraged.
3. Most investments have some "good" and some "bad" ratios. Consequently, it is often difficult to tell whether the investment is financially feasible.

Ratio analysis is useful despite these problems, but investors should make adjustments where necessary. Conducted with good judgment, this type of analysis can provide useful insights into an investment's operations. A number of published sources provide data on ratios for numerous types of investments, including shopping centers, apartments, and office buildings.

COMPARISON OF PAYBACK PERIOD AND IRR

The use of payback period measures continues to be an intuitive set of checks or guidelines for many seasoned real estate investors. However, it can be shown that these calculations are imprecise measures of return when compared to modern calculations such as the internal rate of return.

One of the tools available to real estate investors is the set of appraisal methods. These techniques have a long tradition that dates back to the early part of this century. Commonly known as "the three approaches to value," the appraisal methods may be useful because investors may be familiar with the techniques from appraisal work, the methods may be applicable for investment purposes, or the methods may be familiar to others associated with the project and may therefore be helpful in communicating ideas about the potential investment.

For example, the *cost approach to value* estimates the value of the site and the improvements based on the concept of replacement cost. Investors who have expertise in development may wish to consider that doing so is less than the market price they will have to pay in order to acquire the property. In this situation, the cost approach provides helpful information to investors about an important option available to them.

The *income approach to value* is often used by investors for income-producing property. In recent years, more and more investors are employing relatively sophisticated income approaches, often using computers and spreadsheet software.

The *sales comparison approach* may provide information to the investor about the relative values of attributes, as well as entire properties in the market in which the investment property under consideration is located. This approach is useful in determining whether the assumptions and estimates made in the financial analysis are consistent with the workings of others in the same market. If market values of similar types of property are vastly different from the results obtained in the financial analysis, this is a danger signal and suggests that the investor needs to reexamine the premises and estimates of the investment analysis.

In many ways, the traditional appraisal methods can be used by investors. These methods can be used to estimate market values for comparison purposes, can demonstrate the market values of attributes in similar properties, or can serve as alternative investment techniques to help the investor do a better job in performing the financial analysis.

A comparison of the payback period (Equation 11–1), its rate of return reciprocal (Equation 11–2), and the internal rate of return (as developed in Chapter 2), has been shown for some time. If the payback period, PB, is equal to the total investment cost, (TI) divided by an equal annual income estimate, (I), then an important relationship can be derived as follows:

$$IRR = (1/PB) - (1/PB)[1/(1 + IRR)]^n \qquad (11-20)$$

where:

$$IRR = \text{internal rate of return}$$

Alternatively, the payback period may be expressed as:

$$PB = IRR/[1 - (1/(1 + IRR))^n] \qquad (11\text{--}21)$$

The results show an important finding: *for all projects with expected finite planning periods, the internal rate of return will always be less than the reciprocal of the payback period.* This is a measure of the error associated with the use of the payback reciprocal (or any other payback measure) as an approximation for the internal rate of return. Further, the shorter the holding period, the larger the difference between the payback reciprocal and the internal rate of return. Finally, the smaller the internal rate of return, the larger the deviation using the payback reciprocal.

One final point: the deviations from the internal rate of return using the payback reciprocals can be quite large. Payback methods might provide investors with some good feelings, but they are often very crude and, therefore, dangerous measures of performance.

TRADITIONAL APPRAISAL METHODS

The three traditional appraisal methods are the market comparison, income, and cost approaches. These methods can also be used, and should be used, as investment criteria by the real estate investor, since he or she is particularly interested in the market value of the property. Real estate appraisal advocates the use of the comparison approach as the best method for value estimation. Obviously the investor does not want to pay more than the market value for the investment, even if it is worth more to him or her.

THE MARKET COMPARISON APPROACH

Using the market comparison (or direct sales comparison) approach, the investor estimates value by comparing the subject property with similar properties in the market. Recently sold comparables are selected, and the appraiser identifies and adjusts for the factors that affect the value. In essence, the skilled interpretation of recent sales in the marketplace of similar property leads to the value estimate.

The comparison approach removes the bias a particular investor might have regarding future income appreciation or depreciation and internal rate of return. The comparison approach gives an indication of the expectations of and the return sought by the "typical" investor. This decision-making process is reflected in the market price of recent sales.

The most serious limitation of the comparison approach is the lack of sales data. The appraiser (investor) must have an adequate number of truly comparable sales in order to estimate the value. Since no two properties are exactly alike, the appraiser (investor) must adjust for differences to arrive at a final value estimate. In general, there are five major categories of adjustments:

1. *Time.* Because sales are historical, the comparables should be adjusted for time. For example, suppose the investor observed a comparable that sold six months ago. How have things changed over this period? Has there been new construction of this type of property? Have factors influencing demand for the property changed? What has the inflation rate been over the period? All of these considerations will influence value, either positively or negatively. Taking these factors into consideration, how much would the property sell for today?

2. *Location.* The location of a property can have a significant impact on the value. Obviously, if the comparable is in the same neighborhood, no adjustment will be necessary. If the comparable is in a different neighborhood, the investor must compare the relative advantages and disadvantages of each neighborhood. An adjustment must be made to reflect these differences.

3. *Financing.* Different methods of financing can have a significant impact on the behavior of investors and on the selling prices in the market. It is important to know what type of financing is available at the present time and the terms of financing on the comparable property as well.

4. *Conditions of sale.* The appraiser (investor) must be certain that the buyers and sellers are motivated by ordinary market motives. Factors such as the inclusion of a significant amount of personal property in the sale, inordinate bargaining strength, unusual pressure, and a poorly informed buyer or seller can render a sale useless as a comparable.

5. *Physical characteristics.* This category of adjustments involves many factors, such as size of building, number of rooms, age of the comparable, and lot size.

The appraiser (investor) should select a set of comparables and adjust these to the five key categories. The investor is asking the question, *What would the comparable have sold for if it were like the subject property?*

❏ **USES OF THE MARKET COMPARISON APPROACH.** The appraiser-investor typically places heavy reliance on the market comparison approach for value estimation. The market comparison approach may be used for investment properties if an adequate number of sales have occurred. It is generally possible to find data on the sale of apartments, office buildings, shopping centers, and other types of income properties.

❏ **MARKET COMPARISON APPROACH PROCEDURE.** There are five steps involved in the market comparison approach:

1. Research the market to identify similar properties for which pertinent data are available.
2. Qualify the comparables according to terms, motivating forces, and authenticity.
3. Compare the attributes of each of the comparable properties in relation to time, location, physical characteristics, conditions of sale, and financing.
4. Consider the disparities between the comparable and the subject. The probable effect on the selling price of each comparable must be determined to derive individual market value indications for the property being appraised.
5. Formulate an opinion of the market value of the property being appraised from this analysis.

Because the sales chosen as comparables have a definite bearing on the value estimate, research of the market should be thorough. As far as the nature of the sale is concerned, the financing, bargaining strength, knowledge of buyer and seller, and other significant details of the transaction should be considered. These factors are as important in establishing comparability as are the physical characteristics of the property. In essence, the appraiser is looking for any market "imperfections" that cause the observed selling price of a comparable to be different from the market value.

In making the comparison between the selected comparables and the subject property, the appraiser must note all significant differences among properties. This provides a basis for adjusting the comparables to give an indication of value of the property being appraised. After considering all the data, the appraiser formulates an opinion of value for the subject property.

❏ **MARKET COMPARISON APPROACH EXAMPLE.** Consider the situation in our earlier example. The investor is interested in buying a four-plex. There are three comparable properties that recently sold and can be used to estimate the value of the subject.

■ Comparable Sales Property No. 1 is a three-unit residential complex similar in age and construction quality to the subject. The complex recently sold for $112,500 or $37,500 per unit. The units are slightly smaller than the subject and require an upward adjustment of 5 percent. In addition, this comparable property is located in a slightly inferior location; if the property were located in the subject location it would have sold for 5 percent more per unit.

- Comparable Sales Property No. 2 is a four-unit residential building located across the street from the subject. The property sold last year for $155,000 ($38,750 per unit); during that year property values were increasing at a rate of 10 percent. The building had recently been renovated just prior to the sale. Had the owner not renovated the property it would have sold for 5 percent less.

- Comparable Sales Property No. 3 is a four-plex located down the street for the subject property and sold two weeks ago for $185,000, which is $46,250 per apartment unit. The seller financed the deal for the buyer at a rate considerably below the market rate. The present value of the below-market financing was determined to be $27,250 or $6,250 per unit. The comparable property was similar to the subject in every other way.

Table 11–16 shows the adjustments necessary for the comparable properties. The comparable properties are adjusted to the subject property.

Based on Table 11–16, the subject value should range from $39,300 to $41,250 per unit. The subject property is a four-unit complex; therefore, the value indicated by the three comparables ranges from $157,200 to $165,000. This value indication is in line with the current asking price of $160,000. The sales comparison approach supports the value of $160,000 for the subject property.

❏ **LIMITATIONS OF THE MARKET COMPARISON APPROACH.** The major limitation of the direct sales comparison approach is that an adequate number of comparable sales may not be available. Even if such sales can be found, changes that have occurred over time may diminish the compa-

TABLE 11–16
ADJUSTMENTS TO COMPARABLE PROPERTIES

	1	2	3
Price of Comparable	$112,500	$155,000	$185,000
Financing Adj.	0%	0%	− 15%
Adjusted Price	$112,500	$155,000	$157,250
Market Conditions	0%	+ 10%	0%
Adjusted Price	$112,500	$170,500	$157,250
Number of Units	3	4	4
Price per Unit	$ 37,500	$ 42,625	$ 39,300
Physical Characteristics	+ 10%	− 5%	0%
Indicated Price per Unit	$ 41,250	$ 40,494	$ 39,300
Indicated Price	$165,000	$161,976	$157,200

rability of each sale. Market conditions may have changed due to increases or decreases in supply or demand for a particular type of property.

For example, is it prudent to use an apartment complex sold one year ago as a comparable when operating expenses have increased substantially over the period? In this event, it is difficult to determine what type of adjustment should be made for these differences. Because the direct sales comparison approach may be of little use during times of rapidly changing market conditions, the income approach to value may be better suited to derive the necessary adjustment.

Another problem with the market approach is that it is based on past prices and trends. Adjusting these to reflect current market conditions is difficult. To the extent that sales are lacking or the data used by the appraiser are inadequate, the estimate of the value of the subject property under current market conditions is limited.

THE COST APPROACH

The basic concept on which the cost approach relies is the principle of substitution. According to this argument, no investor would be willing to pay more for a property than the cost of building a property of equal utility. The cost approach may be particularly relevant to the investor who is considering a new project. Suppose the value estimate of the cost approach is lower than the value estimate of the market and both estimates of value are well supported. Such a situation may indicate that a shortage of the particular type of property exists because demand has pushed the price to a level above the cost of construction. In this situation, the prudent action is to build a new structure, so the cost approach is used to make the investment decision.

❑ **USES OF THE COST APPROACH.**   The cost approach is probably the most difficult of the three approaches to apply accurately. Thus the situations in which it is most applicable are those in which data are lacking for the market comparison and income approaches. Churches, public buildings, and special-use properties are often appraised in this manner because the other approaches are somewhat inapplicable. The application of the cost approach to investment property helps to make the "build-versus-buy" decision or helps to determine the feasibility of a renovation or conversion.

❑ **COST APPROACH PROCEDURE.**   Estimate value using the cost approach by following these steps:

1. Estimate the land (site) value as if vacant.
2. Estimate the reproduction cost new or replacement cost new of the basic improvements and other structures (excluding any that were included as part of the land value).

3. Estimate in dollar amounts the loss in value (depreciation) caused by (a) physical deterioration, (b) functional deficiencies, and (c) adverse economic influences.

4. Deduct accrued depreciation from the improvements' reproduction cost new to arrive at a depreciated cost estimate.

5. Add the land value (from step 1) to the depreciated cost estimate (from step 4) to arrive at a value estimate.

The first step in the cost approach is to estimate the land value. This is typically done using the comparison approach discussed earlier.

The second step is to estimate the cost of the improvements. This is accomplished by using reproduction cost or replacement cost. *Reproduction cost* is the cost of producing an exact replica of the subject property. *Replacement cost* is the cost of producing a building with utility equal to that of the subject property. If reproduction cost is used, problems in cost estimation arise if the building is old and functionally obsolete. Such a building would not be built today, and therefore cost data on such construction are lacking. If replacement value is used, there may be a problem in determining the type of building with the same utility as the subject. Because replacement cost eliminates the functional obsolescence in a structure, a depreciation deduction for this item is inappropriate.

Typically, reproduction cost is estimated by the appraiser according to three major techniques: the *quantity survey method*, the *unit-in-place method*, and the *comparative unit method*.

The quantity survey method involves determining the quantity and costs of materials, supplies, equipment, and labor necessary for construction. This is the most costly and time-consuming method.

The unit-in-place method separates the structure into its major components and estimates what it costs for each of these major components to be "put in place." These components include foundation, floor, plumbing, wiring, heating, cooling, exterior walls, partitions, roof decks, and roof cover.

The unit-comparison method of cost estimation is based on square-foot or cubic-foot units. Reproduction cost is derived in terms of dollars per unit based on known costs of similar structures, adjusted for time, location, and physical differences. These unit cost figures can be obtained from local contractors or cost services such as Boeckh's *Building Valuation Manual* or Marshall's *Valuation Service.* To the extent that the subject varies from the benchmark structure, adjustments are necessary to the cost figure.

Once the cost is estimated, allowances for accrued depreciation must be figured. Depreciation—the loss in value—is commonly measured by the *straight-line method* and the *breakdown method.*

The straight-line method depreciates property based on its age and expected life. There are various ways in which to apply this method. Physical life or economic life may be used as the basis for measurement. Physical age is an easily quantifiable measure, but it may not accurately reflect the condition of the property if maintenance and repairs are either better or worse than average. If effective age is used, the appraiser must make a subjective decision regarding the appropriate age of the property.

Because of its simple concept, the straight-line method usually does not reflect the actual market situation. Too many factors affecting accrued depreciation cannot be accounted for by this method. Therefore the breakdown method of depreciation estimation is generally used.

In the breakdown method of depreciation, there are three types of depreciation: (a) physical deterioration, (b) functional obsolescence, and (c) economic obsolescence. *Physical depreciation* is the adverse effect on value caused by deterioration of condition as a result of wear and tear. *Functional obsolescence* is the adverse affect on value resulting from problems in design, structure, or material that causes a loss of utility. *Economic obsolescence* is due to adverse influences outside the property itself.

Both physical deterioration and functional obsolescence may be curable or incurable. *Curable* items are those that can be economically corrected, such as painting and outdated plumbing fixtures. *Incurable* items are those that cannot be corrected physically or are not economically feasible to correct at present.

The depreciated value of the improvements is calculated by deducting the depreciation estimate from the estimated cost. If there are any site improvements on smaller structures, the depreciated cost of these should be estimated using the same procedures. Items such as parking lots, fences, landscaping, and swimming pools should be considered in this step.

❏ **COST APPROACH EXAMPLE.**   To illustrate value estimation using the cost approach, continue with the four-plex example. The investor has a four-plex building that comprises 3,750 square feet. The estimated reproduction cost from comparable properties recently constructed is $40 per square foot. The cost of constructing drives, walks, landscaping, and parking is $8,000. The building is only two years old, so it is estimated that the loss in value from physical depreciation is only $10,000. There is no economic or functional loss in value. The land value is estimated at $15,000.

Using these assumptions, the value under the cost approach would be as shown in Table 11–17.

❏ **LIMITATIONS OF THE COST APPROACH.**   There are certain limitations of the cost approach to value with which the investor should be familiar.

COST EQUALS VALUE.   One limitation is that the cost approach assumes that cost minus depreciation is equal to value. Even with newly constructed improvements, this may not be true. In some instances, the market value may be greater or less than the cost. This is possible if the improvements do not make the best use of the site or if market demand is in equilibrium and additional properties of a particular type are not re-

TABLE 11-17
COST APPROACH

Reproduction Cost:	
3,750 sq. ft. times cost of $40 per sq. ft.	$150,000
Drives, walks, landscaping, parking	8,000
Loss in value:	
Physical depreciation	10,000
Economic depreciation—none	0
Functional depreciation—none	0
Depreciated value of building and other improvements:	
$150,000 + $8,000 − 10,000	148,000
Estimated land value	15,000
Total value = land value + depreciated building value	163,000

quired at that time. Because it costs $163,000 to build the four-plex does not necessarily mean that this is its total value.

Another problem with the cost-equals-value assumption is that the cost is difficult to measure accurately. If several contractors are asked to bid on the same job, variations in these estimates may be as high. So which is the best cost estimate? Obviously, this is not easily resolved. Additional problems regarding the cost estimate may arise depending on the method the appraiser uses.

DEPRECIATION ESTIMATES. Another problem in the application of the cost approach concerns the estimate of depreciation. Depreciation in the cost approach is the loss in value between a new and a used structure, and because the estimation of depreciation is highly subjective, it is open to substantial error.

Identification of the various forms of depreciation is one problem, but proper measurement is an even greater shortcoming of the cost approach. Reliance on the cost approach should be limited to cases in which the property is relatively new and does not suffer from significant functional or economic obsolescence. In the final analysis, we simply do not know very much about estimating depreciation in appraising theory or practice.

THE INCOME APPROACH

The major objective of real estate investors is to maximize their wealth from investments. *Value* is defined as the present worth of the expected future stream of income received from ownership of the property. The amount an investor is willing to pay to acquire a property takes into account the expected annual cash flow as well as the reversion at the end of the holding period.

Operationally, the definition of value is expressed in the following equation:

$$V = \frac{I}{R} \qquad\qquad (11\text{--}22)$$

where:

V = value

I = expected income stream

R = rate of capitalization

☐ **USES OF THE INCOME APPROACH.** The income approach can be applied to all properties that generate an income stream. Information regarding the type of return investors are seeking can usually be obtained through market research or various methods of rate synthesis. Traditionally, appraisers develop an estimate of the net operating income and the appropriate rate of capitalization from which an estimate of value is made from market analysis.

The income approach also is able to adjust for changes in market factors more rapidly than the cost or direct sales comparison approaches. Because these latter approaches depend on historical data, they may not reflect changes in financing, income, expenses, or appreciation. With the income approach, it is possible to make appropriate changes to income and expenses as soon as they are known. If market comparison methods are used to develop a capitalization rate, they will also reflect any changes in market expectations.

☐ **INCOME APPROACH PROCEDURE.** The steps outlining the traditional income approach to value estimation are as follows:

1. Estimate potential gross income.
2. Estimate and deduct a vacancy and bad debt loss allowance to derive effective gross income.
3. Estimate and deduct expenses of operation to derive net operating income.
4. Estimate remaining economic life (or the duration) and pattern of the projected income stream.
5. Select an applicable capitalization method and technique.
6. Develop the appropriate rate or rates.
7. Select the method to derive a value estimate using the income approach.

The basic premise of the income approach is expressed as shown in Equation (11–22). Because the income referred to in this relationship is net operating income (NOI), the first three steps in the procedure are designed to estimate it.

Once NOI is determined, the appropriate rate must be derived. Step 4 indicates that economic life and pattern of the income stream should be considered before selecting a capitalization method.

There are three traditional methods used to derive capitalization rates. The first method extracts the rate from sales in the market. Table 11–18 illustrates three recently sold properties that are similar to the four-plex investment being valued. The rate is derived from the market (as shown in Table 11–18) using Equation (11–22).

When deriving a rate from the market, it is important that the properties be highly similar in terms of age, location, quality, condition, and other significant factors, as are these properties. Because these sales occurred at the same point in time, market and financing conditions should be very similar.

The second method of rate derivation is called the *band of investment*, or mortgage-equity analysis. This method considers the return required by the mortgage, as indicated by the annual mortgage constant (MC), and the return required by equity, as indicated by the equity dividend rate (EDR). Mortgage and equity returns are weighted by the proportion they contribute to total value. The rate (R) is derived using the following:

$$R = L/V(MC) + E/V(EDR) \qquad (11–23)$$

Recall that the investor in our example obtained an 80 percent loan-to-value, the EDR was 23.02 percent, and the monthly mortgage constant on a 12 percent rate compounded monthly for 25 years equals 0.0105322 (0.1263869 annually). The overall capitalization rate is calculated as follows:

$$.80 \times 0.1263869 = 0.1011095$$

$$.20 \times .2302 = 0.04604$$

$$R = 0.1471495 \text{ or } 14.71\%$$

TABLE 11–18
FOUR-PLEX EXAMPLE: A CAPITALIZATION RATE RANGE

		1	2	3
	PGI	$ 36,960	$ 38,400	$ 36,000
minus	VB	1,848	1,920	1,800
equals	EGI	35,112	36,480	34,200
minus	OE	8,426	8,756	8,550
equals	NOI	$ 26,686	$ 27,724	$ 26,650
	SP	$180,000	$177,000	$175,000
Indicated $R =$		$ 26,686	$ 27,724	$ 26,650
		$180,000	$177,000	$175,000
	$R =$	14.83%	15.66%	14.66%

To satisfy the requirements of the mortgage and equity, the investor would pay the price indicated by capitalizing the NOI of the property at a rate of 14.71 percent. Because the information used in the band of investment is taken from the market, the rate derived by this method should be an indication of the overall capitalization rate in the market.

A third method of deriving the capitalization rate is called the *Ellwood technique*. In addition to cash flow, this method takes equity buildup into account through mortgage amortization and increases (or decreases) in value as sources of holding period for the investment.

While the mathematical derivation of the Ellwood method for the overall rate is beyond our present discussion, the Ellwood equation for determining the overall rate is

$$R = y - mc_{-\text{app}}^{+\text{dep}}(\text{SFF}_{y,n}) \qquad (11\text{--}24)$$

where:

R = overall rate

y = equity yield rate, the required before-tax rate of return to equity

m = ratio of mortgage to value (loan-to-value ratio)

c = mortgage coefficient ($c = y + p\,(\text{SFF}_{y,n}) - f$)

dep = proportion depreciation in the property value for the holding period

app = proportion appreciation in the property value for the holding period

$\text{SFF}_{y,n}$ = sinking fund factor at a rate y for the holding period

p = proportion of loan paid off over the holding period

n = length of holding period

f = annual mortgage constant

EXAMPLE 11–2 ESTIMATING VALUE WITH DIRECT CAPITALIZATION: BAND-OF-INVESTMENT APPROACH

An investor is given the following data:

Net Operating Income (NOI) for the subject property = $190,000

Equity Dividend Rate (EDR) from comparable sales = 8.5 percent

Mortgage Constant (MC) from local banks = 13.1 percent

Loan-to-value ratio from local banks = 75.0 percent

The investor's best estimate of the value of the subject property is desired.

Using a composite rate, a band-of-investment approach to develop R as the weighted average of the required mortgage and equity yields. To obtain R using a band-of-investment, the return on equity and the return on debt and equity must be calculated. Recall $R = (L/V)MC + (E/V)EDR$, where

L/V = loan-to-value ratio

MC = mortgage constant

E/V = equity-to-value ratio

EDR = equity dividend rate

$$(L/V) \times MC = .75 \times .131 = .09825$$

$$(E/V) \times EDR = .25 \times .085 = \underline{.02125}$$

$$R = .11950$$

Capitalizing, the investor obtains a value, as defined by the ratio of NOI to R as:

$$V = \$190{,}000/.1195 = \$1{,}589{,}590$$

$$\text{say} \quad \$1{,}590{,}000$$

The band-of-investment procedure is one of the most commonly used in the valuation of income-producing properties. An equity dividend rate that is significantly lower than the mortgage constant suggests that the equity investor anticipates additional benefits not reflected in the immediate rate of return on equity capital, such as, future increases in income and/or value.

☐ **INCOME APPROACH EXAMPLE.** The four-plex example illustrates application of the income approach to value, using the Ellwood method to develop a capitalization rate.

The investor is considering an investment with an NOI of $23,540 in the first year. As stated earlier, the loan is obtained for 80 percent of the property value at an interest rate of 12 percent for 25 years with monthly payments. The property is expected to depreciate in value by 1.25 percent

(1 -$158,000 net sales proceeds/$160,000 purchase price) over the five-year holding period, and the investor requires an equity yield rate of 20 percent.

The overall capitalization rate is calculated as follows, using Equation (11–24):

$$R = y - mc_{-app}^{+dep}(\text{SFF}_{y,N})$$

$$R = .20 - .80(.0794543) + .0125(.13438)$$

$$R = .20 - .0635634 + .0016798$$

$$R = .1381164$$

Using the NOI of $23,540, the value of the quadraplex is

$$V = I/R$$

$$V = \frac{\$23,540}{.1381164}$$

$$V = \$170,436$$

According to the Ellwood method, the estimated value is $170,400. The investor could pay $170,400 for the property, given the assumptions, and earn a before-tax rate of return of 20 percent on the equity investment.

☐ **COMPARISON BETWEEN ELLWOOD CAPITALIZATION AND DCF.** L. W. Ellwood, a practicing appraiser with a keen mathematical bent, showed that the income approach to real estate valuation could be extended beyond direct capitalization from the market, the band of investment approach, and others. In particular, this method permitted the analyst to modify the capitalization rate to be applied to net operating income for two factors: (1) debt financing and (2) changes in property values over time. In the 1960s, Ellwood's technique became a new educational requirement for real estate appraisers and, more importantly, it changed the way of thinking about the income approach in the field.

At the same time, discounted cash flow models were being introduced. These calculations also enabled analysts to integrate financing and appreciation into the analysis. In addition, DCF models permitted even greater flexibility: various types of financing schemes could be evaluated, more appreciation expectations could be examined rather than the relatively few permitted under Ellwood, and tax effects could also be incorporated into the analysis.

An important development occurred when it was shown that under some limiting cash flow assumptions, both Ellwood capitalization and discounted cash flow models provided identical results. This permitted users to be assured of consistent results regardless of which technique was chosen. Over time, discounted cash flow models have been shown to be a more general set of techniques. As a result, cash flow analysis has become the multi-year capitalization method of choice; Ellwood capitalization has become less important, although its contribution to the field should not be forgotten.

EXAMPLE 11–3: ESTIMATING VALUE USING TRADITIONAL INVESTMENT CRITERIA

A real estate investor is considering the purchase of a small office building. The subject property contains 12,000 square feet of net rentable area. Data on recent comparable sales are shown in Table 1.

TABLE 1
RECENT COMPARABLE SALES

Comparable Sale	Sales Price	Gross Income	Vacancy, Rent Loss	Operating Expenses	Rentable Sq. Ft.
1	$570,000	$126,500	$ 6,325	$57,000	12,975
2	$575,000	$126,000	$10,000	$54,180	12,865
3	$640,000	$144,000	$ 8,700	$66,250	14,575
4	$559,000	$130,000	$ 9,100	$59,500	13,500

a. What is the rent per square foot for each comparable?
b. What is the vacancy rate for each comparable?
c. What is the gross income multiplier for each comparable?
d. What is the overall rate for each comparable?
e. What is the operating expense ratio for each comparable?
f. What is the sale price per square foot of rentable area for each comparable?
g. What is the value of the subject property using:
1. The gross income multiplier approach?
2. Direct capitalization using a market extracted overall rate?
3. The price per square foot of rentable area?

For each comparable sale, the investor provides the calculations in Table 2.

TABLE 2
COMPARABLE SALE DATA

Comparable Sale	Rent per Square Foot	Vacancy Rate	Gross Income Multiplier	Overall Rate	Operating Expense Ratio	Sale Price per Square Ft.
1	$9.75	5.00%	4.74	11.08%	.4743	$43.93
2	$9.79	7.94%	4.96	10.75%	.4671	$44.69
3	$9.88	6.04%	4.73	10.79%	.4897	$43.91
4	$9.63	7.00%	4.62	10.98%	.4921	$41.41

Thus, using the data from the comparable sales, the market rent per square foot is about $9.75. The estimated potential gross income for the subject property is:

$$PGI = 12,000 \ (\$9.75) = \$117,000$$

The effective gross income with 6.5 percent vacancy is:

$$EGI = \$117,000 - (.065) \ (117,000)$$

$$EGI = \$109,395$$

The net operating income, with an operating expense ratio of 47.5 percent, is:

$$NOI = \$109,395 - .475 \ (109,395)$$

$$= \$57,432 \ (say \ \$57,500)$$

Using these calculations, the investor estimates the value of the investment as follows:

1. Gross income multiplier approach:

$$Value = \$109,135 \ (4.8)$$

$$Value = \$523,848 \ (say \ \$524,000)$$

2. Direct capitalization approach:

$$Value = \$57,500 / .109$$

$$Value = \$527,523 \ (say \ \$527,500)$$

3. Price per square foot approach:

Value = $12,000 (43.50)

Value = $522,000

While the three approaches yield slightly different estimates, the indicated value of the subject property is about $525,000.

❐ **LIMITATIONS OF THE INCOME APPROACH.** The main limitation of the income approach is that its application is precluded if a property does not produce income, as in the appraisal of single-family residential housing. However, most properties purchased by investors have some expected cash flow, so the use of the income approach is possible in these cases.

Another limitation of the income approach is the development of appropriate "cap" rates. Any of the methods for developing rates are subject to question. In many instances, the appraiser is forced to use rates that are not taken directly from the market, so it is important that the method the appraiser uses to derive the rate parallel the method used by the investor.

Another problem in the development of rates is the projection of future change in the property value. Perhaps the appraiser can gain some insight regarding expectations through a market study. On many smaller investments, appreciation may be expected to provide a significant portion of the overall return. Since an investor is not sure if properties will appreciate in the future, there is likely to be a divergence of opinion among appraisers, investors, brokers, and developers about the proper rate of appreciation or depreciation. Therefore the selection of a rate deemed to be appropriate will often spark controversy, since a subjective element is introduced into the capitalization process.

SUMMARY

This chapter introduces the "traditional" investment criteria, including rules of thumb, ratio analysis, and the basic real estate appraisal techniques. All of these criteria make it possible to calculate the expected rate of return from an investment that is then compared to the required return *or* the calculation of the value of an investment that is then compared to its costs. The advantages of these criteria are that they are easy to calculate and simple to understand. They do, however, have several disadvantages when compared to the more advanced discounted cash flow techniques discussed in the next chapter.

QUESTIONS

11–1. What are the general characteristics of the rules-of-thumb criteria?

11–2. What is the relationship between the overall capitalization rate and the net income multiplier?

11–3. What are average rate of return measures?

11–4. How can the reversion be included in the average rate of return calculations?

11–5. "A major problem using the rules-of-thumb criteria is that they lack sound decision rules." True or false? Explain.

11–6. What are the typical ratios used in analyzing real estate investments?

11–7. What is another name for the "return on equity" ratio?

11–8. What are the limitations of ratio analysis?

11–9. Traditional appraisal approaches can also be used in real estate investment analysis. Illustrate how the three appraisal approaches can be used by investors.

11–10. What is the "income approach to value"?

PROBLEMS

11–1. "Market value is an interesting and useful input to the investment decision process, but more importantly, the investor is concerned with the present worth of the partial interest that represents the investor's planned investment interest." Demonstrate why market value estimation is a useful input to the investment decision.

11–2. Demonstrate how appraisal techniques can be used by investors.

11–3. An investor is considering the purchase an apartment building for $1,000,000. This investment, has the following projected characteristics:

Loan-to-value ratio	70 percent
Net operating income	$185,000
Allowance for vacancy and bad debt	5 percent of PGI
Potential Gross Income	$225,000
Before tax cash flow	$ 65,000
After-tax cash flow	$ 51,000

Calculate the following:
a. Gross income multiplier (GM). Use both PGI and EGI.
b. Net income multiplier (NIM)
c. Before-tax cash flow multiplier (BTCFM)
d. After-tax cash flow multiplier (ATCFM)
e. Overall capitalization rate (R)
f. Equity dividend rate (EDR)

g. After tax return (ATR)

11–4. You have been given the assignment to appraise a single-family house. The house has 1,500 square feet of living area. Analysis of construction costs indicates a per-square-foot cost of $30. The house has an effective age of 50 years and an estimated economic life of 50 years. Changing neighborhood characteristics have had a negative influence of $1,000 on the value. An examination of similar lots indicates a value of $10,000 for the land value. What is the market value estimate of the property?

11–5. For the appraisal assignment in Problem 11–3, you also observe that an analysis of the market indicates the following:

Characteristic	Subject Property	Comparable 1	Comparable 2
Sale price	—	$50,000	$48,000
Time	11/85	9/85	7/85
Location	—	Same	Same
Financing	Conventional	Same	Same
Size	1,500 sq. ft.	1,650 sq. ft.	1,400 sq. ft.
Age	10 yrs.	12 yrs.	8 yrs.
Garage	2-car	Same	None

a. Housing prices have been increasing at the rate of 0.8 percent per month.
b. Each additional square foot is valued at $25.
c. Each additional year of age reduces value by $250.
d. A two-car garage is valued at $5,000.

What is the estimate of value of the subject property?

11–6. Using the following information, estimate the value using the Ellwood valuation model:

NOI	$100,000
L/V	75 percent
Interest rate	9 percent
Maturity	20 years/annual payments
Holding period	8 years
Change in value	20 percent appreciation
Before-tax equity yield	16 percent

11–7. Using the unit comparison method of the cost approach, you are asked to value a 100,000-square-foot industrial building. The land that the building is on is valued at $555,000. The reproduction cost of the building is estimated at $36.50 per square foot. The cost of replacing the parking lots, drives, walks, and landscaping is estimated at $50,000. The previous owner was lax in maintaining both the building and other site improvements, and, as a result, physical deterioration is estimated at $130,000. Further, because the building is 40 years old, some areas of the building are not structurally strong enough to carry some of the heavier new machines. As a result of this functional obsolescence, the building should be devalued by $750,000. Finally, there is no evidence of economic obsolescence.

SELECTED REFERENCES

Ambrose, Brent W., and Hugh O. Nourse, "Factors Influencing Capitalization Rates," *Journal of Real Estate Research,* 8 (Spring 1993), 221–237.

Appraisal Institute, *The Appraisal of Real Estate,* 10th ed. Chicago: Appraisal Institute, 1992.

Boykin, James H., and MARGARET T. GRAY, "The Relevance and Application of the Gross Income Multiplier," *The Appraisal Journal,* 62 (April 1994), 203–208.

Eppli, Mark J., "The Theory, Assumptions, and Limitations of Direct Capitalization," *The Appraisal Journal,* 61 (July 1993), 419–425.

Fisher, Jeffrey D., "Ellwood After Tax—New Dimensions," *Appraisal Journal,* 45 (July 1977), 331–342.

Gettel, Ronald E., *Real Estate Guidelines and Rules of Thumb.* New York: McGraw-Hill, 1976.

Lusht, Kenneth M., "Measuring Rate of Return: Two Rules of Thumb versus the Internal Rate," *Appraisal Journal,* 46 (April 1978), 245–256.

Martin, W. B., "Direct Capitalization or Discounted Cash Flow Analysis?" *The Appraisal Journal,* 61 (July 1993), 390–393.

Sirmans, C. F., and JAMES R. WEBB, "Mortgage Equity Analysis, Again?!," *Appraisal Journal,* 47 (January 1979), 44–52.

Wang, Ko, Terry V. Grissom, and Su Han Chan, "The Functional Relationships and Use of Going-in and Going-out Capitalization Rates," *Journal of Real Estate Research,* 5 (Summer 1990), 231–245.

Wendt, Paul F., *Real Estate Appraisal—Review and Outlook.* Athens, Ga: University of Georgia Press, 1974.

CHAPTER **12**

DISCOUNTED CASH FLOW MODELS

PRINCIPLES

1. Discounted cash flow (DCF) models have become the key measures in modern real estate investment analysis.
2. DCF calculations permit the analyst to evaluate all of the benefits and costs facing real estate investors on a time-adjusted basis.
3. The net present value (NPV) and the internal rate of return (IRR) methods are the basic DCF criteria.
4. There are key and sometimes, critical differences between NPV and IRR.
5. Extensions to the basic DCF methods offer some specialized measures.
6. Recent surveys show DCF models are often used in actual real estate investing.

In the preceding chapter we summarized many of the traditional methods that investors use to make investment decisions. We also explained why these methods are often faulty and prone to inconsistent investment choices. A more rigorous method is described in this chapter. This method, called *discounted cash flow models,* has been used for some time by financial analysts but has only recently been applied to real estate investment analysis.

After the analyst forecasts cash flows, these measures are used to choose projects that are consistent with the investor's personal objectives. However, the possibility of changing cash flow streams, growth or decline in the expected future selling price, and various other concerns regarding financing policy and tax planning may dramatically affect the investment choice. Therefore, any acceptable approach must address these issues. This chapter examines the two discounted cash flow models typically used in practice: the *net present value* approach and the *internal rate of return* method. Both of these capital-budgeting techniques have been designed for the real estate equity investor. In addition, we compare the two techniques, and we show that if the investor's objective is to maximize investment wealth, the use of net present value as an investment criterion will ensure that the best projects will be selected. This implies that at least in some cases, the use of the internal rate of return as an investment criterion will lead to suboptimal choices. Finally, some alternative discounted cash flow models are presented. These represent modifications of the basic models. Based on recent survey results, many investors seem to prefer some of the modified models. The chapter concludes with a brief discussion of the importance of discounted cash flow models.

The Discounted Cash Flow Approach

Modern real estate investment analysis has generally adopted the discounted cash flow approach to valuation. There are many reasons why this approach is favored. First, it can measure cash flows throughout the life of the investment as well as the impact of the reversion at the time of sale. Second, the measure of benefits used—after-tax cash flows—is selected because this measure takes into account factors such as operating expenses, financial expenses, depreciation, interest, tax shelter, and taxation. Third, the after-tax equity reversion takes into account the selling expenses, if any, and the repayment of outstanding principal. Fourth, this approach permits any or all of these variables to change over time, at individual rates of change, if the analyst believes such changes are necessary. Fifth, since expected cash flows in the future and the expected equity reversion at a future selling date are not received by the investor *today*, this technique incorporates a consideration of the time-value of money to permit the adjustment of actual dollars into present value, time adjusted dollars. Finally, the various types of risk may be incorporated into the discounted cash flow approach. In addition, changing risk levels may also be treated, although this may become a difficult task. Therefore, for these and other reasons, the discounted cash flow approach enjoys a prominent place among investment criteria for real estate investment analysis.

The use of discounted cash flow models requires the understanding of more technical methods of analysis, additional data requirements and estimates, and additional time and effort on the part of the analyst. We believe that familiarity with the basic approach and an understanding of the concept of discounted models can help investors improve their analysis of potential real estate investment, and in many cases, eliminate reliance on the traditional rules of thumb.

THE MODELS

The real estate investment process provides a framework for systematically analyzing information to use when choosing among alternative investment opportunities.

Recall from Chapter 2 that the equity valuation model measures the investment value of equity, the net present value of equity, and/or the internal rate of return on equity. The investment value of equity (E) is defined as

$$E = \sum_{t=1}^{n} \frac{ATCF_t}{(1 + k_e)^t} + \frac{ATER_n}{(1 + k_e)^n} \tag{12-1}$$

The net present value of equity (NPV_e) is defined as

$$NPV_e = \sum_{t=1}^{n} \frac{ATCF}{(1 + k_e)^t} + \frac{ATER_n}{(1 + k_e)^n} - (MV - MD) \tag{12-2}$$

The internal rate of return on equity (IRR_e) is the value that satisfies the following equation:

$$0 = \sum_{t=1}^{n} \frac{ATCF_t}{(1 + IRR_e)^t} + \frac{ATER_n}{(1 + IRR_e)^n} - (MV - MD) \tag{12-3}$$

These models constitute basic discounted cash flow analysis.

The calculation of the investment value of equity (E) is equal to the discounted value of after-tax cash flows from operations over the expected holding period and the discounted value of the after-tax equity reversion at the time of sale, discounted by the required rate of return on equity. The result represents the greatest amount that the specific investor is justified in paying to acquire the property rights of the investment. This amount must be compared with the amount of equity required of the investor, which when added to the presumed amount of mortgage debt, equals the acquisition price.

The net present value of equity (NPV_e) is equal to the difference between the investment value of equity and the down payment required of the equity investor. In effect, the investment value of equity represents the benefits from the investment, and the down payment represents the costs. Thus the net present value is the difference between costs and benefits.

The internal rate of return on equity (IRR_e) is the rate of return such that the discounted value of after-tax cash flows and the discounted value of the after-tax equity reversion are equal to the required equity investment. This expected rate of return is compared with the required rate of return on equity to evaluate the investment's attractiveness.

SOME ISSUES IN DISCOUNTED CASH FLOW ANALYSIS

Real estate investment is basically a capitalization process: investors give up a known, certain amount in exchange for an expected, but uncertain, stream of future cash flows. *Capitalization* is the conversion of an expected future stream of benefits into a present-value sum. Therefore, capitalization of income or cash flow is an integral part of investment analysis.

There are four major reasons why discounted cash flow models are superior to the traditional methods discussed in Chapter 11: (1) changing income (and cash flow) streams, (2) changing levels of risk, (3) differing size and types of expected future benefits, and (4) the time-value of money concept.

❐ **CHANGING BENEFIT STREAMS.** Unlike other investments such as corporate bonds and some common stocks, the financial benefits of real estate investments vary each period. In the case of apartment houses, for example, despite the fixing of contract rent and the predominance of level-payment amortized mortgages, operating expenses may vary significantly throughout the leasing period. This causes net operating income to vary. As net operating income varies, so does before-tax cash flow with the fixed debt service payment.

Furthermore, discounted cash flow techniques rely on after-tax cash flow payments in calculating value and return. Chapters 1 and 11 showed that after-tax cash flow differs from before-tax cash flow by the amount of income tax to be paid each period. Since income taxes are calculated by the investor's tax rate times the amount of taxable income, changes in taxable income (or the tax rate) will result in changes in after-tax cash flow. The cash flow statement in Chapter 1 also showed that taxable income varies according to changes in interest payments and depreciation allowances (if an accelerated depreciation method is used). Therefore, since the equity valuation model uses after-tax cash flow as a measure of benefits, changes in net operating income, interest payments, depreciation allowances, or tax rates expected in the future will result in the changing benefit stream from the investment.

Finally, if rental and income payments vary due to monthly lease agreements, or if vacancies vary, or if bad debt problems are particularly relevant, effective gross income and potential gross income will vary. If multiple financing options are used, causing financial expenses to vary from period to period, measures relating to the equity position also may be altered. These possibilities suggest that changing benefit streams are more likely to occur than not, and, as a result, discounted cash flow models are much more suited to handling these problems.

❐ **CHANGING LEVELS OF RISK.** Since financial and economic markets are dynamic in nature, events frequently occur that affect the risk/return opportunities of investments. For example, at the time the investment is being evaluated, there is a certain amount of market risk associated with the investment, as discussed in Chapter 4. If the amount of risk is expected to vary over the expected holding period of the investment, the analyst is concerned with the fact that as the riskiness of the investment increased (decreased), the investment value would fall (rise) in response to the change in risk. Similarly, changes in the required rate of return on equity would occur in proportion to changes in the riskiness of the investment.

Discounted cash flow models are better suited to handle this measurement problem than direct capitalization or other single-period rules-of-thumb. In some cases, the necessary adjustment can be made to income estimates when risk is expected to increase. Other models show that expected increasing risk levels result in falling values of income or cash flows. Finally, complex models may be used to account for expected changes in future risk levels in a discounted cash flow approach. Although this development is beyond the scope of this book, it demonstrates the fact that discounted cash flow models can be extremely flexible and therefore are valuable for real estate analysts.

Some investors suggest that increasing the capitalization rate by using traditional rules-of-thumb has the same effect as raising the risk-adjusted discount rate used in discounted cash flow models. In some cases, it may be possible to get consistent or identical results. However, in view of other limitations and problems with the earlier techniques, the measurement of expected changes in risk is best handled in the discounted cash flow approach

☐ **DIFFERING SIZES AND TYPES OF BENEFITS.**   Another advantage is the ability to accurately account for income or cash flow figures that are expected to vary significantly from year to year. Traditional techniques have either disregarded future benefit streams that were expected to be significantly different from the current one, averaged the expected income or cash flow for the next few years, or stabilized the benefits in some fashion. The ability of discounted cash flow models to reflect the expected size of the income or cash flow in the year in which it is expected to occur is a major improvement over other techniques. Real estate investment analysis often involves property where an income is earned over the holding period and appreciation in value is expected to be realized at the time of sale. Thus the investor actually expects to receive two types of benefits: periodic cash flow receipts and a lump-sum cash flow at the end of the holding period. These benefits cause significant problems for investors using rules-of-thumb. Discounted cash flow models can adequately account for both types of benefits. Furthermore, estimates of benefit sizes can be made without specifying the capitalization rate or investment value. Discounted cash flow procedures also help the investor to account for rising property values, equity build-up, or rising income levels due to changes in demand.

The investor who uses rules-of-thumb either takes rough averages of the changing variables, assumes the changes have no effect on the investment and does nothing about them, or is unable to evaluate the effects of these changes on income-producing real estate.

❒ TIME-VALUE OF MONEY.   Finally, discounted cash flow techniques are important due to the existence of the time-value of money in productive market economies. The concept of the time value of money is critical to investment decisions because returns from the investment often occur at various intervals throughout the holding period. The present value of all the expected income or cash flow payments is less than the sum of the payments, even without inflation or risk, and the analyst must evaluate investments on a time-adjusted basis. Discounted cash flow models help the investor to take into account the *timing* and the amount of payments and receipts. Then this factor is incorporated into the decision criteria.

The traditional single-period measures either ignore the time-value of money or assume these are consistent with discounted cash flow models. However, the former action leads to inferior investment choices while the latter is more general and flexible and therefore preferable.

Discounted cash flow models were developed due to the effect of declining values of future benefits. As we will see, comparisons based on total dollar receipts (income, cash flows, and so on) disregard the measurement of the time-value of money and therefore result in a wrong choice. This point is demonstrated in the following example. An investor wishes to decide between investments G and H. Each costs the same amount. Investment G is expected to yield $100 per year for 10 years. Investment H is expected to yield $1,000 at the end of the tenth year. Each investment is believed to be in the same risk class. Should the investor assume that these two are similar? Obviously, the answer is no. Although both yield the same "total dollars" of benefits, $1,000, investment G will yield some return each year. Since investment H is not expected to return any dollars until the end of 10 years, the time-value of money theory says that investment G is preferred to investment H at any positive discount rate.

Therefore discounted cash flow analysis can be a powerful and useful tool for analysts. It forms the framework for most modern real estate investment analysis and is flexible enough to permit adjustments according to market changes. Finally, it permits a treatment of the time-value of money considerations that are so crucial in making financial decisions.

UNCERTAINTY, FUTURE CASH FLOWS, AND MARKET EFFICIENCY

If we lived in a world in which we knew with certainty *what* and *when* future cash flows would occur, making investment decisions would be much easier. In such a world, however, there would not be any investment problems. The investor would simply calculate rates of return and values of various choices and *know* what each alternative was truly worth. But, in such a world, *everyone* would know what each asset would be worth. Although investment analysis might still exist, investment values would always equal market values.

In the real world, future cash flows from real estate investments and changes in those cash flows are *not* known with certainty. Therefore, investment analysis is risk analysis. But it is possible to view it as the analysis of the quality of data as well as the acquisition of technical skill to identify, measure, and evaluate the uncertainty. As we will see in Chapter 13, there are various ways to incorporate risk into the discounted cash flow framework.

If we believe that the analysis of data will yield valuable information about prospective investments, this implies that other analysis might also learn about the risk and possible returns from the investment by analyzing the same data. If so, there may be little reason to believe that one side of the market has more information than the other. Therefore, the determination of market values may reflect the information available to the market. If this is the case, it may be impossible for investors using market information to outperform others in the market unless the investor has (1) particular or unusual skills, (2) unusual investment requirements, (3) an exceptionally quick response time, or (4) a short-run string of luck.

Of course, the availability of information depends on *market efficiency*, or the rate and extent to which information is incorporated into market prices. If the market is very efficient, the available information is quickly reflected in selling prices of assets in that market. If inefficient, the acquisition of superior information about market activity suggests opportunities for *arbitrage returns,* or the identification of undervalued assets available for sale. Discounted cash flow analysis is often deemed useful whether markets are efficient or not. In inefficient markets, this technique can be used to identify projects that are undervalued. In efficient markets, discounted cash flow analysis can be one of the techniques that assists investors in maintaining market efficiency.

CALCULATING THE INVESTMENT VALUE OF EQUITY (E)

We can now develop the *investment value of equity (E)* model. This model provides the investor with an approach that can then be compared with the market (or asking) price to see if it is an acceptable investment. This measure emphasizes the equity position of the investor and values two major components: *after-tax cash flow* and *after-tax equity reversion.* Of course, emphasis is also placed on the decision rules for making the analysis.

PRESENT VALUE OF AFTER-TAX CASH FLOW

The preceding example calculated investment values using cash flows as measures of benefits. In valuing the portion attributable to the equity holder, the analyst can choose which type of cash flow measure to use. However, there are many reasons why an investor would prefer to use an after-tax cash flow figure.

Chapter 1 defined *after-tax cash flow* as net operating income less debt service less tax payments. This can be represented as

$$ATCF_t = NOI_t - DS_t - T_t \tag{12-4}$$

where:

$ATCF_t$ = after-tax cash flow in the tth period

NOI_t = net operating income in the tth period

DS_t = debt service in the tth period

T_t = income tax liability in the tth period

Furthermore, we can split debt service into two components: interest expense and principal amortization:

$$DS_t = I_t + A_t \tag{12-5}$$

where:

I_t = interest expense in the tth period

A_t = principal amortization in the tth period

Recall that income taxes are calculated by multiplying the investor's marginal tax rate times net operating income plus the replacement reserve less interest expense less depreciation, or

$$T_t = \tau(NOI_t + RR_t - I_t - D_t) \tag{12-6}$$

where:

τ = investor's marginal tax rate

RR_t = reserve for replacement in the tth period

D_t = depreciation allowance in the tth period

By substituting Equations (12–5) and (12–6) into Equation (12–4), we get:

$$ATCF_t = NOI_t - (I_t + A_t) - \tau(NOI_t + RR_t - I_t - D_t) \tag{12-7}$$

Note that the depreciation allowance affects the after-tax cash flow only in the last term of Equation (12–7). The benefits of depreciation result from a reduction in income tax liability and, in this way, depreciation allowances increase the after-tax cash flow to the investor.

Therefore, we can calculate the discounted value of the after-tax cash flows with this basic model:

$$\text{PV of ATCF} = \frac{\text{ATCF}_1}{(1 + k_e)^1} + \frac{\text{ATCF}_2}{(1 + k_e)^2} + \frac{\text{ATCF}_3}{(1 + k_e)^3} + \cdots + \frac{\text{ATCF}_n}{(1 + k_e)^n}$$

$$= \sum_{t=1}^{n} \frac{\text{ATCF}_n}{(1 + k_e)^t} \qquad (12\text{--}8)$$

where:

PV of ATCF = present value of after-tax cash flow stream

k_e = required rate of return on equity

This formula represents the discounted value of after-tax cash flows for the expected holding period. It permits after-tax cash flow estimates to be constant each period as in an annuity or permits the cash flows to vary from year to year as in the typical investment.

PRESENT VALUE OF AFTER-TAX EQUITY REVERSION

However, Equation (12–8) fails to take into account *the expected selling price at the end of the nth year, the satisfaction of the unpaid mortgage note, or taxes due at the time of sale* (capital gains, recapture, or minimum taxes). A better valuation model would take account of these factors, since these affect the cash flow to the investor at the time of sale. Therefore the analyst needs to incorporate these considerations into one model. Equation (12–9) provides the necessary measure: the after-tax equity reversion:

$$\text{ATER}_n = \text{SP}_n - \text{SE}_n - \text{UM}_n - \text{GT}_n \qquad (12\text{--}9)$$

where:

ATER_n = after-tax equity reversion at the end of the nth period

SP_n = estimated net selling price at the end of the nth period

UM_n = unpaid mortgage balance at the end of the nth period

GT_n = taxes on total gain at the end of the nth period

SE_n = selling expenses

Since ATER does not result in a positive cash flow for the investor until the nth period (year), the value of this component can be found as follows:

$$\text{PV of ATER} = \frac{\text{ATER}_n}{(1 + k_e)^n} \qquad (12\text{--}10)$$

where:

> PV of ATER = present value of after-tax equity reversion

Therefore, by combining Equations (12–8) and (12–10), we get the complete equity valuation model:

$$E = (\text{PV of ATCF}) + (\text{PV of ATER}) - \text{TC}_0$$

$$= \frac{\text{ATCF}_1}{(1 + k_e)^1} + \frac{\text{ATCF}_2}{(1 + k_e)^2} + \frac{\text{ATCF}_3}{(1 + k_e)^3} + \cdots + \frac{\text{ATCF}_n}{(1 + k_e)^n} + \frac{\text{ATER}_n}{(1 + k_e)^n} - \text{TC}_0$$

$$= \sum_{t=1}^{n} \frac{\text{ATCF}_t}{(1 + k_e)^t} + \frac{\text{ATER}_n}{(1 + k_e)^n} - \text{TC}_0 \qquad (12\text{--}11)$$

Whenever ATER_n is positive, analysts who neglect the impact of the after-tax equity reversion and rely solely on the after-tax cash flow benefits will calculate a lower value than desirable. Therefore, the inclusion of the reversion is important to valuing income-producing real estate, and Equation (12–10), which measures the investment value of equity (E), is a more realistic model. TC_0 are the equity cash outflows at time 0.

As an example, suppose we wish to value an investment given the assumptions shown in Table 12–1. Assume that the reserve for replacements is $0.00 per year, interest payments vary according to a level-payment amortization schedule of $300,000 borrowed at 12 percent annually for 25 years, and depreciation is deducted on the basis of $400,000 over a depreciable life of 39 years using the straight-line method. The investor's marginal tax rate is .28.

Using these data, we can calculate the annual tax liability, using Equation (12–6), and the results are shown in Table 12–2.

Table 12–3 can then be developed to calculate the annual after-tax cash flow, using Equation (12–7). Finally, the after-tax equity reversion can be calculated, using Equation (12–9) and is shown in Tables 12–4 and 12–5.

If we assume k_e equal to 11 percent, we can get the two components of E:

$$\text{PV of ATCF} = \frac{\$5,508.72}{(1.11)^1} + \frac{\$6,841.67}{(1.11)^2} + \frac{8,222.23}{(1.11)^3} + \frac{\$9,649.23}{(1.11)^4} + \frac{\$1,333.41}{(1.11)^5}$$

$$= \$23,675.25$$

$$\text{PV of ATER} = \frac{\$150,036.00}{(1.11)^5}$$

$$= \$89,039.06$$

TABLE 12–1
INVESTMENT ASSUMPTIONS

Input	Assumption
Building size	Ten offices totaling 8,900 square feet of net rentable area
Purchase price	$400,000
Acquisition costs	$2,500
Rents	$8.00 per square feet in year 1; expected to increase 5% per year
Vacancy and bad debt losses	6% per year
Operating expenses	$21,752 in year 1; expected to increase 6% per year
Financing	
Loan-to-value ratio	75%
Interest rate	12%
Maturity	20 years with monthly payments
Financing costs	$10,000
Prepayment penalty	6% of amount outstanding
Depreciation	
Percent depreciable	85%
Useful life	39 years
Method	Straight-line
Holding period	5 years
Expected selling price	$480,000
Selling expenses	6%
Marginal tax rate	28%
After-tax ROR (rate-of-return)	11%

TABLE 12–2
ANNUAL TAX LIABILITY

	Year	1	2	3	4	5
	Net operating income	45,176	47,217	49,348	51,571	53,890
(+)	Replacement reserves	0	0	0	0	0
(−)	Interest	35,793.03	35,305.25	34,755.61	34,136.26	*49,952.34
(−)	Depreciation	8,782	8,782	8,782	8,782	8,782
(−)	Amortized financing costs	500	500	500	500	500
(=)	Taxable income	101	2,630	5,310	8,153	(12,844)
(×)	Marginal Tax rate	.28	.28	.28	.28	.28
(=)	Tax liability	28.27	736.33	1,486.91	2,282.77	(3,596.42)

*Includes a prepayment penalty.

Therefore, the investment value of equity (E) is $100,214.31, using Equation (12–11).

$$E = \$14{,}050.05 + \$89{,}039.06 - \$12{,}500$$

$$= \$100{,}214.31$$

TABLE 12-3
ANNUAL AFTER-TAX CASH FLOW

Year	1	2	3	4	5
Net Operating Income	45,176	47,217	49,348	51,571	53,890
(−) Interest	35,793.03	35,305.25	34,755.61	34,136.26	*49,952.34
(−) Amortized principal	3,845.97	4,333.75	4,883.39	5,502.74	6,200.64
(−) Tax liability	28.27	736.33	1,486.91	2,282.77	(3,596.42)
(=) After-tax Cash flow	5,508.72	6,841.67	8,222.09	9,649.23	1,333.42

*Includes the prepayment penalty.

TABLE 12-4
AFTER-TAX EQUITY REVERSION

Expected Cash Flow from Sale of Investment

	Expected selling price (SP)	$480,000
minus	Selling expenses (SE)	$ 28,800
equals	Net sale proceeds (NSP)	$451,200
minus	Unpaid mortgage balance (UM)	$275,233
equals	Before-tax equity reversion (BTER)	$175,967
minus	Taxes due on sale (TDS)	$ 25,931
equals	After-tax equity reversion (ATER)	$150,036

TABLE 12-5
EXPECTED TAXES DUE ON SALE

Taxable Income

	Expected selling price (SP)	$480,000
minus	Selling expenses (SE)	$ 28,800
equals	Amount realized (AR)	$451,200
minus	Adjusted basis (AB)	$358,590
equals	Capital gain on sale (CG)	$ 92,610

Taxes Due on Sale

	Capital gain on sale (CG)	$ 92,610
times	Investor's marginal tax rate (τ)	0.28
equals	Taxes due on sale (TDS)	$ 25,931

*See p. 344.

The analyst would be willing to pay up to $100,214.31 in equity for the property. The following discussion examines the decision rules in more detail.

THE NET-PRESENT-VALUE DECISION RULES

When using investment models, it is important to decide whether an investment is acceptable or not and, if so, how attractive it is relative to other alternatives, especially if some of these are mutually exclusive. In fact, one of the major criticisms of the rules-of-thumb has been the lack of consistent decision rules. For example, how short a payback period should the minimally acceptable project have if payback methods are used? How high can the gross income multiplier become before the investment ceases to be attractive? Clearly, there are no objective answers to these questions. The traditional answers often result in more rules-of-thumb.

Using the investment value of equity model developed in this section, we can define an acceptable investment project as one that, minimally, earns the required rate of return. Using Equation (12–11), we get a value for E. Since the initial amount of mortgage debt, MD, must be known in order to calculate the debt service, we next develop an investment value for the total *investment* by adding E and MD. Then this sum is compared with the market value. If this value (E + MD) is greater than market's sales price (or market value), the investor should invest in the project because it would earn more than the required rate of return and increase the investor's wealth. If the market value is greater than the sum of E and MD, the investor would not be able to achieve the required rate of return and should reject it.

Therefore, if the investment value for the total capital is greater than the market value, this excess value is the *net present value* of the investment. As long as the net present value is greater than zero, investment in the project will increase the investor's wealth, and the investor should accept all projects with positive net present values.

Decision Rule 1: Using investment value of equity and mortgage debt, if

$$(E + MD) \geq MV, \text{ then NPV} \geq 0, \text{ and if}$$

$$(E + MD) < MV, \text{ then NPV} < 0.$$

Following the example, E is calculated to be $100,214.31 and MD is $300,000. Since $400,214.31 is greater than $400,000, the decision rule tells the investor to accept the investment (NPV is equal to $214.31).

An alternative approach is to develop a decision rule using E directly. Since Equation (12–11) calculates E, some analysts might prefer a decision rule using E, which indicates whether or not to accept the investment. This can be accomplished by modifying Decision Rule 1 as follows:

Decision Rule 2: Using investment value of equity, if

$$E \geq (MV - MD), \text{ then NPV} \geq 0, \text{ and if}$$

$$E < (MV - MD), \text{ then NPV} < 0.$$

Using the numbers from the example, $100,214.31 is greater than $100,000, so this decision rule also tells the investor to accept the investment.

Obviously, Decision Rules 1 and 2 are consistent. Both provide identical measures of net present value. Both indicate whether or not the wealth of the investor will increase if the investment is acquired.

EXAMPLE 12–1 BEFORE-TAX VALUATION

A basis has been established to calculate the NPV and IRR for a project with a specified set of cash flows. What if the investor knew the NOI and the required rate of return, but wanted to know the value of the project?

The following formula can be used to calculate a value for a project:

$$V = L/V(V) + PVAF_{y\%,n \text{ yrs.}}[NOI - (MC)(L/V)(V)]$$
$$+ PVF_{y\%,n \text{ yrs.}}[(1 + g)^n(V) - L/V(V)(PO)]$$

Consider an investor who wants to calculate the value of a project with the following assumptions:

Property values expected to increase at growth rate (g) of 2 percent per year (10.41 percent over the five-year holding period).

L/V = 75 percent

i = 12 percent, 20 year amortization, monthly payments

Annual mortgage constant (MC) = .13212

Proportion of mortgage outstanding (PO) at end of holding period = .91742

NOI = $45,000 (NOI remains constant over holding period)

N = 5 years

y = 15 percent

$$V = .75(V) + PVAF_{15\%,5 \text{ yrs.}}[45,000 - (.13212)(.75)(V)]$$
$$+ PVF_{15\%,5 \text{ yrs.}}[1.1041(V) - .75(V)(.91742)]$$

$$V = .75(V) + 3.352155[45,000 - (.13212)(.75)(V)]$$
$$+ .497177[1.1041(V) - .75(V)(.91742)]$$

$$V - .75(V) + .332165(V) - .5489331(V) + .34209(V) = 150,847$$

$$.375322(V) = 150,847$$

$$V = \$401,914$$

Thus, the value of this project is $401,914. This represents the maximum that the investor could pay and earn the 15 percent required rate of return on equity.

CALCULATING THE INTERNAL RATE OF RETURN ON EQUITY (IRR$_e$)

An alternative framework for making real estate investment decisions uses a measure called the *internal rate of return*. It is similar to net present value but potentially inconsistent with the foregoing techniques. The *internal rate of return* is defined as the annual rate that equates the present value of the cash inflows with the present value of the cash outflows. In real estate investment analysis, the *internal rate of return on equity* (IRR$_e$) is the measure preferred by most investors.

THE INTERNAL RATE OF RETURN CALCULATION

The internal rate of return on equity, IRR$_e$, in equation form is represented follows:

$$0 = \frac{ATCF_1}{(1 + IRR_e)^1} + \frac{ATCF_2}{(1 + IRR_e)^2} + \frac{ATCF_3}{(1 + IRR_e)^3}$$

$$+ \cdots + \frac{ATCF_n}{(1 + IRR_e)^n} + \frac{ATER_n}{(1 + IRR_e)^n} - (MV - MD) \quad (12\text{--}12)$$

$$= \sum_{t=1}^{n} \frac{ATCF_t}{(1 + IRR_e)^t} + \frac{ATER_n}{(1 + IRR_e)^n} - (MV - MD)$$

Using the numbers from the example discussed earlier, we get the following internal rate of return on equity:

$$0 = \frac{\$5,508.72}{(1 + IRR_e)^1} + \frac{\$6,841.72}{(1 + IRR_e)^2} + \frac{\$8,222.09}{(1 + IRR_e)^3} + \frac{\$9,649.23}{(1 + IRR_e)^4}$$

$$+ \frac{\$1,333.42}{(1 + IRR_e)^5} + \frac{\$150,036.00}{(1 + IRR_e)^5} - (\$400,000 - \$300,000)$$

$$IRR_e = 13.99\%$$

In this case, 13.99 percent represents the yield or time-adjusted rate of return to the equity investor.

Technically, however, a multiperiod internal rate of return cannot be calculated directly. The analyst must (a) approximate the internal rate of return by trial-and-error and center in on the value, (b) use a calculator or computer to approximate the answer using one of several mathematical techniques, or (c) find the rate of return, IRR$_e$, that makes E equal to (MV $-$ MD) (that is, where NPV $= 0$). This last suggestion is actually the condition under which the internal rate of return on equity is derived.

THE INTERNAL RATE OF RETURN DECISION RULE

After a value for IRR_e is derived, the analyst must evaluate the attractiveness of the investment. The following decision rule can be quite helpful.
Decision Rule 3: Using internal rate of return on equity, if

$$IRR_e \geq k_e, \text{ then NPV} \geq 0, \text{ and if}$$

$$IRR_e < k_e, \text{ then NPV} < 0.$$

In this example, 13.99 percent is greater than 11.00 percent, so the investor should invest in the project.

A few words of clarification are in order. First, although the use of the investment value of equity model and the internal rate of return on equity are closely related, there are some important differences. A comparison of Decision Rules 1 and 2 with Decision Rule 3 reveals that in all the rules, a favorable project is indicated by a positive net present value. Whenever one of the rules indicates an "accept" signal, the other two will indicate it as well. Therefore it is impossible to get conflicting "accept-reject" signals between the net present value (investment value of equity) and internal rate of return (on equity) techniques. Second, although the decision rules are consistent about final outcomes, they do not rank projects identically. Finally, despite the close relationship between these two approaches, there is much to lose if the analyst chooses the internal rate of return as a "matter of preference."

WHICH DCF TECHNIQUE SHOULD BE USED?

One of the most frequently discussed issues in the capital budgeting is the comparison between net present value and the internal rate of return. There are several areas in which NPV and IRR have been compared. These are discussed in this section.

EITHER TECHNIQUE CHOOSES AN IDENTICAL SET OF INVESTMENTS

It is possible to decide whether an investment is acceptable by using either the internal rate of return method or the net-present-value method. Consider an investment that has a net present value greater than zero. This means that the discounted value of the benefits, *at some discount rate*, is greater than the investment outlay. At a higher discount rate, the net present value will be lower.[1] Suppose further that the net present value is still positive at the higher discount rate. At some discount rate, the net present value is equal to zero. This rate is also equivalent to the internal rate of return.

Therefore, whenever the net present value is greater than zero, the internal rate of return will be greater than the discount rate used to calculate the NPV. In these cases, both criteria indicate "accept." For conventional cash flow streams, this result will always hold. A similar demonstration can be made when net present values are negative. If the internal rate of return is less than the discount rate, both criteria indicate "reject." The conclusion is important: Since both criteria provide the same results with respect to choosing attractive investment opportunities, either may be used to make the accept-reject decision. Either technique will choose the identical set of investments because the criteria provide identical decisions. However, *both techniques will not rank projects identically*. When considering mutually exclusive projects, this observation is essential to avoid selecting investments that conflict with the goal of wealth maximization.

EXAMPLE 12-2 AFTER-TAX VALUATION

A real estate investor is considering the purchase of an apartment complex. The following assumptions are made:

[1] An exception is if the cash flow stream is nonconventional (that is, if negative cash flows are expected to occur during the life of the investment after one or more positive cash flows). Therefore, throughout our discussion, a conventional cash flow stream is assumed and defined as a cash outflow followed by a series of cash inflows.

$$\text{NOI} = \$47{,}600 \text{ per year}$$

$$\text{Equity investment} = 100 \text{ percent (no mortgage)}$$

$$\frac{\text{Required after-tax rate of}}{\text{return on equity } (k)} = 12 \text{ percent}$$

$$\text{Holding period } (n) = 5 \text{ years}$$

Net selling price at end of holding period is expected to be 20 percent higher than today's price.

$$\text{Marginal tax rate (MTR)} = 28 \text{ percent}$$

$$\text{Building-to-value ratio (B/V)} = 80 \text{ percent}$$

$$\text{Depreciable Life (L)} = 27.5 \text{ Years}$$

$$\text{Depreciation Method} = \text{Straight-Line}$$

What is the maximum price that the investor could pay for this investment?

$$V = \text{PVAF}_{k,N}\left[\text{NOI}_t - \text{MTR}_t(\text{NOI}_t) + \text{MTR}_t(\text{B/V})(V)\left(\frac{1}{L}\right)\right]$$

$$+ \text{PVF}_{k,N}\left[\text{NSP}_N - \text{MTR}_N(\text{NSP}_N) + \text{MTR}_N\left[V - N(\text{B/V})(V)\frac{1}{L}\right]\right]$$

$$V = 3.604776\left[47{,}600 - .28(47{,}600) + .28(.8)(V)\left(\frac{1}{27.5}\right)\right]$$

$$+ .5674\left[1.2(V) - .28(1.2)(V) + .28(V) - .28\left(5(.8)(V)\left(\frac{1}{27.5}\right)\right)\right]$$

$$V = 171{,}587 - 48{,}044 + .0294(V)$$
$$+ .5674(1.2(V) - .336(V) + .28(V) - .04073(V))$$

$$V = 171{,}587 - 48{,}044 + .0294(V) + .6260(V)$$

$$.34464(V) = 123{,}543$$

$$V = 358{,}472$$

The investor would be willing to pay \$358,472 for this investment at a 12 percent rate of return on equity.

RANKING PROBLEMS BETWEEN THE TECHNIQUES

If two (or more) alternative investments are mutually exclusive or if capital is limited, ranking problems may occur when comparing the results under the net present value and internal rate of return criteria. These problems can occur when the projects are of different sizes or when the timing of the cash flows is substantially different. However, these conditions are insufficient to obtain ranking differences between the investments.

For example, suppose we are considering two mutually exclusive alternatives: investments A and B.[2] Each requires outlays of $25,000 in equity. (Table 12–6 compares their expected after-tax cash flows and estimated after-tax equity reversions.) Each has an expected holding period of three years. Upon examination of each project's cash flows, we see that investment A's are higher in the beginning of the holding period and the equity reversion is relatively small. Investment B has minimal cash flows but a large equity reversion.

Using the discounted cash flow model, we can calculate the net present value at various discount rates. It is also possible to calculate the internal rate of return for each investment (shown in Table 12–7). These results indicate that the net present value of each investment declines as the required rate of return on equity increases. However, due to the difference in timing of the cash flows, the net present value of investment B falls more quickly. Figure 12–1 presents different net present values as a function of the discount rate. Both investments A and B are plotted on the graph. Note that when k_e is relatively low, the net present value of B is greater than the net present value of A. If the discount rate is greater than about 15 percent, the net present value of A is greater than that of B.[3] Since the internal rate of return is equal to the rate of discount when the net present value is equal to zero, the IRR_e for investment A is 28.68 percent and the IRR_e for investment B is 24.32 percent. Therefore, the IRR_e for A is greater than that for B, independent of the value of the required rate of return on equity.[4]

TABLE 12–6
EXAMPLE OF TWO MUTUALLY EXCLUSIVE INVESTMENTS

	Investments			
	A		B	
Year	ATCF	ATER	ATCF	ATER
0	$(25,000)		$(25,000)	
1	15,000		1,000	
2	5,000		2,000	
3	$ 2,000	$20,000	$ 4,000	$40,000

[2]As an example of two investments being mutually exclusive, consider the case in which both investments are considered for the same site.
[3]Actually, the specific value for the "crossover point" is 15.10 percent in this example.
[4]Recall that if $k_e > IRR_e$, then NPV < 0 and the investment would be rejected. This is shown at rates higher than 28.68 percent and 24.32 percent for investments A and B, respectively.

TABLE 12–7
RESULTS OF NET PRESENT VALUE AND
INTERNAL RATE OF RETURN ANALYSES

	Investments	
k_e	A	B
0%	$ 17,000	$ 22,000
5	12,825	15,775
10	9,298	10,620
15	6,290	6,313
20	3,704	2,685
25	1,464	(392)
30	(489)	(3,020)
35	(2,204)	(5,278)
40	(3,717)	(7,230)
IRR_e	28.68%	24.32%

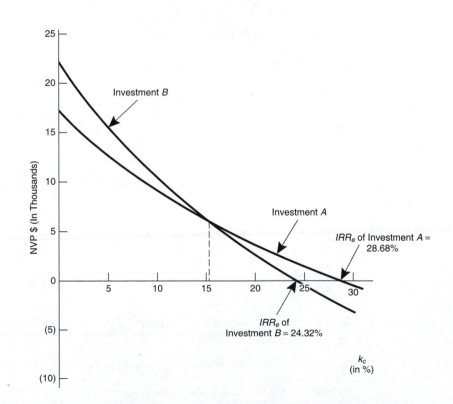

FIGURE 12–1 *NPV as a Function of k_e for Investments A and B*

	Investments	
	A	B
Net Present Value*		✔
Internal Rate of Return	✔	

*At certain required rates of return on equity.

But suppose the required rate of return for investments of this type is 12 percent. Using the net present value criterion, the investor finds the net present value is higher for investment B than for investment A. At the same time, the internal rate of return is higher for investment A. This is the ranking problem that can develop when using net present value and the internal rate of return to compare alternatives. Table 12–8 summarizes the problem. The net present value method favors investment B over A, if $k_e <$ 15.10 percent. The internal rate of return method favors investment A over B in all cases. Given that these investments are mutually exclusive, the investor is forced to choose either A or B even though there is a conflict between the criteria. So which investment should be acquired and why?

Thus the investor would choose one investment if the net present value method is used and the other if the internal rate of return is used. What can the investor do?

One way to solve this problem is to evaluate the investor's wealth position under each alternative. In choosing B, the investor is better off because the net present value is greater. By choosing A, the internal rate of return is higher, but the net present value is lower. Therefore, following the internal rate of return rule results in the selection of a project that is less valuable for the investor *despite its higher rate of return*. This result may shock those who prefer the internal rate of return approach. Nonetheless, the investor would not benefit by choosing the investment with the lower net present value, even if it has a higher internal rate of return.

THE REINVESTMENT RATE ISSUE

One of the most misunderstood issues in the "battle of the DCF techniques" is the presumption of a reinvestment rate difference between NPV and IRR. Some analysts believe that an implicit reinvestment rate exists when one uses these models. Specifically, followers of this tradition argue that the user of the IRR criteria implicitly assume that cash flows from the investment are or can be reinvested at the internal rate of return percentage, while reinvestment is similarly presumed at the discount rate when one uses the net present value calculation. Thus, for any potentially attractive project, (that is, where NPV > 0), the reinvestment rate assumption for the IRR exceeds the reinvestment rate assumption for the NPV, according to this approach. The fundamental question is whether there is a difference in reinvestment rate assumptions between these models? If so, what is the basis for the difference?

The tradition is to argue that the difference exists because the mathematics work out that way. A failure to reinvest at the appropriate rate, either IRR or (k_e), will not achieve a sufficiently high enough future, accumulated value. As a result, proponents of this tradition argue that *there must be a reinvestment rate assumption* and *the difference between IRR and NPV stems from a difference in the reinvestment rate applied in the calculations.*

This question has been examined in detail for several years already, including in the real estate literature.[5] Despite our earlier efforts to settle much of the dispute, some issues never die. Perhaps the reinvestment rate controversy is one of those issues.

In our earlier (1982) textbook, we viewed the reinvestment rate controversy as a series of competing hypotheses.[6] Fundamentally, the issue hinges on whether or not a reinvestment rate assumption even *exists*, and if it does not exist, but the analyst wishes to reinvest, what, then, would be the appropriate rate at which to measure reinvestment?

We prefer to view reinvestment as a choice rather than as a phantom reinvestment assumption.[7] What one investor does with the periodic cash flows is entirely separable from the valuation of the real estate investment project. In effect, the value assigned by the analyst to the investment is silent about the choice the investor possesses regarding what to do with periodic cash flows. After all, the cash flows belong to the equity investor and reinvestment is one of the ongoing options the investor obtains at the time of purchase.

---

[5]See Austin J. Jaffe, "Is There a 'New' Internal Rate of Return Literature?" *American Real Estate and Urban Economics Association Journal* 5 (Winter 1977), 482–502. In addition, professional real estate publications continue to debate these points even in the 1990s.

[6]These ideas are captured as sequential hypotheses. They are: *Hypothesis 1:* Implicit reinvestment rate assumption within the project. *Hypothesis 2:* Implicit reinvestment rate assumption outside the project. *Hypothesis 3:* Explicit reinvestment rate assumption within or outside the project. *Hypothesis 4:* There is no reinvestment rate assumption. *Hypothesis 5:* If a "valuation rate" is desired, the appropriate rate is the required rate of return on equity. See Austin J. Jaffe and C. F. Sirmans, *Real Estate Investment Decision Making.* (Englewood Cliffs, N.J.: Prentice Hall, 1982), pp. 419–425.

[7]For example, it is quite impossible to "see" where the reinvestment rate assumption is within the mathematical formulation of the calculation, or within a graphical presentation, such as Figure 12–1. Some argue that it simply does not exist!

To appeal to a well-employed example, an investor who chooses to spend the annual cash flow on ice cream rather than setting aside these funds for future accumulations might be perfectly rational; it is the investor's money. The economic choice is to give up future monetary accumulations (via consumption of ice cream) versus the building up of future pile of funds through a reinvestment program (via accumulation of money). This choice says *nothing* about the rate of return from the real estate asset. This decision says *something* about the investor's preferences for consumption now (that is, ice cream) or postponed consumption until the future (that is, perhaps ice cream would be preferred at the end of the project). In either case, reinvestment is a investment choice, not a requirement of higher mathematics.[8]

If reinvestment is desired (that is, the investor wishes to postpone consumption of the resources until the future), the appropriate reinvestment rate should be the opportunity cost for equity funds. In this case, it is k_e, the required rate of return on equity. As such, the net present value measures opportunity costs much better than does the internal rate of return.

NONEXISTENT OR MULTIPLE RATES OF RETURN

It is possible to have two or more internal rates of return that are *each mathematically correct.* These occur when negative cash flows are expected to appear in a future period with positive cash flows expected the period(s) before and after the negative one(s). This condition renders the calculation of internal rate of return useless.

In the event that more than one value for IRR_e solves the formula, the investor would have a difficult time deciding the investment's rate of return. Is it the higher one (30 percent) or the lower one (10 percent) or both? Let us assume that the required rate of return is in between (20 percent). If the "right" rate of return is 30 percent, the investor rejects the investment. However, it could be either. The analyst cannot determine what to do if a multiple solution is found.

Some analysts suggest solving for E, using the required rate of return on equity of 20 percent in this case. If the net present value is greater than zero, accept the investment and the problem is solved. What this means is that one must use the net present value approach to make the decision because the internal rate of return method will not result in a solution in this case.

---

[8]If one consumed ice cream each year from the cash flow, would it make any sense to conclude that there were no financial benefits from the investment, even if the value at the end of the holding period was identical to the price paid at the beginning? Of course not; each year the investor earned a rate of return and consumed the benefits annually rather than waiting until the end.

OTHER ISSUES

There are other areas of comparison. For example, what happens when projects have different sizes (that is, is it biased to compare net present values for big and small projects)? What happens when mutually exclusive projects have different planning horizons (that is, it is fair to compare short and long projects)? What happens if projects are inter-related (that is, what assumption needs to be made regarding the degree of independence of investments)? If nothing else, it is important to know how to handle these problems if you are doing financial analysis, especially in real estate markets.

WHAT HAVE WE LEARNED?

The research on DCF models has revealed similarities between NPV and IRR, but also many differences. It is a gross oversimplification to conclude that these measures can be used interchangeably; they cannot be treated synonymously without peril to the financial health of the investor. We have also learned that the application of capital budgeting methods to real estate investment analysis is an old tradition. However, many analysts appear to think that they need not be experts in one of the fundamental tools of their trade. Real estate financial analysis requires expertise for proper application. Finally, if real estate is a "numbers game," analysts must know what the numbers mean. There is no other way.

ADVANCED TECHNIQUES AND MEASURES OF PERFORMANCE

Additional methods have been developed to improve previous measures or to evaluate different problems. This brief section introduces some of the concepts and techniques typically found in more advanced books.

PROFITABILITY INDEX (PI)

One of the criticisms of the internal rate of return techniques is that comparisons on the basis of values of IRR_e failed to consider the size of the investments. To deal with this problem, analysts relied on the *benefit-cost ratio* (sometimes called the profitability index). This provided a measure of "benefits per dollar of cost" and corrected a shortcoming of the internal rate of return.

For real estate investments, the *profitability index* (PI) is defined as

$$PI = \frac{E}{MV - MD}$$

$$= \frac{\sum_{t=1}^{n} \frac{ATCF_t}{(1 + k_e)^t} + \frac{ATER_n}{(1 + k_e)^n}}{MV - MD} \qquad (12\text{-}13)$$

The profitability index, therefore, is the ratio of the investment value of equity, E, to the required equity outlay (MV − MD) for investment alternatives. When the investment value of equity is greater than or equal to the equity outlay, the investor should accept the investment. When the investment value of equity is less than the equity outlay, the investment should be rejected.

Another way of specifying the decision rule follows.

PI Decision Rule: Using the profitability index, if

$$PI \geq 1.00, \text{ then NPV} \geq 0, \text{ and if}$$

$$PI < 1.00, \text{ then NPV} < 0.$$

ADJUSTED INTERNAL RATE OF RETURN (AIRR)

The *adjusted internal rate of return* (AIRR) category contains a number of techniques that were motivated by dissatisfaction with the original internal rate of return measure. The typical adjustments deal with either the reinvestment rate problem or the possibilities of the multiple rate of return problems. Some models deal with both.

The results vary, although some of the advanced models avoid some of the internal rate of return problems. Much of this work was done by analysts such as Strung,[9] who sought to construct a rate of return method free of the problems outlined in the previous section.

The major difficulty with these models is that for the most part, no new information is derived by a "perfected internal rate of return." After all, if there are ranking problems compared to net present value, differences will remain between the investment value of equity approach and the adjusted internal rate of return approach. If a particular model solves all the inconsistencies with wealth-maximization criteria (that is, maximizing net present value), then nothing new is gained because the net-present-value result is already available. The point is that this argument raises some serious questions about the benefits to be gained by investors using these measures.

FINANCIAL MANAGEMENT RATE OF RETURN (FMRR)

One of the more highly regarded measures is the *financial management rate of return* (FMRR). Developed in 1975, it has attracted a wide following in a very short time.[10] It is basically a rate of return model that purports to solve the reinvestment presumption problem and the possibility of multiple rates of return. It uses a holding-period rate-of-return measure that may result in differences from an internal rate of return calculation.

[9]Joseph Strung, "The Internal Rate of Return and the Reinvestment Presumptions," *Appraisal Journal*, 44 (January 1976), 23–33.
[10]Stephen D. Messner and M. Chapman Findlay III, "Real Estate Investment Analysis: IRR versus FMRR," *Real Estate Appraiser*, 41 (July–August 1975), 5–20.

There are many attractive elements about the FMRR model. However, much of the conceptual basis and the reinvestment presumptions have been questioned in recent years. Still, it is too early to judge the degree of acceptance and the amount of reliance placed on this technique.

DISCOUNTED CASH FLOW MODELS IN PRACTICE

In Chapter 11, several rules of thumb and traditional valuation methods were discussed. Conceptual and practical limitations of these measures has led to calls for the adoption of discounted cash flow models to replace the more simpler methods of analysis. While it is interesting to consider new models from a theoretical standpoint, it is also important to see whether such models are successfully used in real world investment decisions.

There have been several surveys of usage of discounted cash flow measures. A recent review and new survey of many of these studies indicates that the use of discounted cash flow models has become increasingly widespread, especially among institutional real estate investors.[11]

Table 12–9 indicates the findings of a few of the well-known surveys of capital budgeting practice in real estate. Those studies cited are thought to be representative of practice among institutional real estate investors.[12]

In general, there are three conclusions regarding the use of discounted cash flow models in practice. First, discounted cash flow analysis in real estate has grown in popularity among real estate investors since the early 1970s and continues to the present day. Not only have the use of these methods become commonplace among analysts, but the relative importance of rules-of-thumb methods has probably decreased. Second, technological developments in the 1980s, including the widespread use of computerized spreadsheets and generic templates, has dramatically reduced the cost of performing financial analysis in this field. Even small-scale investors can perform detailed and sophisticated financial analysis without a large capital investment or expensive start-up costs. Third, while there are numerous conceptual advantages to discounted cash flow models compared to traditional single-period measures,

[11]See W. Jan Brzeski, Austin J. Jaffe, and Stellan Lundström, "Institutional Real Estate Investment Practices: Swedish and United States Experiences," *Journal of Real Estate Research* 8 (Summer 1993), 293–323.

[12]The studies in Table 12–9 are Robert J. Wiley, "Real Estate Investment Analysis: An Empirical Study," *The Appraisal Journal* 44 (October 1976), 586–92; Edward J. Farragher, "Investment Decision-Making Practices of Equity Investors in Real Estate," *The Real Estate Appraiser and Analyst* 48 (Summer 1982), 36–41; Donald E. Page, "Criteria for Investment Decision Making: An Empirical Study," *The Appraisal Journal* 51 (October 1983), 498–508; James R. Webb, "Real Estate Investment Acquisition Rules for Life Insurance Companies and Pension Funds: A Survey," *American Real Estate and Urban Economics Association Journal* 12 (Winter 1984), 495–520; and Brzeski, Jaffe, and Lundström, "Institutional Real Estate Investment Practices," 293–323.

Study (Date)	Wiley (1976)	Farragher (1982)	Page (1983)	Webb (1984)	Sweden (1993)
Number of Respondents (Insurance Company)	68	66	45	96	20
Before-tax measures					
(% using BT)	93	NA	97	92	86
Payback period	11	15	17	18	33
Gross income multiplier	13	6	5	18	33
NOI/Equity	40	NA	17	60	67
Overall rate	NA	15	66	NA	50
Cash-on-cash return	54	73	39	59	25
IRR on equity	40	76	66	64	50
After-tax measures					
(% using AT)	60	NA	87	51	14
Payback period	7	NA	13	13	100
Cash-on-cash return	24	49	29	10	50
IRR on equity	29	NA	61	56	50
Net present value	7	24	18	31	50
Risk analysis					
(% evaluating risk)	87	NA	70	76	86
Raise discount rate	29	29	28	54	67
Sensitivity analysis	12	23	20	13	58
Simulation/prob. mod.	16	10	5	7	50
Holding period					
(Most frequent in years)	Various	NA	10	6–10	6–10
Diversification strategy					
(None)	NA	NA	NA	34	43
By property type	NA	NA	NA	59	63
By geog. location	NA	NA	NA	61	63

*Figures refer to proportions of respondents using measures.
Source: W. Jan Brzeski, Austin J. Jaffe, and Stellan Lundström, "Institutional Real Estate Investment Practices: Swedish and United States Experiences," *Journal of Real Estate Research* 8 (Summer 1993), 318.

investors continue to calculate their traditional measures. Whether these older measures are used as rough guidelines or as decision rules remains uncertain; it is apparent that many investors in the 1990s continue to supplement discounted cash flow models with their predecessors in this field.

SUMMARY

Discounted cash flow models are fundamental to modern real estate investment analysis. Since they are more flexible and robust than traditional appraisal techniques and investment rules-of-thumb, they are likely to provide more and, in some cases, better information. However, the use of these techniques does not imply that the analyst can foretell the future. Although the analyst is required to estimate what cash flows will be in the future, this is done with available information at the time he or she is making the investment decision. It is presumed that there is uncertainty associated with the valuation estimate. It is for this reason that risk analysis is required in order to better decide whether or not the investment should be purchased.

Thus the investor does not predict the future using discounted cash flow models. Discounted cash flow models permit the analyst to evaluate systematically several economic effects on the investment choice in a world of uncertainty. Since the basic discounted cash flow models imply that risk analysis can be captured through the use of the appropriate discount rate or the required rate of return on equity, net present value and internal rate of return models can be used as shown. However, on the issue of risk analysis, the analyst begs the question if the measurement of risk is presumed at the start of the analysis. Therefore, it is necessary to explicitly incorporate risk analysis into discounted cash flow models. This is done in the next chapter.

QUESTIONS

12–1. What are the basic discounted cash flow models?

12–2. "Discounted cash flow models are useful whether real estate markets are efficient or inefficient." True or false? Explain.

12–3. The text lists four reasons why discounted cash flow models are better tools for real estate investors than traditional methods. What are these reasons?

12–4. What is the investment value of equity? How is it used to make investment decisions?

12–5. What is the internal rate of return on equity? How is this rate of return used?

12–6. What is the relationship between Decision Rules 1 and 2 using the investment value

of equity? Between Decision Rules 1, 2, and 3?

12–7. There are several issues involved in comparing the internal rate of return and the net present value methods. What are the issues?

12–8. What is the profitability index? How does it compare with the other discounted cash flow models and criteria?

12–9. What is the FMRR? Describe how it is calculated and compare it with the other models, especially the internal rate of return.

12–10. Do investors who use discounted cash flow models need to predict the future? Why or why not?

PROBLEMS

12–1 Consider the following set of cash flows and reversion:

	Investment	
Year	ATCF	ATER
0	($80,000)	
1	10,000	
2	20,000	
3	20,000	
4	25,000	$50,000

a. What is the net present value of equity if k_e equals 10 percent?
b. What is the net present value of equity if k_e equals 15 percent?
c. What is the present value of equity if k_e equals 25 percent?
d. What is the internal rate of return on equity?
e. Should the investment be accepted under all cases?

12–2. A real estate investor is considering an investment with the following expected cash flows and reversion:

	Investment	
Year	ATCF	ATER
0	$10,000	
1	10,500	
2	12,000	
3	11,000	
4	13,000	
5	13,000	
6	10,000	$140,000

What is the maximum that the investor can pay and earn a 15 percent rate of return?

12–3. An investor is considering an investment that has a total cost of $500,000. The following information is obtained from analyzing the market:

a. Rent = $200 per unit per month
b. Number of units = 50
c. Vacancies = 7 percent
d. Operating expenses = $48,000
e. Loan-to-value ratio = .80
f. Interest rate on mortgage = 10 percent
g. Maturity of mortgage = 25 years (with annual payments)
h. Depreciable basis = 85 percent of total cost
i. Depreciation method = straight-line
j. Useful life = 27.5 years
k. Expected reversion growth = 10 percent over holding period
l. Holding period = 5 years
m. Tax rate = .28
n. Required rate of return on equity = .16
o. Rental growth rate = 5 percent per year
p. Operating expense growth rate = 5 percent per year
q. Financing costs = $16,000 amortized over life of mortgage
r. Prepayment penalty = .06 of outstanding balance

Should the investor buy the project? Why or why not?

12–4. Consider the following set of cash flows and reversion:

	Investment	
Year	ATCF	ATER
0	$(100,000)	
1	10,000	
2	8,000	
3	19,000	
4	20,000	
5	15,000	
6	−10,000	
7	30,000	
8	15,000	$140,000

a. What is the net present value, using k_e = 15 percent?
b. What is the profitability index?
c. What is the adjusted internal rate of return, using r = 8 percent?
d. What is the adjusted internal rate of return, using r = 12 percent?
e. What is the FMRR, using r = 10 percent?
f. What is the net terminal value, using r = 15 percent?
g. What is the net present value of the net terminal value of equity, using r = 14 percent?

12–5. There is an office building for sale at a price of $3 million. The building is 60,000 square feet of which one-sixth is common area. The building leases space at $12 per square foot, per year, and is operating at a 90 percent occupancy rate. Rents are expected to grow at a rate of 5 percent per year and the occupancy rate should remain constant over the next 10 years. The building is currently divided into 50 units with each renting five parking spaces per month at $5 per month, per space. In addition, each of the tenants at the end of the year must contribute $15,000 to common area maintenance costs. The building currently has operating expenses of 40 percent of effective gross income, and these are expected to increase by 5 percent each year. Financing available to the investing company consists of two mortgages. The first mortgage is $2 million at a 12 percent interest rate of 25 years. Financing costs will be 5 percent with an additional 5 percent prepayment penalty on the outstanding balance. In addition, the seller will offer the buyer a second mortgage of $500,000 of the purchase price at a rate of 15 percent over the investor's seven-year expected holding period. Assume a 20 percent land to value ratio with a 39-year depreciable life. The selling price at the end of 7 years will be $4,000,000. Selling expenses are 8 percent of the selling price. Should the investing company purchase the building if it has a

34 percent marginal rate, a 28 percent capital gains rate and requires a 14 percent return?

12–6. An apartment building is available for purchase for a price of $3,500,000. The complex contains a total of 225 units in which 100 are one-bedroom units and 125 are two-bedroom units. The following additional information is available.

One bedroom:
  Rent = $350/month
  Vacancy rate = 6%
Two bedroom:
  Rent = $400/month
  Vacancy rate = 8%
Rental growth rate = 5%
Replacement Reserve Account
  # of refrigerators = 10
    Cost per unit = $350
    Expected economic life = 15 years.
  # of stoves = 10
    Cost of unit = $300
    Expected economic life = 15 yrs.
  # of carpets = 25
    Cost per unit = $500
    Expected economic life = 6 yrs.
Operating expenses in the first year = $426,060
Operating expense growth rate = 7%
Land-to-value = 20%
Depreciable life = 27.5 years
Financing:
  1st mortgage = $2,000,000
    Interest rate = 13%
    Term = 25 yrs. (monthly payments)
    Points = 4
    Prepayment penalty = 6% of outstanding balance
  2nd mortgage = $800,000
    Interest rate = 16%
    Term = 15 yrs. (monthly payments)
The investor believes that in six years the building will increase in value approximately 14 percent to an expected selling price of $4,000,000. Selling expenses are expected to be 8 percent. The investor is currently subject to a 28 percent marginal tax rate which is expected to remain constant throughout the holding period.

If the investor requires a 14 percent rate of return, should the projected project be accepted?

12–7. Suppose an investor is considering two mutually exclusive alternatives: Investments A and B. Each has the following cash flows:

Year	A ATCF	A ATER	B ATCF	B ATER
0	$(50,000)		$(50,000)	
1	30,000		2,500	
2	15,000		4,000	
3	4,000		10,000	
4	2,500	$40,000	20,000	$70,000

Given a four-year holding period and a discount rate equal to 12 percent for each:
a. Calculate the NPV and IRR_e for each investment.
b. Which option should the investor choose? Why?

SELECTED REFERENCES

Cooper, James R., and Stephen A. Pyhrr, "Forecasting the Rates of Return on an Apartment Investment: A Case Study," *Appraisal Journal*, 41 (July 1973), 312–337.

Dilmore, Gene, "Internal Rate of Return and the Reinvestment Concept," *The Real Estate Appraiser*, 39 (July–August 1973), 29–38.

Hanford, Lloyd D., Jr., "The Use of Discount Cash Flow Analysis," *Real Estate Appraiser*, 39 (November–December 1973), 31–34.

Jaffe, Austin J., "Is There a 'New' Internal Rate of Return Literature?" *American Real Estate and Urban Economics Association Journal*, 5 (Winter 1977), 482–502.

_____ , and C. F. Sirmans, *Real Estate Investment Decision Making*. Englewood Cliffs, N.J.: Prentice Hall, 1982.

Ling, David C., "The Valuation of Income Property in Overbuilt Markets," *The Appraisal Journal*, 63 (July 1993), 332–341.

Messner, Stephen D., and M. Chapman Findlay III, "Real Estate Investment Analysis: IRR versus FMRR," *Real Estate Appraiser*, 41 (July–August 1975), 5–20.

Strung, Joseph, "The Internal Rate of Return and the Reinvestment Presumptions," *The Appraisal Journal*, 44 (January 1976), 23–33.

Young, Michael S., "FMRR: A Clever Hoax?," *The Appraisal Journal*, 47 (July 1979), 359–369.

Zerbst, Robert H., "Evaluating Risks by Partitioning the IRR," *Real Estate Review*, 9 (Winter 1980), 80–84.

CHAPTER 13

RISK ANALYSIS

PRINCIPLES

1. The introduction of risk into DCF models is an important extension to the basic DCF calculations.
2. The use of alternative investment scenarios can be an effective method for evaluating risk.
3. While there are several historical methods of accounting for risk, modern analysis has tended to concentrate on the use of the variance as a measure of riskiness of investments.
4. The use of expected values and standard deviations together permits the analyst to develop a powerful method of analysis of both risk and return.
5. There are several important risk analysis methods, including decision trees, sensitivity analysis, and Monte Carlo simulation.
6. Portfolio analysis is the next generation of risk analysis and is rapidly becoming one of the latest developments to affect real estate markets.

The preceding chapter developed and illustrated the two basic discounted cash flow models. This chapter explicitly introduces risk into the analysis. The importance of the analysis of risk cannot be overemphasized. Discounted cash flow analysis in a world of certainty is relatively straightforward and simple once the mechanics have been learned. After the costs and benefits have been estimated, the outcome of the investment becomes a function of the likelihood of success or failure. It is not surprising that the analysis of risk has occupied the minds of numerous financial writers for the past 30 years as they have attempted to identify, measure, and analyze the effects of risk on rates of return and values.

This chapter begins with a brief discussion of the importance of risk analysis in real estate discounted cash flow models. It then reviews the various generations of risk analysis beginning with the early methods of analysis, the traditional and standard techniques, and the modern risk measures. All of these techniques can be viewed as extensions of the basic discounted cash flow models.

Introducing Risk into Discounted Cash Flow Models

Because we live in an uncertain world, investors cannot forecast future cash flows with complete accuracy. However, the development of better information, techniques of analysis, and an understanding of the conceptual relationships between parameters in the world can reduce the risk the investor faces when making investment decisions. This is one of the primary motivations for analyzing real estate investment projects.

Given that all investment decisions are made with an element of risk, risk analysis is very relevant. Without it, the decision might easily be less favorable. Also, since all decisions involve risk, it is impossible to avoid it. Therefore these next two chapters provide various measures, decision rules, and analysis for decision makers who want to choose between alternatives in an uncertain world.

Why Risk Analysis Is Essential

In a world without risk, all outcomes would be known with certainty. Therefore, the probability of receiving an amount of cash flow in a future year would be 100 percent certain. Real estate investment analysis in such a world would be a relatively easy pursuit: select those projects with the highest discounted after-tax cash flows and after-tax equity reversions over the required investment costs.[1] This is the precise method of investment analysis suggested by Chapter 12. However, once we allow for the fact that few cash flows or reversions *are* known with certainty, the problem of risk is introduced. The following demonstrates why risk analysis is so important.

Imagine an investor who is faced with deciding which, if any, of three mutually exclusive investments to acquire. Suppose the investor estimates the after-tax cash flows for each alternative as shown in Table 13–1.[2]

[1]Note that in a world of certainty, the future benefits (or costs) would be discounted by the risk-free rate. This is the rate at which consumers and producers have to be compensated annually in order for them to give up their respective consumption and investment plans.
[2]For illustrative purposes, Table 13–1 ignores the after-tax equity reversion and assumes that each after-tax cash flow for each "state of the world" is constant for each year of the expected holding period.

TABLE 13-1
AFTER-TAX CASH FLOW ESTIMATES FOR INVESTMENTS X, Y, AND Z
FOR DIFFERENT STATES OF THE WORLD*

Investment X	
$ATCF_X$	$1,000
Investment Y	
$ATCF_{y1}$ (if factory does not locate in city)	500
$ATCF_{y2}$ (if factory locates in city)	1,500
Investment Z	
$ATCF_{z1}$ (if city passes rent control ordinance)	−250
$ATCF_{z2}$ (if city defeats rent control ordinance)	0
$ATCF_{z3}$ (if city defeats rent control ordinance *and* adopts a "no-growth" policy)	4,500

*Assume that the after-tax cash flow for each state of the world of each investment is constant each year.

Assuming that the acquisition cost of each of these investments is identical, the investor might initially decide on investment X, which promises to yield $1,000 per year *regardless of the state of the world.* On the other hand, investment Y promises to return $500 per year if the factory does not locate in the city, *but* $1,500 per year if it does. (The presumption, of course, is that the location decision of the factory owners will increase the demand for investment Y, which may be an apartment building to house workers.) Investment Y may be preferable to investment X, since a positive decision by the factory owners would increase the after-tax cash flow by $500 per year under this alternative. Finally, the investor may be interested in investment Z *despite* the low estimates of after-tax cash flow under two outcomes, since the third has such a favorable impact. (The presumption is that without rent control and with a restrictive growth policy, the investor would receive higher cash flow payments than if rent control or urban growth were permitted.)

However, the investor would be unable to make a very effective decision without considering whether these different states were likely to occur. The following cases demonstrate why.

In scenario I, suppose the investor is suspicious of the announcement that the factory will locate in the city. Also, suppose rent control is likely, although adoption of a no-growth policy is remote. Given these beliefs, the investor can make *probability estimates* about the likelihood of the occurrence of the events. Alternatively, suppose the investor has more faith in the announcement. The investor could assign a higher probability to the estimate of after-tax cash flows if the factory is expected to locate in the city, and assuming everything else is the same, the investor would view alternatives differently. We can call this situation scenario II.

Finally, imagine scenario III, where the factory owners convince the investor that there is a strong possibility of locating in the investor's city, the possibility of rent control legislation in the city is reduced, and the prospects for restrictive land-use controls through a no-growth policy are greater than before. The investor could analyze these effects as well.

Table 13–2 shows that investment X might be favored in scenario I, investment Y might be preferred in scenario II, and investment Z might be selected in scenario III. The word "might" is important, as we will see.

To understand the results in Table 13–2, a few terms must be defined. *Probability* is defined as the chance or likelihood that an event will occur. Thus, if there is no chance of this happening, the probability is zero. If the likelihood of an event occurring is certain, the probability is 100 percent. Therefore any probability of occurrence must be between zero and 100 percent.

Mathematically, we can represent probabilities as p_i, so that $0 \leq p_i \leq 1$ for all values of i (that is, the states of the world). In addition, the sum of all probabilities must equal one:

$$\sum_{i=1}^{m} p_i = 1.00 \tag{13–1}$$

where:

$$m = \text{number of occurrences or states of the world}$$

To account for the various probabilities and their effects on the outcome, we must compute *expected values.* An expected value is the sum of each possible outcome multiplied by their probability of occurrence. Mathematically, the *expected after-tax cash flow* for each year is:

$$\overline{\text{ATCF}_t,} = \text{ATCF}_{1t} \times p_t + \cdots + \text{ATCF}_{mt} \times p_{mt}$$
$$= \sum_{i=1}^{m} \text{ATCF}_{it} \times p_{it} \tag{13–2}$$

where:

$$\overline{\text{ATCF}_t} = \text{expected after-tax cash flow for the } t\text{th year}$$

$$\text{ATCF}_{it} = \text{after-tax cash flow if the } i\text{th state of the world occurs in the } t\text{th year}$$

$$p_{it} = \text{probability of the } i\text{th state of the world in the } t\text{th year}$$

Table 13–2 demonstrates how expected after-tax cash flow estimates change as a result of shifts in probabilities. This, of course, affects the attractiveness of investment opportunities. In scenario I, the uncertainty

Scenario I: Factory Favors Alternative City; No-Growth Policy is Unlikely

Investments

X		Y		Z	
ATCF	p(ATCF)	ATCF	p(ATCF)	ATCF	p(ATCF)
$1,000	1.00	$ 500	.75	$−250	.40
		1,500	.25	0	.50
				4,500	.10
$\overline{\text{ATCF}}$ = $1,000		$\overline{\text{ATCF}}$ = $750		$\overline{\text{ATCF}}$ = $350	

Scenario II: Factory Favors Investor's City: No-Growth Policy is Unlikely

Investments

X		Y		Z	
ATCF	p(ATCF)	ATCF	p(ATCF)	ATCF	p(ATCF)
$1,000	1.00	$ 500	.40	$−250	.40
		1,500	.60	0	.50
				4,500	.10
$\overline{\text{ATCF}}$ = $1,000		$\overline{\text{ATCF}}$ = $1,100		$\overline{\text{ATCF}}$ = $350	

Scenario III: Factory Favors Investor's City; Rent Control is Unlikely; No-Growth
Policy is More Likely

Investments

X		Y		Z	
ATCF	p(ATCF)	ATCF	p(ATCF)	ATCF	p(ATCF)
$1,000	1.00	$ 500	.40	$−250	.20
		1,500	.60	0	.50
				4,500	.30
$\overline{\text{ATCF}}$ = $1,000		$\overline{\text{ATCF}}$ = $1,100		$\overline{\text{ATCF}}$ = $1,300	

about the location decision results in investment X having the highest after-tax cash flow estimate. In scenario II, investment Y has the highest estimate of after-tax cash flow. With scenario III, the highest estimate of after-tax cash flow is found in investment Z.

At this point, the problem is to decide which of these investments, if any, should be chosen. Given the goal of wealth maximization, it seems logical that decision rules similar to the NPV decision rules in Chapter 12 could be developed to account for expected values. However, will this modification be sufficient to enable the investor to select the one consistent with personal goals?

The answer is no. However, the use of expected after-tax cash flows is a step in the right direction. The next logical step is to develop a method for estimating the *expected net present value of equity*, using expected after-tax cash flows and the expected after-tax equity reversion as calculation inputs. As we will see, the expected net present value and its subsequent decision rules will not solve the problem of risk because there is no reason to believe that all projects are equally risky.

To develop a measure of expected net present value of equity, we must define the *expected after-tax equity reversion*. When the discounted value of the expected after-tax equity reversion is added to the expected after-tax cash flow stream, discounted for the time value of money, the result is the expected net present value of equity. The expected after-tax equity reversion is equal to the possible after-tax equity reversion values for each state of the world times the probability of occurrence:

$$\overline{ATER}_n = ATER_{1n} \times p_{1n} + ATER_{2n} \times p_{2n} + \cdots + ATER_{mn} \times p_{mn}$$

$$= \sum_{i=1}^{m} ATER_{in} \times p_{in} \qquad (13\text{--}3)$$

where:

$\overline{ATER}_n$ = expected after-tax equity reversion in the nth year

$ATER_{in}$ = after-tax equity reversion if the ith state of the world occurs in the nth year

p_{in} = probability of the ith state of the world in the nth year

Therefore the discounted value of each expected after-tax cash flow and the discounted value of the expected after-tax equity reversion are equal to the expected net present value of equity when the required equity outlay is subtracted.[3]

$$\overline{NPV} = \frac{ATCF_1}{(1 + k_f)^1} + \frac{ATCF_2}{(1 + k_f)^2} + \cdots + \frac{ATCF_n}{(1 + k_f)^n} + \frac{ATER_n}{(1 + k_f)^n} - (MV - MD)$$

$$= \sum_{i=1}^{m} \frac{\overline{ATCF_f}}{(1 + k_f)^t} + \frac{\overline{ATER}_n}{(1 + k_f)^n} - (MV - MD) \qquad (13\text{--}4)$$

[3]This equation assumes that the after-tax cash flows in each year are statistically independent of each other and of the after-tax equity reversion.

where:

$$\overline{NPV} = \text{expected net present value of equity}$$

$$k_f = \text{risk-free rate}$$

Returning to the example involving investments X, Y, and Z, if each expected after-tax cash flow is anticipated for a period of ten years, if each has a $5,000 required equity outlay, and if the risk-free rate is assumed to be 4 percent, we get the results reported in Table 13–3.

As we observed before, the expected cash flow outcomes vary as a result of the changes in probabilities and, now, as a result of the discounting process. It should be pointed out that the risk-free rate is chosen in the calculation of expected net present value of equity because risk is now accounted for by the probability distributions that affect the expected after-tax cash flows. As a result, the risk-free rate is the appropriate discount rate.

The results of expected net present values of equity in Table 13–3 for each investment under each scenario indicate preferences identical with the earlier analysis (Table 13–2). However, this is due to the assumption that each expected cash flow stream is an annuity, each requires the same amount of equity outlay, and each has an identical expected holding period. The fact that investment X under scenario I, investment Y under scenario II, or investment Z under scenario III might not be preferred for non-annuity expected cash flow streams or for investments with differing holding periods is not germane to this discussion. Instead we are primarily concerned with whether the development of expected net present values of equity will permit us to choose one alternative over another.

Unfortunately, it will not. We cannot be sure, for example, that investment Y is preferable to investments X and Z in scenario II because we do not know whether or not investment Y is a riskier investment. As *a result, adopting the goal of maximization of expected net present value of equity may be an improvement over the goal of maximization of net present value of equity independent of the likelihood of various states of the world occurring, but only if we are confident that risk is consistent for all projects under consideration.*

What we need is a method of analyzing risk in relation to expected net present value in order to compare projects on a sound basis. This requires the use of measures of risk based on the variability or dispersion of values. Two well-known measures of this type are the *variance* and *standard deviation*. These techniques were introduced in Chapter 4 and are discussed later in the chapter when they are used to measure risk. At this point, it is sufficient to understand the problem of risk and why it is essential that investors explicitly take it into account when making investment choices.

Scenario I

$$\overline{NPV}_X = \sum_{t=1}^{10} \frac{\$1{,}000_t}{(1 + .04)^t} - \$5{,}000 = \$3{,}110.90^*$$

$$\overline{NPV}_Y = \sum_{t=1}^{10} \frac{\$750_t}{(1 + .04)^t} - \$5{,}000 = \$1{,}083.17$$

$$\overline{NPV}_Z = \sum_{t=1}^{10} \frac{\$350_t}{(1 + .04)^t} - \$5{,}000 = -\$2{,}161.19$$

Scenario II

$$\overline{NPV}_X = \sum_{t=1}^{10} \frac{\$1{,}000_t}{(1 + .04)^t} - \$5{,}000 = \$3{,}110.90$$

$$\overline{NPV}_Y = \sum_{t=1}^{10} \frac{\$1{,}100_t}{(1 + .04)^t} - \$5{,}000 = \$3{,}921.99^*$$

$$\overline{NPV}_Z = \sum_{t=1}^{10} \frac{\$350_t}{(1 + .04)^t} - \$5{,}000 = -\$2{,}161.19$$

Scenario III

$$\overline{NPV}_X = \sum_{t=1}^{10} \frac{\$1{,}000_t}{(1 + .04)^t} - \$5{,}000 = \$3{,}110.90$$

$$\overline{NPV}_Y = \sum_{t=1}^{10} \frac{\$1{,}100_t}{(1 + .04)^t} - \$5{,}000 = \$3{,}921.99$$

$$\overline{NPV}_Z = \sum_{t=1}^{10} \frac{\$1{,}300_t}{(1 + .04)^t} - \$5{,}000 = \$5{,}544.16^*$$

*Designates the preferred investment.

ACCOUNTING FOR RISK IN DISCOUNTED CASH FLOW MODELS

There are many ways of accounting for risk and uncertainty using discounted cash flow models. Although others could be added, we include some of the well-known techniques: (a) conservatism, (b) risk-adjusted discount rates, (c) certainty-equivalent approach, (d) measures of variability, (e) decision trees and sensitivity analysis, (f) probabalistic modeling and simulation, and (g) modern capital market measures.

CONSERVATISM

A rudimentary method of assessing risk is to choose low estimates of cash benefits, choose high estimates of cash outflows (costs), and evaluate the net benefits using a relatively high discount rate. These actions result in a low value estimate or a high required rate of return estimate. If the analyst accepts the project as a good investment, he or she feels even more anxious to make the purchase because this analysis assumed bad outcomes in every case. So a conservative outlook regarding benefits and costs limits potential projects to the best alternative.

The problem with this method is that if the estimates used are more conservative than what the analyst believes will occur, and if the analyst seeks to maximize his or her wealth, conservative action results in the exclusion of some projects that would be acceptable under "normal conditions."

RISK-ADJUSTED DISCOUNT RATES

We noted in an earlier chapter that as the risk associated with an investment rises, the nominal (or market) interest rate (or required rate of return) on that investment increases as the risk is incorporated into the discount rate. The analyst accomplishes the same thing by applying higher risk-adjusted discount rates in order to lower the investment value of the project.

Conceptually, this approach is not difficult. However, some analysts find it hard to assess discount rate levels for each type of risky investment as well as the relevant increase in rates due to the perceived increase in risk levels.

THE CERTAINTY-EQUIVALENT APPROACH

The certainty-equivalent approach offers an alternative to the risk-adjusted discount approach. This approach argues that it is conceptually equivalent and operationally easier to account for the risk associated with the likelihood of the cash flows than it is to account for the time value of money using the risk-free discount rate.

Here the analyst applies a *certainty-equivalent coefficient* to each income or cash flow payment. This coefficient may vary from 0.00 to 1.00 depending on the degree of certainty associated with the receipt of the payment. Typically, one expects cash flows in the immediate future to be more easily estimated than those in the distant future. In the instance of one year, a certainty-equivalent coefficient of almost 1.00 would be multiplied by the expected cash flow. Those expected five years hence may warrant a coefficient of .50. The final year's cash flow is far less certain, so .20 may be used. Obviously, the analyst must decide on the relative sizes of the certainty equivalents based on when the cash flow will occur. In this sense, the risk of the cash flow not occurring is accounted for independently of the consideration of the time value of money.

The certainty-equivalent approach is attractive for a number of reasons. First, it provides a conceptual basis for accounting for risk which is consistent with more traditional methods. Second, it may be easier to use because risk and the time-value of money are treated separately. This may be important depending on the risk characteristics of the project in question. Third, the certainty-equivalent approach requires no new information over the risk-adjusted discount rate approach. Finally, it is easier to derive investment results when risk is not constant over time. Since risk tends to be resolved over time, this last condition offers a strong argument for its adoption.

MEASURES OF VARIABILITY

Traditionally, measures of risk and uncertainty in finance measure the expected variability of cash flows from the expected value. The most common of these measures are the *variance* and the *standard deviation*. There are many reasons why these measures are useful. First, both are operationally consistent with each other because, by definition, the standard deviation is the square root of the variance. Second, both use deviations of outcomes from expected values to measure the degree of variability around the mean. If the expected values are identical, we use variability in the distribution of outcomes to measure risk.

Finally, modern statistical analysis demonstrates that *confidence intervals* and *hypothesis testing* are possible using these measures of variability. Confidence intervals permit analysts to develop a range of possible outcomes based on the expected value and the variance (or standard deviations) of outcomes. Hypothesis testing permits the analyst to statistically investigate the likelihood of achieving certain goals or objectives. Although these techniques are complex, they are very useful in providing information about risk. However, they are also beyond the introductory nature of this book (see the "Selected References" at the end of this chapter).

DECISION TREES AND SENSITIVITY ANALYSIS

Two additional well-known techniques for measuring risk are *decision trees* and *sensitivity analysis*. Decision trees require the analyst to estimate the likelihood of each outcome at every expected decision point in the future. In this manner, the analyst will grasp an understanding of the relationships between each decision and the probabilities of occurrence. Sensitivity analysis is the estimation of investment values by systematic alteration

Current Issue 13–1
Risk Analysis Is What Investment Analysis Is All About
Real estate students and novice investors often seem to have peculiar pre-conceptions about the main objective of real estate investment analysis. Many believe that tax planning is the major part of the analysis. Others treat the financing decision as the primary focus. Still others regard the forecast-ing of income, cash flows, and property value growth rates as the chief ele-ments in the process. While all of these activities have major roles, none gets at the actual crux of the real estate investment process. The real basis of investment analysis is the identification, measurement, and assessment of risk and the ways the investor can deal with risk. This activity is called *risk analysis.*

Risk analysis is fundamental because the calculation of cash flows (includ-ing income, expenses, financing costs, depreciation, future selling prices, and other items) would be a more mechanical exercise if risk did not exist. In such a world, all properties would easily and precisely be priced, and own-ers would know exactly what their rates of return would be for each invest-ment. Competition would force prices of properties to their correct levels and the net present values of all investments would be zero; investors would pur-chase properties and would earn the market rate of return on each property. In this case, the rate of return would equal the risk-free rate.

In the real world, risk is an element in everyday life. The explicit specification of cash flow items attempts to provide the analyst with as much fundamental information as possible so that he or she can identify differences in proper-ties and differences in their expected levels of risk. If the investor is suc-cessful, only "superior" projects will be purchased and less attractive ones will be rejected. Risk analysis may help investors sort out the array of avail-able investment vehicles based on their expected returns and levels of risk.

This does not suggest that if an investor purchases a property, he or she is guaranteed to obtain an increase in investor wealth. Since all investment analysis is based on expectations, investors do the best they can with the information, skills, and judgment they possess *before* the project is se-lected. In a world with risk, the best analysis will not always ensure a suc-cessful venture; sometimes things go wrong, economic conditions change, or new information that is detrimental to the investment becomes available subsequent to the purchase. Note that this does not mean that the investor made any mistakes in performing the risk analysis prior to the acquisition of the investment. It merely means that, in retrospect, the analyst's best ef-forts did not result in a successful investment.

Risk analysis is what the investor needs to concentrate on once the me-chanical aspects of investment analysis are understood. Computers are for calculating; investors are for thinking and analyzing. Real estate investment analysis is actually risk analysis.

of the inputs. This technique is characterized by the question "What if . . . ?" In other words, the analyst might ask, "What if effective gross income fell by 10 percent?"

These techniques are helpful in judging the linkages and inputs of various investment decisions (decision trees) and the sensitivity of value of return to changes in certain input values (sensitivity analysis). Furthermore, this type of analysis is available to most analysts in real estate investment.

PROBABILISTIC MODELING AND SIMULATION

A logical extension of decision trees and sensitivity analysis is the incorporation of random elements directly into the decision-making process. *Probabilistic modeling* involves the use of subjective probability distributions around various input variables. For example, the analyst estimates the distribution of outcomes around effective gross income, operating expenses, debt service, growth rates in income and expenses, growth rate in property values, and others. The probabilistic model then uses this information to make a valuation estimate. *Simulation* is an integral part of this process, since the distributions of inputs for a large set of observations are typically generated by a computer program. Many computer services now offer these types of programs to investors.

MODERN CAPITAL MARKET MEASURES

The final method measures risk by integrating risk and return into a modern capital market approach. This involves measuring the risk of an asset as a function of variability with other investments ("covariability"), or with the real estate market in general rather than variability of its own possible outcomes. This *covariance* is essential to modern portfolio theory.

To the extent that the risk of real estate investments is viewed as a function of the relationship between the expected returns of one investment and the expected returns of other investments in the market, the development of market measures of risk incorporating principles of diversification, portfolio theory, and capital market theory may be useful. Recent attempts to modify financial models for real estate investments have made some gains in this direction, although more development is expected.

EXAMPLES OF RISK ANALYSIS

THE CERTAINTY-EQUIVALENT APPROACH

The certainty-equivalent approach incorporates risk separately from the consideration of the time value of money by accounting for it in the *numer-*

ator (the cash flows) rather than the denominator of the discounted cash flow model. This factor is the *certainty equivalent of the expected cash flow*.

Following traditional analysis, the certainty-equivalent factor is derived by answering the question, *What is the smallest certain after-tax cash flow (ATCF*) for which the investor would be willing to give up the expected, risky, after-tax cash flow (ATCF) and still be indifferent?* Mathematically, we can represent this factor by the symbol α:

$$\alpha = \frac{\text{ATCF*}}{\text{ATCF}} \text{ (so that } 0 < \alpha \leq 1) \tag{13–5}$$

where:

$$\alpha = \text{certainty-equivalent factor}$$

$$\text{ATCF*} = \text{certain after-tax cash flow}$$

$$\text{ATCF} = \text{expected (but risky) after-tax cash flow}$$

If we allow values of α to vary over all t periods, the investment value of equity can be written as follows:

$$E = \sum_{t=1}^{n} \frac{\alpha_t \text{ATCF}_t}{(1 + k_f)^t} + \frac{\alpha_n \text{ATER}_n}{(1 + k_f)^n} \tag{13–6}$$

where:

$$\alpha_t = \text{certainty-equivalent factor in the } i\text{th year}$$

$$k_f = \text{risk-free rate}$$

If the use of the certainty-equivalent approach also provides an estimate of the investment value of equity, then for some values of α_t and $(k_e - k_f)$:

$$E = \sum_{t=1}^{n} \frac{\alpha_t \text{ATCF}_t}{(1 + k_f)^t} + \frac{\alpha_n \text{ATER}_n}{(1 + k_f)^n} = \sum_{t=1}^{n} \frac{\text{ATCF}_t}{(1 + k_e)^t} + \frac{\text{ATER}_n}{(1 + k_e)^n} \tag{13–7}$$

It also follows that for some values of α_t and $(k_e - k_f)$, the net present values are equivalent in these models:

$$\text{NPV}_e = \sum_{t=1}^{n} \frac{\alpha_t \text{ATCF}_t}{(1 + k_f)^t} + \frac{\alpha_n \text{ATER}_n}{(1 + k_f)^n} - (\text{MV} - \text{MD}) \tag{13–8}$$

$$= \sum_{t=1}^{n} \frac{\text{ATCF}_t}{(1 + k_e)^t} + \frac{\text{ATER}_n}{(1 + k_e)^n} - (\text{MV} - \text{MD})$$

As an example, suppose an investor wishes to compare the risk-adjusted discount rate technique with the certainty-equivalent approach for the following expected after-tax cash flow and after-tax equity reversion stream (investment Q in Table 13–4).

If cash flows in the near future are believed to be less risky than cash flows in the distant future, the investor would be more willing to accept lower, certain, after-tax cash flows (ATCFs*) in the distant future than in the near future. This is identical to saying the investor believes that $\alpha_1 > \alpha_2 > \alpha_3$.

Suppose that by the method presented earlier, the investor determines the following values for α_t: $\alpha_1 = 0.95$, $\alpha_2 = 0.90$, and $\alpha_3 = 0.85$. The net present value, using the certainty-equivalent approach, would be $1,756.97, assuming a risk-free rate of 4 percent:

$$NPV_e = \frac{0.95(\$2,000)}{(1.04)^1} + \frac{0.90(\$4,000)}{(1.04)^2} + \frac{0.85(\$6,000)}{(1.04)^3} + \frac{0.85(\$12,000)}{(1.04)^3}$$
$$- \$17,000$$

$$= \$1,756.97$$

According to the NPV decision rules, any positive value indicates that the investment should be accepted.

Suppose the risk premium $(k_e - k_f)$ is equal to 11 percent. The appropriate discount rate to be used is the sum of the risk-free (k_f) and the risk premium $(k_e - k_f)$ or the required rate of return on equity (k_e). To calculate the net present value using the risk-adjusted discount rate approach, k_e is equal to 15 percent:

$$NPV_e = \frac{\$2,000}{(1.15)^1} + \frac{\$4,000}{(1.15)^2} + \frac{\$6,000}{(1.15)^3} + \frac{\$12,000}{(1.15)^3} - \$17,000$$

$$= -\$401.00$$

TABLE 13–4
EXAMPLE FOR CERTAINTY-EQUIVALENT
AND RISK-ADJUSTED DISCOUNT
RATE COMPARISONS

	Investment Q	
Year	ATCF	ATER
0	$(17,000)	
1	2,000	
2	4,000	
3	6,000	$12,000

However, using the risk-adjusted discount rate approach, the investor would reject the investment. In this case, a comparison between the risk-adjusted discount rate approach and the certainty-equivalent approach results in a conflict about whether to accept the investment.

Proponents of the certainty-equivalent approach argue that acceptance of the investment makes sense, since the net present value is positive. However, users of risk-adjusted discount rates argue that at a 15 percent discount rate, the investment should be rejected because the net present value is negative. The resolution of this matter depends on the investor's ability to estimate certainty-equivalent factors.

THE VARIANCE AS A RISK MEASURE

In the example of investments X, Y, and Z developed earlier in this chapter, the analysis of alternative investments using expected after-tax cash flows presumed all of the projects were equally risky. Because all sets of cash flows were of the same risk class, any differences in the expected after-tax cash flow were a function of the probabilities of occurrence of different states of the world. The *variance* is a measure of dispersion, or deviation away from the expected value.

As an example, suppose the investor must choose between three mutually exclusive projects: investments E, F, and G, as shown in Table 13–5. The investor estimates various after-tax cash flows for each state of the world and assigns subjective probability estimates to the likelihood of occurrence.

A review of the table indicates that the expected after-tax cash flow of each investment is identical. Therefore a measure must be developed to determine the relative riskiness of each investment. The variance of the expected after-tax cash flow is one such measure.

TABLE 13–5
EXPECTED AFTER-TAX CASH FLOWS FOR INVESTMENTS E, F, AND G WITH
VARIOUS STATES OF THE ECONOMY*

| State of the Economy | Probability of of State Occurring | Investments | | |
		E	F	G
Recession	.20	$ 500	$ 750	$ 900
Normal	.60	1,000	1,000	1,000
Boom	.20	1,500	1,250	1,100

$ATCF_t$ of investment E $= \$500(.20) + \$1,000(.60) + \$1,500(.20) = \$1,000$
$ATCF_t$ of investment F $= \$750(.20) + \$1,000(.60) + \$1,250(.20) = \$1,000$
$ATCF_t$ of investment G $= \$900(.20) + \$1,000(.60) + \$1,100(.20) = \$1,000$

*Note that these after-tax cash flows are for the *t*th year.

TABLE 13–6

σ_t^2 of investment E $= (\$500 - \$1,000)^2.20 + (\$1,000 - \$1,000)^2.60 + (\$1,500 - \$1,000)^2.20$
$= \$100,000$

σ_t^2 of investment F $= (\$750 - \$1,000)^2.20 + (\$1,000 - \$1,000)^2.60 + (\$1,250 - \$1,000)^2.20$
$= \$25,000$

σ_t^2 of investment G $= (\$900 - \$1,000)^2.20 + (\$1,000 - \$1,000)^2.60 + (\$1,100 - \$1,000)^2.20$
$= \$4,000$

*Note that these variances are for the tth year and that the dimension of the variance is in "dollars squared."

The variance is defined as σ_t^2, so that:

$$\sigma_t^2 = \sum_{i=1}^{m} (\text{ATCF}_{it} - \overline{\text{ATCF}_t})^2 p_{it} \qquad (13\text{–}9)$$

where:

$\sigma_t^2 =$ variance of expected after-tax cash flows for the tth year

$\text{ATCF}_{it} =$ after-tax cash flow if the ith state of the world occurs in the tth year

$\overline{\text{ATCF}_t} =$ expected after-tax cash flow for the tth year

$p_{it} =$ probability of the ith state of the world in the tth year

The variances for investments E, F, and G can be calculated by using this equation (Table 13–6). It is not surprising that the tighter the probability distribution around the expected after-tax cash flow, the smaller the variance. As a measure of risk, the lower the variance, the lower the risk.

Graphically, we can see the probability distributions of investments E, F, and G in Figure 13–1. Here the distribution is "widest" for investment E and "tightest" for investment G, which corresponds to the magnitudes of our risk measure.

Recall that earlier in the chapter, we showed that projects could be ranked on the basis of expected after-tax cash flow if risk was presumed constant for all projects. However, if the expected after-tax cash flows for projects under consideration are equivalent, as in the cases of investments E, F, and G (see Table 13–5), the investor will be neutral about these investments only if the risk is the same for all. In this example, the risk varies with the project (see Figure 13–1) and a new measure is needed. The variance of the after-tax cash flow shows that investment G would be preferred over investment F, and investment F over investment E (see Table 13–6).

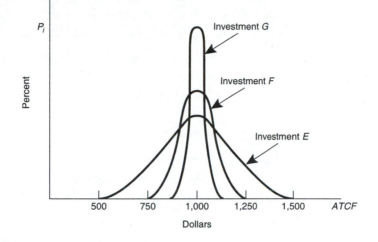

FIGURE 13–1
Probability Distributions for Investments E, F, and G

These results indicate that the investor can now analyze expected values and risk together when making investment choices. This ability, as we will subsequently show, is useful in forming a very robust criterion.

THE STANDARD DEVIATION AS A RISK MEASURE

A popular measure of risk, the *standard deviation,* is the square root of the variance:

$$\sigma_t = \sqrt{\sigma_t^2} \qquad\qquad (13\text{–}10)$$

where:

σ_t = standard deviation of expected after-tax cash flows for the *t*th year

The standard deviations of investments E, F, and G are shown in Table 13–7. Note that the greater the variance, the greater the standard deviation. So it does not matter whether the investor calculates variances or standard deviations in order to identify the investment with the lowest risk; either will provide the same information.

❑ **SOME SIMPLE EXAMPLES.** As a review of the use of the expected value, variance, and standard deviation criteria for choosing investments, it may be useful to consider a few simple examples. In each case, the in-

TABLE 13–7
STANDARD DEVIATIONS OF EXPECTED
AFTER-TAX CASH FLOWS FOR
INVESTMENTS E, F, AND G*

σ_t of investment E $= \sqrt{100,000}$
$= \$316.23$

σ_t of investment F $= \sqrt{25,000}$
$= \$158.11$

σ_t of investment G $= \sqrt{4,000}$
$= \$63.25$

*Note that these standard deviations are for
the tth year and note that the dimension of
the standard deviation is in "dollars."

vestor's task is to choose the investment that is consistent with the goal of expected wealth maximization, taking risk into account.

EXAMPLE 1. An investor is confronted with a choice between investments A and B, with the expected values, variances, and standard deviations shown in Table 13–8. Since the expected after-tax cash flow in year t of investment A is greater than that of investment B and the risk, as measured by the variance (and the standard deviation) of the cash flows in year t, is the same for each investment, it is safe to conclude that the investor would prefer investment A over B. Since the risk is identical, the investor would choose the investment with the higher expected after-tax cash flow.

TABLE 13–8
EXPECTED VALUES, VARIANCES,
AND STANDARD DEVIATIONS FOR
INVESTMENTS A AND B

	Investment	
	A	B
$\overline{\text{ATCF}_t}$	$200	$100
σ_t^2	25	25
σ_t	$ 5	$ 5

EXAMPLE 2. Imagine an investor who is confronted with a choice between two other investments, C and D, with the expected values, variances, and standard deviations shown in Table 13–9.

In this case, since the expected after-tax cash flows are the same, the investor must consider possible differences in risk. It is clear that since the variance (and the standard deviation) are greater for investment D than for

TABLE 13-9
EXPECTED VALUES, VARIANCES,
AND STANDARD DEVIATIONS FOR
INVESTMENTS C AND D

	Investment	
	C	D
$\overline{ATCF}_t$	$200	$200
σ_t^2	25	36
σ_t	$ 5	$ 6

investment C, the investor would prefer investment C. In cases where the expected values are the same, the investor would always prefer less risk, and therefore the investment with the lower variance (and standard deviation) is chosen.

EXAMPLE 3. Imagine that the investor is given yet another choice between investments E and F, with the expected values, variances, and standard deviations shown in Table 13–10. In this case, the expected after-tax cash flow in year t is greater for investment F than for investment E. However, the risk is also greater. Although investment F expects to return a higher after-tax cash flow than does investment E, the cash flow stream is more risky. So which investment should be selected?

Although the analysis was quite straightforward in Examples 1 and 2, it is more difficult in Example 3. Specifically, we need the theory of utility to decide the issue. However, some authors have advocated the use of the coefficient of variation to choose between investments E and F.

TABLE 13-10
EXPECTED VALUES, VARIANCES,
AND STANDARD DEVIATIONS FOR
INVESTMENTS E AND F

	Investment	
	E	F
$\overline{ATCF}_t$	$200	$200
σ_t^2	25	36
σ_t	$ 5	$ 6

THE COEFFICIENT OF VARIATION AS RISK MEASURE

The *coefficient of variation* is defined as the standard deviation divided by the expected value:

$$v_t = \frac{\sigma_t}{ATCF_t} \qquad\qquad (13\text{–}11)$$

where:

> v_t = coefficient of variation of expected after-tax cash flows for the
> tth year

The coefficient of variation can be used to evaluate choices when the expected value *and* risk of one alternative are greater than those of another. In the case of investments E and F, the coefficients of variation are equal to .05 and .03, respectively (as shown in Table 13–11).

TABLE 13–11
COEFFICIENTS OF VARIATION FOR INVESTMENTS
E AND F

	Investment	
	E	F
v_t	\$5 ÷ \$100 = .05	\$6 ÷ \$200 = .03

Using the coefficient of variation, the investor concludes that the "risk per dollar of expected value" is greater for investment E than for investment F, and therefore investment F is preferred over investment E. The coefficient of variation may be viewed as an attempt to standardize the amount of risk per unit of value.

The trouble with the coefficient of variation as an investment decision rule for risky investments is that *it may not always work*. So it must be discarded, as the next example will show.

EXAMPLE 4. An investor is given a choice between two final investments, G and H, with the probability distributions shown in Table 13–12.

TABLE 13–12
EXPECTED PROBABILITY DISTRIBUTIONS FOR
INVESTMENTS G AND H

	Investment		
G		H	
$ATCF_i$	p_i	$ATCF_i$	p_i
\$100	1.00	\$200	.50
		400	.50

TABLE 13–13
EXPECTED VALUES, VARIANCES,
AND STANDARD DEVIATIONS FOR
INVESTMENTS G AND H

| | Investment | |
	G	H
ATCF$_t$	$100	$300
σ_t^2	0	10,000
σ_t	$ 0	$ 100
v_t	.00	.33

Given the probability distributions for each after-tax cash flow, variances, standard deviations, and coefficients of variation can be calculated for year t. These are shown in Table 13–13.

It is clear that the expected after-tax cash flow and the variance (and standard deviation) of one alternative (investment H) are greater than those of the other (investment G). Therefore this example is a possible candidate for using the coefficient of variation.

However, a review of the probability distribution of investment H indicates that something is wrong with the measure if investment G is preferable to investment H. The proof is, of course, that no matter which outcome occurs (that is, whether it is $200 or $400), either would be preferable to the outcome under investment G ($100). Therefore, despite the fact that the coefficient of variation criterion indicates otherwise, investment H will always be preferred.

Therefore, the coefficient of variation fails as a useful criterion for choosing among risky alternatives. However, it *is* possible to develop useful decision rules for making these choices, as we will see.

THE MEAN-VARIANCE DECISION CRITERION

Since an investor must be able to evaluate risky investment opportunities in a manner consistent with his or her goals and risk preferences, a decision rule would be useful for this purpose. The rule developed here is commonly called the *mean-variance decision criterion*. It says that investment 1 is preferable to investment 2 if:

a. The expected after-tax cash flow of investment 1 is greater than or equal to the expected after-tax cash flow of investment 2, and the variance of the expected after-tax cash flow of investment 1 is less than the variance of the expected after-tax cash flow of investment 2, or

b. The expected after-tax cash flow of investment 2 and the variance of the expected after-tax cash flow of investment 1 are less than or equal to the variance of the expected after-tax cash flow of investment 2[4]

To demonstrate the applicability of the rule, refer to Examples 1 through 4 in the previous section. In Example 1, investment A is preferable to investment B because A's expected cash flows are greater than B's and the variances are equal. Investment C is preferable to investment D in Example 2 because C's variances are less than D's and their expected cash flows are equal. However, for Examples 3 and 4, the decision rule cannot indicate which is preferred. In both investment F and investment H, the expected cash flows *and* variances are greater than for investment E and investment G, respectively. As a result, this decision rule cannot decide the outcomes based on the criterion established.

MODERN RISK ANALYSIS

DECISION TREES

Decision trees are a quantitative technique useful for mapping out complex decisions.[5] Some real estate investments may require several types of decisions which may not be obvious without a more careful analysis. This technique enables the analyst to specify various options, their pay-offs, and the possible outcomes, given a set of choices.[6]

All decision trees must have the following elements:

- Action nodes: decision points between alternative choices.
- Event nodes: critical events at which time various outcomes occur from a course of action.
- Payoffs: the results of choosing a course of action.
- Probabilities: the likelihoods of future outcomes occurring.

---

[4]The validity of this rule here depends on (a) investments 1 and 2 having annuity after-tax cash flow streams, (b) after-tax equity reversion values being equal to zero or an annuity payment, and (c) each investment being of equal length. If these conditions are not satisfied, the investor must modify the parameters used to account for the differences between the investments. This is done by using expected net present value instead of expected after-tax cash flows and expected variance of the net present value of after-tax cash flows instead of the expected variance of the after-tax cash flows.

[5]Actually, financial applications using decision trees had been suggested as long ago as the 1950s.

[6]A good description, with detailed examples of the use of decision trees for real estate can be found in Stephen E. Hargitay and Shi-Ming Yu, *Property Investment Decisions*. (London: E & FN Spon, 1993). Much of the discussion in this section has been adapted from this excellent source.

Using these elements, the analyst is able to model alternative choices at critical times during the investment process. Various payoffs are associated with each event. Subjective probabilities are assigned to each payoff. Once a criterion is selected, the analyst is able to calculate the "best" route, or path through the decision tree.

Choosing a decision criterion is not simple. Attitudes toward risk and uncertainty are important, but there are several criteria which have frequently been used. These include:

- Choose a decision path which minimizes the worst outcome (the "minimax" rule),
- Choose a decision path which maximizes the best outcome (the "maximax" rule),
- Choose a decision path which maximizes the expected payoff (the "expected monetary value" rule), and
- Choose a decision path which minimizes the expected loss (the "minimum regret" rule).

In addition, there are other variants.

For some real estate applications, decision trees can be quite valuable, especially for those in which a series of complex decisions make it difficult to see the eventual outcomes. With the development of recent application software, it is also easier than ever to construct and use decision trees. We might see the use of decision trees among real estate analysts grow in the future.

SENSITIVITY ANALYSIS

Sensitivity analysis is defined as the repetition of multiple estimations of calculations using a known model, by systematically varying the inputs to the model to evaluate the impact of changes on the expected results. This technique can be viewed as a set of questions in the following form:

If _____ is changed from _____ to _____ , what impact does this change have on the net present value of equity?

As an example, suppose we consider investment S with the expected cash flows and reversion given in Table 13–14. The net present value of equity, ΔE, for investment S is $4,730.60, using a required rate of return on equity, k_e of 15 percent.

To see what impact a change in after-tax cash flow has on net present value, study the results in Table 13–15. These show various estimates of after-tax cash flow each period (t) when the net present value of equity is equal to 15 percent. Note that a small increase in the estimated after-tax cash flow stream substantially increases the net present value of equity.

TABLE 13-14
EXPECTED CASH FLOWS FOR
INVESTMENTS

Year	ATCF	ATER
0	$(25,000)	
1	5,000	
2	5,000	
3	5,000	
4	5,000	
5	5,000	
6	5,000	$25,000

TABLE 13-15
RESULTS OF SENSITIVITY ANALYSIS: ATCF$_t$

Estimated ATCF$_t$	Net Present Value of Equity*
$1,500	$(8,515.09)
4,000	946.12
5,000	4,730.60
6,000	8,515.09
8,000	16,084.05

*Assuming ATER$_n$ = $25,000 for n = 6.

Thus, for investment S, the investor is "sensitive" to changes in the level of after-tax cash flows.

The analyst might also want to test various growth rates for the after-tax cash flow stream. Since investment S is estimated to return $5,000 in after-tax cash flow per year, it has a zero percent annual growth rate in after-tax cash flows (Table 13–16).

TABLE 13-16
RESULTS OF SENSITIVITY ANALYSIS: GROWTH RATE IN ATCF$_t$

Estimated Growth Rate in ATCF$_t$	Net Present Value of Equity*
$ 0	$4,730.60
1	5,133.83
3	5,966.65
5	6,841.49
10	9,219.16
20	14,900.69

*Assuming ATCF$_t$ = $5,000 for t = 1 and ATER$_n$ = $25,000 for n = 6.

TABLE 13–17
RESULTS OF SENSITIVITY ANALYSIS: GROWTH RATE IN $ATER_n$

Estimated Annual Growth Rate in $ATER_n$	Net Present Value of Equity*
0%	$ 4,730.60
3	6,827.96
6	9,254.04
12	15,255.87
15	18,922.41
20	26,195.50

*Assuming $ATCF_t$ = $5,000 for $t = 1, 2, \ldots , 6$.

In this case, as the expected growth rate increases, the net present value of equity climbs at a decreasing rate. Therefore the analyst is less concerned about estimating the correct growth rate in after-tax cash flow than about the magnitude of the cash flow each period ($ATCF_t$), since the impact on net present value is lessened in this case.

Also, the analyst could examine the sensitivity of net present value to different annual growth rates in property values to see how these affect the values of the after-tax equity reversion. Obviously, changes in the after-tax equity reversion will affect the net present value of equity. Table 13–17 gives the results of this sensitivity analysis for investment S. It is easy to see that changes in the expected growth rate in after-tax equity reversion exert a sizable impact on the net present value of equity for investment S given an expected holding period of six years in this case. Note, however, that the slope of this sensitivity function is less steep than that for estimated after-tax cash flow each period, but greater than for the growth rate in after-tax cash flow.

Finally, an analyst may want to examine these changes in combination with each other. For example, taking an initial cash flow of $1,500 with a 1 percent growth in cash flows and no growth in the reversion, the estimated net present value of equity would be − $8,395.60, using 15 percent as the required rate of return on equity. On the other hand, if the analyst wanted to calculate the net present value of equity with an initial cash flow of $8,000 and an expected growth rate of 20 percent in the after-tax cash flow and after-tax equity reversion, this can be done as well. In this case, the net present value of equity is $53,820.81, using k_e, equal to 15 percent.

Sensitivity analysis, therefore, demonstrates the impact of misestimating cash flows, equity reversions, the required rate of return on equity, or any combination of parameters.[7] It is quite valuable to investors and analysts for this reason.

[7]The reader should keep in mind the types of inputs that would cause ATCF and ATER to vary. These include rents, vacancies, operating expenses, financing terms, tax rates, depreciation rules, and others.

Whether sensitivity analysis is valuable as a method for analyzing risk is another matter. Its advocates generally feel that, as a risk measure, this technique minimizes the risk of low rates of return (and low net present values) by examining a number of outcomes with various types of inputs.

EXAMPLE 13–1 SENSITIVITY ANALYSIS

In Chapter 12 we calculated the NPV and IRR for an office building case under certain anticipated assumptions. What would happen if any of the various assumptions changed? How would this effect the NPV and IRR of the investment being considered? Do a sensitivity analysis for the office example based on the following assumptions. Change the inputs one at a time.

Growth Rate in Rents	NPV	IRR	Rents: $ Sq Ft	NPV	IRR	Depreciation (basic)	NPV	IRR
4%	$ (3,259)	10.28%	$7.75	$(5,875)	9.72%	90%	$ 318	11.07%
6	3,751	11.81	8.10	2,649	11.58	80	109	11.02
7	7,355	12.58	8.25	6,304	12.38	70	(100)	10.98

Vacancy	NPV	IRR	Tax Rate	NPV	IRR	Reversion Price	NPV	IRR
4%	$ 4,359	11.95%	25%	$1,978	11.43%	$470,000	$(3,803)	10.16%
5	2,286	11.50	31	98	11.02	490,000	4,230	11.91
7	(1,859)	10.59	35	(56)	10.99	500,000	8,247	12.74

Operating Expenses	NPV	IRR	Growth Rate In Operating Expenses	NPV	IRR	Selling Expenses	NPV	IRR
$19,000	$ 8,370	12.83%	3%	$3,600	11.78%	4%	$ 4,316	11.93%
20,000	5,406	12.18	5	1,363	11.30	5	2,265	11.49
23,000	(3,485)	10.24	7	(958)	10.79	7	(1,837)	10.60

Financing: Interest Rate	NPV	IRR	ROR (After-Tax)	NPV	IRR
10%	$15,653	14.38%	10%	$4,918	11.05%
11	7,967	12.73	12	(4,252)	11.05
13	(7,596)	9.33	15	(16,357)	11.05

Several of the assumptions result in either a negative NPV or an IRR less than the investor's required rate of 11 percent. Any combination of these assumptions could take place. The investor must evaluate this risk when deciding whether or not to invest in this project.

EXAMPLE 13–2 SENSITIVITY ANALYSIS USING SPREADSHEETS

Suppose we wished to consider how sensitive our potential real estate investment was to changing mortgage interest rates. It is possible to evaluate the impact of, say, higher interest rates on the net present values and internal rates of return for any project as traditionally described above. However, the power of spreadsheets such as Lotus 1-2-3 or Excel can be harnessed to do a better job.

As an example, we wish to consider an apartment investment with 5 efficiency units, 10 one-bedroom apartments, and 12 two-bedroom units. The monthly rent is expected to be $350, $450, and $600 respectively. Vacancy allowances are estimated at 2, 3 and 4 percent respectively. The initial operating expense ratio is 42 percent.

The property is expected to be financed with a $900,000 mortgage at 8.00 percent percent annually for 30 years (annual payments only) and $200,000 equity. Seventy percent of the purchase price is attributable to the building for depreciation purposes over 27.5 years. The marginal tax rate is 28 percent.

Rent is expected to grow for all units at 3.5 percent annually, vacancy losses at 2.0 percent annually, operating expenses are estimated to grow at 3.0 percent, and property values are expected to grow at 4.0 percent annually. Selling expense are estimated at 7 percent of the gross sale price.

Using a holding period of seven years and a 14 percent discount rate for equity capital, we get the result shown in Table 1.

TABLE 1

Year	ATCF	ATER
1	$13,161	
2	15,557	
3	18,037	
4	20,603	
5	23,259	
6	26,007	
7	28,849	$393,272

The before-tax IRR on equity for this project is 21.2877 percent and the after-tax IRR on equity is 17.6177 percent. The net present value is $40,511. Using a 14 percent after-tax discount rate, this project appears to be a very good one.

If the investor wishes to consider the effects of alternative mortgage interest rates, it is possible to calculate various impacts all at once. The results are displayed in Table 2.

TABLE 2

Inputs (Mort. Rates) %	Outputs					
	ATCF(1)	ATCF(7)	ATER(7)	BTIRR/E	ATIRR/E	NPV/E
5.00	$26,999	$42,703	$432,677	29.89%	24.15%	$115,565
6.00	22,681	38,341	417,938	27.08	22.06	91,107
7.00	18,058	33,715	404,836	24.21	19.87	66,061
8.00	13,161	28,849	393,272	21.29	17.62	40,511
9.00	8,023	23,764	383,131	18.35	15.30	14,533
10.00	2,674	18,486	374,290	15.40	12.94	(11,805)
11.00	(2,857)	13,035	366,624	12.45	10.55	(38,441)
12.00	(8,544)	7,433	360,008	9.53	8.13	(65,322)
13.00	(14,364)	1,699	354,321	6.64	5.70	(92,403)
14.00	(20,297)	(4,148)	349,451	3.79	3.28	(119,644)
15.00	(26,325)	(10,092)	345,293	0.98	0.85	(147,015)

In this case, we show the impact on various mortgage interest rates on after-tax cash flow for years 1 and 7, the after-tax equity reversion, both before- and after-tax IRRs, and on NPV. For this example, the project remains a good investment until mortgage rates go above 9.00 percent. Notice also that at very high interest rates, cash flows become increasingly negative and lenders may not approve such loans with low debt coverage ratios.

Data Tables are very powerful tools within spreadsheets. Many users do not seem to know they are available, even though sensitivity analysis is often performed on an ad-hoc basis. Data tables should be a part of almost all financial analysis where there is uncertainty about the input estimates used in the analysis.

SIMULATION

Sometimes termed "probabilistic modeling" or "Monte Carlo simulation," there is a well-established tradition of assigning probabilities to input op-

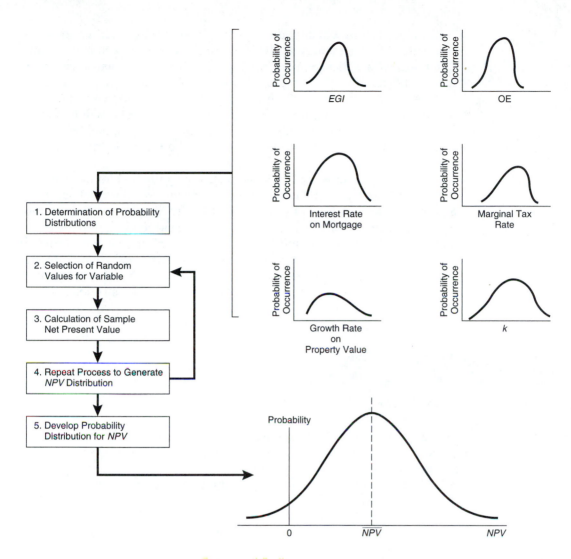

FIGURE 13–2
Illustration of Probabilistic Modeling

tions and generating a set of simulated results for the financial analysis of real estate. Begun in the early 1970s, this type of analysis is now generally available on microcomputers as well as mainframes.[8]

Simulation differs from sensitivity analysis in that there is a random element at work when the calculations are performed in simulation. This randomness is used to better capture likelihoods in the uncertain real world.

[8]For a working example within a Lotus 1-2-3 template, see "simulate.wk1" on the advanced set of real estate investment templates from JS & Associates in Appendix B.

Subjective probability distributions are required for various inputs critical to the financial analysis. Through random selection, the computer draws a series of parameter values and a calculated result is recorded. This process is repeated numerous times, each time recording the result. Ultimately, the investor obtains a cumulative probability distribution to evaluate the likelihood that the investment will be favorable (that is, say the probability that the net present value will be greater than zero). If this probability is estimated to be high, the investment is favorable.

Figure 13–2 shows the basic Monte Carlo simulation for a real estate investment. First, probability distributions are developed for inputs. Next, a random value is selected from each probability distribution and used to calculate a sample NPV. This process is repeated several times to obtain a cumulative distribution of NPVs. Finally, the distribution is standardized and a probability is estimated based upon the samples. While there are some criticisms of this method, over the past decades, Monte Carlo simulation has been used to estimate the outcomes of various problems in a wide range of arenas.

EXAMPLE 13–3 MONTE CARLO SIMULATION

Using one of the templates as described in Appendix B, it is possible to perform a complete Monte Carlo simulation in a Lotus 1-2-3 spreadsheet environment.

In this model, the analyst is permitted to enter probability distributions for several variables:

Potential gross income	Selling expenses
GPI growth rates	Discount rates
Vacancy rates	Holding periods
Operating expense ratios	Mortgage amounts
Growth in operating expenses	Mortgage terms
Income tax rates	Mortgage interest rates (by year)
Property value growth rates	

For each input, up to five "states-of-the-world" are permitted with their own unique probability of occurrence. For example, in the analysis performed for this example, the distribution of gross possible income was:

GPI	Probabilities
$122,000	.27
149,000	.34
162,000	.15
180,000	.12
199,000	.12

Note that the distributions need not be symmetric, but the probabilities must add to 100 percent.

Several types of results are available, including detailed cash flow analyses. Summaries of sample runs are also available. In this case, the results shown in Table 1 were generated for a sample of 15 calculations.

TABLE 1

Potential Gross Income	Income Tax Rate	Holding Period	Expected Return	Mortgage Term	IRR	NPV
$149,000	0.35	9	0.15	20	0.12	− 47,092
122,000	0.28	7	0.14	20	0.11	− 52,054
122,000	0.35	7	0.13	20	0.12	− 25,723
162,000	0.35	6	0.12	25	0.12	2,875
122,000	0.28	9	0.13	20	0.11	− 41,778
149,000	0.28	6	0.15	20	0.16	15,865
199,000	0.35	10	0.13	20	0.21	184,698
149,000	0.28	9	0.14	20	0.17	64,238
149,000	0.35	8	0.12	20	0.12	− 3,006
149,000	0.35	6	0.12	20	0.11	− 11,699
162,000	0.28	8	0.13	20	0.19	132,809
149,000	0.35	7	0.13	20	0.16	48,197
122,000	0.35	7	0.12	30	0.13	12,049
149,000	0.28	9	0.13	20	0.17	74,564

For the run with 15 sampled NPVs, the output shown in Table 2 is produced:

TABLE 2
ANALYSIS OF NET PRESENT VALUES

Max NPV	$184,698	Variance	4.64E + 09
Min NPV	($ 60,999)	Std. Dev.	68,140
Average NPV	$ 19,530	Z-Value (NPV = 0)	−0.29

TABLE 2
CONTINUED

| Range | | | | | Probability of Positive Net |
From	To	FRQ.	Prob.	Mid. Points	Present Value
$$-$ 60,999	$$-$ 44,893	3	20.00%	$$-$ 52,946	61.79%
$-$ 44,892	$-$ 28,788	1	6.67	$-$ 36,840	
$-$ 28,787	$-$ 12,682	1	6.67	$-$ 20,734	
$-$ 12,681	3,424	3	20.00	$-$ 4,628	
3,425	19,530	2	13.33	11,477	
19,531	52,563	1	6.67	36,047	
52,564	85,597	2	13.33	69,081	
85,598	118,631	0	0.00	102,114	
118,632	151,664	1	6.67	135,148	
151,665	184,698	1	6.67	168,182	
	Total	15	100.00%		

Notice that the cumulative probability of net present value being greater than zero is 61.79 percent.

The same analysis was rerun 30 times, using the same probability distributions on the inputs, the cumulative probability estimate changed to 57.93 percent. For a run of 100 estimates, the probability changed to 72.57 percent; at 200 times, it was estimated at 61.79 percent again. Clearly, the analysis produced different answers with different runs. This was not unexpected, since the random drawing from the input distributions gives rise to unique answers each type the analysis is performed.

The standard way to reduce these differences is to increase the size of the runs. At a sample of 450, the cumulative probability was 65.54 percent and is shown in Table 3.

TABLE 3
ANALYSIS OF NET PRESENT VALUES

Max NPV $299,141	Variance .... 4.89E + 09
Min NPV ....($ 93,422)	Std. Dev. 69,896
Average NPV .... $ 30,090	Z-Value (NPV = 0) .... −0.43

| Range | | | | | Probability of Positive Net |
From	To	FRQ.	Prob.	Mid. Points	Present Value
$$-$ 93,422	$$-$ 68,720	28	6.22%	$$-$ 81,071	65.54%
$-$ 68,719	$-$ 44,017	34	7.56	$-$ 56,368	
$-$ 44,016	$-$ 19,315	61	13.56	$-$ 31,665	
$-$ 19,314	5,388	56	12.44	$-$ 6,963	
5,389	30,090	62	13.78	17,740	
30,091	83,900	116	25.78	56,996	

TABLE 3
CONTINUED

83,901	137,711	55	12.22	110,806
137,712	191,521	34	7.56	164,616
191,522	245,331	2	0.44	218,426
245,332	299,141	2	0.44	272,236
	Total	450	100.00%	

It was run again at 450 samples and 65.54 percent was obtained again. However, notice in Table 4 that there are differences in the resulting range and frequency distribution.

TABLE 4
ANALYSIS OF NET PRESENT VALUES

Max NPV $306,531	Variance . . . . 4.09E + 09
Min NPV . . . .($ 96,459)	Std. Dev. 63,966
Average NPV . . . . $ 27,708	Z-Value (NPV = 0) . . . . −0.43

Range		FRQ.	Prob.	Mid. Points	Probability of Positive Net Present Value
From	To				
$− 96,459	$− 71,626	21	4.67%	$− 84,042	65.54%
− 71,625	− 46,792	26	5.78	− 59,208	
− 46,791	− 21,959	47	10.44	− 34,375	
− 21,958	2,874	71	15.78	− 9,542	
2,875	27,708	84	18.67	15,292	
27,709	83,472	119	26.44	55,591	
83,473	139,237	59	13.11	111,355	
139,238	195,002	16	3.56	167,120	
195,003	250,766	5	1.11	222,885	
250,767	306,531	2	0.44	278,649	
	Total	450	100.00%		

Finally, a simulation was run for 1,000 samples; the same probability results were obtained (Table 5).

TABLE 5
ANALYSIS OF NET PRESENT VALUES

Max NPV $295,739	Variance . . . . 4.67E + 09
Min NPV . . . .($100,964)	Std. Dev. 68,325
Average NPV . . . . $ 30,528	Z-Value (NPV = 0) . . . . −0.45

TABLE 5
CONTINUED

Range					Probability of Positive Net
From	To	FRQ.	Prob.	Mid. Points	Present Value
$-100,964	$- 74,666	38	3.80%	$- 87,815	65.54%
- 74,665	- 48,367	81	8.10	- 61,516	
- 48,366	- 22,069	122	12.20	- 35,218	
- 22,068	4,229	158	15.80	- 8,919	
4,230	30,528	152	15.20	17,379	
30,529	83,570	232	23.20	57,049	
83,571	136,612	135	13.50	110,092	
136,613	189,654	67	6.70	163,134	
189,655	242,697	10	1.00	216,176	
242,698	295,739	5	0.50	269,218	
	Total	1,000	100.00%		

We can be reasonably assured that 65.54 percent is a good estimate that the net present value will be positive for this project with its assigned probability distributions.

Current Issue 13–2
Portfolio Analysis in Real Estate Markets
Portfolio analysis for real estate investors was once thought to be a dream or a futuristic concept. The truth is that portfolio analysis has become reality in a very short time. Developing a portfolio of investments using diversification of risk as a principle rather than constructing a portfolio by acquiring individual assets is an important step in the development of real estate investment analysis as a field of study and a professional practice.

For students, instructors, and practitioners, this step is also a major challenge—to our traditional ways of thinking, to our methods of analysis, and to our decision-making operations in real markets. Further recognition of these developments came recently from the Nobel Prize in Economics Committee when they selected Harry Markowitz and William Sharpe (and Merton Miller) for their seminal contributions in the 1950s and 1960s, which changed the world of investment.

Institutional investors in real estate are actively pursuing diversification strategies based upon this type of analysis. Small investors may also be following this strategy, even if they are unaware of the changes—the rise of

> index mutual funds can be viewed as a direct result of the "portfolio revolution". The use of *covariance* as a measure of risk is the next generation of risk analysis in the long line of analysis in real estate.

INTRODUCTION TO PORTFOLIO ANALYSIS FOR REAL ESTATE INVESTORS

Real estate investment analysis has also been affected by the revolution in capital markets involving the concept of market risk. Specifically, a new method of analysis is in the process of taking over: portfolio analysis and the selection of investments based upon the risk-reduction potential investments possess when considered in an investment portfolio. Rather than evaluate investments based upon their own riskiness, this method looks at how the risk characteristics of any investment *co-vary* with the existing holdings. In this sense, diversifying by type, location, size, or style of investment has taken on new meaning.

WHY DIVERSIFICATION MATTERS

One of the more intuitive notions in the investment process is that an investor will diversify holdings to reduce the risk of unexpected losses. The general feeling is that by "spreading out" investments, the "risk" will be considerably lower, although the "returns" might be less than by "plunging" into one specific investment. If this naive approach is at all correct, it would seem that proper real estate investment theory should provide a framework for these "gains from diversification."

An analytical view of the problem suggests that diversification *can* reduce risk whenever the *portfolio of assets* are less than *perfectly positively correlated*. A portfolio of assets is a set or combination of assets selected according to some investment criteria. If the criteria uses principles of *portfolio theory*, the portfolios chosen will be *efficient*, or those with the greatest return for a certain degree of risk or the lowest level of risk for a specified rate of return.

Correlation is the degree of statistical relationship between two variables. *Perfectly positive correlation* is a positive one-to-one relationship, *perfectly negative correlation* is a negative one-to-one relationship. *Statistical independence* exists when there is no relationship between the values of the variables (that is, *zero correlation*).

To demonstrate why diversification matters, consider investments A and B in Table 13–18.

A		B	
R_i (%)	p_i	R_i (%)	p_i
−15	.50	−15	.50
35	.50	35	.50

Similarly, in Chapter 9, the expected rate of return, $\bar{R}$, is equal to the estimated return for each ith state of the world, R_i, times the probability of occurrence of each state, p_i.

$$E(R) = R_1 p_1 + R_2 p_2 + \cdots + R_m p_m$$
$$= \sum_{i=1}^{m} R_i p_i \qquad (13\text{–}12)$$

where:

$E(R)$ = expected rate of return

R_i = estimated return for ith state of the world

Similarly, the variance σ^2_R, and standard deviation σ_R, of the distribution of rates of return can be derived.

$$\sigma^2_R = \sum_{i=1}^{m} [R_i - E(R)]^2 p_i \qquad (13\text{–}13)$$

$$\sigma_R = \sqrt{\sigma^2_R} \qquad (13\text{–}14)$$

where:

σ^2_R = variance of expected rate of return

σ_R = standard deviation of expected rate of return

For investments A and B, we get the following results:

$$E(R_A) = E(R_B) = -15(.50) + 35(.50) = 10.00$$

$$\sigma^2_{R_A} = \sigma^2_{R_B} = (-15 - 10)^2\,.50 + (35 - 10)^2\,.50 = 625.00$$

$$\sigma_{R_A} = \sigma_{R_B} = 25.00$$

TABLE 13–19
EXPECTED RETURNS AND
PROBABILITIES FOR
INVESTMENT C

R_i (%)	p_i
−15	.25
10	.50
35	.25

Since the distribution of returns for both investments are identical, they possess the same expected values, variances, and standard deviations.

Now suppose that an investor knows about the benefits of diversification and decides to form a new alternative, investment C, which consists of an amount equal to one-half of investment A and one-half of investment B. Investment C will have the following returns and associated probabilities (Table 13–19), assuming that the returns on investments A and B are statistically independent of each other.[9]

The probabilities for investment C are computed as follows. The outcome of −15 percent is expected to occur 50 percent of the time with investment A and 50 percent of the time with investment B. Since investment C is really one-half of each investment, the probability is the product of the likelihoods, or 25 percent. The outcome of 35 percent follows a similar pattern. But it gets more complex for the outcome of 10 percent. Perhaps the easiest way to see the results is that the expected return of 10 percent will occur for both investments A and B if—15 percent or 35 percent did not. In this case, it would be 50 percent of the time.[10] Therefore,

$$E(R_C) = 10.00$$

However, the main point of this example is that *the variance and standard deviation for investment C are lower than for investments A or B.*

$$\sigma^2_{R_C} = (-15 - 10)^2 \,.25 + (10 - 10)^2 \,.50 + (35 - 10)^2 \,.25$$

$$= 312.50$$

$$\sigma_{R_C} = \sqrt{312.50}$$

$$= 17.68$$

Therefore, investing in a portfolio of investments, even with identical distributions, reduces risk. This is important since it suggests that in-

[9]This is equivalent to saying that the correlation between the investments as measured by the correlation coefficient, ρ_{AB}, is equal to zero.
[10]The outcome of 10 percent is also calculated as follows: $- 15_A$ (.25) $+ 35_A$ (.25) $^+ - 15_B$ (.25) $+ 35_B$ (.25) $= 10.00$.

vestors who diversify with uncorrelated investments (or as we shall see, less than perfectly positively correlated investments) will gain from it. Stated differently, investors who fail to diversify are implicitly giving up investment opportunities (investment C) that promise the same expected return $[E(R_A) = E(R_B) = E(R_C)]$ but lower risk $(\sigma_{R_A} > \sigma_{R_C}$ and $\sigma_{R_B} > \sigma_{R_C})$.

PORTFOLIO THEORY AND THE MEASUREMENT OF RISK

The previous example presumed that there was no statistical relationship between investments A and B. If this condition does not hold, the variance of portfolios would be calculated incorrectly.

In general, we can use the following equation for a two-asset portfolio:

$$\sigma_p^2 = w_A^2 \sigma_{R_A}^2 + w_B^2 \sigma_{R_B}^2 + 2w_A w_B Cov_{AB} \qquad (13\text{--}15)$$

so that

$$w_A + w_B = 1\sigma_R^2$$

where:

$$\sigma_p^2 = \text{variance of portfolio of investments A and B}$$

$$w_A = \text{proportion of portfolio in investment A}$$

$$w_B = \text{proportion of portfolio in investment B}$$

$$Cov_{AB} = \text{covariance between investments A and B}$$

Similarly, the standard deviation of the portfolio is the square root of the variance

$$\sigma_p = \sqrt{\sigma_p^2} \qquad (13\text{--}16)$$

where:

$$\sigma_p = \text{standard deviation of the portfolio of investments A and B}$$

The *covariance* between investments is a measure of the relationship between the distributions of the investments. Specifically, the covariance is a function of the correlation between the returns and the standard deviation of each investment.

The covariance is defined as:

$$Cov_{AB} = \rho_{AB}\sigma_{R_A}\sigma_{R_B} \qquad (13\text{--}17)$$

where:

ρ_{AB} = correlation coefficient between the returns on investments A and B

Substituting Equation (13–17) into Equations (13–15) and (13–16), respectively, we get:

$$\sigma_p^2 = w_A^2 \sigma_{R_A}^2 + w_B^2 \sigma_{R_B}^2 + 2w_A w_B \rho_{AB} \sigma_{R_A} \sigma_{R_B} \qquad (13\text{–}18)$$

$$\sigma_p = \sqrt{w_A^2 \sigma_{R_A}^2 + w_B^2 \sigma_{R_B}^2 + 2w_A w_B \rho_{AB} \sigma_{R_A} \sigma_{R_B}} \qquad (13\text{–}19)$$

As an example, consider Table 13–20, a portfolio consisting of investments M and N.

The standard deviation of this portfolio is determined as follows, given various values for ρ_{MN}, the correlation coefficient.

$$\sigma_p = \sqrt{.0625(625) + .5625(225) + 2(.25)(.75)\rho_{MN}(25)(15)}$$
$$= \sqrt{165.625 + 140.625\rho_{MN}}$$

Table 13–21 shows that the standard deviation of the portfolio varies with the value of the correlation coefficient between returns on investments M and N.

Therefore, the more negatively correlated the investments, the lower the overall portfolio risk. In the example of investment C, the value of the correlation coefficient was presumed to be zero, since statistical independence was assumed. Even with the zero correlation coefficient for investments M and N, the risk of the portfolio is less than the risk of the individual investment. Note also that the covariance varies directly with the correlation coefficient.

These examples contain many implications for real estate investment analysis. First, riskiness is different for assets considered in port-

TABLE 13–20
EXAMPLE OF WEIGHTS AND RISK
MEASURE FOR A TWO-ASSET PORTFOLIO

	Investment	
	M	N
w	.25	.75
w^2	.0625	.562
σ_p^2	625%	225%
σ_R	25%	15%

TABLE 13–21
FUNCTION OF THE
CORRELATION COEFFICIENT

ρ_{MN}	σ_p
+1.00	17.50
+0.50	15.36
0.00	12.87
−0.50	9.76
−1.00	5.00

folios.[11] Second, portfolio risk varies with the relationship between the expected distributions of the individual investments. The more positive the correlation, the greater the risk. Third, as a result of the direct relationship between the risk of the portfolio and the correlation or covariance between the investments, the investor can reduce the risk by selecting investments with negative correlations. Finally, portfolios with more than two investments use the same diversification principles to reduce risk.[12]

As a final note, the portion of risk that can be "diversified away" is called *diversifiable* or *nonsystematic risk.* The remainder is *nondiversifiable* or *systematic risk.* The theory suggests that a competitive market will not pay a premium for any diversifiable risk that could be eliminated by adding less than perfectly correlated investments to the portfolio. So the implication is that the market will only compensate the investor for systematic risk. A well-known measure of systematic risk is *beta* (β) in the *capital asset pricing model (CAPM).*

THE CAPITAL ASSET PRICING MODEL

With diversification, the riskiness of a portfolio of investments will be less than the riskiness of the individual investments. Therefore, if real estate investments are valued in a portfolio, it seems reasonable that investors would want to analyze the impact of each investment in terms of how the investment's risk contributes to the overall riskiness of the portfolio. The

[11]Note that if $w_M = 1.00$ in the example, the entire portfolio consists of investment M, and Equation (13–19) reduces to $\sigma_p = \sqrt{625} = 25\%$, which is identical to σ_{R_M}, the risk of the individual asset.

[12]For example, for three investments: A, B, and C, the standard deviation of the portfolio would be:

$$\sigma_p = \sqrt{W_A^2 \sigma_{R_A}^2 + W_B^2 \sigma_{R_B}^2 + W_C^2 \sigma_{R_C}^2 + 2W_A W_B Cov_{AB} + 2W_A W_C Cov_{AC} + 2W_B W_C Cov_{BC}}$$

For a portfolio with n investments, see Eugene F. Fama and Merton H. Miller, *The Theory of Finance* (Hinsdale, Ill.: The Dryden Press, 1972).

capital asset pricing model (CAPM) allows the investor to do this. The measure of systematic (or nondiversifiable) risk is *beta* (β).

If we diversify away all risk by selecting investments with negative covariances of returns, the expected return for the *j*th investment is:

$$E(R_j) = R_f + (\bar{R}_m - R_f)\beta_j \qquad (13\text{--}20)$$

where:

$E(R_j)$ = expected return on investment J

R_f = risk-free rate

$\bar{R}_m$ = expected rate of return for the market portfolio

β_j = beta coefficient for investment J

An inspection of Equation (13–20) reveals that the expected return can be divided into a risk-free rate and a risk premium. The risk-free rate is a function of economic productivity. The risk premium, in a portfolio sense, is the excess market return over the risk-free rate times the level of market risk for the specific investment.

Figure 13–3 graphs the relationship between the expected return for investment J as a function of the risk, measured by beta. This function is frequently called the *security market line (SML)*.[13]

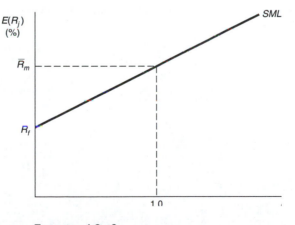

FIGURE 13–3
The Security Market Line for Investment J

[13]Note that Figure 13–3 is similar, but not identical to Figure 2–1, which shows the risk-return relationship for the entire market. In this context, Figure 2–1 is called the *capital market line (CML)*.

The security market line is the expected rate of return on an investment consisting of a riskless rate of return plus a risk premium equal to the premium paid on the "average" investment, adjusted upward or downward according to this investment's risk in relation to its covariance of returns with others in the market. For example, if R_f equals 6 percent and $\bar{R}_m$ equals 15 percent, the expected return will vary with beta values (Table 13–3).

Therefore, the higher the risk, β_j, the higher the expected return, $E(R_j)$, from investment J. If β_j is less than 1.00, the expected return will be less than the expected rate of return for the market. If it is greater than 1.00, the expected return on investment J will be higher than the expected return on the market portfolio.

Finally, it is possible to relate the covariance of expected returns for individual investments and the market with beta. Beta can also be defined as the ratio of the covariance of the expected returns for investment J with the expected return for the market portfolio to the variance of the market portfolio:

$$\beta_j = \frac{Cov_{JM}}{\sigma_m^2} \qquad (13\text{--}21)$$

where:

$$Cov_{JM} = \text{covariance between investment J and market portfolio}$$

$$\sigma_m^2 = \text{variance of expected rate of return of market portfolio}$$

By substitution, we get the following results:

$$E(R_j) = R_f + (\bar{R}_m - R_f)\frac{Cov_{JM}}{\sigma_m^2} \qquad (13\text{--}22)$$

By algebra, we can rewrite the expected return on investment J equal to the risk-free rate plus the "market price of risk," λ times the covariance between the investment J and the market portfolio.

$$E(R_j) = R_f + \lambda Cov_{JM} \qquad (13\text{--}23)$$

where:

$$\lambda = \text{market price of risk, or } \frac{(\bar{R}_m - R_f)}{\sigma_m^2}$$

Stated as Equation (13–12), the expected rate of return may be more easily derived by calculating λ for the market portfolio, which will not vary with each investment. This latter factor is accounted for by the covariance.

In summary, the *CAPM* approach is a potentially robust framework for real estate investment analysis. However, the required assumptions and data requirements in terms of real estate applications cast serious doubts on whether this approach is useful, *even* if it is proven to be theoretically attractive, a task not yet accomplished.

REAL ESTATE INVESTMENTS AS PORTFOLIO ASSETS

The preliminary evidence regarding portfolio approaches to real estate has been increasingly promising. Initially, skeptics and disbelievers tended to chuckle as researchers and some analysts struggled to find sufficient data to measure the market return or to calculate portfolio allocations that reasonably matched practice in the real world. However, the proponents of portfolio analysis as a tool for real estate investors may yet prove to have the last laugh.

Recent researchers indicate that with the development of new data sources and continual empirical knowledge about risk and return experiences in commercial real estate markets, portfolio analysis for real estate is becoming a reality. While just in the preliminary stages, one would expect that over the next few years, this method will become a standard extension to the measurement of real estate risk as has DCF methods. In addition, the valuation of individual properties will inevitably be affected by portfolio considerations of institutional investors. In the end, real estate investment analysis will no longer be performed on a project-by-project basis as has been the tradition. The future seems to be moving in a different direction.

SUMMARY

In a world of uncertainty, the ability to measure risk or the uncertainty of future benefits and liabilities of an investment can be the difference between the success and failure of an investment. This chapter illustrates methods of risk analysis used in making investment decisions. We begin by introducing risk into the discounted cash flow models developed in Chapter 12. Next, we illustrate how variance and standard deviation are used to measure risk through the use of the mean-variance decision criterion. The chapter concludes by introducing modern methods of measuring risk such as decision trees and sensitivity analysis (including an example of the Monte Carlo Simulation) and the benefits of diversification through portfolio theory in the measurement of risk, as well as the capital asset pricing model.

QUESTIONS

13–1. Why is risk analysis essential to real estate decision making?

13–2. What is the expected net present value of equity? Why is it more useful than the net present value of equity, assuming certainty?

13–3. There are several traditional methods of accounting for risk. What are these methods and what are their shortcomings?

13–4. This book illustrates the certainty-equivalent approach. How does this method compare with the more traditional risk-adjusted discount rate method?

13–5. What are the variance and standard deviation measures of risk?

13–6. "The tighter the distribution around the expected value, the lower the risk." True or false? Explain.

13–7. Show that if two investment opportunities have the same expected values, the investment with the lower variance and lower standard deviation will be preferred.

13–8. What is the coefficient of variation? Why does it fail as a risk measure?

13–9. What is sensitivity analysis and how is it used in real estate investing?

13–10. Do you think risk analysis is useful in actual real estate investing? Why or why not?

PROBLEMS

13–1. An investor is offered the following three investments:

	Investment		
	S	T	U
p	ATCF	ATCF	ATCF
.25	$1,000	$2,000	$2,500
.50	3,000	3,000	3,000
.25	5,000	4,000	3,500

a. What are the expected after-tax cash flows for each investment in each *t*th year?
b. Which investment would an investor prefer?
c. Prove why certain investments are preferable to others.

13–2. Using a numerical example, demonstrate how the certainty-equivalent approach can be inconsistent with the risk-adjusted discount rate model.

13–3. Calculate the coefficient of variation for the investment chosen in Problem 13–1. Is this a useful measure? Explain.

13–4. An investor is considering the purchase of a parcel of land.
a. If the investor pays $45,000 for the land, what will be the rate of return if the land sells for $50,000 one year from purchase?
b. Suppose the investor formulates the following expectations:

State of the World	Probability	Expected Selling Price
1	.05	$48,500
2	.80	50,000
3	.15	55,000

What is the expected rate of return? What is the standard deviation of the expected rate of return?

13–5. Suppose an investor is considering investing in three projects with the following estimated returns and probabilities:
a. Calculate the expected rate of return, variance of the expected rate of return, and standard deviation of the expected rate of return.

A		B		C	
$R_i\%$	P_i	$R_i\%$	P_i	$R_i\%$	P_i
−10	.25	−10	.25	−10	.25
10	.50	10	.50	20	.75
18	.25	18	.25		

Calculate the portfolio standard deviation when the value of the correlation coefficient is − .50; 0.0; and + .50. Explain why it would make sense to diversify by investing in all three projects rather than any one individually.

b. Assuming that these projects are mutually exclusive, which would the investor choose if his goal was to maximize wealth, minimize risk?

13–6. Using the information from Problem 13–5, and the following:

	A	B	C
w	.40	.35	.25
w^2	.16	.1225	.0625

SELECTED REFERENCES

Clauretie, Terrence M., and James R. Webb, *The Theory and Practice of Real Estate Finance*. Fort Worth, Tex.: The Dryden Press, 1993.

Cooper, James A., and Cathy A. Morrison, "Using Computer Simulation to Minimize Risk in Urban Housing Development," *Real Estate Appraiser*, 39 (March–April 1973), 15–26.

Corgel, John B., "On Improving Interpretations of Simulated Investment Values," *The Real Estate Appraiser and Analyst*, 46 (November–December 1980), 16–22.

Findlay, M. C., S. D. Messner, and R. Tarantello, "Risk Analysis in Real Estate", *Real Estate Appraiser and Analyst*, 45 (July–August 1979), 27–38.

Frew, James, and G. Donald Jud, "A Simulation Model of Commercial Real Estate Development," *The Real Estate Appraiser and Analyst*, 54 (Fall 1988), 23–49.

Friedman, Harris C., "Real Estate Investment and Portfolio Theory," *Journal of Financial and Quantitative Analysis*, 4 (April 1970), 861–874.

Grissom, Terry V., James L. Kuhle, and Carl H. Walther, "Diversification Works in Real Estate, Too," *Journal of Portfolio Management*, 13 (Winter 1987), 66–71.

Gyourko, Joseph, and Peter Linneman, "Analyzing the Risk of Income-Producing Property," *Urban Studies*, 27 (1990), 497–508.

Hargitay, Stephen E., and Shi-Ming Yu, *Property Investment Decisions: A Quantitative Approach*. London: E & FN Spon, 1993.

Hartzell, David, John Hekman, and Mike Miles, "Diversification Categories in Investment Real Estate," *American Real Estate and Urban Economics Association Journal*, 14 (Summer 1986), 230–254.

Hoag, James W., "Toward Indices of Real Estate Value and Return," *Journal of Finance*, 35 (May 1980), 569–580.

Kapplin, Steven D., "Financial Theory and the Valuation of Real Estate under Conditions of Risk," *Real Estate Appraiser*, 42 (September–October 1976), 28–37.

Martin, William B., Jr., "A Risk Analysis Rate-of-Return Model for Evaluating Income-Producing Real Estate Investments," *Appraisal Journal*, 46 (July 1978), 424–242.

Miles, Mike, and Michael Rice, "Toward a More Complete Investigation of the Correlation of Real Estate Investment Yield to the Rate Evidenced in the Money and Capital Markets: The Individual Investor's Perspective," *Real Estate Appraiser and Analyst*, 44 (November–December 1978), 8–19.

Ratcliff, Richard U., and Bernhard Schwab, "Contemporary Decision Theory and Real Es-

tate Investment," *The Appraisal Journal*, 39 (April 1970), 165–187.

Wofford, Larry E., "A Simulation Approach to the Appraisal of Income Producing Real Estate," *American Real Estate and Urban Economics Association Journal*, 6 (Winter 1978), 370–394.

Part V

Applications

Chapter 14

Applying the Investment Process: A Case Study

Principles _____

1. Given the real estate investment process and its expansion throughout the book, it is possible to apply this approach and its supporting calculations when making actual investment decisions.
2. This chapter provides an extensive illustration using a detailed case study.
3. The real estate investment process and the tools and techniques throughout this approach permit the investor to develop a comprehensive real estate investment strategy.

In the previous chapters we outlined and discussed the real estate investment process. In this chapter we apply this decision-making process in a detailed case format. The investment situation involves a young married couple, John and Judy Smith, considering the purchase of a small apartment building.

We first review some of the basic elements of a real estate investment strategy. Then we "walk" the investor step by step through the decision-making process. The reader is encouraged to work all the numerical calculations and use the text as an answer key. Only by such a detailed analysis will the mechanics of real estate investment decision making be understood.

Obviously, a case study cannot examine in detail all the relevant elements. Any decision-making situation contains judgmental aspects. Thus our interpretation and judgment (decisions) may be different from yours. Indeed, this is a key concept in investment decision making. Decisions are based on expectations. How to formulate the expectations and "judge" our expectations is the important learning element in any case study.

Elements of an Investment Strategy

Investment analysis involves identifying the factors that influence risk and return of alternative investments. There are several key elements in the development of an investment strategy. These include diversification, legal environment, choices of ownership entity, choices of management strategy, choices of financing options, tax planning, choices of decision criteria, and inflation expectations. Let us discuss each of these elements.

Diversification

To make optimal decisions, resources must be allocated to real estate in consideration with other types of investments, such as stocks and bonds. This area of investment analysis is referred to as *portfolio analysis*. A portfolio is a combination of different types of investments or investments with different characteristics. Through diversification, investors can lower the overall risk to which they are exposed.

Diversification involves investing equity into a number of different investments. An ideal portfolio of investments is one in which the returns for each investment are inversely related to each other.

One method of diversification would be to choose the same type of real estate investment but in a spatially varied fashion. A particular investor, for example, may prefer residential investments. The real estate portfolio could be diversified by spreading investments across different housing markets.

An investor could also diversify equity capital into different types of real estate investments (residential and commercial) *and* different locations for the various investments (that is, different neighborhoods, cities, or even states). In this case, the investor may be able to improve the investment portfolio by carefully analyzing different expectations regarding the type and location of property.

Legal Environment

The development of a real estate investment strategy must include an understanding of the legal environment. The legal environment affects the investment decision in a number of ways. For example, the type of legal estate involved in the transaction can dramatically affect the value of the investment. The value of real property can significantly differ depending on the estate's limitations, duration, and conception. Therefore, the investor must understand the legal implications involving investing and making a real estate investment strategy.

To analyze an investment strategy, the investor has two choices: accept the legal environment as a constraint and work within it to achieve the desired financial outcome or adopt a more active stance regarding the legal environment and use the law to the investor's best interests.

While the first is a more passive approach, it should not be viewed as less aggressive or less ambitious. It seeks to achieve financial results, given a set of expectations and legal outcomes that legal counsel will support.

The second approach views the legal environment as a changing area which can be molded to fit the particular situation and requirements. In this case, the analyst seeks legal counsel as an active participant in the decision-making process.

OWNERSHIP ENTITY

Another important issue is the choice of business entity for ownership. Since this choice can mean the difference between the achievement of financial objectives or bankruptcy, or between fixed (or limited) liability and complete (or unlimited) liability in the event of suit against the owner, the choice of ownership entity is not to be overlooked. Furthermore, the choice of ownership varies according to the rights of control and operation which may lead to problems concerning the ownership of property.

MANAGEMENT STRATEGY

Another important consideration is an analysis of the managerial decisions during the period of ownership. Many things occur during this time that affect the value of the property.

Because many operating decisions are delegated to the property manager when one is employed, the property manager may be one of the most important participants in the real estate investment process. Many of the production, operations, and financial decisions made by this person (or firm) may determine an investment strategy for the owner.

FINANCING OPTIONS

Financing is another major area. The investor must answer some important questions such as, What is the appropriate level of debt? Is there an appropriate time to refinance in the case of a level-payment amortized loan? Should second mortgage sources be sought in order to expand the holdings of real estate investments when an attractive property becomes available? The answers to these and other questions involve dealing with financing policy, and the solutions are not easily derived.

TAX PLANNING

Income taxation has a great impact on real estate investment decisions. The cash flow on which to make investment decisions is the amount after taxes. The amount of taxes depends on the taxable income and the investor's tax rate. A real estate investment strategy for income-producing property must involve considerable tax planning. The tax implications at the time of sale are also important.

In general, since income taxation remains one of the basic ways in which federal and state governments collect money, tax planning is a necessary prerequisite for maximizing the equity investor's wealth. Those who choose to analyze projects on a before-tax basis can select inferior projects over better ones or in many cases overstate values or expected returns.

DECISION CRITERIA

There are various methods of measuring expected returns and investment values. The more traditional criteria are called rules-of-thumb because they are more easily used and require fewer data for analysis. The more sophisticated criteria require more data and more complex estimation procedures, and they employ a stronger conceptual basis. The investor interested in developing a real estate investment strategy must decide on which criterion (or criteria) the decision will be made. For some investors, many measures and criteria will be used to provide as much relevant information as possible. For others, experience may show that only a select few are needed. Finally, a few investors may rely only on one or two approaches to make the investment decision.

Effective real estate investment decision making requires that the investor make the best choice, given the established objectives and a set of alternatives. Implicit in this statement is the presumption that a wrong choice is costly in terms of giving up expected income, cash flow, or wealth.

THE INVESTMENT STRATEGY: A CASE STUDY

To illustrate the development of the real estate investment strategy, we will use a detailed case study of an apartment building investment. While it is impossible to illustrate all the problems faced by an investor, this example is a step-by-step discussion of an investment strategy based on the investment process discussed in the preceding chapters.

The subject property is a 10-year-old apartment building with an asking price of $500,000. There are 16 rentable units with an average of 1,125 square feet per unit. Currently, demand is strong and is expected to continue to grow steadily. The location of the property is excellent relative to shopping and employment centers. The building is in good condition with little deferred maintenance.

STEP 1: IDENTIFYING INVESTOR OBJECTIVES

The initial step is to identify the objectives of the investor. There are several different reasons for investing, such as inflation hedge and cash flow.

John and Judy Smith decide that they want to earn a 12 percent rate of return per year on their equity investment on an after-tax basis over the anticipated holding period of eight years. The Smiths anticipate selling the property at the end of year 8. This desired rate of return is determined after considering the other investment opportunities and the relative risk of the project. The Smiths' major objective is to decide whether the project is expected to generate the required return of 12 percent.

STEP 2: ANALYSIS OF THE INVESTMENT ENVIRONMENT

The second step is to analyze the environment in which the investment decision is made. This consists of three categories: market, legal, and sociopolitical.

❏ **MARKET ANALYSIS.** Two major categories of risk include the possibility that an investment will not generate the expected level of net income (business risk) and the possibility that income increases will not keep pace with inflation (purchasing-power risk). Market analysis is designed to aid the investor in identifying the factors that influence these categories of risk.

The basic components of a market study include

1. Definition and delineation of the market area for an investment.
2. Analysis of the demand factors. Demand for housing is dependent on the number of households, income levels, and other demographic aspects, such as sex, age, and education.
3. Analysis of supply factors. This includes the existing competition in the market area, a survey of projects currently under construction, and an understanding of projects under consideration. It is most difficult to obtain information about this latter category. However, real estate lenders, appraisers, brokers, developers, and other real estate professionals can provide this type of information. Vacancy rates for existing competition should be carefully considered along with rent levels and operating expenses.
4. The physical aspects of any proposed or existing project must be reviewed. Such factors as the compatibility with existing uses, size, shape, topography, zoning regulations, density requirements, and deed restrictions must be analyzed.

The market study must also provide information about such items as anticipated rent levels, vacancy rates, and forecasts of future property values.

To analyze the market for the investment, the Smiths collect data for a sample of comparable properties. Table 14–1 summarizes some of this information. The Smiths have information on the comparable properties in the price range similar to the subject property. Information on the date of sale, sale price, number of apartments, number of vacant apartments, average square footage per apartment, number of rooms, effective gross income, and operating expenses can be found in Table 14–1. Research at the county records office and other inquiries revealed the information (found in Table 14–1) regarding the financing of the 10 comparable properties.

Table 14–2 summarizes various units of comparison for each of the comparable properties. We have calculated the price per apartment, price per room, price per square foot, gross income multiplier, average rent per unit per month, average rent per room per month, average rent per square foot per month, operating expense ratio, overall rate, vacancy rate, loan and equity information, net operating income, and equity dividend rate for each comparable sale. From this information, the Smiths formulate expectations about the marketplace. Note that rent for the comparables ranges from $453 to $578 per month per unit. Note also that the vacancy rate is between zero and 18.18 percent. Table 14–3 summarizes the assumptions based on this comparison.

❑ **LEGAL ANALYSIS.**   A second major category of risk is legislative (legal) risk. This is the possibility that the government will change the laws and introduce restrictions and regulations that cause incomes and/or property values to decline. Examples of this type of change would be increased taxation, change in zoning ordinances, and the exercising of the right of eminent domain.

Legal risk can also arise from the relationships between the other participants in the investment process (see Figure 1–2 in Chapter 1). For example, there may be deed restrictions that limit the use of the property or outstanding mortgage liens against the property that create a "cloud" in the title. The investor must realize that *property rights* are bought and sold in the real estate market.

The investor must be certain that the seller possesses the property rights. The buyer (investor) cannot acquire more rights than the seller has to sell. Table 14–4 illustrates the assumptions from the legal analysis.

❑ **SOCIOPOLITICAL ANALYSIS.**   Another area to be analyzed involves potential social constraints related to an investment. While a project may be legally permissible, it may not be feasible from society's point of view. Social controls in real estate investment analysis have received increased attention in recent years.

A real estate investment creates *external* effects on the neighborhood and society in general. Some of these external effects are *positive* while others are *negative.* Potential external effects and their possible benefits and costs affect the risk and return expected from an investment. Examples of these effects include increased traffic and lowered (or increased) property values.

In this case, the apartment building's value should reflect these external effects. If it were a proposed project, the investor would be more

TABLE 14–1
COMPARABLE APARTMENT SALES

Comparable	Date of Sale (Months Ago)	Sale Price	Number of Apartments	Number of Vacant Apartments	Number of Rooms	Average Square Feet per Apartment	Effective Gross Income	Operating Expenses	Financing
1	2	$300,000	10	1	38	1,000	$54,000	$24,000	75% L/V; FRM; 25 yr.; interest rate 10%; 2 pts.; 3% AC costs.
2	6	330,000	11	2	40	950	62,400	29,900	70% L/V; 9.75% interest only annual pmts.; balloon in 10 years; 3 pts.; 3% AC costs.
3	8	475,000	14	1	60	925	86,900	39,000	80% L/V; FRM, 20 yr.; interest rate 9.5%; 3 pts.; 2% AC costs.
4	1	545,000	17	0	66	1,100	92,400	38,900	Assumption of $425,000 loan; 15 yr. maturity; interest rate 9%; 0 pts.; 2% AC costs.
5	5	525,000	18	2	72	1,050	105,800	52,000	Seller financed; $450,000 at 8%; interest only annual pmts.; balloon in 10 yrs.; 0 pts.; 3% AC costs.
6	6	510,000	15	1	63	1,125	86,400	38,000	75% L/V; FRM; 25 yr.; interest rate 10.25%; 2 pts.; 2% AC costs.
7	3	500,000	16	0	63	1,100	93,600	42,100	Seller financed $400,000 loan at 10% for 25 yrs.; 0 pts.; 2% AC costs.
8	10	410,000	13	2	58	1,000	69,600	29,000	Assumption of $350,000 loan; 10 yr. interest only annual pmts.; 8.75% interest rate; 0 pts.; 2.5% AC costs.
9	5	590,000	22	3	84	1,025	120,500	59,500	70% L/V; 20 yrs.; interest rate 9.75%; 3 pts.; 2% AC costs.
10	1	800,000	24	3	102	1,100	142,000	60,500	50% L/V 1st mort. @ 9.75%, 1 pt., 25 yr.; 30% L/V 2nd mort, interest only, 0 pts., 12% interest rate, 3% AC costs.

Note: Acquisition cost is % of S.P. and points are % of loan.

TABLE 14–2
UNITS OF COMPARISON FOR APARTMENTS*

Comparable	Price per Apartment	Price Per Room	Price per Sq.Foot	Gross Income Multiplier	Average Rent per Unit/ Month	Average Rent per Room/ Month	Average Rent per Sq. Foot/ Month	Operating Expense Ratio	Overall Rate	Vacancy Rate	Equity Div. Rate	Net Oper. Income	Loan Monthly Pmt	Equity Inv.
1	$30,000	$7,895	$30.00	5.56	$500	$131.58	$0.5000	44.44%	10.00%	10.00%	6.18%	$30,000	$2,045	$ 88,500
2	30,000	8,250	31.58	5.29	578	158.89	0.6082	47.92	9.85	18.18	8.61	32,500	1,877	115,830
3	33,929	7,917	36.68	5.47	557	129.98	0.6022	44.88	10.08	7.14	4.65	47,900	3,542	115,900
4	32,059	8,258	29.14	5.90	453	116.69	0.4118	42.10	9.82	0.00	1.35	53,500	4,311	130,900
5	29,167	7,292	27.78	4.96	551	137.76	0.5248	49.15	10.25	11.11	19.61	53,800	3,000	90,750
6	34,000	8,095	30.22	5.90	514	122.45	0.4571	43.98	9.49	6.67	4.04	48,400	3,543	145,350
7	31,250	7,937	28.41	5.34	488	123.94	0.4432	44.98	10.30	0.00	7.17	51,500	3,635	110,000
8	31,538	7,069	31.54	5.89	527	118.12	0.5273	41.67	9.90	15.38	14.20	40,600	2,552	70,250
9	26,818	7,024	26.16	4.90	529	138.55	0.5156	49.38	10.34	13.64	6.95	61,000	3,917	201,190
10	33,333	7,843	30.30	5.63	563	132.47	0.5123	42.61	10.19	12.50	5.28	81,500	5,965	188,000
AVG.	31,156	7,717	30.03	5.46	525	131.03	0.5061	45.19%	10.04%	9.38%	7.80%	50,070	3,439	125,667

*Calculated from Data in Table 14–1.

421

TABLE 14–3
ASSUMPTIONS FROM MARKET ANALYSIS

1. Investment type: Apartments
2. The asking price is $500,000
3. The total number of rentable units is sixteen. The average number of square feet per unit is 1,125. The total number of rooms is 70.
4. The holding period of the investment is 8 years.
5. Rents are expected to range from $540 to $560 per unit per month.
6. Vacancy and bad debt losses are expected to be between 6 and 8 percent per year.
7. Rents are expected to increase at an annual rate between 3 and 7 percent.
8. Demand is expected to be strong. Evidently there is a growing demand.
9. The location is excellent relative to shopping and employment centers.
10. The building is in good condition with little deferred maintenance. This should help keep demand strong.

TABLE 14–4
ASSUMPTIONS FROM LEGAL ANALYSIS

1. The property conforms to current building code and zoning restrictions.
2. There is no threat of rent control in the community.
3. Property rights to be acquired are fee simple, subject to existing easements and government restrictions.
4. Current easements do not appear to have a significant impact on the value.
5. The current liens are property taxes (not in arrears) and an existing mortgage (nonassumable) that will be paid off on sale.

concerned with the sociopolitical constraints. Is there any adverse neighborhood reaction to the investment? Table 14–5 indicates no expected sociopolitical problems with the investment.

STEP 3: FORECAST OF CASH FLOWS

The third step in the development of the investment strategy is to forecast the expected cash flows (both in and out) for the expected holding period (length of ownership). The cash inflows are derived from two sources: the annual cash flows from rental collections and the cash flow from the disposition (typically sale) of the investment. The investor is interested in the expected after-tax cash flow from these two sources. This represents the amount of cash that the investment is expected to generate after all obligations, including income taxes, have been met.

Cash flows are those that the project is *expected* to generate. The investor will not know the *actual* cash flows until the investment has been acquired, operated, and sold. This is what investing is all about—sacrificing

TABLE 14-5
ASSUMPTIONS FROM SOCIOPOLITICAL ANALYSIS

1. There appear to be no sociopolitical problems associated with this investment.
2. The comprehensive zoning ordinance has been in effect and there do not appear to be any major developments in this area.
3. Local citizen groups are supportive of this type of investment.
4. Landlord-tenant law should not impose any problems on this investment.

outflows for expected inflows. There is always the possibility that an investment will not produce the investor's expected level of cash flow. To formulate the expected cash flows, the investor must make decisions and assumptions regarding operations, financing, reversion, and tax planning.

☐ **OPERATING DECISIONS.** To formulate the expected cash inflow, the investor must make assumptions regarding the operation of the investment. This operating plan should include expenses such as maintenance, repairs, utilities, property taxes, insurance, and replacement reserves. Replacement reserves are estimated by allocating $6,000 over an 8-year period for items such as refrigerators and stoves. Table 14–6 shows the projected level of operating expenses in the first year. Total operating expenses are forecasted to be $47,520 in the first year. These expenses are expected to increase at a rate between 3 and 7 percent each year.

In the first year, the expected operating expenses require approximately 49 percent of the effective gross income (EGI). The Smiths must compare this expected level of expenses with that of the competition. After doing so, the Smiths decide that the operating expense ratio (OER) will probably vary between 47 and 50 percent (see Table 14–2).

☐ **FINANCING DECISIONS.** The next area of analysis of formulating the expected cash flows is the financing decisions. Financing involves two

TABLE 14-6
FORECAST FIRST-YEAR OPERATING EXPENSES

Expense Category	Amount	% of Most Likely EGI (Rounded)
Real estate taxes	$10,717	11%
Replacement reserves	750	1
Insurance	2,915	3
Utilities	11,692	12
Administrative (management)	7,806	8
Maintenance and operation	10,725	11
Miscellaneous	2,915	3
Total operating expenses	47,520	49%

TABLE 14-7
FINANCING DECISION ASSUMPTIONS

Debt Financing

1. The investor can borrow $375,000 from a local lender. This results in a loan-to-value ratio of about 75 percent.
2. The mortgage interest rate is 9 percent.
3. The mortgage maturity is 25 years with monthly payments.
4. Financing costs, including points and fees, are 3 percent of the amount borrowed, or $11,250 ($375,000 times .03).
5. Prepayment penalties are 4 percent of the outstanding balance.

Equity Financing

1. The equity investment is $125,000 plus the $11,250 financing costs and $10,000 in acquisition costs. Total equity is thus $146,250.
2. The desired rate of return on the equity position is 12 percent after tax.

sources: debt and equity. Table 14–7 summarizes the financing decision assumptions. Total mortgaged debt is $375,000 and the equity required is $146,250. Note that the equity is the sum of the down payment ($500,000–$375,000) plus the cost of replacing the mortgage ($11,250) and other acquisition costs in the amount of $10,000. The acquisition costs are estimates for legal fees and various transfer taxes.

The required rate of return on the equity is 12 percent. This rate reflects the risks to which the equity position is exposed (business risk, inflation risk, legal risk, and financial risk).

Table 14–8 gives the mortgage amortization schedule. This shows the distribution between interest and principal for each year of the holding period. The debt service is expected to be $37,764 per year.

❏ **REVERSION DECISIONS.** The second category of cash flow is that from the expected sale of the investment. The investor must forecast the expected changes in the property value over the expected holding period. The investment horizon is eight years. Table 14–9 summarizes the reversion decision assumptions.

❏ **TAX-PLANNING DECISIONS.** The last major area of analysis in forecasting the expected cash flows is tax planning. Table 14–10 lists the assumptions for tax planning. The important elements are the tax rate and the depreciation deduction. The amount of the depreciation deduction depends on the depreciable basis, useful life, and depreciation method. Table 14–11 gives the depreciation schedule based on the assumptions in Table 14–10.

TABLE 14-8
MORTGAGE AMORTIZATION SCHEDULE

Asking price: $500,000   Payments: Monthly
Amount borrowed: $375,000   Annual mortgage constant: .100703
Interest rate: 9%   Debt service: $37,764
Maturity term: 25 years

Year	Proportion Outstanding	Amount Outstanding	Debt Service	Principal Payment	Interest Payment
0	1.0	$375,000			
1	0.988843	370,816	$37,764	$4,184	$33,580
2	0.976640	366,240	37,764	4,576	33,188
3	0.963293	361,235	37,764	5,005	32,759
4	0.948693	355,760	37,764	5,475	32,289
5	0.932724	349,772	37,764	5,988	31,775
6	0.915257	343,221	37,764	6,550	31,214
7	0.896151	336,057	37,764	7,165	30,599
8	0.875253	328,220	37,764	7,837	29,927

TABLE 14-9
REVERSION DECISION ASSUMPTIONS

1. Property values are expected to increase between 3 and 4 percent per year.
2. Selling expenses (brokerage fees, legal fees, etc.) are estimated to be 10 percent of the selling price.

TABLE 14-10
TAX-PLANNING ASSUMPTIONS

1. The investor is in a 31 percent marginal tax bracket that is not expected to change over the holding period. Capital gains are taxed at a 28 percent rate.
2. The building has a value of $425,000 (or about 85 percent of the total cost). Acquisition costs are $10,000. The depreciable basis is thus $435,000.
3. The useful life of the building for tax purposes is 27.5 years .
4. The investor will use the straight-line depreciation method.
5. The alternative minimum tax is not applicable.
6. Tax losses can be taken in the year they occur.

Table 14–12 summarizes the assumptions necessary to forecast the expected cash flows. These assumptions are based on the market, financing, operations, reversions, and tax-planning analyses. The Smiths have formulated expectations on three possible "states of the world": most likely, optimistic, and pessimistic. These three possible outcomes provide information regarding the "sensitivity" of the investment decision based on the assumptions. It is obvious that the Smiths will not know the actual

TABLE 14-11
DEPRECIATION SCHEDULE

Asking price: $500,000   Land value: $75,000
Acquisition costs: $10,000   Useful life: 27.5 years
Depreciable amount: $435,000   Depreciation method: Straight-line method

Year	Building	Amount	Cumulative
0	$435,000		
1	419,182	$15,818	$ 15,818
2	403,364	15,818	31,636
3	387,545	15,818	47,455
4	371,727	15,818	63,272
5	355,909	15,818	79,090
6	340,091	15,818	94,908
7	324,273	15,818	110,726
8	308,455	15,818	126,544

state of the world until they buy, operate, and sell the property. The Smiths must, however, make a decision today based on the expectations. The next section develops the expected after-tax cash flows from operations and sale under these three possible outcomes.

❒ THE EXPECTED CASH FLOW FROM OPERATIONS.   Using the assumptions from the preceding analysis, the expected after-tax cash flows from operations, under the most likely, optimistic, and pessimistic outcomes, are given in Tables 14–13 through 14–18.

Tables 14–13 and 14–14 show that for the most likely outcome, the investment generates a positive taxable income each year. Note that using these most likely assumptions, rents are estimated to be approximately $774 per unit per month at the end of eight years, up from the initial $550.

Table 14–15 gives the ATCF for the optimistic assumptions. Under these assumptions, rents after eight years are estimated to be approximately $899 per month per unit. Since rents are rising much faster than operating expenses, NOI, and thus ATCF, more than doubles over the eight-year projected holding period.

Table 14–17 gives the expected ATCF from operations under the pessimistic assumptions. Here, rents are forecast to be approximately $664 per unit per month at the end of the holding period. Also, note that the investment generates a tax shelter for each year of the holding period and that in the last year the BTCF is negative. The investment does have a declining expected ATCF for each year.

TABLE 14–12
SUMMARY OF ASSUMPTIONS FOR INVESTMENT INPUTS

Input		Assumptions
Purchase price		$500,000
Acquisition costs		$10,000
Number of units		16
Rents	Optimistic:	$560 per month expected to increase 7% per year
	Most Likely:	$550 per month expected to increase 5% per year
	Pessimistic:	$540 per month expected to increase 3% per year
Vacancies	Optimistic:	6%
	Most Likely:	8%
	Pessimistic:	10%
Operating expenses	Optimistic:	$47,520 in the first year expected to increase 3% per year
	Most Likely:	Expected to increase 5% per year
	Pessimistic:	Expected to increase 7% per year
Financing		$375,000 mortgage; 9% interest rate; monthly payments for 25 years; prepayment penalties of 4% of outstanding balance; 3% financing costs
Depreciation		Straight-line; useful life of 27.5 years
		Depreciable basis of $435,000
Holding period		8 years
Reversion price	Optimistic:	Selling price is expected to be $685,000
	Most Likely:	Selling price is expected to be $675,000
	Pessimistic:	Selling price is expected to be $665,000
Selling expenses		10% of selling price
Tax rate		31% marginal tax rate; the alternative minimum tax is not applicable. Capital gains tax rate is 28%
Equity		Total equity investment of $146,250; desired after-tax rate of return on equity is 12%

The declining ATCF results from the fact that rents are not rising as fast as operating expenses, which causes NOI to decline. We are assuming the investor can benefit from the tax losses by reducing his ordinary taxable income. Tax laws regarding how much one can use this type of loss to offset ordinary income vary by the employment of the investor. These passive activity losses could also offset passive activity gains.

❏ **THE EXPECTED AFTER-TAX CASH FLOW FROM SALE.** The expected after-tax cash flow from sale (ATER) is given in Tables 14–19, 14–21, and 14–23 for the most likely, optimistic, and pessimistic assumptions regarding fu-

TABLE 14–13
EXPECTED CASH FLOW FROM OPERATIONS: MOST LIKELY ASSUMPTIONS

		1	2	3	4	5	6	7	8
						Year			
	Potential gross income (PGI)	$105,600	$110,880	$116,424	$122,245	$128,357	$134,775	$141,514	$148,590
minus	Vacancy and bad debt allowance (VBD)	8,448	8,870	9,314	9,780	10,269	10,782	11,321	11,887
plus	Miscellaneous income (MI)	0	0	0	0	0	0	0	0
equals	Effective gross income (EGI)	97,152	102,010	107,110	112,466	118,089	123,993	130,193	136,703
minus	Operating expenses (OE)	47,520	49,896	52,391	55,010	57,761	60,649	63,681	66,865
equals	Net operating income (NOI)	49,632	52,114	54,719	57,455	60,328	63,344	66,512	69,837
minus	Debt Service (DS)	37,764	37,764	37,764	37,764	37,764	37,764	37,764	50,893†
equals	Before-tax cash flow (BTCF)	11,868	14,350	16,955	19,691	22,564	25,581	28,748	18,945
minus	Taxes (savings) from operation (TO)*	165	1,056	1,997	2,991	4,041	5,150	6,322	1,120
equals	After-tax cash flow (ATCF)	$ 11,703	$ 13,293	$ 14,958	$ 16,700	$ 18,523	$ 20,431	$ 22,426	$ 17,824

*See Table 14-14 for tax computations.
†This includes a prepayment of $13,129 on the mortgage.

TABLE 14-14
TAXES FROM OPERATIONS: MOST LIKELY ASSUMPTIONS

		Year							
		1	2	3	4	5	6	7	8
	Effective gross income (EGI)	$97,152	$102,010	$107,110	$112,466	$118,089	$123,993	$130,193	$136,703
minus	Operating expenses (OE)	47,520	49,896	52,391	55,010	57,761	60,649	63,681	66,865
equals	Net operating income (NOI)	49,632	52,114	54,719	57,455	60,328	63,344	66,512	69,837
minus	Interest on debt (I)	33,580	33,188	32,759	32,289	31,775	31,214	30,599	43,056*
minus	Depreciation deduction (D)	15,818	15,818	15,818	15,818	15,818	15,818	15,818	15,818
minus	Amortized financing costs (AFC)	450	450	450	450	450	450	450	8,100
plus	Replacement reserves (RR)	750	750	750	750	750	750	750	750
equals	Ordinary taxable income (OTI)	534	3,408	6,443	9,648	13,034	16,613	20,394	3,613
times	Investor's marginal tax rate (τ)	0.31	0.31	0.31	0.31	0.31	0.31	0.31	0.31
equals	Taxes (savings) from operations (TO)	$ 165	$ 1,056	$ 1,997	$ 2,991	$ 4,041	$ 5,150	$ 6,322	$ 1,120

*This includes a prepayment penalty of $13,129.

429

TABLE 14–15
EXPECTED CASH FLOW FROM OPERATIONS: OPTIMISTIC ASSUMPTIONS

		Year							
		1	2	3	4	5	6	7	8
	Potential gross income (PGI)	$107,520	$115,046	$123,100	$131,717	$140,937	$150,802	$161,359	$172,654
minus	Vacancy and bad debt allowance (VBD)	6,451	6,903	7,386	7,903	8,456	9,048	9,682	10,359
plus	Miscellaneous income (MI)	0	0	0	0	0	0	0	0
equals	Effective gross income (EGI)	101,069	108,144	115,714	123,814	132,481	141,754	151,677	162,294
minus	Operating expenses (OE)	47,520	48,946	50,414	51,926	53,484	55,089	56,741	58,444
equals	Net operating income (NOI)	53,549	59,198	65,300	71,887	78,996	86,666	94,936	103,851
minus	Debt service (DS)	37,764	37,764	37,764	37,764	37,764	37,764	37,764	50,893†
equals	Before-tax cash flow (BTCF)	15,785	21,434	27,536	34,123	41,233	48,902	57,172	52,958
minus	Taxes (savings) from operations (TO)*	1,380	3,253	5,277	7,465	9,828	12,379	15,134	11,664
equals	After-tax cash flow (ATCF)	$ 14,405	$ 18,182	$ 22,259	$ 26,659	$ 31,405	$ 36,522	$ 42,038	$ 41,294

*See Table 14–16 for tax computations.
† This includes a prepayment of $13,129 on the mortgage.

430

TABLE 14–16
TAXES FROM OPERATIONS: OPTIMISTIC ASSUMPTIONS

				Year				
	1	2	3	4	5	6	7	8
Effective gross income (EGI)	$101,069	$108,144	$115,714	$123,814	$132,481	$141,754	$151,677	$162,294
minus Operating expenses	47,520	48,946	50,414	51,926	53,484	55,089	56,741	58,444
equals Net operating income (NOI)	53,549	59,198	65,300	71,887	78,996	86,666	94,936	103,851
minus Interest on debt (I)	33,580	33,188	32,759	32,289	31,775	31,214	30,599	43,056*
minus Depreciation deduction (D)	15,818	15,818	15,818	15,818	15,818	15,818	15,818	15,818
minus Amortized financing costs (AFC)	450	450	450	450	450	450	450	8,100
plus Replacement reserves (RR)	750	750	750	750	750	750	750	750
equals Ordinary taxable income (OTI)	4,450	10,492	17,023	24,080	31,703	39,934	48,818	37,627
times Investor's marginal tax rate (τ)	0.31	0.31	0.31	0.31	0.31	0.31	0.31	0.31
equals Taxes (savings) from operations (TO)	$ 1,380	$ 3,253	$ 5,277	$ 7,465	$ 9,828	$ 12,379	$ 15,134	$ 11,664

*This includes a prepayment penalty of $13,129.

431

TABLE 14–17
EXPECTED CASH FLOW FROM OPERATIONS: PESSIMISTIC ASSUMPTIONS

		Year							
		1	2	3	4	5	6	7	8
	Potential gross income (PGI)	$103,680	$106,790	$109,994	$113,294	$116,693	$120,194	$123,799	$127,513
minus	Vacancy and bad debt allowance (VBD)	10,368	10,679	10,999	11,329	11,669	12,019	12,380	12,751
plus	Miscellaneous income (MI)	0	0	0	0	0	0	0	0
equals	Effective gross income (EGI)	93,312	96,111	98,995	101,965	105,023	108,174	111,419	114,762
minus	Operating expenses (OE)	47,520	50,846	54,406	58,214	62,289	66,649	71,315	76,307
equals	Net operating income (NOI)	45,792	45,265	44,589	43,750	42,734	41,525	40,105	38,455
minus	Debt service (DS)	37,764	37,764	37,764	37,764	37,764	37,764	37,764	50,893†
equals	Before-tax cash flow (BTCF)	8,028	7,501	6,825	5,987	4,971	3,761	2,341	(12,437)
minus	Taxes (savings) from operations (TO)*	(1,025)	(1,067)	(1,143)	(1,258)	(1,413)	(1,614)	(1,864)	(8,608)
equals	After-tax cash flow (ATCF)	$ 9,053	$ 8,568	$ 7,968	$ 7,244	$ 6,384	$ 5,375	$ 4,205	$ (3,829)

*See Table 14–18 for tax computations.
†This includes a prepayment of $13,129 on the mortgage.

432

TABLE 14-18
TAXES FROM OPERATIONS: PESSIMISTIC ASSUMPTIONS

				Year				
	1	2	3	4	5	6	7	8
Effective gross income (EGI)	$93,312	$96,111	$98,995	$101,965	$105,023	$108,174	$111,419	$114,762
minus Operating expenses	47,520	50,846	54,406	58,214	62,289	66,649	71,315	76,307
equals Net operating income (NOI)	45,792	45,265	44,589	43,750	42,734	41,525	40,105	38,455
minus Interest on debt (I)	33,580	33,188	32,759	32,289	31,775	31,214	30,599	43,056*
minus Depreciation deduction (D)	15,818	15,818	15,818	15,818	15,818	15,818	15,818	15,818
minus Amortized financing costs (AFC)	450	450	450	450	450	450	450	8,100
plus Replacement reserves (RR)	750	750	750	750	750	750	750	750
equals Ordinary taxable income (OTI)	(3,300)	(3,441)	(3,688)	(4,057)	(4,559)	(5,207)	(6,013)	(27,269)
times Investor's marginal tax rate (τ)	0.31	0.31	0.31	0.31	0.31	0.31	0.31	0.31
equals Taxes (savings) from operations (TO)	$(1,025)	$(1,067)	$(1,143)	$(1,258)	$(1,413)	$(1,614)	$(1,864)	$(8,608)

*This includes a prepayment penalty of $13,129.

433

TABLE 14–19
EXPECTED CASH FLOW FROM SALE IN YEAR 8:
MOST LIKELY ASSUMPTIONS

	Expected selling price (SP)	$675,000
minus	Selling expenses (SE)	67,500
equals	Net sales proceeds (NSP)	607,500
minus	Unpaid mortgage balance (UM)	328,220
equals	Before-tax equity reversion (BTER)	$279,280
minus	Taxes due on sale (TDS)*	62,733
equals	After-tax equity reversion (ATER)	$216,547

*See Table 14–20 for calculation of taxes due on sale.

TABLE 14–20
TAXES DUE ON SALE IN YEAR 8: MOST LIKELY ASSUMPTIONS

	Expected selling price (SP)	$675,000
minus	Selling expenses (SE)	67,500
equals	Amount realized (AR)	607,500
minus	Adjusted basis (AB)	383,455
	Total gain on sale	224,045
minus	Investor's marginal tax rate (τ)	0.28
equals	Taxes due on sale (TDS)	$ 62,733

TABLE 14–21
EXPECTED CASH FLOW FROM SALE IN YEAR 8:
OPTIMISTIC ASSUMPTIONS

	Expected selling price (SP)	$685,000
minus	Selling expenses (SE)	68,500
equals	Net sales proceeds (NSP)	616,500
minus	Unpaid mortgage balance (UM)	328,220
equals	Before-tax equity reversion (BTER)	$288,280
minus	Taxes due on sale (TDS)*	65,253
equals	After-tax equity reversion (ATER)	$223,027

*See Table 14–22 for calculation of taxes due on sale.

ture values of the property. Tables 14–20, 14–22, and 14–24 give the taxable income and the taxes due on sale for these three possible outcomes.

STEP 4: APPLYING THE DECISION-MAKING CRITERIA

The preceding section developed the expected cash flow from operations and sale. We now turn to the decision-making criteria: rules-of-thumb, appraisal methods, and discounted cash flow models.

TABLE 14–22
TAXES DUE ON SALE IN YEAR 8: OPTIMISTIC ASSUMPTIONS

	Expected selling price (SP)	$685,000
minus	Selling expenses (SE)	68,500
equals	Amount realized (AR)	616,500
minus	Adjusted basis (AB)	383,455
	Total gain on sale	233,045
minus	Investor's marginal tax rate (τ)	0.28
equals	Taxes due on sale (TDS)	$65,253

TABLE 14–23
EXPECTED CASH FLOW FROM SALE IN YEAR 8:
PESSIMISTIC ASSUMPTIONS

	Expected selling price (SP)	$665,000
minus	Selling expenses (SE)	66,500
equals	Net sales proceeds (NSP)	598,500
minus	Unpaid mortgage balance (UM)	328,220
equals	Before-tax equity reversion (BTER)	270,280
minus	Taxes due on sale (TDS)*	60,213
equals	After-tax equity reversion (ATER)	$210,067

*See Table 14–24 for calculation of taxes due on sale.

TABLE 14–24
TAXES DUE ON SALE IN YEAR 8: PESSIMISTIC ASSUMPTIONS

	Expected selling price (SP)	$665,000
minus	Selling expenses (SE)	66,500
equals	Amount realized (AR)	598,500
minus	Adjusted basis (AB)	383,455
	Total gain on sale	215,045
minus	Investor's marginal tax rate (τ)	0.28
equals	Taxes due on sale (TDS)	$ 60,213

❐ **RULES-OF-THUMB.** Some alternative rules-of-thumb are shown in Table 14–25. These include the gross income multiplier (GIM), overall rate (R), equity dividend rate (EDR), after-tax rate (ATR), debt-coverage ratio (DCR), and operating-expense ratio (OER). Each is calculated using the most likely, optimistic, and pessimistic assumptions.

How does the investor decide whether or not to invest, using these rules-of-thumb? Obviously, the investor needs a standard of comparison.

To illustrate, the GIM for each of the comparable properties is shown in Table 14–26. These can be used as the standard by which to make the decision. By comparing the gross income multiplier of the subject property

TABLE 14-25
RULES OF THUMB USING FIRST-YEAR CASH FLOW FROM OPERATIONS*

| | | State of the World | |
Rule-of-Thumb	Most Likely	Optimistic	Pessimistic
1. Gross income multiplier (GIM)	5.15	4.95	5.36
2. Overall rate (R)	9.93 %	10.71 %	9.16 %
3. Equity dividend rate (EDR)	9.5 %	12.6 %	6.4 %
4. After-tax rate (ATR)	9.36 %	11.52 %	7.24 %
5. Debt-coverage ratio (DCR)	1.314	1.418	1.213
6. Operating expense ratio (OER)	48.91 %	47.02 %	50.93 %

*Calculated using cash flows in Tables 14–13, 14–15 and 14–17.

TABLE 14-26
RULES-OF-THUMB FOR COMPARABLE SALES*

Comparable	Gross Income Multiplier	Overall Rate	Equity Dividend Rate	Debt-Coverage Ratio	Operating Expense Ratio
1	5.56	10.00%	6.18%	1.22	44.44%
2	5.29	9.85	8.61	1.44	47.92
3	5.47	10.08	4.65	1.13	44.88
4	5.90	9.82	1.35	1.03	42.10
5	4.96	10.25	19.61	1.49	49.15
6	5.90	9.49	4.04	1.14	43.98
7	5.34	10.30	7.17	1.18	44.98
8	5.89	9.90	14.20	1.33	41.67
9	4.90	10.33	6.95	1.30	49.38
10	5.63	10.19	5.28	1.14	42.61

*Calculated using data in Table 14–2.

(5.15) with those of the comparables, we see that the subject property appears to be in the lower end of the range. This indicates that the property may be somewhat underpriced relative to the market. The market GIM appears to be around 5.5. Using this and the subject property most likely EGI of $97,152, we get a value estimate of

$$\text{Value} = 5.5 (\$97,152) = \$534,336$$

The debt-coverage ratio (DCR) is widely used by mortgage lenders. It is the ratio of the NOI to the debt service. In this case, the DCR in the first year is 1.314 in the most likely outcome. This would probably fall in the acceptable range for most mortgage lenders. The various other rules-of-thumb shown in the table are used in the same manner as the GIM or the DCR. The investor compares these with a standard and accepts or rejects the investment. Note that the rules-of-thumb do not always lead to the same accept/reject decision. An investment that may be acceptable using the GIM may be unacceptable using the EDR method. The investor should compute all the various rules of thumb and arrive at the investment decision after analyzing each one.

❒ **APPRAISAL METHODS.** A second set of decision-making criteria consists of the traditional appraisal methods discussed in Chapter 11. These methods of valuation are the direct sales comparison approach, the cost approach, and the income approach. Each of these methods provides the investor with an estimate of value for the subject property. These estimates can be used in making the investment decision.

Table 14–27 gives the estimated value of the property using the *cost approach.* The Smiths estimate the land market value at $75,000. The apartment buildings have a reproduction cost (new) of $33 per square foot for a total of $594,000. However, given the physical condition, the depreciated value is estimated at $431,950. The total indicated value of the property using the cost approach is $507,000.

Under the *direct sales comparison approach,* the value of the property is estimated using the comparable sales obtained in the market. As we noted in Chapter 11, there are various units of comparison. Table 14–28 gives the unadjusted prices per room, unit, and square foot for each comparable and

TABLE 14–27
COST APPROACH SUMMARY: 16-UNIT APARTMENT

Property Component	Reproduction Cost	% Depreciation	Depreciation	Market Value
		Land		
3 acres @ $25,000 per acre, or 16 apartment units @ $4,688 per unit				$ 75,000
		Building components		
Foundation/Frame	$119,000	15%	$ 17,850	
Floor	77,000	40	30,800	
Walls/Partitions	137,000	20	27,400	
Roof structure	71,000	35	24,850	
Plumbing/Electrical wiring	107,000	30	32,100	
Heating/Air conditioning	83,000	35	29,050	
Total	$594,000		$162,050	$431,950
Indicated value from cost approach			(rounded)	$507,000

TABLE 14-28
UNADJUSTED MARKET COMPARISON APPROACH ESTIMATES

Comparable	Unadjusted Price per Room*	Indicated Value— Subject Property	Unadjusted Price per Unit*	Indicated Value— Subject Property	Unadjusted Price per Square Foot*	Indicated Value— Subject Property
1	$7,895	$552,632	$30,000	$480,000	$30.00	$540,000
2	8,250	577,500	30,000	480,000	31.58	568,421
3	7,917	554,167	33,929	542,857	36.68	660,232
4	8,258	578,030	32,059	512,941	29.14	524,599
5	7,292	510,417	29,167	466,667	27.78	500,000
6	8,095	566,667	34,000	544,000	30.22	544,000
7	7,937	555,556	31,250	500,000	28.41	511,364
8	7,069	494,828	31,538	504,615	31.54	567,692
9	7,024	491,667	26,818	429,091	26.16	470,953
10	7,843	549,020	33,333	533,333	30.30	545,455

*Calculated from sales data.

the unadjusted indication of the value for the subject property. These unadjusted estimates provide a fairly wide range in the value of the subject property.

Table 14–29 gives the adjustment grid for selected comparable sales. Given the data in Table 14–1, the Smiths decide that comparable numbers 2, 3, 6, and 9 were the most similar to the subject property. In addition, analysis of the various units of comparison (price per unit, price per room, price per square foot) indicates that price per unit is probably the best unit of comparison.

The adjustment grid (Table 14–29) indicates an adjusted price per unit of $31,783. This results in an estimated value of about $508,528 ($31,783 times 16 units). Note that the comparables have been adjusted for time, location, and building condition. Using the direct sales comparison approach, it appears that the property's market value is within the $494,000 to $515,000 range.

The third appraisal method is the *income approach*. Under this approach, the value is estimated by capitalizing the property's income stream. As we noted in Chapter 11, there are three major income methods: direct capitalization of NOI using a market-extracted overall rate, direct capitalization using a weighted-average capitalization rate, and the mortgage-equity method. Table 14–30 gives the *market-extracted overall rate* for each comparable and the indicated value for the subject property. The overall rate was calculated for each comparable by dividing the NOI by the

TABLE 14–29
ADJUSTMENT GRID FOR COMPARABLE SALES

	Comparable Sale			
Factor	2	3	6	9
Sales price	$330,000	$475,000	$510,000	$590,000
Number of units	11	14	15	22
Price per unit	30,000	33,929	34,000	26,818
Time adjustment	+4%	+5%	+4%	+3%
	1,200	1,696	1,360	805
Condition of building	0	−15%	−10%	+5%
		(5,089)	(3,400)	1,341
Location	+3%	+5%	0	+7%
	900	1,696	0	1,877
Net adjustment	2,100	(1,696)	(2,040)	4,023
Value per unit	32,100	32,232	31,960	30,841
Indicated value of subject property (16 units)	$513,600	$515,714	$511,360	$493,455

*See Table 14–1.

TABLE 14–30
VALUE USING MARKET-EXTRACTED OVERALL RATE

Comparable*	Overall Rate†	Indicated Value—Subject Property‡
1	10.00%	$496,320
2	9.85	503,956
3	10.08	492,175
4	9.82	505,597
5	10.25	484,327
6	9.49	522,982
7	10.30	481,864
8	9.90	501,210
9	10.33	480,047
10	10.19	487,185

*See Table 14–1.
†This is the NOI of each comparable divided by its sale price, as reported in Table 14–2.
‡This is the subject property's estimated NOI ($49,632) divided by the rate from each comparable.

sale price. For example, comparable number 1 had an NOI of $30,000 and a sale price of $300,000.

This results in an overall rate of 10 percent ($30,000/$300,000). Using this rate and the subject property's estimated NOI of $49,632 in year 1, the indicated value is $496,320. This process was repeated for each comparable. Using this approach, it appears that a value estimate of $480,000 to $520,000 would be reasonable. Since the subject is most similar to 2,3,6, and 9, we can estimate an overall rate from these comparables of 10 percent. This indicates a value of $496,320 as a direct capitalization.

Another income approach method is to capitalize the NOI using a *weighted-average overall rate (R)*, defined as

$$R = L/V \, (MC) + E/V \, (EDR) \qquad (14\text{–}1)$$

where:

R = overall rate

L/V = loan-to-value ratio

MC = annual mortgage constant

E/V = equity-to-value ratio

EDR = equity dividend rate

Using the loan-to-value ratio of 75 percent, an interest rate of 9 percent with a maturity of 25 years (monthly), and an equity dividend rate of 9.5 percent (see Table 14–26):

$$R = .75(.100703) + .25(0.095)$$

$$R = .0755 + .0238$$

$$R = .0993$$

The indicated value would be:

$$V = \$49,632/.0993$$

$$V = \$499,819$$

Thus the asking price of $500,000 appears to be reasonable using these appraisal methods.

Recall from our discussion of the appraisal model in Chapter 11 that the total value of an investment can be defined as the value of the mortgage plus the present value of the cash flows to the equity. This is called the *mortgage-equity method*. In equation form:

$$V = V_M + V_E \qquad (14\text{--}2)$$

where:

V = total value

V_M = value of the mortgage

V_E = value of the equity

Using the before-tax cash flows, the value of the equity position (V_E) can be written as

$$V_E = \sum_{t=1}^{n} \frac{\text{BTCF}_t}{(1 + y)^t} + \frac{\text{BTER}_n}{(1 + y)^n} \qquad (14\text{--}3)$$

where:

BTCF_t = expected before-tax cash flows in year t

BTER_n = expected before-tax equity reversion in the year of sale

y = required rate of return on equity (before tax)

Returning to our example, suppose the Smiths required (before-tax) return is 20 percent. Using the "most likely" forecasts of the BTCF and BTER shown in Table 14–31, the present value of these cash flows is approximately $134,180. Since the mortgage value (amount) is $375,000, the total value of the investment would be

$$V = \$375{,}000 + \$134{,}180$$

$$V = \$509{,}180$$

This means that the Smiths could pay up to $509,180 for the investment and earn an expected yield of 20 percent. A price more than this would mean that the expected yield would be less than 20 percent, and vice versa. Using this mortgage-equity valuation approach, the investment seems to be acceptable to the investor. Note that if the investor-required before-tax yield on equity was increased (decreased), the value of the investment would decrease (increase).

❏ DISCOUNTED CASH FLOW MODELS.   The third major set of investment criteria consists of the discounted cash flow (DCF) models. As the name implies, the DCF models take the forecast cash flows and discount them back to the present. Thus the investor has the present worth of the expected cash flows.

The best DCF model is called the *net present value* (NPV) technique, in which the investor calculates the total present value of the cash flows and compares this with the cost of investing. Under the NPV criterion, the investor invests if the NPV is positive. The investor does not invest if the NPV is negative. These decision rules make sense intuitively. They say: Compute the present worth of the expected cash flows at the desired rate of return; compare this present worth with how much it costs to invest; if

TABLE 14–31
PRESENT VALUE OF EQUITY USING BEFORE-TAX CASH FLOWS

Year	BTCF	BTER	Present-Value Factor at 20%	Present Value
1	$11,868		.83333	$ 9,890
2	14,350		.69444	9,965
3	16,955		.57874	9,813
4	19,691		.48225	9,496
5	22,564		.40188	9,068
6	25,581		.33490	8,567
7	28,748		.27908	8,023
8	18,945	$279,280	.23257	69,358
			Total equity value =	$134,180

the costs exceed the present worth of the cash flow, do not invest; if the present worth of the cash flows exceeds the costs, do invest.

Tables 14–32, 14–33, and 14–34 give the net present value of the ATCF from operation and the ATER from the sale at the end of eight years. Recall that the equity investment was $146,250. These present values were calculated using a 12 percent rate of return. These cash flows are taken from the most likely, optimistic, and pessimistic outcomes. The after-tax cash flows represent the amount going to the equity position after all expenses, debt service, and taxes have been paid.

Column 5 of Tables 14–32, 14–33, and 14–34 contains the present-value factor at the desired 12 percent rate of return on equity. Recall that the Smith's objective is to decide whether or not the investment would yield a 12 percent rate of return on the equity investment of $146,250. The present-value factors were taken from the present-value tables in Appendix A. These factors, when multiplied by the expected cash flows in the respective years, give the present value of these cash flows, as shown in column 6.

To interpret the present value numbers in column 6, look at Table 14–32. This table gives the ATCF for the most likely assumptions. In year 5, the investment is expected to generate $18,525 in ATCF. However, the present value of this $18,525 is $10,511.64. This means that at the desired rate of return of 12 percent, the Smiths are willing to pay $10,511.64 for the right to receive $18,525 five years later.

The net present value of the cash flow is found by adding the numbers in column 6. Note that the net present value for the most likely as-

TABLE 14–32
PRESENT VALUE OF AFTER-TAX FLOWS AT 12% RATE: MOST LIKELY ASSUMPTIONS

Year	Equity*	ATCF†	ATER‡	Present-Value Factor at 12%	Present Value
0	$(146,250)			1.0	$(146,250)
1		$11,703		.89286	10,449
2		13,293		.79719	10,597
3		14,958		.71178	10,647
4		16,700		.63552	10,613
5		18,525		.56743	10,511
6		20,431		.50663	10,351
7		22,426		.45235	10,145
8		17,824	$216,547	.40388	94,658
				Net present value =	$21,721

*This is the asking price ($500,000) minus the mortgage ($375,000) plus the financing costs ($11,250) plus acquisition costs of $10,000.
†See Table 14–13.
‡See Table 14–19.

TABLE 14–33
PRESENT VALUE OF AFTER-TAX FLOWS AT 12% RATE: OPTIMISTIC ASSUMPTIONS

Year	Equity	ATCF*	ATER†	Present-Value Factor at 12%	Present Value
0	$(146,250)			1.0	$(146,250)
1		$14,405		.89286	12,862
2		18,182		.79719	14,495
3		22,259		.71178	15,844
4		26,659		.63552	16,942
5		31,405		.56743	17,820
6		36,522		.50663	18,503
7		42,038		.45235	19,016
8		41,294	$223,027	.40388	106,754
				Net Present Value = $	75,986

*See Table 14–15.
†See Table 14–21.

TABLE 14–34
PRESENT VALUE OF AFTER-TAX FLOWS AT 12% RATE: PESSIMISTIC ASSUMPTIONS

Year	Equity	ATCF*	ATER†	Present-Value Factor at 12%	Present Value
0	$(146,250)			1.0	$(146,250)
1		$9,053		.89286	8,083
2		8,568		.79719	6,830
3		7,968		.71178	5,671
4		7,244		.63552	4,604
5		6,384		.56743	3,622
6		5,375		.50663	2,723
7		4,205		.45235	1,902
8		(3,829)	$210,067	.40388	83,295
				Net Present Value =	$(29,520)

*See Table 14–17.
†See Table 14–23.

sumptions is $21,721. The net present value of the cash flows under the optimistic assumptions is $75,986. Likewise, the net present value is − $29,520 for the pessimistic assumptions. Under the most likely assumptions, the investment is acceptable, since the NPV is positive. This means that the present value of the cash inflows at a rate of 12 percent is greater than the equity outflow. Thus the investment is "worth" $21,721 more than it "costs."

A second discounted cash flow method is the internal rate of return (IRR). Recall from Chapter 12 that the IRR is the rate that will make the present value of the cash inflows equal to the present value of the cash outflows. Using the most likely estimates of the cash flows (see Table 14–32), the IRR is 14.54 percent. Under the optimistic forecasts, the IRR is 20.31 percent. With the pessimistic forecasts, the IRR falls to 8.3 percent.

To make the investment decision using the IRR method, compare the calculated IRR using the expected cash flows with the required rate. If the expected rate of return exceeds the required rate, then the investment is acceptable. In the case for the most likely forecasts, the calculated (expected) IRR is 14.54 percent. The required rate is 12 percent. Thus the project appears acceptable.

☐ **SENSITIVITY ANALYSIS.** The assumptions made should reflect expectations about the future based on the best available information. Suppose the investor believes rents may drop due to a declining economy or that operating expenses may be much more than expected. What was once a potentially profitable investment may not be beneficial anymore. Table 14–35 illustrates the sensitivity of the IRR and NPV results, given different assumptions. This analysis was performed by using the most likely assumptions as a base. The inputs are changed one at a time and changed back when proceeding to the next variable.

Table 14–35 indicates that rents, operating expenses, vacancy, and interest rate are particularly sensitive, while the tax rate and reversion price don't seem to have much of an affect on the NPV and IRR. For example, if operating expenses increase from $47,520 to $55,000, the NPV drops from $21,721 to a negative $8,013. The NPV increases 50 percent when the interest rate drops 1 percent from 9 percent to 8 percent.

STEP 5: THE INVESTMENT DECISION

Now that the Smiths have established the objective and the investment environment, forecasted the cash flows, and applied the investment criteria, should they pay $500,000 for the investment?

Table 14–36 summarizes the results of the various investment criteria. Note that some of these indicate an accept decision, whereas others indicate a reject decision. The rules-of-thumb recommend acceptance. The appraisal methods result in both acceptance and rejection, but the rejection outcomes are quite close to being acceptable. Generally, the direct sales comparison approach is the most widely advocated. The more sophisticated discounted cash flow models, using the most likely forecasts of cash flow, recommend acceptance.

For the most likely outcome, the NPV of the investment is $21,721. Using the NPV decision rules, the Smiths should make the investment.

TABLE 14-35
SENSITIVITY ANALYSIS

Rents	NPV	IRR	Operating Expenses	NPV	IRR	Vacancy	NPV	IRR
$525	$ 4,167	12.49%	$ 40,000	$51,615	18.03%	15%	$ (7,663)	11.10%
540	14,700	13.72	45,000	31,739	15.71	10%	13,326	13.56
560	28,743	15.36	50,000	11,863	13.39	6%	30,117	15.52
575	39,276	16.59	55,000	(8,013)	11.06	2%	46,908	17.48

Tax Rate	NPV	IRR	Reversion Price	NPV	IRR	Interest Rate	NPV	IRR
25%	$24,146	14.81%	$650,000	$15,178	13.82%	8%	$33,454	15.88%
28	22,934	14.68	665,000	19,104	14.26	8.5%	27,616	15.22
35	20,105	14.35	685,000	24,338	14.82	10%	9,774	13.15
38	18,893	14.21	700,000	28,264	15.22	11%	(2,357)	11.72

TABLE 14-36
SUMMARY OF INVESTMENT CRITERIA

Criterion	Proposed Investment	Market Rate	Acceptable
Rule-of-Thumb			
GIM	5.15*	5.5	Yes
DCR	1.31*	1.15	Yes
EDR	9.5%*	5%	Yes
Appraisal methods			
Cost approach	$500,000	$507,000	Yes
Direct sales comparison	500,000	508,528	Yes
Income approach			
Direct capitalization	500,000	496,320	No
Weighted-average capitalization	500,000	499,819	No
Mortgage equity method	500,000	509,180	Yes
Discounted cash flow models			
Net present value	$ 21,721*	$ 0	Yes
IRR	14.54%*	12%	Yes

*Using the most likely estimates of the expected cash flows.

    The investment would be made under the optimistic outcome. The investment should not be undertaken under the pessimistic assumption.

    Suppose the Smiths assigned the probabilities in Table 14–37 to the three possible "states of the world." They believe that there is an 80 percent chance of the most likely assumption occurring. There is a 10 percent probability of the optimistic or pessimistic outcomes. Multiply these prob-

TABLE 14-37
EXPECTED NET PRESENT VALUE

State of the World	Probability	NPV	NPV
Optimistic outcome	.10	$75,986	$ 7,599
Most likely outcome	.80	21,721	17,377
Pessimistic outcome	.10	(29,520)	(2,952)
			Expected NPV = $22,024

abilities times the net present value of each state in order to find the expected net present value. Thus it would appear that the project is one worth considering as an investment. The Smiths could obviously reassess the likelihood of the various states of the world and recalculate the expected NPV.

What should the Smiths do? Obviously, many assumptions have been made. This, however, is what investing is all about. Investment is giving up cash today (equity) in return for expected, but risky, cash inflow in the future. The investor must formulate the expectations explicitly. While no investor knows the actual outcome, this does not mean that expectations cannot be formed about the future. The critical question is, How certain is the investor that the expectations are correct? Obviously, under some possible outcomes the investor should invest, whereas under others the investor should not. The important lesson for the investor is to examine each assumption and expectation carefully, thus reducing the risk as much as possible. The investment decision is only as good as the expectations on which it is based.

THE OFFER

Using the analysis, the Smiths decide to make an offer on the property of $475,000. Other factors in the offer are as follows:

1. The offer is contingent on the investor being able to obtain a $375,000 mortgage at an 9 percent rate with monthly payments over 25 years.
2. Property taxes, of $4,900 for the current year, are to be prorated between the seller and the buyer at closing.
3. The seller is to provide the buyer with a termite inspection at a cost of $250.
4. The buyer is to obtain a title insurance policy at a cost of $1,000 (to be paid by the buyer).
5. Transfer tax, estimated at $6,000, is to be split 50/50 between the seller and the buyer.

6. Hazard insurance policy at a cost of $2,000, paid in advance for the current year, is to be prorated at closing.

7. Loan origination fees of $11,250 are to be paid by the buyer.

8. The seller has 72 hours to accept the offer.

9. Closing is set for January 1,19XX.

10. The seller is to deliver a general warranty deed.

11. The seller is to provide evidence of marketable title.

12. The buyer is to make an earnest money deposit of $5,000. This will become part of the buyer's equity if the offer is accepted.

13. Other costs of the transaction will be as follows:

Buyer:

Document preparation	$ 500
Appraisal fees	1,000
Survey	500
Recording fees	100
Legal fees	2,000

Seller:

Legal fees	$750
Broker's commission	25,000
Termite inspection	250
Mortgage balance	275,500

THE COUNTEROFFER AND ACCEPTANCE

The seller reviews the offer and decides to accept all items except the price. The seller counteroffers at a price of $490,000.

This appears acceptable to the buyer, who accepts the counteroffer. Now the buyer and the seller have a binding sales contract.

CLOSING THE TRANSACTION

Table 14–38 contains the closing statement for this transaction. Note that the purchase price is $490,000. The buyer has deposited $5,000 and will borrow $375,000 on the first mortgage. The real property taxes have been paid by the seller, but since the closing is taking place at the beginning of the year, the buyer essentially reimburses the seller. The buyer is incurring a total cost of the transaction of $136,250. Basically the buyer is putting down $115,000 ($490,000 − 375,000) and incurring acquisition costs of about $10,000 and financing costs (see item 9) of $11,250. This represents about 4.3 percent ($21,250/ $490,000) of the purchase price. The buyer needs about $136,250 to close the transaction. The resulting equity investment is $10,000 less than expected because the purchase price decreased by $10,000.

TABLE 14-38
THE CLOSING STATEMENT

Seller Sam and Mary Jones   Buyer John and Judy Smith
Address 3928 Gourrier   Address 405 Ave. F
         Somewhere, USA   Anywhere, USA
                                                             Ph (523) 555-2345
Phone (251) 555-8575   Mortgagee American Bank   Lender Union Federal   Ph (523) 555-2798
Attorney Walt Smith   Phone (251) 555-6442   Attorney Neal Vincent Ph (523) 555-9417

| | Buyer | | Seller | |
Item	Debit	Credit	Debit	Credit
1. Consideration	$490,000			$490,000
2. Earnest money deposit		$ 5,000		
3. Real property taxes	4,900			4,900
4. Buyer's mortgage		375,000		
5. Preparation of loan documents	500			
6. Loan fees	11,250			
7. Real estate transfer tax	3,000		3,000	
8. Appraisal fee	1,000			
9. Termite certificate			250	
10. Agent's commission			25,000	
11. Survey	500			
12. Fire insurance	2,000			2,000
13. Legal fees	2,000		750	
14. Title insurance	1,000			
15. Recording	100			
16. Seller's mortgage			275,500	
Debit/credit totals	516,250	380,000	304,500	496,900
Balance needed to close		136,250		
Balance to seller			192,400	
Totals	516,250	516,250	496,900	496,900

A more likely outcome would be that the buyer could only borrow 75 percent of the purchase price. The criteria analyzed in the previous section would then not be precise. However, viewing the previous analyses, we know that the investment would still be attractive.

SUMMARY

In this chapter we presented a detailed case study of how to apply the real estate investment process. We analyzed each of the various components involved in making the investment decision. Applying the process requires analysis of various options and assumptions available to the investor. To understand the complexity of decision making, it is necessary to work all the numerical calculations. We encourage you to try your skill by working the problems at the end of this chapter.

QUESTIONS

14–1. What are the elements of developing an investment strategy?

14–2. In the case study, the first item the investor does is specify an investment objective. Why is this important?

14–3. In the case study, the analysis of the market environment is given careful consideration. In the real world, this is frequently overlooked. What are the dangers of neglecting this aspect of real estate investing?

14–4. In the case study, what other issues might be raised under the sociopolitical analysis?

14–5. In the case study, results are presented from the income and expense analysis, the financing choices, and the tax-planning decisions. Do you think the options chosen are reasonable? Why or why not?

14–6. In the case study, three scenarios are shown: most likely, optimistic, and pessimistic forecasts. What is the purpose of this presentation? How can the results help to make better investment decisions?

14–7. In the case study, the results of the rules-of-thumb calculations and appraisal methods are presented. What can you conclude from these calculations?

14–8. In the case study, the discounted cash flow models are analyzed. What do the results indicate for the investment under consideration?

14–9. Should the project be accepted as analyzed in this chapter? Why or why not?

14–10. What changes in assumptions and inputs might be interesting to improve the attractiveness of the investment?

PROBLEMS

14–1. Using Table 14–2, explain how the following were calculated:
a. Price per apartment
b. Price per room
c. Price per square foot
d. Operating expense ratio
e. Vacancy rate.
What, in your opinion, is the best unit of comparison for this example?

14–2. What would happen to the expected equity rate of return if the investor decided to use 100 percent equity in the most likely case?

14–3. Suppose the investor could split the financing assumed in the chapter in the most likely case into the following scenario:

	First Mortgage	Second Mortgage (Interest Only)
Mortgage amount	$200,000	$175,000
Interest rate	9%	9%
Maturity	25 yrs./ monthly payments	25 yrs./ monthly payments
Financing costs	3%	3%
Prepayment penalty	None	None

Which capital structure would the investor prefer? Why? How do NPV and IRR change?

14–4. Suppose the investor had the choice of debt financing assumed in the chapter on the following:

Mortgage amount	$375,000
Interest rate	12.5%
Maturity	25 years/ monthly payments
Financing costs	2%
Prepayment penalty	None

Which is the optimal choice?

14–5. Suppose the investor's marginal tax rate is not expected to be constant over the holding period. How would this be taken into account in the example?

SELECTED REFERENCES

Institute of Real Estate Management, *Income/ Expense Analysis: Conventional Apartments,* (Chicago: Institute of Real Estate Management, 1993.)

Sirmans, G. Stacy, and John D. Benjamin, "Determinants of Market Rent," *Journal of Real Estate Research,* 6 (Fall 1991), 357–380.

CHAPTER 15

ADDITIONAL
CASE APPLICATIONS
OF THE INVESTMENT PROCESS

PRINCIPLES

1. It is also possible to apply the investment framework to other real estate decisions.
2. This chapter illustrates some alternative decisions which investors are often asked to make.
3. By applying the principles and methods, investors should be able to evaluate other situations as well.

In the previous chapters of this text, we learned how to apply various financial tools to solve decision making problems. The purpose of this chapter is to provide four case studies that illustrate these tools.

The first case involves analysis of a small office building that has four tenants. The investor must determine whether the purchase of the property is justified, given the required rate of return on equity. The second case entails an investor who owns an existing apartment building; he must decide whether to sell the property today, operate it "as is" with no renovations, or operate it after renovating it. The third problem offers a discounted cash flow analysis of whether a firm should lease or purchase additional industrial warehouse space. Finally, the fourth case involves a tax-deferred exchange; the investor must decide whether to exchange a property with another investor or sell the property and use the sales proceeds to acquire the other investor's property.

CASE I: ACQUISITION OF AN OFFICE BUILDING

Businesses need office space. While some small companies are operated out of the owners' houses, the vast majority must lease or purchase commercial space. Tenants provide cash inflows to investors who acquire commercial real estate for investment purposes. In turn, investors are able to operate and maintain the property, service debt, pay property and income taxes, and hopefully provide themselves with a positive return on their equity investment.

The primary risk to investors is that the investment, ex post, may be a negative net present value project. In the following case study, an investor must decide whether to invest in a commercial property. Provided the NPV, based on his projection and required rate of return, is greater than or equal to zero dollars, he should purchase the office building.

AN OFFICE BUILDING EXAMPLE

An investor has just inherited $605,000. A local commercial real estate broker has presented her with the following opportunity to purchase a small office building for $1,500,000.

There are four existing leases. A bank rents the 9,500 square feet on the first floor for $10,500 per month with level payments for three more years. Thereafter, the bank is expected to renew for 10 years at $12,000 per month. An insurance company rents 6,200 square feet on the second floor for $12.85 per square foot per year. The lease will expire at the end of two years. She expects to rent this space for the market rental at that time. Current market rent is $14.00 per square foot of rentable space per year. Market rents are expected to increase at 4 percent per year for the next five years and then zero percent per year for the following seven years. A lawyer leases the 2,500 remaining square feet on the second floor at $2,750 per month for the next 10 years with annual increases based on 50 percent of the increases in market rents. An accounting firm rents 9,950 square feet on the third floor at $.94 per square foot per month. These payments will increase 1 percent for year two, followed by a 2 percent per year increase for years three and four, and then 3 percent per year increases for the remaining six years on the lease.

Office buildings in the area typically have 5 percent vacancy. The building is currently 100 percent leased but there is still the possibility of a tenant leaving before the lease expires. Thus, she projects a vacancy and credits an allowance of 3 percent in the first two years and 5 percent in the years thereafter.

Projections for operating expenses include management fees based on 7 percent of effective gross income. Property taxes are $20,000 for the first two years with a 15 percent increase in the third year with no further increases thereafter. Utility expenses are based on $1.50 per square foot of gross building area increasing at 5.5 percent per year. Insurance is based on $.18 per square foot of net rentable area increasing at 4 percent per year. Janitorial expenses are projected at $.75 per square foot of gross area increasing by 6 percent per year. Maintenance allowances of $.25 per square foot of gross area is projected with a 4 percent annual increase. Other expenses total $39,000 per year and are expected to increase at 3 percent per year for three years, 2.5 percent for the following year, and 2 percent thereafter.

The parking lot likely will need repaving on a rotating basis every 12 years at a cost of $12,000. Therefore, a yearly reserve replacement account of $1,000 per year should be established.

Other information important to the analysis is presented in Table 15–1.

THE SOLUTION

Discounted cash flow analysis requires calculating after-tax cash flows from operation for each year, after-tax equity reversion in the year of sale, and discounting these inflows to the present at the investor's required rate of return on equity. Should the present value of these inflows exceed outflows when the property is purchased, the investor can earn a positive return on his equity investment.

Table 15–2 reports the expected cash flow from operations for each year. The first calculation is potential gross income (PGI), which equals the gross rent to be received from all tenants, assuming no vacancies. Because there are four tenants, the expected rent on each lease must be determined separately. Then they can be summed for each year's PGI *for the entire office building*. Table 15–3 shows the lease-by-lease PGI calculation for the bank, insurance company, lawyer, and accountant. For example, first year rent for the bank is simply $10,500 per month for 12 months, or $126,000. Likewise, the insurance company's rent is 6,200 square feet multiplied by $12.85 per foot, or $79,670. This amount then increases in year three to $93,883, or 6,200 square feet multiplied by $14.00 per foot multiplied by the growth rate of 4 percent per year for two years.

Vacancy is projected to average 3 percent of PGI, or $10,527 in year one. This is expected to grow to 5 percent after year 2. Miscellaneous income is $56,400 in the first year. This is 30 parking spaces rented at $150 per month plus $200 per month in vending income. This income is projected not to change over the 10-year holding period. Effective gross income (EGI) is calculated as PGI less vacancy plus miscellaneous income.

Management fees are estimated to be 7 percent of EGI, or $27,775 in year 1. Operating expenses are reported separately in Table 15–4, consisting of property taxes, utilities, insurance, janitorial, maintenance, and other expenses. For example, year-1 maintenance expenses are $0.25 per square foot of gross area of 31,150, or $7,788. This grows at a 4 percent annual rate,

TABLE 15-1
ADDITIONAL INFORMATION FOR OFFICE BUILDING ANALYSIS

Building gross area (square feet)	31,150
Non-financing acquisition costs	$135,000
Other income	
Paid parking spaces	30
Monthly rent per space	$150
Monthly vending income	$200
Growth rate for other income	0%
Financing information	
First mortgage (fixed rate with monthly payments)	
Loan-to-value ratio	50%
Interest rate	9.50%
Term (years)	20
Financing costs	2%
Prepayment penalty (% of O. Bal.)	3%
Second mortgage (Interest-only with monthly payments)	
Loan-to-value ratio	20%
Interest rate	8%
Term (years)	10
Financing costs	1%
Prepayment penalty (% of O. Bal.)	0%
Depreciation information	
Land-to-value ratio	15%
Depreciable life	39 years
Tax rate information	
Ordinary income marginal tax rate	31%
Capital gains tax rate	28%
Future selling information	
Expected yearly appreciation	2%
Selling expenses	9%
Expected holding period (years)	10
Required rate of return on equity (after tax)	15%

so year 2 is $7,788 multiplied by 1.04, or $8,099. Summing the six operating expenses obtains total annual expenses. Subtracting management fees and operating expenses from EGI gives net operating income (NOI).

To find before-tax cash flows (BTCF), annual debt service on both mortgages must be subtracted from NOI. The first mortgage has a debt service of $83,892 and the second mortgage payment is $24,000. Notice in the year of reversion that the first mortgage has a 3 percent prepayment penalty of $16,208. This is 3 percent of the outstanding balance ($540,272) at the end of year 10. The second mortgage is an interest-only loan, so no principal is repaid until the year of reversion; debt service is equal to interest paid each year. There is no prepayment penalty on this junior mortgage. Summing the annual debt service of each mortgage results in the

TABLE 15–2
EXPECTED CASH FLOW FROM OPERATIONS FOR EACH YEAR: OFFICE BUILDING EXAMPLE

		Years									
		1	2	3	4	5	6	7	8	9	10
	Potential gross income (PGI)*	$350,906	$352,688	$369,842	$394,596	$402,740	$406,384	$410,138	$414,004	$417,986	$422,088
minus	Vacancy and bad debt allowance (VBD)	10,527	10,581	18,492	19,730	20,137	20,319	20,507	20,700	20,899	21,104
plus	Miscellaneous income (MI)	56,400	56,400	56,400	56,400	56,400	56,400	56,400	56,400	56,400	56,400
equals	Effective gross income (EGI)	396,779	398,508	407,750	431,266	439,003	442,465	446,031	449,704	453,487	457,384
minus	Management fees	27,775	27,896	28,542	30,189	30,730	30,973	31,222	31,479	31,744	32,017
minus	Other operating expenses (OE)†	141,942	147,598	156,535	162,767	169,098	175,527	182,278	189,370	196,819	204,647
equals	Net operating income (NOI)	227,062	223,014	222,672	238,310	239,175	235,966	232,531	228,855	224,924	220,720
minus	Debt service (DS)	107,892	107,892	107,892	107,892	107,892	107,892	107,892	107,892	107,892	124,100
equals	Before-tax cash flow (BTCF)	119,170	115,123	114,781	130,418	131,283	128,074	124,639	120,963	117,032	96,620
minus	Taxes (savings) from operations (TO)**	29,814	28,965	29,306	34,645	35,452	35,051	34,638	34,216	33,785	25,999
equals	After-tax cash flow (ATCF)	$ 89,357	$ 86,157	$ 85,475	$ 95,774	$ 95,830	$ 93,023	$ 90,001	$ 86,748	$ 83,247	$ 70,621

*See Table 15–3.
†See Table 15–4.
**See Table 15–5.

TABLE 15–3
LEASE BY LEASE RENTAL INFORMATION: OFFICE BUILDING EXAMPLE

					Years					
	1	2	3	4	5	6	7	8	9	10
Lease #1-Bank	$126,000	$126,000	$126,000	$144,000	$144,000	$144,000	$144,000	$144,000	$144,000	$144,000
Lease #2-Insurance Company	79,670	79,670	93,883	97,638	101,544	101,544	101,544	101,544	101,544	101,544
Lease #3-Lawyer	33,000	33,660	34,333	35,020	35,720	35,720	35,720	35,720	35,720	35,720
Lease #4-Accountant	112,236	113,358	115,626	117,938	121,476	125,120	128,874	132,740	136,723	140,824
Potential gross income	$350,906	$352,688	$369,842	$394,596	$402,740	$406,384	$410,138	$414,004	$417,986	$422,088

457

TABLE 15–4
OPERATING EXPENSES: OFFICE BUILDING EXAMPLE

					Years					
	1	*2*	*3*	*4*	*5*	*6*	*7*	*8*	*9*	*10*
Property taxes	$ 20,000	$ 20,000	$ 23,000	$ 23,000	$ 23,000	$ 23,000	$ 23,000	$ 23,000	$ 23,000	$ 23,000
Utility	46,725	49,295	52,006	54,866	57,884	61,068	64,426	67,970	71,708	75,652
Insurance	5,067	5,270	5,480	5,700	5,928	6,165	6,411	6,668	6,935	7,212
Janitorial	23,363	24,764	26,250	27,825	29,495	31,264	33,140	35,129	37,236	39,470
Maintenance	7,788	8,099	8,423	8,760	9,110	9,475	9,854	10,248	10,658	11,084
Other expenses	39,000	40,170	41,375	42,616	43,682	44,555	45,447	46,355	47,283	48,228
Total expenses	$141,943	$147,598	$156,534	$162,767	$169,099	$175,527	$182,278	$189,370	$196,820	$204,646

gross debt service. For example, debt service for each year except year 10 is $107,892, or $83,892 plus $24,000. Year 10 is greater because the prepayment penalty of $16,208 is added to the $107,892 to obtain $124,100.

After-tax cash flow calculations require forecasting taxes from operations; these are reported in Table 15–5. The interest on debt is calculated for each year. Depreciation of $36,154 is the sum of acquisition costs of $135,000 and the building-to-value ratio of 85 percent multiplied by the purchase price of $1,500,000, all divided by the useful life of 39 years $\{[135,000 + (1,500,000 \times .85)]/39\}$.

Although there are financing costs paid at the beginning of the first year, tax rules require that they be amortized over the life of the loan(s). Because the 10-year holding period is less than the 20-year amortization of the first mortgage, the unamortized portion of the loan is accelerated in the year of reversion, as reported in Table 15–6; however, the second mortgage term equals the holding period, so there is no acceleration. Finally, replacement reserves are estimated to be $1,000 per year. With all of these calculations, ordinary taxable income is derived. This is multiplied by the investor's marginal tax rate of 31 percent to obtain taxes from operations, which is the final entry in Table 15–2 to determine after-tax cash flow for each year.

After-tax equity reversion equals the expected selling price at the end of year 10, less selling expenses, less the unpaid mortgage balance, less taxes due on sale. In essence, the investor must satisfy the real estate brokers, the mortgage lenders, and the government *before* she receives any proceeds at the time of sale. Recall the investor is the residual claimant.

Table 15–7 reports taxes due on sale. The expected selling price equals the purchase price multiplied by a 2 percent compounded growth rate, or $1,828,492 [1,500,000 $\times$ (1.02)^{10}]. Selling expenses are 9 percent of the expected selling price, or $164,564. This difference results in the amount realized of $1,663,927. The investor's adjusted basis of $1,273,462 equals the purchase price of $1,500,000 plus acquisition costs of $135,000, less accumulated depreciation over the 10 years of $361,538. Subtracting the adjusted basis from the amount realized yields the capital gain on sale of $390,466. At a 28 percent capital gain tax rate, the investor's taxes due on sale equal $109,330.

Table 15–8 reports expected cash flow from the sale of the office building. Net sales proceeds equal the amount realized of $1,663,927. From this is subtracted the unpaid mortgage balances on the first and second mortgages ($540,272 and $300,000) to obtain before-tax equity reversion. Subtracting taxes due on sale of $109,330 results in after-tax equity reversion of $714,325.

Now that the expected after-tax cash flows from operation and after-tax equity reversion from sale have been calculated, the investor is able to determine whether this is a positive net present value (NPV) project. Note that the equity investment of $603,000 is the sum of the downpayment

TABLE 15–5
TAXABLE INCOME AND TAXES FROM OPERATIONS FOR EACH YEAR: OFFICE BUILDING EXAMPLE

		Years									
		1	2	3	4	5	6	7	8	9	10
	Effective gross income (EGI)	$396,779	$398,508	$407,750	$431,266	$439,003	$442,465	$446,031	$449,704	$453,487	$457,384
minus	Total operating expenses (OE)	169,717	175,493	185,077	192,956	199,829	206,499	213,500	220,849	228,563	236,664
	Net operating income (NOI)	227,062	223,014	222,672	238,310	239,175	235,966	232,531	228,855	224,924	220,720
minus	Interest on debt (I)	94,685	93,374	91,933	90,349	88,608	86,694	84,591	82,278	79,736	93,150
minus	Depreciation deduction (D)	36,154	36,154	36,154	36,154	36,154	36,154	36,154	36,154	36,154	36,154
minus	Amortized financing costs (AFC)	1,050	1,050	1,050	1,050	1,050	1,050	1,050	1,050	1,050	8,550
plus	Replacement reserves (RR)	1,000	1,000	1,000	1,000	1,000	1,000	1,000	1,000	1,000	1,000
	Ordinary taxable income (OTI)	96,174	93,437	94,535	111,757	114,362	113,068	111,736	110,373	108,984	83,867
times	Investor's marginal tax rate (τ)	.31	.31	.31	.31	.31	.31	.31	.31	.31	.31
equals	Taxes (savings) from operations	$29,814	$28,965	$29,306	$34,645	$35,452	$35,051	$34,638	$34,216	$33,785	$25,999

TABLE 15-6
SCHEDULE OF AMORTIZED FINANCING COSTS: OFFICE BUILDING EXAMPLE

Year	1st Mortgage	2nd Mortgage	Total
1	$ 750	$ 300	$ 1,050
2	750	300	1,050
3	750	300	1,050
4	750	300	1,050
5	750	300	1,050
6	750	300	1,050
7	750	300	1,050
8	750	300	1,050
9	750	300	1,050
10	8,250	300	8,550
Total	$15,000	$3,000	$18,000

TABLE 15-7
TAXES DUE ON SALE: OFFICE BUILDING EXAMPLE

	Taxable Income	
	Expected selling price (SP)	$1,828,492
minus	Selling expenses (SE)	164,564
equals	Amount realized (AR)	1,663,927
minus	Adjusted basis (AB)	1,273,462
equals	Capital gain on sale (CG)	390,466
	Taxes Due on Sale	
	Capital gain on sale (CG)	$390,466
times	Investor's marginal tax rate (τ)	0.28
equals	Taxes due on sale (TDS)	$109,330

TABLE 15-8
EXPECTED CASH FLOW FROM THE SALE: OFFICE BUILDING EXAMPLE

	Expected selling price (SP)	$1,828,492
minus	Selling expenses (SE)	164,564
equals	Net sales proceeds (NSP)	1,663,927
minus	Unpaid mortgage balance (UM)	840,272
equals	Before-tax equity reversion (BTER)	823,656
minus	Taxes due on sale (TDS)	109,330
	After-tax equity reversion (ATER)	$714,325

TABLE 15–9
NET PRESENT VALUE OF EQUITY:
OFFICE BUILDING EXAMPLE

Year	ATCFs	Present Value at 15%
0	$(603,000)	$(603,000)
1	89,357	77,702
2	86,157	65,147
3	85,475	56,202
4	95,774	54,759
5	95,830	47,645
6	93,023	40,217
7	90,001	33,835
8	86,748	28,358
9	83,247	23,664
10	784,947	194,023
	IRR = 15.59%	NPV = $18,552

($450,000), the financing costs ($18,000), and the acquisition costs ($135,000). Discounting at an after-tax required rate of return on equity of 15 percent, Table 15–9 reports an NPV of $18,552, so this is a viable project. The internal rate of return on the investment is 15.59 percent; thus any investor with an after-tax required rate of return on equity of less than 15.6 percent would invest, *given the assumptions*.

SUMMARY AND CONCLUSIONS

This case study illustrates how discounted cash flow analysis can be used by investors to determine whether to invest in a project, given a set of assumptions and the investor's required rate of return on equity. Regardless of how complicated the leases may be, the equity valuation model is still the appropriate technique to use.

In the next case, we investigate whether an apartment owner should renovate a property.

CASE II: RENOVATION OF AN APARTMENT

Apartment complexes wear out just as any other capital asset; consequently, the investor is faced eventually with the choice of whether to operate and/or sell the property with or without renovations. Should he choose to renovate, the outflows to "update" the property must not exceed the present value of expected increased inflows.

An Apartment Renovation Example

A real estate investor (in a 31 percent ordinary income tax bracket and 28 percent capital gains bracket) owns an apartment investment that was purchased five years ago for $1,500,000. The depreciable basis was $1,200,000. The investor has been using the straight-line depreciation method with a 27.5 year life. The investment was financed with a $1,125,000 fixed-rate mortgage at an interest rate of 9 percent with monthly payments for 20 years. The investor estimates that the current selling price is $1,875,000, and selling expenses would be 8 percent of the selling price.

The investor is trying to decide whether to sell the investment now, continue to operate for five more years "as is" and then sell, or continue to operate for five more years with renovations and then sell, if his required after-tax rate of return on equity is 15 percent.

The net operating income (NOI) next year is expected to be $206,250 and is expected to increase 3 percent per year if operated "as is." The value of the investment is expected to be $2,025,000 at the end of this additional five years with selling expenses of 8 percent.

The investor could invest equity to renovate the project for a cost of $150,000. These costs would be depreciated over 27.5 years using the straight-line method. If the investor does so, the NOI next year would be $225,000 and would increase 3 percent per year. The value of the investment at the end of the additional five years would be $2,250,000 with selling expenses of 8 percent.

A summary to the analysis is presented in Table 15–10.

The Solution

□ **Option 1: Sell Today "As Is."**   The investor's first choice is simply to sell the apartment today without any renovations. If this is the option exercised, then the after-tax equity reversion must be calculated; the steps are reported in Tables 15–11 and Table 15–12.

Table 15–10 reports the current selling price to be $1,875,000, with 8 percent selling expenses; therefore, net sales proceeds are $1,725,000 [$1,875,000 × (1 − 0.08)]. To calculate the unpaid mortgage balance at the end of five years (which is today), recall the investor borrowed $1,125,000 at 9 percent compounded monthly for 20 years. This yields a monthly debt service of $10,122, or $121,463 annually. The proportion outstanding currently equals 88.70705 percent of the original loan amount, or $997,954. (See Appendix A, Table 3). Subtracting the unpaid mortgage balance from the net sales proceeds results in before-tax equity reversion of $727,046 ($1,725,000 − 997,954).

To find ATER, however, taxes due on sale must be determined. Table 15–12 reports this calculation. To find the capital gain to be taxed at the 28 percent rate, the investor's adjusted basis needs to be computed. The ad-

TABLE 15–10
SUMMARY OF THE "AS IS" VS. RENOVATE ANALYSIS

Capital gains tax rate	28.00%
Tax bracket	31.00%
Purchase price	$1,500,000
Depreciable basis	$1,200,000
Depreciation time	27.5 years straight-line
Loan amount	$1,125,000
Loan interest rate	9.00%
Loan term	20 years paid monthly

Sell Today

Current selling price	$1,875,000
Selling expenses	8.00%

Hold 5 Yrs. "As Is" & Sell

Selling price in 5 years	$2,025,000
NOI	$ 206,250
NOI increase	3.00%

Renovate, Hold 5 Yrs., & Sell

Additional equity investment	$ 150,000
Depreciation time	27.5 years straight-line
Selling price in 5 Years	$2,250,000
NOI	$ 225,000
NOI Increase	3.00%

TABLE 15–11
AFTER TAX CASH FLOW IF SELL TODAY: APARTMENT EXAMPLE

	Current selling price (SP)	$1,875,000
minus	Selling expenses (SE)	150,000
equals	Net sales price (NSP)	1,725,000
minus	Unpaid mortgage balance (UM)	997,954
equals	Before-tax equity reversion (BTER)	727,046
minus	Taxes due on sale (TDS)	124,091
equals	After-tax equity reversion (ATER)	$ 602,955

justed basis equals the purchase price five years ago, less accumulated depreciation. The depreciable basis is given as $1,200,000 to be depreciated over a 27.5 year useful life, or $43,636 per year. Because five years have passed, the accumulated depreciation is $218,182; hence, the investor's adjusted basis today is $1,281,818 ($1,500,000 − 218,182). Therefore, the capi-

TABLE 15-12
TAXES DUE ON SALE TODAY: APARTMENT EXAMPLE

	Net sales price (NSP)	$1,725,000
minus	Adjusted basis (AB)	1,281,818
equals	Capital gain on sale (CG)	443,182
times	Investor's marginal tax rate (τ)	.28
equals	Taxes due on sale (TDS)	$ 124,091

tal gain is $443,182 ($1,725,000 − 1,281,818) and the taxes due on sale are $124,091 ($443,182 × 0.28). Substituting this into Table 15–11 yields ATER of $602,955 ($727,046 − 124,091).

☐ **OPTION 2: CONTINUE TO OPERATE "AS IS" FOR FIVE YEARS AND THEN SELL.** Rather than sell the apartment today, the investor could choose to operate the property "as is" for an additional five years and then sell it. To evaluate this alternative, the after-tax cash flows and equity reversion must be calculated, given today's information.

Table 15–10 reports that under this alternative, the future selling price at the end of year 5 (10 years from the original purchase) is expected to be $2,025,000, selling expenses are projected to be 8 percent of the selling price, and NOI is expected to be $206,250 in year 1 (next year) and grow at a compounded rate of 3 percent.

Table 15–13 shows the after-tax cash flow under this option. Recall annual debt service is $121,463, so BTCF equals $84,787 (NOI of $206,250 less debt service of $121,463) in year 1. With NOI increasing 3 percent each year, but debt service not changing, BTCFs are increasing, also.

To calculate ATCF for each year, taxes from operations must be determined. Table 15–14 reports the taxes for each year. The interest on debt is calculated for each year. Notice depreciation of $43,636 does not differ from the first option. So, taxable income equals $74,137 (NOI of $206,250 less interest of $88,477 less depreciation of $43,636) in year 1. Therefore, taxes from operations are $22,982 ($74,137 times 0.31) in year 1. Notice the

TABLE 15-13
AFTER TAX CASH FLOW IF CONTINUE TO OPERATE "AS IS": APARTMENT EXAMPLE

		1	2	3	4	5
	NOI	$206,250	212,438	218,811	225,375	232,136
minus	Debt Service (DS)	121,463	121,463	121,463	121,463	121,463
equals	Before-tax cash flow (BTCF)	84,787	90,975	97,348	103,912	110,673
minus	Taxes (Savings) from operations (TO)	22,982	25,860	28,885	32,067	35,418
equals	After-tax cash flow (ATCF)	$ 61,805	65,115	68,463	71,845	75,255

TABLE 15–14
TAXES FROM CONTINUING TO OPERATE "AS IS": APARTMENT EXAMPLE

		1	2	3	4	5
	NOI	$206,250	212,438	218,811	225,375	232,136
minus	Interest (I)	88,477	85,383	81,998	78,296	74,247
minus	Depreciation (D)	43,636	43,636	43,636	43,636	43,636
equals	Taxable income	$ 74,137	83,419	93,177	103,443	114,253
times	Investor's marginal tax rate (τ)	.31	.31	.31	.31	.31
equals	Taxes from operations (TO)	$ 22,982	25,860	28,885	32,067	35,418

marginal tax rate of 31 percent is greater than the capital gains rate of 28 percent. Substituting taxes from operations into Table 15–13 yields ATCF for years 1–5.

The expected selling price of $2,025,000, minus 8 percent selling expenses, yields net sales proceeds of $1,863,000 [$2,025,000 × (1 − 0.08)], as shown in Table 15–15. To calculate the unpaid mortgage balance at the end of year 5 (which is 10 years from the original purchase), recall the debt service is $121,463 annually. The proportion outstanding at the end of year 10 equals 71.02589 percent of the original loan amount, or $799,042. (See Appendix A, Table 3). Subtracting the unpaid mortgage balance from the net sales proceeds results in before-tax equity reversion of $1,063,959 ($1,863,000 − 799,041).

To find ATER, however, taxes due on sale must be determined. Table 15–16 reports this calculation. To find the capital gain to be taxed at the 28 percent rate, the investor's adjusted basis needs to be computed. Recall that depreciation is $43,636 per year. Because 10 years have passed, the accumulated depreciation is $436,364; hence, the investor's adjusted basis today is $1,063,636 ($1,500,000 − 436,364). Therefore, the capital gain is $799,364 ($1,863,000 − 1,063,636) and the taxes due on sale are $223,822 ($799,364 times 0.28). Substituting this into Table 15–15 yields ATER of $840,136 ($1,063,958 − 223,822).

TABLE 15–15
ATCF FROM SALE IN 5 YEARS "AS IS": APARTMENT EXAMPLE

	Selling price (SP)	$2,025,000
minus	Selling expenses (SE)	162,000
equals	Net sales price (NSP)	1,863,000
minus	Unpaid mortgage balance (UM)	799,042
equals	Before-tax equity reversion (BTER)	$1,063,958
minus	Taxes due on sale (TDS)	223,822
equals	After-tax equity reversion (ATER)	$ 840,136

TABLE 15-16
TAXES DUE ON SALE IN 5 YEARS: APARTMENT EXAMPLE

	Net sales price (NSP)	$1,863,000
minus	Adjusted base (AB)	1,063,636
equals	Capital gain on sale (CG)	799,364
times	Investor's marginal tax rate (τ)	.28
equals	Taxes due on sale (TDS)	$ 223,822

❑ **OPTION 3: CONTINUE TO OPERATE FOR FIVE YEARS AFTER RENOVATIONS AND THEN SELL.** Another alternative for the investor is to renovate the apartment, hold it for five more years, and sell it. After-tax cash flows and equity reversion will differ under this option because such items as the depreciable and adjusted bases will change.

Table 15–10 reports that under this alternative, the future selling price at the end of year 10 (five years from today) is expected to be $2,250,000, selling expenses are projected to be 8 percent of the selling price, and NOI is expected to be $225,000 in year 1 (next year) and grow at a compounded rate of 3 percent.

Table 15–17 shows the after-tax cash flow under this option. Recall debt service is $121,463, so BTCF equals $103,537 (NOI of $225,000 less debt service of $121,463) in year 1. With NOI increasing 3 percent each year, but debt service not changing, BTCFs are increasing, also.

To calculate ATCF for each year, taxes from operations must be determined. Table 15–18 reports the taxes for each year. The interest on debt is calculated for each year. Notice depreciation differs from the first two options because the improvements must be depreciated, also. The renovation cost of $150,000 divided by a 27.5-year useful life equals an annual depreciation deduction on the improvement of $5,455; this, added to the depreciation on the original improvements of $43,636, equals $49,091. So, taxable income equals $87,432 (NOI of $225,000 less interest of $88,477, less depreciation of $49,091) in year 1. Therefore, taxes from operations are $27,104 ($87,432 × .31) in year 1.

TABLE 15-17
AFTER-TAX CASH FLOW FROM OPERATIONS WITH RENOVATIONS: APARTMENT EXAMPLE

		1	2	3	4	5
	NOI	$225,000	231,750	238,703	245,864	253,239
minus	Debt service (DS)	121,463	121,463	121,463	121,463	121,463
equals	Before-tax cash flow (BTCF)	103,537	110,287	117,240	124,401	131,776
minus	Taxes from operations (TO)	27,104	30,156	33,360	36,728	40,269
equals	After-tax cash flow (ATCF)	76,433	80,131	83,880	87,673	91,507

TABLE 15–18

TAXES FROM OPERATIONS WITH RENOVATIONS: APARTMENT EXAMPLE

		1	2	3	4	5
	NOI	$225,000	231,750	238,702	245,864	253,239
minus	Interest (I)	88,477	85,383	81,998	78,296	74,247
minus	Depreciation (D)	49,091	49,091	49,091	49,091	49,091
equals	Taxable Income (TI)	$ 87,432	97,276	107,613	118,476	129,902
times	Investor's marginal tax rate (τ)	.31	.31	.31	.31	.31
equals	Taxes from operations (TO)	$ 27,104	30,156	33,360	36,728	40,269

Table 15–10 reports the selling price to be $2,250,000, with 8 percent selling expenses; therefore, net sales proceeds are $2,070,000 [$2,250,000 × (1 − 0.08)], as shown in Table 15–19. The unpaid mortgage balance at the end of year 10 (which is five years from today) is still $799,042, so subtracting the unpaid mortgage balance from the net sales proceeds results in before-tax equity reversion of $1,270,958 ($2,070,000 − 799,042).

To find ATER, however, taxes due on sale must be determined. Table 15–20 reports this calculation. To find the capital gain to be taxed at the 28 percent rate, the investor's adjusted basis needs to be computed. Recall from Option 2 that the accumulated depreciation is $436,364; however, the accumulated depreciation on the improvement at the end of year 5 must be added, also, or $27,272 ($5,455 × 5 years) to obtain aggregate depreciation of $463,636 ($436,364 + 27,272). Hence, the investor's adjusted basis is $1,186,364 ($1,500,000 + 150,000 − 463,636). Therefore, the capital gain is $883,636 ($2,070,000 − 1,186,364), and the taxes due on sale are $247,418 ($883,636 × .28). Substituting this into Table 15–19 yields ATER of $1,023,541 ($1,270,959 − 247,418).

☐ **PRESENT VALUE OF THE THREE OPTIONS.** Now that the ATCFs and ATERs have been calculated for the three options available to the investor, a capital budgeting statement can be derived. Table 15–21 reports the cash

TABLE 15–19
AFTER-TAX CASH FLOW FROM SALE IN 5 YEARS WITH
RENOVATIONS: APARTMENT EXAMPLE

	Selling price (SP)	$2,250,000
minus	Selling expenses (SE)	180,000
equals	Net sales price (NSP)	2,070,000
minus	Unpaid mortgage balance (UM)	799,041
equals	Before-tax equity reversion (BTER)	1,270,959
minus	Taxes due on sale (TDS)	247,418
equals	After-tax cash flow (ATER)	$1,023,541

TABLE 15–20
TAXES DUE ON SALE IN 5 YEARS: APARTMENT EXAMPLE

	Net sales price (NSP)	$2,070,000
minus	Adjusted basis (AB)	−1,186,364
equals	Capital gain on sale (CG)	883,636
times	Investor's marginal tax rate (τ)	× .28
equals	Taxes due on sale (TDS)	$ 247,418

TABLE 15–21
PRESENT VALUE OF THE THREE OPTIONS: APARTMENT EXAMPLE

Year	1 Sale Today	2 Continue "As Is"	3 Operate with Renovations
0	$602,955		$ (150,000)
1		$ 61,805	76,433
2		65,115	80,131
3		68,463	83,879
4		71,845	87,673
5		915,391	1,115,048
PV @ 15%	$602,955	$644,184	$ 636,709

inflows and outflows under the three alternatives today. At a 15 percent required after-tax rate of return on equity, Option 2 yields the highest present value of $644,184. Option 3, to renovate, is the second-best alternative at $636,709, and Option 1 is the least desirable choice with a present value of $602,955. Hence, the investor should continue to operate the apartment for an additional five years "as is" and then sell.

SUMMARY AND CONCLUSIONS

This case study illustrates how investors can make rational decisions as to whether they should make capital improvements to their properties or simply operate/sell them "as is." While one may think that it is always easier simply to operate or sell "as is," it sometimes makes financial sense to renovate the property because the incremental cash inflows may more than offset the additional cash outflows to improve the real estate.

In the next case, an investor must decide whether to lease or purchase a warehouse.

CASE III: PURCHASING VERSUS LEASING A WAREHOUSE

Business owners are faced with a real estate decision as soon as they decide to become a viable concern: Should we purchase the commercial property where we intend to operate the business or should we lease the property? Purchasing any real estate provides for tax breaks because the improvements are depreciable, and if the property appreciates in value, the owner reaps the rewards. Leasing, on the other hand, can be attractive if the owner of the business has a short-term need or projects that his or her company will expand or contract to the point that the current space being utilized will be sub-optimal in the future. Also, leasing protects the lessee against the downside risk of property devaluation. Of course, the tenant may have to pay higher rent to compensate the landlord for this risk.

In the following case study, an investor must decide whether to purchase or to lease additional warehouse space.

A PURCHASE-VERSUS-LEASE EXAMPLE

RSG Company needs additional warehouse space for its operations. It has found a small industrial warehouse building that can be either purchased or leased. You have been hired to advise the company in its decision making. Table 15–22 illustrates the facts of the case.

As RSG's personal adviser, you must decide which is the best choice. And, you have been asked to solve for the rent that would make RSG Company indifferent between owning and leasing. To make these decisions, the after-tax cash flows and after-tax equity reversion from owning will be differentiated with the after-tax cash flows from leasing. The option with the least negative outflow is the one that should be exercised.

THE SOLUTION

❑ OPTION 1: PURCHASING THE WAREHOUSE.   Because RSG is a "user" of the proposed property, there is no net operating income (NOI); however, borrowing 75 percent of the $1,250,000 purchase price ($937,500) at 11.5 percent with interest-only payments and a 10-year balloon payment results in annual debt service of $107,812 [($937,500 × 0.115], as reported in Table 15–23. This is constant throughout the 10-year term. Because there is no NOI, before-tax cash flows equal debt service of $107,812.

To calculate ATCF for each year, taxes from operations must be determined. Table 15–24 reports the taxes for each year. The interest on debt is calculated for each year; because this is an interest-only loan, the interest payment equals the debt service.

Depreciation equals the depreciable basis of $875,000 [purchase price of $1,250,000 × (1 minus the land-to-value ratio of 0.30)] to be depreciated over a 39-year useful life, or $22,436 ($875,000/39). So, taxable income equals −$130,248 (interest of −$107,812 less depreciation of −$22,436). Therefore, taxes from operations are −$44,284 × (−$130,248 × 0.34). Substituting taxes from operations into Table 15–23 yields ATCF of −$63,528 for the 10 years.

TABLE 15-22
PURCHASING VERSUS LEASING

	Company Purchases the Building
Purchase price	$1,250,000
Financing	75% L/V at 11.5%, interest-only payments with a balloon payment in 10 years.
Holding period	10 years
Selling price at end of 10 years	$1,650,000
Selling expenses	9% of sales price
Marginal tax rate	34%
Capital gains tax rate	28%
Depreciable life	39 years, Straight-line method
Land-to-value	30%
Required rate of return	14%

	Company Leases the Building
Lease Term	10 years
Rent	$11,000 per month net to the owner for the first 5 years with a 15% increase in the 2nd 5 years. RSG Company bears all the operating expenses.
Marginal Tax Rate	34%
Required Rate of Return	14%

The selling price in ten years is expected to be $1,650,000, with 9 percent selling expenses; therefore, net sales proceeds are $1,501,500 [$1,650,000 × (1 − 0.09)], as shown in Table 15-25. The unpaid mortgage balance at the end of year ten is simply the loan amount at the inception of the loan of $937,500 ($1,250,000 purchase price × .75 loan-to-value ratio). Subtracting the unpaid mortgage balance from the net sales proceeds results in before-tax equity reversion of $564,000 ($1,501,500 − 937,500).

To find ATER, however, taxes due on sale must be determined. Table 15-26 reports this calculation. To find the capital gain to be taxed at the 28 percent rate, the investor's adjusted basis needs to be computed. Annual depreciation is $22,436; because 10 years have passed, the accumulated depreciation is $224,360. Hence, the investor's adjusted basis today is $1,025,640 ($1,250,000 − 224,360). Therefore, the capital gain is $475,860 ($1,501,500 − 1,025,640) and the taxes due on sale are $133,241 ($475,860 × .28). Substituting this into Table 15-25 yields ATER of $430,759 ($564,000 − 133,241). Notice the marginal tax rate of 34 percent is greater than the capital gains rate of 28 percent.

Thus, if RSG Company owns the building, it must pay $312,500 down ($1,250,000 × .25) and has ATCFs of −$63,528 for each of the 10 years. At

TABLE 15–23
AFTER-TAX COST OF OWNERSHIP: WAREHOUSE PROPERTY

					Year					
	1	2	3	4	5	6	7	8	9	10
NOI	0	0	0	0	0	0	0	0	0	0
minus Debt service (DS)	$107,812	$107,812	$107,812	$107,812	$107,812	$107,812	$107,812	$107,812	$107,812	$107,812
equals Before-tax cash flow (BTCF)	107,812	107,812	107,812	107,812	107,812	107,812	107,812	107,812	107,812	107,812
minus Taxes from operations (TO)	44,284	44,284	44,284	44,284	44,284	44,284	44,284	44,284	44,284	44,284
equals After-tax cash flow (ATCF)	$ 63,528	$ 63,528	$ 63,528	$ 63,528	$ 63,528	$ 63,528	$ 63,528	$ 63,528	$ 63,528	$ 63,528

TABLE 15–24
TAXES FROM OPERATIONS: WAREHOUSE PROPERTY

					Year					
	1	2	3	4	5	6	7	8	9	10
NOI	0	0	0	0	0	0	0	0	0	0
minus Interest (I)	$107,812	$107,812	$107,812	$107,812	$107,812	$107,812	$107,812	$107,812	$107,812	$107,812
minus Depreciation (D)*	22,436	22,436	22,436	22,436	22,436	22,436	22,436	22,436	22,436	22,436
equals Taxable income (TI)	(130,248)	(130,248)	(130,248)	(130,248)	(130,248)	(130,248)	(130,248)	(130,248)	(130,248)	(130,248)
times Investor's marginal tax rate (τ)	.34	.34	.34	.34	.34	.34	.34	.34	.34	.34
equals Taxes from operations (TO)	$(44,284)	$(44,284)	$(44,284)	$(44,284)	$(44,284)	$(44,284)	$(44,284)	$(44,284)	$(44,284)	$(44,284)

*Depreciation = $1,250,000 (1 − .30)/39 = $22,436.

473

TABLE 15-25
AFTER-TAX CASH FLOW FROM SALE: WAREHOUSE PROPERTY

	Selling price (SP)	$1,650,000
minus	Selling expense (SE)	148,500
equals	Net sales price (NSP)	1,501,500
minus	Unpaid mortgage balance (UM)	937,500
equals	Before-tax equity reversion (BTER)	564,500
minus	Taxes due on sale (TDS)	133,241
equals	After-tax equity reversion (ATER)	$ 430,759

TABLE 15-26
TAX EFFECT OF SALE: WAREHOUSE PROPERTY

	Net sales price (NSP)	$1,501,500
minus	Adjusted basis* (AB)	1,025,640
equals	Taxable income (TI)	475,860
times	Capital gains rate**	.28
equals	Taxes due on sale (TDS)	$ 133,241

*AB = $1,250,000 − ($22,436 × 10 yrs) = $1,025,640.
**CGR = Capital gains tax rate.

the end of year 10, the company would realize $430,759 in cash inflows from the expected sale.

❒ **OPTION 2: LEASING THE OFFICE BUILDING.** RSG Company has no debt service when leasing; however, its rental payments are treated as cash outflows of NOI. The company would pay $11,000 per month, or $132,000 annually, for the first five years. Then the rent escalates 15 percent to $151,800 ($132,000 × 1.15). So, BTCFs equal NOI of −$132,000 for the first five years and −$151,800 for the last five years, as reported in Table 15–27.

To calculate ATCF for each year, taxes from operations must be determined. Table 15–28 reports the taxes for each year. Under the leasing alternative, finding taxable income is quite simple because there are no interest or depreciation deductions. In fact, NOI equals taxable income in this example because there are no financing costs or replacement reserves. Therefore, taxes from operations are −$44,880 (−$132,000 × 0.34) for years 1–5 and −$51,612 for years 6–10. Substituting this into Table 15–27 yields ATCFs of −$87,120 for the first five years and −$100,188 for the last five years.

❒ **PRESENT VALUE OF OWNERSHIP VERSUS LEASING.** Now that the ATCFs and ATERs have been calculated for the two options available to the company, the present value of each alternative can be derived. The pre-

TABLE 15-27
AFTER-TAX COST OF LEASE: WAREHOUSE PROPERTY

					Year					
	1	2	3	4	5	6	7	8	9	10
NOI*	−$132,000	−$132,000	−$132,000	−$132,000	−$132,000	−$151,800	−$151,800	−$151,800	−$151,800	−$151,800
minus Debt service (DS)	0	0	0	0	0	0	0	0	0	0
equals Before-tax cash flow (BTCF)	− 132,000	− 132,000	− 132,000	− 132,000	− 132,000	− 151,800	− 151,800	− 151,800	− 151,800	− 151,800
minus Taxes from operations (TO)	− 44,880	− 44,880	− 44,880	− 44,880	− 44,880	− 51,612	− 51,612	− 51,612	− 51,612	− 51,612
equals After-tax cash flow (ATCF)	−$87,120	−$ 87,120	−$ 87,120	−$ 87,120	−$ 87,120	−$100,188	−$100,188	−$100,188	−$100,188	−$100,188

*Rent = $11,000 × 12 = $132,000 in years 1–5; then rent = $132,000 × 1.15 = $151,800 in years 6–10.

TABLE 15–28
TAX EFFECT OF LEASE: WAREHOUSE PROPERTY

						Year					
		1	2	3	4	5	6	7	8	9	10
	NOI	−132,000	−132,000	−132,000	−132,000	−132,000	−151,800	−151,800	−151,800	−151,800	−151,800
minus	Interest (I)	0	0	0	0	0	0	0	0	0	0
minus	Depreciation (D)	0	0	0	0	0	0	0	0	0	0
equals	Taxable income (TI)	−132,000	−132,000	−132,000	−132,000	−132,000	151,800	−151,800	−151,800	−151,800	−151,800
times	Investor's marginal tax rate (τ)	.34	.34	.34	.34	.34	.34	.34	.34	.34	.34
equals	Taxes from operations (TO)	(44,880)	(44,880)	(44,880)	(44,880)	(44,880)	(51,612)	(51,612)	(51,612)	(51,612)	(51,612)

476

sent value of ownership at a 14 percent required after-tax rate of return equals -$527,674, while the present value of leasing is $-$477,729, as calculated below.

$$PV\ of\ Ownership\ at\ 14\% = (\$312,500)$$
$$+ [-\$63,528]PVAF_{(.14,\ 10)}$$
$$+ [\$430,759]PVF_{(.14,\ 10)}$$

$$= (\$312,500) - \$63,528\ (5.2161156)$$
$$+ \$430,759\ (.2697438)$$

$$= (\$527,674)$$

$$PV\ of\ lease\ at\ 14\%: = [-\$87,120]PVAF_{(.14,\ 5)}$$
$$+ [-\$100,188]PVAF_{(.14,\ 5)}PVF_{(.14,\ 5)}$$

$$= -\$87,120\ (3.433081)$$
$$- \$100,188\ (3.433081)\ (.5193687)$$

$$= (\$477,729)$$

Because the ATCFs do not change under the ownership alternative, they can be treated as an annuity for 10 years discounted at the required rate of 14 percent. Also, the ATER at the end of year 10 is a lump sum. Similarly, the ATCFs under the lease alternative can be treated as two five-year annuities. Note that because the second annuity (that is, years 6–10) is calculated as a lump sum *as of the end of year 5*, this lump sum must then be discounted to today using a present value factor for five years at a 14 percent rate.

Table 15–29 summarizes the after-tax cash flows and reversion under the two options. These result confirm the above calculations, showing that RSG Company should lease the warehouse, rather than purchase because the net present value is greater under the lease option.

◻ **CALCULATION OF RENT THAT MAKES THE COMPANY INDIFFERENT BE-TWEEN PURCHASING VERSUS LEASING.** Clearly, at some rental amount, the company would be indifferent between owning and leasing. The present value of purchasing equals an outflow of $527,674. Setting this equal to the present value of leasing, with NOI or rent (R) as the unknown, we can solve the following equation, where MTR equals the marginal tax rate and g equals the change in rent.

$$\$527,674 = Rent(1-MTR)(PVAF_{14\%,\ 5\ yrs.})$$
$$+ Rent(1-MTR)\ (1 + g)(PVAF_{14\%,\ 5\ yrs.})\ (PVF_{14\%,\ 5\ yrs.})$$

$$\$527,674 = Rent(1-MTR)\ PVAF_{14\%,\ 5yrs.}\ [1 + (1 + g)\ (PVF_{14\%,\ 5\ yrs.})]$$

$$\$527,674 = Rent\ (1 - .34)\ 3.433081\ [1 + (1.15)\ (.5193687)]$$

TABLE 15-29

Year	Cost of Owning	PV of Owning @14%	Cost of Leasing	PV of Leasing @14%	PV of Differential
0	($312,500)	($312,500)	$0	$0	($312,500)
1	(63,528)	(55,726)	(87,120)	(76,421)	20,695
2	(63,528)	(48,883)	(87,120)	(67,036)	18,153
3	(63,528)	(42,880)	(87,120)	(58,803)	15,923
4	(63,528)	(37,614)	(87,120)	(51,582)	13,968
5	(63,528)	(32,994)	(87,120)	(45,247)	12,253
6	(63,528)	(28,942)	(100,188)	(45,644)	16,702
7	(63,528)	(25,388)	(100,188)	(40,039)	14,651
8	(63,528)	(22,270)	(100,188)	(35,123)	12,853
9	(63,528)	(19,535)	(100,188)	(30,809)	11,274
10	(63,528) + 430,759	99,058	(100,188)	(27,025)	126,083
Net Present Value		($527,674)		($477,729)	($49,945)

$$\$527{,}674 = .66\,(\text{Rent})\,(5.483571)$$

$$\text{Rent} = \$145{,}800 \text{ per year}$$

$$\text{Rent} = \$145{,}800/12 = \$12{,}150 \text{ per month initial rent.}$$

Rental payments are tax deductible; thus, the after-tax cost of rent is one minus the marginal tax rate. Hence, R is multiplied by (1-MTR). Again, rents are an annuity, so the present value of an annuity formula can be used for both five-year periods of nonchanging rents. $(1 + g)$ is included in the second term on the right-hand-side of the equation because rents are assumed to grow by 15 percent for the second five-year period.

Solving for rents, we obtain $145,800 in annual rent that could be charged to make the company indifferent between purchasing and leasing the property. Thus, at an initial rent of $12,150 per month, RSG Company is willing either to purchase or to lease.

SUMMARY AND CONCLUSIONS

This case study has shown that the purchase-versus-lease decision is similar to other financial decisions; discounted cash flow analysis allows the informed investor to make prudent choices of whether or not to purchase real estate.

CASE IV: EXCHANGE VERSUS SALE-BUY

Chapter 10 presented an example in which an investor chooses to exchange his apartment for an eight-plex, rather than sell his property and then use the proceeds to purchase the eight-plex. This case is provided as an extension of that problem. Several of the facts contained in Chapter 10 are repeated so that this case is all-inclusive and does not require the student to return to the chapter for additional information.

TAX DEFERRED EXCHANGE VERSUS SALE-BUY EXAMPLE

❐ **A TWO-PARTY EXCHANGE.** Assume that a two-party exchange is being considered by Mr. Dunn and Mr. Roe. Mr. Dunn owns an eight-plex residential building with a market value of $660,000 and an outstanding mortgage of $240,000. The adjusted basis of the property is $300,000. Mr. Roe owns an apartment building with a market value of $750,000 and an outstanding mortgage debt of $450,000. The adjusted basis of the property is $525,000.

Mr. Dunn and Mr. Roe have decided to exchange their investments. Mr. Dunn's transaction costs are $49,500, while Mr. Roe's are $57,000. This includes brokerage fees, legal fees, appraisal fees, and other costs of the exchange. The differences in equities will be balanced by cash.

BALANCING EQUITY POSITIONS. Tables 15–30 and 15–31 explain the method of balancing the equities. The first table lists the pertinent data on each property. The second table computes the equity for both parties by deducting the mortgage debt from the market value. The net equity position is then computed for both parties by subtracting the equity received from the equity given. Note that Mr. Roe owes Mr. Dunn $120,000.

CALCULATION OF REALIZED GAIN. Table 15–32 shows how to calculate the realized gain. The realized gain is the gain that the investor would have had if the property had been sold rather than exchanged. It is the market

TABLE 15–30
EXCHANGE PROPERTY DATA

Property 1	Mr. Dunn's Property
Market value	$660,000
Mortgage debt	240,000
Adjusted basis	200,000
Transaction costs	49,500

Property 2	Mr. Roe's Property
Market value	$750,000
Mortgage debt	450,000
Adjusted basis	525,000
Transaction costs	57,000

TABLE 15–31
BALANCE EQUITIES ON EXCHANGE

Mr. Dunn's Equity	
Market value	$660,000
minus Mortgage debt	240,000
equals Equity	$420,000

Mr. Roe's Equity	
Market value	$750,000
minus Mortgage debt	450,000
equals Equity	$300,000

Net Equity Position
Mr. Roe owes Mr. Dunn the difference in equity of
$120,000, to be paid in cash:

		Mr. Dunn	*Mr. Roe*
	Equity given	$420,000	$ 300,000
minus	Equity received	300,000	420,000
equals	Net equity	$120,000	$(120,000)

TABLE 15–32
REALIZED GAIN ON EXCHANGE

Mr. Dunn's Realized Gain		
	Market value	$660,000
minus	Adjusted basis	300,000
minus	Transaction costs	49,500
equals	Realized gain	$310,500

Mr. Roe's Realized Gain		
	Market value	$750,000
minus	Adjusted basis	525,000
minus	Transaction costs	57,000
equals	Realized gain	$168,000

value minus the adjusted basis and the transactions costs. The realized gain is computed in Table 15–32 for both parties.

CALCULATION OF RECOGNIZED GAIN. The recognized gain and taxable gain are calculated in Table 15–33 by subtracting the boot (or cash) given and the transactions costs, and adding the net loan relief to (or from) the boot (or cash) received. The net mortgage relief is considered unlike property only to the extent that the difference between the two mortgage bal-

TABLE 15-33
RECOGNIZED GAIN ON EXCHANGE*

Mr. Dunn's Recognized Gain

	Boot (or cash) received	$120,000
minus	Boot (or cash) given	0
plus	Net loan relief	0
minus	Transaction cost	49,500
equals	Recognized gain	$ 70,500

Mr. Roe's Recognized Gain

	Boot (or cash) received	$ 0
minus	Boot (or cash) given	120,000
plus	Net loan relief	210,000
minus	Transaction costs	57,000
equals	Recognized gain	$ 33,000

*The recognized gain is the taxable gain because it is less than the realized gain.

ances is positive. Thus there is no "negative" net mortgage relief. *The investor pays tax on the lower of the recognized gain or the realized gain.*

ATCF AND POSITION AFTER EXCHANGE. The ATCF is computed in Table 15–34. Mr. Dunn receives a positive cash flow of $50,760 while Mr. Roe pays out $186,240. Table 15–35 shows the amount of taxes both investors owe as a result of the exchange.

The equity positions after the exchange are shown in Table 15–36. Mr. Dunn received an apartment building with a market value of $750,000, with equity of $300,000, and an after-tax cash inflow from the exchange of

TABLE 15-34
CASH FLOW FROM EXCHANGE

		Investor	
		Mr. Dunn	Mr. Roe
	Cash outflow	0	120,000
minus	Transaction costs	49,500	57,000
plus	Cash inflows	120,000	0
minus	Tax on gain (28% bracket)*	19,740	9,240
equals	Net cash flow (ATCF)	$ 50,760	$186,240

*See Table 15–35.

TABLE 15–35
TAXES DUE ON EXCHANGE

		Mr. Dunn	Mr. Roe
	Taxable gain	$70,500	$33,000
times	Marginal income tax rate	.28	.28
equals	Tax on gain	$19,740	$ 9,240

TABLE 15–36
EQUITY POSITION AFTER EXCHANGE

		Investor	
		Mr. Dunn	Mr. Roe
	Market value of property given	$660,000	$750,000
minus	Mortgage debt	240,000	450,000
equals	Original equity	$420,000	$300,000
minus	Transaction costs	49,500	57,000
minus	Tax on recognized gain	19,740	9,240
plus	Cash given	0	120,000
equals	New equity position	$350,760	$353,760

$50,760. Thus, his new equity position is $350,760 after the exchange. Mr. Dunn has deferred taxes on the unrecognized gain (the realized gain minus the recognized gain). Had the investment been sold outright, Mr. Dunn would have had to pay tax on the total recognized gain of $310,500.

And, after the exchange, Mr. Dunn's adjusted basis has risen from $300,000 to $510,000. This adjusted basis would be allocated to the land and building; since Mr. Dunn's adjusted basis has increased, he will have a larger depreciation deduction after the exchange, thus generating more tax shelter. The new adjusted basis is the value of property received, plus taxable gain, minus realized gain.

Mr. Roe has acquired an eight-plex building from the exchange with a market value of $660,000, with equity of $420,000. His original equity position in the apartment building was $300,000. His new equity position is shown in Table 15–36.

❑ EXCHANGE VERSUS SALE-BUY. The most important motivation for exchange is the availability of income tax deferral. That is, taxes that would be paid on an outright sale may be postponed under the use of the exchange. However, the avoidance of taxes may not necessarily maximize wealth. The investor must also look at the property's after-tax cash flows over the holding period. Although taxes are deferred in an exchange, the depreciation basis will also be lower in an exchange. Will the benefits of the tax deferral in the exchange outweigh the benefits of increased basis in an outright sale?

To illustrate, assume that rather than exchange his apartment building with Mr. Dunn, Mr. Roe chooses to sell his property to Mr. Dunn, and use the sales proceeds to acquire Mr. Dunn's eight-plex. Mr. Roe plans to hold Mr. Dunn's eight-plex for five years, at which time he expects to sell it to Mr. James for $725,000. Selling expenses will be $50,000.

Mr. Roe's apartment building is valued at $750,000, with an existing mortgage of $450,000. Net operating income is estimated at $67,500 per year. The adjusted basis of the property is $525,000. Transaction costs from sale will be $57,000.

Mr. Dunn's eight-plex is valued at $660,000 with an existing mortgage of $240,000. Net operating income is estimated to be $65,000, increasing 2 percent per year. Transaction costs from sale will be $49,500. Mr. Roe can borrow $464,040, amortized over a 25-year period at 10 percent with annual payments of $51,122. The land-to-value ratio is 25 percent, and the improvement will be depreciated on a straight-line basis over a 27.5-year period.

Assume that should Mr. Roe exercise the exchange option, financing available to him is for 20 years at a 10 percent interest rate compounded annually.

Mr. Roe must calculate the benefits of exchanging-selling versus selling-buying-selling. Should Mr. Roe exchange-sell or sell-buy-sell?

THE SOLUTION

☐ SALE ALTERNATIVE.

ATER FROM SALE TODAY. Table 15–37 computes the after-tax equity reversion from the sale of Mr. Roe's apartment complex to Mr. Dunn. Net sales proceeds are $693,000 ($750,000 − 57,000). The expected taxes due on the sale are computed in Table 15–38 to be $47,040 or 28% of the capital gain of $168,000.

TABLE 15–37
EXPECTED CASH FLOW FROM APARTMENT SALE TODAY

	Expected selling price (SP)	$750,000
minus	Selling expenses (SE)	57,000
equals	Net sale proceeds (NSP)	693,000
minus	Unpaid mortgage balance (UM)	450,000
equals	Before-tax equity reversion (BTER)	243,000
minus	Taxes due on sale (TDS)*	47,040
equals	After-tax equity reversion (ATER)	$195,960

*See Table 15–38.

Table 15-38
Expected Taxes Due on Apartment Sale Today

		Taxable Income
	Expected selling price (SP)	$750,000
minus	Selling expenses (SE)	57,000
equals	Amount realized (AR)	693,000
minus	Adjusted basis (AB)	525,000
equals	Capital gain on sale (CG)	168,000
		Taxes Due on Sale
equals	Taxable income from sale (TIS)	168,000
times	Investor's marginal tax rate (τ)	.28
equals	Taxes due on sale (TDS)	$ 47,040

EIGHT-PLEX ACQUISITION. Mr. Roe uses the ATER of $195,960 (Table 15–37) as a downpayment to purchase Mr. Dunn's eight-plex for $660,000. The remaining $464,040 is financed under the previously mentioned terms.

ATCF FROM SALE-DAY. Table 15–39 shows the expected after-tax cash flows from operations for the five-year holding period. The annual debt service is subtracted from the expected NOI each year. Tax savings from operations are subtracted from this figure to find annual after-tax cash flows. Expected tax savings are computed in Table 15–40. Interest and depreciation are deducted from NOI to find ordinary taxable income. This is multiplied by the investor's marginal tax rate (.28) to get taxes from operation.

ATER FROM SALE IN YEAR 5. Table 15–41 computes Mr. Roe's expected cash flow from sale of the eight-plex to Mr. James in year 5 for $725,000.

Table 15-39
Expected Cash Flow from Eight-Plex Operation on Sale-Buy

		Year				
		1	2	3	4	5
	Net operating income (NOI)*	$65,000	$66,300	$67,626	$68,979	$70,358
minus	Debt service (DS)	51,122	51,122	51,122	51,122	51,122
equals	Before-tax cash flow (BTCF)	13,878	15,178	16,504	17,857	19,236
minus	Taxes (savings) from operations (TO)	167	663	1,180	1,718	2,280
equals	After-tax cash flow (ATCF)	$13,711	$14,515	$15,324	$16,139	$16,956

*NOI is increasing 2% per year.

TABLE 15-40
EXPECTED TAXES FROM EIGHT-PLEX OPERATIONS ON SALE-BUY

		Year				
		1	2	3	4	5
	Net operating income (NOI)	$65,000	$66,300	$67,626	$68,979	$70,358
minus	Interest on mortgage (I)	46,404	45,932	45,413	44,842	44,214
minus	Depreciation deduction (D)*	18,000	18,000	18,000	18,000	18,000
plus	Replacement reserves (RR)	0	0	0	0	0
equals	Ordinary taxable income (OTI)	596	2,368	4,213	6,137	8,144
times	Investors marginal tax rate (τ)	.28	.28	.28	.28	.28
equals	Taxes (savings) from operations	$ 167	$ 663	$ 1,180	$ 1,718	$ 2,280

*$18,000 = [$660,000 purchase price times $(1 - 0.25$ B/V ratio)]/27.5 years.

TABLE 15-41
EXPECTED CASH FLOW FROM SALE IN YEAR 5

	Expected selling price (SP)	$725,000
minus	Selling expenses (SE)	50,000
equals	Net sale proceeds (NSP)	675,000
minus	Unpaid mortgage balance (UM)	435,234
equals	Before-tax equity reversion (BTER)	239,766
minus	Taxes due on sale (TDS)*	29,400
equals	After-tax equity reversion (ATER)	$210,366

*See Table 15-42.

The ATER is $210,366. The expected taxes from sale (Table 15-42) are computed to be $29,400. The proportion outstanding at the end of year 5 equals 93.79235 percent of the original loan amount, so the unpaid mortgage balance is $435,234.

The adjusted basis of $570,000 equals the original basis of $660,000 less accumulated depreciation of $90,000.

☐ **EXCHANGE ALTERNATIVE.** Mr. Roe's exchange of his apartment building for Mr. Dunn's eight-plex, and subsequent sale in 5 years results in different ATCFs and ATER than had he sold his apartment to Mr. Dunn, purchased and held Mr. Dunn's eight-plex for five years, and then sold it.

ATCF FROM EXCHANGE. Table 15-43 computes the expected after-tax cash flow from operations for the five-year holding period. The annual debt service is subtracted from the expected NOI each year. Taxes from operations are subtracted from this figure to find annual after-tax cash flows. Expected taxes are computed in Table 15-44. Interest and depreciation are

TABLE 15–42
EXPECTED TAXES DUE ON SALE IN YEAR 5

	Taxable Income	
	Expected selling price (SP)	$725,000
minus	Selling expenses (SE)	50,000
equals	Amount realized (AR)	675,000
minus	Adjusted basis (AB)	570,000
equals	Total gain on sale (TG)	$105,000
	Taxes Due on Sale	
equals	Total gain on Sale	105,000
times	Investor's marginal tax rate (τ)	.28
equals	Taxes due on sale (TDS)	$ 29,400

TABLE 15–43
EXPECTED CASH FLOW FROM OPERATIONS ON EXCHANGE

		Year				
		1	2	3	4	5
	Net operating income (NOI)	$65,000	$66,300	$67,626	$68,979	$70,358
minus	Debt service (DS)	48,981	48,981	48,981	48,981	48,981
equals	Before-tax cash flow (BTCF)	16,091	17,319	18,645	19,998	21,377
minus	Taxes (savings) from operations (TO)*	2,859	3,426	4,022	4,647	5,305
equals	After-tax cash flow (ATCF)	$13,160	$13,893	$14,623	$15,351	$16,072

*See Table 15–44.

TABLE 15–44
EXPECTED TAXES FROM OPERATIONS ON EXCHANGE

		Year				
		1	2	3	4	5
	Net operating income (NOI)	$65,000	$66,300	$67,626	$68,979	$70,358
minus	Interest on first mortgage (I)	41,700	40,972	40,171	39,290	38,321
minus	Depreciation deduction (D)	13,091	13,091	13,091	13,091	13,091
plus	Replacement reserves (RR)	0	0	0	0	0
equals	Ordinary taxable income (OTI)	10,209	12,237	14,364	16,598	18,946
times	Investor's marginal tax rate (τ)	.28	.28	.28	.28	.28
equals	Taxes (savings) from operations (TO)	$ 2,859	$ 3,426	$ 4,022	$ 4,647	$ 5,305

deducted from NOI to find ordinary taxable income. This is multiplied by the investor's marginal tax rate (.28) to find taxes from operation. Note that the differences between the cash flows from sale-buy versus exchange are due to mortgage and depreciation differences.

Mr. Roe borrows $417,000 ($660,000 purchase price − $300,000 equity downpayment + $57,000 transaction costs) for 20 years at a 10 percent interest rate compounded annually; annual debt service is therefore $48,981. The depreciation deduction of $13,091 is calculated as follows. Mr. Roe's new basis in Mr. Dunn's eight-plex is $525,000 ($660,000 purchase price + $33,000 recognized gain − $168,000 realized gain). Recall the land allocation is 25 percent, or $165,000 ($660,000 × .25), so Mr. Roe's depreciable basis in the eight-plex is $360,000 ($525,000 − 165,000). Based on a 27.5 year useful life, annual depreciation using a straight line basis is $13,091 (360,000/27.5). Notice this is less than the $18,000 from Table 15–40 because of Mr. Roe's lower adjusted basis in the new property. This illustrates an important point about exchanging: while the investor might owe less taxes at the time of exchanging (versus an outright sale), typically the investor's adjusted basis, and thus depreciation deduction, will be lower under the exchange alternative.

ATER IN YEAR 5 FROM SALE (EXCHANGE).   Table 15–45 computes Mr. Roe's expected cash flow from sale of the eight-plex acquired via the exchange with Mr. Dunn five years before. The ATER is $242,122. The expected taxes from sale (Table 15–46) are $60,327. The adjusted basis is $459,545 [$525,000 new basis − ($13,091 depreciation times five years)]. The proportion outstanding at the end of year 5 equals 89.34077 percent of the original loan amount, so the unpaid mortgage balance is $372,551.

❒ NPV AND IRR OF SALE/BUY VS. EXCHANGE.   Table 15–47 compares the cash flow under the two choices. Also, it reports the NPV and IRR for both the sale-purchase and the exchange. Assuming a required after-tax rate of return of 10 percent, the exchange alternative is a positive NPV project

TABLE 15–45
EXPECTED CASH FLOW FROM SALE (EXCHANGE)

	Expected selling price (SP)	$725,000
minus	Selling expenses (SE)	50,000
equals	Net sale proceeds (NSP)	675,000
minus	Unpaid mortgage balance (UM)	372,551
equals	Before-tax equity reversion (BTER)	302,449
minus	Taxes due on sale (TDS)*	60,327
equals	After-tax equity reversion (ATER)	$242,122

*See Table 15–46.

TABLE 15-46
EXPECTED TAXES DUE ON SALE

	Taxable Income	
	Expected selling price (SP)	$725,000
minus	Selling expenses (SE)	50,000
equals	Amount realized (AR)	675,000
minus	Adjusted basis (AB)	459,545
equals	Total gain on sale (TG)	$215,455
	Taxes Due on Sale	
equals	Total gain on sale (TG)	$215,455
times	Investor's marginal tax rate (τ)	.28
equals	Taxes due on sale (TDS)	$ 60,327

TABLE 15-47
NPV AT 10% AND IRR OF SALE-BUY VERSUS EXCHANGE

(1) Year	(2) Exchange	(3) Sale/Buy	[(2) − (3)] Difference
0	$(195,960)	$(195,960)	$0
1	13,160	13,711	(551)
2	13,893	14,515	(622)
3	14,623	15,324	(701)
4	15,351	16,139	(788)
5	16,072	16,956	(884)
	242,122	210,366	31,756
	NPV = $9,275	NPV = −$7,814	NPV = $17,089
	IRR = 11.15%	IRR = 8.98%	

($9,275), while the sale/buy alternative is a negative NPV project ($7,814). Therefore, the difference in the NPVs is $17,089. Note that the IRR of the exchange (11.15 percent) is higher than the IRR of the sale/buy (8.98 percent).

Because the differential cash flow analysis results in a positive NPV, Mr. Roe should exchange his apartment for Mr. Dunn's eight-plex, operate it for five years, and sell, rather than sell his apartment to Mr. Dunn, use the net sales proceeds to purchase Mr. Dunn's eight-plex, operate it for five years, and sell.

SUMMARY AND CONCLUSIONS

This final case study illustrates the use of discounted cash flow analysis to determine whether exchanging real estate for other like-kind property is preferable to selling real estate outright and using the proceeds to acquire other property. This particular example resulted in the exchange being the better option; however, selling and purchasing simultaneously the same properties that are considered for exchange can be optimal when the sum of the present value of the ATCFs exceeds the present value of the ATER. ATCFs are greater under the sale-buy option because of larger depreciation deductions, while ATER is greater under the exchange alternative because of the lower adjusted basis in the property received in the exchange.

SUMMARY

The purpose of this case study chapter has been to demonstrate that discounted cash flow analysis can be utilized in many applications of real estate decision making. Whether the property be an office building, an apartment, a warehouse, a multifamily residential property, or any other property type, comparing the after-tax cash flows and after-tax equity reversion of alternative decisions allow the investor to make an informed decision about such things as whether to purchase, lease, sell, exchange, operate "as is," or renovate.

PROBLEMS

15-1. Using the information from Case I in the chapter, assume that the 6,200 square feet that the insurance company is currently leasing can only be leased for $13.00 per square foot in two years. Further, assume that market rents will increase by 4 percent for only the next two years, and then by 2 percent for the following three years, and then 0 percent for seven years. If the investor still requires a return on equity of at least 15 percent, would she still accept the project?

15-2. Using the information from Case I, assume that the expected yearly appreciation is 1.5 percent rather than 2 percent as forecasted. Would the investor still accept the project if her required rate of return was still 15 percent?

15-3. Using the information provided in Case II in the chapter, assume that if the investor were to make the improvements, NOI would increase by 3.5 percent annually, and the selling price in five years would be $2,500,000. Which option would the investor choose if her required rate of return were still 15 percent?

15-4. Assume the facts from Case III are true except that RSG is able to obtain financing with interest-only payments at 9.75 percent with a balloon payment in 10 years.
   a. Compute the NPV of the ATCFs.
   b. Which option would you now advise them to pursue?

15-5. Assume that all the facts from Case III are still true except that the expected selling price in 10 years is now $2,000,000.
   a. Calculate the net present value of the after-tax cash flows.
   b. Which option would you now recommend to RSG?

15-6. Assuming the facts from Case IV, calculate the net equity position of Mssrs. Dunn and Roe if the market value of Mr. Dunn's property is $725,000.00 and the mortgage debt is $250,000.00.

SELECTED REFERENCES

Institute of Real Estate Management, *Income/Expense Analysis: Office Buildings.* Chicago: Institute of Real Estate Management, 1993.

White, John R. *The Office Building.* Chicago: Appraisal Institute, 1993.

PART VI

CONCLUSION

CHAPTER 16

REAL ESTATE INVESTMENT DECISION MAKING: AN OVERVIEW

PRINCIPLES

1. Real estate investment decision making has its own set of fundamental principles.
2. Despite recent developments, a number of unanswered questions remain within the field of real estate investment analysis.

The literature on real estate investments has expanded rapidly during the past 25 years.[1] Since the publication of Wendt and Cerf's book in 1969,[2] which developed the discounted cash flow model for real estate on an after-tax basis, it is fair to say that this field has developed and matured considerably. Numerous articles and studies continue to be performed by academics, practitioners, and laymen. While real estate continues to fascinate many people as an investment vehicle and as a method for achieving financial success[3], it appears that by the 1990s, real estate investment analysis is no longer characterized by the "get-rich-quick" tradition from which it came.

[1]See Austin J. Jaffe and C. F. Sirmans, *Real Estate Investment Decision Making* (Englewood Cliffs, N.J.: Prentice-Hall, 1982), for detailed review of the history of real estate investment analysis.

[2]See Paul F. Wendt and Alan B. Cerf, *Real Estate Investment Analysis and Taxation* (New York: McGraw-Hill, 1969).

[3]As a testimonial, consider the fact that several books of the how-to-get-rich genre continue to make the best-selling list each year.

In the previous editions of this book, we laid out the fundamental principles of this field and also noted the major questions which were unresolved. Specifically, these two lists were as follows:

THE FIVE PRINCIPLES OF REAL ESTATE INVESTMENT DECISION MAKING (CA. 1986)

1. *Real estate investment analysis is a systematic type of economic analysis.*
2. *Risk and return are closely related.*
3. *The goal of wealth maximization will ensure the optimal set of investments.*
4. *The analysis of the institutional environment of real estate is essential.*
5. *Real estate investment analysis is risk analysis.*

THE FIVE UNRESOLVED ISSUES OF REAL ESTATE INVESTMENT DECISION MAKING (CA. 1986)

1. *How efficient are real estate markets?*
2. *Why do investors like real estate as an investment vehicle?*
3. *What affects net operating income?*
4. *How sensitive are investments to changes in financing and tax policy?*
5. *Is there a future for real estate and portfolio analysis?*

With the recent changes in real estate investment markets with the conclusion of the turbulent times of the 1980s and the changing investment environment of the 1990s, it is time to revisit "what is known" and "what is unknown" about real estate investing. As before, we have restricted our list to five points in each category in the interests of brevity. The study of real estate is sufficiently complex that there may be a larger number of first principles governing these markets than many others. Similarly, despite our enhanced knowledge as a result of the experiences in the 1980s, there are perhaps as many unanswered questions now as in the past. In the final section of this book, we make a few observations about the future of real estate investment analysis.

THE FIVE NEW PRINCIPLES OF REAL ESTATE INVESTMENT DECISION MAKING

1. *While real estate investment analysis remains a systematic type of economic analysis, increased attention from the institutional investment community is transforming the meaning of real estate financial analysis.* The fundamental analysis of real estate projects remains the focus of most real estate in-

vestors. However, institutional investment activity has meant that a number of traditional practices have come under attack and are being challenged. Individual investors can compete with financial institutions in the market place, but at least in some markets, investment decision making is becoming increasingly more competitive. As outlined throughout the book, the individual investor still has economic incentive to identify all the factors that are likely to affect the investment in the future and decide how influential these factors will be. In addition, the small investor has incentive to rank each potential investment according to its attractiveness to him or her as an investment vehicle. Finally, the individual investor still has incentive to revise original estimates of parameter values in response to changes in the investment environment or changes in his or her perspective or economic position.

What has changed a bit in recent years are several factors. First, real estate markets are probably becoming more competitively priced as excess returns are squeezed out of the market a lot sooner, more often, and more aggressively. Second, technological changes in information and data processing has meant that the level of technical competence among investors in the market has risen. This fact has meant that what once was thought to be sophisticated financial modeling may, by today's standards, be nothing more than normal. We may be coming to a time when deal making via the investment rules-of-thumb will be a rare event.

Third, changes in the financial system throughout the 1980s has changed the rules for many real estate investment decisions. This observation refers not only to changes due to highly visible tax reform acts; it also refers to a fluid legal environment, with the beginning of a return to the protection of private property rights rather than a continuing expansion of the power of the state, or a vast number of new and sophisticated financing vehicles for real estate markets. Finally, all of these changes has given strong credence to the claim that real estate, despite its problems at the end of the last production/financing cycle, is now taken seriously as an institutional investment on a scale not seen previously in the United States. The integration of real estate and financial markets is clearly underway on a national and even international scale.

Note that all investors must carefully evaluate the relationship of the project to the various environments. In the new environment, investors are more likely than ever to be worse off if they carelessly select a real estate project at random or by failing to consider the impact of a change in the institutional arrangement within which the project is located. Therefore, investors will ensure that their decisions are the best possible by systematically evaluating the choices available at every point in time. One elaborate paradigm to accomplish this task has been outlined in Chapter 1 and serves as the basis for this book: the *real estate investment process*. Implicit in this approach is the belief that real estate investors can benefit from a careful and critical analysis of the economic factors that affect the investment. Institutional real estate investors regularly devote sizable resources to ensure that the best projects are chosen with the information available at the time.

2. Risk and return are closely related; in the future, they will be even more so. Theoretically, there is little doubt about the relationship between expected risk and expected return. If these two factors were not strongly positively related, investors would act such that the market prices of competing investments would change until they were. If one investment offered higher returns and lower levels of risk than other investments, every investor would attempt to buy the high-return, low risk investment. Since such demand for the investment would bring pressure to the price, it is likely the price of the investment would rise. In subsequent periods, the expected rate of return would fall, since a higher acquisition price would be required.

Similarly, the market prices of other investments would fall, as few investors would find these investments attractive relative to the first investment. It may be that more individuals would enter the market (if we have been talking about a subset of possible investors), but they, too, would prefer the other investment to the remaining several.

The basic principles that underscore the positive relationship between risk and return are the notion of investor risk aversion and the opportunity for economic returns through arbitrage. *Risk aversion* refers to the belief that investors will demand high returns for high levels of risk. If high returns are not expected, they will seek other investments with lower levels of risk for the same level of return, or low returns in compensation for lower levels of risk undertaken by the investor.

Risk aversion implies that an investor will insist on an added amount of return if he or she is forced to bear added risk, since the presumption is that less risk is preferred to more and that high returns are preferred to low returns. *Arbitrage* is a term that describes an economic process in markets where participants will act in the interest of wealth maximization to exploit market opportunities without risk. Such opportunities arise as a result of market inefficiencies, inside information, or for other reasons. In all cases, arbitrage opportunities imply a violation of the risk and return relationship. As a result, investors will always accept arbitrage opportunities in real estate markets because, by definition, there is no risk and some expected return.

As markets become more competitive, the risk-return relationship is expected to sharpen. This has implications for the ability of investors to earn abnormal returns in real estate markets. Following these principles, one would expect that it will be increasing difficult to outperform the real estate market in the absence of superior information, skills, or expertise.

3. *While the goal of wealth maximization will ensure the optimal set of investments for individual investors, portfolio selection principles will be required to ensure that nonsystematic risk is diversified away.* One of the most widely debated topics in the popular business literature is the question of what is the appropriate goal or objective of the investor. One of the more intuitive notions advocated by many real estate writers is that investors should adopt several investment goals, based on personal preferences, needs, and special objectives. We have argued that the basic objective of the individual equity investor in real estate "should" be to maximize the value of the equity position. This objective is identical with what has been called the "goal of wealth maximization" earlier in the book.

If the individual investor is willing to accept the goal of wealth maximization as desirable, there are likely to be several benefits. For example, the investor can proceed comfortably with the knowledge that accepting any real estate investment that maximizes the value of the equity claim on the investment, will be the best individual investment choices. This means the investor can be confident that any investment chosen will be expected to increase his or her wealth as much as or more than any other project available at the time.

Finally, if the goal of wealth maximization is accepted by the investor, he or she can be confident with the use of a *single* method if the method proves to be consistent with the goal: net present value. This method is ideal, since it gives the investor estimates of how much the equity position would increase (or decrease) by accepting the investment. If the investor ranks potential investments by this calculation and chooses those with the highest net present values, he or she can be assured that no other set of investments will provide a greater increase to his or her wealth position. In addition, the model developed in Chapter 12 was all-inclusive in that it analyzed income, vacancies and bad debts, operating expenses, financing expenses, depreciation, growth in property values, amortization, and settlement of the mortgage at the time of sale. In addition, it permitted an evaluation of the time value of money. As a result, the calculation of the net present value of equity contained all the items most investors believe are fundamental to selecting the best real estate investment projects.

On the other hand, the ability to diversify away unnecessary risk means that real estate investors may find that the evaluation of real estate investments in a portfolio will be different than collecting individual investments with positive net present values. The revolution of Markowitz, Lintner, and Sharpe has changed the way of thinking about real estate investment acquisitions. In the future, as databases continue to grow and the costs of managing real estate data fall further, real estate investment analysis will increasingly become a type of portfolio selection method, using fundamental real estate investment methods as a basis. What seemed like a dream a few years ago is in the process of become a reality now.

4. The analysis of the institutional environment of real estate is more essential than ever. There are two major points of departure for the financial analysis of real estate compared with the financial analysis of any other enterprise or asset. The first is that real estate values are determined not only by their physical location vis-à-vis other real estate down the block and in the same neighborhood but also in relationship to the urban area. There is no doubt that location affects the value and hence the analysis of real estate as much as or more than any other attribute. In addition, the distance from choice economic property is also an important variable. It affects the economic rent the location commands, the clientele interested in the real estate, and the likely infrastructure surrounding the asset.

The second reason for the unique characteristics of real estate investment analysis is the set of real estate institutions affecting the real estate participants. These institutions have been categorized in this book in terms of their environments: market, legal, financing, and taxation. Real estate investments have specialized environments in each category. Society has long treated land and improvements on the land differently from other assets.

Because real estate values are based on their unique locations and institutions, the analysis of real estate is fundamentally an analysis of the value of locations and institutions. In this sense, real estate investment decision making requires critical analyses of the economic relationship between specific parcels of land and their location and an understanding of the environments that have been created by forces in society to use, direct, and maintain the asset called real estate.

With some practice, performing cash flow analysis becomes relatively straightforward. With the ability to computerize the financial calculations, it is even easier.[4] What remains considerably more difficult is the proper assessment of the impacts of complicated institutional arrangements affecting most real estate markets. It is this type of expertise which will likely be in demand in the years ahead.

5. Real estate investment analysis remains risk analysis. During the past several years, people learned how to "do the numbers" when analyzing real estate investments. Indeed, a careful reading of this book will enable you to join this club of evaluating investment projects by systematically representing the important attributes of real estate in an organized

---

[4]For those readers who are skeptical, Appendix B lists several real estate templates which are currently available. A review of these computer models should convince most skeptics about the "new information age" which is taking over and how relatively easy it is to generate cash flow numbers.

process. The good news is that this approach is better and more time-tested than several others. The bad news is that investment analysis is far more difficult in real life.

If successful investing in real estate were as simple as calculating a few numbers and choosing the largest one, everyone would be instantly rich. The difficulty comes about in deciding on which of the attractive projects is likely to pay off. In other words, it is the *risk* associated with investment that is fundamental to an analysis of which investment is more attractive than others. Since risk analysis is so fundamental, it follows that the investor with the most sophisticated real estate computer software is unlikely to be more successful than numerous competing investors *if* he or she fails to evaluate risk.

As a result, risk analysis is what real estate investment analysis is all about. Those who are superior in identifying and measuring risk are likely to be those who make the most money as real estate investors. Those who neglect risk are likely to earn the same returns as everyone else, including those who never calculate anything but the interest earned on their passbook savings accounts at their local banks.

As indicated earlier in this chapter, as markets become more competitive, the relationship between risk and return will become even stronger. This observation emphasizes that real estate as risk analysis will also become more important in the future. It is also implied that the methods of risk analysis will develop and expand using methods unknown today but perhaps quite common to the next generation of investors in the future.

THE FIVE UNRESOLVED ISSUES OF REAL ESTATE INVESTMENT DECISION MAKING IN THE 1990S

1. Studies in real estate markets indicate a fair amount of informational inefficiency. Are these markets truly inefficient, or are there alternative explanations? Previously, we wondered: How efficient are real estate markets? This was held as an important question of theoretical and practical significance because the answer would determine, among other things, the type and method of analysis useful for investors. If studies showed that real estate markets were relatively efficient in the sense that market prices reflected available public information about the bundle of rights for sale, then investors would not likely earn superior returns by investing in real estate, despite all of the mythology about real estate as a great investment. If the market prices information quickly and accurately, "news" to the investor would be of little benefit in an attempt to outperform the market.

On the other hand, if valuable information was slow to affect market prices, investors would be able to identify properties for sale with positive net present values and could take advantage of others in the market. In effect, if market prices are inefficient, there will be violations of the risk-return relationship and, thus, opportunities for abnormal returns to accrue to the investor. When inefficient markets prevail, superior returns to real estate may be likely for investors who are able to take advantage of the mispricing.

The notion of market efficiency is well known in much of the real estate literature. However, considerable confusion exists regarding what the efficient market hypothesis (EMH) means for investors. Some have argued that the EMH suggests that all real estate investments must be efficiently priced. Others have presumed that the EMH implies that abnormally high rates of return are not possible in any real estate investment. Still others seem to believe that advocates of the EMH are unaware that many well-known and not-so-well-known individuals have made fortunes by investing in real estate.

None of these arguments imply that the EMH is incorrect or useless. In each case, there is a defect in the application of the EMH to the experience in real estate markets. For instance, the EMH suggests that in the absence of insider information, there is no reason to believe that systematically higher returns would accrue to one individual over another unless the market mechanism was precluded. If so, high returns could accrue to investors relative to risk. If not, the typical investor would probably earn a typical rate of return, the market rate of return.

The important point is that the EMH is a mere, albeit important, hypothesis. Ten years ago, what had not been resolved is a good sense of the degree of market efficiency that characterizes real estate markets. This question could only be resolved empirically (that is, by looking at the specific numbers). Previously, we knew very little about the degree of efficiency in real estate markets. Now, we know a bit more.

Research has shown a fair amount of empirical evidence, at least in some markets. Relative to a decade ago, we know a great deal more about the rate-of-return experiences in real estate markets. Generally, the conventional wisdom from these studies is that real estate returns are often abnormally high relative to risk and compared with other investment markets. This has remained a paradox for many researchers.

Recent researchers have tried to explain this persistent finding generally in one of two ways: either a) methodological criticism has been launched against the research methods, so that with this or that correction, the results often conform to the efficient pricing paradigm, or b) the state of our databases are sufficiently poor that enhanced data sources would be expected to find contrary results. Some have also rejected the EMH, especially in real estate markets, and concluded that market prices are set chaotically or based upon alternative principles. Whatever is taken as reasonable, we cannot presently resolve this matter.

2. If real estate investments are becoming more integrated with world capital markets, what continues to make investors like real estate as an investment vehicle? This question continue to perplex us. The answer does not appear to the authors to be obvious. According to most observers and social commentators, investors have traditionally favored real estate for investment purposes. The interesting question is why is this so, given increasingly well-established markets, some of the disadvantages associated with the ownership of real estate, and a growing integration and new generation of investment vehicles.

Some of the answers are unsatisfactory on a theoretical level. For example, such answers as "land is fixed in nature," "improvements on the land are long-lived and durable," or "individuals need space as population expands" are clearly not acceptable reasons for real estate as a favored investment vehicle. As long as competing investors are aware of these factors, including current owners of real estate and subsequent sellers of the asset, the prices charged for ownership interests are likely to reflect these characteristics. It is only when the "market" does not perceive the attribute such that only a few parties in the market are aware of a certain characteristic is it likely that real estate investments will be preferred, since the returns associated with these assets are likely to be higher for a given level of risk.

It is difficult, indeed, to determine why real estate remains so highly favored. (Of course, many institutional investors wish, in retrospect, that they did not favor real estate so much!) Perhaps market prices are slow to reflect information and, as a result, investors make money if they are early into the market and sell it to a later entrant. Perhaps real estate investors are confident that social policy will always favor real estate and are really in the market for government subsidies. Perhaps investors can delineate themselves into narrow tax clienteles, given the progressive nature of the federal tax system and the complex nature of tax calculations. Perhaps real estate is best viewed as a safe haven for international capital. Whatever the reason, we remain unable to explain why real estate is such a preferred investment form.

3. What is the relationship between macroeconomic policy and real estate investment? Every textbook on real estate investment analysis (including this one) as well as every textbook on real estate appraising devotes a considerable amount of space to market analysis. This area is generally recognized as essential in the modern analysis of real estate valuation. The problem is that the linkages between the macroeconomic activities in the market place and the impact on the individual investment are simply unknown.

Some analysts devote considerable effort in trying to identify keys to effective and successful investments by examining the market environments where successful investments have been made. While this "case approach" is useful as a teaching device and is often interesting, it is not always successful in identifying what the functional relationship is between, for example, the growth in census population and the market rent of a two-bedroom apartment. It is this type of relationship that would be extremely useful when making income estimates for new investments or income projections for future years of the investment.

It has been argued that if students of markets actually knew how markets worked, such functional relationships could be designed and verified through empirical testing. It is fair to say that despite a considerable amount of interest in this area, few studies, if any, have satisfactorily provided many of the linkages we need. The linkages exist; it is up to students and researchers of the future to identify and discover them. In the last five years, some progress in this area has been made, especially in the area of office markets. However, more work is needed.

4. How important are changes in financing and tax policy for real estate markets? In other words, this question asks, If changes in financing and/or tax policies are critical to real estate investment decision making, how sensitive are investment projects to such changes? For example, if the tax law affecting real estate investments is changed again by Congress as was recently done in 1990, what is the likely impact on the market for real estate investments?

While numerous studies have shown the direction of the change in policy as a result of new programs, the estimate of the magnitude of the change is a particularly difficult and complicated problem. However, the issue is critical for investors as well as policy makers. If the change in policy is expected to have a dramatic impact but, in actuality, the impact is minimal, the effectiveness of the policy is brought into question. On the other hand, if the change in policy is expected to have a minimal impact but the impact is dramatic, the policy may do considerable harm. Clearly, the magnitude of the change in social policy is an issue of serious consequence.

It is now commonly held that removal of tax benefits resulting from the Tax Reform Act of 1986 led, or at a minimum, lengthened the deep recession of real estate markets at the end of the 1980s and the beginning of the 1990s. With the continuing evolution of the capital markets and capital market instruments and the prospect of changing tax policies in the future, much is unknown in this area.

5. How expansive will portfolio analysis be for institutional and other real estate investors? Five years ago, we pondered whether there would be a future for real estate portfolio analysis. This question has been answered by pension fund managers, real estate investment trust officers, life insurance real estate managers, and Wall Street. The move toward portfolio approaches for real estate asset management began to take shape over the past several years, and by now, it is taken as given that it will be a part of the future. This is true despite continuing difficulties in making the applications using the standard models and methods. As the institutional real estate investor continues to look at real estate opportunities, portfolio analysis will become a larger part of this field.

However, it remains unclear how portfolio methods need to be altered for real estate investments. It remains unknown what is the best pricing model for the real estate asset class. It also remains uncertain who will benefit most from these applications: institutional investors, as is generally presumed, or the growing set of sophisticated individual investors who are playing the same analytical games on a smaller scale.

If "the time for real estate portfolio theory has finally arrived," there remains many problems to be worked out. Data problems still loom large. Information about properties is often privately held, precluding the opportunity for a wider dissemination of market information. Existing models may not capture enough of the heterogenous characteristics of real estate investments. Some researchers have reached the conclusion that real estate portfolio analysis is still far away. They may be correct; the proper analysis of a real estate market may prove to be a very tough nut to crack. As such, for many people, the valuation of real estate is likely to remain a single-asset analysis.

THE FUTURE OF REAL ESTATE INVESTMENT DECISION MAKING

What can we expect in the future? There are several developments currently under way that point the path of the future. First, real estate markets are rapidly becoming integrated into the overall capital market. This is a major development that is expected to continue in the future. Despite the difficulties in most real estate markets in recent years, an increasingly large number of investors remain interested in real estate as an investment, although some are expected to remain on the sidelines for some time.

Second, it seems that the future will require ever greater levels of financial expertise in the area of real estate investment decision making than we predicted five years ago. This means that not only will computerized real estate investment analysis be commonplace, but increasingly, higher levels of financial analysis will be required for students seeking entry-level positions and for consultants seeking work with financial institutions. As an example, students can now evaluate real estate using sophisticated models such as Monte Carlo simulations within a spreadsheet environment. Previously, such a program was thought to be only suitable for experienced computer users or those with considerable knowledge in the field. The world is changing rapidly; it is difficult to keep up. "Real estate as a numbers game" has been overtaken by "real estate as financial analysis" in the modern world.

Third, it seems unlikely that the environment in which real estate financial decisions are made will become less complex. In the areas of legal and tax policy, the relationship between real estate and the rest of the environment is becoming more and more complicated. In the area of financing, real estate has enjoyed an explosion in development and creative new instruments. We expect this trend to continue. As a result, the institutions that affect real estate are becoming more and more distinctive. This is an area to be watched in the future.

Finally, the prospects for the future in providing opportunities for success as an investor remain favorable. However, increased competition and higher standards of analysis are likely to transform real estate investment analysis into a much more specialized activity than it already is. For some, this is welcome news because it will enable them to try out their new technology and modern training. For others, it implies that making money in real estate will become that much more difficult. To be sure, the future is likely to be different from the past; it always is. In the area of real estate investing, this is almost a certainty.

SELECTED REFERENCE

Jaffe, Austin J., and C. F. Sirmans, "The Theory and Evidence on Real Estate Financial Decisions: A Review of the Issues," *American Real Estate and Urban Economics Association Journal*, 12 (Fall 1984), 378–400.

REAL ESTATE INVESTMENT TABLES

The tables presented in this appendix are used in making real estate investment decisions. There are three tables:

Table 1—Present Value of $1.00 Factors (Annual)

Table 2—Mortgage Constant (Monthly Payments)

Table 3—Proportion Outstanding on Mortgages

Table 1 provides the factor for finding the present value of a payment to be made in the future at various rates of discount. Table 2 provides the mortgage constant factors for monthly payments. The mortgage constant, when multiplied by the amount borrowed, tells the investor the payment necessary to fully amortize the loan. Table 3 contains the proportion outstanding on mortgages at various interest rates, mortgage maturities, and holding periods.

TABLE 1
PRESENT VALUE OF $1 FACTORS (ANNUAL)

			Interest Rate				
Years	10.00%	12.00%	14.00%	16.00%	18.00%	20.00%	Years
1	0.909091	0.892857	0.877193	0.862069	0.847458	0.833333	1
2	0.826446	0.797194	0.769468	0.743163	0.718184	0.694444	2
3	0.751315	0.711780	0.674972	0.640658	0.608631	0.578704	3
4	0.683013	0.635518	0.592080	0.552291	0.515789	0.482253	4
5	0.620921	0.567427	0.519369	0.476113	0.437109	0.401878	5
6	0.564474	0.506631	0.455587	0.410442	0.370432	0.334898	6
7	0.513158	0.452349	0.399637	0.353830	0.313925	0.279082	7
8	0.466507	0.403883	0.350559	0.305025	0.266038	0.232568	8
9	0.424098	0.360610	0.307508	0.262953	0.225456	0.193807	9
10	0.385543	0.321973	0.269744	0.226684	0.191064	0.161506	10
11	0.350494	0.287476	0.236617	0.195417	0.161919	0.134588	11
12	0.318631	0.256675	0.207559	0.168463	0.137220	0.112157	12
13	0.289664	0.229174	0.182069	0.145227	0.116288	0.093464	13
14	0.263331	0.204620	0.159710	0.125195	0.098549	0.077887	14
15	0.239392	0.182696	0.140096	0.107927	0.083516	0.064905	15
16	0.217629	0.163122	0.122892	0.093041	0.070776	0.054088	16
17	0.197845	0.145644	0.107800	0.080207	0.059980	0.045073	17
18	0.179859	0.130040	0.094561	0.069144	0.050830	0.037561	18
19	0.163508	0.116107	0.082948	0.059607	0.043077	0.031301	19
20	0.148644	0.103667	0.072762	0.051385	0.036506	0.026084	20
21	0.135131	0.092560	0.063826	0.044298	0.030937	0.021737	21
22	0.122846	0.082643	0.055988	0.038188	0.026218	0.018114	22
23	0.111678	0.073788	0.049112	0.032920	0.022218	0.015095	23
24	0.101526	0.065882	0.043081	0.028380	0.018829	0.012579	24
25	0.092296	0.058823	0.037790	0.024465	0.015957	0.010483	25
26	0.083905	0.052521	0.033149	0.021091	0.013523	0.008735	26
27	0.076278	0.046894	0.029078	0.018182	0.011460	0.007280	27
28	0.069343	0.041869	0.025507	0.015674	0.009712	0.006066	28
29	0.063039	0.037383	0.022375	0.013512	0.008230	0.005055	29
30	0.057309	0.033378	0.019627	0.011648	0.006975	0.004213	30
31	0.052099	0.029802	0.017217	0.010042	0.005911	0.003511	31
32	0.047362	0.026609	0.015102	0.008657	0.005009	0.002926	32
33	0.043057	0.023758	0.013248	0.007463	0.004245	0.002438	33
34	0.039143	0.021212	0.011621	0.006433	0.003598	0.002032	34
35	0.035584	0.018940	0.010194	0.005546	0.003049	0.001693	35
40	0.022095	0.010747	0.005294	0.002640	0.001333	0.000680	40
45	0.013719	0.006098	0.002750	0.001257	0.000583	0.000273	45
50	0.008519	0.003460	0.001428	0.000599	0.000255	0.000110	50

TABLE 2
MORTGAGE CONSTANT (MONTHLY PAYMENTS)

	Interest Rate						
Years	7.00%	8.00%	9.00%	10.00%	11.00%	12.00%	Years
1	0.086527	0.086988	0.087451	0.087916	0.088382	0.088849	1
2	0.044773	0.045227	0.045685	0.046145	0.046608	0.047073	2
3	0.030877	0.031336	0.031800	0.032267	0.032739	0.033214	3
4	0.023946	0.024413	0.024885	0.025363	0.025846	0.026334	4
5	0.019801	0.020276	0.020758	0.021247	0.021742	0.022244	5
6	0.017049	0.017533	0.018026	0.018526	0.019034	0.019550	6
7	0.015093	0.015586	0.016089	0.016601	0.017122	0.017653	7
8	0.013634	0.014137	0.014650	0.015174	0.015708	0.016253	8
9	0.012506	0.013019	0.013543	0.014079	0.014626	0.015184	9
10	0.011611	0.012133	0.012668	0.013215	0.013775	0.014347	10
11	0.010884	0.011415	0.011961	0.012520	0.013092	0.013678	11
12	0.010284	0.010825	0.011380	0.011951	0.012536	0.013134	12
13	0.009781	0.010331	0.010897	0.011478	0.012075	0.012687	13
14	0.009354	0.009913	0.010489	0.011082	0.011691	0.012314	14
15	0.008988	0.009557	0.010143	0.010746	0.011366	0.012002	15
16	0.008672	0.009249	0.009845	0.010459	0.011090	0.011737	16
17	0.008397	0.008983	0.009588	0.010212	0.010854	0.011512	17
18	0.008155	0.008750	0.009364	0.009998	0.010650	0.011320	18
19	0.007942	0.008545	0.009169	0.009813	0.010475	0.011154	19
20	0.007753	0.008364	0.008997	0.009650	0.010322	0.011011	20
21	0.007585	0.008204	0.008846	0.009508	0.010189	0.010887	21
22	0.007434	0.008062	0.008712	0.009382	0.010072	0.010779	22
23	0.007299	0.007935	0.008593	0.009272	0.009970	0.010686	23
24	0.007178	0.007821	0.008487	0.009174	0.009880	0.010604	24
25	0.007068	0.007718	0.008392	0.009087	0.009801	0.010532	25
26	0.006968	0.007626	0.008307	0.009010	0.009731	0.010470	26
27	0.006878	0.007543	0.008231	0.008941	0.009670	0.010414	27
28	0.006796	0.007468	0.008163	0.008880	0.009615	0.010366	28
29	0.006721	0.007399	0.008102	0.008825	0.009566	0.010324	29
30	0.006653	0.007338	0.008046	0.008776	0.009523	0.010286	30
31	0.006591	0.007281	0.007996	0.008732	0.009485	0.010253	31
32	0.006533	0.007230	0.007951	0.008692	0.009451	0.010224	32
33	0.006481	0.007184	0.007910	0.008657	0.009421	0.010198	33
34	0.006433	0.007141	0.007873	0.008625	0.009394	0.010176	34
35	0.006389	0.007103	0.007840	0.008597	0.009370	0.010155	35
40	0.006214	0.006953	0.007714	0.008491	0.009283	0.010085	40
45	0.006097	0.006856	0.007635	0.008429	0.009234	0.010047	45
50	0.006017	0.006793	0.007586	0.008391	0.009205	0.010026	50

TABLE 3
PROPORTION OUTSTANDING ON MORTGAGES WITH MONTHLY COMPOUNDING: VARIOUS INTEREST RATES, MORTGAGE MATURITIES, AND HOLDING PERIODS

Mortgage Maturity	Holding Period	Interest Rate					
		7.00%	8.00%	9.00%	10.00%	11.00%	12.00%
15 Years (180 Months)	1	0.960902	0.964022	0.966947	0.969683	0.972236	0.974614
	2	0.918978	0.925057	0.930793	0.936191	0.941260	0.946008
	3	0.874023	0.882858	0.891247	0.899192	0.906699	0.913774
	4	0.825818	0.837157	0.847992	0.858319	0.868138	0.877452
	5	0.774128	0.787663	0.800679	0.813166	0.825116	0.836523
	6	0.718702	0.734060	0.748928	0.763285	0.777115	0.790404
	7	0.659269	0.676009	0.692323	0.708181	0.723559	0.738436
	8	0.595539	0.613139	0.630407	0.647306	0.663806	0.679877
	9	0.527203	0.545052	0.562683	0.580058	0.597138	0.613891
	10	0.453926	0.471313	0.488606	0.505767	0.522755	0.539536
25 Years (300 Months)	1	0.984702	0.986909	0.988844	0.990530	0.991991	0.993250
	2	0.968298	0.972731	0.976641	0.980068	0.983054	0.985644
	3	0.950708	0.957377	0.963293	0.968510	0.973084	0.977073
	4	0.931846	0.940748	0.948694	0.955742	0.961960	0.967415
	5	0.911622	0.922739	0.932724	0.941638	0.949549	0.956532
	6	0.889935	0.903236	0.915257	0.926056	0.935701	0.944269
	7	0.866680	0.882113	0.896151	0.908843	0.920251	0.930451
	8	0.841744	0.859238	0.875253	0.889827	0.903013	0.914880
	9	0.815005	0.834464	0.852395	0.868820	0.883781	0.897335
	10	0.786334	0.807633	0.827392	0.845614	0.862322	0.877564
30 Years (360 Months)	1	0.989842	0.991646	0.993168	0.994441	0.995499	0.996371
	2	0.978949	0.982599	0.985695	0.988300	0.990477	0.992282
	3	0.967270	0.972801	0.977521	0.981516	0.984873	0.987675
	4	0.954745	0.962190	0.968581	0.974022	0.978622	0.982483
	5	0.941316	0.950699	0.958801	0.965743	0.971646	0.976632
	6	0.926916	0.938253	0.948105	0.956597	0.963864	0.970040
	7	0.911474	0.924774	0.936405	0.946494	0.955181	0.962611
	8	0.894917	0.910177	0.923607	0.935332	0.945494	0.954241
	9	0.877162	0.894368	0.909609	0.923002	0.934685	0.944808
	10	0.858124	0.877247	0.894297	0.909380	0.922626	0.934180

USING SPREADSHEETS FOR REAL ESTATE INVESTMENT ANALYSIS

Real estate investment analysis has enjoyed a long history of computerized financial analysis. As long ago as 1974, Dasso noted that there were at least 112 articles written about computerized real estate analysis in actual practice using mainframes and canned software.[1] Now, with the development of microcomputers, a new generation of real estate computer users has arrived. In particular, it was the development of the computerized spreadsheet in the late 1970s that has had a major impact on real estate investment analysis.

There are several advantages of spreadsheets over hand-calculated analyses for real estate investors. These include the ability to perform long sets of mathematical calculations, the rapid speed of computers, accuracy and reliability, extensive storage capabilities, and the very inexpensive cost of processing.[2] And, spreadsheets are considerably easier to learn and use than any of the other computer software that preceded them. In effect, once an investor understands the benefits and power of spreadsheets, it is unlikely that the investor will revert to hand calculations again.

This real estate investment book contains numerous calculations. A set of templates has been developed that can be used with Lotus 1-2-3, the best selling and most widely used spreadsheet program. With the use of this specially prepared diskette and Lotus 1-2-3, or Excel, the reader can

[1]See Jerome Dasso, "Computer Applications in Real Estate," *CREUES Real Estate Report*, No. 13. (Storrs, Conn.: Center for Real Estate and Urban Economic Studies, June 1974).
[2]For more discussion, see Austin J. Jaffe, "Computer Technology and Real Estate Education: Some Observations," *Proceedings of the Real Estate Educators Association Annual Conference* (August 1985), pp. 15–31.

calculate all of the important analyses found in this book. In fact, use of the diskette may simplify some of the concepts taught in the book, and the investor may be able to concentrate on the investment choices rather than on performing the calculations. If so, this is the real value of computerized real estate investment analysis!

DESCRIPTION OF COMPUTER SOFTWARE

The real estate software that accompanies this book consists of two diskettes of Lotus 1-2-3, or Excel, templates. Each diskette is available on IBM or 100-percent compatible hardware using modern versions of Lotus 1-2-3 orExcel 4.0 (or other spreadsheets which can read Lotus- or Excel-formatted files). Each diskette contains a special file which will automatically welcome you when you initially load Lotus or Excel.[3] The introductory file will provide an overview of all of the computerized applications and provide instructions for access and usage. (Written instructions are also provided.)

Each application also contains its own menu so that usage, even for computer novices, is quite easy. It is also easy to print or graph your results if you have the proper hardware.

Readers interested in software can choose between either or both sets. These sets are described below.

SET I: BASIC REAL ESTATE INVESTMENT TEMPLATES[4] (5 APPLICATIONS)

The following fundamental real estate investment questions may be answered by users of these templates:

- How do I evaluate the timing and size of mortgage payments?
- How much will it actually cost me to borrow?
- What are the expected cash flows from a real estate investment?
- How much can I expect to earn from an investment?
- How do the investment risks of each alternative project compare?

---

[3]It should be noted that Excel 4.0 requires Windows 3.1, while Lotus 2.x or higher runs in a DOS environment. In addition, Lotus 1-2-3 for Windows will also work with these templates, since they can read ".wk1" files.

[4]Do not be fooled by the "basic" adjective in the name. These five templates are full-automated applications for novice as well as sophisticated real estate investors. This set may be sufficient for your needs, even if you are reasonably experienced.

- What is the relationship between my property and the market comparables?
- How much is my property worth?

Specifically, the five templates are as follows:

1. *Present Value* (pv.wk1). This template calculates a detailed table of present values or present value factors for one or up to several discount (interest) rates and for one to many years. The template is completely automated to provide as large a table as the user indicates based upon only the few required inputs.

2. *Effective Cost of Borrowing* (effcost.wk1). The calculation of the borrower's actual, or effective cost of borrowing is no longer a mystery for the real estate decision maker. This application includes all of the leading mortgage and other loan provisions found in most modern mortgages. These provisions are usually hidden as additional costs to the borrower. These costs include closing fees and costs, early repayment of the outstanding balance of the loan with and without penalties, prepaid interest for construction loan financing, discount points and mortgage placement fees, and mortgage insurance.

3. *After-Tax Financial Analysis* (cashflow.wk1). A complete discounted cash flow analysis is provided for any type of real estate investment from simple rental houses to multiple purpose structures. Users can input up to five types of rental units, up to three different mortgages with or without prepayment penalties and amortized financing costs, various growth rate estimates, depreciation and capital gains (appreciation) treatment for projects on an after-tax basis for up to 10 years. This template uses the current tax law following changes in the tax law from 1986 and 1993. Various criteria are also reported including many financial ratios, net present value, and the internal rate of return.

4. *Risk Analysis* (risk.wk1). This application calculates the expected rates of return, variances, and standard deviations of returns for up to ten different investments. Users are then free to compare all types of investments on the basis of risk and return. Since both risk and return are merged into the analysis, in many cases, investors can evaluate which investment would be preferred to meet the investors' objectives and long-term goals.

5. *Comparable Sales Analysis* (comp.wk1). This template calculates several units of comparison for up to twenty market comparables. It also provides several rules of thumb and employs regression analysis to provide an indicated value for the subject property. The results of the traditional sales comparison adjustment grid are

compared with the regression analysis using the same data, often with interesting conclusions.

SET II: ADVANCED REAL ESTATE INVESTMENT TEMPLATES[5] (5 APPLICATIONS)

The advanced set of templates answer the following questions:

- By which of several investment criteria should an investment be judged?
- How sensitive are the cash flows to errors in input estimation?
- What is the Financial Management Rate of Return for an investment?
- When and under what conditions should an investment be refinanced?
- How can Monte Carlo simulation for real estate investments be used by investors?
- How can portfolio theory be used in actual real estate investing?
- How do the results of sophisticated investment and risk modeling compare with more traditional investment methods?

Specifically, these five templates are as follows:

6. *Cash Flow and Sensitivity Analysis* (cf2.wk1). This template enables users to perform a complete and detailed discounted cash flow analysis especially designed for investments in income-producing rental units. Several well-known investment criteria are presented and the use of sensitivity analyses is an automatic feature of the spreadsheet. This template may be sufficient for some investors to acquire the set all by itself!

7. *Financial Management Rate of Return* (fmrr.wk1). This rate of return calculation was invented and popularized over the past 20 years. Heralded as one of the best investment measures of return, the financial management rate of return (FMRR) can be cumbersome to calculate by hand. This template permits cash flows up to ten years with specified safe and required rates of return. The FMRR solution is compared with the IRR, AIRR, and NPV. Sensitivity analyses are shown for various reinvestment and discount rates.

[5]This is a new set of templates containing some sophisticated methods of analysis. We are pleased to provide applications such as a complete Monte Carlo simulation and portfolio analysis for real estate within Lotus 1-2-3 and Excel 4.0 environments. Real estate investment analysts should be able to take advantage of the computational power of modern computers, and users can do so with these templates.

8. *Refinancing Decision* (refin.wk1). The refinancing decision is one of the most common financing decisions for real estate investors. This template permits the analyst to compare new financing options for existing mortgages with loan origination fees, prepayment penalties, and for fixed-rate mortgages (FRMs) or adjustable-rate mortgages (ARMs). The year of refinancing is also an input parameter. Tables are presented to show how the results vary with the planned holding period. The template also analyzes the decision to sell or continue to operate as an added feature!

9. *Monte Carlo Simulation* (simulate.wk1). This technique is undoubtedly one of the most sophisticated real estate modeling procedures in the field. Known in real estate circles as the *most advanced risk analysis method*, typically developed for mainframe or mini-computer users in the past, this template is an actual, comprehensive Monte Carlo simulation for real estate investment analysis. Probability distributions for up to 15 different inputs are provided. A complex menu structure permits users easy access. The simulation can be set for up to 1,000 runs (with modern computers, this takes two to three minutes rather than the two to three hours it took only a few years ago!). At the conclusion of the runs, the complete results are provided including the probability of the project under analysis being successful. You will want to see this template as soon as you open the package!

10. *Portfolio Selection Model* (port.wk1). One of the important developments in financial markets has been the use of portfolio selection methods for investment purposes. Now, this sophisticated template permits real estate analysts to apply portfolio theory principles to choosing a real estate investment portfolio. These selections are based upon technical portfolio rules (three alternative rules are available for users) and the analysis can be performed with or without risk-free assets. Perhaps for the first time, real estate investors will now be able to construct portfolios without bearing unnecessary risks.

Instructions for Obtaining Software

These diskettes containing the sets of real estate templates are currently available according to the following schedule:

Lotus 1-2-3 Templates

Set I: Basic Real Estate Investment Templates	$29.95
Set II: Advanced Real Estate Investment Templates	$69.95
For Both Sets I and II:	$89.95

EXCEL TEMPLATES

Set I: Basic Real Estate Investment Templates $ 99.95
Set II: Advanced Real Estate Investment Templates $ 99.95
For Both Sets I and II: $189.95

Please add $2 shipping and handling to each order. Send a check or money order to:

> JS & Associates
> Calder Square
> P.O. Box 10262
> State College, PA 16805
> USA

These diskettes are available in either the 3.5 inch or 5.25 inch formats. Pennsylvania residents must add 6 percent sales tax. You will need an IBM or 100-percent compatible computer and either Lotus 1-2-3 (Release 2.x, 3.x or later) or Excel (4.x or later). Note that Excel and Lotus 1-2-3 for Windows both require Microsoft Windows 3.1 or later. Please allow three to four weeks for delivery. Thank you for your interest in JS & Associates.

INDEX